D1600173

Country of the Cursed and the Driven

Early American Places is a collaborative project of the University of Georgia Press, New York University Press, Northern Illinois University Press, and the University of Nebraska Press. The series is supported by the Andrew W. Mellon Foundation. For more information, please visit www.earlyamericanplaces.com.

Borderlands and Transcultural Studies

Series Editors Pekka Hämäläinen, Paul Spickard

Country of the Cursed and the Driven

Slavery and the Texas Borderlands

Paul Barba

University of Nebraska Press
Lincoln

Library of Congress Control Number: 2021936392

To all my family

Contents

Maps and Tables

Acknowledgments

This book emerged from an enormity of labor, attention, support, care, and love from others. I'm indebted to the people of UC MEXUS, whose institution subsidized my early research as a mostly unfunded graduate student at the University of California, Santa Barbara. With their dissertation grant, I was able to travel to Austin on numerous occasions to conduct critical research at the Texas State Library and the University of Texas, where I met the wonderful people of those institutions. Special thanks go out to Kathryn Kenefick, Sarah Cleary, and the many others who welcomed me to the Dolph Briscoe Center for American History. My project also benefited greatly from two very generous grants at Bucknell University, the C. Graydon and Mary E. Rogers Faculty Fellowship and the Andrew W. Mellon Bridge to Retirement Research Grant. These awards allowed me to return to Texas, where I explored more local archives, including the Austin History Center and the Bexar County Spanish Archives. The two grants also financed my acquisition of materials from various digital archives, which pushed me into new interpretive directions.

I will always be fond of the people of UCSB. The Black Studies Department laid the philosophical groundwork of my larger research endeavors as an undergrad and then continued to cultivate my intellectual passions in the years that followed as a graduate student. Chris McAuley generously offered his guidance throughout my (long) student career at UCSB, and others from the department, especially the late great Otis Madison, Jude Akudinobi, Douglas Daniels, and Earl Stewart, kept me reeled in. The UCSB History Department, of course, was my academic home. Pat Cohen, Salim Yaqub, Randy Bergstrom, Sarah Cline, Ann Plane, Mhoze Chikowero, and Beth Digeser supported me during those pivotal moments of my graduate career, and Pekka Hämäläinen and James Brooks kindly humored me when I shared my mostly half-baked research aspirations with them during the earliest stages of this project. John Majewski never hesitated to offer his assistance or encouragement, and Verónica Castillo-Muñoz taught me to reach for the stars in academia. Without my two primary mentors, Carl Harris and Paul Spickard, neither this book nor my scholarly career would exist. Paul rescued me from my aimless wanderings of early graduate school and then carried me across the doctoral finish line, all while balancing committee work for a million other graduate students. Carl was the first person to tell me that I belong in academia; I only wish he were still around to read this book, the payoff of all the faith he put in me as a young student of history. Thank you, Paul and Carl. I'd be remiss to ignore the formative support and care of Jeff Landeck, Olivia Walling, Ryan Abrecht, David Baillargeon, Hanni Jalil-Paier, Chris Kegerreis, Eric Massie, Ross Melczer, Brian Tyrrell, and (my man) Jackson Warkentin, who, in their own unique ways, all provided motivation, recommendations, provocative discussion, sounding boards, and, above all, friendship.

My time at Bucknell has been short but no less important. Colleagues from all over campus have transformed how I think about not just my research but my place in academia at large. Khalil Saucier and Jaye Austin Williams of the Africana Studies Program have pressed me to rethink many of my interpretations at a fundamental level. I'm immensely indebted to both for their intellectual generosity. Obed Lira and Adam Burgos are professionals at indulging me in fascinating philosophical conversations, which certainly helped to fine-tune various aspects of this book, and Anthony Stewart's mentorship kept me propped up amid the trials of early professorship. Luyang Ren, Bucknell's GIS and Web application specialist, went above and beyond her job obligations to transform my rough map ideas into legible cartographic representations. I'm especially grateful for my (current and former) colleagues in the History Department, who have welcomed me with open arms since day one. Beeta Baghoolizadeh, Casey Bohlen, Claire Campbell, David Del Testa, Mehmet Dosemeci, John Enyeart, Cymone Fourshey, Jay Goodale, Jennifer Kosmin, Mark Sheftall, Jennifer Thomson, and Ann Tlusty all offered critical, constructive feedback on some portion of this book (and Liz Loss coordinated many of my research efforts), with John and Casey especially dedicating extra labor to my manuscript. I couldn't have asked for a better group of people to work with.

The University of Nebraska Press staff are the best. Matt Bokovoy is a stellar, super-accommodating acquisitions editor, who kept up my confidence throughout the entire publication process, and others, including Heather Stauffer, were equally supportive. Of course, UNP reached out to my excellent readers, whose close, generous parsing of my manuscript offered me a strong foundation for imagining a path to finalizing this book. I'm particularly grateful for Todd Wahlstrom's detailed analysis of my work and his many astute recommendations, as well as Alan Gallay's early encouragement and feedback. UNP also connected me to the great people of the Early American Places Initiative, who guided me through the final stages of publication. Thank you all for making my publishing aspirations a reality. And as I made final revisions, I was also fortunate to cross paths with Max Flomen, who kindly offered his own expert perspective and supportive input.

Although this book asks some tough questions about the nature of family, I have only affection and admiration for mine. I want to thank my extended kin, including my many aunts, uncles, and cousins, for keeping me grounded in general. It's easy to get lost in the worlds of books, essays, and old documents, but relatives are great at reminding me that I can't forget about this world. I especially want to make a shoutout to my in-laws, Cindie Grisso, Chet Grisso, Cyla Fisk, Ryan Fisk, and Sherri McMackins; my cousin Daniel Martin; and my godparents, Mina Tacata and Robert Tacata, who have all been unwavering in their love and support. *Quiero agradecer a mis abuelas,* Socorro Chávez *y* Domitila Barba, *quienes con mucho sacrificio cementaron la base de todos mis logros.* I'm appreciative of all the sacrifices of my foremothers, who, for generations, have endured colonialism and its many legacies. *Muchas gracias.*

Elva Chávez Barba and Carlos Barba ("just two poor kids from the projects") taught me how to be the best person I could be, and my brothers, Michael and David Barba, continue to challenge me. I'm still a work in progress, but I'm certainly proud to be the son of such hardworking, committed, and loving parents and the brother of two brilliant but down-to-earth men. Michael deserves a special thanks for offering his journalistic expertise during my final stages of writing, and David for fathering my awesome nephews, Gabriel and Julian. I love you all!

I'm forever grateful for the companionship of Catri Grisso Barba. She has stood by me every step along the way, patiently, lovingly. She is my rock, my anchor. And she took more than her share of photographs of rare books and archival materials. Of course, she also brought into this world my *little* rock (star), Elyse Susana-Quinn. Thank you, Elyse, for inspiring me in ways I couldn't have imagined. I love you both.

Country of the Cursed and the Driven

Introduction: "Cursed and Driven, Traded, as Slaves . . . O, What a Country"

In the mid-1920s, Abner J. Strobel wrote, at the pestering of R. M. Farrar, an account of the pre–Civil War plantation society of Brazoria County, Texas. In his essay, Strobel waxed eloquent about "noble men and women," happy, well-treated "Negroes," and the splendor of "a civilization . . . that has no counterpart in the annals of Time." To him, the slave-based plantations of Texas flourished under the guidance of a "people without peer," men and their honorable wives who dedicated their lives to the labor of building "a civilization in the wilderness." If, by the time he published his history in 1926, the past felt distant to Strobel, it was because most of these plantations had vanished or lay "practically a ruin." But his narrative, he hoped, could be a means to bridging that gap, a way for "the present generation" to connect to this heroic past and "to realize what a happy and contented lot was the portion of the early settlers" of Texas. According to Strobel, preserving their memory in writing was the least he could do for the true defenders of this Texan legacy, "the survivors of the Confederate Army, who stood like a stone wall for white supremacy and preserved and gave us our present civilization, to whom we owe a debt of gratitude the can never be repaid."[1]

In other words, Strobel was invested in rewriting plantation history to resurrect the racist causes of White Texans before, during, and after the U.S. Civil War. And in this regard, he aligned himself with a generation of White supremacist authors who also were writing about the supposed backwardness of a postemancipation society, with lamentations for what had been lost.[2] There was, nonetheless, one notable difference in Strobel's Texas account of the world enslaved people had built. Unlike his sentimentalist counterparts stationed elsewhere in the country, Strobel was determined to fuse his White supremacist sentimentalism with a heavy dose of Texas exceptionalism. "Ours is not like the history of any other state of the Union," Strobel declared. "Texas history, taken as a whole, is unique."[3]

This point was about all Strobel got right in his essay on slave-based plantation society in Texas. *Taken as a whole*, with an appreciation of the experiences of Hispanic, Lipan Apache, Comanche, Tonkawa, Mexican, Kiowa, Anglo-American, and Black people (as well as others), Texas history *was* rather unique—just not how Strobel, an Anglo-Texan chauvinist, understood it to be. To comprehend more fully the history of nineteenth-century Texas, we must broaden our scope of analysis well beyond the likes of the McNeels, Groces, Perrys, and Whartons of Texas—the plantation owners—to include the histories of people like Sarah Ashley and Abelino Fuentes, whose trials and tribulations reveal a Texas that was neither romantic nor heroic. Indeed, from them we glean a Texas that was remarkable only because it was home to over a century and a half of diverse, colonialism-spawned, cross-ethnic slaving violence. Their stories strip the veneer from the triumphalist and heroic accounts of Texas pasts, exposing the violence and exploitation that was fundamental to the making of Texas.[4]

For Ashley, an enslaved Black woman, Texas was a living hell. Born into Anglo-American slavery, she experienced the full force of slaver exploitation and torture—in the service of developing a mid-nineteenth-century Anglo cotton kingdom. She and her Black counterparts endured brutal whippings that did not stop "till dey have blister on 'em," agonizing displays of cruelty, like the pouring of "salt and red pepper" on open wounds, and severe deprivation of food and clothing. When she and others did not face these "punishments" for insubordinate behavior or low productivity in the cotton fields, they still feared the violence of separation, because their slaver, Henry Thomas, was "a spec'lator [who] buys up lots of niggers and sells 'em."[5] Amid the daily terrors of Anglo slaveholders and their proxies, she, like so many of her enslaved Black neighbors, built the Anglo-Texas Strobel missed so dearly.

For Fuentes, Texas was neither a plantation fantasy world nor a cotton hellscape; it was, rather, Comanchería, the land of the Comanches. Fuentes's experiences in Texas were, like Ashley's, framed by the violence of Texas slavers, but unlike Ashley's subjugators, Fuentes's slavers were

Comanche. Born free in the outskirts of Monclova, Coahuila, Fuentes first fell victim to Comanche slaver violence in 1838, at the age of seven, when a party of thirty or so Comanches attacked Fuentes and his family, capturing him and killing his older brother, Pedro. "Taking the route to the north," Fuentes later remembered, the Comanche slavers marched him to their Texas homeland, located hundreds of miles away from the young boy's family and community. It was there, in the southern portion of Comanchería, that Fuentes would toil for nine long years as a slave, "caring for the horse herds of the Indians."[6] His forced labor, like that of Ashley, would sustain the economic vitality of his slaver hosts.

From the perspectives of Ashley and Fuentes, Texas was the source of their suffering, not a glorious place where Christian civilization met the great bounties of nature. Instead, Texas was where forced migration and familial displacement came into sharp relief, where violence, coercion, and the reverberating imperatives of colonial extraction worked hand in hand to forge slaver dominion across vast, varied, and contested landscapes. Yet few chroniclers of Texas have had interest in weaving together the histories of people like Ashley and Fuentes in the service of spotlighting and bridging Texas's diverse slaving pasts. Because the slavers of Ashley and Fuentes did not share the same ethnic or political origins, historians have tended to relegate their histories to separate fields of inquiry. Conventionally, Ashley's story belongs to the history of Anglo-America's expansion of the cotton frontier; Fuentes's story belongs to Native American, "frontier," or Tejano history. The net effect is a neatly partitioned Texas history, with clean boundaries between topics and fields that mirror the fixed borders of the modern state. Although Texas history may not appear as chauvinistic as during Strobel's time, it continues to struggle with nation- and ethnicity-based teleologies and approaches.[7]

Country of the Cursed and the Driven aspires to offer a more comprehensive history of Texas during the eighteenth and nineteenth centuries.[8] Specifically, it seeks to move beyond the conventional partitioning of Texas history by taking a cue from Elijah Hicks, a Cherokee man whose reflections on the mid-nineteenth-century Texas borderlands enunciated the tangled forces of cross-ethnic slaving in the region. When Hicks traveled to Comanchería in 1846, he expected to witness the treaty powers of a freedom-espousing U.S. federal government at work, but instead he observed the legacies of generations of colonialism, large-scale population transfer, intercommunity violence, personal exploitation, and dominion-building in the Texas borderlands:

> Camanchee girls & prisoners taken at a treaty of peace [in] St. Antonio and elsewhere by the Texans have been brot to camp by the agents employed by [U.S.] Com[missione]rs. to be returned to their people. This is the Country of Captives: the weeping Camanchee girls, held in duress by the Texans; the silvan face of anglo Saxon Sons & daughters and the Sons of the Montezumas & Guatimozin, cursed and driven, traded, as slaves by the roving & haughty Camanchee. O, what a country of freedom in name, a nation's birthright to two miles of African Slaves.[9]

As Hicks's comments illuminate, few communities of the Texas borderlands were shielded, as either victims or perpetrators, from the violence of slavery. Hispanic, Comanche, Anglo-American, and African-descended people were all implicated in Texas borderlands slavery to varying degrees, and for some the roles of slaver and slave could switch at a moment's notice. The century and a half from 1700 to 1860 ebbed and flowed between competing visions of Native and colonial Euro-American rule, and shifting geopolitics often dictated who could perpetrate slaver violence—as well as who would be forced to endure it. By 1860, an Anglo-American colonial order, with anti-Blackness and Native annihilation as its credos, would emerge supreme in the borderlands, but it was only after generations of colonialism-induced multiethnic struggle and dominion building. And even then, the Anglo-American regime would have to withstand both internal and external attacks on their supremacy during and after the U.S. Civil War.

Driven and ambitious were the slavers of the Texas borderlands and their counterparts. In Texas, slaving and the quest for dominion regularly operated in conjunction with one another. Spaniards were among the first to transform the Texas borderlands through widespread slaving violence. For Spaniards, Texas always represented the vast reaches of empire, and the conquest of *la tierra de las Tejas*, the land of the Tejas, was a foregone conclusion in their minds. Early efforts, including those of Álvar Núñez Cabeza de Vaca and Francisco Vázquez de Coronado, beset as they were with many failures, may have betrayed that conceit, but the slow march of Spanish colonialism—a process built on the violence of slave raiding, trading, and exploitation—fortified Spanish resolve, just as it penetrated and destabilized an untold number of Native communities across North America.[10] When another European empire, France, threatened to undermine Spanish authority in the present-day Texas-Louisiana border region during the latter part of the seventeenth century, Spanish Texas—which to this point remained on the northeastern edge of the Spanish slaving frontier—emerged as an urgent arena for Spanish settler colonialism.[11] By the 1710s, Spanish officials had planted, with the acquiescence of various Native groups, colonists at San Antonio, Nacogdoches, and La Bahía.

As it turned out, however, French saboteurs were the least of the Spaniards' worries in Texas. The Ndé, or "Apache," people of present-day Texas exercised considerable dominion over much of the western, central, and northern parts of the region. Spaniards quickly discovered that if they were to succeed in colonizing their far northeastern territories, they had to contend with Ndé power and influence. As newcomers to Texas, Spaniards knew little of the geopolitical intricacies of the region, but they learned and adapted quickly. With guidance from local populations of Xarames, Payayas, Ervipiames, Caddos, and others, Spanish colonists challenged Ndé regional authority and emerged as one of the dominant military, economic, political, and cultural communities of Texas. In this hotly contested geopolitical context, slaving became a critical component of Spanish articulation of dominion.

The eighteenth-century migration of Nʉmʉnʉʉ, or Comanche, people would disrupt and ultimately undermine the new Spanish-oriented colonial order in Texas.[12] Comanches, a recently transformed equestrian people, began their rapid migration to modern-day western and northern Texas as late as the 1740s and continued to expand across Texas throughout the next several decades. Once in the western and northern Texas borderlands, Comanches anchored themselves as the foremost economic, political, and cultural body of the broader region. Taking a cue from and building off of the violently destructive and extractive Spanish colonial invasion of the North American southwest, Comanches wielded slaving violence to reconfigure life in the Texas borderlands yet again. Specifically, the violence of Comanche slave raiding displaced and destroyed many of the Ndé communities of the region, and Comanche slave trading operated as an important complement to their larger system of commerce and market penetration. Over the course of about a century and a half, Comanches rearranged geopolitics, dismantled longtime local alliances, disrupted European colonial machinations, and asserted spectacular economic influence.[13]

In many respects, the unyielding regional power of Comanches accounts for yet another mass movement of expansionist people into the Texas borderlands. The ability of Comanche communities to marshal and to control horse, mule, and other livestock resources drew

Anglo-American colonizers ever westward from nearby U.S. territories. A flowering commerce between Comanche and Anglo-American traders provided the initial impetus for an Anglo-American reorientation toward Texas, but Comanche disregard for and outright rejection of Spanish—and later Mexican—colonial prerogatives opened the door for massive Anglo investment in Texas, as desperate Hispanic leaders turned to Anglo-Americans for the "civilized" colonization of Texas. And colonize they did. Starting as little more than a trickle in the opening years of the nineteenth century, the Anglo-American colonial invasion grew by the 1830s and 1840s to torrential proportions. Anglo-American settler colonists brought with them both enslaved Black people and the collective desire to develop the agricultural, commercial, and (eventually) political infrastructures of the region. The only barrier they could foresee was the pesky influence of Native people. Fortunately for them, their disdain for Indians was shared by most of the Hispanic locals. Immediately they got to work clearing their newly appropriated lands, a process that removed or destroyed plant, animal, and Native life.

From a broad perspective, these larger forces of population transfer, regional assertion, and community consolidation gave Texas an amorphous shape throughout the eighteenth and nineteenth centuries. Space, resources, and dominion were constantly under contestation in Texas, and, despite frequent claims to the contrary, no single group of people or state held total sway over the region. Instead, the geography of Texas was dictated only by the limits of imagination and power. Depending on point of view, Texas was variously Kónitsąąhįį gokíyaa,[14] Tejas, Nʉmʉnʉʉ Sookobitu,[15] Coahuila y Tejas, the Republic of Texas, or Texas. With travelers, traders, diplomats, fighters, spies, surveyors, slavers, and enslaved people regularly undermining or circumventing territorial boundaries in Texas, it was only through widespread, continual violence that the larger, usually encroaching, communities of Texas were able to assert any measurable control over their territorial holdings. Even then, this control was often fragile and tentative.

The amorphous shape of Texas was also a function of the many overlapping historical claims and connections of the longtime Native inhabitants of the region. Up until the second half of the nineteenth century, although wracked by centuries of colonial infiltration and disruption, Texas was, above all, Native country.[16] The ancient trade routes and long-held alliances that crisscrossed much of present-day Texas gave the region a sense of cohesion, even before Euro-American imperialists and others attempted to impose one. The Southern Plains and their

Map 1. Spatial arrangement of select communities in the Texas borderlands, ca. 1700–1860. Cartography by Luyang Ren.

periphery—which included northern Mexico, parts of New Mexico, and Texas—were characterized by a distinct regional political economy, with various centers of production and diverse exchange networks. Trade in this context not only homogenized consumption patterns; it also forged intergroup alliances and distinct political hierarchies. Even if Native country often operated in indiscernible ways for European and Euro-American observers, a broader logic to it was undeniable.[17]

This is not to suggest that Native people saw themselves as uniformly—or racially—"Native." Quite to the contrary, group identity was dictated more by the respective economic, political, and cultural histories of each community of people rather than some preconceived, racialized notion of Nativeness.[18] In fact, the Native communities of Texas had their own conceptualizations of place and dominion that sometimes operated in opposition to other, neighboring Native communities, because Native notions of space and place often were tied to interpretations of and claims over resource domains, which included both ecological systems and human trade networks.[19] As other scholars have noted, the redrawing of Native borders onto Euro-American-oriented maps is in many ways a futile—and rather colonial—exercise. The limits of Native homelands in Texas shifted according to larger patterns of resource acquisition, such as when communities tracked the seasonal changes of animal migration or gathered wild foodstuffs from different parts of the region during different times of the year. Thus, territoriality—how a group defines "a set of spaces . . . in which a strategy of integrated management of the land is observed"—was the governing mechanism of spatial articulation in Native Texas.[20] Although Euro-American intruders would seek to undermine this system by attempting to impose their own interpretations of boundaries upon Texas, Native territoriality would remain salient and continue to govern community relations well into the middle decades of the nineteenth century. Prior to the latter half of the nineteenth century, Texas was, at its core, a series of Indigenous homelands, the home of Conchos, Sumas, Cocoyames, Mesquites, Cacalotes, Opoxmes, Conejos, Polacmes, Puliques, Poxsalmes, Payayas, Pastias, Pampopas, Cacaxtles, Pacuaches, Ijiabas, Apaysis, Apes, Yoricas, Ocanas, Sampanals, Xarames, Ervipiames, Avavares, Cantonas, Mandones, Chalomes, Sanas, Emets, Cavas, Tohos, Mariames, Tohahas, Pansius, Panequos, Apasams, Muruams, Manams, Naamans, Caisquetebanas, Mayeyes, Biskatronges, Kironas, Palaquechares, Teaos, Yojuanes, Simaomas, Tusonibis, Cascosis, Coapites, Cujanes, Clamcoehs, Temerlouans, Querechos, Escanjaques, Vaqueros, Llaneros, Natagés, Lipanes, Mescaleros, Hasinais, Nabedaches, Nacogdoches, Nadacos, Neches, Nasonis, Caddohadachos, Natchitoches, Adais, Guascos, Tonkawas, Taovayas, Tawakonis, Wichitas, Iscanis, Cocos, Orcoquizas, Bidais, Deadoses, Attacapas, Opelousas, and others.[21]

Contested dominion building, a persistent regional political economy, and the enduring prevalence of Native territoriality meant that Texas existed as *borderlands*. Borderlands are, generally speaking, "contact zones . . . of mobility, spaces where individuals might elude domination." In this sense, fixed, state-oriented boundaries and categories tell only part of the story. Borderlands are places where "face-to-face relationships could . . . trump centrist power and orthodoxies." In the borderlands, membership and power were usually the outcomes of family ties, patron-client relations, and local alliances. At least in these regards, Texas was made of borderlands. Imperial and national prerogatives had a measured influence on life in Texas, but local, intercommunal, and interpersonal relationships often framed the day-to-day terms of living. Moreover, too many historical figures and forces crossed and recrossed the boundaries of modern-day Texas for the boundaries to be given deterministic value. To the contrary, a strict adherence to boundaries handicaps analysis of the many ways people experienced and shaped history in the Texas borderlands. As Samuel Truett has argued, to appreciate borderlands history is to appreciate "the story of many peoples, shaped in distinct ways at the continental crossroads of empires, nations, markets, and cultures."[22]

An appreciation of "continental crossroads," particularly the historical trajectories of Hispanic, Comanche, and Anglo-American people in Texas, alerts us to the fact that the contact zones of the borderlands were not just areas of creative interaction and reinvention; they were also places of pervasive violence. If the dominion-extending drive of slavers was the impetus for Hispanic, then Comanche, and then Anglo-American expansion into the Texas borderlands, slave driving of a very personal sort was the engine of that expansion. Although Strobel's romanticized narrative sought to hide this reality, the testimonies of formerly enslaved people could not; both the day-to-day and the spectacular violence that slavers and their proxies wielded against enslaved people sustained the slaving regimes of the Texas borderlands. As the memories of Ashley and Fuentes reveal, how enslaved people experienced that violence generally reflected the nature of their exploitation. Hispanic slavers typically forced their slaves to toil in their homes and on their ranches, while Comanche slaveholders often subjected their slaves to manufacturing, pastoral, and reproductive labor. Anglo-American slavers, meanwhile, generally committed most enslaved people to torture-driven agricultural production.

Although slavery in the Texas borderlands may not have existed across communities as a uniform economic system, the Hispanic, Comanche, and Anglo-American iterations of slavery resonated throughout the borderlands, sometimes coalescing and overlapping at particular historical moments.[23] A definition of slavery is thus useful for tracking the unique kind of violence that thousands upon thousands of enslaved victims experienced for over a century and a half in Texas. For the purposes of this book, I define slavery as *a personal condition of subjugation that is (1) sustained by the use and threat of violence and by sociocultural stigma and (2) forced upon victims for the purposes of enhancing the disposition (social, psychic, economic, or otherwise) of the slaver.*[24] I borrow from the work of sociologist Orlando Patterson and contend that host societies understood slaves to be "natally alienated and generally dishonored." In other words, it was the initial (and sometimes ongoing) intention of slavers and host communities to strip slaves of any genealogical or historical roots and to exclude them from a sense of respectability or social regard.[25] In this sense, person-to-person coercion and violence worked in conjunction with sociocultural conventions designed to subordinate, to Other-ize, and (especially for Black people) to make fungible. Nonetheless, slaves always served some sort of social, psychic, or economic function within their host communities. Whether it be to locate field or herd laborers, to enhance the productive and reproductive capacities of a household, or to assert personal social worth, slavers procured slaves to fulfill specific community- or individual-based material, psychic, or social needs.[26]

Slavery in the Texas borderlands was never a static institution or system of practices; it was, rather, part of a web of ever-changing processes.[27] Broader economic, political, and cultural changes—including interactions with other forms of slavery—influenced how slavery looked and took shape within and across various communities.[28] As such, *Country of the Cursed and the Driven* tracks the transformations of slaving practices in the Texas borderlands over the course of more than a century and a half. From this historical approach, we can see how *slavers* and *slaving*, terms I employ to emphasize the active, processual nature of slavery in the Texas borderlands, responded to and drove an oft-changing colonial world.[29] Naturally, Hispanic, Comanche, and Anglo-American slaver regimes themselves morphed and mutated over time as well. During the earliest period, Spanish and then Comanche slave raiding (the subject of part I) served as a force of population transfer, simultaneously displacing and relocating communities.[30] When Hispanic and Comanche dominion building came to a head during the latter part of the eighteenth century, transformations across the broader region spawned new impetuses for slaving. Spaniards and Comanches, and then Mexicans and Anglo-Americans, forged surprising, uneasy alliances, with shared if unequal commitments to violence and slavery (the subject of part II) as major terms of their agreements. As Texas became inexorably linked to the expanding Anglo-American cotton frontier in the East, a new era of Anglo-American slaving supremacy emerged. Amid this new era of Anglo power (the subject of part III), slaving would reach unprecedented heights, but shifting power relations did not necessarily foreclose other forms of slavery. Amid the ever-consuming shadow of Anglo-Americans' anti-Black colonial project, Comanche slaving reached its own pinnacle, and some Hispanic residents would reinvent themselves as slavers and slaver proxies too. What is important to note is that slavery's forms emerged not necessarily from some essential set of core cultural attributes (i.e., ownership rights over others, legal institutions of subjugation, and structural racism) but from the nexus of various, ever-changing human networks, prerogatives, and decisions. To understand the full complexion of slavery in the Texas borderlands, we must concede the possibility that slaving systems with unique cultural and historical roots could influence the character of one another. And as this book seeks to demonstrate, the histories of Hispanic, Comanche, and Anglo-American slavery were undeniably interwoven.

With an eye toward the processual, historical character of slavery, it becomes easier to discern how slavery in the Texas borderlands coalesced around two culturally resonant impulses: manly violence and kin incorporation. In a region where states (and their laws) had a limited hold on the day-to-day life of borderlands inhabitants, other social structures—specifically patriarchy and constructs of family—prevailed. In Hispanic, Comanche, and Anglo-American communities alike, manly violence was often the measure of social worth. Men who proved themselves capable of subjugating outsiders generally accrued esteem and standing—honor—within their home societies. For Hispanic people, this ethos was perhaps older than the conquest of the Americas itself, but it certainly flowered in the violent crucible of the Texas borderlands. For Comanches, the celebration of manly violence developed amid the growth and penetration of European colonialism at large, and it would continue to grow well into the nineteenth century. In the Anglo-American slaver-colonial world, manly violence was all too familiar, especially in those sections where people had intimate ties to genocidal frontier warfare and the enslavement of African people and their descendants.

This celebration of manly violence buttressed slaving practices in the Texas borderlands. Slaving violence was, after all, always a mode of domination, and for Hispanic, Comanche, and Anglo-American people, domination was largely a male prerogative.[31] It was perhaps only natural that the family, where men in patriarchal societies typically exercise a very personal, if not intimate, kind of domination, became an important social mechanism for the functioning of Texas slavery.[32] Why and how the integration of enslaved people as kin became a prominent mechanism of slavery varied across Hispanic, Comanche, and Anglo-American communities, but the pervasiveness of kin incorporation is striking. From the earliest days of Spanish colonization, Spaniards integrated enslaved people into their communities by adopting captives as *criados* and godchildren. As the enslavement of Native people was technically illegal in Mexico, Spanish colonists skirted such proscriptions by baptizing captured individuals into what they considered the larger family of Christ. The act may have been embedded in feelings of goodwill and paternalistic benevolence, but baptism also meant that Spaniards could never willingly return these newly minted "Christians" to their supposedly heathen communities, thereby justifying their enslavement. Furthermore, Spaniards sometimes took kin making more literally by sexually exploiting enslaved people, who eventually bore children to further enhance the productive capacities of their households. At least in this regard, the experiences of enslaved Native and Black people in Spanish Texas overlapped. Thus, when enslaved Native and Afro-Mexican people carried the surnames of their slavers, it was not just an expression of imagined paternalistic prerogative; sometimes the phenomenon spoke to real, painful, and traumatic processes of family making.

In Comanche society, slave integration emerged less out of attempts at subterfuge and more in response to changing technological, economic, and demographic imperatives. With ever-expanding livestock herds (the primary vehicle for Comanche reinvention amid a destructive colonial world), Comanche men were able to meet labor demands by incorporating young enslaved children into their households—as opposed to selling them away as trade commodities. Comanche men also forcefully brought enslaved women into their households through marriage. As polygynists, Comanche men undoubtedly exploited their new enslaved wives for economic purposes. Because Comanche women were among the principal producers of manufactured goods in Comanche communities, in addition to maintaining the livability of Comanche households, Comanche slave-wives were responsible for bearing and rearing the children of their slaver-husbands. Although forced reproduction necessarily boosted the economic and demographic vibrancy of Comanche communities by introducing new, productive members, the bearing of children also came with the burdens of forced child rearing. For women enslaved by Comanches, family making was a central aspect of their condition as slaves.

Anglo-American slavery in Texas also functioned according to mechanisms of kin incorporation. The most obvious was the system of paternalism that created fictions of family between enslaved people and their slavers. Anglo-American slavers considered slaves subordinate members of their male-headed families and sometimes forced them to take their surnames. The notion that slaves were members of Anglo-American slaveholding families grew especially popular as Anglo-American colonists defended their institution against attempted Mexican governmental sanction. Fictitious and rhetorical as it may have been, it allowed for the normalization of the sexual and reproductive exploitation of enslaved people. Enslaved Black people suffered not only from the direct sexual violence of their slavers (and their proxies) but also from the pain associated with bringing their children into a world of slavery. Moreover, the familial ties that Anglo-American slaveholders forced on their slaves made fugitive escape *also* the abandonment of metaphorical and literal family members—a heartbreaking and potentially disorienting alternative to life as a slave.

Slaver violence and forced incorporation effectively cursed the enslaved people of the Texas borderlands. Although practically incorporated into their host communities, enslaved people regularly bore the stigmas of a debased, outsider status. For enslaved Black people, their Blackness—as defined by Hispanic and Anglo-American slaving societies—was their curse, and like many curses, it was transgenerational, passed on from parent to child. Non-Black enslaved people were less likely to suffer from heritable stigmas, but their stigmatized status could leave them similarly isolated and vulnerable to personal violence. Yet the fact that the dishonor of Blackness remained so enduring—if not entirely monolithic in meaning—amid the instability of the borderlands reinforces the notion that anti-Blackness has often thrived wherever European-driven colonialism has extended its long tentacles.[33] Evidence even suggests that some Comanches learned to discern Blackness from their colonial encounters. In this sense, the curse of slavery, transgenerational and ever-translatable, was most poignant and unrelenting for the Black population of Texas. Revealingly, in a land where slaving victimizers sometimes became slaving victims, only on the rarest of occasions did Black inhabitants become the victimizers of slavery.[34]

But if enslaved people faced stigmatization and dishonor in their host communities, why did the slavers of Texas so often feel compelled to incorporate their slaves as literal and figurative members of their families? Although paradoxical, kin incorporation of the generally dishonored was rooted in a very practical problem: the *inclusion* of "the stranger while continuing to treat him as a stranger."[35] The family structure provided one of the most important and expedient ways to incorporate exploited outsiders into the slaver societies of Texas. On a logistical level, households were convenient settings for controlling and monitoring individuals who generally resented or challenged slaver and host authority. On an ideological level, the slaver-slave relationship paralleled the other patriarchal relationships of Hispanic, Comanche, and Anglo-American people. Submission to male authority was the basis for social organization at multiple levels across these societies, and in the borderlands, where states had minimal to no control over the everyday lives of people, the family unit offered a pliable apparatus for the manipulation, exploitation, and surveillance of enslaved bodies.[36]

Appreciation of slavery's ties to kin making also helps us to overcome the historiographical gulf that persists between the literatures on Euro-American and Native American slaveries. Until relatively recently, there has been a tendency for scholars to draw rather hard distinctions between the kind of slavery practiced by Anglo-Americans and that practiced by Native people.[37] According to these formulations, Native slavery—and to an extent, the enslavement of Native people by Euro-American agents—is better characterized as *captivity*, while the Anglo-American enslavement of Black people deserves the title of *slavery* proper.[38] In the literature on anti-Black slavery in North America, scholars generally affix the term "slavery" to a state of bondage with economic, property-centered underpinnings. Certainly, scholars have examined the social, political, cultural, psychic, and ontological foundations of Anglo-American slavery, but the historiographical consensus is that Anglo-American slavery was at its core a mode of economic production. According to this line of reasoning, slaves would not have existed had slavers not found commercial outlets for the output of their labor. Furthermore, the fact that slaves were owned legally by their slavers meant that they and their children existed as chattels, theoretically outside of the social structures that governed host communities. In this way, slaves were almost identical to domesticated animals.[39]

On the flip side, a sizable contingent of scholars has been reluctant to characterize Native slavery as anything like Anglo-American slavery.[40] To many, *captivity* better describes Native slaving practices because the state of bondspeople under Native rule was more precarious, ever-changing, and less tied to economic relations. According to this formulation, captivity was above all enmeshed in sociocultural and political meaning rather than economic significance.[41] Thus, when a captor traded a captive for goods or other captives, the exchange was to facilitate or to ease diplomacy, not to extract or to produce wealth. In this sense, these captives were more akin to *prisoners* or *detained outsiders* than to slaves.[42] Finally, in making the case that captivity better describes the condition of slaving victims, scholars have highlighted the importance of adoption and marriage. Captives could not have been slaves, the reasoning goes, because, unlike Black chattels (the victims of hereditable slavery), these individuals and their children could be incorporated as "full members" of their host communities.[43]

Interpretations of captivity that identify kin incorporation as evidence of captivity's inherent difference from slavery have missed an important aspect regarding the adoption and marriage of captured people: such relationships were, regardless of their captor's intentions, still defined by the unilateral violence that captors could dispense against their victims. Without question, significant differences existed between slavery's roles within diverse slaving societies; depending on a number of factors, the enslavement of others could serve economic, geopolitical, religious, social, and psychic purposes. But what of the enslaved herself? If her enslavement was meant to contribute to the demographic viability of the host community, was the exploitation of her reproductive capacities somehow less cruel or burdensome? Did the time and energy that the forcefully incorporated person put into her new "family" not count as slave labor? *Country of the Cursed and the Driven* challenges these assumptions. Substantial disjunction of perspective *must* have existed among enslaved people and their slavers. The fact that captured people were adopted or married into the host societies simply meant that *their slavers* desired to embed them within a familial setting. The interpretations of enslaved people were still structured by their sense of loss, natal alienation, and personal suffering.[44]

An examination of slavery's ties to kin making not only opens up our broader understanding of how slaving systems sometimes operate; it also helps us to locate enslaved people in places that scholars generally have overlooked. Specifically, the household, where the everyday practices of slavery were often located, becomes a critical unit of analysis.[45] This has not always been the case in studies of slavery in Texas. In fact, appropriation of the kin-making-is-not-slavery model has hidden and obscured much of the history of slavery in Texas prior to the 1820s.[46] Because both contemporary historical actors and generations of scholars have subsumed the violence of slave incorporation under notions of adoption, marriage, and other forms of kin integration, "slaves" literally have disappeared in the historical record. Yet, once we interrogate the assumption that family making was inherently benevolent and mutually advantageous for all parties involved, we begin to see how kin incorporation could be—and often was—a mechanism of enslavement. Moreover, it becomes somewhat easier to locate these enslaved family members in the documentary record. Thus, *Country of the Cursed and the Driven* argues that family and slavery were not diametrically opposed. In many ways, they could be two sides of the same coin.

Finally, a book about enslaved people, violence, and Native communities requires at least a brief rumination on representations of violence. First and foremost, it is *not* my intention to reproduce narratives of slaving violence and suffering carelessly or unwittingly. As Saidiya Hartman has argued, it is imperative that scholars call attention to "the ease with which . . . scenes [of brutality] are usually reiterated [and] the casualness with which they are circulated." When it comes to brutality against enslaved bodies, she has explained, the consequences of such a "routine display" can be disturbing: "Rather than inciting indignation, too often they immure us to pain by virtue of their familiarity—the oft-repeated or restored character of these accounts and our distance from them are signaled by the theatricality of language usually resorted to in describing these instances—and especially because they reinforce the spectacular character of black suffering."[47] Rightfully so, Hartman has emphasized how narratives of violence against enslaved people have cultivated—and continue to cultivate—the fungibility of Black bodies, yet her warning is also pertinent when it comes to the history of Native people in the Americas. Over the course of half a millennium Native people have been the victims of what we might think of as rhetorical violence—that is, systems of discourse that are aimed at justifying the administration of violence against a group of people—and I do not seek to perpetuate such violence. Instead, with this book I hope to underscore the fact that Native people are just that: people. There is nothing innately different about Native people, and as a descendant of the tangled genealogical webs of a colonized Native America, I have no desire to deny my own personhood. What I want to make clear is that Native people in the Texas borderlands were capable of every human attribute, even the capacity to administer terrible violence over the course of many decades. The violence of Native people, however, was not devoid of a larger sociocultural or economic logic, nor was it divorced from the larger context of European colonial invasion and extraction. Like the violence of Euro-Americans, Native violence was complex and historical in nature. In my estimation, this study reveals more about male propensities to violence and the reverberations of European colonialism, which "tended to have an accelerant effect on . . . preexisting indigenous violence," than anything else. But in the Texas borderlands, patriarchy and the legacies of colonialism were not exclusive to a single group; they were cross-cultural.[48]

Above all, my intention is to contextualize violence, to construct a historical narrative that illuminates the specific geopolitical, economic, social, and cultural circumstances that gave rise to separate but imbricated slaving systems. *Country of the Cursed and the Driven* is a study of violence as process and as structure, a "link-chain . . . [that is] always and everywhere subject to change." As a scholar with a forum to speak about violence, I offer my analysis of these violent worlds in hopes of shedding light on some of the ways in which people envision, practice, react to, build from, conceal, and justify violence.[49] If we are to learn from the consequences of violence, it is imperative that we spotlight the origins and "instrumentality" of violence, that we challenge the assumption that violence is simply natural or essential to human experience. Therefore, this book endeavors to explain how both communities and individuals—historical agents—are at the heart of violence.[50]

But inherent limitations persist. As the late Comanche historian Francis Joseph Attocknie declared in the preface to his sketch of his people's history, "It would be beyond the capability of any modern researcher to properly present the great and adventuresome Comanches of the past."[51] The same could be said for all of the Native people of the eighteenth- and nineteenth-century Texas borderlands, who left few contemporary documents of their own creation. Likewise, it is an equally gargantuan task to represent adequately the experiences of the tens of thousands of Black people enslaved in Texas, whose vast silences in the historical record betray their expressions of outrage as well as their day-to-day enunciations of personhood, agency, and resistance. Mostly built on a documentary record derived from or filtered through Euro-American colonial lenses, *Country of the Cursed and the Driven* is necessarily beset with analytical shortcomings. Nonetheless, this book operates according to the belief that a more nuanced *historical* account of slavery's diverse story in the Texas borderlands, one that charts change over time, can help modern readers to approach a fuller understanding of those experiences. Theoretical modeling is of only limited utility in re-creating these past worlds. "No timeless ethnographic categories or political definitions," Ned Blackhawk has argued, "characterize . . . Native peoples."[52] Life in the Texas borderlands ebbed and flowed for its inhabitants according to changing relations of violence, exploitation, resource allocation, and community movement. *Country of the Cursed and the Driven* seeks to elucidate those changing relations, as well as the places of the diverse Texas inhabitants within them.

Part I
Slave Raiders and Their Cycles of Violence, 1500s–1760s

On May 12, 1745, a party of Spanish colonists marched into the church of San Fernando de Béxar, located in the heart of Spanish Texas, with fourteen Native children, most of them Apache, and all ten years or younger. The Spanish escorts were predominantly soldiers, men such as Luis Menchaca, Martín Flores, and Luis Maldonado, but a few women, including Juana de Urrutia, also accompanied the group. On the surface, this was supposed to be a holy day, a day on which these fourteen young children were to be received, through rituals of prayer and holy oil, into the comfort of a great Christian family. As *padrinos* and *madrinas*, godfathers and godmothers, the accompanying Spaniards made promises before the observing priest and the larger Christian community to protect and cherish these new converts, for their souls belonged to God above. Demonstrating the new, Christian beginnings for these children, all but one were given new names. A seven-year-old girl became "María." A five-year-old was made "Francisca." And a two-year-old was now "Joseph Antonio."[1]

In the realm of Spanish colonial discourse, this was more evidence of the righteousness of the Spanish conquest of the Americas, evidence that Spanish colonists were doing the work of God Almighty. But for those fourteen children, whose biological families were nowhere to be seen during these rituals of kin and community incorporation, this was the start of a new life of slavery. Only weeks earlier had they, along with their friends and families, fallen victim to a massive, "punitive" Spanish-led slave raid on their Ypande and Natages communities.[2] Ripped from their homes, alienated from their customs of living, these children were, according to the colonial record, becoming Christianized. Yet on a practical level, their baptism meant that they were forever tethered to the Hispanic world, destined to a life of abuse, exploitation, and possibly even sexual violence.

The experiences of these fourteen children, and the systems of violence that circumscribed their experiences, have often eluded the analysis of Texas slavery scholars. To a large extent, this exclusion has been a function of a strict definition of slavery. When Randolph Campbell wrote in his 1989 seminal study that the "nature of Texas's historical experience with slavery" was "limited," what he meant by *slavery* was *anti-Black chattel slavery*. Like so many others who have written about the history of slavery in North America, Campbell's understanding of slavery was rooted in the prevailing legal structure that defined the conditions and existence of enslaved people. As Campbell has argued, "Slavery, wherever it existed, needed protective laws."[3] Although his comment partly reflects his concern with how Anglo-Texans sought to solidify slavery's standing in a new colonial context, the enunciation of the relationship between law and slavery remains one of the guiding frameworks of North American slavery's analysis. Even Jason Gillmer, who has characterized the history of Texas slavery as "messy," has attributed this messiness to the fact that "the *law* was flexible and fluid and able to adapt to everyday experiences."[4]

Many scholars have ignored the early, pre-nineteenth-century history of slavery in Texas because their formulations of slavery, like those of Campbell and Gillmer, depend upon recognition of state power.[5] Because the state—manifested through the legal structures of Spaniards, Mexicans, Texians, and U.S. Americans—established the parameters of a slave's existence, the thinking goes, all explorations of slavery in Texas necessarily track the history of state-building in the region. Thus, historians generally have mapped out the changes in Texas slavery according to distinct political eras: the Spanish-Mexican period, the Republican period, and the Statehood period.[6]

But this approach misses an important point: the state did not always exercise totalizing influence in Texas. *Texas* itself—as a political construct—changed over time as state power waxed and waned, especially prior to the mid-nineteenth century. Texas was made of borderlands, where local, intercommunal, and interpersonal relationships often framed the terms of day-to-day living more so than imperial and national prerogatives.[7] In this context, slavery is better understood as *borderlands slavery*. During the eighteenth century, the primary state apparatuses, the Church and the Spanish Crown, asserted only limited influence on slaving practices. Although the state established laws to dictate slavery's existence, Texas borderlanders regularly ignored or circumvented them. In some cases, Spanish colonists even co-opted institutional practices, like baptism, to subvert the dictates of the state. Ultimately, the borderlands communities themselves established the meanings of experiences of enslavement in Texas. In short, to appreciate the role of slavery in Texas, especially during the early years, scholars must expand both their definitions of slavery and their interpretation of Texas geography.

Part I elaborates the mass relocation of Spaniards and Comanches into the Texas borderlands, from the sixteenth into the eighteenth century, highlighting the roles of slave raiding and violence as engines of community movement. It advances the argument that the history of slavery in Texas can be explained only by connecting it to larger historical processes that began beyond the geographical limits of modern-day Texas. During these early decades, both Spaniards and Comanches—the principal actors in these chapters—enmeshed themselves in colonialism-spawned cycles of violence. For Spaniards, colonial settlement in Texas drew energy from the larger conquest of Mexico, where slaving violence and exploitation spread the Spanish colonial reach far and wide, including the current U.S. Southwest. During the seventeenth century, Spaniards struggled to overcome their reputation as slavers, but by the 1710s Spaniards managed to establish a solid foothold in the heart of Texas, partly by convincing locals of their military utility. Within a few years of settler colonization, these military alliances against Ndé *naciones* would serve as the basis for their new slaving regime—and thus their assertion of Spanish dominance in the region. For Comanches, their great sweep toward Texas, which became readily apparent to Spaniards by the mid-eighteenth century, echoed the violence of their Spanish predecessors and operated according to a series of slave raids against many of the same Ndé victims. Although Comanches were successful at expanding their influence—incorporating transformative technologies and integrating themselves in a broad, cross-regional network of commerce—they did so at a great cost. Their slave-raid-based expansion, like that of their Spanish counterparts, necessarily made them the enemies of certain peoples who already claimed the borderlands as their homelands.

It was also during these decades that the seeds of later, more totalizing forms of Texas slavery were sown. Although evidence regarding the quotidian character of slavery is especially sparse during these decades, some patterns are discernable. The larger thread of anti-Blackness, for instance, remains visible, even in the thin documentary record. Anti-Blackness—the association of Blackness with slavery and dishonor that makes Black bodies fungible, accumulable, and extinguishable—gained greater currency during the formidable years of the Spanish conquest of the Americas, and as Spaniards forged their path toward Texas, Spanish colonialism would continue to implicate Black (i.e., African-descended) people, as slaves and as colonists.[8] Even as the ostensibly Black population of Texas was relatively small, Blackness retained its salience as a symbol of dishonor.[9] Equally important, if not more so during this period, was the Spanish antagonizing of Indigeneity, or as Spaniards termed it, Indian savagery. Like anti-Blackness, Spanish discourses of Indian savagery simultaneously emerged out of and were fueled by Spanish slaving violence. Spanish colonizers Other-ized Native people (i.e., as non-Christian and uncivilized) as they subjugated local populations and entrenched their settler colonial project.[10] When Native people resisted with violence of their own, Spanish claims of victimhood became the justifications for new waves of "punitive" slaving violence. In this way, Spanish slaving in the Texas borderlands was part of a larger feedback loop of Spanish colonial violence.[11]

In the context of Comanche slavery, extant evidence from this early period provides few clues regarding the social status of enslaved people. Yet some inferences can be made regarding the importance of kin incorporation as a significant mode of enslavement within Comanche communities. Comanche slavers seemed to have preferred to enslave children and women, who, as enslaved fictive kin, offered special, gendered economic and demographic contributions to their host communities. The same could be said for the Spanish slavers of the Texas borderlands, who also favored enslaved women and children. As was likely the case within Comanche contexts, slavers in Spanish Texas forcefully integrated those they enslaved, supposedly as family, to help sustain the fledgling Spanish communities. For Spanish colonists, Christian rituals, particularly baptism and the familial relationship of *compadrazgo*, or godparenthood, were the mechanisms, along with violence, through which Spanish slavers solidified their control of enslaved bodies.

1 / "Obliged to Punish and Conquer These Indians": Slavery and the Hispanic Path to Colonization in Texas, pre-1717

On March 9, 1707, Sargento Mayor Diego Ramón departed from San Juan Bautista del Norte presidio, a military outpost on the far northern frontier of Mexico, along with Fray Isidro de Espinosa, thirty-one soldiers and *vecinos*[1] from nearby colonial settlements, and a Native guide from Mission San Juan Bautista. Their mission, as decreed by Governor Martín de Alarcón, was to punish the rebellious *ladino*[2] Indians who had been stealing horses and killing Spaniards across Nuevo León, and their journey from the western banks of the Río Grande took them across the great river into Texas, as far northeast as the modern-day city of Cotulla. Along the way, the party encountered a number of Native bands, who in exchange for tobacco, knives, and other goods offered both safe passage and important military intelligence about *los indios enemigos*, the enemy Indians of the region. With a little inducement, Ramón was even fortunate enough to recruit several of them as spies.[3]

The Spanish forces reached a *ranchería*, or encampment community, belonging to the rebellious Pelones on March 26. But before attacking, Ramón gave to his followers an express order not to kill a single Indian "if they do not offer much resistance, because they are only to be taken alive." Invoking the name of the apostle Santiago, Ramón and his men charged the Native gathering with great fury, exchanging blows with the defenders. Nearby Native fighters rallied to the defense of the Pelones, but their efforts were no match for the well-armed Spanish soldiers. In the end, the expeditioners killed ten Native fighters and enslaved twenty-five

Native men, women, and children. After investigating the remains of the large *ranchería*, Ramón counted a total of fifteen huts crafted from the hides of horses he assumed the Pelones had stolen. The presumed evidence of contraband was confirmation of a job well done.

After Ramón and his men returned to San Juan Bautista, Ramón distributed the *presas*, or prisoners, "into equal parts." With this act, Ramón gave voice to an impulse that for generations had undergirded many similar kinds of Spanish campaigns on Mexico's northern frontier: the impulse to enslave. By passing his prisoners into the hands of Spanish colonists, who were to educate them in the Christian way of life, Ramón had sentenced these unfortunate men, women, and children to a life of slavery. His conditions of possession, which stipulated their instruction in "the Mysteries of the Holy Faith," were more than a bureaucratic gesturing to an all-pervasive Catholic ideology; they were critical to the legitimation of the prisoners' enslavement by Spanish colonists. Once baptized, the Native *presas* were made part of the holy Christian family and were never to return to their purportedly godless homeland. This last step of metaphorical kin incorporation ensured a life of subjugation in the Spanish world of the Mexican Northeast.

Although Ramón's 1707 expedition may not have been a watershed moment in Texas history, it did mark the arrival of the Spanish slaving frontier in the Texas borderlands. For nearly two centuries, Spanish colonial expansion from the heart of Mexico into the North proceeded according to cycles of violence. The desire to acquire slaves, coupled with Spanish mineral obsessions and religious fervor, drove Hispanic people northward. When Native people resisted, subsequent Spanish slave-raiding measures, couched in the language of Christianization and "punishment," expedited colonial expansion outward. With each Native attack upon the budding Spanish communities along the ever-shifting northern frontier, Spaniards responded with equally intense violence, for in the eyes of Spanish colonists, the Indians' intransigence and bellicosity justified their enslavement. Even as Spanish officials attempted to curb *la esclavitud de los indios* through various legal means, the cycles of violence that engulfed the northern frontier—in tandem with a general Spanish willingness to subsume slavery under the umbrella project of Christianization—ultimately fueled slavery's perpetuation for decades to come. Unfortunately for Native resistors, the violence that was meant to check Spanish expansion in effect drew Spaniards ever closer to previously unexposed Native populations. By the time Spanish colonial operatives began making sustained forays into the heart of Texas during the second half of the seventeenth century, their frontier violence already had reverberated well beyond their colonial gaze.[4] Spanish slaving had been so prominent for so long that the various Native peoples of the far Northeast were often skeptical of Spaniards, if not actively hostile.

Here we begin our sweeping narrative of slavery in the Texas borderlands by situating the Spanish Texas colonial project within a longer history of Spanish slaving practices. When Spain finally began to invest energy and resources into Texas during the late seventeenth and early eighteenth centuries, slavery already had been woven into the fabric of Spanish colonialism. The individuals who built Spanish Texas during the eighteenth century, like Ramón and his followers, were veterans of Spanish slaving violence elsewhere along the frontier. It was such men who laid the rhetorical groundwork for future generations of slaving violence, conflating the quest for power, dominance, and exploitable labor with paternalistic notions of "punishment" and Christianization—as so many of their predecessors had done in previous frontier contexts. Just as important, they were also men (and women) who brought with them the legacies of anti-Black slavery. As scholars have noted, more enslaved Africans were sent to Mexico than any other Spanish-ruled colony in the Americas prior to 1640, and the introduction of enslaved African men, women, and children during the sixteenth and seventeenth centuries contributed to the diversity of slavery and people in the budding Spanish colonial outposts of the Northeast.[5] In the context of Spanish-induced cycles of violence, the enslavement of Black people generally complemented Spanish subjugation efforts, with enslaved Black people serving as both an exploitable labor force and symbols of Hispanic domination. Although the prominence of anti-Black slavery receded as the Spanish frontier extended northward, by the eighteenth century *la esclavitud de los negros* still persisted and would remain salient in Spanish Texas.

This chapter thus builds on the growing scholarship of slavery in Mexico by exploring how Spanish practices of anti-Native and anti-Black slaving violence colored the slow colonial advance of Spaniards toward the Texas borderlands.[6] When Hispanic colonists finally arrived in Texas, they did not abandon their expectations regarding Native and Black subjugation, nor did they suddenly invent new institutions of bondage and exploitation. Instead, they adapted their colonial knowledge and practices to the unique circumstances of the borderlands, where no single group of people had yet asserted—or cared to assert—total dominion over the region. Their conversion to the borderlands context would prove to be a difficult, arduous process, but many remained convinced that their drive for mineral, religious, and military conquests were to be buoyed by the enslavement of Native and Black bodies.

"We Would Make Them Slaves": The Origins of Spanish Slaving in Mexico

The Spanish slaving practices that surfaced in Texas during the eighteenth century were part of a long history of Spanish violence against Native and African peoples in the Americas. The initial catalyst for Spanish northern migration after the conquest of the Aztecs in central Mexico was the quest for quick riches. In the aftermath of the fall of Tenochtitlán, Spanish colonists searched far and wide for duplications of the great mineral wealth served up by the conquered Mexican empire. The expeditions led by Pánfilo de Narváez (1527), Hernando de Soto (1539), and Francisco Vázquez de Coronado (1540) left destructive, indelible marks on both the Native landscapes of North America and the imaginations of their European contemporaries; yet, for over two decades, such wide-reaching Spanish exploration efforts yielded only small mineral discoveries.[7] Moreover, by 1540 a surge in Spanish-Native warfare indicated that subsequent expeditions north would have to contend with Indigenous resistance. Spaniards remained ambitious and oppressive, but events suggested that the future was bleak.[8]

This all changed with Juan de Tolosa's discovery of silver at Zacatecas in 1546, as the prospects of mineral riches revitalized Spanish efforts to populate the northern frontier of New Spain. Occurring only four years after the close of the Mixtón War, the discovery of silver unleashed the collective energies of Spanish entrepreneurialism and evangelism, energies that would thrust Spanish colonial endeavors northward for the next two and a half centuries.[9] Within a few years, Zacatecas would develop into a rich mining town, home to dozens of mining companies, bands of soldiers, hundreds of Spanish mine workers, muleteers, and more than a hundred enslaved *negro*[10] people. Mine owners built stamp mills and ore-refining plants and imported mine workers from Michoacán and the central valleys of Mexico. Soon Zacatecas was surrounded by villages of Tarascan, Mexican, Tlaxcalan, and Texcocan laborers. From this colonization also emerged generations of wealthy and widely influential Spanish families, including the Oñates, the Zaldivars, and the Ibarras, as well as inspiration for further colonial exploration. Soon more mining towns appeared farther north, including Guanajuato (1552–53), San Martín

(1556–57), Sombrerete (ca. 1558), Avino (ca. 1558), Mazapil (1560), Santa Bárbara (1567), and Cerro de San Pedro (1583). Thus, by the end of the sixteenth century, the Spanish mining frontier was rapidly approaching the southern border of the modern-day United States.[11]

But this is not to suggest that the northward advance of Spanish colonialism was an uncontested process. From the earliest days of Spain's mining frenzy, Native people resisted.[12] Zacatecas, for instance, was located in the interior of the Gran Chichimeca, a vast territory that stretched across the modern states of Jalisco, Aguasclientes, Nayarit, Guanajuato, and Zacatecas, where a number of diverse groups of Pames, Guamares, Zacatecos, and Guadichiles resided. As the roads that led to Zacatecas (and the subsequently established mining centers) cut through the hunting grounds of the various Chichimecan[13] peoples, the colonial caravans, mule trains, and travelers that trekked along El Camino Real became the object of Chichimeca assaults. Localized violence on the royal roadways quickly escalated to full-scale warfare, and for the next four decades Native people battled Spaniards for preservation of their homelands in northern Mexico. And although a clear-cut Spanish policy was slow to develop in response to this violence, Indigenous attacks along the silver highways and at nearby colonial estates eventually were countered with Spanish fortification efforts and direct reprisals. Thus, by the mid-1550s, general hostility characterized Native-Spanish relations on New Spain's northern frontier. Warfare had become virtually continuous, and as Spanish colonial ambitions continued unabated, few could anticipate an end to the struggle. It was against this backdrop of *la guerra Chichimeca*, the Chichimeca War, that the broader outlines of Spanish practices and policies regarding anti-Native slavery took a lasting shape.[14]

The enslavement of the Indigenous peoples of the Americas had been part and parcel of Spanish conquest and colonization since the arrival of Cristobal Colón in 1492. As Andrés Reséndez has argued, Colón actually "intended to turn the Caribbean into another Guinea" by re-creating in the New World the Portuguese slave-trading system he had participated in on the coasts of western Africa. Although Colón's transatlantic slave-trading goals proved to be too ambitious for the Catholic monarchs who financed his Caribbean enterprise, their reservations did not prevent him and his men from exploiting the local populations on the islands themselves, where enslaved Native people were forced to mine and pan for gold, dive for pearls, and meet every other desire of the Spanish invaders. From the Caribbean such coercive practices leapfrogged onto the continental mainland during Hernán Cortés's conquest of the Aztecs.[15] Cortés himself was a major slaver during the early wars in central and southeastern Mexico (1520s), and Spaniards enslaved people from a number of different locales, including Cholula, Cachula, Texcoco, Cuernavaca, and Guastepeque. Even the Spanish monarchs ultimately took part in the proliferation of anti-Native slavery, receiving a *quinto*, or fifth, of all slaves taken. During the early days of Spanish colonialism in the Americas, conquest was often indiscernible from wholesale enslavement.[16]

Slavery was a direct and justifiable byproduct of war in the minds of Spanish conquerors. For the early Spanish colonists of Mexico, warfare necessarily yielded material rewards, and some of the more coveted prizes were *esclavos de guerra*, slaves of war. Slave acquisition through warfare was a practice justified by appeals to European Just War theory, which demanded that war be conducted "in order that the peoples shall increase their faith and that those who would combat it shall be destroyed." Theorists like the sixteenth-century Juan López de Palacios Rubios argued that Indians were to embrace the Christian faith voluntarily, but they could not refuse Christian (Spanish) rule. Those who refused Christian subjugation were condemned—by the will of God—to face enslavement. Buttressed by such logic, "just" warfare thus accounted for the enslavement of thousands of Indigenous resistors. As one of Cortés's soldiers explained, "If they [the Indians] did not come in peace but wished to give us war, we would make them slaves; and we carried with us an iron brand like this one to mark their faces."[17]

But warfare was not the only means of slave accumulation; Spaniards also obtained slaves through the *rescate*, or ransoming, of captives held by Native nations. The practice of *rescate* originated during the Spanish Reconquista of earlier centuries, when Christians of the Iberian peninsula were susceptible to Muslim enslavement. Because enslaved life in a Muslim world appeared horrifying to Christians, Redemptionist Orders collected funds to purchase the freedom and repatriation of enslaved Christians. *Rescate* was intended to be a noble practice, but it was not long before Spaniards employed the language of *rescate* to obscure the nature of their slave-trading practices, particularly along the coasts of Africa. In the context of Mexico, Spaniards justified the purchase of enslaved Indians from Native slavers by claiming honorable intentions—that is, the redemption of Native souls from the grips of heathenism. The practice of *rescate* was immediately legitimated in Mexico when the king issued a royal *cédula* on October 15, 1522. Upon hearing of the royal declaration, Cortés prophesied that with the influx of new Indian slaves, New Spain would produce more gold than all of the American islands combined.[18] In this way, Cortés and his Spanish successors tethered acts of enslavement to a broader Christianizing mission.

Nuño Beltrán de Guzmán was perhaps the most notorious slaver of the sixteenth century. Made governor of Pánuco in 1525 and president of the highest Spanish court in New Spain (the Real Audiencia de México) four years later, Guzmán oversaw the vast expansion of *la esclavitud de los indios* on the continental mainland. In Pánuco, he sanctioned and regulated the *rescate* of Native captives, justifying the practice of *rescate* as a means to protect enslaved individuals from the supposed cannibalism of their captors. Guzmán was also instrumental in the Spanish advance northward. Unsatisfied with his exploration of the Río de las Palmes, Guzmán took it upon himself to expand the northern frontier of New Spain, journeying to far-off places like present-day Jalisco, Zacatecas, Nayarit, and Sinaloa. With him, of course, came his lust for slave hunting and violence, and he left a trail of bloodshed and destruction along the Pacific Coast of New Spain. In Michoacán alone, Guzmán enslaved several thousand Native people, many of whom were forced to march in chains for miles upon miles. Perhaps as transformative as Guzmán's personally led conquests were his cavalry detachments of soldiers, whose principal task was to seek out and enslave the Native people of the northwestern frontier. These detachments did much to engender fear and desperation across the North, but they also paved the way for further Spanish colonization, each incursion enhancing Spanish knowledge of the region.[19]

Thus, by the mid-sixteenth century and the start of the Chichimeca War, at least tens of thousands of Native people already had fallen prey to Spanish slaving operations.[20] With enslaved people serving as laborers and trade commodities, slave wealth had proven to be one of the most alluring enticements of New Spain, and Spaniards of all ranks continuously pressed for an expansion in both the scope and frequency of slaving. Their slaving ambitions were not, however, left unchecked, as various critics, including Bartolomé de las Casas, challenged the practices of Indigenous enslavement and exploitation. Las Casas's appeals to the Spanish Crown began as early as the second decade of the sixteenth century, and by 1542 he had secured enough influence among royal authorities to effect the passage of las Leyes Nuevas, the New Laws. Signed by King Carlos II, the New Laws called for vast reforms, including the elimination of anti-Indian slavery, the curtailment of the tribute and forced labor system known as the *encomienda*, and the prohibition of wars of conquest.[21] These laws infuriated the *encomenderos* (the grantees of *encomiendas*) and conquistadors of the Americas, but they did not effectively end *la esclavitud de los indios*. As before, the enslavement of Native people continued during wars and interactions with vilified, non-Christian *indios*.[22]

Las Leyes Nuevas and the ideological assaults of Las Casas and others also contributed to the rise of another form of slavery in New Spain: anti-Black slavery. Enslaved African men, women, and children had been forced to make their way to Spanish America as early as 1501, but a strong emphasis on African slave labor—as opposed to Native slave labor—emerged as Spanish commentators began to condemn Spanish abuses against Indigenous people. As one of the more tragic ironies of the era, Las Casas, the theologian most responsible for the intellectual attack against the enslavement of Native people, may have been among those most responsible for the ideological defense of African-based slavery. According to Las Casas, the importation of enslaved Africans was the "solution" to the problem of anti-Native slavery in the Americas. But Las Casas was not alone in espousing the benefits of anti-Black slavery. In 1518, one Spanish high official, Alonso Zuazo, argued, "This land is the best that there is in the world for negroes, for the women, for the old men, [and] it is a great marvel when one sees any of these people die."[23]

Thus, enslavement of Native and Black people was inextricably intertwined in the early history of New Spain. Laws and prohibitions designed to limit and curtail the enslavement of Native people jump-started the mass enslavement of Africans in Spanish America. Statistical figures tell part of the story. In 1553, about three and a half decades after Cortés's arrival in the Mexican mainland, Spanish officials estimated that there were some 20,000 African individuals living in New Spain. By 1643, 80,000 Afro-Mexicans were said to be living as slaves in Mexico. Three years later, a census indicated that 151,618 Black people were residing in the region. Some of this population growth can be explained through natural processes of reproduction, but much of it was rooted in one of the largest American slave-trading enterprises of its time. From 1521 to 1639, over 110,000 enslaved individuals, most from central and eastern parts of Africa, were imported into Mexico, with about 50,500 during the years 1595 to 1622 and another 23,500 during the years 1623 to 1639. "From New Spain's inception," Herman L. Bennett has argued, "Africans had a discernable presence."[24]

The ideological expediency of anti-Black slavery notwithstanding, Spaniards were interested in accumulating African men, women, and children in Mexico to meet labor demands. Enslaved Africans toiled under the harsh conditions of *obrajes* (factory workshops), worked as land clearers, tillers, and harvesters on great sugar plantations, and regularly labored in the dangerous mines spread out across Mexico. In the highly urbanized centers of New Spain, enslaved Black people were especially coveted as domestic and personal servants. And across Mexico, enslaved Afro-Mexicans could be found employed as teamsters, artisan assistants, and even soldiers.[25]

An emphasis solely on the labor of enslaved Africans and their descendants nonetheless obscures the remarkable fungibility of Black bodies in Spanish America. Corporeal violence against enslaved Black people established the conditions of a slave's personal subjugation and, as Bennett has noted, also "reminde[d] both previous arrivals and those born into slavery that domination daily constructed their debased status." In this way, cross-generational violence created Blackness as a unique, self-reinforcing stigma of dishonor for the populations of Spanish Mexico that descended from Africa. It also meant that the enslavement of Afro-Mexican people generated anti-Blackness, as it sought to curtail and deny the personhood of Black people while simultaneously lifting the Spanish ruling class to levels of higher social respectability. Yet even as anti-Blackness probably remained most potent as a platform for perpetual personal domination, Spaniards still exploited Black bodies for other purposes. As Bennett has argued in his study of seventeenth-century Mexican ecclesiastical proceedings on Black sexuality, the Catholic Church also attempted to use Black bodies in ways that would have resonated among their subjugated Native contemporaries—as sites for testing the power of its broader civilizing program. Like Native "neophytes," Hispanicized Black people provided Spanish observers with evidence of the efficacy of Christian domination. Black bodies could be made into whatever slavers and their proxies wanted them to be.[26]

Given the importance of African-based slavery in colonial Mexico, it is somewhat surprising that enslaved Afro-Mexicans were not as numerically prevalent on the northern frontier as they were in the metropolitan centers of New Spain. Colin Palmer has attributed this to the instability of colonial rule in the region and to the continued emphasis on the enslavement of Native people:

> The frontier parts of the north formed one of the few areas which did not receive these [Black] slaves in any appreciable numbers. The absence of enslaved blacks on the northern frontier was due largely to the unsettled nature of Indo-Spanish relations there in the post-Conquest years. Spanish attempts to subjugate the Indians in the north encountered strong resistance for a number of years. Many of the Indians who were captured in these frontier wars were enslaved under the pretext that they were taken in a "just" war. The continued enslavement of Indians in these areas, therefore, had the effect of reducing the demand for African slaves.[27]

Documentary evidence from Nuevo León during the seventeenth century (briefly discussed below) lends some credence to this interpretive emphasis on the influence of Native-Spanish warfare on the character of anti-Black slavery in the North. Nevertheless, despite the small number of enslaved Afro-Mexicans, Black people still figured prominently in the Spanish colonization of New Spain's northern frontier, especially as colonists, soldiers, and symbols.[28]

Most Spanish colonists in the North did not feel obligated to conform to the more ideologically palatable form of enslavement that was anti-Black bondage. In the context of violent conquest and the immense mineral possibilities of the northern frontier, the enslavement of intransigent and supposedly barbarous Indians remained most convenient and lucrative, and prohibitions against anti-Native slavery carried less weight on distant frontiers.[29] Spaniards, moreover, continued to find more rhetorical cover for the enslavement of Native populations. Spaniards reported, for instance, hyperbolic incidents of appalling Native violence, such as Chichimeca warriors ripping still-pumping hearts out of Spanish victims and the enslavement of small Spanish children. For Spanish settlers, soldiers, and officials alike, such behaviors could not go unpunished. To them, enslavement served as the proper punitive response.[30]

In general, the retaliatory violence of Chichimecas gave Spanish authorities the rhetorical ammunition they desired to reframe the Chichimecan conflict as a *guerra a fuego y a sangre*, an all-out war of blood and fire. In the context of a *guerra a fuego y a sangre*, soldiers who already preferred payments for their military service in enslaved bodies were permitted to distribute among themselves all Indian enemies captured during battle. Rules were to govern this form of enslavement, as those captured were to be registered and educated as God-fearing Christians, but it was these same rules that also offered slavers legal reassurance for their slaving activities. Similar to the *rescate* cases earlier in the century, spreading Christianity was ostensibly the impulse behind the forced incorporation of captured Native people, but it also meant that enslaved Chichimecan individuals could never return to their communities of origin. Effectively, this was natal alienation through Christ.[31]

The Chichimeca War was thus a critical moment in the history of both Spanish slavery in the Americas and Spanish expansion to the north. First, the Chichimeca War resulted in the establishment of a far-reaching infrastructure for future commerce, mineral extraction, and defense across the north of Mexico. The back-and-forth violence between Spaniards and Chichimecan people heightened Spanish awareness of both demographic patterns and resource allocation on the frontier. Moreover, the emphasis on the establishment of defensive posts planted along trade and communication routes, as opposed to full-scale settler colonies, points to both the importance of soldier-settlers and the concerns of high officials to limit spending for expansion northward. Spanish authorities were befuddled by the more mobile characteristics of frontier Native peoples, and private resources became essential to most punitive and exploratory measures. The limited willingness of the Spanish government to invest its own resources into these operations also proved to be instrumental in motivating Spanish soldiers to seek out slaves; if soldiers were to risk their personal property and well-being, they wanted to be paid in enslaved bodies.[32] Finally, the war highlighted the self-propelling potential of violence. Widespread and continuous conflict instigated and justified further violence. Violence ping-ponged back and forth between Spaniards and Chichimecas, and given the pervasiveness of this violence, anti-Native slavery thrived. Spaniards ultimately effected "peace" with Chichimecan peoples during the final decade of the sixteenth century—but only after a complete reevaluation of frontier policy, as diplomacy, Native-based (e.g., Tlaxcalan) colonization, and gift-giving took center stage in this peace process.[33] In any case, peace arrived well after the Chichimeca War had set in motion various forces that drove Spaniards farther and farther north.

The Cycles of Spanish Slaving Expansion

The cycles of violence unleashed by Spanish instigation of the Chichimeca War were to replay themselves with stunning frequency for decades. After the conquest of Zacatecas, Spanish expansion northward progressed according to three broad trajectories: (1) up the western coast to the Californias, (2) across the great central plateau known today as the Mesa del Norte, and (3) along an eastern route near the Sierra Madre Oriental. Per the western course, Spaniards followed the trails of Guzmán's bloody Pacific Coast conquests, which by 1531 had extended as far north as modern-day Culiacán, Sinaloa.[34] Along the central plateau route—and more pertinent to this study—Spaniards vaulted from mining community to mining community. The founding of Santa Bárbara, Nueva Vizcaya, in 1567 was key to this progression, as the town served as the principal staging ground for future exploratory and colonization missions, including the notorious Juan de Oñate expedition in 1598 into Pueblo country in current-day New Mexico. Santa Bárbara was also important because it was in this vicinity that Spaniards came into contact with the far-reaching, Jumano-oriented trade and kin networks that extended from Chihuahua to Pecos and even to present-day Texas-Louisiana.[35]

The push into Nueva Vizcaya and New Mexico foreshadowed many of the issues Spaniards would face for centuries on the northern frontier. On the one hand, it was illustrative of the Spanish Crown's renewed emphasis on a "spiritual," assimilative (as opposed to military) conquest of the Americas. In 1573, King Felipe II issued the Comprehensive Orders for New Discoveries, which prohibited unauthorized exploration—a crime punishable by death—and demanded a change in semantics, as the term "conquest" was officially replaced by "pacification." Issued to prevent a repeat of the rebellion-inducing excesses of the conquistadors and fortune seekers from earlier in the century, these orders thrust the religious into the forefront of Spanish colonial efforts. From the end of the sixteenth century through the seventeenth (and into the eighteenth), clergymen were thus charged with stretching the northern limits of the Spanish Empire, and it would be men of the cloth from New Mexico and Nueva Vizcaya who resurrected Spanish interest in the Texas borderlands.[36]

Yet the renewed role of spiritual leaders in Spanish colonialism did not end the enslavement of Native people. In Nueva Vizcaya, the *encomienda* was modified to accommodate the labor demands of mining centers and their surrounding industries.[37] In New Mexico, Franciscans fantasized about establishing a Christian utopia, but the New Mexican conqueror Oñate and his men treated the Pueblo inhabitants as little more than fodder for the Spanish mining complex to the south. Oñate sent off many Acomas as slaves to the mining frontier during his initial conquest in 1599, and others were enslaved to serve Spanish masters locally. By the

1630s, after Luis de Rosas became governor of the province, Spaniards were actively launching slave raids into the outskirts of Pueblo country. As was the custom during the Chichimeca War, Spanish soldiers fought "just" wars against the more mobile Native groups who inhabited the margins of Spanish-controlled towns, all for the sake of acquiring slaves to ease the burdens of life on the rugged, isolated frontier or, in the case of the Rosas-led operations, to procure workers for local *obrajes* and southern mining centers.[38] Thus, by 1680, the central migratory trajectory north had proceeded rather methodically, and even as Native peoples resisted Spanish incursions with violence of their own, Spaniards had established strongholds in and around Santa Bárbara, Parral, San Juan del Río, Guanaceví, San Andrés de la Sierra, Valle de San Bartolomé, and Santa Fe.[39] Continuous slave hunting satiated a Spanish lust for labor and subservience, but as Spaniards in Texas would come to learn, it would leave a lasting legacy of strained relations among Native communities, unconventional and surprising alliances, modified subsistence arrangements, and a general Native distrust of Spanish people.

The eastern route to the northern frontier of New Spain had a much more direct effect on Spanish colonial progression to Texas. As was the case for the western and central routes, the advance of the Spanish frontier in the East was largely the product of slave-hunting endeavors. Guzmán set the stage in the 1520s with his slaving in Pánuco (located along the eastern coast of Mexico), where Native people were captured and rerouted to the goldfields of the Caribbean. With the silver rushes of the 1540s and 1550s, slaving networks veered westward, and by the 1570s veterans of the Chichimeca War began formal colonization of New Spain's far Northeast, founding Saltillo and Monterrey. Led by Alberto del Canto, these Basque and Portuguese soldiers and entrepreneurs sought great riches in the faraway lands of the North, searching for both silver and individuals to enslave. Canto's wholesale slaving practices were so atrocious that the Audiencia of Guadalajara formally condemned his behaviors and ordered his arrest. Canto managed to flee from Spanish authorities, but his official absence from the Northeast did not stop Spanish slave hunting. In fact, only a few years later, Luis de Carabajal y Cueva resumed slave raiding on an even greater scale. As seasoned veterans of the Chichimecan conflicts, these enterprising Spanish representatives of diverse Iberian origin saw slaving as a natural outgrowth of Spanish military advancement on the frontier. Yet again, Spanish colonizers situated their violence within the context of "just" warfare, considering slaves as appropriate payment for their military

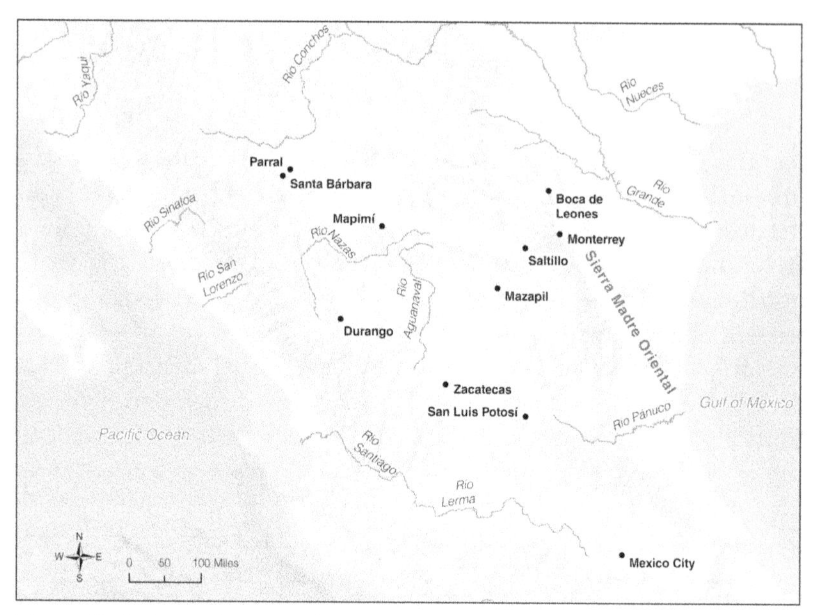

Map 2. Early Spanish colonial centers, outposts, and terminals. Cartography by Luyang Ren.

service. And slave capital could be lucrative: an average slave was worth about 75 pesos during the last quarter of the sixteenth century.[40]

Carabajal's career also highlights the persistent historical connections between the enslavement of both Native and African people. Before Carabajal ever crossed the Atlantic to wreak havoc on the Native populations of Mexico's Northeast, he served as a Portuguese trading agent and royal accountant on the Cape Verde Islands off the coast of West Africa. There he gathered enslaved Africans (from the Islands and the mainland) and sold them to slaver captains heading to the Americas. Eventually, Carabajal returned to Iberia and then made his way to the Americas, bringing with him his slaving proclivities. His transfer of slaving operations to the Americas mimicked the career of Colón, and it brought into relief the merging interests of Iberian leaders. Portuguese merchants had offered their slave-trading services to the Spanish Crown since the latter part of the fifteenth century, and such connections would flourish in the closing decades of the sixteenth century with the union of the Spanish and Portuguese Crowns. With Felipe II as head of both monarchies, Spanish leaders were able to direct and reorganize the African slave trade to the Americas much more efficiently. Portuguese men like Carabajal took advantage of this cooperation and involved themselves in the similarly profitable business of enslaving Native people in the Americas.[41]

It is difficult to overestimate the influence of slavery when explaining the Spanish colonization of the Northeast. Significantly, slave hunting provided early colonists with quick access to capital, as Spaniards sold slaves to the mines of Zacatecas, Fresnillo, and Sombrerete, and until the middle of the seventeenth century slaves were the principal export of Nuevo León. But enslaved people also met local labor demands. Throughout the entire seventeenth century, enslaved Native people—women and children especially—worked as domestic servants in the homes of Saltillo and Monterrey *vecinos*. And as José Cuello has argued, the *encomienda* practices of Nuevo León residents operated in tandem with the enslavement of Native locals. Because *encomenderos* generally did not want to provide basic subsistence for their workers all year long, the principal difference between *encomienda* and slavery was the brief reprieve from labor that individual *encomienda* workers experienced during slow labor seasons. From a larger perspective, however, *encomienda* Indians were hunted like slaves, traded like slaves, chained like slaves, and always subject to the iron fist of the Spanish *encomendero*.[42]

As elsewhere in Mexico, Native people were not the only group held in bondage by Spanish slavers in the Northeast. During the early decades of Spanish colonization of the Northeast, enslaved Afro-Mexicans were among the bands of Spanish colonists and soldiers who carved out colonial communities in the territories of Native peoples. Like their Native counterparts, enslaved Black people symbolized economic opportunity for the colonial invaders of the region. In Monterrey, for instance, a diverse lot of military officers, cart owners, ranchers, farmers, and even priests claimed ownership of Black bodies, revealing the flexibility of anti-Black slavery in Mexico.[43] Although very few slaveholders had more than a few slaves, the more prosperous Spanish colonists owned up to ten or more enslaved people. Men like Antonio López de Villegas, whose property inventory included two multistory houses, a silver-extracting *hacienda*, two other ranching and agricultural *haciendas*, two mines, and twelve enslaved people, proved that economic diversification and slavery could be highly compatible, even on the frontier. Thus, a small market in Black bodies existed in colonial Monterrey, where a Black man in his prime laboring years could fetch about 400 pesos from an eager Spanish buyer. Most frontier people may have been cash-strapped, but the exploitative possibilities of anti-Black slavery were enticing.[44]

This is not to say that anti-Black slavery thrived in the Northeast. Rather, as Palmer has argued, African-based slavery existed haphazardly there, largely as a result of the pervasive cycles of violence between Spanish and Native people. With Native people constantly threatening to attack encroaching Spanish settlements and with Black slave prices reaching hundreds of pesos per slave, such an investment in slave property was inherently risky. As Native attackers did not necessarily discriminate between enslaved Afro-Mexicans and their slavers, Black residents often shared with their Spanish oppressors the experience of Native anticolonial violence.[45] Desperation could lead to unlikely alliances. Juan de Mendiola, for instance, "without regards for his early age and the risk involved," took an arrow "through his body" for his slaver, Capt. Hernando de Mendiola, when Native attackers stormed the captain's ranch. Although the piercing shot "almost caused him his death," Juan de Mendiola survived, and his service of "loyalty" and labor ultimately motivated his slaver to manumit him upon his own death, a delayed but profound victory for a man embedded in a world of violence.[46] Such acts of bravery in the face of possible death may not have been common, but the willingness of some slaveholders to manumit their slaves further undermined the institution of anti-Black slavery in a place where it already operated uneasily.[47]

Juan de Mendiola's defense of his slaver also hints at another reality of the northward-moving Spanish slaving frontier: after generations of conquest and warfare, Native resistance to colonial expansion was hardly waning. By the time Spaniards had reached the southern boundaries of present-day Texas during the mid-seventeenth century, the decades of slave hunting and general violence had begun to catch up with the colonists. Spanish slaving had inspired a great Native exodus northward, and many of the Native communities that Spaniards would encounter along the edges of the northern frontier had been refugees of disease, warfare, and destitution.[48] Moreover, they were hardly willing to capitulate to Spanish subjugation. For these Native exiles, life in the North was not necessarily more economically secure or environmentally friendly, but it did offer a brief reprieve from Spanish violence. Although largely displaced peoples, these refugees responded creatively to such dire circumstances, banding together with new groups, shifting their subsistence strategies, and engaging in the broad trade networks of the region. When Spanish colonists pushed their way into Texas, they would have to contend with these highly adaptive—yet cautious—communities.

Surmounting "the Deadly Hatred" and into the Texas Borderlands, 1650–1716

The second half of the seventeenth century was an era of widespread Native unrest across Mexico's northern frontier. In Nueva Vizcaya, New Mexico, Coahuila, and Nuevo León, Spanish officials reported violent, coordinated Native uprisings. To a large extent, the wave of Native rebellion stemmed from changing geopolitical and economic circumstances. As horse populations grew rapidly in the North, Native communities transformed horses into major tools of economic production, commerce, and defense. Native people also adjusted their subsistence patterns, integrating livestock raiding into existing methods of resource accumulation, an adaptation that appeared as little more than "theft" in the eyes of Spanish observers.[49] Compounding Spanish frustrations were the attacks on herders and ranchers that sometimes accompanied such resource-extraction operations. Yet Native anticolonial violence was also explicitly political and retributive. When in 1651 a force of some six hundred Native fighters descended on the home of Capt. Alonso de León (the elder), located about twenty miles from the town of Cadereyta, Nuevo León, their motives were rather clear. By this time, de León had earned for himself the reputation of a slave raider, and many of the Native attackers had been formerly enslaved in Spanish mines. The fact that Native people from multiple ethnic groups banded together to attack a known slaver suggests that resistance to Spanish slavery was the rallying cry of many Native groups at the time.[50] The Frenchman René Robert Cavelier, Sieur de La Salle, confirmed as much when he visited the Texas borderlands in the 1680s, claiming that the locals "have a deadly hatred for the Spaniards because they enslave them."[51]

Native raids and attacks became quite frequent during the second half of the seventeenth century. As Native forces swept across the northeastern Spanish settlements, few Spanish colonists escaped this concert of anticolonial action, and with uprisings involving hundreds of Native warriors, panic sometimes overtook Spanish observers. As one provincial governor explained in the aftermath of a major pan-Native revolt in the San Antonio Valley (south of the Río Grande), "The valley would be depopulated, because it was not possible to continue the war or to defend against so many nations that had joined to harm the Spaniards."[52] To some Spanish colonists, Native violence made life unbearable and unsustainable on the northern frontier. But to others, it provided the rhetorical ammunition they needed to embark on punitive campaigns.

A call to violence thus became a common refrain in Mexico's Northeast. Even clergymen like Fray Francisco de Ribera advocated an aggressive war of extreme force and slave taking. Ribera asserted, "We have lived incautiously with the Indians. We have pardoned them many times and have tried to go on by gentle means (in case they might get tired and settle down)." A benevolent, fatherly touch, he argued, had yielded nothing; instead, it had backfired, creating a hopeless Christian dilemma: "For once the Spaniards are exterminated, there will be no one to preach good to the enemy Indians in the mountains." Incorporation through slaving violence, he claimed, was the only way to save defiant Native people from the depths of their heathenism: "Although some Indians may be killed in the war, it is more advantageous for the other Indians even to be made slaves for a few years than to spend their whole life in the mountains and woods, with their insults and thievery, as public enemies of their neighbors and of the Divine Majesty." This was the Spanish defense of *la esclavitud de los indios*, established over a century earlier, that would persist well into the eighteenth century. As Ribera argued, Spaniards were "obliged to punish and conquer these Indians and to subject them by any necessary means, even if it means to destroy and exterminate them." And "because they, as declared enemies, are trying to destroy and exterminate the Spaniards," such violence could be executed "with a clean conscience."[53] So it was with a clean conscience that Spanish soldiers attacked and raided the Native communities of the Northeast, on the margins of modern-day Texas, where Papagayos, Cacaxtles, and others resided. During a series of mid-seventeenth-century sweeps, Spaniards left hundreds of Native people dead, while enslaving hundreds more "of all ages and both sexes," some of whom "were exiled to Zacatecas . . . [and] condemned to personal service in shackles."[54]

This was the historical context that set the stage for Spanish colonization of Texas in the mid-1680s. Up until then, cycles of Spanish mineral extraction, Native resistance, and Spanish campaigning slowly carried Spaniards northeastward toward the Texas borderlands. Glory-filled dreams of wealthy peoples and lands remained just below the surface of the empire's collective consciousness, but it was the exigencies of anti-Native exploitation and warfare that brought Spaniards to the edges of the Texas borderlands. By the 1680s, although not perceived as Texas per se, the trans–Río Grande region had materialized into an area of significant concern for Spaniards. Resurgent Native attacks had proven that the region had become the destination for various Native rebels and refugees, and intercommunity contact had offered Native people opportunities to ally and consort with similarly displaced groups from other areas. Spaniards may not have viewed the trans–Río Grande region solely as a zone for slave raiding, but they believed that military vigilance remained a necessity along this northern frontier of vast mineral wealth. Slavery was, at the very least, a byproduct of this vigilance—if not the prime instrument of it.

By the final two decades of the eighteenth century, the thirst for riches, souls, and slaves had pulled the Spanish Empire cautiously toward the land they soon would call Tejas. Spanish authorities were for the most part content with the scattered mission-settlements and presidios near the lower Río Grande region, and regular Native opposition dissuaded most Spaniards from pursuing an expansionist colonization program deep into Texas. But news of French machinations along the Gulf Coast, where La Salle attempted to establish a colony for the French Empire, changed all of this. La Salle's short-lived colony at Fort St. Louis near Matagorda Bay during the early 1680s exposed to Spanish authorities the imperial vulnerabilities of their northern frontier. For Spaniards, no longer did the northern mining frontier of New Spain seem secure; instead, the threat of a French invasion loomed large.[55] Quickly, Spanish officials initiated several fact-finding excursions by land and by sea. The first two sea-based expeditions, launched in January and September 1686, were both failures, so officials turned to the northeastern native Alonso de León to lead a number of expeditions by land. The son and namesake of the famed chronicler of Nuevo León (mentioned above), de León eventually would prove to be a worthy candidate, but his initial efforts yielded very little evidence of La Salle and his French followers. In fact, after a total of three expeditions under the leadership of de León, Spanish surveyors had found only the remains of a French sailing vessel and a French deserter by the name of Jean Géry, a colorful character who claimed to have gained a degree of influence among the local people of the region.[56] Such were the inauspicious beginnings to the sudden Spanish obsession with Texas.

But Spanish authorities were persistent. During the entire nine-year period from 1685 to 1693, officials directed their attention and energies toward Texas in unprecedented fashion. Several expeditions marched across the varied terrain of Texas, and with each expedition Spanish officials compiled and catalogued more knowledge of the Texas landscapes and peoples. Predictably, some of the Native people whom Spaniards encountered, such as the Cacaxtles, were former victims of Spanish slaving violence, but others had not yet encountered Spaniards directly.[57] The

Caddos of eastern Texas—specifically, the Hasinai, or Tejas—were most impressive to Spanish observers, as their densely populated settlements, discernibly hierarchical communities, and vast commercial connections reminded Spaniards of the great Indian civilizations of the South. The Caddos, they believed, were nothing like the Native peoples of the lower Río Grande region, who, in Spanish discourse, were fragmented, nomadic, and barbarous; rather, the Caddos depended upon farming, and their great farmlands required the cooperation of large, interconnected communities. Spanish observers even convinced themselves that the Caddos intended to worship the one true God—if only they could escape the oppressive influences of their nefarious priests.[58] In short, the Caddos invigorated the Spanish colonial imagination.

By the time Spaniards had learned that Karankawas had destroyed the French colony in 1688, Spanish concerns in Texas had shifted toward conversion of the local people of the region. Recognizing the relative weakness of nearby French colonial operations, Spanish authorities now believed that subjugation of the Native populations would provide the necessary buffer against a future French invasion into Mexico. Thus in 1690, officials from Mexico City ordered de León to take possession of Caddo territory in northeast Texas and to establish mission settlements among the Indians. This was de León's final expedition into Texas, but it did result in the establishment of two mission-settlements near Nabedache, Neche, Hainai, and Nacono villages, one named San Francisco de los Tejas and the other Santísimo Nombre de María. A year later, Domingo Terán left for the eastern Texas mission-settlements with reinforcements, and with the conclusion of both expeditions, the settlements housed an unremarkable total of eighteen people: four missionaries, three lay brothers, eight soldiers, two boys, and a servant.[59] Nevertheless, the two expeditions marked the official beginnings of Spanish colonial settlement in the heart of the Texas borderlands.

At the time, the eastern Texas mission-settlements represented the culmination of Spanish missionary efforts on Mexico's far northeastern frontier. Since the mid-seventeenth century, Franciscans had worked tirelessly to introduce the Native peoples of the lower Río Grande area to the Christian way of life. Talk of mission-settlements began in Coahuila as early as 1658, but significant inroads were not made until 1674, when Franciscans, under the leadership of Fray Juan de Larios, established Mission Santa Rosa and Mission San Ildefonso de la Paz near the Río Sabinas. These missions were created principally for Gueiquezales and Boboles, but Spaniards reported over thirty different Native groups in the settlements. It is also worth noting that many of these groups had banded together in an effort to combat the deleterious effects of disease and Spanish slaving. Thus, the mission-settlements existed more as places for Native communities to establish new resource channels and to regroup politically than as permanent homes where Native residents could receive an education in Hispanic "civilization."[60] In any case, after such arduous yet fruitless work among the predominantly mobile populations of the lower Río Grande region, the missionaries were enthusiastic about the opportunity to preach to the sedentary Caddo peoples of northeast Texas. Fray Damián Mazanet could not wait to begin evangelizing among the Caddos, believing, "Our Lord suffers more for each soul lost due to the lack of ministers than everything he endured in his passion and death."[61]

Missionary self-congratulatory declarations notwithstanding, the mission-settlements were an utter failure. An epidemic hit the villages near Mission Santísimo in 1691, taking the lives of some three hundred Native residents. Naturally, the Caddos blamed the Spaniards, and conditions at the mission-settlements rapidly deteriorated. Compounding the devastation of disease was the Spanish proclivity for domination and abuse. Missionaries regularly attempted to undermine the authority of the Caddo religiopolitical leadership (the *xinesí*), and Spanish soldiers capitalized on their close proximity to Native women. As Juliana Barr has argued, the rape of Caddo women by Spanish soldiers was the principal cause of the Spanish expulsion in 1693.[62] In October of that year, Mazanet and company decided to set their mission structures aflame and flee Caddo country, bringing with them the few items they could carry on their backs. The missionaries returned to San Juan Bautista broken and defeated, with a clear sense that the Texas borderlands remained an impenetrable Native country.[63]

In the context of the late seventeenth-century Northeast, the expulsion of the Franciscans from eastern Texas should not have been surprising. Despite decades of involvement in the affairs along the lower Río Grande, disease and ubiquitous violence had made the Spanish hold on the region considerably unstable. As Mazanet understood his people's ejection from Caddo country, Spanish colonists "thought they were to be made rulers of the Tejas" when they should have learned to appreciate their hosts' generosity.[64] Even though Franciscans managed by 1703 to build three missions along the Río Grande at San Juan Bautista, San Francisco Solano, and San Bernardo, missionaries had limited success finding willing Native converts. Native residents generally came and went at will, and victims of Spanish violence regularly passed word along to others that Spanish involvement also meant the burdens of violence and exploitation. In 1674, Fray Juan Dionysio de Peñasco, for example, struggled to recruit the Yoricas who lived north of the Río Grande because of this very concern regarding Spanish "tyranny."[65] Such an example suggests that Spaniards had at least some awareness of the extent to which their abuses had crippled Native-Spanish relations, but their awareness obviously did little to curb their behaviors when it mattered most.

Thus, violence continued to characterize Spanish-Native interactions during the late seventeenth century. De León, for instance, was often occupied with the onslaught of Native attacks on the missions, towns, and haciendas of the Northeast during his tenures as governor of Nuevo León (1682–84) and Coahuila (1687–91), and his campaigning activities were so extensive that the seventeenth-century Spanish chronicler of Nuevo León, Juan Bautista Chapa, believed that the people of New Spain were forever indebted to him for "the pacification of the northern region."[66] After de León's death in 1691, others took up the mantle of Native "pacification." Diego Ramón was among such leaders, and his body of work included a number of campaigns against the Tobosos of the region. The details of each expedition varied, but as was the custom, Spaniards often resorted to slave raiding to subjugate locals. In one punitive campaign organized by de León, Maj. Carlos Cantu attacked an encampment of Janambres, enslaving twenty people, many of whom were shipped off "to exculpate their crimes in the mines of Mazapil and Bonanza."[67] Colonial violence became so endemic, so entrenched within Spanish colonial culture, that even men of the cloth—those tasked by the Crown in 1573 to not conquer but bring "peace" to the frontier—faced accusations of abuse and enslavement of Native victims.[68] Given such practices, there is little wonder early Spanish missionary efforts failed miserably in Texas.

What ultimately emerged from the new Spanish interest in Texas during the 1680s and 1690s was, if anything, an increased awareness of Spanish weakness in the Texas borderlands. With each expedition, Spanish authorities sought to make real their claims of dominion over the territory that would eventually be known as Texas (and Louisiana), but despite such efforts all they gained was a better sense of how tenuous their hold over the region truly was. Spaniards lacked the trust of the Native communities closest to their strongholds south of the Río Grande, and all expeditions into the heart of Texas were subject to the vagaries of Native assistance or disruption. Colonial violence had destabilized the trans–Río Grande region, and Spaniards were now reaping what they had sown. Moreover, the failures of Spanish colonial efforts in Texas during the 1690s deterred Spanish authorities from exploring further colonization opportunities for nearly two decades.

When Spanish high officials turned their attention back toward Texas in the 1710s, it was again in response to French maneuverings. From 1693 to 1716, only a handful of Spanish expeditionary parties ventured past the Río Grande region, and when they did, they were generally of the missionizing or slave-raiding variety, like Diego Ramón's slaving foray discussed in the opening of this chapter.[69] In the meantime, however, French colonists continued to plant themselves in the lower Mississippi Valley. Since the 1690s, French traders had sought out commercial relations with the Caddos of Texas-Louisiana, and French efforts accelerated during the second decade of the eighteenth century. In 1713, Antoine de la Mothe, Sieur de Cadillac, became governor of Louisiana, and his task was explicit: make Louisiana into a profitable colony. At that time, much of western Louisiana was Caddo territory, and immediately upon the colony's establishment French traders got to work strengthening commercial ties with the locals. French commercial ambitions were broadly inclusive, so Louis Juchereau de St. Denis, a relative of Louisiana colony founder Pierre Le Moyne d'Iberville, traveled to San Juan Bautista on the Río Grande in hopes of opening direct trade lines with Spaniards in Mexico's Northeast. Upon reaching San Juan Bautista in 1714, St. Denis set off a chain reaction of events that eventually would lead to Spanish viceregal support of full-scale colonization of Texas.[70]

With St. Denis's arrival, Spanish officials in the capital once again feared a French invasion. The fact that St. Denis could travel so easily to the Spanish outposts on the Río Grande frightened Spanish authorities. All of a sudden, mass colonial settlement became much more palatable, and in 1715 a general *junta*, or council meeting, in Mexico City authorized the reoccupation of eastern Texas. Within a year, Domingo Ramón (the son of Diego Ramón) and seventy companions—including nine priests, three lay brothers, twenty-five soldiers, three Frenchmen, and a few dozen civilians—were off to the lands of the Hasinais. Impressively, after just one month Ramón and company were able to establish four missions among the Caddos. Within a year, two more missions were erected, and a total of six Spanish missions dotted northeastern Texas.[71] Although Spanish colonists finally seemed to have gained a foothold in Texas, the Ramón expedition was only the beginning of full-scale Spanish colonization.

Fray Antonio de San Buenaventura y Olivares was among the more vigorous proponents of settler-based colonization. In his November 1716 appeal to the viceroy, he advocated the colonization of both soldier- and citizen-settlers, and in mid-December the viceroy ordered Martín de Alarcón to settle *vecinos* on a site near the San Antonio River. Together with Olivares, Alarcón was to draw his soldiers from across the Mexican Northeast and then march into the heart of Texas. The colonial scheme excited Olivares, but the new governor of Coahuila and Texas, Alarcón, did not share the friar's enthusiasm.[72] Fray Olivares would have to wait a year and a half before witnessing the departure of Alarcón and company. Until then, colonization of Texas would remain an imaginative activity, best suited for the workings of far-off bureaucrats and administrators.

Given the history of Spanish failures in Texas, colonization plans were certainly imaginative. The most extensive colonization schemes advocated a line of fortifications, buttressed by settler colonies, which would serve as a defensive perimeter against foreign invasion. Juan de Oliván Rebolledo, the *auditor general*,[73] argued that several fortifications, spread out from the Río Grande to the Mississippi, were in fact necessary for total colonization of Texas. In his December 1717 plan, Oliván suggested the settlement of two separate colonies of Spanish families and "families of *Yndios* either from Tlascala or from Mexico" to serve as the basis for further expansion. These colonists were to begin the arduous tasks of planting and field cultivation, and after some time these same settlers were to branch out into new colonies, creating a chain of Spanish settlements "successively linked with one another." "Within a short time," Oliván predicted, "those territories [of Texas] may be settled, and their *vecindades* can approach ours."[74] Oliván's plan was to overpower the Native communities of the Texas borderlands through sheer volume of Hispanic settlements, which over time would regenerate themselves as they cumulatively devoured Native lands.[75]

The colonization plans of the 1710s only partially addressed the history of Spanish violence in the Texas borderlands, even though colonial violence had proven so debilitating in the past. In his proposals, Oliván recommended the migration of soldiers who "have prerequisites of being farmers and married" but also "will be aided by the military experience they have acquired in dealing with the bordering *Yndios*." In emphasizing the colonization of married men, Oliván hoped to prevent the sexual exploitation of local women, which "caused much resentment among the Asinaiz" during the 1690s. Married men, he believed, "will not vex either [Indian women] who have recently adopted Catholicism or *las gentiles*."[76]

He also warned expeditionary leaders not to use violence to induce Indians to join mission-settlements, declaring that Native people "shall not be compelled by the force of arms; for arms should be resorted to only in self-defense or in [defense] of those who have been reduced."[77]

Overall, these Texas colonization schemes appeared to have exhausted the creative capacities of Spanish authorities. Although high officials had reservations about the earliest wave of colonial migrants, no class or *casta*[78] seemed to be exempt from possible participation in the colonization of Texas. Christianized Indians, Spanish war veterans, "vagrants," "idle men and women," married women, "dissolute women," mixed-race *mestizos*, and Afro-Mexicans eventually were all included in the instructions and recommendations from capital officials.[79] On the surface, colonial officials indicated that they were most concerned with an increased French influence, but it is not difficult to discern their anxieties regarding Native reticence and hostility toward a revived Spanish presence. Most officials during this time agreed that a concerted Spanish settlement program was key to strengthening the Spanish hold on the Texas borderlands. By the late 1710s, Spanish authorities would begin to put these ideas into practice.

For the prospective Texas colonists who had some familiarity with the longer history of Spanish-Native interactions on the northeastern frontier, the task of Texas colonization must have seemed daunting. Talk of great settler transfer suggested a new approach to northeastern colonization, but violence still captured the collective imagination of northeastern residents. The diverse groups of Native peoples scattered across the Texas borderlands were well aware of Spanish abuses and slave raids; for many, their relocation into the Texas borderlands was part of this legacy of Spanish slaving violence. The intermittent alliances between Spaniards and Native peoples in the region suggested that future partnerships were not entirely beyond the realm of possibility, but they did not provide a clear-cut method for productive, cooperative interaction. Rather, the sporadic alliances often illustrated how, in the context of the broad sweep of European colonialism, the interests of Spaniards and Native people were diametrically opposed to one another.

But by the opening decades of the eighteenth century, despite all of their efforts, Spaniards had not established a monopoly on violence and domination in the greater southwest region of the modern-day United States. After two centuries of colonial shockwaves reverberating across the Americas, Native communities had adapted to changing geopolitics, demographics, technologies, and economic systems. Within the Texas borderlands, refugees of Spanish slavery and colonialism converged, from the West and the South, with longtime residents forced to accommodate relatively recent arrivals. In such a context, conflict over resources was virtually inevitable, and it was this very conflict that opened the door for a precarious collaboration between certain Native communities in Texas and Spanish colonizers. Specifically, an Ndé consolidation of power in Texas had alienated a number of other communities, and Spaniards' willingness to contribute their services in the fight against Apache rule proved alluring enough to certain Native people across Texas to allow for their active cooperation. Thus, if only in small increments, Spaniards had begun to realize that if they were to build their great wall of defense against a future French invasion, they would have to ally and consort with the Native groups of the region. But would a colonial project dependent upon Native cooperation mitigate the Spanish slaving imperative? The past was foreboding. Despite viceregal warnings (or perhaps *because of* viceregal proscriptions), Spaniards were equipped with a strong rhetorical defense for practices of enslavement, particularly with regard to the so-called savage Indians of the *tierra adentro*, the interior lands. Capital officials demanded Native acquiescence for the establishment of the Spanish-led mission settlements of Texas, and their allowance for so-called defensive violence opened the door for slaving. Not surprisingly, once hostilities between the new Spanish settlers and Ndé communities erupted, Spanish slaving flowered in the borderlands. The collective weight of two centuries of Native slave taking proved too heavy a burden for the Spanish colonists of Texas to cast away so easily.

Summary

The Spanish path to colonization of Texas was long, slow, and hotly contested. Spanish authorities did not see the merits in investing heavily in the far-off northeastern region of Mexico until French colonists appeared to threaten the great mineral holdings of New Spain. It was only then, with one of Spain's principal imperial competitors knocking on the door of their wealthy colony, that Spanish high officials fixed their attention squarely on Texas.

But exactly how Spaniards responded—and how successful their responses would be—depended more on the long history of Spanish colonial expansion northward prior to the late eighteenth century than on actual French activities. When Spaniards advanced northeastward, they did not try to escape the cycles of violence they for so long had perpetrated against Native people. Slavery had become a central part of Spanish colonial development in Mexico, implicating Spanish, Native, and Black people, and slavery, both anti-Native and anti-Black, would continue to color the lives of all involved in the larger process of Spanish colonization in Texas. Furthermore, Spanish slaving had contributed to the changing demographic and geopolitical circumstances of the Texas borderlands by the second half of the seventeenth century. Many of the Native people of Texas either were refugees of Spanish slaving or had learned of Spanish violence from others. This was the historical setting for the eighteenth-century Spanish emergence in Texas; this was the legacy of the Spanish slave raider's expansion.

2 / "Blinded by the Craving for Slaves": Slavery and the Quest for Spanish Dominion in Native Country, 1718–1760

Governor Jacinto de Barrios y Jáuregui's task appeared much simpler on paper than in practice: reconnoiter the San Sabá River area and prepare to move the San Xavier presidio to this new location. The year was 1756, and although relations with their Ndé enemies had cooled substantially over the past several years, Spaniards still harbored much ill will and distrust toward them. San Sabá was the heart of Ndé country, and few Spanish men knew much about it. But those who had traveled through Apachería, the land of the Apaches, were more than happy to relate their experiences to the authorities.[1] In search of such key information, Governor Barrios turned to these men, and their reports offered the governor a window into the cultural and geopolitical circumstances of the Texas borderlands.[2]

The men whom Barrios interviewed were both soldiers and *vecinos* of Spanish Texas. They all agreed that the San Sabá region had no good roads leading into it and that the surrounding area was a veritable no-(White)man's land. The men also recalled their important contributions to pivotal skirmishes against Apaches over the years, those from the Juan Antonio Bustillo y Ceballos campaign of 1732 and the Pedro de Rábago y Terán expedition of 1748 as well as several others. Just as important, they boasted about their slaving activities and how they only wished that they had taken more prisoners. Above all, they wanted the governor to know that it was the soldiers and *vecinos* of Texas, more so than anyone else from the Mexican Northeast, who were responsible for punishing and pacifying the dangerous Apaches. As Phelipe Muñoz de Mora explained,

"All the campaigns that had been made had been [manned] by troops of this province without other help." Their violence, they believed, was deserving of praise and commendation. Without their efforts, Texas would have been lost to *los indios bárbaros*—the savage Indians.[3]

Their testimony helped Barrios to recalibrate his plans for the relocation of the San Xavier presidio to the San Sabá area, and within several months the new presidio, San Luis de Las Amarillas, stood tall near the San Sabá River. Yet beyond the immediate utility of their testimony, the declarations of the men also revealed much about the history of Spanish slaving during the first four decades of Spanish colonization in Texas. As they made evident, violence and the enslavement of Native enemies were central parts of their colonial experiences in Texas, and the pacification of the frontier—the defeat of a great Apache menace—was their legacy to bear. Here was the tale of the Spanish conquest, localized for the Texas context but still reverberating with the assumption that Christian civilization was to prevail over Indian savagery. Significantly, the soldiers and *vecinos* felt no obligation to hide their slaving tendencies, even though Spanish law explicitly prohibited the enslavement of Native people. As far as they were concerned, their actions were righteous, the work of God-driven men. Slaving subjugation was justified because they were *the* stabilizing, civilizing force of the Texas borderlands.[4]

This chapter details the first four decades of Spanish colonization in Texas, highlighting the centrality of slaving violence and coercion in the colonial settlement of Hispanic people. Slavery in the Texas borderlands was geopolitical in character, violently tying disparate peoples together through cross-community slaver brutality and exploitation. The enslavement of outsiders sometimes spawned diplomacy, as the kin of victims reached out to their leaders to recover stolen family, but it also sowed the seeds of generations-long anger and resentment. Just as important, slavery operated as a tool of economic gain and social control. In the context of Spanish Texas, the exploitation of enslaved people eased the economic hardships of frontier life, while the subjugation of perceived outsiders, both Native and Black, was essential to the intracommunal forging of *español*-ness, or Whiteness. Although the custom of raiding enemy communities for slaves provoked frequent reprisals and counterattacks, Spaniards were persistent in their slaving. To them, nothing demonstrated the power of the Spanish Empire and the prerogatives of their settler colonial community better than the conquest of their enemies. Violence was the measure of their social worth.[5]

The contest over Texas during this period resulted in the enslavement or deaths of hundreds—and probably thousands—of mostly Native people, as well as the pillaging of countless horses, livestock, and other goods. Certainly, Native people were contributors to the violence of this era, but the men, women, and children who suffered at the hands of Spanish slaving operations were the principal victims of these cycles of violence. Enslaved people experienced the exploitation of Spanish slaving on multiple levels, toiling on behalf of their slavers on their estates and in their homes and enduring forced incorporation into slaveholding families. Both literally through sexual violence and metaphorically through ritual, Spanish slavers integrated their slaves into their Texas communities as kin. The lines between slave and nonslave in Spanish Texas were sometimes blurry, but the opacity of enslaved status (and the general weakness of the Spanish state on the frontier) allowed anti-Native slavery to persist despite royal prohibitions.

Scholars generally have discounted the economic and social value of slavery in Spanish Texas, but close examination of slavery in Spanish San Antonio reveals that slavery was woven into the socioeconomic fabric of the colony.[6] Although few Spanish colonists cared to discuss their slaving practices openly, many important families in Spanish Texas involved themselves in the enslavement of Native and Black people. The advantages of an extra domestic worker, farmhand, or livestock herder proved too alluring for many Spanish colonists, even when they knew that the enslavement of Native people was contrary to Spanish law. Moreover, enslaving, violating, and destroying Native enemies had important social implications: those who proved themselves on the battlefield lived up to settler colonial expectations and thus claimed Whiteness with greater ease. Slavery during the opening decades of Spanish colonization in Texas would not measure up—at least in terms of scale—to the slaving systems that would prevail during the nineteenth century, but it laid the groundwork for another century of slaving violence. By the late 1750s, the Spanish colonial quest for power and dominion in the Texas borderlands had implicated them in a rapidly expanding web of cross-community violence and personal domination.

Extending "the Protection of the Spaniards": Spanish Colonial Settlement in Native Country, 1718–1722

The colonizing expeditions of two veteran Indian-fighting frontiersmen set the stage for Spanish slavery's emergence in the Texas borderlands. The first expedition, led by Martín de Alarcón in 1718, ushered in a new age of Spanish colonization. It brought to Texas the first substantive wave of Spanish soldiers, settlers, horses, and livestock and established or marked off key posts for possible Spanish development. Significantly, the expedition party rejuvenated Spanish-Native relations in the region, crafting a handful of critical alliances that would prove instrumental in the shaping of Spanish dominion.[7] With the conclusion of the expedition, the Spanish population of Texas would never drop below 160 residents during the period of Spanish rule—not a small feat, considering the three decades' worth of operations prior.[8]

Appointed *governador y teniente de capitán* of the province of Texas nearly a year and a half prior to his party's departure from the Río Grande, Alarcón typified the leadership of Texas-bound expeditions. Like his predecessors, he had built his reputation in part through the zealous persecution of *indios bárbaros* as *capitán a guerra* in San Diego del Mazapil and then governor of Coahuila. Having served "with such Christian zeal, application, and fidelity" against "irreducible" communities of Native people, Alarcón was an attractive candidate for the unwieldy task of colonizing Texas, especially as his colonial followers, a motley group of seventy-two soldiers, craftsmen, and muleteers, also came from the war-torn frontier of the Northeast.[9] Their expeditionary mission was not to conquer the local populations of Texas outright, but the men were prepared for destructive conquest, if it came to that.

Governor Alarcón departed from Mission San Juan Bautista del Río del Norte with his party of seventy-two soldiers and settlers, several hundred horses, cattle, sheep, and chickens, and "six droves of mules laden with clothing and provisions" on April 9, 1718. After marching for two weeks, the colonial travelers arrived at their first destination: a spring of water near the San Antonio River. Here, "adjoining a small thicket of live oaks," Fray Antonio de San Buenaventura y Olivares met up with the Alarcón party and established Mission San Antonio de Valero. A few days later, on May 5, the governor took possession of a nearby site in the name of the Spanish king, "and fixing the royal standard with the requisite solemnity, the father chaplain having previously celebrated mass . . . it was given the name of villa de Béjar." For the next several months, this location on the San Antonio River became the principal base of operations for Governor Alarcón, as he detached and led various subexpeditions from this outpost, including a reconnoitering mission to the old French fort near La Bahía del Espiritu Santo (Matagorda Bay). It was also here at San Antonio that the governor later met with the representatives of the Hasinais and the leaders of some twenty-three Native *naciones*, including the man "whom all the nations recognize as a superior," El Cuilón. El Cuilón, also known as Juan Rodríguez, and the other leaders were from the Ranchería Grande, a large multiethnic encampment of Native people located northeast of San Antonio, and their guidance aided the Spaniards on their way to Caddo country, where Alarcón and Caddo leaders exchanged rituals and promises for mutual aid. On his return from Caddo country, Alarcón met with members of the Xarame, Payaya, and Pamaya *naciones*.[10] Slowly but surely, the Spanish expeditioners were laying the groundwork for future colonial prospects.

By the end of the expedition, Alarcón and his Spanish followers had encountered an impressive array of Native peoples, including the Pacuaxin, Caocose, Mallaye, Huyugan, Xanac, Emet, Too, Curmicai, Caddo, Biday, Cabdacho, Xarame, Payayas, Pamaya, Ervipiames, Hasinai, and Aname *naciones*. Alarcón's mission was to secure local alliances, and in this regard his expedition was a success. Everywhere he traveled, Alarcón distributed gifts to Native people, regaled perceived Native leaders with special luxury items, and negotiated military alliances. He so impressed one Hasinais *capitán* that he became fictive kin in his eyes, "as if born among them." This paved the way for the crowning achievement of Alarcón's expedition: a military alliance with the historically reticent Caddo people, who promised to "help him [Alarcón] and his people in anything that might present itself . . . defending them with the Spaniards against the enemies who were harassing them."[11]

With the completion of the Alarcón expedition, Spanish colonization of the Texas borderlands finally had come into greater focus. As before, a Spanish presence was to exist in eastern Texas, but unlike earlier efforts two more stations also were to receive attention and investment: San Antonio and La Bahía. Missionaries worked assiduously to reach the hearts of the local Native people and to transform them into their version of hardworking, God-fearing subjects of the Spanish Crown. At San Antonio and La Bahía (where the prominent frontiersman Domingo Ramón was made commander), the newly arrived Spanish soldier-settlers sowed the seeds of Spanish settler colonialism: they built irrigation canals, planted maize, beans, and corn, raised livestock, shored up presidio defenses, established local government, and traded with Native locals.[12] Now, with dozens of Spanish soldier-settlers stationed at key outposts and the tacit support of thousands of Indigenous inhabitants, for once the future of a Spanish regime in Texas appeared bright.

The Alarcón expedition probably would have been the extent of Spanish colonial operations for years to come had French machinations not forced the cautious hand of the Spanish Crown yet again. Throughout the first quarter of the eighteenth century, with Spanish and French authorities fighting over the legitimate successor to the Spanish Crown, Spanish-French relations vacillated between war and peace, and by the late 1710s war had erupted again. In June 1719, Lt. Philippe Blondel and seven Frenchmen brought the conflict to the Texas-Louisiana borderlands by attacking the Spanish mission-settlement at Los Adaes. News of the French attack swept across Mexico and excited many, especially José de Azlor y Virto de Vera, the Marqués de San Miguel de Aguayo, who took it upon himself to rescue Spanish Texas from the grips of French domination. Aguayo's efforts would represent the second major wave of settler colonists into Texas.

The *marqués* was a highly ambitious man. Already the descendant of a noble family from Spain, José de Azlor expanded his influence by marrying Ignacia Xavier, the daughter of the first Marqués de San Miguel de Aguayo, Agustín de Echevers. The second *marqués* left Spain with his wife in 1712 to oversee their great landed estates in Coahuila, making the *hacienda* of Patos their home. From 1713 to 1720, Aguayo defended the Coahuila frontier against Native rebellion, supplying and maintaining Spanish soldiers at his own expense. Even as Aguayo was rounding up troops and supplies for his massive expedition to Texas, he still made time to secure his reputation as a frontier defender, personally leading and financing slave-raiding operations against hundreds of Native rebels in Coahuila. Like that of Alarcón, Aguayo's record in the Northeast demonstrated a strong history of anti-Native violence.[13]

The *marqués* had long dreamed of leading a Spanish expedition into the North American interior in search of the mythical Gran Quivira, the site of the famed Seven Cities of Gold that Francisco Vázquez de Coronado had heard about in the sixteenth century, but all early requests fell on deaf ears. Despite repeated rejections, however, Aguayo continued his posturing, and in late October 1719 the *marqués* acquired the governorship of Coahuila and Texas. Upon hearing news of the French attack on Los Adaes, Aguayo became moved by "insatiable zeal and desires" and quickly prepared a force of 580 individuals, many veterans of the frontier, for an expedition to rid Texas-Louisiana of the French presence once and for all.[14] Delays prevented the Aguayo expedition from heading toward central Texas until early 1721, but by April of that year he and his men had reached San Antonio. For the next several months, the Aguayo party would traverse much of modern-day Texas, from the San Antonio River to the Trinity, meeting with important leaders (including Louis Antoine Juchereau de St. Denis) as they resupplied and revamped the existing Spanish settlements. By the end of 1721, after depositing six cannons and one hundred soldiers at Los Adaes and reestablishing Mission San Francisco de los Neches, Mission Nuestra Señora de la Concepción, Mission San José de los Nazonis, and Mission Nuestra Señora de Guadalupe de los Nacogdoches, Aguayo had made his way to La Bahía, where he and his followers founded another mission (Espíritu Santo de Zúñiga) and built a fort inland from Matagorda Bay. One year and 130,000 pesos later, Aguayo retreated from the Texas field, but his efforts had left an indelible mark on Texas: by spring 1722, Spanish Texas (sans the Río Grande establishments) consisted of nine missions, four presidios, 269 soldiers, and dozens of families, boasting an estimated total of 640 Spanish colonists.[15]

With the conclusion of the Aguayo expedition, finally the ambitious dreams and visions of Spanish colonialists were coming to fruition. Forever the great wilderness beyond—the *tierra adentro*—had eluded Spanish efforts to control and to dominate it, but the Spanish-led peopling of Texas had opened up the northeastern frontier to new possibilities. Perhaps most important was the active support of Native people. As the *marqués* traversed the disparate landscapes of the Texas borderlands, he schemed with a number of Native leaders and, like Alarcón, distributed gifts to thousands of accommodating Native residents. El Cuilón, the prominent *capitán* of the Ranchería Grande, resurfaced again, voicing his desire for a mission-settlement for his people. At Mission San Antonio de Valero and the newly founded Mission San José y San Miguel de Aguayo, the *marqués* passed out clothing and "dressed" hundreds of Indians, "including maidens and children." Among the Hasinais, the *marqués* offered silver-handed batons and "dress of distinction" to their leaders. Almost everywhere Aguayo and company went, the Native people they encountered were, per Spanish accounts, "pledging their obedience to Our Lord the King," for they were now "under the protection of the Spaniards."[16]

This active support from Native peoples was the key difference between previous expansionist efforts to the Northeast and the colonial

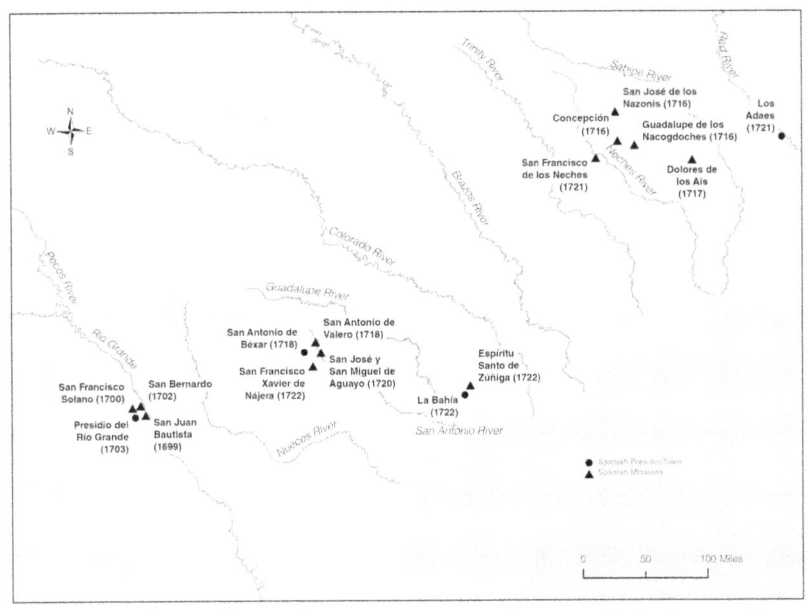

Map 3. Spanish presidios and missions, ca. 1720. Cartography by Luyang Ren.

activities from 1718 to 1722. Slave raiding had pushed the northeastern frontier of New Spain farther and farther north throughout the seventeenth century, and Native people in Texas were aware of this legacy. A handful of Native groups had made early attempts to recruit Spaniards for defensive or economic purposes, but Spaniards too often proved unreliable, burdensome, and exploitative. As Sieur Derbanne discovered during his trip through Texas in 1717, "All the Indian nations, who are in those parts [Texas], thoroughly hate the Spaniards because they abuse them badly." Thus, when Alarcón and Aguayo arrived starting in 1718, the Spanish expeditionary leaders went to great lengths to demonstrate the material and defensive advantages of a Spanish alliance. Only then—after the likes of Alarcón and Aguayo had professed their intentions "to defend them from all their enemies"—did Native leaders seriously consider an intimate relationship with Spaniards.[17] Although the writings of Spanish observers speak of purportedly desperate Indians in dire need of Spanish defensive, material, and spiritual aid, future Spanish success in Texas was to be dependent upon Native consent.[18]

But the successes of the two expeditions were also a function of fortuitous timing, as there would have been no desire for Spanish assistance at all had they sought support at a different historical moment. From east to west and from north to south, various Native communities were in the process of restructuring political alliances, commercial relations, subsistence patterns, and slaving practices. To the east, the Caddo communities were reaping the benefits of a rejuvenated commercial alliance with the French settlements of the Mississippi. French colonists had sought out greater access to the vast trade networks of the North American Southwest, and the Caddos were desirous of trade that yielded vast quantities of guns and other manufactured items.[19] An expanding slave trade was integral to this Caddo-French alliance, as it permitted the Caddos to transform conflicts with their principal enemies, Apaches, into a highly lucrative trade with Frenchmen who, in the southern reaches of New France, had participated in the enslavement of locals as early as the 1680s.[20] The trade was so voluminous that even members of the Alarcón expedition, during their short 1718 stay in Caddo country, had become familiar with it. "The Cabdachos . . . are the ones through whose hands the French acquire slaves and other things of that land from the Indians," reported Fray Francisco de Céliz. "Since the Indians are so interested in muskets, powder, bullets, and clothing, which they exchange for young slaves, wars are maintained and even brought about among the Indians themselves, causing many tribes to be destroyed who would otherwise be converted to Christianity." By 1720 French officials were claiming that the Indian-French commerce in slaves, horses, and skins was the most profitable enterprise in Natchitoches.[21]

In the southern and central parts of Texas, Native communities were trying to cope with the changing ecological conditions of the region and the end of a centuries-long Jumano trade complex. A series of droughts, combined with the deleterious effects of the Spanish introduction of cattle, significantly limited access to food supplies, and from 1700 to 1720 various Native groups sought out new modes of subsistence.[22] Some, such as the Yojuanes, moved north to ally and integrate with the Tonkawas of the Red River region. Others, such as the Payayas, sought out Spanish assistance. Finally, some, particularly the Ervipiames, confederated to create new communities, including the multiethnic encampment known to Spanish observers as the Ranchería Grande. A mobile, trade-oriented community, the Ranchería Grande became home to a diverse group of Native residents, including former Christian converts, traders, and anti-Spanish rebels. In 1707, Spaniards encountered the Ranchería Grande, consisting of Tobosos, Tripas Blancas, Jumanos, and Ervipiames, not too far to the east of the Río Grande, but by 1720 the community of some two thousand individuals had moved to the Brazos Valley.[23] By then, various Tonkawa bands had integrated with them, and Caddos, Bidais, Orcoquizas, and Deadoses were among the groups with whom they traded. It seems evident that at the time of Spanish settler colonization in Texas, the leaders of the Ranchería Grande, principally those from the Ervipiames population, were debating whether or not to seek out Spanish or French assistance. It was not until the late 1740s, however, that the members of the Ranchería Grande committed to Spanish missionary assistance. Even then, this relationship was short-lived, as the Ranchería Grande people abandoned the missions soon after.[24]

The main players in this rapidly changing arena were the so-called Apache peoples of the northern and western Texas borderlands. While Ndé groups ("Ndé" is the self-referent of Apaches and means "the people") had long been the source of fear and consternation for the smaller *naciones* that were spread across the Texas borderlands, by the turn of the eighteenth century the Apaches of the region had begun to supplant the long-held Jumano trade orientation. This commercial expansion to the south was in part tied up with Comanche hostility from the north, but much of the Ndé success in elevating themselves as a strong force in the region was the result of Apache adaptation to changing economic, political, and demographic circumstances—the vast consequences of European colonialism.[25] Four broad adaptation strategies accounted for Ndé power and dominance during the first half of the eighteenth century: (1) new methods of economic production, (2) flexible sociopolitical structures, (3) the incorporation of outsiders into their kin networks, and (4) a willingness to wield violence.[26]

The four strategies overlapped to a considerable extent.[27] New methods of economic production, such as farming and pottery making, emerged principally from the Ndé-Pueblo exchange in the eastern part of the Southern Plains during the second half of the seventeenth century. Prior to this period, most of the Athapaskan-speaking groups of the Southern Plains seem to have been primarily hunter-gatherers and assiduous traders, but by the eighteenth century Spaniards noted the increasingly sedentary characteristics of Ndé plains communities. Along with subsistence practices, Pueblo communities exchanged people with their Ndé neighbors. Sometimes these exchanges were violent and forced, such as the trade in captured individuals, but Pueblos also regularly fled to Ndé territory in hopes of escaping Spanish colonial violence and exploitation. Here a flexible sociopolitical organization was imperative, as Ndé bands permitted—to varying degrees—the incorporation of outsiders, which in turn supported healthy demographic levels and the introduction of new economic practices. More specifically, because Ndé bands were growing in size, their communities gained a greater capacity to breed and care for larger herds. With larger herds, Ndé villages in turn could sustain more people and enhance trade relations.[28]

Ndé embrace of "heterogeneity and admixture" reinforced their territorial and political sway across the North American Southwest (including parts of present-day northern Mexico). Along the lower Río Grande, they incorporated and confederated with Native groups, including many of the longtime foes of Spanish frontiersmen in Coahuila and Nuevo León. In fact, it was likely through their integration of Native refugees and rebels that Ndé communities strengthened their commercial ties to the Jumano trade center at La Junta. Ultimately, the Ndé commitment to farming, resource confiscation, and trading proved for some groups to be an attractive alternative to the more fragile existence of independent life in the rather fragmented southern and western portions of Texas. By the second decade of the eighteenth century, the Jumanos had disappeared from European records, but they seem to have been replaced by (and incorporated into) the Ndé communities of the region.[29]

Ndé slaving practices grew within the context of the development of these new economic operations, incorporation strategies, and flexible sociopolitical structures. Ndé dependence upon livestock encouraged frequent hunting and raiding, practices that often manifested in identical fashion. Raiding would become more important over time as European colonialism extended its tentacles deeper into Native country throughout the eighteenth and nineteenth centuries, but reports of Apache raids certainly were common during and before the earliest days of settler colonialism in Texas. The principal targets for these resource "harvesting" operations were large animals such as mules and horses, and sometimes Ndé raiders stole people too. Given the expanding spheres of colonial fur, arms, and slave commerce, across both Spanish and French domains, Ndé violent participation in "commodified human exchange systems," through slave taking and trading, is unsurprising.[30] But it is also evident that they sometimes treated stolen people as exploited labor, enslaved individuals who contributed to the economic vitality of Ndé communities. The labor of enslaved people was particularly important to changing Ndé economies as many worked with herded animals or labored with animal skins.[31]

Slave taking also had geopolitical ramifications, as bondspeople who became trade goods were integral to diplomatic relations and bonds of reciprocity. The Ndé-Toboso slave trade along the Conchos River, for example, partially explains the flowering of the Ndé influence at La Junta during the eighteenth century.[32] The act of slave taking, however, had the potential to undermine intercommunity relations, as enslaving outsiders scarred both the victims and their communities. Many of the Native groups living near the lower Río Grande in particular were victimized by Ndé slaving, and the Spaniards of central Texas seem to have lived in constant fear of similar attacks during the first half of the eighteenth century as well. So although the people stolen by the various parties of the region personified the broader conflict over resources and territory that had been initiated with the onset of European colonialism during the mid-sixteenth century, Ndé slaving contributed to the violence that permeated the Texas borderlands and became a rallying cry for European colonists and Native communities alike. As St. Denis claimed, the Apaches were "at war with all the world."[33]

The Ndé *naciones* that the Spaniards encountered in Texas were thus collections of highly adaptive and economically inventive people by 1720. Their willingness to incorporate outsiders allowed them to grow in the face of widespread epidemics, but their commitment to raiding made them the antagonists, if not enemies, of many of the Native groups of Texas.[34] When Alarcón and Aguayo courted the diverse Native communities of Texas, they were able to promise defense against a perceptible Ndé threat. Ostensibly, these Spanish leaders were bringing Native peoples under the fold of Spanish rule, but the appeals from Native representatives made the terms of their relationships crystal clear: the Native-Spanish alliances of Texas were to provide material and military benefits for the Native parties against Ndé provocation.[35] The Spanish mission-settlements offered access to goods, and access to goods helped forge obligations of reciprocity. Just as important, the mission-settlements—which Pedro de Rivera Villalón noted in the late 1720s were so "close to the presidio"—served as fortresses against Ndé attacks.[36] Thus, both Alarcón and the Marqués de Aguayo made protection a critical component of their declarations to their new allies. Ndé raiders would put these alliances to the test immediately, offering the Spanish newcomers ample opportunity to prove their worth in the eyes of their Native allies.

If, in the aftermath of the Alarcón and Aguayo expeditions, Spanish colonization had finally turned the corner, the context for a Spanish emergence in the Texas borderlands was hardly an unfamiliar one. As before, violence and Spanish colonial intrusion were to be inextricably intertwined. Although slave raiding had receded into the backdrop of Spanish colonial imperatives in Texas, Spaniards secured their future prospects in the region by inserting themselves into—and exacerbating—cycles of violent interaction across the Texas borderlands. Ultimately, Spanish encounters with the Ndé peoples of the region served as an opportunity for the rise of a new slaving regime in Texas.

The Ndé-Spanish Collision: Spanish Slaving in Texas Takes Shape, 1721–1740

According to Margo Tamez, it is erroneous to interpret Ndé interactions with Spanish colonists outside of the centuries-long Ndé traditions of anticolonial rebellion, which strove to "release . . . sites of conquest back to sites of *diyin* (an Ndé concept of spiritual autonomy and 'power')."[37] Certainly, the first Ndé attacks on the rising Spanish settler colonial apparatus in Texas bear out that argument. Beginning in April 1721, Ndé rangers disrupted colonial operations by sabotaging lines of commerce, injuring or killing colonists, and confiscating dozens of horses in the vicinity of the Spanish presidio at San Antonio. But regardless of Ndé intentions, these same attacks unleashed the first wave of Spanish slaving violence out of the newly established San Antonio settler colonial hub. Nicolás Flores y Valdés led two campaigns, one in 1722 and another in 1723, and both military responses illustrated the iron-fisted impulses of Spanish endeavors. With the help of dozens of Native allies, the Spanish soldier-settlers traversed the Ndé homeland, ventured across the northern range of hills known as La Lomería, and mercilessly hunted Ndé rangers and their families. They returned to San Antonio with scores of horses, news of mass killings, and even the severed heads of Ndé rebels, bloody trophies that signaled to other colonists and their Native neighbors that Spaniards were to rule supreme in the Texas borderlands. Flores and company also brought back plenty of plunder: Ndé saddles, bridles, knives, spears, and other manufactured goods. And of course, the Spanish colonists took slaves, specifically twenty women and children, who were "distributed among the soldiers" upon their return to San Antonio.[38] With the early 1720s Flores campaigns, a new era of Spanish slaving had arrived in the Texas borderlands.

Yet the full expansion of Spanish slaving into the San Antonio sphere was not necessarily a foregone conclusion. Upon the return of Flores and his men from their 1723 expedition, one of the local religious, Fray José

González, protested to officials that the women and children enslaved by the campaigners were not to be distributed among the Spanish residents of San Antonio to live out their lives in bondage, but instead to be used as conduits for peace. This particular course of action (i.e., captive diplomacy), if successful, might have steered Spaniards toward less violent relations with Ndé people down the road, and it would have allowed the Spanish colonists to claim fidelity to the dictates of the Spanish Crown regarding the enslavement of Indians. But even though Flores sent a forty-year-old Ndé woman back to her *ranchería* in October 1723, when Ndé diplomats visited San Antonio three weeks later to discuss the terms of their people's release, Flores convinced himself—after speaking with two individuals who were formerly enslaved by Apaches—that the Ndé leadership had no interest in suppressing their anticolonial efforts, caring only for the liberation of their friends and family. So when a second Ndé diplomatic party arrived at San Antonio in early 1724, Flores refused to return their kin. Disgusted, the emissaries departed, leaving behind a twelve-year-old girl. The gesture was both symbolic and illustrative. As the Ndé *capitán* dramatically handed over the girl, he said to Flores, "Take *muchacho*," insinuating, "This is what you want, not peace."[39] In the eyes of the Ndé, Spanish prisoner-taking was all about slave accumulation. And given the long history of Spanish colonialism in the Northeast, where violence, coercion, and exploitation were a sanctioned part of Hispanic life, this Ndé analysis was astute.[40]

Predictably, Ndé resistance to Spanish settler colonialism in Texas persisted, and Apache attacks escalated over the years. From 1724 to 1726, Spaniards reported Apache raids at San Antonio, at El Almagre (near the Llanos River), on the upper Medina, along the Nueces, and near the Guadalupe River. In these raids, Ndé fighters cast a wide net, attacking and even enslaving individuals from Spanish, Mesquite, Paquache, and Sana communities.[41] Spanish officials did not leave accounts of any specific anti-Apache reprisals, but in 1728 Brig. Pedro de Rivera Villalón reported, "The only enemies of the area [of San Antonio] are a few *indios* Apaches living in *la lomería grande*, who . . . [are] usually punished for their boldness."[42] But those "*indios* Apaches," in tandem with widespread Native rebellion across the Spanish frontier, acted like a specter in the Spanish mind. Rivera, who at the time was touring the Mexican North at the behest of the viceroy, would go on to craft proposals to reform the administration of Spain's frontier colonies, and his recommendations (codified in the Reglamento de 1729) explicitly recognized how anti-Native violence was to serve as the fulcrum of Spanish colonial successes there. Presidial collaboration and strategic, conscientious incursions, his orders explained, were necessary to free the colonies, especially the Texas borderlands settlements, "from the ravages wrought by *los indios enemigos.*" Changes to Spanish slaving practices, moreover, seemed necessary, and the Reglamento outlawed the tradition of distributing prisoners among the local Spanish population in favor of a policy that deported all of those enslaved "to the outskirts of Mexico." The final piece to the reimagined Texas puzzle was consolidation of the San Antonio field, with the relocation of the Querétaro-run missions of eastern Texas to the San Antonio River and the importation of dozens of Canary Island settlers. Collectively, Rivera's reconfiguration called for greater Spanish punitive power, the elimination of Native dissidents and rebels, and the strengthening of settler communities. In other words, Spanish authorities sought a reinvigoration of the settler colonial project in Texas.[43]

The events of 1731–32 would put Rivera's new program to the test. After a months-long wave of Ndé attacks on Spanish travelers, mule trains, and herds in 1731, local Spaniards lamented that only the Native residents of Mission Valero, who were said to have "dispersed the Apaches with great shouts," had any success repelling these Apache rangers. Then on September 18, 1731, some forty Ndé raiders stole sixty horses from the presidio, leading a small group of Spanish soldiers away from presidial defenses. By the time Capt. Juan Antonio Pérez de Almazán arrived at the scene of the skirmish, about five hundred Ndé fighters had come to reinforce their compatriots, now outnumbering the Spaniards about fifty to one. Luckily for the Spanish soldiers, after a two-hour showdown a large group of armed San Antonio mission-settlement Indians came to the rescue and chased away the Ndé war party. The missionary Fray Mariano de los Dolores y Viana later recalled, "If the *Yndios* of this mission had not entered the conflict, all would have been killed and the Presidio of San Antonio ransacked and destroyed."[44]

Unfortunately for the Ndé communities living in the broader vicinity of San Antonio, their 1731 anticolonial sweeps served as the kind of rallying cry the Spaniards desired to resume their violent campaigning. In his report to the viceroy in December 1731, Captain Almazán claimed that the extent of Apache hostility toward San Antonio that year had been unprecedented, frightening so many Spaniards that soldiers were ready to relocate their families elsewhere. For the *capitán*, it was time to punish these intractable enemies. His primary impediment was securing enough military aid, as he could mobilize only sixty soldiers, and the *vecinos* of the settlements were willing to fight only if compensated with slaves. Fortunately for Almazán, viceregal support quelled his fears, and even Pedro de Rivera—in his role as advisor to the viceroy—rubber-stamped a settler-soldier license for slaving, provided the prisoners were relocated to other provinces after the battles concluded. On January 6, 1732, the viceroy ordered the campaign against the Apaches of Texas to be carried out.[45]

Although administrative quarreling delayed the punitive expedition, a joint Spanish-Native force of two hundred to three hundred campaigners departed from San Antonio into Ndé country on October 22, 1732. Led by a new governor, Juan Antonio de Bustillo y Ceballos, the large party hoped to recruit the aid of Caddos located near the San Gabriel River. Unfortunately, their slave-raiding reputation had proceeded them; one of the *capitanes*, El Francés, had cautioned his people that the Spaniards were planning to enslave their women and children while their warriors were away fighting Apaches, so they declined to help.[46] Undeterred by the Caddo refusal, Governor Bustillo and company pressed on and eventually found four *rancherías* in the vicinity of the San Sabá River. The seven hundred warriors they encountered there were purportedly from four different *naciones* (Apaches, Ypandis, Yxandis, and Chentis), and the following battle lasted about five hours. Bustillo later reported that Spanish forces had killed some two hundred enemy Indians, enslaving thirty-eight women and children—a number so small only because most had fled immediately upon seeing the Spanish threat. Additionally, the Spanish soldiers seized several hundred horses and mules. With only one reported casualty and seven Spaniards wounded, the 1732 campaign was a smashing success for the Spanish-led party.[47]

Back-and-forth violence would continue throughout the 1730s, with Ndé rangers descending upon Spanish outposts, traveling parties, and herds, and Spaniards responding with attacks of their own. In July 1733, after soldiers, friars, and civilians sent petition after petition to Spanish authorities, help seemed to have arrived in the form of an old frontier veteran: José de Urrutia. Urrutia, who supposedly had led thousands of Native people to war against Ndé communities in Texas during the 1690s, became captain of the San Antonio presidio in July 1733, and officials in Mexico City explicitly ordered him to lead an expedition of "pacification" against unrelenting Ndé anticolonial resistance.[48] Urrutia's leadership was not as decisive and transformative as Spanish locals had hoped, but under his watch Spaniards still successfully captured the prominent Ndé *capitán*, Cabellos Colorados, who during the mid-1730s forged a trade relationship with some San Antonio residents but also enslaved two Spanish *vecinos*.[49] Furthermore, in 1739 Urrutia led a company of men into Apachería, near the San Sabá River, where they attacked a *ranchería*. Enslaving Indians was still illegal according to the dictates of the Spanish Crown, but Urrutia and his men paid no mind. As Fray Fernandez de Santa Ana, who was critical of Urrutia's actions, later explained, slaving was fundamental to the 1739 campaigners: "The expedition was profitable to those only who had horses and other commodities which they sold at exorbitant prices. It is rather ridiculous that these same people claim to be pledged as servants of our King while their intention was, as I have mentioned, to gain a considerable capture of horses, hides, *Yndios* and *Yndias* to serve them. These are the aims of the expedition motivating most of the *vecinos* who join the soldiers for such purposes. Just as the goal is so base, so is the outcome."[50] Extant evidence does not indicate specifically how many Ndé individuals fell victim to Spanish slaving during Urrutia's late 1739 campaign, but Spanish accounts make it clear that after two decades of settler colonialism in Texas, Spanish colonists had normalized the impulse to enslave.

From Slave Raids to Missions: Apache-Spanish Relations, 1740–1760

By 1740, Spaniards had entangled themselves fully within borderlands cycles of slaving and raiding violence. Stationed hundreds of miles away from administrative centers, Spanish colonists in Texas negotiated and manipulated local circumstances to elevate their importance in regional affairs, with and without official state endorsement. They had searched for vulnerable but willing allies and had found locals who believed a Spanish partnership would offer leverage against a common foe. When Ndé fighters attacked the Spanish intruders, the colonists responded with an onslaught of slaving fury. For many Spanish soldiers and *vecinos*, slaving had emerged as a forceful, manly response to the tribulations of a harsh frontier life, an articulation of Spanish dominion in a Native-dominated world. Just as important, of course, was the reality that enslaved individuals provided labor and economic reprieve in a place where poverty and hardship prevailed.[51] If Spanish authorities truly believed that their empire was effectively curtailing anti-Native slavery, the Texas arena offered a plethora of evidence that they were fooling themselves. To the contrary, the Spanish enslavement of Native people in the Texas borderlands was only becoming more prevalent.

The 1740 replacement of José de Urrutia with his son, Toribio Urrutia, as captain of the San Antonio presidio all but guaranteed that slaving would continue to drive Spanish colonial interactions with Ndé locals. Like his father, Toribio Urrutia embraced slaving violence as a solution to Apache resistance. The only problem was that Ndé communities were beginning to diversify their responses to Spanish aggression at the same time that Urrutia ascended to the Béxar captaincy, making it more difficult for Spanish colonists to justify all-out war against Apaches. In December 1740, for instance, San Antonio officials reported that the Ndé leader Cuero de Coyote had visited the presidio, asking for permission to settle his people on the banks of the Guadalupe River, some eighty miles northeast of San Antonio. According to the report, the "primary reason" Cuero de Coyote and his followers reached out to the Spaniards was that they "want to live there with the Spaniards and Father Missionaries." This was an obvious olive branch on the part of Ndé diplomats, a blueprint to move toward long-term peace with the Spanish colonial invaders, but Spaniards could interpret it only as overdue capitulation to the holy project of missionary Christianization—if not further evidence of Apache mendacity.[52] Spaniards not far to the south, nonetheless, continued campaigning against eastern Ndé communities, and Urrutia plotted his own deadly operations against their rebellious foes.[53]

Urrutia's moment came in the spring of 1745, when he led a force of about fifty soldiers and auxiliaries from San Antonio north toward Apachería. According to Fray Benito Fernández de Santa Ana, who accompanied the men on the expedition, the Spanish forces ultimately found and attacked a *ranchería* of some two hundred Ypandes and Natagés near the San Sabá River. It is unclear exactly how many people the Spaniards enslaved, but the baptismal records from San Fernando de Béxar indicate that the Spaniards seized at least fourteen children. Fray Juan Domingo Arricivita claimed that Urrutia "had such good success that not only did he subdue them, but also he made prisoners of many of their leaders and most respected elders." Soon after the slaving expedition, four Ndé women traveled to San Antonio, alerting the Spanish colonists that they had just squandered any chance for peace.[54]

Ndé retribution was swift and severe. Only a couple of months after the Urrutia campaign, on June 30, 1745, two groups of Ypandes and Natagés led a massive attack on the San Antonio presidio. The Apache forces totaled some 350 individuals (including women and children), so many that the Spaniards believed "they could have attacked the presidio mercilessly and without fear of much opposition." About one hundred

Native residents from Mission Valero came to the rescue of the presidio and attacked the encroaching Ndé party "with such impetus and shouting that at first discharge of the guns, they killed several and forced the others to withdraw." Nevertheless, the show of force demonstrated to the Spaniards the direness of Ndé-Spanish relations and the extent to which slave raiding had infuriated Ndé community members.[55]

What seems to have curbed the fury of the attackers was news that their enslaved kin had not yet suffered much abuse at the hands of the Spaniards. Although evidence suggests that Captain Urrutia and his fellow campaigners would have preferred to keep the dozens of Ndé prisoners from the 1745 campaign permanently as slaves, Fray Fernández and others were intent upon using them as pawns for peace talks. According to Fray Fernández, one prisoner was particularly valuable for convincing the Apaches to agree to peace: the seven-year-old daughter of the *capitán grande* of the Ypandes. The missionary likely gained possession of the young girl as a member of the slave-raiding expedition, and immediately upon returning to San Antonio he baptized her, declaring, "I . . . will not give her up until her father submits to royal authority."[56]

Certainly, the friar's declaration struck a chord. As Fray Fernández would later note, "What they [the Apaches] value most—more than any gift or courtesy I could give them—is the liberty of the *presas* from their *nación*."[57] In addition to the seven-year-old child, the Spaniards had enslaved other kin of the Ypande *capitán grande*. The friar and his supporters were effectively holding these Apaches hostage in hopes of forcing the hand of their leaders. Essentially, the Spaniards offered them an ultimatum: either submit to Spanish authority or abandon their family to a life of perpetual slavery. Slowly, requests for mission-settlements began to filter into San Antonio.[58] For Fray Fernández and company, this was captive diplomacy at its finest: not only were Ndé leaders willing to talk peace; they were also talking about missions.

Yet other difficulties in securing the peace continued to surface during the latter part of the 1740s, particularly as the enemies of Ndé communities began petitioning for Spanish aid. Several weeks after Urrutia's slave-raiding expedition returned to San Antonio, a delegation of Yojuanes, Deadoses, Mayeyes, and Ervipiames arrived at San Antonio, requesting a mission-settlement. Requests for missions continued to pour in throughout the year from the leaders of these *naciones*, and even the Cocos of the Gulf Coast, who actively had resisted European colonization for generations, expressed interest in Spanish missionary assistance. In February 1746, Spanish clergymen got to work building

Mission San Francisco Xavier de Horcasitas along the San Xavier (now San Gabriel) River with dozens of Ervipiames, Mayeyes, and Yojuanes. Nearly three years later, Spanish missionaries were able to convince a number of Orcoquizas, Bidais, and Deadoses to relocate to nearby Mission San Ildefonso, and by spring 1749 Cocos and Topes were gathering at a third mission-settlement, Mission Nuestra Señora de la Candelaria. On July 7, 1749, capital officials sanctioned plans for the construction of a presidio on the San Xavier River, named Presidio San Xavier de Gigedo. Finally, after decades of negotiation, Spanish officials were bringing the Ranchería Grande people into the fold of Spanish rule.[59]

But the new Spanish alliances with the Yojuanes, Ervipiames, Mayayes, Orcoquizas, Bidais, Deadoses, and Cocos frustrated Ndé leaders, as these groups had been adversaries of their people for decades and were currently implicated in the Caddo-French trade in enslaved Apaches.[60] Additionally, the location of the new mission-settlements along the San Xavier River, known as Apache Pass, had long been a key thoroughfare for Ndé travelers, if not part of Ndé country proper. Peace talks with Spanish officials, if infrequent, at least had signaled to the Ndé leaders some commitment to a new era of qualified amity. The San Xavier mission-settlements, however, were a show of bad faith on the part of the Spaniards, undermining their budding peaceful relationship. Thus, it was not long before Ndé raiders were descending upon the new San Xavier mission-settlements, and soon they were turning their attention back to the San Antonio settlements.[61] So after a large group of Ndé raiders killed four Spanish soldiers from the presidio there, Coahuila's Governor Pedro de Rábago y Terán led a punitive expedition, which included twenty soldiers from San Antonio and about ten *vecinos* from San Fernando de Béxar, north from Monclova, past San Antonio, and into Apachería. Over the course of several days, the expeditioners devastated various Ndé communities, seizing dozens of mules and horses and as many captives as they could find. Years later, Juan Antonio Moraín remembered the campaign as being "not as successful as he had anticipated," but the expedition still yielded slaves for the residents of San Antonio, San Juan Bautista, and Monclova.[62]

The Rábago y Terán campaign of 1748 did not, however, quench the Spanish thirst for retributive submission, and Captain Urrutia proceeded to conduct two more campaigns during the winter of 1749. Before leading the expeditions, Urrutia gave specific orders regarding appropriate conduct, explicitly advocating (benevolent) enslavement over slaughter: "Neither the soldiers nor the auxiliary *indios* were to kill any *indio*, except in self-defense. They were simply to capture those they could, of both sexes, and any captives were to be treated with great kindness."[63] The first punitive expedition consisted of about seventy Spaniards and 130 Native auxiliaries and ultimately sacked a small, undefended Ndé *ranchería* in February, taking three women and five children. During the campaign, however, Ndé rangers had taken advantage of the absence of Spanish forces at San Antonio and had raided Mission Concepción. When Urrutia and company learned of the attack upon their return to San Antonio, they immediately gathered an additional hundred fighters and set out in pursuit of the raiders. Near the Guadalupe River, about fifty miles from San Antonio, the pursuers found another vulnerable Apache *ranchería*. The Spanish forces routed the Ndé community and seized an additional thirty men, ninety women, and forty-seven children. With 175 total captives taken, this campaign represented the largest slave raid in Spanish Texas to date.[64]

Once the expedition party returned to San Antonio, the missionaries moved quickly to stake a claim in the future of these newly enslaved Apaches. As in the past, the friars were adamant about using the prisoners as pawns for opening up diplomatic talks with Ndé leaders. Fray Dolores y Viana selected one woman taken during the campaigns to serve as a messenger, telling her and others that "the missionary fathers wished them the greatest spiritual good for their souls and much happiness for all their people." He then sent the woman to relay this message to her people, also letting them know that if they gathered in mission-settlements, "the missionaries would intercede with the Spaniards to return all the prisoners." Such a promise would have resonated with the Ndé leaders because the Spaniards had made various efforts to distribute the prisoners across Spanish Texas as slaves soon after they arrived at San Antonio. As Fray Arricivita claimed, "The cravings for servants was such that even the governor of the province, using his absolute power, took several of them to Adais." Only word of the viceroy's explicit orders stalled the Spanish residents' slaving impulses: "When the viceroy was informed of this, he wrote him [the governor] a letter ordering him to return them immediately and without delay to the presidio of San Antonio, calling his attention to the abuse he had committed in carrying them away. This strong eyewash was necessary to open the eyes of those who had been blinded by the craving for slaves."[65]

It was not long before Ndé representatives began to stream into San Antonio, some making promises to settle in Spanish-run mission-settlements, others expressing interest in establishing new lines of diplomacy by marrying the Native women of the San Antonio missions. According to Fray Arricivita, "Their perseverance in asking for them [mission-settlements] . . . was like an arrow that penetrated [the] heart with inconsolable grief." But the missionaries were uncertain of how to settle the many Ndé bands that were spread out across Texas. Fray Dolores y Viana was worried that the congregation of too many people in one locale would undermine missionizing efforts, as the sheer numbers would overwhelm the few missionaries. Moreover, the missionaries were afraid that these Apaches, longtime adversaries of Spanish colonialism, would sway the missionized Indians of San Antonio away from Spanish influence: "[The missionaries] had to prevent the neophytes from becoming contaminated by the wretched habits and diabolical ceremonies observed by the Apaches or by the dances and beverages that they use in their great fiestas." Thus by 1749, Spanish missionaries had a lot to be optimistic about, but it was a cautious optimism.[66]

Missionary claims notwithstanding, Ndé requests for Spanish support were less about a spiritual longing for Christian guidance and more about an exploration of alternative means for survival. By the latter part of 1749, the sum of Spanish slave raiding, a budding Comanche-Wichita-Caddo alliance, and the rapid depletion of regional bison had forced Ndé leaders to reevaluate their standing within their Texas homelands. One Spanish soldier, Ygnacio de Zepeda, remarked several years later, "They [the Apaches] were suffering so much hunger and were so intimidated by the Comanches that they were compelled to live among the Spaniards." Thus, Ndé diplomats, including Boca Comida, reached out to both Spanish missionaries *and* military men. According to Governor Domingo Cabello in his 1784 report, the peace deliberations of August 1749 led to the release of many enslaved Apaches and to a number of shared ceremonies between Spanish leaders, Ndé *capitanes*, and mission Indians. The peace talks culminated on August 19 with a great dance at the plaza of the San Antonio presidio, where the large group of Apaches, Spaniards, and Native locals buried a live horse, a hatchet, a lance, and six arrows. With these celebrations, the Ndé and Spanish participants promised "to treat each other as friends and brothers."[67]

The new peace treaty was the impetus the Spanish missionaries needed to push forward their long-held designs for Ndé mission-settlements. On February 23, 1750, Fray Fernández de Santa Ana wrote to the viceroy, Conde de Revillagigedo, with plans for the foundation of an Apache mission-settlement. According to Fray Fernández, Apache enthusiasm for Spanish support was at an all-time high. Key to the friar's plan was a program that would cover the material well-being of the new recruits, which would reduce even "the most rebellious *nación* . . . to civilized life." And when bribes failed, an accompanying presidial force would coerce the new mission residents to "sow their fields and maintain them until the harvest." Everything was falling into place, Fray Fernández argued; even the decades-long animosity between Ndé communities and other Native peoples of central and southern Texas—who were now residing in or near mission-settlements on the San Antonio River—was coming to an end. He claimed, "Although they are very old enemies of the Apaches, they [the San Antonio mission Indians] say, 'We always thought that the Apaches would never be our friends nor come to be Christians, but today we know that their friendship with us comes from the heart. They speak the truth, that they desire a mission, and the priests can believe them.'"[68]

Not all Spanish colonists were enthusiastic, though, as nearly three decades of violence between Ndé rangers and Spanish colonists had created a lingering sense of fear and bitterness, particularly for San Antonio *vecinos*. According to Fray Dolores, the settlers of San Antonio were generally opposed to Apache missions "because their children and women were handed over to the Apaches and some of them do not want to be deprived of the quickest advantages that come to them in having in their possession some *Yndizuelos* whom they deprive of speaking with their relatives."[69] *Vecino* reservations notwithstanding, missionizing efforts prevailed. During the first half of the 1750s, Spanish officials dispatched a number of representatives to investigate prospective sites for Apache missions-settlements along the Pedernales, Sanas (Llano), and San Sabá rivers, and the final exploratory mission, under the command of Pedro de Rábago y Terán, struck gold when they encountered the *ranchería* of the Ndé leader Tacú, known also as Chiquito, just past the Pedernales River. Tacú claimed that he and his 467 followers were longing for Spanish assistance and that he knew of ten more *capitanes* on the Concho River who were also looking to ally with Spaniards. Unilaterally, Rábago y Terán decided to move the San Xavier mission-settlements to the San Marcos River, deeper into Apachería, to begin the long process of incorporating Ndé families into the mission system.[70]

The slow pace of Ndé mission development during the 1750s was more the result of the crawling speed of Spanish colonial bureaucracy than of the purported treachery or indolence of Ndé petitioners, as Spaniards often claimed. Along the Río Grande, other Ndé leaders, including Pastellano, started requesting missionary aid in 1750, and over the next five years thousands of Ndé men, women, and children would flow in and out of a makeshift and constantly moving Ndé-serving mission system, with minor "successes" at Pueblo San Lorenzo, where a number of influential Ndé *capitanes*, including El Gordo, El de Godo, and Bigotes, spent some time. The most promising mission-settlement during the era, from the perspective of Spanish missionaries, was Mission Santa Cruz de San Sabá, which was built along with Presidio de San Luis de Las Amarillas near the San Sabá River. With Diego Ortiz Parrilla commanding the presidio and Fray Terreros heading the mission, the San Sabá complex drew considerable favor from various Ndé bands, including that of El Chico and his Lipan kinspeople. By the summer of 1757, Spaniards counted some three thousand Ndé residents in the San Sabá vicinity. Although the Ndé presence was often fleeting and uneven during the subsequent fall and winter months, the amiable response the Spaniards received was more than a welcome reprieve from the previous three decades of explicitly anticolonial violence. As never before, a lasting peace appeared within the realm of possibility.[71]

But Spanish authorities underestimated the geopolitical ramifications of their new Ndé collaboration. Although the Spaniards had been aware of the prevalence of anti-Ndé animosity across the Texas borderlands for decades, the opportunity to subdue Apaches through missions was, in the minds of Spanish leaders, too good to pass up. A long-term mission-based Spanish-Apache alliance, they reasoned, would put an end to the cycles of violence that had cursed the borderlands for decades while simultaneously asserting Spanish supremacy. Unfortunately for the Spanish colonists of Texas, their Ndé plans were severely shortsighted. By allying with a people who remained the adversaries of numerous other Native groups, Spaniards declared *themselves* the enemy. Perhaps Spanish officials simply miscalculated the utility of an Apache peace, or perhaps Spanish colonists were too blinded by their drive for glory and regional power to recognize the dangers of their actions. Either way, the Ndé collaboration, particularly the San Sabá project, would prove to be one of the greatest oversights in the history of Spanish Texas, not only transforming the geopolitics of the region but also marking the beginning of a new era of slavery.

The immense folly of the Spanish decision to declare allegiance to the Ndé communities of Texas became readily apparent when, on March 16, 1758, some two thousand Native warriors descended upon the recently constructed San Sabá mission. The scene of so many well-armed Native fighters horrified the few Spanish residents of the mission, as "most of the enemy carried firearms, ammunition in large powder horns and pouches, swords, lances, and cutlasses." Even the younger boys carried bows and arrows. Just as ominous, many of the attackers rode up on horses, their faces covered with red and black war paint and their bodies clothed in French uniforms. "Some were disguised as various kinds of animals," reported Fray Miguel de Molina, "and some wore feather headdresses." At the head of the party was a Comanche *capitán grande*, who left quite the impression upon Fray Molina: "His dress and his red jacket were well-decorated, after the manner of French uniforms, and he was fully armed. His face was hideous and extremely grave." When the friars approached the leaders of the war party, they made generous offerings of tobacco and other items, only to be rejected and humiliated. The attackers wanted no part of the missionaries and their tribute; they "had no intention other than to fight the Apaches." Spanish overtures thus failed to sway the commanders, and soon Native fighters were raiding the mission grounds for anything of value. After shooting a friar and a soldier in the back as they rode off, the attackers sacked the mission. Andres de Villareal, a guard at the San Sabá Mission, recalled, "At once the barbarians loosed their cruelty on all our people, killing and wounding them."[72]

News of the "Norteño" assault swept across New Spain, and along the northern frontier fear spread like wildfire. The Spaniards were unsure where to lay the blame. Some pondered the role of foreign agents, possibly Frenchmen; others found Spanish military weakness culpable.[73] And even though the Ndé residents were the obvious targets of the siege, a number of Spanish leaders in the Northeast, including Governor Ángel de Martos y Navarrete of Coahuila, wanted to blame Apaches for the violence at San Sabá, because "although they are our friends (or so they say), they . . . [did not] warn us that the Comanches were plotting against us." But firsthand witnesses were crystal clear when it came to identifying the culprits of the attack and their motives: the so-called Norteños, or Northerners, were out for Apache blood.[74] Equipped with horses and French firearms, Comanches, Wichitas, Tonkawas, and Caddos had allied by the 1750s, and at San Sabá this confederation of Norteños continued their decades-long wars with the Ndé peoples of Texas.[75]

After the panic subsided and concerns over culpability evaporated, a familiar refrain emerged: Native violence could not go unpunished. Colonel Ortiz Parrilla, whose honor had taken a significant hit during the entire fiasco at San Sabá, pushed to lead the obligatory punitive campaign against the Norteños. The captain outlined his intentions in a letter to the viceroy, the Marqués de las Amarillas, on April 8, 1758: "I shall carry out the just punishment of the barbarians at the proper time and in their own land whenever you consider it advisable. . . . I shall be most happy to punish severely the audacity of these false and treacherous heathen and teach them that their low opinion of our settlements in these parts is mistaken. If I have the same good fortune that I have had in the other enterprises I have undertaken, I assure you that nothing will be left to be desired."[76] Amid a sea of bad news, such bold predictions must have arrived as a breath of fresh air for Ortiz Parrilla's superiors, and plans for a counterattack against the Norteños gained momentum over the course of the year.

The Ortiz Parrilla expedition set out for Norteño country from San Antonio in late August 1759 and arrived at the San Sabá River on September 1. The campaign forces were composed of about five hundred members, including fighters from the Río Grande, Nuevo León, San Luis Potosí, San Antonio, San Sabá, La Bahía, and Coahuila outposts.[77] One hundred thirty-four Ndé fighting men assisted the Spanish-led forces throughout the expedition, with numerous other Apaches accompanying the troops from time to time. From the San Sabá, the campaigning party traveled north toward the Red River, and after following the tracks of various mobile Native communities, they found a Yojuan *ranchería* at Arroyo de la Emboscada. The campaigners assaulted the encampment and after about three hours of fighting defeated the Yojuanes. The attackers seized 149 Yojuan men, women, and children, leaving fifty Yojuanes dead. According to the diarist of the expedition, who was critical of his Ndé allies' performance, "Five children and five women . . . perished by the barbarous rigor of the Apaches, who used their arms only on the children and the women."[78]

With help from the Ndé auxiliaries, the Spanish soldiers chained together the enslaved Yojuanes and interrogated a handful of them. From these interrogations, the Spaniards learned of a village of Taguayas, Yscanes, Taguacanas, Quichais, and Paises on "the river of the French presidio of Natchitoches, which they call the Red," and the expeditionary forces continued their march. On October 7, several dozen Norteño warriors surprised the Spanish-led forces but ran away into nearby woods before fully engaging them. The retreat, however, was tactical; the Norteño skirmishers had led the campaigners into a trap. Upon exiting the wooded area, Ortiz Parrilla and his followers discovered a highly fortified Taovaya village, "consisting of tall oval-shaped huts enclosed by a stockade and moat." Behind the fortress, bands of Comanches had made camp. As Juan Angel de Oyarzun reported it, "the entire front of the stockade was crowned with Indians armed with muskets." A French flag flew in the center of the fort, and sentinels shouted from afar, mocking the Spanish and Native onlookers. It was not long before the two sides exchanged gunfire.[79]

The Norteño warriors impressed the Spanish soldiers with both their weaponry and their discipline. The Spanish troops, on the other hand, were less impressive. According to the campaign diarist, the Spanish campaigners, "discouraged, confused, and without any remedy whatsoever, failed entirely in obedience and in the sustained vigor with which the engagement began." And as the fighting continued, the Ndé auxiliaries lost interest as well, "protesting that in the entire afternoon they have not been able to find a way to steal the enemy's horses or other effects or to take prisoners." As casualties continued to mount, the Spanish captain finally decided to retreat. With fifty-four Spanish soldiers and auxiliaries killed and two cannons lost, Colonel Ortiz Parrilla and his remaining followers marched back to San Antonio with their proverbial tail between their legs.[80] The one silver lining was the fact that the campaigners had managed to drag along with them the chain gang of enslaved Yojuanes. At San Antonio, the Apaches sold off most of the enslaved Yojuanes, and a few received the holy waters of baptism—a ritual that guaranteed them a life of bondage in Spanish Texas.[81]

The 1759 campaign was an apt bookend to the first four decades of Spanish colonization.[82] For about forty years, Spaniards fought with resistant Ndé peoples across the Texas borderlands to secure their place as rulers of the region, and for about forty years, Native communities foiled these attempts. Violence and slavery, moreover, characterized much of the interaction between Spaniards and their Native enemies. The enslavement of 149 Yojuan men, women, and children was a last-ditch effort to demonstrate to the geopolitical players of the region that Spaniards were still the dominant force of Texas. Although tragic, it was fitting that the slave raid targeted a vulnerable community that was only partly complicit in the San Sabá attack. Spanish violence certainly had its flair, but unfortunately for the Spaniards, their violence was often more efficient at demonstrating insecurity than at articulating dominion.

"These Prisoners Were Their Slaves": The Contours of Spanish Slavery, 1720–1760

The closing years of the 1750s marked the beginning of the end to the brief Spanish heyday in Texas. For decades, Spaniards slowly forged alliances with the diverse communities of the Texas borderlands, usually by means of shared violence against Ndé peoples. Through such warfare, the Spaniards sought to demonstrate their dominance over the Indigenous people of the borderlands, and for some time Spanish raiding and missionizing successfully managed to reorient regional power along a Spanish-centered axis. San Antonio—while not the Texas paradise Spaniards had dreamed of decades earlier—had become a hub of Native reinvention where Native people gathered to reorganize, marry, subsist, and trade. Mission-building efforts were virtually unceasing, and even though it was clearly not the intention of Spanish authorities, the mission-settlements of Texas provided loci for revitalization of broken or splintered Indigenous populations.[83] Furthermore, by the 1740s the mission-settlements along the San Antonio River had achieved a level of economic prosperity unmatched in the region.[84] Thus, while the Native communities of Texas continued to function with respect to non-Spanish prerogatives, Spanish assistance based along the San Antonio River operated as an undeniably magnetic force; the frequent engagement of Native people with Spanish institutions was evidence that many of the Native peoples of Texas were making efforts to incorporate themselves into a Spanish-oriented world.

But mission-settlements were only one part of Spanish plans to dominate the Texas borderlands. Settler colonization was equally integral to Spanish schemes, and the soldiers and civilians who built the colonial outposts served as the arms of the Spanish Empire. Unfortunately for central government officials, the Spanish colonists they sent to Texas often acted, as settler colonists often do, according to their own concerns and imperatives rather than the dictates of Spanish authorities.[85] The conditions of the northeastern frontier were often isolating, cruel, and unforgiving, and Spanish colonists regularly sought to exploit, through violence, the seemingly untapped labor supplies that were Native communities. Yet it was only the continuous military conflicts with Ndé peoples that offered eager Spanish soldiers and settlers any real opportunities to gather bodies to exploit. From about 1720 to 1760, the world of Spanish Texas was rather small and insulated, and the demand for enslaved people never reached the proportions of the Caribbean colonies, central

Mexico, or even other outposts in the North. Nevertheless, calls for slaves frequently surfaced in Spanish Texas. As Fray Arricivita claimed, "No edict was sufficient to prevent the soldiers of the different presidios from wanting to take prisoners, nor the settlers from insisting on selling them. They were all stubborn in their claim that these prisoners were their slaves."[86]

Spanish Texas was not equipped for the agriculture-based slavery that prevailed in some parts of New Spain, and despite frequent rumors of Texas's great mining potential, Spaniards in Texas had no need for enslaved mine workers.[87] Instead, Spanish colonists sought out slaves to assist them in the daily drudgeries of life on the frontier. The handful of legally recognized slaves in Spanish Texas likely worked as domestic or artisanal servants. These enslaved people were always Black, and their status was framed by a legal structure designed to protect and to coordinate the transactions of slave buyers and sellers. Since the days of Álvar Núñez Cabeza de Vaca, enslaved Black people accompanied Spanish travelers into Texas, and these early bondsmen shared in many of the struggles (and sometimes intrigue) of life on the northeastern frontier. Their roles were diverse, some serving as personal servants and others as trumpeters, but just as important all enslaved Black people—unlike enslaved Native individuals—were chattel property.[88] This point was made clear in the eighteenth-century bills of sale that declared Black slaves "subject to servitude, free from contract, mortgage, and debenture, or lien." And like *ganado mayor* (large livestock such as cows and horses), Black bodies had monetary value and could be sold and traded according to the desires of their owners.[89] In short, anti-Black slavery functioned with respect to the economic imperatives of purchasers and traders, a harsh reality that made life under slavery in Spanish Texas especially unpredictable and oppressive (and similar to the slavery endured by other Black men, women, and children throughout the Atlantic world).

Enslaved Afro-Mexicans were not, of course, the only enslaved people in Texas; enslaved Native people lived with and worked alongside Black bondspeople. And even though enslaved Black people were among the earliest Hispanicized migrants to Texas, enslaved Native people generally outnumbered them from 1720 to 1760. In the poor reaches of Mexico's Northeast, few Spanish colonists had the capital to purchase enslaved Black people, so many turned to the enslavement of Native people for alternative sources of labor. The switch to anti-Native slavery, nonetheless, was not a simple, seamless process, and neither was it absolute. Because the Spanish Crown had outlawed *la esclavitud de los indios*, Spanish slavers either had to become ideological acrobats to justify their slaving practices or keep their slaving hidden from administrative view (a feat that was not too difficult in the borderlands). Ultimately, most slavers agreed that if the enslavement of Native people could be couched in the language of punishment, protection, and Christianization, the question of anti-Native slavery's legality was moot. As Spanish slaving escalated throughout the eighteenth century, many slavers saw their violence simply as a natural outgrowth of their colonial presence.

Statistics offer some insight into the broader outlines of Spanish slavery in Texas. From 1720 to 1760, Spaniards and their Native auxiliaries enslaved at least five hundred to six hundred Native men, women, and children. This does not mean, however, that every enslaved individual was kept long term as a slave within Spanish Texas. Some were sent south to the mining districts of the Mexican Northeast, while others were charged with crimes (e.g., rebellion) and served out their sentences in Mexico City. Still others were returned to their home communities at the conclusion of diplomatic talks.[90] These qualifications aside, a comparison of the number of people enslaved during Spanish campaigns with the numbers from contemporary Spanish population counts provides some sense of the magnitude of slaving in Spanish Texas. In 1723, when Nicolás Flores and several other soldiers enslaved twenty Ndé women and children, the total Spanish population in San Antonio was approximately 150 colonists—a ratio of two enslaved Apaches per fifteen Spaniards. Nearly ten years later, after the Bustillo y Ceballos slaving expedition in 1732, the Spanish population of San Antonio (including the newly founded villa of San Fernando de Béxar) had more than doubled to about 350 residents, and the ratio of Ndé bondspeople to Spanish colonists was about one to nine. It is unclear exactly how many Ndé captives were seized during the 1745 Toribio Urrutia punitive campaign, but Spaniards baptized at least nineteen Ndé prisoners in San Antonio. With this figure, an average of one in twenty-six Spanish residents (of a total of 490) could have made claim to one of the Apaches Captain Urrutia and his followers enslaved that year.[91]

In the years 1748, 1749, and 1759, Spanish slaving operations peaked. After Coahuila's Governor Rábago y Terán's long campaign in 1748, which yielded a total of one hundred slaves, the ratio of enslaved Native individuals to colonists in San Antonio would have been as high as two for every eleven Spanish colonists. Of course, as Rábago y Terán was the governor of Coahuila at the time, the enslaved people were not

Table 1. Estimates of enslaved individuals, Spanish colonists, and Spanish households, 1723–1759

Campaign	*No. of Enslaved Individuals*	*San Antonio Population*	*Spanish Households*
1723	20	150	50
1732	38	350	60
1745	19+	490	108
1748	100	560	125
1749	175	560	125
1759	149	660	148

Note: I have used the same 4.5 multiplier employed by de la Teja and Meacham to calculate rough population estimates from available household estimates. De la Teja, *San Antonio de Béxar,* 19–20; Castañeda, *Our Catholic Heritage in Texas,* 2:278–300; Meacham, "The Population of Spanish and Mexican Texas," 78, 80, 85, 99–100, 102.

distributed only among San Antonio residents; thus, the slave-to-colonist ratio would have been much lower (probably closer to one enslaved person for every nineteen colonists). In 1749, however, all 175 enslaved individuals were funneled through San Antonio channels. Many were returned to their original communities by the end of 1749, but the slave-to-colonist ratio may have reached a high of one enslaved person for every three Spanish colonists in San Antonio. Finally, the slave-to-colonist ratio was equally remarkable after the 1759 Ortiz Parrilla campaign. The Red River–bound punitive expedition resulted in 149 captives against a San Antonio Spanish population of about 660 residents, a ratio of two enslaved people per nine colonists.[92]

The picture presented by these figures and ratios is still rather opaque when we factor in the forced mobility of these enslaved people and the uncertainty of their fate after their initial enslavement. But if we also consider the fact that the slaving campaigns did not simply replenish the enslaved population, and that the seizing of five hundred to six hundred individuals had somewhat of a cumulative effect on the enslaved population of Spanish Texas, we might assume conservatively that the population of enslaved people in San Antonio hovered around 10 percent of the total population of San Antonio (not including missionized Native residents).[93] Put another way, about one in ten people in Spanish San Antonio may have been enslaved at any given point during these four decades. This percentage does not seem unreasonable, particularly if we relate it to the number of households in San Antonio during that same period. From 1726 to 1762, San Antonio consisted of between 60 and 148 households. Thus, if the enslaved Native and Black population remained between thirty and fifty people at any given time (there were at least twenty-one enslaved Black individuals living in Texas during this period), on average, at least one in three homes would have benefited from the labor of an enslaved person. It is also worth noting that there was at least one instance in which the soldiers of San Antonio sent enslaved Native people to the missions because they "were not wanted by anyone in the presidio"—possibly a result of their homes being oversaturated with slaves (i.e., slavers feared they would be unable to control them adequately).[94]

Because *la esclavitud de los indios* was technically illegal—and few contemporaries were willing to admit their involvement in slaveholding—it is difficult to determine with certainty which San Antonio colonists held enslaved Native people in their households. There is some evidence, however, that there were a handful of influential San Antonio families that invested a lot of time, energy, and resources in slavery. Most of these individuals were military men or belonged to one of the extended military families of San Antonio. Capt. Nicolás Flores and his family, for instance, were especially invested in slaveholding. Flores, born ca. 1670, likely began his frontier military career in the Spanish army around 1690. Stationed at Monclova in 1693 and at San Juan Bautista in 1701, he was a veteran of Native-Spanish warfare by the time he settled in San Antonio as a member of the Aguayo expedition. His slaving days in Texas began as early as 1707 (as part of the Diego Ramón expedition) and continued through 1723 with his controversial campaign into Ndé country that year.[95] His daughter, María Josepha Flores y Valdés, followed in his footsteps, holding a number of slaves through her marriage with Miguel Nuñez Morillo. It seems that María Josepha Flores was actually one of the few Spanish residents to have possessed both Native and Afro-Mexican bondspeople, as she sold two Black people in October 1743. After Miguel Nuñez Morillo (and her subsequent husband) passed away, she married for a third time, to none other than Capt. Toribio Urrutia, one of the most prolific slavers in the history of Spanish Texas. In addition to leading one of the largest slave raids in Spanish Texas history in 1749, Urrutia owned at least two enslaved Black people in 1744, a *negra* and her child. Baptismal records also indicate that Flores owned two Black individuals in 1750 and another Black man and his Ndé partner, María de Jesús, in

1758.[96] For the Flores and Urrutia families, marriage, military service, and slavery were the ties that bound them together.

Measuring the economic influence of slavery in Spanish Texas is an equally difficult task. Slave labor's contribution to agricultural and manufacturing output likely tracked the productive capacity of the Spanish Texas communities at large during this period. The residents of Spanish Texas were dependent upon subsistence agriculture, and the farming labor of enslaved people would have paralleled that of other, nonslave farm laborers—which, in San Antonio, produced little to no surplus for market exchange.[97] Slave contributions to manufacturing were probably minimal as well, because very few Spanish Texas residents participated in the production of manufactured goods during the first period of settler colonization. Most goods were imported from Mexico's frontier commercial centers, like Saltillo, but some were smuggled in from French Louisiana. Either way, there would have been few opportunities and little reason for Spanish slavers to force their slaves to work as full-time farm workers or manufacturers.[98]

Slave labor probably was most important as domestic work and in the context of the herding industry. The home was the central site of slavery in Spanish Texas, so there can be no doubt that enslaved people aided in the maintenance of the household economy. Their daily tasks would have been mundane and probably included cleaning, cooking, and other domestic activities, but slave work in the home likely freed up time and energy for slavers and their families to engage in other activities. Slaveholders with multiple bondspeople or other forms of domestic help, such as female family members or paid servants, probably forced some of their slaves to work as herders of the many horses, mules, and cattle, making them indispensable to the vitality of a budding pastoral economy.[99] In sum, if we think broadly about economic production and contribution, we might consider slave labor to be significant to the functioning of Spanish Texas—even if quantifying slave labor output remains an impossible task.

Baptismal records are the best sources available for understanding the social dynamics of slavery in Spanish Texas from 1720 to 1760.[100] At a minimum, baptismal entries confirm the existence of enslaved people in the vicinity of San Antonio, as the records serve as a catalogue of nearly every birth in Spanish San Antonio. Most entries include details regarding the perceived identity of a baptized individual, her age, her parents, her godparents, and other details regarding her status. Some, but not all, explicitly identify the child as an *esclavo* (slave), while others indicate that the baptized individual was *del servicio de* ("in the service of") a specific resident of San Antonio.[101] In the San Antonio baptismal records from 1731 to 1760, there are six clear entries of Black *esclavos* and another forty-six entries that strongly suggest the enslavement of a Native individual. Regarding Native individuals, baptismal entries imply enslaved status if (1) the individual is identified as an enemy *indio* (i.e., Apache, Jumano/Wichita, Comanche, or Yojuan); (2) the baptized Native individual's parents are left unidentified; (3) the status of the mother or father of the baptized individual is that of an enslaved Native person; (4) the Native individual was baptized soon after a documented slave raid; or (5) the Native child was baptized by one Spaniard, usually a man and a soldier. It also should be noted that the very existence of an *indio* in the San Antonio baptismal records is contrary to the proscriptions of Spanish authorities and missionaries, who made great efforts to segregate Native mission residents from Spanish colonists.[102] Thus, the baptism of a Native individual at the Spanish town church generally means that the baptized individual was living in a Spanish household.

Just as important, the baptismal records hint at the operations of one of the key mechanisms of enslavement in Spanish Texas: the baptism of an enslaved person. The baptism of seized Native individuals was instrumental to the processes of enslavement because the act discursively alienated captured people from their communities of origin. Once baptized, the Native recipient of the holy ritual became a recognized member of a greater Christian family and subject to Spanish rule within a (usually) male-headed household. For Spaniards, this meant that they could no longer return the baptized individual to her Native community—whether through barter or through diplomacy—as it would be immoral to abandon her, now a "Christian," to a world of heathenism. It also meant that Spaniards had the right, if not the moral obligation, to chase after so-called fugitive converts and to force them to live under Spanish subjugation.[103] It was thus at this moment that Spanish processes of enslavement dovetailed with Spanish ideologies regarding Christian missionizing and civilization. Here religious leaders, authorities, soldiers, and *vecinos* could agree that bondage was for the greater good; it was one way to bring the fruits of civilization and spiritual enlightenment to "savage" people. The logic was as old as the Spanish conquest of the Americas itself, but it was especially comforting for those who knew *la esclavitud de los indios* had long been outlawed by the Spanish Crown.[104]

Beyond establishing a justification for the forced bondage of Native people, the ritual of baptism also meant that the baptized individual was to receive the spiritual guidance of chosen individuals from her host community. Under the spiritual and material supervision of *padrinos* (godparents), the newly incorporated *ahijado* (godchild) could reap the supposed benefits of the relationship and set of obligations known as *compadrazgo* (godparenthood). The baptismal records indicate that dozens of enslaved Native people were incorporated into specific Spanish families through *compadrazgo*. It is not clear that the establishment of a *compadrazgo* relationship necessarily (i.e., by definition) bound the *ahijada* to her *padrinos* as a slave, but in some instances that may have been the case. Of the estimated forty-six baptized slaves in the records, for instance, twenty-four were baptized without indication of parents but with a single godparent, usually a male soldier. If a single Spaniard was held responsible for the upbringing of an enslaved individual, his or her authority would have been left relatively unchecked; parentless, single-godparent slaves had few, if any, other advocates or supporters in the host community. At the very least, the implication was clear: the creation of the *compadrazgo* relationship formalized Spanish control over an enslaved Native person and ensured the forced incorporation of the individual into a Spanish household. Some Spanish slaveholders even went as far as to force their surnames upon their slaves, solidifying their status as enslaved "kin."[105] Spaniards involved in this process would not have found any of these impulses contradictory. More likely, they would have seen the incorporation of enslaved people into their households as natural, because Spaniards had long understood that the "perfect" male-headed Spanish family included enslaved people. As Michelle A. McKinley has argued, in the Spanish colonial world, "household labor relations were couched in the discourse of protection, dependency, kinship, reciprocity, and discipline."[106]

Baptismal records also provide a few details regarding relationships *among* enslaved people. Once in the home of a Spanish colonist, baptized individuals likely were subject to the authority of the household head. It is not clear how slaveholders viewed their Indian slaves in relation to Black slaves, but enslaved Black and Native people may have identified with one another to some extent. The baptismal records lend credence to this interpretation. It is apparent, for instance, that both Native and Afro-Mexican bondspeople struggled to find "legitimate" marriage partners who were not enslaved themselves. Of the six unions noted in the records that included at least one enslaved partner, in all but one both partners were enslaved. María de Jesús, an enslaved Ndé woman, and Francisco Arendando, an enslaved Black man, for instance, gave birth to Joséph Fulgencio de la Trinidad in 1758. Both lived in the household of their slaver, Doña Josepha Flores, and because their son was *legítimo* (legitimate) Flores likely approved and orchestrated their union. The authority of their slaver almost certainly would have factored into their ability to stay together and have a child. Nevertheless, the existence of slave unions should not be dismissed, as their partnerships would have helped to ease the physical, psychological, and spiritual burdens of life under Spanish slavery.[107]

Finally, the baptismal records offer some clues regarding enslaved women's susceptibility to sexual violence. Sexual violence may explain the several entries that identify enslaved mothers with "unknown" partners. María, the *mulata* (part-Black) slave of Joséph Antonio Rodrígues, gave birth to two children during the 1740s, and in each case the father could not be identified. During the 1750s, Margarita Menchaca, an enslaved Ndé woman, baptized two supposedly fatherless, "illegitimate" children: Antonia and Joséph Mateo de la Trinidad. Revealingly, Margarita Menchaca shared the last name of her owner, Luis Menchaca. Like other slaveholders, Luis attempted to incorporate Margarita as kin by forcing his family name upon her—a metaphorical incorporation.[108] It is possible, however, that Antonia and Joséph Mateo are evidence of attempts to incorporate Margarita as kin in a literal fashion (i.e., through rape).

Aside from the baptismal records, few documents hint at what it was like to live under Spanish slavery. The recorded testimony of Antonia Lusgardia Hernándes, however, is a notable exception. According to Lusgardia, living conditions in the household of Miguel Nuñez Morillo, the patriarch of one of the few known slaveholding households, were especially harsh. Identified as a *mulata libre* (a free, part-Black woman), Lusgardia was by law not a slave, but her testimony in a civil suit still revealed the expansiveness of slaver oppression. According to her testimony, Lusgardia "suffered so much from lack of clothing and from mistreatment of my humble person" that she moved out of the home of Nuñez and into the residence of another man. Apparently Lusgardia's departure infuriated Nuñez, and he stole one of her two children, a young boy named Ignacio. It is unclear if the child was the illegitimate offspring of Nuñez, but Lusgardia noted that she "gave birth to [Ignacio] in [Nuñez's] home." "Just for this reason," argued Lusgardia, "and because his wife baptized the said creature, he, exercising absolute power, snatched away from me my son—the only man I have and the one who I hope will eventually support me." Nuñez interpreted the situation a bit differently, however. According to Nuñez, the fact that his wife, Josepha Flores, acted as godmother to the boy when he was born entitled them to the child. He claimed that Lusgardia had "renounced her rights" to Ignacio and that "she should not have any grounds to ask for him back again, since the said Lusgardia has failed to comply with any of her part of the agreement." If Nuñez could be a tyrant toward the legally free residents of his household, it would not be hard to imagine that his treatment of enslaved people was similarly severe. The fact that Nuñez explained his supposed entitlement to Lusgardia's son by invoking his wife's credentials as godmother also adds credence to the argument that Spaniards sometimes interpreted the *campadrazgo* relationship as an important slaving mechanism for control and coercion.[109]

The Social Reverberations of Slaving Violence, 1720–1760

In the borderlands, the personal slavery of Native and Black men, women, and children was the harrowing embodiment of the cycles of colonial violence that afflicted the multicultural communities spread out across the Texas countryside. To some extent, Spanish slavers projected onto the bodies of enslaved people the anger, frustration, and uncertainty born of years of war with Native peoples. The geopolitical conflicts of the region were continuous, turbulent, and often disempowering for Spanish colonists, but the enslavement of outsiders and their subsequent forced incorporation into individual households provided the generally impoverished Spaniards of Texas with a degree of power and control. In this context, *negro* and *indio* slaves served as symbols of Spanish opportunity, stability, and dominance, if not settler colonial raisons d'être. Yet, Spanish slaving came with a steep price, for violence begot violence. Reflecting on the turmoil of the 1730s, Fray Arricivita lamented the conditions created by Spanish slave raiding: "In proportion as the Apache suffered harm, so did their hatred and the revenge they took increase. This makes it clear that the campaigns have only resulted in notable losses and expense."[110]

In Spanish Texas, violence was ubiquitous. It was the principal tool for conquest, a means of diplomacy and interethnic interaction, and, of course, an expression of personal and regional power. Not surprisingly, the preponderance of violence also had the potential to reconfigure the mechanisms of social control that Spaniards had brought with them to

Texas. Hispanic racial ideologies, built upon notions of social segregation and stratification, morphed and mutated over time, and although Spanish colonists continued to perceive the social makeup of their communities as racially diverse and hierarchical, racial boundaries sometimes shifted and blurred. While Spanish officials had always hoped that *españoles* (White people) would bring civilization to the supposed wilderness of Texas, the ever-changing racial composition of Spanish Texas made such aspirations illusory and fantastical. By midcentury, Spaniards were beginning to content themselves with the racially mixed lot of colonists who had laid the foundations for the small Spanish settlements of Texas. What mattered most to them in the context of the borderlands, they discovered, was the subjugation of independent Native communities. As long as they shared in the violence of the region, local Spaniards were becoming more willing to share the privileges of *español*-ness. Thus by 1760, even though Spanish Texas was composed of a hodgepodge of multiethnic individuals, Spanish community members increasingly forged their identities along axes of frontier violence and slavery rather than the traditions that emanated from a central Mexican (or European) core. In the face of a rebellious *indio* enemy, ancestral origins meant less than the ability to conquer and civilize through violence.

Since the earliest years of committed Spanish settler colonization, Spanish authorities imagined the expansion of Spanish dominion through the work of racially pure and trustworthy Spanish agents, equipped with both a moral (Catholic) compass and a passion for service to the Crown. Although a few Spanish officials hinted at the absurdity of such an imprudent impulse, colonial schemers generally identified *españoles* as the ideal candidates for soldier-settler colonization in Texas. The viceroy's *fiscal*, or Crown attorney, for instance, recommended in November 1716 that Alarcón's colonization expedition into Texas be composed of "*españoles*, not *mulatos*, *coyotes*, or *mestizos*." The *auditor general*, Juan de Oliván Rebolledo, believed that only at a later date, after the young *español*-led colonies had time to develop and prosper, should government authorities make plans to send "all vagrants and persons of both sexes without a trade found in Mexico [City] and other cities, persons sentenced to presidio without dishonor, and any women taken into custody by court action."[111] Such concerns were repeated in subsequent colonization formulations, and during preparations for the impending Aguayo expedition of the early 1720s officials declared similar preferences for a racially pure body of colonists.

Of course, Spanish dreams of a lily-white Texas were better suited to the realm of the imagination. The first soldiers and settlers were anything but "pure-blooded" *españoles*; rather, it was the consensus of many contemporary observers that the first wave of Hispanic colonists was a multiethnic bunch, which included "*mulatos*, *lobos*, *coyotes*, and *mestizos*."[112] The proclaimed ethnic makeup of 117 members of the Aguayo expedition recruited from Celaya exemplified the diversity of these early colonists. According to one report, of the 117 recruits, there were seventeen *mestizos*, twenty-one *coyotes*, forty-four *españoles*, thirty-one *mulatos*, two *castizos*, one free *negro*, a Sapotlán *indio*, and one *lobo*. Moreover, most of the soldiers and their families who joined Alarcón and Aguayo were drawn from the mixed-race populations of the Northeast. By the 1730s, even residents from San Antonio—who had a vested interest in declaring the racial makeup of their colonial outposts as strictly *español*—were representing their population as racially diverse. In his testimony regarding the performance of Governor Bustillo y Ceballos, for example, Juan Curbelo claimed "that he had not failed to protect and favor the *españoles*, *mulattos*, and *mestizos* who had desired to live in these provinces and sought out all possible benefits for all [of them]."[113]

The government-directed settlement of Canary Islanders during the early 1730s—although ostensibly consisting only of *español* families—did little to dilute the non-*español* element in Spanish Texas. The Isleños, like their predecessors, were of uncertain heritage. Manuel Angel de Villegas Puente's descriptive report on the Isleño families, drafted in the city of Cuautitlán in November 1730, offers some clues regarding the racial identities of the Isleño settlers. According to the report, most of the fifty-four transplanted colonists were of "dark complexion" with "black curly hair," and few families demonstrated consistent physical characteristics among all family members. The family of Antonio Santos, for instance, was typical of these Isleño families. Villegas Puente described Santos as being "medium height, broad-shouldered, [with] round face, dark complexion, large nose, black eyes, thin beard, black beard, and hair, rather grey and curled, [and] black eyebrows." His wife, Isabel Rodríguez, was reported as "tall, [with] fair complexion, thin nose, round face, light brown eyes, [and] black eyebrows and hair." Although three of their four children had dark skin, their other physical traits varied considerably.[114]

Afro-Mexicans also contributed to the racial diversity of Spanish Texas during the first four decades of Spanish settler colonization. Even though few remarks were left regarding the Black population in Texas prior to the last third of the eighteenth century, the presence of

Black people in Spanish Texas was not an insignificant social reality for Spanish residents. Afro-Mexicans were members of the earliest Spanish parties that navigated the Texas borderlands during the sixteenth and seventeenth centuries, and Spanish authorities even contemplated establishing a Black colony to help expedite Spanish colonization of the province.[115] The plan never came to fruition, but Afro-Mexicans inevitably made important contributions to the Spanish colonization of Texas. Undoubtedly, African-descended people were among the hundreds of Hispanic individuals who made their way to Texas as settler colonists of the Spanish Crown.

But even as Afro-Mexicans actively participated in Spanish colonial efforts, anti-Blackness—as a set of ideas, assumptions, and practices—remained potent within Spanish society. Since the sixteenth-century, when Spanish colonists began to import great numbers of enslaved Africans into New Spain, Spaniards had associated *negro*-ness with forced servitude.[116] This association followed Spanish colonists to Texas during the eighteenth century; thus, to be *negro* in Spanish Texas was to be marked by the legacy of slavery. In terms of identity markers, the descriptors *esclavo, negro*, and *mulato* were often synonymous with one another, and baptizing friars—operating with a keen sense of the heritability of Blackness—usually felt the need to indicate explicitly the free (*libre*) status of a child when a *mulato* or *negro* child was not legally enslaved. Therefore, the marker *mulato* rarely was written without the word *libre* or *esclavo* next to it.[117] Also illustrative of the debased status of Black people in Texas was the use of the more derogatory terms *negro* and *mulato* instead of *moreno* and *pardo*, terms that Afro-Mexicans elsewhere in Mexico seem to have preferred.[118] In these ways, Spaniards preserved anti-Blackness within the documentary record of the era. At least at a discursive level, the inscription of anti-Blackness into contemporary texts sustained its currency, providing Spaniards with a vocabulary and grammar for its local interpretation and implementation.

This did not mean, however, that Spanish Texas was a strictly stratified society with impenetrable racial boundaries. On the contrary, the turbulent conditions of the Texas borderlands helped to ease—at least for the nonslave population—some of the social stigmas that were more pronounced in the metropolitan parts of Mexico.[119] In the borderlands, biological and ancestral origins sometimes had less significance than a strong anti-*indio* service record; in other words, bravery and honor in the face of a barbarous Indian enemy could erase the dishonor of a lower *casta* status. Spanish officials believed that *español, indio, negro, mestizo,* and *mulato* colonists, to varying degrees, were all capable of expanding the influence of the Spanish Crown by civilizing the *indios bárbaros* of the region. And although they may have preferred the stark dividing lines of a segmented, racialized community, Spanish authorities could not control the extent to which the shared experience of anti-Native violence often brought these diverse Hispanic people together, thereby undermining attempts at top-down racial stratification while simultaneously forging a more capacious sense of settler colonial entitlements. It is not a coincidence that by midcentury, after decades of cross-community conflict, the shedding of blood on the battlefield began to emerge as a metaphor for both shared military violence and the cleansing of ancestral impurity. As Bernardo de Miranda explained, "[Texas's] soldiers and *vecinos* had shed their blood in the many and continuous campaigns, forays, and incursions which have been made since [the time of] Captain Don Nicolás Flores until the year of [seventeen] forty-nine." And although by 1760 Spaniards could tout a Spanish-Ndé peace agreement, "the glory [for this] was due only to the forces of this province without the help of any other province."[120] Put succinctly, Spanish colonists were becoming more White, more socially esteemed and entitled, through warfare against Native enemies. This was why the men whom Governor Jacinto de Barrios y Jáuregui interviewed in 1756—mentioned at the opening of this chapter—wanted to spotlight their own personal contributions to the conquest of the Texas borderlands. They believed that their performance in war trumped any racial concerns that their superiors may have had. Conquest of the *indio* was their reason for existence, and they had proven themselves worthy.[121]

Summary

From 1718 to 1760, Spaniards sought to recalibrate Texas affairs according to their own colonial priorities and concerns. They forged military alliances with local residents, established mission-settlements and presidio communities, and battled over resources and territory with new enemies. The enslavement of these enemies—usually women and children—was an articulation of Spanish colonial power, and their slave labor offered Spaniards a reprieve from the poverty of frontier life, as well as a boost to their sense of social worth and colonial importance. The costs of Spanish slavery, however, were high even for Spaniards, as slaving had a boomerang effect, enmeshing these colonists in devastating cycles of violence that would color the lives of Spanish community members for decades. Enslaved people themselves were hardly an insignificant part of Spanish San Antonio, accounting for about one in ten residents. And although Spanish residents couched their slaving practices in the language of family and Christianization, life for enslaved Black and Native people was certainly harsh and oppressive, for it was through the violation and exploitation of their bodies that Spaniards sustained their colonial project.

Yet by the late 1750s, Spanish influence had come under attack. Powerful *naciones* from the North and Northeast, including the recently confederated Wichitas, Caddos, and Comanches, were beginning to articulate their control over much of Texas through commercial expansion and violence. Their coordinated siege of the San Sabá mission-presidio complex was the acute expression of such dominance, and for the next several decades Texas affairs would reflect changes emanating from the heart of Comanchería as much as from any other center, including Mexico City. Even the soldiers and *vecinos* interviewed by Governor Barrios in 1756, who wanted to take credit for conquering the Apaches of Texas, could not ignore the rising power of Norteño communities. As Ygnacio Hernández recalled, "The *Yndios* had been reduced by the troops of this province without the help from any other province. . . . Not only this but also . . . the great depredations perpetrated upon them by the Comanche *Yndios* had caused them to declare themselves at peace."[122] In the Texas borderlands, a new day was dawning.

3 / "Reduced to Peace . . . by the Attacks of the Comanches": Slavery and the Comanche Emergence in the Texas Borderlands, 1706–1767

The Ndé *náshneta*[1] awoke in a cold sweat, his body trembling from the horrors he had witnessed in his sleep. The scene he could not shake loose from his dream world was that of enemy men surprising defenseless Ndé women and children and rounding them up to begin their long trek to a life of enslavement. Anguish washed over him as he considered the troubling implications of this scenario. His people had suffered greatly for decades at the hands of slave raiders, and the idea of losing hundreds more to slavery was unbearable. Perhaps he was feeling guilty for leaving his kinspeople alone and vulnerable on the upper Nueces River while he and his compatriots were out hunting near the San Sabá. It was, after all, 1762, and for over a dozen years he and his people had worked tirelessly to forge a lasting peace with their borderlands neighbors. If orchestrated by their supposed allies, the enslavement of his people was an obvious breach of conduct, an unequivocal act of treachery. Had the prospects of peace made him foolish? Had his people become weak? Was his terrible dream actually a terrifying premonition? What would he discover when he finally reunited with his people?[2]

The purported villains of this man's nightmare were Spanish soldiers and missionaries, but they might as well have been Nʉmʉnʉʉ–Comanches. Spanish and Comanche slaving and violence were ubiquitous to the past few generations of his people's history, and it must have been difficult for him to untangle the threads of war, diplomacy, trade, and slavery when it came to interacting with Spaniards and Comanches. Precedents suggested that his dream-world intuition would lead him to the scene of a dreadful silence—the kind of silence that emerges only in the aftermath of widespread desperation, violence, and trauma. But upon returning to his people's settlement, located at the newly established Spanish mission, San Lorenzo, the *náshneta* was comforted by familiar sights: women hard at work and children at play. Even the vast horse herds remained unharmed and intact. Most important, his people were not enslaved.

That slavery was on the Ndé leader's mind during the early 1760s would not have come as a surprise to anyone living near the young mission-settlement at San Lorenzo. As previously discussed, slavery was an integral part of Ndé-Spanish relations for much of the first half of the eighteenth century, with hundreds of Ndé men, women, and children falling victim to Spanish slave raids and attacks. But by the 1750s, peace talks preoccupied Ndé and Spanish diplomats, and the threat of slave raids was arriving not from Spanish strongholds but from Comanche and Norteño centers to the north and northeast. Since the 1740s or earlier, Comanches had waged a devastating war against the Ndé *naciones* of Texas, expanding Comanche dominion ever southward. Like the colonial invasion of Spaniards decades earlier, the movement of Comanche communities into the Texas borderlands was driven in part by extensive slave raids, and as Comanche fighters and slavers pushed Comanchería's frontiers progressively outward, the displacement of Ndé communities paved the way for further Comanche territorial development. Sadly, the unidentified Ndé leader's fears proved prescient, because in the spring of 1762 his people *did* fall victim to slave raids, in this case at the hands of Comanches. By the late 1760s, many of the Ndé communities that had called the greater part of Texas home for countless generations had retreated southward to and across the Río Grande or west to the mountainous terrain of the Chihuahuan deserts of present-day southern New Mexico and western Texas, just beyond the reach of Comanche war parties. The Comanche conquest of the Southern Plains may not have been complete by the 1760s, but clearly the forced removal of Ndé people, particularly Lipan Apaches, had ushered in a new era in Texas borderlands history. Slave raids and violence against the Esikwita, or "the gray-rumped," as Comanches derisively called Lipanes, had remade the Texas plains into the southern portion of Comanchería.[3]

The history of the long-term movement of Comanche people from the Great Basin–Rocky Mountain region of the Northwest into the Texas borderlands from 1706 to 1767 thus reveals slavery's role as a unique force of migration and economic development in a world continuously wracked by European colonial forces.[4] Slavery provided Comanches with both a mechanism and an impetus for continued expansion onto the Southern Plains. Within Comanche communities, enslaved people supplied much of the domestic and pastoral labor necessary to sustain Comanche mobility while also contributing directly to the production of tradable, manufactured goods. As commodities themselves, enslaved people also expanded market and diplomatic opportunities for Comanche slavers in the borderlands. The drive to procure more captured people was itself an engine of expansion, with each Comanche slave raid simultaneously stimulating outward territorial growth. By the middle decades of the eighteenth century, slave raiding brought Comanches right into the thick of Texas borderlands geopolitics, and almost immediately Comanches emerged as major regional players.[5] The massive Comanche-led attack on the Spanish mission at San Sabá in 1758, which bookended the narrative portion of the previous chapter, was thus symbolic of this heightened Comanche influence, as Comanches and their allies declared to the Spanish colonists that they had overstepped their bounds by consorting with their avowed Ndé enemies.

Of course, Comanche slaving practices, like other forms of Texas borderlands slavery, did not exist in stasis during these long, formidable years. Extant written evidence from the first two-thirds of the eighteenth century is rather scarce, but enough survives for scholars to contemplate the changing character and functions of slavery during each phase of the Comanche sweep across the Southern Plains into Texas. As was the case for the Spanish colonists of Texas during the first several decades of the eighteenth century, violence, exploitation, and slavery colored the lives of Comanche people and were integral to Comanche political, economic, and cultural expansion.[6] Although slave commerce and slave labor seemed to mesh seamlessly with eighteenth-century Comanche equestrian-based expansionism, Comanches—like all slaveholding people—had to reconcile the tensions inherent to the violent exploitation and social incorporation of enslaved people. What Comanches came to discover was that the integration of conquered people as enslaved laborers and kin—the essence of borderlands slavery—helped to sustain Comanche population growth in an age of war, a broadening nexus of colonial penetration, and debilitating disease epidemics. Increasingly, to be Comanche meant to be an innovator and a survivor—and sometimes a ruler—in a world of violence and slavery.

Northwestern Beginnings, Pre-1719

Scholars generally place the origins of the Nʉmʉnʉʉ among the Shoshones of the northeastern Great Basin and central and northern Rocky Mountains, who during the sixteenth century had lived in culturally vibrant communities across the region.[7] Life in the sixteenth-century Shoshone world revolved around the economic activities of hunting, fishing, and gathering, and the resource wealth of the region offered great community stability. With such natural resources at their disposal, Shoshones might have remained content in their sixteenth-century homeland, but sometime during that century (and possibly earlier), Shoshones found themselves drawn to the ecological riches of the Great Plains. Prior to this era, dry conditions on the Great Plains had encouraged most communities to avoid the wildlife-scarce region; yet, in time, new environmental transformations were setting in motion the massive migration of Shoshone people, a process that began slowly but soon snowballed into vast relocation efforts. The cooler temperatures and heavy rainfalls of the Little Ice Age (ca. 1500 to ca. 1850) were resurrecting the lushness and abundance of the Great Plains, and the region over time became an attractive destination for various groups.[8] With so many fresh resource opportunities available, particularly bison, a new age of prosperity seemed inevitable.

For Shoshones, however, life on the central parts of the Great Plains did not last beyond the late seventeenth century. Toward the end of the century, the Shoshone people broke off into two different groups, one heading north to prosper from the great bison populations of the Yellowstone Valley and the other migrating south to seek out Spanish horses along the northern borderlands of New Mexico. The latter group of migrants, whom Pekka Hämäläinen and Dan Flores have termed "proto-Comanches," eventually made their way toward the territory of the powerful Ute people, located northwest of the Spanish colonies of New Mexico, where they forged a highly lucrative military alliance with their hosts. Scholars also have theorized that it was among these Utes that this group of migrant people became known as *Comanche* from the Ute term *kumantsi*. There is considerable uncertainty as to the original meanings of the term, but scholars seem to agree either that *kumantsi* meant "enemy" (or "those-who-are-always-against" in *nʉmʉ tekwapʉ*), or that it was a term reserved for people who were distant relatives. The first interpretation (i.e., that *Comanche* meant "enemy") suggests that the early Comanche-Ute encounters were characterized by violence, while the second insinuates a common origin for the Comanche and Ute people, who spoke similar Shoshone dialects. In any case, the political and military relationships that ultimately developed between the Comanches and Utes would prevail for decades, lasting well into the middle years of the eighteenth century.[9] It was also during this period of alliance that early manifestations of Comanche slavery likely emerged.

With the assistance of their Ute allies, the Nʉmʉnʉʉ thrived in the diverse ecological environments of their new home. From roughly 1700 to 1740, Comanches spread out across a territory loosely bounded by the upper Arkansas River Valley to the east, the western foothills of the Rocky Mountains to the west, the Big Timbers of the Arkansas to the north, and the Llano Estacado to the south. The ecological variety of their territory made for diverse economic activity, and local Comanche economies benefited greatly from an abundance of antelopes, jack rabbits, and bison, not to mention the various berries, nuts, and roots that populated the region. Control of this territory offered Comanches and Utes access to other sources of economic wealth as well—namely, Spanish markets in manufactured goods, agricultural products, and horses. At the great fall fairs of Taos and San Juan, Comanche traders regularly bartered the meat and hides they collected during their hunts in exchange for maize, horses, pottery, cotton blankets, and even firearms. And as Comanches joined their Ute partners in extensive raids into Navajo, Ndé, and Pawnee territories, Comanches traded stolen people to the residents of New Mexico.[10] Thus, it was here, in the New Mexican sphere of Spanish colonialism, where Comanches learned of the immense commercial value of enslaved people.[11]

The slave-raiding and -trading networks of New Mexico's northern borderlands had originated well before Comanches entered the scene ca. 1706. Since the earliest days of the Spanish conquest and colonization of New Mexico, Spaniards made great efforts to enslave the local people of the region, and by 1637 their slaving operations had expanded northward into the Tierra de los Yutas, the Land of the Utes, where Spanish raiders procured slaves to be funneled into the nascent textile workshops of colonial New Mexico.[12] Although most Native people experienced Spanish slavery as direct victims, the Spanish creation of markets in enslaved bodies offered opportunities for those willing to trade in human commodities. Thus by the 1650s, Spanish observers were reporting Apache trading parties with "captive Indians from Quivira" (in modern-day Kansas), and in the few decades prior to the Pueblo Revolt many of these Apache traders were supplying Spanish buyers with bondspeople taken from the Caddo villages to the southeast.[13] In 1694, as Spaniards completed their reconquest of the Pueblos, the slave trade—now more explicitly couched by Spaniards in a discourse of Christian salvation and "rescue"—resumed, and the Spanish colonists of New Spain's northern frontier were once again able to stock their homes, mining facilities, and workshops with enslaved Native people.[14] It is unclear the extent to which Utes engaged in the supplying of slaves for the Spanish markets, but the brief periods of peace during the latter half of the century would have provided Utes with the opportunity to sell enslaved individuals if they so desired.[15] Either way, throughout most of the seventeenth century Utes generally found themselves not slavers but the victims of slavery, as the collective devastation of disease, Spanish technologies, and pervasive violence rendered them perpetually vulnerable and defenseless. Only with time and through significant social, political, economic, and technological adaptations did Utes reemerge as power players in the New Mexican slave networks.[16]

By the time Comanches arrived at the outskirts of colonial New Mexico at the turn of the eighteenth century, the massive extractions of enslaved people from the northwestern Ute homelands more or less had come to an end. That Comanches entered the New Mexican slave-based commercial economy principally as suppliers instead of victims was testament to their ability to reinvent themselves as equestrians. It had only been a generation or so, in the aftermath of the great New Mexican uprisings against Spanish colonialism, since the Comanches had first gained access to horses, but by the 1710s Comanches already had become masters of this technology. Horses revolutionized the Comanche way of life, offering new economic, military, social, and political capabilities. With horses, Comanches could transport goods at faster speeds and in greater quantities; they could expand their raiding operations, in terms of both distance and frequency; and they could harness the resource wealth of the region like never before. Hämäläinen has described Comanche integration of horse technology eloquently: "A horse . . . represented a new way to tap energy. Horses drew their strength directly from plant life, allowing their masters to eliminate the arduous phase of searching for animals to feed their other animals (dogs). A conduit between immense, abstract solar energy and concrete, immediately available muscle power, the horse redefined the realm of the possible."[17] With horses, Comanches did not have to suffer the fate that their Ute counterparts had suffered years earlier as victims of the colonial New Mexican slave markets; to the contrary, horses gave Comanches the power to be the enslavers.

With limited documentary evidence, it is difficult for historians to pinpoint the first Comanche slave raids in the region, but we do know, per the diary of Juan de Ulibarri, that Comanche raids had already begun by 1706. In his diary, Ulibarri noted that the residents of Taos feared an imminent joint Ute-Comanche attack on their communities, and according to one Ndé informant, Utes and Comanches were also on their way to raid a number of Apache communities scattered along the rivers and streams of the region. On August 27, 1706, Ulibarri received confirmation that Ndé suspicions were well founded, as "the Utes and Comanches had attacked two rancherías; one of the Carlana and Sierra Blanca [Apache] tribe, the other of the Penxayes [Apache] tribe." Unfortunately, Ulibarri did not leave further details of these attacks, and it is unclear how many (if any) slaves were acquired by Comanches and Utes during these assaults.[18] We may assume, however, that it was sieges like these which yielded the bondspeople that Comanches and Utes brought to the slave markets of New Mexico during the first decade of the eighteenth century.[19]

By the 1710s, the coordinated assaults of Comanches and Utes had moved beyond the geographical outskirts of Spanish New Mexico toward the heart of the Spanish colony, and by the end of the decade Spanish officials were clamoring for all-out war against Utes and Comanches. In 1719, New Mexico governor Antonio Valverde Cosio ordered the convening of a war council to gather expert opinions regarding the prevalence of Ute-Comanche violence over the past several years, and the testimonies of various Spanish settlers, soldiers, and officials made it evident to the governor that Ute-Comanche raids were devastating the New Mexican borderlands. Up to that time, Ute-Comanche attacks generally had been confined to the surrounding areas of the region, but now the raiders were growing bolder by the day, threatening to smash the poorly defended Spanish colonies. According to Capt. Joséph Naranjo, Spanish officials needed to move quickly against the Ute-Comanche threat because "if they are not punished this insolence will fall upon the settlements and the people will not be secure in their own homes." Capt. Joséph Truxillas agreed, declaring, "They will cripple the neighborhood in such a manner that the settlers will not be able to march out in defense."[20]

But beyond the sheer violence of the assaults, Spanish residents were also frustrated with the now discernably exploitative quality of Ute and Comanche interactions with Spanish colonial settlements. Spanish observers accused Utes and Comanches of deceit and treachery, claiming that their raids were conducted under the veneer of peace. Alejo Martín declared, "Although up to the present they have shown themselves friends of the Spaniards, yet under this friendship they have carried off some animals. They have been tolerated in order to conserve friendly relations. But now they have dishonored themselves and have begun to commit murder."[21] What these Spanish critics were noticing, however, was not so much evidence of the betrayal or treachery of Comanche and Ute traders but rather a broader strategy of exploitation. As Hämäläinen has argued, Comanches and Utes were "treat[ing] the [Spanish] colony itself as an exploitable resource depot," cutting off their competitors to the markets of Spanish New Mexico in an effort to monopolize the commerce of the region. This was how Comanches and Utes made certain that they were the principal suppliers of trade goods, including slaves.[22]

The baptismal records of Spanish New Mexico from 1700 to 1720 provide some evidence regarding the extent of early Ute-Comanche slave trading. According to David Brugge's baptismal record tabulations, of the 114 enslaved Native individuals baptized during the first three decades of the eighteenth century only 5 were of Ute origin and not one was Comanche. Moreover, 73 were Apaches, 22 were Navajos, 7 were Pawnees, 5 were Jumanos, and 2 were Hopis. Of course, it would be inappropriate to assume that all of the slaves were procured initially by Ute-Comanche slavers, but the lopsidedness of the distribution (5 enslaved Ute-Comanches versus 109 others) implies that Utes and Comanches generally controlled the supply side of the slave trade in Spanish New Mexico in comparison to their Native rivals.[23]

What the baptismal records do not account for is the extent to which Comanches and Utes incorporated enslaved people into their own communities. The rest of the Spanish colonial record fails in that regard as well, instead only suggesting that the slave networks northwest of New Mexico extended well beyond the limits of Spanish administrative awareness by the eighteenth century.[24] But given Comanche economic development during this period, particularly the rapid accumulation of horse herds, it does not seem unreasonable to assume that changing Comanche economic activity created incentives for the integration of exploited outsider labor. After all, the Spanish colonial record *does* reveal that Comanche horse herds expanded dramatically from 1700 to 1720 as a result of their frequent raids on the borderlands settlements of New Mexico.[25] Although the surge in horse acquisitions offered Comanches remarkable political, military, and economic opportunities, the increase also came with new responsibilities—namely, the sustenance of such horses. Comanches would not become full-scale pastoralist people until later in the eighteenth century, but the sudden influx of horses certainly created new labor demands. Considering the fact that Comanches were already in the business of collecting and selling outsiders, enslaved people could have helped to maintain such horses if Comanche slavers did not wish to sell to Spanish traders the men, women, and children they acquired during their raids.[26]

Slave Raids and Migrant Communities, 1719 to 1740

For the next two decades, Comanches escalated their devastating war against the Ndé people of the New Mexican borderlands and beyond. By the late 1710s, the pursuit of horses and slaves had lured many Comanches away from the homeland of their Ute allies and toward new economic and geopolitical opportunities to the east. Thus, when Governor Valverde led an anti-Comanche campaign onto the Southern Plains during the late summer of 1719, the scene they witnessed was one of "depopulated rancherías" made possible by Comanche conquest.[27] Along the way, he and his men learned from various Ndé informants "that their enemies, the Comanches, were persecuting and killing their kinsmen and others of their nation" and that Comanches had "carried off their women and children captives until they now no longer knew where to go to live in safety." Ndé representatives, including an Apache *capitán*, Carlana, reached out to Valverde for assistance against their Comanche enemies, but Valverde could offer little more than ostentatious promises to "punish their wickedness." Even with a concerted Ndé diplomatic effort afoot, the Comanche descent on Ndé *rancherías* continued.[28]

Although Spanish observers could hardly discern what they were witnessing, the Ndé testimony was clear evidence of a rising Comanche model of dominion building. On the one hand, Comanche slave raids buttressed Comanche economic opportunities, providing marketable goods and possible labor to sustain their growing society; on the other hand, slave raids displaced local Ndé communities, paving the way for a Comanche takeover. As Carlana explained to Valverde, "he had come fleeing from his country, the Sierra Blanca, with half of his people to get the help of the Apaches of La Jicarilla. The rest of his people, he said, had gone for protection farther into a land of Apaches whom Chief Flaco governed, because of the continual war that the Ute and Comanche enemy made upon them."[29] But his homeland was not the only Ndé-controlled territory suffering from a Ute-Comanche onslaught; El Cuartelejo, an Ndé-Pueblo refuge located in a resource-rich valley of present-day southeast Kansas, also was under siege. According to Governor Valverde's Ndé informants, "those of their tribe who were settling in el Cuartelejo had deserted the spot and were dispersed among the other rancherías of their tribe because they were molested and persecuted."[30] Rapidly, the vacuum created by Ute-Comanche attacks was pulling these same Ute and Comanche raiders and their families toward new territories.[31] It was thus around 1719 that the contours of a broader Comanche migration paradigm were becoming more apparent—a paradigm that fused an impulse for slave raiding with the long-term movement and relocation of communities.

Comanche slave raids continued to displace Ndé communities living on the Southern Plains throughout the 1720s. In November 1723, New Mexico governor Juan Domingo de Bustamante received word from Carlana and two other Ndé leaders that "the heathens of the Comanche nation, their enemies, had attacked them with a large number in their rancherías . . . carrying off their women and children." Apparently, the three Ndé diplomats were so frightened by the efficiency and coordination of the Comanche attack that they promised to accept "the sacrament of holy baptism . . . and to come together to live in their pueblos in the same form in which the Christian Indians of this kingdom dwell" in exchange for assistance.[32] Spanish-Ndé military deliberations notwithstanding, Comanches struck again the following spring, and like the previous recorded attack, the Comanches "abducted their women and children." The victimized Apaches responded with violent campaigns of their own, but their efforts did little to curb the Comanche offensive.[33] The violence of the mid-1720s escalated to such an extent that Comanche-Ndé warfare grew to mythic proportions, with Governor Domingo Cabello of Texas recalling a 1723 "battle so hard-fought that it lasted nine days." According to the governor, who was writing in 1784, the epic battle left Ndé communities devastated and wandering: "Having lost [the battle], the Lipanes and Apaches were forced to abandon their homeland and seek their safe haven, where their enemies would not persecute them; so they headed toward these territories [of Spanish Texas]." By 1727, the condition of the Jicarilla and Cuartelejo Apaches had become unquestionably desperate.[34] According to Brig. Pedro de Rivera, many had fled to Taos, and although some Spanish officials were optimistic that Comanche violence was bringing Apaches inadvertently into the fold of Spanish dominion, such was not the case: "They have no other aim than the purpose of their safety—to be secure from the enemies who attack them."[35]

With slave raids continuing to serve as an engine of Comanche migration, the 1720s were thus a period of remarkable territorial accumulation and consolidation for the Comanches. After decades of expansion, by 1730 Comanches had carved out an impressive territorial range for themselves. Stretching from the Arkansas River in the North to the Cimarron in the South and from the Sangre de Cristo Mountains in the West to the plains region near present-day Oklahoma City in the East, Comanchería had now come into clearer focus. For the next decade, Comanches would concentrate on optimizing their relatively novel way of life on the plains. From roughly 1730 to 1740, Comanche accumulation of horse herds accelerated to the point that the Comanches were, at least in theory, capable of mounting their entire population on horseback. Yet such a buildup—which had reached "the critical threshold of mounted nomadism," as Hämäläinen has argued—had political, social, and cultural ramifications. More specifically, the Comanches were forced to break into smaller bands in an effort to locate adequate foraging grounds. These bands, termed *rancherías* by Spanish observers, consisted of several smaller groupings of extended families, known as *nʉmʉnahkahnis* by Comanches. *Nʉmʉnahkahnis* were the fundamental unit of Comanche social organization and were often united with other *nʉmʉnahkahnis* through kin relations. Such collections of *nʉmʉnahkahnis*, which included anywhere from twenty to several hundred people, were headed by a single headman, or *paraibo*, and generally operated according to their own prerogatives.[36] This prevailing autonomous social structure might also explain the fissure between Comanches and Utes, which seems to have been underway around this time.[37]

Comanches also strengthened their commercial ties to the New Mexican borderlands economy. During the 1730s they reinvigorated the slave trade along the upper Río Grande, and by 1735 seasonal trade fairs had become "regular" and "customary" for New Mexico residents, particularly those living at Taos. As Fray Miguel de Menchero explained, Comanche dominance in the slave trade, which mostly victimized Ndé communities, signified Comanche territorial sway: "In the course of the year they [the Comanches] travel more than a thousand leagues from New Mexico, according to what I was told by an Indian who was among those that came to the sale and ransom of the captives in the year 1731." The exchange of enslaved people was such a key component of New Mexico–Comanche commerce that Spanish officials felt compelled to establish official regulations for the conduct of the *rescate*, or ransoming, of enslaved people brought in by Comanches.[38] By 1740, the slave trade

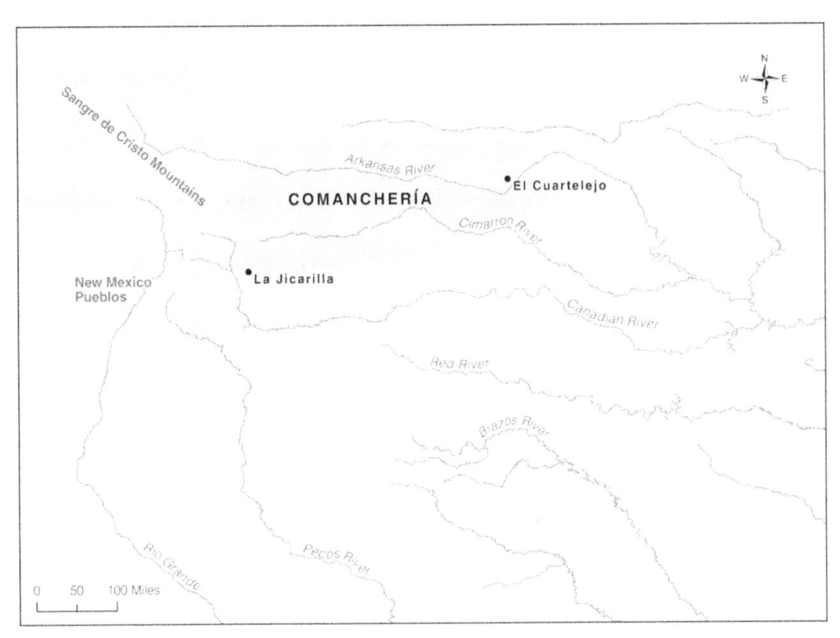

Map 4. Comanchería, ca. 1730. Cartography by Luyang Ren.

had grown so extensive in New Mexico that Spanish authorities gave permission to *genízaros*, or formerly enslaved Native people, to build their own settlement on the margins of Spanish New Mexico so as to not overcrowd the Spanish-controlled towns.[39]

Like the previous twenty-year period, the 1720s and 1730s left little documentary evidence relating to the conditions of enslaved people within Comanchería. One document that offers some clues, however, is the testimony of two French traders, Pierre and Paul Mallet, who traveled to Santa Fe from Pawnee territory toward the end of the period, in 1739. According to the Mallet brothers' testimony, an "Arikara Indian" was living as a slave in a Comanche village located on the Arkansas River. The Arikara warned the French travelers—perhaps in an effort to secure their trust—that "this tribe [of Comanches] wanted to attack them." The Mallet brothers sent the man back to his Comanche slavers, but he returned to them soon after. Apparently, he offered his services as a guide in exchange for his freedom, and the Frenchmen "hired him . . . with the promise to procure his liberty." According to their new traveling companion, he "knew the road to the Spaniards . . . as he had been a slave among them and had been baptized there." For the Mallets, his services were without a doubt invaluable.[40]

The Mallet brothers' discussion of their encounters with the enslaved Arikara man was certainly brief, but the account offers clues of what Comanche slavery might have been like during the 1730s. The most significant conclusion that can be derived from their testimony is that Comanches maintained an enslaved population within their communities, and not all enslaved individuals were sold immediately to buyers in New Mexico. Because the enslaved man had once lived, enslaved, among Spaniards in New Mexico, he may have been traded to Comanches or acquired during a Comanche raid. The testimony also suggests that enslaved people sometimes acted as diplomatic intermediaries. The decision to contact the French traders may have been of his own volition, but it is hard to imagine that his Comanche slavers would have permitted him to return to the Frenchmen a second time if he had escaped during the first encounter. The "promise to procure his liberty" also implies that the Mallet brothers believed that the man was still bound to the authority of Comanche slavers, even if he was to serve as their guide. Significantly, the unnamed Arikara man's desire to aid the Frenchmen in exchange for his freedom makes it apparent that he interpreted his condition as oppressive.

Broader demographic and economic changes may also help us to discern the character of slavery in Comanchería during this period. By 1740, the total population of Comanchería had ballooned to some ten thousand people, and given the occurrence of at least one major epidemic during the 1730s, it would be difficult to imagine that the Comanche population boom happened by natural means only.[41] Rather, Comanches likely had begun to absorb into their communities many of the people they enslaved instead of selling them—although the nature of this integration is mostly indiscernible. The few clues left by the Mallet brothers' account of the enslaved Arikara suggest that at least some Comanche slaves retained outsider status. The late-1720s comments of Pedro de Rivera, the first European contemporary description of Comanches, implies that Comanche slavers had a preference for enslaved children "because they kill the older ones."[42] Comanches may have attempted to incorporate some of their slaves as kin, either as adopted children or as wives, but there is no reason to believe that this process of kin incorporation lacked physical or psychological trauma. If enslaved women were made the sexual "partners" of Comanche men, sexual violence would have been a central part of their experiences as enslaved kin. And in light of the demographic uncertainties of the eighteenth century (i.e., the conditions created by unpredictable epidemics and waves of colonial violence), enslaved women would have been valued especially for their reproductive labor. Evidence from the late eighteenth and nineteenth centuries, when Euro-Americans accumulated a more extensive documentary record of Comanche interactions, supports these conclusions.[43]

Large-scale slave incorporation also may have been a result of the Comanches' broad conversion to mounted nomadism. With their perfection of mounted hunting, the carrying capacities of their communities expanded immensely. Massive bison hunts provided subsistence resources for Comanches both directly (through bison materials, such as meat and skins) and indirectly (through the trade in bison-derived goods), and no longer would Comanche communities have to worry about regulating population levels out of fear of starvation or deprivation. In this context, Comanches would not have been burdened by new (enslaved) mouths to feed; rather, enslaved people would have offered tremendous potential to contribute to the economic vitality of Comanche communities, perhaps aiding in the tanning of skins or participating in other laborious activities.[44] A byproduct of the Comanches' transformation into mounted mobile people, however, was a systematic devaluation of female, plant-based economic activity. The turn toward a polygynous, patriarchal society was a long time in the making for Comanches, but the great (colonial and noncolonial) resource wealth of the Southern Plains, in addition to the vast accumulation of horse herds during the first few decades of the eighteenth century, offered Comanche men unprecedented opportunities to assert male dominance within their communities. Wealth in enslaved bodies would have buttressed that influence and authority.[45]

Finally—and as was the case for Spaniards in Texas around the same time—the collective experience of decades of slaving probably had begun to leave its mark upon social configurations within Comanche society. Violent conflict seems to have been a recurring reality for Comanche communities during the 1730s, but Comanche warriors were not leading the same sorts of vast slave raids into new, unchartered territories as before. Instead, warfare likely had been reduced to a series of small, undocumented skirmishes, making the 1730s a relatively quiet decade for Comanches. Yet, by the middle third of the eighteenth century, social status and honor had become tied to military performance. As Governor Francisco Marín del Valle noted in his report on Comanches in the New Mexican sphere, leadership responsibilities were allocated to "the one who killed the most enemies."[46] Moreover, material benefits like access to new sources of horses and slaves, which contributed to a warrior's capacity to conduct further campaigns and demonstrate his value to the community, also resulted from regular participation in violent conflict. So if for a period of ten or so years Comanche men had few opportunities to earn social prestige through frequent warfare and cross-community violence, a whole generation of young men were left waiting, possibly with considerable anxiety, for an opportunity to prove their social worth.[47]

Thus by the 1740s, the two historical trajectories of Comanche and (Texas) Spanish violence veered ever closer toward convergence. With Comanche communities spreading southward toward the modern-day Texas panhandle and Spaniards establishing a foothold within the central, southern, and eastern sections of Texas, the stage was set for an explosive encounter. Both sets of communities had remade their broader locales through slaving violence, reconfiguring geopolitics and economic landscapes. Enslaved people, integrated as exploited kin, buttressed the growing regional influence of both Comanches and Spaniards, and within each society the violent enslavement of outsiders bolstered the standing of Comanche and Spanish men, who generally believed that violence was the measure of a man. Whether the collision of these two systems of violence would result in combustion or covalence remained to be seen. But before Comanches made their exceptional push into the heart of the Texas borderlands, they would devote a decade or so to enlarging their already bourgeoning commercial network. Only then, with new Native allies at their side, would Comanches be prepared to remake much of the Texas borderlands into parts of Comanchería. Slaving, of course, would continue to act as a significant engine of Comanche dominion building.

Securing a Comanche-centric Commerce, 1740–1752

The 1740s arrived at a critical point in the history of Comanche expansion. After about a decade of steady geopolitical consolidation, equestrian optimization, commercial stabilization, and outsider integration, Comanches were on the verge of moving toward yet another era of growth, dominance, and affluence. Fully mounted, Comanches had fostered an unprecedented level of mobility, allowing them to rearrange and reallocate resource domains according to grander, expansionist imperatives. The broader limits of Comanchería had become somewhat fixed throughout most of the 1730s, but such geographic stasis was only temporary, as Comanches continued to adjust to the diverse ecological areas of a new territory. Access to ever-growing horse and bison herds provided Comanche communities with the technologies and commodities necessary for a trade in essential agricultural foodstuffs. Militarily, Comanches faced few real threats; instead, Comanche slavers only seem to have conducted small-scale raids against others, particularly Apaches. Although such Comanche slave raids did not have the same migratory effect that previous slave raids had, slaving continued to supply Comanche traders with highly valuable goods for the New Mexico markets to the west. Finally—and, quite possibly, as never before—Comanches were learning how to incorporate enslaved people into their communities on a wider scale. At the very least, slave integration had helped Comanche population figures rise to new heights. The limits of Comanchería may not have shifted much during the 1730s, yet many changes had cut through Comanche society. By 1740, Comanchería was poised for further transformation.

Resource pressures and external threats nonetheless checked further Comanche ascendancy on the Southern Plains (and beyond). Significantly, Comanches suffered from limited access to European-manufactured firearms, the result of a deeply entrenched Spanish fear of armed Native peoples. Ever since the first quarter of the sixteenth century, Spanish authorities had expressed grave concerns regarding Native access to a trade in firearms, and Spaniards regularly made efforts to curtail and stifle the trade in guns to Comanches.[48] To the east, however, French authorities had fewer qualms about trading guns and ammunition with prospective Native allies. In fact, most Native-French alliances across the North American West were anchored by commercial ties in weaponry. From the end of the seventeenth century through the first half of the eighteenth, French colonists labored indefatigably to open up and profit from new trade networks, and by midcentury French merchants had built commercial relationships with Osage, Pawnee, Wichita, and even Ndé communities.[49] And as Spanish officials were noticing, guns were the fulcrum upon which these trading partnerships rested.[50] It was becoming increasingly clear that if Comanches were to continue their expansionist thrust southward and eastward, a more stable access to firearms, ammunition, gun powder, and other manufactured goods was to be a prerequisite.

Threats also arrived from the North and Northeast. Although Comanches and Pawnees had been longtime competitors over the resource domains of the Great Plains, Comanche-Pawnee violence intensified during the 1740s, with Pawnee war parties raiding Comanche communities for horses and Comanche slavers routing Pawnee villages for slaves.[51] The Pawnees of the lower Platte River Valley, like their Comanche enemies, probably first became acquainted with horses toward the end of the seventeenth century, and by 1714 Euro-Americans were regarding Pawnee riders as good horsemen. By the 1720s, the Pawnee demand for horses grew so great that Pawnee representatives were traveling to Ndé communities on the Southern Plains to establish new modes of commerce. It is unclear if and how long the Pawnee-Ndé agreements lasted, but by midcentury Pawnees had turned their attention toward Comanche communities for opportunities to extract horses.[52] But Pawnees were not the only northern peril of Comanches; by 1749, Spaniards had received news that Comanches were campaigning against the "Aa Nation" of the North. Scholars are uncertain of the identity of this group of people, but it is likely that the Aas were either the Arapahoes or Crows of the Northern Plains.[53] In any case, it is clear that during the 1740s life on Comanchería's northern borders was regularly violent and tumultuous.

The Arapaho/Crow and Pawnee threats of the North and Northeast, however, must have paled in comparison to the dangers presented by the powerful Osages of the lower Missouri and Arkansas river valleys. The Osages of the eighteenth century were a culturally and economically inventive people, who, like the Comanches of the Southern Plains, had gained considerable influence across the trans-Mississippian region by adapting to diverse resource domains and fluctuating commercial opportunities. Adjusted to both the grasslands and the woodlands of the lower Missouri and Arkansas valleys, Osage communities consisted of efficient horticulturalists, savvy traders, resourceful hunters, and seasoned warriors, which made the Osage people one of the more influential Indigenous nations of eighteenth-century North America. During the first half of the century, Osages established exchange networks with the French traders stationed along the Mississippi River, and with French firearms in hand Osage fighters often swept across the territories of various plainspeoples, extracting bison, horses, mules, and enslaved people.[54] The Osage midcentury sweep reconfigured the geopolitics of the Southern Plains, and after pushing all but two Wichita villages southward to the Red River, Comanchería stood as the last barrier to an unencumbered Osage access to the North American Southwest at large.[55]

Along Comanchería's western border, tensions were also escalating, as the interactions between New Mexico residents and Comanche visitors shifted from amiable to destructive. According to Hämäläinen, the goodwill built throughout the 1720s and 1730s with New Mexican traders evaporated during the early years of the 1740s, when Spanish merchants "violated Comanche codes of proper behavior by haggling over prices, pushing inferior commodities, and refusing to sell certain goods, such as guns." Prior to the 1740s, New Mexicans and Comanches had established peaceful relations through trade, which for Comanches meant the establishment of fictive, or metaphorical, kinship ties. From a Comanche perspective, the exchange of goods was an articulation of political and social attachments as well as a commitment to providing for the material needs of both trading communities. During the latter part of the 1730s, however, Spaniards began disrupting such an arrangement by enforcing laws that excluded Pueblos from the Comanche trade and by imposing European-based trade practices. Thus, the violation of Comanche exchange protocols was likely the principal cause of the great Comanche raids of the early 1740s, thereby adding yet another front of violence for midcentury Comanches. By the late 1740s, the conflict would prove especially costly, as New Mexican governors unleashed two devastating expeditions against Comanche communities. The first, in 1747, left 107 Comanches and their Ute allies dead as campaigners seized 206 slaves and approximately a thousand horses. During the second campaign in 1750, the expeditioners broke up a Comanche *ranchería* and massacred nearly one hundred fleeing men, women, and children. In short, Comanches were beginning to experience the victimization of mass slaving violence for themselves.[56]

With mounting pressure coming from nearly every direction, Comanches must have felt increasingly isolated on the Southern Plains. Yet, it could not have been clear that seeking external support would have been the best course of action. With their long history of violence against neighboring communities, the decision to look for new allies was risky. Who would have welcomed an alliance? To what extent had Comanche slave raids crippled diplomatic relations? Were some communities inherently excluded from such a cooperative relationship? Fortunately for the Comanches, they found willing partners to the south in the Taovayas, Guichitas, and Iscanis—collectively known as Wichitas—and their decision to unite with these peoples from the Arkansas and Red River valleys would prove transformative. Not only were Wichita traders willing to barter the guns, powder, and ammunition that they collected from French colonists; they also were prepared to train the Comanches in the art of handling firearms.[57] For their part, Comanches supplied Wichitas with horses from their vast herds as well as enslaved people.[58]

The commercial partnership was both timely and mutually beneficial: Comanche expertise in the acquisition and managing of horses complemented the Wichita access to manufactured goods and agricultural products. And soon the Comanche-Wichita alliance would extend even to the battlefield, with Comanches and Wichitas fighting alongside one another.

As early as 1748, the Wichita alliance began paying huge dividends, as French traders brought vast quantities of firearms into Comanchería in exchange for horses and mules. According to New Mexico's Governor Joaquín Codallos y Rabál, news that thirty-three Frenchmen were selling "to the aforesaid Cumanches plenty of muskets in exchange for mules" in 1748 was a good "reason to fear some conspiracy." Governor Codallos had difficulty fathoming the Comanche-French commerce as a rational, economic arrangement between two autonomous, enterprising parties, and to the governor the commercial alliance could have been little more than a great French plot to subvert Spanish rule. But the governor's Euro-centrism betrayed him; the Comanche-French trade was in reality evidence of a broader Comanche impulse to capitalize, prosper, and expand. As Governor Tomás Vélez Cachupín noted a few years later, Comanche political and commercial posturing was making them stronger: "By joining with the Jumanos [Wichitas], they [the Comanches] may be too powerful to resist."[59] Thus by mid-1752, Spanish authorities were calling for an end to the aggressive anti-Comanche campaigns orchestrated by Spanish military leaders during the past several years. Instead, Spanish officials were warning New Mexican residents to be more mindful of their dangerous neighbors, offering free access to the New Mexican markets while respecting Comanche cultural protocol. The viceroy's *auditor* expressed the new approach in no uncertain terms: "The best policy is always to make them liberal gifts and permit them free entrance and trade for their hides and for ransoming individuals of other tribes whom we customarily ransom to be catechized among our people."[60]

For Wichita communities, the Comanche alliance offered significant defensive benefits, and throughout the early 1750s joint parties of Comanche and Wichita warriors campaigned against Osage villages to help curb the violence Wichitas were facing from their Osage enemies.[61] The peace brokered between Wichitas and Comanches also seems to have spread into Pawnee country, as Spanish authorities began learning of military alliances between Wichitas, Comanches, and Pawnees as early as August 1752.[62] Finally, the material and defensive benefits of the Comanche alliance partly inspired the Wichitas of the Red River Valley to establish themselves more permanently between their Comanche partners to the northwest and their French allies to the east. The site the Taovayas, Guichitas, and Iscanis chose was located on the north bank of the Red River in present-day Jefferson County, Oklahoma, and the fort they constructed was awe-inspiring. Built to accommodate large populations of both residents and visitors, the fort was highly defensible and equipped to withstand lengthy attacks and barrages. The Taovayas seem to have manned the fort, while the Guichitas and Iscanis established their villages immediately adjacent to it.[63] By the latter part of the 1750s, various groups of Tonkawas, Caddos, and Comanches had begun to station their *rancherías* nearby as well.[64] Together, Wichitas, Comanches, Tonkawas, and Caddos would be known as the infamous Norteños by the Spanish observers of Texas.[65]

The Comanche-Wichita alliance also coincided with the beginning of sustained Comanche migration into the heart of Texas. Prior to the 1740s, Comanches had forged their identities as equestrians, traders, and slavers according to the historical currents emanating from New Mexico, the Great Plains, and the Mississippi River. The Comanche-Ndé wars had drawn Comanche communities closer and closer to Texas, but by 1730 Comanches had grown mostly content with the southern limits of their territory, located along the Canadian River. With their new commercial and political allies to the southeast, however, Comanches began to discover new, highly lucrative opportunities springing from another direction. In 1743, just as conflicts were about to break out along the various borders of Comanchería, Spaniards began receiving news of a Comanche presence in Texas. According to Antonio Bonilla, officer of the Secretaria de Cámara of Mexico, it was in 1743 that Comanches ratcheted up their war effort against the Ndé plainspeople of Texas: "The Apaches dared to attack them in their own territory, but were valiantly repelled, and from that day to this retain a servile fear of them."[66] From 1743 on, Comanche and Ndé communities would compete with one another along the northern and western portions of Texas, but the Comanche-Wichita alliance of 1746 was the death knell of an unfettered Ndé influence over the Texas plains. For the next several decades, Apachería's Texas holdings rapidly deteriorated in favor of an expanding Comanchería. And as both Ndé and Spanish borderlanders would come to discover, slavery would play a pivotal role in the Comanche ascendance in the Texas theater, just as it had in New Mexico.

The War for Texas: The Comanche-Ndé Conflicts of the 1750s and 1760s

Although scholars know that the Comanche-Ndé wars resumed in Texas as early as 1743, Euro-American observers left few written details about the conflicts during the ten-year period following the 1743 incident. This dearth of source material may have been the result of a lull in violence, but it is also likely that few Euro-Americans commented on the conflicts because they occurred beyond the administrative range of Spanish or French colonists.[67] Moreover, we might assume that the other crises that both Comanche and Ndé communities faced during the period from 1743 to 1753 (i.e., Osage pressures from the East, Spanish slaving campaigns, and disease epidemics) limited the fighting capacities of Comanches and Apaches. In any case, by 1753 Spaniards were again reporting Comanche-Ndé violence in Texas. Lt. Juan Galván, who was charged with the task of exploring the San Sabá River Valley in 1753, was among the first to break the documentary silence, claiming that "the Lipanes do not have relations with the Comanches, who are their enemies and continue to cause them harm."[68] Within a year, Spanish officials were receiving requests from Ndé leaders to establish buffers along the San Sabá River to block the Comanche spread into Texas. Spanish authorities interpreted such petitions as evidence of their desire to live in mission-settlements, but it would not be long before they realized that Ndé leaders were primarily concerned with checking Comanche expansion. As Juan Antonio Moraín declared in November 1756, "The Apaches had been reduced to peace . . . by the attacks of the Comanches."[69] Comanches were forcing Apaches into the fold of the Spanish Empire.

The year 1755 seems to have been a critical moment in the history of Comanche-Ndé relations. By that time, Ndé communities still exercised considerable control over the hunting ranges of the San Sabá River region, with at least ten *rancherías* stationed north of the San Sabá at the start of the year. Moreover, Comanche attacks into Apachería had not been devastating enough to arouse the concern of Spanish officials nearby. If cooler heads had prevailed at this time, or if Comanche and Ndé leaders had elected to ally with one another against a common enemy, perhaps the Spanish colonists of the region, the violence of the next dozen or so years might have been averted. Surprisingly, amity had become a real possibility in 1755 when Spanish missionaries were able to broker a brief peace between Ndé and Comanche diplomats near the San Xavier mission on the San Gabriel River. According to Fray

Francisco Aparicio, the peace talks were initially so successful that they culminated in a joyous celebration, as "all the Indians sang together and touched weapons in token of friendship."[70] But a Comanche-Ndé peace was not to last. Comanches had bigger aspirations, and the Ndé communities of the Southern Plains appeared more of a burden than an asset to Comanche expansionist endeavors. By February 1756, Comanches were in the midst of yet another explosive thrust southward, and this time the thrust would not halt until most Ndé communities had abandoned their Texas homelands in favor of the lower Río Grande Valley or the western mountains of the present-day New Mexico–Texas border region.[71] Comanche migrants were determined to make the bison- and horse-rich countryside of Texas the southern portion of Comanchería.

The attacks of Comanche rangers in 1756 drew into the fray Ndé communities from all over the northern frontier of Mexico. In September 1756, the Ndé *náshneta*, Bigotes, and some five hundred followers set out from San Fernando de Austria, located in modern-day Zaragoza, Coahuila, to campaign against marauding Comanches to the north.[72] By the end of the year, other Ndé groups, including Natages, Mescaleros, Pelones, Come Nopales, and Come Caballos, also had found themselves engaged in war with the Norteños.[73] And even though Comanche communities were generally stationed along the northern portions of Texas, "a long distance" from the San Sabá, Colorado, and Concho rivers, Comanche raiders apparently traveled as far south and west as San Felipe, the capital of Chihuahua.[74] Certainly not all Comanche attacks were effective or entirely destructive, but they undoubtedly disrupted the hunt-heavy subsistence cycles of most Ndé communities in Texas. According to the *sargento mayor* of Coahuila, Bernardo de Miranda, Comanches "compelled them [the Apaches] to abandon a great part of their land by their continuous and frequent depredations."[75] By the latter part of 1757, Spanish officials were even hearing rumors that Norteños were preparing to attack them, particularly at the newly established mission-presidio complex for Ndé plainspeople on the San Sabá River.[76] It was not long before Spaniards themselves would feel the wrath of Comanche military power as well.

The signs of an impending attack were there, if only Spanish authorities had been willing to pay close attention. Rumors continued to swirl throughout the winter of 1757–58, and on February 25, 1758, Norteño raiders made their presence known by driving off fifty-nine horses from the presidio of San Sabá. Several days later, on March 2, another group of Norteños stole an additional sixty-two animals from San Sabá. If the thefts of animals were not enough to convince Spanish officials of imminent danger, the attack of four mining prospectors on the Pedernales River on March 9 should have indicated the Norteños' hostile intentions. Moreover, the Ndé leaders who frequented the mission-settlement throughout 1757–58 regularly explained to the Spanish missionaries and officers that their unwillingness to settle there was a direct result of their war with Comanches. As the Lipan *náshneta*, Tacú, told Col. Diego Ortiz Parrilla in May 1757, too many of his kinspeople had fallen victim to Comanche violence and slave raids. The San Sabá location was poorly defensed and extremely vulnerable to a Comanche attack; thus, he and his people were willing to settle nearby only after the Comanche threat had been dissolved.[77] Yet on March 16, when some two thousand war-ready Norteños arrived at the San Sabá mission, the Spanish residents were still taken by surprise. Only later did the Spaniards recognize the error of their blind obstinacy.[78]

The Norteño descent upon the San Sabá mission-settlement on the morning of March 16 was one of the most spectacular events in the history of the eighteenth-century North American West. The huge party of Comanches, Wichitas, Tonkawas, and Caddos was led by a distinguished Comanche *paraibo*, who alerted every observer of his esteemed status by touting a red French uniform jacket, armor, a musket, war paint, and, of course, his personal steed. Others followed suit with their display of prestige goods and advanced fighter technology, and an untold number were mounted. Perhaps as many as a thousand were armed with firearms, while the remaining equipped themselves with pikes, bows and arrows, and cutlasses. These Norteños had come with one clear purpose: to annihilate their Ndé foes. Although missionaries begged the Norteño leaders to accept tribute in exchange for peace, it did not take long for the Norteño warriors to lose patience with the pleading missionaries. After briefly surveying the mission defenses, the Norteños unleashed an onslaught of violence and destruction. On most occasions, Comanches and their allies might have sought out in the fray individuals to enslave, but not on this day. After raiding for animals and other valuable goods, the Norteño fighters set the mission ablaze. Only those who managed to escape during the early stages of the siege survived. Over the next several months, Spanish observers and authorities quibbled over the meaning and ultimate purpose of the attack, but there can be little doubt that the sack of San Sabá was as much a punitive action as it was a demonstration of Norteño power, with a great Comanche *paraibo* leading the way. Comanches used the

San Sabá episode to signal to the people of the Texas borderlands that they were ready to run the show.[79]

If the San Sabá siege was the climactic declaration of a Comanche emergence in Texas, the next several years were a slow but methodical articulation of Comanche expansion. And unlike the San Sabá episode, which did not include the enslavement of any of the Norteños' enemies, the next phase of Comanche territorial consolidation witnessed the resumption of Comanche slave raiding. News of Comanche aggression first arrived in June 1758, after Comanche raiders finally tracked down the Ndé *náshneta*, Tacú, on a hill near the Concho River, sacking his pitched encampment and pillaging it for all of the tents, arms, and horses abandoned by the fleet-footed Tacú. Unfortunately for his comrades, "a number were left dead" and nineteen were enslaved by the Comanche raiders.[80] Various Ndé leaders mobilized their followers soon after and in November that year launched a series of broad attacks against the Comanche migrants. The countercampaigns, however, failed to recover much of the territory lost to Comanches over the past handful of years, and once again Ndé diplomats were seeking assistance from Spaniards in Texas.[81] But this time, Ndé leaders were bent on convincing Spanish authorities that they needed to be more strategic in the site they chose. By 1760, Comanche communities had positioned themselves as far south as the San Sabá River, not far from the mission-presidio complex, and Apaches wanted no part of those troubles.[82] The location that several Ndé ambassadors preferred was in a narrow canyon along the upper Nueces River. Known to Spaniards at the time as both El Valle de San José and El Cañón, this site eventually became the location of two mission-settlements: San Lorenzo de Santa Cruz and Nuestra Señora de la Candelaria del Cañón. By February 1762, several hundred Ndé men, women, and children had relocated to the two mission-settlements.[83]

But the Ndé relocation to the south did not stop the Comanche advance. In May 1762, only a few months after Spaniards and Apaches celebrated the founding of the second mission, Candelaria, Comanches devastated several Ndé *rancherías* posted near San Lorenzo. In June and July, Comanches repeated their attacks, this time stealing horses from the Spanish presidio at San Lorenzo, and although Spanish soldiers were aware of the violence, none was willing to fight back.[84] Even Bigotes, a longtime anti-Comanche fighter, could not escape the wrath of Comanche raiders. In September 1762, he and his followers were attacked on the Frio River—a Norteño raid that resulted in the capture of Bigotes's sister.[85] Toward the end of the year, Comanches attacked and raided the small Ndé communities that bravely, if not audaciously, had chosen to plant their *rancherías* near San Sabá.[86] It is unclear how many people were enslaved during these particular attacks, but the assaults were evidently destructive and demoralizing. Only days after the Comanche raid on Bigotes's *ranchería*, Norteños arrived in San Antonio with sixteen enslaved Apaches in addition to the scalps, skulls, fingers, and ears of twenty-two Ndé victims.[87] It was also around this time that the panicked Ndé *náshneta* mentioned at the opening of this chapter was terrorized by nightmares of Spanish soldiers enslaving his people at the San Lorenzo mission. Needless to say, the Ndé people of the Texas borderlands were feeling vulnerable.

By 1763, Norteño frustrations with the Spanish-Ndé relationship in Texas had reached new heights. From a Norteño perspective, the initial sack of Mission San Sabá in March 1758 was orchestrated with the primary purpose of crippling Ndé influence in the region and not necessarily with the intention of bringing Spaniards into the Comanche-Ndé conflict. But the renewed efforts of Spanish missionaries and officers to collaborate with Ndé communities along the Nueces River signaled to Norteños that the Spaniards had committed themselves to a long-term alliance with their Esikwita enemies. Thus, it was not long before Norteños began plotting joint attacks against the various Spanish outposts in Texas. In April 1763, Spaniards learned of these plans when a formerly enslaved Lipan man arrived at the San Sabá presidio on foot, claiming that fourteen enemy nations, including Tahuacanas, Comanches, and Yojuanes, "were convening in order to advance against this presidio, the new converts [of the missions on the upper Nueces], and the Presidio of San Antonio de Vejar."[88] Little came of these rumors, but by January of the following year Norteños were attacking the supply trains and squadrons that traveled to and from the Spanish outposts at San Antonio and San Sabá.[89] In February and March 1764, Norteño attacks grew bolder, with Norteño raiders attacking the San Sabá presidio and stealing horses from the herds at San Antonio and even La Bahía.[90] By September, circumstances had become so desperate at San Sabá that the viceroy, the Marqués de Cruillas, ordered reinforcements to be sent to assist the rapidly declining presidio.[91]

With San Sabá all but lost to Comanches and their Norteño allies, the Ndé mission-settlements along the upper Nueces River became the last Ndé stronghold in the Spanish Texas sphere of influence, and for at least a brief period the small Ndé communities made the most of the strategic advantages of their new home. Although Comanche attacks had limited

Ndé access to the bison herds of the Texas plains, the security offered by the rugged terrain of the canyons near the upper Nueces strengthened the Ndé resolve to withstand the Norteño onslaught. During the winter of 1764–65, Ndé leaders began plotting extensive hit-and-run strikes against their Comanche enemies. The decision to fight had grown out of both economic desperation and their anger at Comanche slave raids. According to Fray Arricivita, the Apache *capitanes* had decided "to fight until they had exterminated the Comanches who captured their women and children and hindered them from taking advantage of the buffalo, being their enemies in every way." Apparently these attacks were rather successful, as Ndé war parties descended upon the various *rancherías* stationed along the southern reaches of Comanchería, pillaging the vulnerable communities and then retreating to the protective confines of their new settlements. Arricivita outlined the general contours of these strikes:

> Through the information of spies, they [the Apaches] knew which rancherías were isolated and attacked them, doing whatever damage they could. They killed the old men and infants and carried away the women and children, traveling day and night with their prey until they reached the Chanas River, where the hills leading to Los Caño-nes begin. When they reached this place, they considered themselves very secure, relying on the inability of their enemies to penetrate the ridge. Such was the case, for even though the latter followed them, they turned back on reaching this place.[92]

But the wave of Ndé successes was not to last long. Although they had found themselves entangled in conflicts in virtually every direction, Norteños were committed to ridding the borderlands of their Ndé inhabitants.[93] Norteño attacks resumed as early as February 1766, when Capt. Felipe de Rábago y Terán, the nephew of Pedro de Rábago y Terán, reported an assault at El Cañon. According to Rábago y Terán, a large party of well-armed Norteños, including Comanches and Taovayas, attacked the Ndé communities located just beyond the mission-settlements at El Cañon, killing some, enslaving others, and stealing all of their horses.[94] Spanish soldiers and Comanche raiders skirmished throughout the summer, but circumstances quickly turned dire in the fall, when the Ndé *náshneta* El Turnio, sensing an impending Comanche siege, suddenly led his people away from San Lorenzo. The Comanche assault arrived soon after, and the small number of Lipanes who stayed with the thirty Spanish soldiers still stationed there had little chance to repel the war party of some three hundred armed Comanches. Although the missionaries' fears that the women of the mission would "fall into the hands of such ferocious beasts" never came to fruition, the attack successfully robbed the mission of its vast horse herd.[95] In November, Comanche fighters returned to the San Lorenzo mission, but the ingenious decision to bolster the appearance of mission defenses by arming the women of the mission dissuaded the raiders from doing any real damage to the settlement.[96]

After successfully repelling a couple of Comanche-led assaults during the fall of 1766, the Lipanes of the upper Nueces River likely felt confident that the tide was turning in their favor once again and thus began resuming their hunting trips on the bison-rich plains of Texas. Unfortunately for these Lipanes, their confidence would betray them. In late December, a party of Comanche rangers finally outmaneuvered the cautious Ndé residents of El Cañon, attacking a band of Lipanes on their return from a hunt. As Arricivita remembered the attack, the Comanche fighters "struck such a cruel blow when about a league from the mission that they killed and captured more than thirty and took all the meat and over one thousand horses, passing before the very walls of the missions with all the spoils." When Spanish soldiers attempted to rescue the enslaved Lipanes and recover the stolen goods, their efforts proved futile. The Comanche raiders surrounded the pitiful detachment of soldiers and killed eight of them. The defeat was an embarrassment to the Spanish colonists of Texas, particularly as the Comanche victors "ridiculed the cannon [that the Spanish soldiers abandoned] indecently and practiced barbarous excesses with the dead."[97] More important, however, the Comanche victory was a decisive blow against their Ndé enemies. By January 1767, Spanish officials were receiving news that the Apaches staying at El Cañon had abandoned the mission-settlements entirely, relocating to the Río Grande.[98] Thus, Comanche violence and slave raiding had prevailed; El Cañon was also to be part of Comanche country.

Early Comanche Slavery in Perspective

From the 1750s through the 1760s, Comanche slavers tore families and communities apart as they built their broad sphere of influence from the Arkansas River in the North to the Upper Nueces in the South. Undeniably, the impact of Comanche slaving upon victim communities, particularly Ndé *rancherías*, was unforgiving and extreme. As longtime victims of Spanish slavers, the Ndé residents of Texas were not unfamiliar

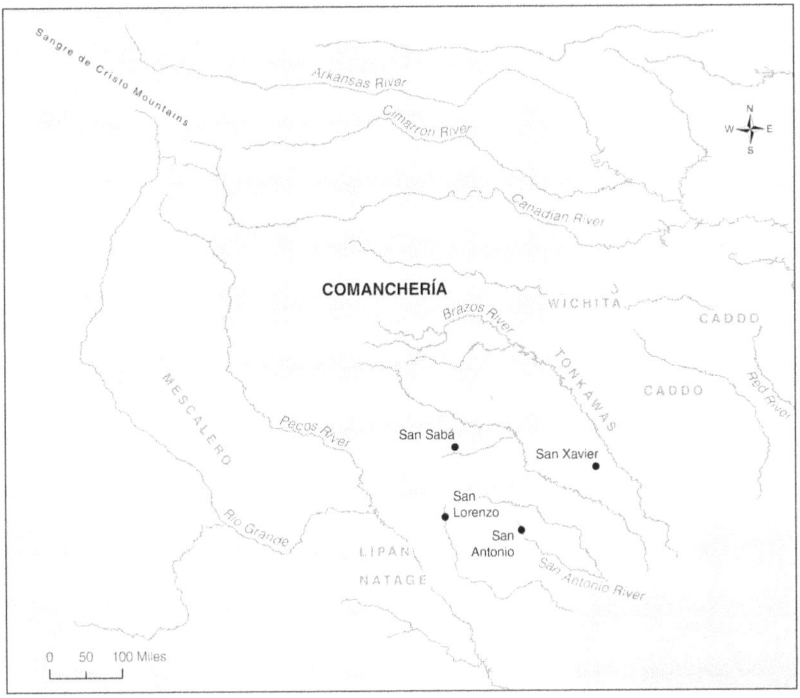

Map 5. Comanchería, ca. 1767. Cartography by Luyang Ren.

with slave raids, but the swiftness and vigor of Comanche attacks during the 1750s and 1760s devastated Ndé communities.[99] Although the precise effects of decades of Comanche slave raiding upon Ndé society are difficult to measure, it is evident that in addition to the widespread displacement of Ndé plainspeople, Comanche pressures forced them to adapt economically, politically, socially, and culturally. At the heart of midcentury Ndé troubles was a fundamental change in resource accessibility. The seventeenth- and eighteenth-century Ndé dominance of the Southern Plains was made possible by their collective ability to manipulate and adapt to the diverse resource domains of the region, as they creatively combined the various technologies, commercial networks, and foodstuffs available. The result was a conglomeration of mounted, semisedentary, and commercially oriented peoples who were simultaneously feared and admired by many. Yet, Comanche aggression, in tandem with Spanish colonialism, dismantled this influential way of life for the Ndé plainspeople. As was the case for the Jicarillas and Cuartelejos earlier in the eighteenth century, some Ndé groups sought assistance and refuge among unusual allies. To the south, the violent encroachment of Comanche raiders during the 1740s, 1750s, and 1760s motivated the Lipanes, Natagés, and other Ndé *naciones* to consider by midcentury an alliance with the Spanish-influenced peoples of Texas—an unthinkable proposition during the previous three decades. Finally, other Ndé groups fled to the more desolate areas in the Southwest, finding protective cover in the hill and desert country of the modern-day shared-border region of Texas, New Mexico, Chihuahua, and Coahuila. According to Enrique Gilbert-Michael Maestas, a number of *rancherías* became obvious "defensive refuges." And Lipanes, who traditionally had adorned themselves with a white alkali paste to signify their identity as the "Light Gray People," more regularly wore red, symbolizing the constant state of warfare they faced.[100]

Comanche-induced relocation, along with Spanish colonial pressures, also required Ndé plainspeople, especially those accustomed to the vast quantities of bison and the dependability of annual crop yields, to reevaluate community subsistence patterns. As equestrians, most were intimately familiar with the various technological possibilities of horses, but it was during this era of displacement that Ndé communities generally became more dependent upon horses as a direct source of food and consumption. The lives of most Ndé residents of the Texas borderlands thus became intimately tied to horses, with hunting and resource confiscation becoming their defining economic behaviors. Slaving does not seem to have been nearly as prolific among them as it was among Comanches at this time, but the portability of enslaved bodies provided mobile Ndé communities with much-needed labor in a time of great demographic decline and uncertainty. Overall, the new emphases in Ndé economy certainly caused friction with neighboring horse- and cow-herding communities, but they offered Ndé *naciones* new opportunities to thrive and to prosper amid harsh regional and historical circumstances.[101]

Of course, slaving was a two-way street: just as Comanche slaving violence transformed mid-eighteenth-century Ndé life and society, slavery was also reconfiguring Comanche society from within. The available documentary evidence provides virtually no clues regarding the number of enslaved individuals living within the confines of Comanchería during the 1750s and 1760s, but given the great preponderance of intercultural conflict and the frequent colonial reports of slave raids, we can assume that Comanches had many opportunities to incorporate enslaved people into their society. A comparison of figures from reported slave raids with Euro-American purchase or ransom records might offer some hints about the number of enslaved outsiders integrated within Comanche society. Nevertheless, even if scholars could recover every single accurately reported slave raid and compare them to what we would presume to be representative purchaser documents, we would not be accounting for the enslaved people traded *among* those who generally left no written record (i.e., Pawnees, Wichitas, and Caddos). What scholars do know, however, is that Comanches were prolific slave raiders and traders and at least sometimes integrated enslaved people as commodified possessions and exploited laborers. Such interactions with slavery were without question enough to familiarize Comanches with the singular violence of slavery, and evidence suggests that slavery bled into many other aspects of Comanche society.

The violence that was fundamental to Comanche slavery—while rather opaque in the limited documentary evidence during the previous decades—became clearer to Euro-American observers by the middle part of the eighteenth century. One particular—and supposedly common—slaveholding behavior stands out as an example of the violence that had become entrenched within Comanche slavery. Fray Andrés Varo detailed this behavior in a report he wrote in 1751 to discredit the work of the local Spanish authorities of New Mexico:

> Among many other infamies there is one of such a nature that if I did not so desire a remedy I would remain silent, since it is so obscene and unfit for chaste ears. It is the truth that when these barbarians bring a certain number of Indian women to sell, among them many young maidens and girls, before delivering them to the Christians who buy them, if they are ten years old or over, they deflower and corrupt them in the sight of innumerable assemblies of barbarians and Catholics (neither more nor less, as I say), without considering anything but their unbridled lust and brutal shamelessness, and saying to those who buy them, with heathen impudence: "Now you can take her—now she is good." The laws that are broken in this hellish ceremony or exhibition alone I have already cited . . . but the consequences that follow from it can only be wept for, for it is impossible to fathom them and much less to tell them.[102]

His general disdain for the populations of the New Mexican borderlands notwithstanding, Varo's hyperbolic description of Comanche rape speaks to the importance of violence in the Comanche slaving system. Even if scholars ignore Fray Varo's moralizing and his employment of a racist, civilization-barbarism discourse, the performed acts of sexual violence remain as visceral indicators of how totalizing the power of individual slavers could be. In the context of a slaver-slave relationship, basic human decency was by no means a requirement; instead, personal power dictated interactions.

Yet, Fray Varo's report does more than illuminate the gendered violence of Comanche slavery; it also speaks to its complexities. As Hämäläinen has argued, the violence of Comanche slavery had strong economic underpinnings, and even in the case of the public rapes of enslaved women—which would have been cruel acts of patriarchal brutality—Comanche slavers were articulating an economic vision born of their Spanish colonial encounter: their violation of women created a demand for Spanish buyers who were more likely to purchase slaves if they could justify the exchange as an act of heroism and honorable, manly virtue.[103] But the acts of sexual violence were not just expressions of Comanche market and colonial awareness; they were also the logical conclusion of a system of slavery built upon violent integration. For at least two or three decades, Comanche communities expanded in part by means of the forced incorporation of enslaved people. Children, it seems, were valued for their potential as current and future contributors to Comanche society, and enslaved women offered reproductive labor. Thus, in addition to domestic work, women had the potential to make Comanche communities grow in the literal sense—and such a capability cannot be divorced from other forms of labor in terms of scope or importance.[104] The theatricality of the public rapes probably muddles scholars' ability to evaluate the quotidian violence suffered by enslaved people within Comanche communities, but there is no reason to believe that the forced removal and integration of people from their home community to another foreign community was painless, benign, or nontraumatic. In some ways, we might even consider the staged performance of sexual violence as a message directed toward other Comanche slaves as well. If they also had to witness the violence, it would have served as a harrowing reminder of their slavers' ultimate power over them.[105]

More traditional understandings of exploitation also account for Comanche slavery's economic character. While I have found no direct contemporary references to Comanche slavers forcing their slaves to work in the manufacturing of hides or hide-based products during this period, the sheer volume of the Comanche trade in manufactured goods suggests the prominence of slave labor during production.[106] Furthermore, substantial labor was required to build and to maintain the domestic structures of the mobile Comanche communities. Bison, for instance, served as the principal building resource for Comanche housing, but converting the raw materials of bison to usable construction materials for domiciles that were "good and well suited for defense" was an arduous, labor-intensive process.[107] Later Euro-American observers noted that the building and transportation of Comanche lodges was primarily a female task, and as many of the integrated slaves were women, slave labor probably was integral to the maintenance of Comanche domestic life.[108] Finally, Comanche equestrianism certainly benefited from slave labor. By midcentury, Comanche horse herds had swollen to unprecedented levels, and with new trade demands springing from both New Mexico and the Red River Valley, controlled access to a steady supply of horses had become as important as ever. For the task of monitoring and herding horses, enslaved boys would have been ideal candidates, which partly explains why Comanche raiders were so keen on enslaving children.[109]

In addition to its clear commercial and economic value, Comanche slavery had begun to take on an obvious sociopolitical character by midcentury. Since the earliest days of Euro-American–Comanche interactions, Comanche slavery had been characterized by a geopolitical orientation: the Comanche redistribution of enslaved bodies enhanced Comanche foreign relations with some groups while simultaneously crippling their relations with others.[110] By the 1750s and 1760s, Spanish officials in New Mexico actively had begun to strengthen diplomatic ties by requiring the exchange of enslaved people as prerequisites to alliance, and it is not unreasonable to assume similar arrangements also occurred between Comanche communities and other Native groups, especially as Comanches made peace agreements with other Indigenous nations.[111] In any case, detailed Euro-American descriptions from the mid-eighteenth century, which offer glimpses of the internal workings of Comanche politics, provide some insights into how slavery operated in conjunction with Comanche social structures. And as these midcentury documents also include the earliest identification of named Comanche historical figures, scholars can glean some understanding of how slavery affected Comanches (and their slaves) on an individual level.[112]

One particularly revealing incident occurred during peace talks between Comanche leaders and Spanish authorities in New Mexico during the winter of 1751–52. During this round of negotiations, Governor Vélez Cachupín demanded that the Comanche visitors return several enslaved Spanish women and children if they hoped to resume their commerce. According to a Kiowa informant who was formerly enslaved by Comanches, the request caused a rift between two *paraibos* because one leader, Nimiricante, wanted to acquiesce, while another, who owned one of the desired Spanish women, refused. Nimiricante even offered his counterpart an Apache woman in exchange, but the steadfast slaver would not surrender his Spanish slave. As a result, Nimiricante "told him [the slaveholder] to leave his rancherías or suffer their punishment." As the Kiowa woman understood it, the *paraibos* "do not always have all of their people under their eyes and . . . there are some Comanches so perverse that they even steal horses from their own people and sell them to other rancherías." Apparently Nimiricante decided to hold off trading at Taos until he dealt with the matter to his liking.[113]

This incident is important for our purposes because it offers a glimpse of Comanche power structures relative to slavery. The fact that Nimiricante believed he had the power to direct the distribution of enslaved individuals (even if he was willing to barter for them) suggests that positions of political authority influenced the control of enslaved bodies. Moreover, by refusing to part with his slave, the man who possessed the enslaved Spanish woman was articulating his political (and possibly economic) independence from the Comanche *paraibo*, Nimiricante. It is unclear if part of the slaver's ability to resist Nimiricante's authority was directly rooted in his possession of an enslaved person, but we can assume that the claim of ownership during such tense times was testament to his confidence in his entitlement to the enslaved woman as well as his influence in the broader Comanche society. In short, he believed that what he did with his slave was his prerogative and that nobody had the power to tell him otherwise.[114]

The incident also hints at the democratizing aspects of raiding in Comanche society. Although *paraibos* were vested with the power to lead their communities, especially in diplomatic affairs, Comanche men more or less had the freedom to pursue economic independence and an enhanced social status on their own. As the Kiowa woman claimed, Comanche *paraibos* did not always monitor the behavior of their male followers. In this scenario, even though Nimiricante considered his fellow slaveholder an equal of sorts, he could do little to enforce his will, even if he so desired. This was the case with the so-called rogue raiders who attacked outposts in search of booty without permission from their leaders. But this was a necessary reality for Comanche leaders, because to curtail raids was to limit access to horses, the most important resource in Comanche society. Thus, for those who were seeking to build their horse wealth, the loose political structure provided greater economic opportunities. Eventually, the accumulation of horses would result in a need for more laborers, and further raiding offered access to slave labor. It was through this cycle that Comanche horse herds expanded, enslaved populations grew, and political authority remained decentralized.[115]

Even though Comanche society was not characterized by a rigid political hierarchy, social influence was not solely measured in terms of politics. As was the case in Spanish Texas, there can be little doubt that Comanche social status was intertwined with processes of intercultural violence, including slaving. Spanish writers regularly pointed out that Comanche fighters and raiders were extraordinarily courageous and willing to sacrifice their personal safety and well-being for the defeat of their enemies.[116] For instance, in 1763 a party of twenty-three Comanches, including two women, attacked a large Ndé *ranchería* located in the Texas–New Mexico borderlands. According to two Spanish observers, Francisco Romero and Joseph Antonio Miraval, even though the attackers were armed with guns, swords, lances, and bows and arrows, they had no chance to prevail. The raiders, nevertheless, fought to the death, and only one woman survived the skirmish.[117] Evidently, even when attackers were well-armed, slave raiding was an inherently risky business. And while many successful slave raids were conducted against unprotected communities, slavers always risked the chance of miscalculating enemy defenses or of being punished by the furious kinspeople of those they enslaved. Given such dangers, the active accumulation of slave plunder was an honorable endeavor, worthy of social esteem and recognition.[118]

Unfortunately, because scholars have so few contemporary sources regarding the internal dynamics of Comanche society, we can only speculate that the violence inherent in slave raiding extended in a similar fashion to relations between a slaver and his slaves.[119] There probably were key differences given the fact that courage in the face of the enemy was a necessity within the arena of war, while possessing and controlling enslaved individuals did not require bravery or the same risk of death. Therefore, violence may have been required to control enslaved people (and thus was required to maintain the political and social status that was tied to the possession of slaves), but it did not necessarily function as an honor-creating mechanism. If anything, in the slaver-slave context, violence instead served as an instrument of prestige sustenance, as the accumulation of enslaved bodies indicated greater (horse) wealth and influence.

Finally, it is rather apparent that by midcentury Comanches' historical connections to slaving systems had etched into their collective psyche a degree of fear and paranoia regarding the violent possibilities of intercultural interactions. Throughout the first half of the eighteenth century, Comanches interacted with various iterations of slavery as raiders, traders, diplomats, slaveholders, and even slaves themselves. The diversity of Comanche encounters with slavery made slavery a rather fluid institution (if it may even be considered a single institution) for Comanches, but such fluidity did not make the lived conditions of enslavement necessarily any less violent or traumatic. As Comanche rangers enslaved men, women, and children, ripping them away from their communities of origin, they had to have witnessed the inherent pain involved in this process. Observing the exchange in enslaved bodies could not have been any less excruciating, as friends and families were torn apart from one another yet again. And of course, forced labor—whether reproductive or manual—was harsh, tiresome, agonizing, and generally unrewarding. Thus, the prospect of enslavement by enemy forces inspired great fear and trepidation. Such was the case when Governor Vélez Cachupín and his soldiers surrounded a fleeing Comanche *ranchería* near a watering hole in 1751. According to the governor, as the Spanish soldiers and their allies drew closer to the trapped Comanche party, they could hear "the cries of six women and some children . . . [who] feared that they would not be pardoned" and believed that the Spaniards were there "to seize and execute them." Only an agreement to restore individuals they had enslaved in New Mexico in the past assured the Comanche party that peace was a real possibility.[120] Violence and slavery were two of the few languages that both Spaniards and Comanches could understand.

An awareness of slavery's psychological impacts, nonetheless, did not deter Comanche migrants from continuing their own slaving operations. To the contrary, slavery would continue to rise in scope and importance within Comanche society through the eighteenth century. If anything, slavery increasingly offered Comanches new avenues to personal wealth, social prestige, and regional domination. Certainly Comanches understood the geopolitical risks of enslaving their neighbors; yet to many, the rewards of slaving were too attractive.

Summary

For the Nʉmʉnʉʉ, the six-decade period from 1706 to 1767 was an era of great innovation, territorial expansion, migration, and prosperity. As intercultural conflict, widespread epidemics, and geopolitical realignment often tested Comanche resolve, the journey from their ancient homeland of the Northwest to the southern reaches of Texas was not an easy one, but it was certainly impressive. The ability to take advantage of diverse ecological and commercial opportunities made Comanches flexible and resourceful as they made their collective march across the Southern Plains and into the heart of Texas. Although horses were the transformative technology that provided Comanches with a means to dominate the vast resource domains of the Southern Plains, slavery offered Comanches economic and social mechanisms to control and to order their ever-changing world. By supplying enslaved people, Comanches integrated themselves into the prevailing commercial world of the North American Southwest; by raiding for enslaved bodies, Comanches violently articulated their military power and potential. In time, Comanches learned of the value of incorporating into their society enslaved people as stigmatized and exploited laborers. But slave raiding also reverberated on a geopolitical level, as victim communities—namely, Ndé communities—abandoned their homelands in hopes of finding a reprieve from Comanche (and Spanish colonial) violence. Almost simultaneously, Comanches filled the vacuum left by fleeing Ndé *rancherías*, and what was once Apachería became Comanchería. This process repeated itself, almost in cyclical fashion, for decades, well into the latter half of the eighteenth century. By 1767, slave raiding had brought Comanches all the way south to the upper Nueces River in Texas.

Although the Spanish colonists who settled in Texas during the first half of the eighteenth century wanted to view themselves as conquerors and rulers of the region, the Comanche newcomers who arrived during the latter part of the century were more deserving of such titles. Their modes of operation may have been similar, as violence and slavery often took center stage in their respective dramas of dominion building, but Comanche expansion functioned according to a much more innovative and flexible impulse. While Spaniards were juggling the bureaucratic, ideological, and material contradictions inherent to their history of slaving, campaigning, missionizing, and "civilizing," Comanches were adapting, raiding, displacing, trading, and taking. Violence had become a regular part of life in the Texas borderlands; whether one marshaled it in his favor or succumbed to it was a matter of determination, skill, and resource access. During the first two-thirds of the eighteenth century, Comanches did all they could to end up on the forgiving side of violence. For Comanches, "it was better to die than to retreat."[121]

Part II
Strange and Violent Bedfellows, 1760s–1836

In late December 1787, the influential Comanche *paraibo* Oabancem-econequic (or Gordo Cojo to the Spaniards) paraded over seventy men, women, and children into San Antonio. By late 1787, the sight of so many Comanches marching through the heart of Spanish Texas, without resistance or harassment, had become commonplace, as Spanish and Comanche leaders now lived in peace. During this visit, Spaniards met the Comanche travelers with the best hospitality the poor frontier town could offer, and in exchange the Comanche leader shared his good news. He and his fighters had been chasing a mobile Lipan community for weeks, and after trekking hundreds of miles across the Texas borderlands his men finally had caught up with their mutual enemies, striking them near the old mission-settlement at San Sabá. There Oabancemeconequic's men killed numerous Lipanes, stole many horses, and enslaved some of the survivors. The news undoubtedly pleased the Spanish governor, Rafael Martínez Pacheco, because he knew that as long as both Comanches and Spaniards remained committed to the destruction of Apaches, amity between the two groups had a chance.[1]

Yet the Comanche *paraibo* was not finished proving his fidelity to the Spanish-Comanche peace. Before heading back to Comanchería, Oabancemeconequic sold to Martínez Pacheco one of the young *indios* enslaved during their most recent campaign. Because amiable Comanche diplomacy required the exchange of goods, Martínez Pacheco's purchase of the young Lipan demonstrated his dedication to their "brotherly" relationship. That the "good" they exchanged was a commodified person mattered not. If anything, the exchange of an enslaved person reinforced the potency of cross-community collaboration through violence. Both Martínez Pacheco and Oabancemeconequic understood that the Spanish-Comanche peace rested upon the broken backs and fallen bodies of enslaved and deceased Ndé people.

Part II moves our historical narrative of slavery in the Texas borderlands forward through the latter part of the eighteenth century and into the first third of the nineteenth century. During this period, the fate of Spanish Texas hinged upon Spaniards' ability to adapt to widespread Comanche exploitation and violence. Surprisingly, neither Spaniards nor Comanches found it expedient to enslave the other; instead, both groups preferred to channel their slaving energies elsewhere, particularly against the Ndé peoples of the borderlands. Their mutual recognition of the possibilities of camaraderie through anti-Ndé violence ultimately allowed for an enduring Spanish-Comanche peace, which lasted from the mid-1780s through the early 1810s.[2] Oabancemeconequic's 1787 slaving campaign against Lipanes was therefore just the beginning of this violent collaboration.

Peace, however, also depended upon the Spaniards' ability to prove their material commitment to Comanche welfare. On a practical level, this meant constant tribute payments to Comanche visitors. But with the tumult of the War of Mexican Independence, which first reached Spanish Texas in January 1811, Spanish coffers dried up, leaving Comanches feeling betrayed. So what Comanches could not receive voluntarily from the Spaniards they took for themselves. The wave of Comanche violence that spread across Spanish Texas during the 1810s left the Hispanic borderlands communities on the brink of utter collapse. It was thus in this context that Spanish officials began entertaining new plans for colonizing the "barbarous" Texas borderlands. In 1820, as the War of Mexican Independence came to a close, the arrival of Moses Austin and his plan for Anglo-American colonization presented Spanish authorities with an opportunity to secure Mexico's northeastern frontier for good. His plan, taken up by his son Stephen F. Austin soon after he died in June 1821 and then accepted (with modifications) by the new Mexican government, would usher in yet another era of slavery in the Texas borderlands.

Hispanic and Anglo-American colonial collaborators may have dreamed of a liberalized and economically prosperous Texas, but like the Spanish-Comanche peace of the previous era, shared violence undergirded their new partnership.[3] Although Mexican officials hoped to placate Comanches for as long as possible, their long-term vision of Texas did not include the recognition of Comanche dominion. Instead, they expected to revitalize Texas commerce and industry through European and Euro-American settler colonization and economic advancement, which, for Anglo-Americans, meant the expansion of anti-Black slavery into the borderlands. This, of course, could occur only through the displacement or extermination of Native locals, and the earliest years of Anglo-American colonization witnessed concerted mutual efforts by Mexicans and Anglo-Americans to rid Texas of the so-called Indian menace. Although Mexican authorities had reasons to be skeptical of Anglo-American loyalty to Mexico, the urgency of the Indian problem persuaded them to cooperate with these suspicious allies. But when Hispanic and Anglo-American collaborators could no longer see eye to eye on the appropriate use of violence, their partnership dissolved. The Texas Rebellion of 1835 and 1836 was the culmination of this unraveling.[4]

Collaborative violence was at the heart of the changes that occurred throughout the Texas borderlands during this period. From the 1760s through the 1830s, borderlands residents became more and more integrated commercially with neighboring regions, exchanging foodstuffs, cash crops, animals, and various forms of manufactured goods (including firearms).[5] Also included in these vast networks of exchange were enslaved people, who crisscrossed the North American continent, from Mexico to the Great Plains to the Atlantic seaboard. All of these commercial networks, although ostensibly about exchange, were sustained by (and contributed to) violence. Cross-community raids met the demands of livestock markets; commodities like animal skins and horses depended upon the labor of exploited (and often enslaved) individuals; slave labor produced foodstuffs and cash crops (with the help of imported draft animals); the commodification of people transformed enslaved individuals into objects of slaver desire; and firearms fueled further violence. Comanches were masters of commerce in the Texas borderlands, and through them Spaniards would expand their own involvement in borderlands trade, including the traffic in enslaved people. Anglo-Americans in Texas were equally commerce oriented, however, and their quest to expand their ties to the cash-crop-based markets of the Atlantic world inspired them to further entrench themselves in the violent exploitation of Black bodies. The slave trade that Anglo-Americans established in Texas during the 1820s and early 1830s may have not been as extensive as the one that prevailed in the United States at the time, but it added another level of integrative violence to the Texas borderlands.

Anglo-American colonization also breathed new life into anti-Blackness. During the latter part of the eighteenth century, anti-Blackness lived on, cursing both enslaved Black people and nonslave descendants of Africa. All Black people faced stigmatization in Spanish Texas, and only the omnipresent threat of *los indios bárbaros* had the potential to distract Hispanic residents from their obsessions with Blackness as a debased status. Yet with the arrival of Anglo-Americans, who brought thousands of enslaved Black people with them, anti-Blackness gained even more currency. The Anglo-American slave trade principally targeted Black bodies, reinforcing their exchangeability, just as Anglo-American slaver violence fortified Black subjugation. By the mid-1830s, *slavery* and *Blackness* would become more synonymous than ever in the Texas borderlands.

The early nineteenth century also represented renewed efforts to establish state authority in Texas.[6] Turn-of-the-century Spanish plans of settler colonization reinvigorated the imperial imagination in Texas, and Anglo-American colonization was inextricably tied to Mexican ambitions to expand the powers of their young nation-state. Nonetheless, Texas remained a series of borderlands, where local dynamics reigned supreme. Spanish integration into the Comanche-oriented slave trade was evidence of this, as were their continued attempts to legitimate and naturalize the enslavement of others through kin incorporation. Within Comanchería, where internal processes were more visible for Euro-American commentators during this period, family making was also an important instrument of social control. Even Anglo-Americans, whose form of slavery bore a deep legal lineage, reframed their slaving system to accommodate local expectations. Conveniently, Anglo-Americans also argued that their form of slavery was based on familial relations, particularly as Mexican authorities sought to curtail their slaveholding abilities. Thus, even though scholars generally have argued that family making mitigated the severity or violence of slavery in the Texas borderlands during this period, the history detailed in part II challenges this interpretation.[7] Instead, part II elaborates how practices and metaphors of kinship were integral to slavery's existence as integrative systems of violent exploitation.

4 / "Companions on Campaign": The Spanish-Comanche Battle for Texas, 1760s–1820

In February 1786, Governor Domingo Cabello sent thirty-five-year-old Miguel Pérez, a Yojuan slave of Sargento Baltazar Reyes Pérez, to a Tonkawa village located north of the provincial capital of Spanish Texas at San Antonio. His instructions were clear: convince Tonkawa leaders to end their new friendship with the Lipanes, the longtime foes of Spaniards in Texas and Pérez's one-time slavers. The governor selected Pérez because he sought out the favor of Pérez's father and brother, who, although Yojuanes, had worked their way up the leadership ranks of the Tonkawas. The governor would not be disappointed with his choice. Among the Tonkawas, Pérez managed to convince not only their leadership but also the two hundred or so Tawakonis, Iscanis, and Flechazos in their midst to join their campaign against the Lipanes. Soon after, with Pérez by their side, the Tonkawas and their allies attacked a Lipan village near the Colorado River, seizing a number of slaves and more than six hundred horses.[1]

Miguel Pérez's activities during the early months of 1786 illuminate the precarious nature of Texas borderlands geopolitics in the late eighteenth century. Two decades earlier, Spaniards were still committed to an alliance with the Ndé *naciones* of the region, but by the mid-1780s they had reversed course. As the 1760s and 1770s rolled on, Spaniards in Texas came to realize that their fortunes depended upon a greater acquiescence to the rising power of their Comanche neighbors, who during these years were strengthening their economic and political hold on the region. Pérez's recruitment of Tonkawas, Tawakonis, Iscanis, and

Flechazos on behalf of Spaniards in 1786 demonstrated to Comanches that the Spaniards were committed to a shared program of anti-Ndé violence—a commitment that solidified a 1785 agreement of peace between their leaders. Comanches and Spaniards had enslaved Apaches for generations; now they were doing it as partners for the cause of "peace."

Pérez's story also has a personal dimension to it. Lipan slavers initially enslaved him when he was eight years old during the Diego Ortiz Parrilla campaign in 1759. Soon after, they sold him to Baltazar Pérez, who then kept him in bondage for two and a half decades. Suddenly in 1786, after being "so faithful to his master" for so many years, Pérez emerged as a viable diplomatic player in an important cross-cultural borderlands drama. Perhaps this was his moment of vengeance against his former slavers. Or perhaps this was his chance to prove his worth beyond the confines of personal servitude. Or perhaps Pérez just relished the opportunity to reunite with the remaining members of his biological family. Given the paucity of documents regarding his life, we may never know what motivated him to complete his governor-mandated task so well; nonetheless, his experiences with (and alongside) Lipan, Spanish, Tonkawa, Tawakoni, Iscani, Flechazo, and Comanche slaving violence bring into relief, from a personal perspective, the convergence of Texas borderlands slaving practices. In the Texas borderlands, slaving systems did not exist in isolation from one another. Because slavery was at the heart of dominion building for both Spaniards and Comanches, it was virtually inevitable that the slaving systems of each group would come into contact by the latter part of the eighteenth century, entangling many communities in a web of violence, exploitation, and coercive integration. This chapter details Comanche-Spanish interactions from the 1760s to 1820, highlighting how slaving practices converged, fed off each other, and then diverged over time.

Surprisingly, Spaniards and Comanches generally did not resort to the direct enslaving of one another from the 1760s through the opening years of the nineteenth century. Instead, Comanches exploited Spanish Texas for its animal resources (and then tribute), while Spaniards sought to control Comanches and other Norteños through trade. When Comanches and Spaniards agreed to peace in 1785, the two groups channeled their slaving energies toward the Ndé peoples of the region, unleashing a wave of violence against their shared enemies. From a broad perspective, the peace allowed Comanches to continue to enlarge their economic and political influence, even as external pressures began to check their unrivaled dominion in the borderlands. For Spaniards, the peace was a much-needed reprieve, as Spanish Texas witnessed an impressive demographic regeneration from 1785 to 1810, despite their collective submission to Comanche power. But when the War of Mexican Independence reached Texas in the early 1810s, the peace disintegrated, and Spanish Texas teetered on the brink of collapse. Driven to desperation, Spanish officials turned to more ambitious schemes of settler colonization, becoming more receptive to the settlement of agriculture-minded slaveholding colonists.

In James Brooks's examination of New Mexico, he has found that "captive taking and trading represented the most violent and exploitative component of a long-term pattern of militarized socioeconomic exchange between Indian and Spanish societies."[2] The same could be said about the Texas borderlands from the 1760s to 1820, where the martial cultures of Spaniards and Comanches regularly interacted at the nexus of slave raiding and trading. For both groups, personal violence against enslaved people breathed vitality into their economic and social systems. As herders, manufacturers, personal servants, domestic workers, fighters, commodities, and possibly even field hands, enslaved people could be molded and repurposed—by violence—to meet the exigencies of slaver life in the borderlands. Enslaved people also became the family—"mothers," "wives," "sons," "daughters," and "godchildren"—of their slavers. In this chapter, I argue that within both Spanish and Comanche contexts processes of kin incorporation should be read not as benevolent attempts to include outsiders as functional members of host communities but instead as effective ways to control and exploit integrated individuals.[3] They were, in other words, calculated adaptations to the particularities of borderlands circumstances.

Rendered "Barbarous": Spanish Texas in Turmoil in the 1760s

"This is a fortification that is as barbarous as the enemy who attacks it," remarked Cayetano María Pignatelli Rubí Corbera y San Climent, the Marqués de Rubí, after his examination of the grounds of Presidio San Sabá in the summer of 1767. Although harsh, his disdain for Spanish colonial forces in Texas was not confined to the poorly manned presidio that somehow still stood in the middle of Comanche country. When Rubí arrived at San Antonio, he was equally shocked by the appearances of the presidial soldiers. Colorful, mismatched, and disorganized, the soldiers of Béxar looked more like a ragtag militia than the military representatives of a powerful Spanish monarch. And Los Adaes, the easternmost

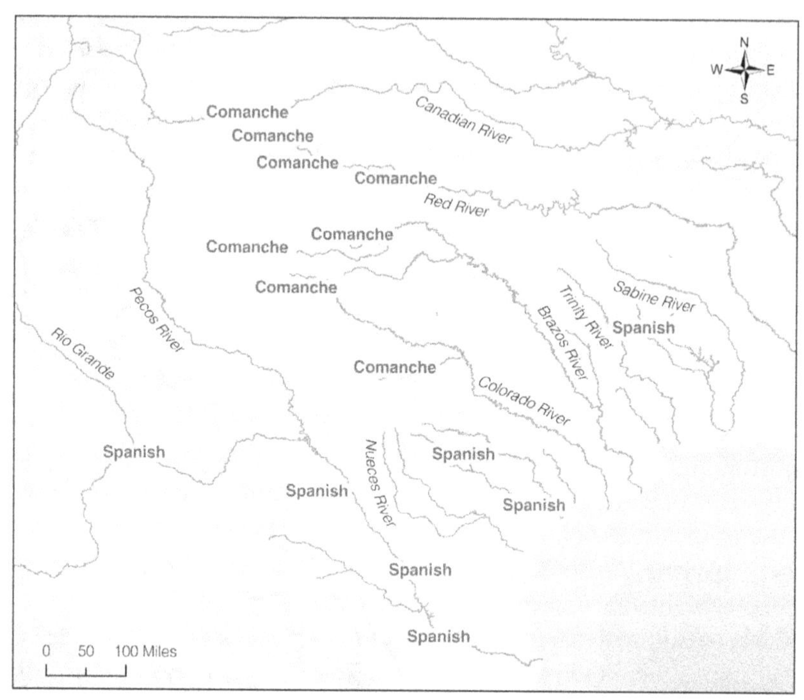

Map 6. Comanche and Spanish communities in the Texas borderlands, ca. 1800. Cartography by Luyang Ren.

outpost of Spanish Texas, was perhaps the most pathetic. The presidio there was "a short hexagonal enclosure with three bastions all built of staked pine, badly constructed and in worse condition." Only twenty-five families, "distributed in various flimsy plank huts," resided in Los Adaes. According to the Marqués de Rubí, wretched were the conditions of the "weak, ill-placed, and incapable" Spanish colonies of Texas.[4]

While Rubí's report on Spanish Texas could not have surprised Spanish officials familiar with the history of La Provincia de las Tejas, its timing, in the aftermath of the Seven Years' War, made his observations especially alarming. The Seven Years' War, which lasted from 1754 to 1763 in the American context, reshaped imperial imaginations on the North American continent. France, defeated in the contest, lost Canada and their Louisiana territories east of the Mississippi to England, and Spain, a late ally of France, was forced to cede Florida to the English. Significantly, amid the chaos of imperial war, diplomatic negotiation, and geopolitical maneuvering, France secretly gave western Louisiana to Spain.[5] This was a critical moment in the history of Spanish Texas: after decades of colonial posturing, the French imperial threat was over. No longer would Spanish colonists have to fear a French invasion of their northern mining territories, nor would they have to keep a watchful eye out for subversive French agents and saboteurs in Texas, because Louisiana was now part of the Spanish Empire. Yet the cession of Louisiana presented a host of new geopolitical problems, none more significant in the eyes of imperial authorities than a fresh threat of English invasion from the East. And Rubí's report, which reflected on his year-long inspection of the northern frontier, did nothing to quell those fears. Texas especially was in a state of "misery."[6]

But Rubí promised solutions. He recommended the reorganization of presidial forces, the reallocation of frontier funds, and the relocation of poorly situated military outposts (particularly the Texas presidios at Los Adaes and Orcoquizá).[7] Mismanagement of colonial forces, he reasoned, was at the heart of Spain's misfortunes on the northern frontier. Just as important, however, Rubí also encouraged the abandonment of Ndé peace talks. While traveling across Texas, he became acquainted with the Wichita leaders of the region, including the Taovaya *capitán*, Eyasiguichi, who convinced him of the expediency of a Spanish-Norteño alliance "in the pacification of the entire northeastern frontier."[8] But as Norteños had long been the enemies of Apaches, an alliance with them meant a repudiation of Ndé peace overtures. In his recommendations, Rubí took the alliance a step further: not only should Spaniards dismantle Ndé peace efforts; they should "extinguish" Apache communities altogether. As Rubí understood the matter, the weight of a Spanish-Norteño partnership would crush the Apache threat: "With this vile nation [of Apaches]—incapable of resisting our presidios in an open war—walled in between our frontier and their enemy Nations of the North, it will suffer a war before and behind it, which it cannot sustain."[9]

Spanning some 7,600 miles, several provincial territories, scores of communities, and two years of travel, the Marqués de Rubí's tour was meant to underscore the ultimate colonial omniscience of the Spanish Empire. One well-respected man and his small team of colonial representatives were all that Spain needed to reassert its geographical claims and geopolitical awareness along the fringes of empire. Or so imperial authorities believed. If the acts of surveying, cataloguing, and reorganizing the northern provinces of New Spain were meant to articulate Spanish dominion, the actual findings of the *marqués*'s reports revealed the fundamental weakness of the Spanish imperial reach. No matter how many Spanish soldiers and settlers relocated to properly situated presidial outposts and no matter how many European territorial claims were ceded to the empire, Spain's North American holdings appeared much more Native than Spanish at the time the *marqués* and his followers made their trek.[10] Thus, the *marqués*'s description of San Sabá as "barbarous" was inaccurate only in its racist, derogatory implications; if Rubí used the term as a synonym for *Native-dominated*, then Texas was certainly "barbarous."

Comanches played no small role in minimizing Spanish influence during the middle decades of the eighteenth century. Through aggressive economic, geopolitical, and migratory strategies, Comanches had spread their territorial dominion across a vast region loosely bounded by the Sangre de Cristo Mountains to the west, the Cross Timbers to the east, the Arkansas River to the north, and the Nueces River to the south. In the Texas borderlands, where Spaniards had worked tirelessly to expand Spanish dominion for decades, Comanches inserted themselves as the up-and-coming rulers of the land. Increasingly, the Native communities of Texas were looking to Comanches for new economic and geopolitical opportunities. Slavery thus took on new meanings and functions. For centuries, the peoples of the broader Texas region primarily had to contend with the slaving practices of Spaniards and their allies. From the 1760s on, Texas slavers were just as likely to be Comanche as Spanish, particularly as Comanches expanded their slave-trading connections within the larger networks of borderlands commerce.

At the forefront of this southern and eastern Comanche expansion was a separate collection of Comanche people known to contemporary observers variously as Kotsotekas, Naitanes, or Comanches Orientales.[11] Although slave raiding was central to the initial Comanche migration to the Texas borderlands, access to the vast herds of bison and horses motivated them to stay. Thus, Comanches Orientales invested much time and energy into the acquisition and maintenance of animals in Texas. They were a mobile people, "never stopping in a place except while it abounds in cattle [bison]," as Athanase de Mézières, the well-traveled lieutenant governor of newly Spanish Natchitoches, noted in July 1772. And although Euro-American observers generally disparaged their mobile lifestyle, Comanche mobility was key to their economic and political influence in the region: they were difficult to find, equally difficult to attack, and primed to make the most of the various resource domains of the Texas borderlands.[12] De Mézières, who learned much about Comanches from his interactions with Wichitas and a handful of Comanche diplomats, could not hide his admiration for Comanche power:

> The Comanche are scattered from the great Missuris River to the neighborhood of the frontier presidios of New Spain. They are a people so numerous and so haughty that when asked their number, they make no difficulty of comparing it to that of the stars. They are so skillful in horsemanship that they have no equal; so daring that they never ask for or grant truces; and in the possession of such territory that, finding in it an abundance of pasturage for their horses and an incredible number of cattle which furnish them raiment, food, and shelter, they only just fall short of possessing all of the conveniences of the earth.[13]

Ranging across a large swath of territory that included both the Llano Estacado and the Edwards Plateau of modern Texas, the Comanches Orientales had positioned themselves well to prosper from a massive North American trade network that stretched hundreds of miles from New Mexico in the West to the Mississippi River in the East. By the 1760s, the great Norteño alliance between Comanches, Wichitas, Caddos, and others—made manifest in the huge San Sabá raid of 1758—was under adjustment, as Wichitas replaced the Hasinais of northeast Texas as the principal middlemen traders of the region and as Tonkawas also saw their influence diminish. But these geopolitical shifts did not disrupt the vitality of Eastern Comanche economic operations. Situated on the Southern Plains, these Comanches now acted as intermediaries between their Western Comanche *hermanos* and their trading partners farther to the east.[14] As farmers and merchants, the Wichita people of the Red River Valley were particularly significant in this trade system, exchanging surplus crops with Comanches Orientales for dried meat and hides. And as Wichita ties to the trans-Mississippi region grew, so did Wichita access to Euro-American manufactured goods. Soon Wichita traders were funneling into Comanche communities firearms, ammunition, and other Euro-American merchandise from French and English traders living to the east. In exchange, Comanches Orientales offered Wichita merchants both horses and slaves, the latter whom Comanches Orientales generally procured through raids on Ndé communities or through a thriving trade in foodstuffs, slaves, horses, and other merchandise with their Western Comanche counterparts.[15]

Animal raiding in Texas lubricated this vibrant trade in people, animals, and goods. Because steady horse acquisition was critical to

Comanche successes, throughout the 1760s Comanches regularly raided Spanish Texas for horses. Typically, a small party of Comanche rangers, consisting of no more than twenty or so men, would attack the outposts and settlements at San Antonio, San Sabá, La Bahía, or Laredo[16] using stealth and guile. The party would strike at night or early in the morning, when few residents were standing watch, and run off with dozens and sometimes hundreds of horses and mules. Their swift retreat would lead them to nearby wooded areas, where the raiders usually found enough cover to escape their angry pursuers. And although largely economic in their orientation and function, Comanche raids were undoubtedly violent, as livestock were slaughtered, homes were sometimes set ablaze, and a significant number of witnesses were maimed or killed. Hispanic servants, herders, and travelers were particularly vulnerable to Comanche violence, as Comanche rangers typically employed the element of surprise. Comanche and Norteño violence became so disconcerting around Béxar by the close of the 1760s that Hugo O'Conor relocated the governor's headquarters from Los Adaes to San Antonio, where the seat of the Spanish government in Texas—now better situated to respond to Comanche violence—would remain until Mexican Independence.[17]

Overall, the 1760s ultimately bore witness to the asymmetry of Comanche-Spanish relations in Texas. Comanche raiding, trading, and diplomatic machinations outmatched and outlasted the limited efforts of Spanish officials, soldiers, settlers, and missionaries to control the Texas borderlands.[18] In the Spanish sphere of Texas, horse herds were rapidly depleting; ranches had been abandoned; people were dying at the hands of Comanches near San Antonio, San Sabá, La Bahía, and Laredo; and even the San Antonio mission settlements—the lifeblood of the Spanish San Antonio economy for decades—were showing signs of poverty and deprivation.[19] In short, the whole of Spanish Texas was under siege. To Spanish observers, the source of their communities' collective devastation was obvious: Comanche depredations.

Given the extent of Comanche violence during the 1760s, the Marqués de Rubí's late 1760s remarks about and recommendations for Texas were notably perceptive. Despite his overly ambitious interpretation of Spanish entitlement to the northern frontier, Rubí understood that Spanish successes still hinged upon capitulation to the Native-dominated political economy of the region. If Spaniards were to remain influential, they needed to forge diplomatic and economic ties that extended beyond the immediate confines of particular colonial outposts. More precisely, Spaniards needed to tie themselves directly to the commercial and political centers of the North, to commit themselves to the logics of Comanche and Norteño societies. Naturally, this recalibration would reshape slaving practices in the Texas borderlands, and from the 1770s onward slavery in Spanish Texas was to be as heterogeneous as ever. Like the rest of Spanish society, even the violence of Spanish slavers would be circumscribed by Native power.

Forging the Comanche-Spanish Slaving Détente in the 1770s

To the credit of both Spanish high officials and colonists, the Spanish colonial system in Texas did not collapse entirely under the weight of Comanche and Norteño pressures during the 1750s and 1760s. Instead, through the implementation of new diplomatic, military, and commercial strategies, Spanish Texas survived the first period of prolonged Comanche onslaught. The Marqués de Rubí's advocacy for a Norteño-Spanish military alliance was the first step in preserving Spanish relevance in the geopolitics of the Texas borderlands. Equally important, however, was the new willingness of Spanish administrators to pursue strategies based on Spanish-Native commerce (in goods and slaves) and to curtail outright slave raiding against Norteño communities.

Since the early eighteenth century, Spanish colonists in Texas had used gift-giving as a means to recruit Native people into the sphere of Spanish influence, but the new emphasis on material exchange was decidedly unique in at least two ways: (1) no longer were missionaries central to the equation, and (2) such exchanges were to be understood as part of a larger, rational system of Spanish colonial rule that pinpointed commerce as the key agent of cultural (i.e., assimilative) change.[20] The failures of the Ndé missions—although doomed from the start—were likely most responsible for Spanish disillusionment with new Texas missionary projects of the period, but a broader, Bourbon Reform–Era concern with "enlightened," reason-based approaches to the so-called Indian problem also inspired Spanish authorities to diminish the role of the religious.[21] Thus by the 1770s, missionaries had lost much of their influence as mediators between Spanish officials and independent Native communities, and in their place emerged a handful of colonial government–appointed military officers, traders, and interpreters, many with ties to Louisiana and the eastern Texas borderlands. These men, such as Athanase de Mézières y Clugny, J. Gaignard, Antonio Gil Ibarvo, Antonio Treviño, Pedro Vial, and Francisco Xavier Chávez, would become critical instruments in the attempted rearticulation of Spanish colonial authority in Texas. Specifically, they were charged with strengthening the Spanish colonial presence by forging Spanish-Native alliances and commercial relationships. Not surprisingly, it was many of these same men who amplified a previously minimal commercial element to Spanish slavery in Texas. In some ways, these men catalyzed an integration of Spanish and Comanche slaving practices.

The new broader emphasis on commercial diplomacy was built on a rather simple assumption: that humans are creatures of consumption. What Hispanic philosophers and administrative officials brought new to this assumption was the idea that human self-interest could be manipulated into a mechanism of subjugation. They theorized that if only Spaniards could lure Indians into their system of commerce and transform their patterns of consumption to depend upon Spanish-derived goods, Indians would be at the mercy of their Spanish distributors. This strategy resonated across the Spanish Empire throughout the latter part of the eighteenth century. A popular publication, *Nuevo sistema de gobierno económico para la América*, said it best: "There is no savage who cannot be dominated by industry and made sociable by a ready supply of all things he likes."[22]

Beyond the abstractions of Spanish political-economic theory, in the context of Texas there was also a strong practical element to this shift in Spanish imperial policy. Since the early eighteenth century, French and Spanish colonists had built close trade and kin relationships with the various Native peoples of the Texas-Louisiana borderlands. At Los Adaes, the capital of Texas for decades, Spanish residents, including the Chirinos brothers (Domingo and Manuel), Agustín Rodríguez, and Fray Francisco Zedano, had established lasting economic and familial bonds with various Caddo people in the region. Even two Texas governors, Jacinto de Barrios y Jauregui and Ángel Martos y Navarrete, fostered (illegal) trade ties between Native communities, Spanish Los Adaes, and French Louisiana. At Natchitoches, Native–Euro-American connections were more extensive, and Natchitoches merchants, soldiers, and citizens often married, traded with, and fought alongside the Caddos and Wichitas who frequented the outpost.[23] Throughout the eighteenth century, Spanish and French officials sought to either regulate or eliminate entirely such connections, but trade, family making, and friendships persisted nevertheless. Significantly, these bonds accounted for Spain's feeble hold on the region; without them, the empire's influence in Texas-Louisiana was all but lost.[24]

The new official emphasis on commerce-based diplomacy was an important step in the transformation of Spanish-Native relations in the Texas borderlands: not only did it encourage Spanish colonists to think beyond violence in their interactions with Native communities; it also provided Spaniards with opportunities to build off and acknowledge their generations-long clandestine trade relationships with Native communities. Just as important, it set the stage for the refashioning of borderlands slavery in Spanish Texas, bridging the personal violence of slavers against slaves with the intercommunity bonds of gift-giving. Specifically, commercial strategies of diplomacy opened up Spaniards to the influences of Norteño and Comanche slave trading.

But commercial diplomacy (which started during the early 1770s) and slave trading between Comanches and Spaniards took time to develop, especially because Spaniards wanted to control the terms of commerce. At the time of Norteño peace talks, the constant horse raids by Comanches and their attacks on Spanish and Ndé-Spanish settlements convinced colonial authorities that Comanches were undeserving of gift offerings, especially when it came to firearms and ammunition, which they knew would be used against them.[25] But the more Spanish officials interacted with Norteño leaders, the more they comprehended the rising political, commercial, and military influence of Comanches in the region. Prior to the 1770s, Spaniards may have felt justified in focusing their attention principally upon the Wichita and Caddo communities of the Red River. As Taovayas, Iscanis, Guichitas, Tawakonis, Kichais, and Caddohadachos generally controlled access to Euro-American manufactured goods coming from the East, Spanish efforts to secure alliances with them offered prospects for the extension of Spanish rule. But as Hämäläinen has argued, Comanches were unsatisfied with their marginal role in the southwestern traffic in guns, powder, and ammunition, interpreting Wichita attempts to limit the flow of guns into Comanchería as violations of kinship-based exchange protocol. Therefore, in an effort to punish their ungrateful allies and to cut out the trade middlemen, Comanches went to war with Wichitas throughout the 1770s, eventually pushing the limits of Comanche dominion beyond the confines of the Wichita settlements on the Red River, all the way to the lower Brazos River region, near Bosque Creek.[26] By the close of the 1770s, de Mézières had anointed Comanches "masters in the region which must be crossed to get to the banks of this large-volumed river [the Mississippi]."[27]

As Wichita influence rapidly declined, Spaniards in Texas more actively turned their attention to the Comanches Orientales. But as with their dealings with other independent Native peoples, Spaniards were opposed to supplying Comanches with firearms, and the early ramifications of this refusal were predictable: Comanche leaders interpreted Spanish obstinacy as an act of unbrotherly hostility—the kind of behavior demonstrated by an enemy, not a prospective ally. In response, Comanches continued to view the settlements of Spanish Texas as exploitable resource centers, and throughout the 1770s and early 1780s they escalated their horse raids and small-scale attacks against Spanish settlements.[28] The early 1780s were particularly harsh for Spanish communities. After Comanches displaced their Lipan enemies living along the Guadalupe River, they unleashed a series of raids on the San Antonio and La Bahía areas, hitting locations as far south as Camargo. Spanish Texas withered as the population dropped by 10 percent, from 3,103 people in 1777 to 2,828 in 1784.[29] Spanish observers like Governor Domingo Cabello could do little more than lament their powerlessness in the face of the Comanche offensive: "Not a moment passes in which news of rapacities and disasters does not reach me. All these *ranchos* find themselves totally helpless and abandoned. And from this will result the total destruction and loss of this province."[30]

This helps to explain why Spaniards did not resort to the familiar practice of raiding Native communities for slaves as "punishment" for rejecting Spanish authority: Spaniards generally were incapable of carrying out such slaving operations. This is not to say, however, that they did not *try* to wield slaving as an instrument of regional authority, because in 1772 Spanish leaders attempted to force Comanche capitulations through captive diplomacy. In this particular episode, a Spanish detachment apprehended three Comanche women and a Comanche girl near San Antonio, and Governor Juan María Vicencio Ripperdá sought to force concessions from Comanches under the leadership of Povea. Although the *paraibo* and his followers indulged the governor for some time, in practice their negotiations were little more than stall tactics for the eventual rescue or escape of their kinspeople. In the end, the Comanche representatives actually failed (and Ripperdá would send the women southward to Coahuila, to live out their days in missions or as slaves), but Comanche attacks in Spanish San Antonio persisted. Overall, the affair proved to the Spaniards that even captive diplomacy—a successful endeavor in the past with other Spanish enemies—was a futile project with Comanches. Holding hostages did not guarantee a stop to Comanche raiding, and individuals easily could circumvent the negotiation process.[31]

Spanish lamentations were only exacerbated by the general failure of their military responses. Just as they did during the 1770s, Spanish officers sent detachments to pursue and punish Comanche raiders, and as before most detachments failed to track down their Comanche targets.[32] Governor Cabello attributed Spanish failures to "the scanty number of troops with which these two presidios [of Béxar and La Bahía] are garrisoned" and to the fact that "the horses of this company [at La Bahía] and the company at Béxar are completely spent and their numbers depleted." But the reality was that the Spaniards in Texas never had a chance in this contest. On a practical level, Comanches were excellent at evading Spanish violence. The mobility of Comanche communities and the small size of their typical raiding parties meant that Spanish campaigners were constantly engaged in a frustrating cat-and-mouse game, one that did not bode well for pursuers who sought out people with advanced equestrian skills.[33] From a broader perspective, Comanches had continued to enhance their political and economic base in the Texas borderlands, essentially replacing Wichitas as the principal suppliers of horses and mules in the Louisiana trade. Coupled with a thriving trade in slaves and livestock *within* Comanchería, access to the Louisiana trade made Comanche raiding in Texas a highly lucrative business. The Comanche system had many moving parts, and Spaniards in Texas were dealing (poorly) with only one of its components.[34]

Notably, Comanches did not find it worthwhile to enslave Spaniards in Texas either. From the Comanche perspective, this was a function of their broader economic prerogatives in the region. The Hispanic settlements of the Texas borderlands at the time did not present the same economic opportunities as those of New Mexico, where a commerce in goods and slaves had been central to interactions between colonial (and colonized) residents and Comanche visitors and raiders for decades. Instead, the settlements of Spanish Texas served as a different kind of exploitable resource center: the breeding grounds for massive herds of domesticated horses, mules, and cattle. If the residents of Spanish Texas, including those living at the San Antonio and La Bahía mission-settlements, were economically adept at anything, it was at growing and maintaining horse and cattle herds. As Comanches had become so dependent upon these animals for their military and economic might, a Comanche-induced depopulation of the Spanish Texas settlements would have introduced a great deal of uncertainty into the broader patterns of Comanche raiding and trading. Moreover, an Eastern Comanche demand for slaves could be fulfilled by other means—namely, through slave raids against other enemies or through a continuous slave trade with their Western Comanche counterparts (and others). Thus, Eastern Comanches likely saw attempts at capturing the residents of the small and unstable Spanish-led settlements of Texas as not worth the risk. It was much easier—and more in line with broader economic patterns—to acquire slaves elsewhere.[35]

Effectively, Comanches and Spaniards had established a slaving détente. The diversified nature of the Comanche economy combined with the general impotence of Spaniards in Texas translated into very few instances of cross-community slaving. Rather, Comanches exploited Spanish Texas for other resources, and Spaniards sought to adapt to the Comanche onslaught by embracing new models of interaction. Commerce, they were discovering, could be a useful way to deflect the violent opportunism of Comanches and other Norteños. Implementing this new model, however, was a struggle, because Spaniards were convinced that they could dictate the terms of engagement. At least they were partly right: Comanches *were* willing to negotiate, and commerce *did* offer an avenue toward peace. But it was not until Spaniards also promised a return to their annihilationist campaign against the Ndé *naciones* of the borderlands—the longtime foes of Comanches—that peace would become a reality. Thus, "peace" hinged upon the potential for shared violence, which in turn would bridge Comanche and Spanish slaving systems.

Peace, Shared Violence, and Subjugation, 1780–1810

Given the opposite trajectories of fortunes in the Texas borderlands, it seems odd that peace between Comanches and Spaniards suddenly arrived in 1785, but larger forces emanating beyond the crucible of Spanish-Comanche relations were at work. Despite the continuing ascendance of Comanche influence, Comanchería found itself under attack from multiple directions yet again in the late 1770s and 1780s. From the North, Comanches faced military pressures from Kiowas, Pawnees, and Spanish New Mexicans; from the East Osages continued their relentless offensive; and from the South, Ndé defenders persistently harassed Comanche communities, especially as Comanches moved their raiding operations farther southward near the lower Río Grande. Comanches also faced significant economic calamities, as Western Comanches lost most of their commercial connections to Kiowas, Pawnees, Kansas, and Iowas, and as Comanches Orientales ostracized the Wichita traders of the Red River Valley. Compounding these troubles was a devastating smallpox epidemic that ravaged Comanchería around 1780. Evidence suggests that Comanches Orientales lost a whopping two-thirds of their total population, or as many as sixteen thousand people. Thus by the first part of the 1780s, Comanches may have been dominating the Texas borderlands, but structural problems still threatened to unravel all of the successes they had achieved.[36]

For Spaniards, peace and stability in the Mexican North became more urgent with the end of the American Revolutionary War in 1783. Even though Spain offered substantial military and economic assistance to the colonists during the war, with the end of the war there was ample reason to believe that the new nation would eventually pose a threat to Spanish imperial holdings on the continent. They especially feared the influences of Atlantic-oriented traders in Comanche country, who, with their vast market connections and access to manufactured goods, would offer Comanches more incentives to plunder Spanish livestock. It was thus the job of Spaniards to draw Comanches away from the Anglo-American economic sphere before it ever blossomed near the Texas borderlands.[37] But how, exactly, could Spaniards forge peace with their Comanche enemies after so many years of violence? What would it take to end—or at least mitigate—Comanche exploitation? What *could* Spaniards offer their borderlands superiors?

Shared anti-Ndé antipathy, it turns out, proved to be the remedy to the Comanche-Spanish conflict. Apaches had long resisted both Comanche and Spanish dominion in the Texas borderlands; thus, the subjugation or destruction of Ndé communities was high on the list of priorities for both peoples. To the Spaniards of Texas, the Ndé alliances of the 1750s and 1760s were not only great failures but also evidence of the supposed untrustworthiness of Apache people. The frequent cattle slaughters and horse thefts of Lipan rangers near San Antonio and La Bahía throughout the 1760s, 1770s, and 1780s—which for Lipanes fit into their seasonal patterns of hunting—proved the disloyalty of Apaches in the minds of Spanish observers, and news that Lipanes were finding more ways to arm themselves with guns terrified Spanish authorities.[38] For Comanches, Ndé communities never stopped being the targets of slave and horse raiding. Comanche rangers hit Ndé *rancherías* throughout the early 1770s, and their attacks increased in intensity and frequency during the late 1770s and early 1780s. After these raids, which resulted in a number of captured horses and slaves, the Lipanes were left "quite terrified and intimidated, so that they dare not leave the land bounded by the presidios of Béxar and Río Grande, this [presidio] of El Espíritu Santo, and the disemboguement of the said river [the Río Grande] into the sea." Yet Lipanes were generally persistent in their attempts to take advantage of the prime hunting grounds of the San Sabá River Valley. Unfortunately for them, their defiant return visits often inspired further Comanche violence.[39]

As noted earlier, Spanish calls for an anti-Ndé alliance first surfaced in colonial discourse with the Marqués de Rubí during the late 1760s. Back then, Rubí's calls likely frustrated Spanish leaders in Texas, who at the time had been working for over a decade to collaborate with the various Ndé communities of the region. But as the years wore on and as the Ndé peace experiments yielded few obvious benefits for the Spanish colonists of Texas, Spanish officials became more vocal about the possibilities of a Norteño alliance against Apaches.[40] Then, during a series of colonial councils that met across the Mexican North from December 1777 to January 1778, the idea received an administrative stamp of approval. Council members were cognizant of Norteño violence, but they figured it would be best to rechannel that energy—embodied by an estimated 7,280 Comanche warriors—rather than resist it. To them, seeking the aid of Comanches was the only logical choice. So although "a proposal to repair to hands which have shed our blood, in order that they may shed the blood of other enemies, seems strange," explained de Mézières in February 1778, "the most effective mode of securing the desired reduction of the Comanches will be to have them as companions on the campaign."[41] Certainly it was an uneasy, awkward alliance they were proposing. But shared violence made strange bedfellows feel less strange.[42]

Formal peace between Spaniards and Comanches was forged in the late summer of 1785, when Pedro Vial and Francisco Xavier Chávez, with a number of horses, provisions, and plenty of gifts, made their way north to Comanchería under the orders of Governor Cabello. There, among a Comanche leadership that included Cabeza Rapada and Camisa de Hierro, the "two great *capitanes* of the nation," Vial and Chávez managed to convince their hosts of a peace treaty based on three conditions: (1) joint warfare against Apaches, (2) the opening of trade between the Comanche and Spanish communities, and (3) regular Spanish payments. To Comanches, the agreement was about as good as could be expected from their Spanish neighbors. Not only had Spaniards pledged themselves to a shared anti-Ndé cause; they also were willing to demonstrate their fictive kinship, their brotherhood, by offering a steady supply of gifts. As Camisa de Hierro explained, "From now on, the war with our brothers the Spaniards has ended. They will not see our footprints around San Antonio, for we will not subject them to any injury or thefts."[43]

With a joint commitment to the destruction of Ndé people as a cornerstone of the Comanche-Spanish peace, the two groups embraced their anti-Ndé mission right away. Across the northern provinces of New Spain, Spanish authorities formalized the macabre policy of offering bounties for pairs of Apache ears and other body parts. Spanish officials also promised Comanche slavers a bridled horse and two hunting knives in exchange for every Ndé captive, effectively tapping into the Comanche slave trade.[44] And starting in January 1786, Comanches and Spaniards launched joint campaigns against their mutually vilified enemies across the Mexican North, fighting side by side in at least five expeditions during a two-plus-year period.[45] During these campaigns, veteran anti-Ndé fighters like Ugalde teamed up with Comanche *paraibos*, such as Sofais, Cota de Malla, and Zoquiné, to "annihilate" Mescaleros, Lipanes, and others. Even enslaved people, like the Yojuan man Miguel Pérez, found ways to insert themselves into this wave of anti-Ndé violence. Collectively, the campaigners chased Apaches all over the borderlands, from Monclova in the South to the Colorado River Valley in the North, killing dozens of Apaches while taking scores of captives. By the 1790s, Spanish officials were reporting that Apaches were reeling from the "full rigor of our arms." The Comanche-Spanish collaboration left the Ndé people of the borderlands displaced and demoralized.[46]

Yet even as Spaniards and Comanches cooperated on a rather equal playing field against their common Ndé foes, from a broader perspective the Comanche-Spanish peace was actually tilted toward the benefit of the Comanches. The peace in Texas was, after all, contingent upon regular Spanish offerings of gifts, and over time Comanches effectively transformed the Spanish settlements of Béxar, Nacogdoches, and La Bahía into tribute depots, where Comanche visitors could receive everything the poor frontier towns could offer: food to eat, tobacco to smoke, face-to-face meetings with officials, parting gifts, and even a stay at a specially constructed 2,160-square-foot *jacalón*, or lodge (at Béxar).[47] At times, the volume and cost of goods distributed to Comanche visitors were astounding. The expenses for August 1790 to August 1792, for instance, totaled 3,468 pesos, and for the period spanning January 1, 1794 to July 27, 1799, Spanish officials estimated that they had distributed to Comanches and other Native visitors gifts worth a total of 11,837 pesos. Spaniards continued their tribute payments well into the nineteenth century: in 1810, for instance, they spent nearly 4,000 pesos on gifts for Native visitors.[48] And when Spanish tribute proved insufficient in quantity or quality, Comanches took what they wanted through small-scale raids.[49] For the Spaniards, peace was certainly a costly business.

Fortunately for the Spaniards, the Comanche peace allowed for the slow rebuilding of their communities. Even though Comanches initially depressed Hispanic populations during the early 1780s, Spanish population figures in the aftermath of peace began to rise slowly but steadily. In 1785, the year of peace, Spanish officials reported a population of 2,919; within six years the population had risen to 3,316. By the late 1790s, Spanish Texas had grown to approximately 3,900 people, and in June 1803 Spanish officials reported a small growth in the total population, with 2,500 at Béxar, 618 at La Bahía, and 770 at Nacogdoches. By the closing years of the peace period, the population of Spanish Texas had grown, through natural means and further transplantation of colonists, by about 48 percent in comparison to the pre-peace figures, with total estimates at over 4,300 people.[50] By no means was Spanish Texas expanding rapidly, but a decades-long halt to Comanche violence gave Spanish settlements the opportunity to recover and even witness some demographic growth. Ironically, Spanish settler colonialism in Texas—including its eliminationist imperative—survived *because* colonists explicitly recognized Native (Comanche) authority in Texas.

Slavery also experienced a sort of renaissance within Spanish Texas. Although enslaved populations did not grow as dramatically as the general Hispanic population, dozens of enslaved people were born or baptized during the peace period. The baptismal records at San Fernando de Béxar indicate the baptism of forty-five enslaved individuals between late 1785 and 1810, but it is possible that another forty-two baptisms involved slave-*ahijados*.[51] Thus, of the 1,545 recorded baptisms from October 1785 through 1810, between 3 and 6 percent involved slave-*ahijados*. If we compare these figures to those of the earliest recorded period of Spanish baptisms in Béxar (1731–60), in which enslaved people accounted for about 10 percent of the baptisms, we may conclude that enslaved population percentages actually declined during the peace period. In raw numbers, however, the enslaved population seems to have grown, with an increase in slave baptisms from fifty-two to as many as eighty-seven. It is also worth noting that these estimates do not include the enslaved populations of the other Spanish settlements in Texas, including Nacogdoches, which in 1809 was home to at least sixteen enslaved Black people and probably numerous enslaved Native people. Spaniards also tended to hide their Native slaves from administrative view, leaving the documentary record necessarily incomplete.[52]

The overall population trends during the 1785–1810 period suggest that peace brought stability to Spanish Texas. No longer did Hispanic residents have to fear constant Comanche attacks, and more prospective settlers were beginning to view Texas as a possible destination for relocation. But as intercommunity violence between Comanches and Spaniards became less commonplace, the personal violence of slavers remained salient. One byproduct of the Comanche-Spanish peace was the expansion of a commerce in slaves between Spanish and Native traders. The Spanish shift toward a Comanche-modeled slave trade began during the 1770s, but it became more apparent in the aftermath of peace in 1785. The baptismal records at San Fernando de Béxar, for instance, show that from 1785 to 1811 Spanish residents at Béxar purchased at least nineteen enslaved individuals from Native sellers.[53] The nineteen baptisms of traded slaves made up 42 percent of the forty-five (evident) slave baptisms during the same period. This trend contrasted with the pattern of slave acquisition during the earlier period of slavery in Spanish Texas (pre-1760), when most enslaved people were acquired directly through slave raids. Notably, at the forefront of this shift toward slave trading were individuals who were active in Comanche diplomacy or who had easier access to Native supplies of slaves. Pedro Vial was one such man. Vial, who frequented Comanchería probably more often than any other person from Spanish Texas during this period, possessed at least one slave, a fifteen-year-old Yojuan girl, whom he baptized "Margarita Vial" in 1788. But men who were more influential than Vial, men like Governors Rafael Martínez Pacheco, Manuel Muñoz, and Juan Bautista Elguézabal, also involved themselves in the slave trade by purchasing enslaved children from Comanche traders, baptizing them as their kin, and forcing them to reside (and work) in their households.[54]

Yet high-ranking Spanish officials did not have a monopoly on the trade. Lower-ranking military men, such as San Antonio presidial sergeant Prudencio Rodríguez, also partook in the Comanche-modeled slave trade. In April 1789, Sergeant Rodríguez baptized a ten-year-old Lipan captive named María Antonia Margarita. According to baptismal records, Rodríguez kept María in his house, probably as a servant. Francisco Galbán was another low-ranking slaver, and from 1802 to 1803 he purchased and baptized three enslaved children. The three individuals—whom Galbán named María Petra, José María de Jesus, and María Gertrudís de la Concepción de la Luz—were all five years old or younger, and in case observers were suspicious of his intentions, Galbán made assurances that he would educate these enslaved children "in the rudiments of the [Catholic] faith."[55]

Spanish involvement in the slave trade makes it apparent that Comanche slavery remained tied to commerce. Prior to the peace era, Spaniards indirectly tied themselves to Comanche slave trading when they purchased former Comanche slaves from Wichita traders.[56] After the 1785 peace, Comanche-Wichita trade relations persisted, but Comanches were more willing to work directly with Spanish traders. It is, nonetheless, quite difficult to estimate the extent of Comanche slave-trading operations in the Texas borderlands, especially because contemporary observers offered no approximations. Beyond the instances documented in the baptismal records, only anecdotal evidence exists. For instance, in January 1786 Domingo Cabello reported the arrival of twenty-three Comanches who were hoping to trade "two small Indian girls they had captured from the Apaches in the province of La Sonora" for horses. Two years later, in June 1788, Comanche leader Josiniquente sold to José Mares an enslaved woman.[57]

Calculating enslaved populations within Comanchería is an equally impossible task, as contemporary Euro-American observers offered conflicting estimates. In 1785, when Spaniards got their first look at Comanche society from within, apparently Comanches Orientales had only "ten men" living among them as slaves. According to the Vial-Chávez report, these ten men "were at full liberty, according to their age. Neither they nor those who had been their masters knew the origin of their captivity, and thus they had become totally Cumanches."[58] This figure seems extremely low when we consider (1) the extensive history of Comanche slaving in Texas, (2) the number and testimonies of escaped slaves from Comanchería, and (3) the common conflation of slaves with so-called full members of host Comanche communities. As detailed above, at the very least dozens of slaves passed through Comanche hands in Texas. According to Euro-American documentation, many slaves were exchanged with Wichita, Spanish, French, and Western Comanche traders, but we also know that some remained enslaved among their slavers. This fact is established by the testimonies of individuals who escaped from slavery in Comanchería. Much of the intelligence Spanish officials collected about Comanches was derived from enslaved informants, such as the testimony of Francisco Xavier Chávez, José Solís, José Manuel Apodaca, and various Native fugitives. The accounts of these escapees indicate that the duration of their enslavement varied from days to several years, so although slavery may not have been a permanent condition for those held in bondage, enslaved people *did* live among Comanches Orientales for extended periods of time.[59]

Vial's final comment about the ten slaves living among Comanches in 1785 also hints at one more possible explanation for the underestimation of Vial and Chávez in their report: Comanche kin incorporation hid slavery from Euro-American view. Vial highlighted the importance of family making in processes of enslavement in Comanche society when he said that the ten slaves he identified "had become totally Cumanches." It is likely that slaves within Comanche society were imperceptible to untrained Euro-American eyes—even those, like Chávez, with some familiarity with Comanche social dynamics. The fact that Vial and Chávez did not report the existence of enslaved women and children lends credence to this interpretation. As women and children were the principal targets of Comanche slave raiding, there would have been a greater likelihood for Vial and Chávez to encounter enslaved women and children living among their Comanche hosts. Where, then, were these people? They probably were distributed among the two thousand or so families who inhabited Eastern Comanchería. In his 1786 report to high authorities, Domingo Cabello—who likely received most of his information regarding Comanches from Vial and Chávez—unintentionally articulated the difficulties Spanish observers had when distinguishing enslaved people from supposedly authentic, full members of Comanche society: "[Comanche men] are so extremely jealous that for quite trivial reasons they kill their women, and even when the latter give them no cause for it, they treat them harshly and without much consideration, *as if they were slaves*."[60]

Although later accounts, such as the April 1805 report of the Anglo-American colonial agent John Sibley, do not provide a much clearer picture of enslaved populations in Eastern Comanchería, they do reinforce the idea that slaves were a significant group within Comanche communities. In his report, Sibley, who gathered all of his information from residents and visitors at Natchitoches, claims that Comanches "have a number of Spanish men and women among them, who are slaves, and who they made prisoners when young." Sibley's comment is also instructive because he makes it clear that Euro-American observers generally were concerned about enslaved *Euro-Americans*; thus, their estimates of enslaved populations usually discounted Native individuals who were enslaved among Comanches. He echoes this bias in 1808, when he notes, "The Complexion of this Nation is fairer than that of Any Other of the Numerous Tribes I have ever seen. Many of the Women have light Brown or Auburn Hair & Blue or light Grey Eyes." That same year a Spanish soldier, Francisco Amangual, also visited Eastern Comanchería, but like the reports of his contemporaries and predecessors, he only made note of the existence of enslaved Euro-Americans in the village of his host, Cordero (specifically, "a Spaniard who had served as cowherd to an Indian under his command").[61]

Even though scholars have no way of calculating the precise number of enslaved individuals living among Comanches Orientales during the peace period, it is apparent that the alliance with Spaniards in Texas did not change their slaving practices in any structural manner. Instead, Comanche slavers simply incorporated Spanish traders into their slave-trading system and continued to enslave enemy groups, like Apaches. Spaniards, on the other hand, adapted to the Comanche model by engaging in the borderlands slave trade with more regularity. Investing in the Comanche commerce in slaves gave Spaniards an alternative means to acquiring enslaved people in an era in which slave raiding in Texas became less prominent. The mutual exchange of enslaved bodies, along with the joint enslaving of Ndé people, also solidified the bonds of alliance and brotherhood between two former enemies. To the dismay of Spaniards in Texas, however, peace became unsustainable by the 1810s, when the alliance of shared violence crumbled.

Desperate Times Call for Desperate Measures, 1811–1820

Although Comanches and Spaniards engaged in considerable cross-cultural collaboration from 1785 to 1810, the Comanche-Spanish peace contained at its heart one essential prerequisite: the Spanish ability to support Comanche economic prerogatives. Comanches and Spaniards understood one another as they pillaged Ndé communities, killed Ndé men, and enslaved Ndé women and children, but such bonds of violence meant little if Spaniards were unable to fulfill their obligation, as fictive kin, to provide for the well-being of Comanches. Whenever Comanches visited the Spanish settlements of Texas, they expected to receive the same generous offerings that Spaniards had been providing for over two decades. A failure to meet these expectations, they believed, was an affront to their declared bonds of brotherhood. So when Spaniards in Texas suddenly were unable to pay their regular tribute during the 1810s, the Comanche-Spanish peace unraveled.

Miguel Hidalgo's revolt in Guanajuato in the fall of 1810—the opening salvo of the Mexican War of Independence—initiated the collapse of peace in Texas. With Spanish authorities channeling their funds, resources, and manpower toward a multiprovince counterinsurgency effort, Spanish Texas's gift distribution infrastructure was hit hard, and Comanches noticed. But nothing could have prepared Spanish Texans for the internal turmoil of the next few years. Revolutionary trouble arrived in January 1811, when Juan Bautista de las Casas, a retired militia captain, attacked Spanish royalists stationed in San Antonio and captured the governor and his staff. Although his reign as revolutionary leader lasted for only a handful of weeks, it ushered in a wave of rebellious activity. In August and September the following year, José Bernardo Gutiérrez de Lara, a rancher and merchant from Revilla, and Augustus William Magee, a former U.S. Army lieutenant, led the so-called Republican Army of the North into Spanish Texas and captured Nacogdoches and La Bahía. A Spanish force under the leadership of Governor Manuel Salcedo and Lt. Col. Simón de Herrera squared off against the Republican Army over the course of several months, first at La Bahía and then at Salado, where Republican fighters ultimately gained the upper hand and slaughtered the royalists. Over three hundred of Herrera's men died in the Battle of Salado, and after the remaining royalists surrendered, Gutiérrez de Lara and his followers brutally executed Salcedo, Herrera, and twelve other officers. The fighting resumed the following summer when Republicans, now under the command of José Alvarez de Toledo, and a revitalized royalist army again met on the battlefield. The royalists administered a smashing defeat, killing 1,300 of the 1,400 men under Toledo's command, while losing only fifty-five of their own men. Joaquín de Arredondo, the rising frontier commander who headed the royalist army, then proceeded to capture 215 suspected rebels on his way to San Antonio, executing some of them. Finally, at Béxar, Arredondo put to death an additional forty suspected insurgents and rebel sympathizers. Arredondo's counterinsurgency effectively ended the Mexican independence movement in Texas for several years, but it came at a high cost: with so much internal violence and so many lives lost, Spanish Texas was left reeling. Gift-giving in this context had become virtually impossible.[62]

Fortunately for Comanches, the implosion of Spanish Texas did not jeopardize the vibrancy of *their* broader economic system. Since the late 1790s, Comanches had been connecting themselves to other economic conduits, specifically those made available by various Anglo-American and Louisiana-based merchants. As traders like the Kentuckian Philip Nolan ventured west in search of Native-groomed horses, they found ready sellers in Comanches. The earliest interactions were often haphazard, indirect, and limited in scope, but by 1807 Comanches were prepared to commit more fully to the Anglo-American trade. That year, Comanches sent diplomats to Natchitoches to meet with the Indian agent John Sibley. Sibley impressed the Comanche contingent, and the following summer Anthony Glass, a prominent merchant from Louisiana, made his way to Comanchería to trade. By the late 1810s, Spanish observers had become convinced that tens of thousands of guns were making their way from Anglo-America into Comanchería. Tremendous were the ramifications of this new commercial relationship. "By establishing exchange ties with Americans, and by linking their pastoral horse-bison economy to the emerging capitalist economy of the United States," Hämäläinen has argued, "eastern Comanches set off a sustained commercial expansion that eventually swept across Comanchería. By the time the Spanish colonial era ended in 1821, the entire Comanche nation had moved out of the Spanish orbit. They commanded a vast commercial empire that encompassed the Great Plains from the Río Grande valley to the Mississippi and Missouri river valleys."[63]

Thus by the 1810s, Comanches had grown tired of the usually generous but stubborn, deluded, and disrespectful Spanish colonists of Texas. And with lucrative economic opportunities available elsewhere, the Spanish alliance had lost its luster. Signs of the Comanche-Spanish peace's demise surfaced in the spring of 1810, when Comanches raided livestock in the San Sabá Valley. By July, Comanches Orientales had extended their raiding to ranchos near San Marcos and Laredo. Around the same time, Western Comanches pushed their raiding frontier well south of the Río Grande to Monclova. In August that year, Spaniards reported Comanche raids along the lower Río Grande, the Frio River, and the Nueces. At La Bahía, residents reported that Comanches took some three hundred horses from their settlements.[64]

Comanche leaders—including Cordero, El Sordo, and another *paraibo*, Paruaquita—gave Spaniards a chance to smooth over relations the following year, in 1811, but Spanish officials badly bungled their opportunity. That September, when El Sordo visited San Antonio with a group of women and children, Spanish officials arrested all of them. News of their captivity traveled across Comanchería, and on April 8, 1812, a Comanche leadership retinue of Cordero, Paruaquita, Pisinampe, and Yzazat arrived at San Antonio. The impressive party of Comanche *paraibos* demanded an explanation of El Sordo's captivity. Yet instead of quelling their anxieties, Governor Salcedo stoked their anger: he met the Comanche leaders with some six hundred fighters by his side. This marked the official end of the Spanish-Comanche peace in Texas.[65]

Spanish Texas quickly unraveled in the aftermath of this final failed attempt at peace. During the winter of 1813–14, Comanche attacks and raids devastated the San Antonio countryside, and in January 1814 Governor Arredondo ordered the abandonment of the surrounding ranches. Comanches also undermined the Spaniards' ability to tap into the rest of the Spanish colonial infrastructure, as they repeatedly struck the supply convoys that moved to and from San Antonio. By August that year, Spaniards in Texas were reporting that nearly all of their livestock had been stolen or destroyed. But as the decade closed, Comanche violence only seemed to escalate. Regular reports of dead *vecinos* and captured children reached the desk of the governor, and in October 1817 the new governor, Antonio Martínez, reported that violence had become quotidian in San Antonio, as "Comanches are threatening us daily in this territory." With each attack, the general outlook in Spanish Texas grew more and more grim. By the summer of 1818, the governor concluded, "There is not a single cow in the surrounding territory."[66]

Under Governor Martínez, Spaniards seem to have had some success in repelling the Comanche offensive. In the aftermath of the March 1818 attack on Mission Refugio, for instance, the presidial commandant at La Bahía set out with a number of troops and *vecinos* to track down the Comanche rangers. He and his forces scored a victory when they managed to overtake the party of thirty-eight Comanches, killing one of them and rescuing a captive child. Equally impressive was the booty they recovered, which seems to have included much more than what Comanches initially had confiscated: forty animals and fifteen guns.[67] In general, however, Spaniards could offer little resistance to the Comanche siege. Soldiers were poorly equipped and regularly spread thin. Governor Martínez even resorted to impressing locals into military action. The governor's frequent requests for guns, ammunition, mounts, and reinforcements bear witness to the ultimate feebleness of Spanish forces during the late 1810s.[68] Martínez's April 1819 comments capture the gravity of the situation in Spanish Texas:

> Rarely a day passes that this capital is not attacked by the Indians, one time by *Tahuacanos* and another by *Comanches* or *Lipanes*, and these, with various evil Spaniards, disorganized or united, are attacking our fortifications almost every night. . . . I predict with

> sadness that this province will be destroyed unwittingly by lack of inhabitants, and I myself by lack of the resources which are necessary for subsistence. This is inevitable because no one wishes to live in the province for fear of danger and because the few inhabitants now existing are being killed gradually by the savages, and the cattle and horses as well.[69]

Overall, death and destitution engulfed the Hispanic populations of Spanish Texas during the 1810s. When Spaniards were not slaughtering their own in contests over internal political authority, Comanches were sweeping down upon the fledgling Spanish colonial settlements, reshaping Spanish Texas into little more than a series of impoverished outposts that "hardly bear comparison to any Indian village."[70] Moreover, the cross-cultural slaving détente that persisted for so many years between Comanches and Spanish came to a crashing halt, and Hispanic residents were now just as vulnerable to Comanche slaving as anybody else in the Texas borderlands. As never before, Spanish Texas had become susceptible to Comanche slaving operations, and the number of slaves from Spanish Texas living among Comanches accelerated during the 1810s. The deterioration of peace in Spanish Texas also had ramifications for slavery in Comanche society: the end of peace would catalyze Comanche slaving in the trans–Río Grande region. After 1820, the whole of northeast Mexico would become the slaving and raiding grounds of Comanches.

It was thus in the context of Spanish Texas's subjugated status and impending demise that schemes of Anglo-American colonization arrived as a possible panacea. From its inception, a Comanche peace built on commercial dependency was meant to serve as a stepping stone to greater endeavors—namely, the conquest of the *indios bárbaros*. Yet for Spanish authorities, progress in this direction moved much too slowly (and ultimately failed) in Texas; the anti–Ndé-commerce-centered peace could suppress Comanche-Spanish violence, but it did little to assert Spanish control over Native Texas. So Spanish officials devised other plans. And as in the past, their schemes relied upon settler colonists. But for the first time in Spanish Texas history, agriculture-based slave labor factored into the new equations of colonization.

Fortunately for these Spanish schemers, they did not have to look hard for prospective colonists. With the rise of Napoléon Bonaparte came the end of Spanish rule in Louisiana, and by 1803 the Louisiana Territory had exchanged imperial hands from France to the United

States. The Louisiana Purchase ultimately offered Spanish authorities many headaches and plenty of anxiety, but it also created a surplus of disgruntled former Spanish subjects within Louisiana. Moreover, Native people from the Lower Mississippi Valley also wanted to escape Anglo-American rule. Thus by late 1803, Spanish officials were receiving numerous requests from various groups to relocate to Spanish territory, and it was not long before the great colonial imagination of Spain had been reawakened in the Texas context. In November 1803, the Crown approved recommendations made by Nemesio Salcedo regarding the emigration of Spanish subjects from Louisiana to the Mexican North, and over the next few years settlement petitions streamed into the offices of Spanish frontier officials. Some petitioners, like John Curon, a native of Ireland but longtime Catholic resident of Louisiana, wanted to settle near Nacogdoches in order to take advantage of the vast trading networks already established there. Others, including Luis Tinza, a Catholic leader of the Apalachee nation, simply wanted to escape what they assumed would be an oppressive Protestant Anglo-American regime.[71] Yet the most convincing schemes were those that were compatible with the larger imperatives of Spanish high officials, those that promised to transform Texas into a thoroughly "civilized," Hispanic province.

Colonization plans with an emphasis on the development of agricultural industries, like that of Fray Juan Brady and Bernardo Martín Despallier, were thus most seductive to Spanish authorities. In April 1804, Brady and Despallier sent to Governor Elguézabal their plans to settle more than two hundred "noble, influential, and rich families, as well as some poor ones, [who] desire to move to the provinces under your command." The benefits for the Crown were numerous, the Louisiana colonial advocates assured the governor, because the relocation of so many loyal, industrious people would simultaneously weaken the neighboring U.S. government as it fortified the Mexican Northeast: "From the industry of these influential and industrious vassals the government can secure supplies for the King's manufactures, since they are all industrious persons, who by application and labor, can give great value to the country because of their extreme numbers, their slaves, their servants, and their goods." The agricultural industries that the new colonists could establish, they argued, would bring riches and stability to the Spanish Empire: "These citizens are coming to develop those branches of agriculture which will bring benefit to the king and to the public. For instance, tobacco, cotton, cane, and other things necessary for the King's navy can be secured by our government without the necessity of making application to foreign countries." In short, these Louisiana colonists would bring agriculture to Texas, and agriculture would save Texas as it buttressed the Spanish Empire.[72]

Although the grand plans of Brady and Despallier never came to fruition, Spanish officials seem to have taken seriously the matter of establishing slave-based, agricultural communities during these early years of the nineteenth century.[73] As José Miguel Ramos de Arizpe explained in his 1812 report on the northern frontier, the lands of Texas were ripe for agricultural development: "The benign sky, the pleasant climate, the extremely fertile terrain, the naturalness of everything, are inviting of the enjoyment of the most innocent and solid prosperity by means of agriculture." As "virtuous, haters of arbitrariness and disorder, just lovers of true freedom," even Hispanic borderlanders could serve as ideal instruments for such development. The only impediments were the *indios bárbaros*, whose frequent depredations had kept Spanish colonists burdened with constant military service and away from their fields. "The principal fruits of that province," claimed Ramos de Arizpe, "are to this day, unfortunately, reduced to those from the planting of maize, a little wheat, and even less sugar cane in the areas surrounding San Antonio de Véjar and La Bahía." Ramos de Arizpe did not comment explicitly on the utility of slave labor, but it is clear that he desired greater integration with Atlantic slavery-based markets. According to him, the Spanish Crown needed to authorize the opening of a port on the Texas coast in order to free the province from the tyranny of a closed commerce: "The mercantile system, which even though it has enriched us a little, has made us poor; it has enveloped all the rest of the Spaniards in misery; it has been the scourge that is most terrible and cruel; and it has made the Americas suffer."[74]

Yet by the close of the 1810s, nothing had come of the push for cash-crop colonization in Texas. As Governor Martínez declared, "Under present conditions in this province, agriculture will soon be retarded because no one wishes to come from other provinces to work in this one at the risk of his life and in a state of dire need."[75] Too violent and unstable were the years leading up to 1820, and too ideologically conflicted and administratively overwhelmed were Spanish authorities to put in motion another program of settler colonization. Ultimately, it would take the persistent efforts of Anglo-American outsiders, with the consent of the Spanish government and its Mexican successor, to prime the engine of renewed settler colonization in Texas. As predicted, slavery and agricultural production would develop in lockstep during this new era. Unfortunately for Hispanic government officials, their urgent drive to reenergize Hispanic civilization in the borderlands effectively sowed the seeds of their own demise in Texas.

Families and Slaves: A Juxtaposition of Comanche and Spanish Slavery, 1760s–1820

During the half-century from the 1760s to 1820, Spanish and Comanche slaving practices in the Texas borderlands shifted according to broader economic, geopolitical, and social changes. The tumultuous years from the 1760s through 1785 were characterized by much violence but little cross-community slaving. In the aftermath of the peace negotiations of 1785, Spaniards and Comanches channeled their slaving energies toward the joint enslavement of their Ndé foes and also began engaging in a more regular slave trade with one another, which partially integrated Spanish slavery into the Comanche model. With the collapse of peace around 1810, however, Comanches abandoned their slaving détente with Spaniards and pushed their slaving frontier even farther south, well beyond the centers of Spanish colonial Texas. Such period variation notwithstanding, longer continuities in the slaving systems of both Comanches and Spaniards existed. Although both iterations of slavery drew from unique lineages, in the Texas borderlands the two forms shared much in common.

Despite scholarly claims to the contrary, both Spanish and Comanche slavers valued their slaves for their labor.[76] In Spanish Texas, most enslaved people performed household labor, which included cooking, cleaning, and attending to the personal desires and needs of their slaver hosts. The household nature of their enslavement was most apparent in baptismal records, where priests continued to identify individuals as being "in the service of" their slavers.[77] In addition to their domestic labor, the work of enslaved people reflected the individual needs of their personal subjugators. Take, for instance, Miguel Pérez, the Yojuan slave who in 1786 successfully recruited Tonkawas to fight in an anti-Ndé campaign. Spanish authorities claimed that he was "so faithful to his master," Baltazar Pérez, "serv[ing] him in anything that occurs to him." Baltazar was a presidial soldier during the period of Pérez's enslavement, so it is possible that Pérez maintained his home while Baltazar was away on campaigns and expeditions. Or perhaps Pérez joined Baltazar as a body servant, a cook, or even an extra fighter on those expeditions. We also know that Pérez was not the only slave in Baltazar's household, as Baltazar's wife, Rosalia Flores, was also a slaveholder. In 1801, Flores owned at least four enslaved Afro-Mexicans: María Policarpia Pérez, José Cristiano Nepumoceno Pérez, Manuela Pérez, and María Damacía Guadalupe Pérez. The Pérez-Flores slaves likely labored on the large parcel of land Flores inherited from her father sometime prior to 1782. It is even possible that Pérez's "faithful" service to the Pérez-Flores household before 1786 helped Baltazar and Flores amass the wealth needed to acquire more enslaved people at the turn of the century. The very fact that the Pérez-Flores household consisted of multiple slaves strongly suggests that enslaved people had economic value; a household of that size on the Spanish frontier would have been untenable without the labor contributions of each member of the household.[78]

It is unlikely that many Spanish slaves engaged in agricultural work, although some may have assisted the handful of Bexareños who planted crops at the time.[79] In 1803, Governor Elguézabal reported that *vecinos* "confine their labor to planting corn, though not in great quantities . . . to the planting of beans, chili pepper and some sugarcane." According to Elguézabal, agricultural development had been limited by "the lack of a market" and because "a loom or a manufactury has never been known" in the town.[80] Because there were at least a few San Antonio colonists who were involved in agriculture *and* owned slaves, we might assume that they exploited their slaves' labor to foster their agricultural endeavors. Among these farmers was Antonio Baca, the slaver of at least one Black woman and an Apache child. Baca, who lived in the vicinity of Mission San Antonio de Valero, owned both land and water and raised sugarcane. It is doubtful that Baca's two slaves accounted for *all* of the labor required to grow sugarcane, but there is no reason to believe that they were not somehow involved in such activities as clearing, tilling, planting, and harvesting. And as Baca was also a merchant, his slaves could have been responsible for collecting and transporting the sugar and other trade goods for sale. Moreover, his Comanche trade connections, which were prominent at the time, would have allowed him to purchase slave-generated goods from Comanche traders in exchange for his own slave-supported merchandise. This would have represented a convergence of Spanish-Comanche slaveholder commerce.[81]

In Comanchería, enslaved people worked in two principal capacities: as herders and as household laborers. By the late eighteenth and early nineteenth century, Comanche horse herds numbered some thirty thousand to forty thousand horses, which made herding the number one economic activity of Comanches.[82] Teenage boys generally were tasked with the arduous labor of herding horses, which involved protecting the horses from animal predators and braving the harsh weather of blistering summers and frigid winters, but women frequently assisted in pastoral duties as well. The economic function of enslaved people helps to explain the Comanche preference for enslaving women and children: the many enslaved women and children procured by Comanches were ideal for the kind of labor needed to manage the great horse herds of Comanche communities. Without their pastoral labor, the Comanche system would not have been able to sustain itself for so long.[83]

The Comanche household, like the Spanish household, was also an important labor domain for enslaved people. Here women were essential, as they reared children, processed meat, cooked, and maintained the tipi. As previously mentioned, Euro-American commentators frequently interpreted the condition of women in Comanche society as harsh and slave-like. Certainly much of the Euro-American disdain for the condition of Comanche women was the result of ethnocentric biases regarding the proper role of women, but it seems apparent that Comanche women actively engaged in domestic work and in the manufacture of hides. Given the fact that Comanches were mobile people, whose mobility required the constant assembling and disassembling of housing units, it is tough to underestimate the importance of domestic labor in Comanche society. Sibley provided some indirect details regarding female slave labor in 1805, when he commented, with a hint of admiration, on the ability of Comanche women to set up (and pack up) camp for their mobile communities:

> They have tents made of neatly dressed skins, fashioned in form of a cone. . . . When they stop, their tents are pitched in very exact order, so as to form regular streets and squares, which in a few minutes has the appearance of a town, raised, as it were, by enchantment; and they are equally dexterous in striking their tents and preparing for a march when the signal is given; to every tent two horses or mules are allotted, one to carry the tent, and another the poles or sticks, which are neatly made of red cedar.[84]

Because Comanche women were active in the production of manufactured goods, enslaved women also would have contributed to Comanche industry. Female manufacturing was another Comanche practice that Euro-American commentators fixated on. In 1786, Domingo Cabello noted that Comanche women "are obliged to dress the meat and hides" of bison and deer. In his 1808 report, Sibley made similar remarks about female manufacturing labor, but with additional details: "The Women seem in the Most Abject & degraded State of Servility, they Appear to be Constantly and Laboriously employ'd In dressing Buffalo Skins, Painting and Ornamenting them with a Variety of Colours & figures, making their own & their Husbands dresses, Collecting fuel, Attending & guarding their Horses & Mules, in Cooking, Making Leather Halters & Ropes, Making & repairing their Tents, & making their riding & Pack Saddles &c. &c."[85] Again, Sibley's comments are colored by his assumptions regarding appropriate gendered behaviors, but they do highlight the remarkable diversity of female labor in Comanche society. Little wonder Comanches so often captured women during slave raids. Their labor kept Comanche society afloat.

As discussed previously, in both Spanish and Comanche society slaves had commercial value. The commercial character of Comanche slavery was often the most visible aspect of the system, something Spanish soldiers and officials often learned about through their encounters with the enslaved people they purchased from Comanche and Norteño traders. The slave trade brought Comanches all sorts of commodities, including "tobacco, knives, axes, and glass beads." Sometimes they traded slaves for horses, which in Texas were already domesticated, and at other times they exchanged them for foodstuffs or manufactured goods. Fray Francisco Atanasio Domínguez, who witnessed the Comanche slave trade in New Mexico, detailed the rates of exchange for Comanche slaves in the 1770s. According to Domínguez, "an Indian girl from twelve to twenty years old" could be exchanged for "two good horses and some trifles" or "a she-mule and scarlet cover." Naturally, enslaved men were "worth less," but Comanche traders were willing to bargain their price as well. The key point is that Comanches interpreted enslaved people as commodities to be traded, owned, and accumulated as transactional goods.[86]

Spaniards in Texas shared this belief in the value of commodified bodies. As the dozens of bills of sale in the Béxar archives indicate, enslaved Black people were particularly vulnerable to the slave market. The anti-Black slave trade in Spanish Texas was connected to all parts of Mexico, but it also tied Bexareños, the residents of Béxar, to other frontier colonial settlements, even Louisiana. Although some enslaved individuals were traded together with their children, some of these slaves undoubtedly were torn from their families as a result of this trade.[87] In addition to the commercial exchange of enslaved Black people, Spaniards sometimes bought and sold Native slaves among themselves. In 1785, for instance, María Gertrudis de la Peña, an *india*, petitioned for her freedom. According to her testimony, de la Peña was purchased and sold by four different men, finally landing in the hands of Ángel Corcio Navarro by means of Antonio Oquillas for 50 pesos. Apparently, by 1785 de la Peña could no longer tolerate her condition, "since under the name of *esclavo* I live in the house of the aforesaid Don Angel, suffering many ill-treatments from all of his family and especially from the referred Don Angel Corzio." De la Peña's story, however, was not entirely unique, as the slave trade had grown so vast during the 1770s—implicating Spaniards from San Antonio all the way to the coastal region just south of the Río Grande in Nuevo Santander—that Spanish officials ordered an investigation.[88] The commodification of enslaved bodies was a practice that transcended Hispanic-Comanche cultural boundaries.

How slavers and host societies meted out personal violence was particularly significant in circumscribing the conditions of slaves under both the Spanish and the Comanche systems. In Comanche society, enslaved people felt the violence of their slavers immediately. Women and children who were captured during a raid often had to suffer the pain of watching their slavers execute or torture the older men of their party. Writing in 1818, David G. Burnet offered a vivid, if not hyperbolic, description of the fate of men when captured by Comanches during battle:

> They take a peculiar delight in torturing the adult male prisoners, who, according to an ancient custom, are surrendered to their fiend-like amusement for three days succeeding their arrival in the village. . . . During the three days of abandonment by the men, the prisoner is stretched on the ground, each extremity pinioned to a stake, where he lies motionless, save in the writhings of fear and anguish, and exposed to the fury of the squaws, who alternately recreate themselves by inflicting on their prostrate enemy every variety of torture that a savage fancy can suggest. . . . Faint with fear and trembling, he is hurled to the centre, while the shouting throng gather around in tumultuous circles, and assail him with clubs, and thongs, and knives, and javelins, and fire-brands, in unmeasured and reckless fury. . . . He is then again staked-out on the earth, to await the diversions of the morrow, and the morrow—when similar scenes are re-acted upon him. If haply, he survives this severe initiation, he is afterwards exempt from corporal punishment, is considered a member, *sub conditionis*, of their society, and is attached as a slave to the family of the warrior who captured him, where he is generally treated with humanity.

There is much to unpack in Burnet's long, lurid description—especially for its rhetorical value in the context of Anglo-American westward colonial expansion—but the broader outlines of the process he details ring true when compared to other contemporary sources. In essence, adult men faced a degree of violence (and possibly torture) upon capture, and if they proved themselves pliable enough, Comanche slavers incorporated them as slaves. That extreme violence was administered to adult males does not seem surprising, given both the context of their acquisition during war and their likelihood to resist enslavement violently. Even though it is obvious that Burnet embellished his description for the sake of painting Comanches as savage or inherently evil, aspects of his account are substantiated by less rhetorical sources.[89]

In any case, Burnet is correct about Comanche tendencies to integrate enslaved children as kin: "When [Comanches] capture boys and girls, as they often do in their excursions to the Spanish provinces, they usually treat them with much lenity and kindness, and retain them in a kind of filial servitude, very little inferior to the condition of native children. It is singular with what facility these ill-fated youths will assimilate themselves to the habits of their new associates."[90] Here Burnet highlights what scholars generally consider to be the most distinctive aspect of Comanche slavery: the kin incorporation of captives. The documentary record is rich with accounts of Comanches adopting young captured children and marrying enslaved women. As early as 1772, Spanish observers in Texas were making this assertion regarding the adoption of children, and the claim surfaces frequently enough from 1772 to 1820 that it would be difficult to refute entirely.[91] Nevertheless, as we interpret these claims about Comanche adoption, we must remember that all of the Euro-American commentators viewed such adoptions as inherently abhorrent. As Burnet declares in his description of Comanche adoption practices, "Spanish boys from 10 to 15 years old will become so reconciled to their captivity in a few weeks after their introduction to this wild and uncultured society, as to be distinguishable only by the slight variations of nature, from their savage companions, and will generally outstrip them in rude and vicious licentiousness."[92] To Burnet and other Euro-American observers, kin incorporation was perhaps *the worst part* of Comanche slavery: the violence of torture, they reasoned, was fleeting; savage adoption, however, was life-long, permanent, and ultimately perverse.

But this is not to deny kin incorporation as a key mechanism of Comanche enslavement processes. To the contrary, the incorporation of young captured children as family served as a stabilizing device within slaving communities. It served at least three purposes: (1) to buttress the economic productivity of Comanche households (which had become especially susceptible to the devastation of epidemics and waves of colonial violence by the last quarter of the eighteenth century), (2) to make the indoctrination of enslaved outsiders easier, and (3) to legitimate the claims of the family members of slaveholders. As enslaved children were forced to labor as both domestic workers and herders, it may seem obvious that they enhanced the economic productivity of Comanche households. Yet in the context of the destructive epidemics of the late 1700s and early 1800s, replacing family members was particularly important for Comanche households, and captured children offered a quick replenishment of depleted populations. It was also easier to assimilate children—or as Juan Antonio Padilla described it, to "teach [them] their wicked customs"—when slaves were assigned to particular households.[93]

The incorporation of slaves as family members also may have offered the kin relations of slavers a sense of shared authority over slaves. José Manuel Apodaca's misgivings about a proposed trip to Comanchería in 1786 reflect this dynamic. As Pedro Vial planned his second trip to Comanchería that year, he hoped to bring along with him Apodaca, a former slave of both Comanches and Wichitas. Vial's thinking was that Apodaca would provide vital insights into Comanche and Wichita society, but Apodaca wanted to stay as far away from his former slavers as possible. Apparently Apodaca "did not dare to travel by the Taboayazes and Cumanches, fearful that some kinsperson of his former masters might want to recapture him." To Apodaca, familial relations served as the bonds of slaver authority. Others agreed. In 1791, a group of Comanches, including Sofais, appealed to Governor Muñoz for news regarding "a captive who had come in flight from their *ranchería*." According to Sofais, "the Comanche acting as his [the slaver's] father was killed" in a recent skirmish with Mescaleros, so they were there to collect him. Evidently, the death of a slave's slaver-father was not enough to sever the bonds of slaver authority; slaver authority extended to all familial relations.[94]

Women probably suffered most from their enslavement under Comanche slavers. By the turn of the nineteenth century, polygyny was expanding within Comanche society, and enslaved women supplied some of the wives required for the growing institution. As Hämäläinen has argued, "the escalation of polygyny went hand in hand with the escalation of slavery. The two institutions had a common genesis—both developed to offset chronic labor shortages arising from market production—and they were functionally linked: many female slaves were eventually incorporated into Comanche families as wife-laborers." Polygyny may have reflected ancient Comanche family-making practices, but its ties to labor systems and to the growing influence of slaveholding men were undeniable. Comanche men acquired wives to expand their household's productive capacity, and the greater the production capacity, the greater the political and social clout of the men.[95] When Comanche men married their slaves, they incorporated them as laboring kin.

Even if enslaved women became the wives of Comanche men, there is no reason to believe spousal status was voluntary or necessarily benign. By definition, forced wifehood meant that coercion and sexual violence were regular parts of the lives of enslaved women.[96] Moreover, sexual violence rendered female slaves vulnerable in a number of ways: not only did they have to suffer from the physical and psychological traumas inherent to the particular acts of sexual violence (i.e., rape); they also had to live with the burdens of reproductive labor and of raising their children under slavery. Forced parenthood was one means by which Comanche slavers could control enslaved women because attempts to escape risked the well-being of the enslaved mothers' children. One incident from 1791 sheds light on how effective forced parenthood was at sustaining female bondage. In January of that year, a Native slave escaped from Comanchería after a Comanche *ranchería* was attacked by Mescaleros. Sadly, the escapee was unable to bring his mother along with him to Béxar. According to Governor Muñoz, "This *Yndio* does not want to return to live among them [the Comanches]. . . . He affirms that his mother is [a captive] but does not know from where, because she herself has told him they would come to live among the Spanish as soon as he was bigger." Clearly, the fugitive's mother had viewed her enslaved status as a burden tied to her son's condition; if she was going to escape, it would be alongside her son once he was old enough to escape with her. Alas, the opportunity for freedom arrived only for her son. Although the woman may have taken solace in the fact that her son was able to escape their shared enslavement, *she* remained enslaved. In this sense, kin incorporation was a form of subjugation.[97]

Comanche vocabulary also reveals the limits of the adoption thesis. According to modern dictionaries, Comanches—as all people—have long made nuanced distinctions between the kinds of members within their society. There are actually multiple variations of *slave* and *captive* in the Comanche lexicon: specifically, slaves or "servants" who "must do work for another" are known as *tiriʔaiwapIs* (or *ʉrʉʔai wapis*), while adopted "captives" are *kwʉhʉpʉs*. From such distinctions, we may assume, at the very least, that not all enslaved people were adopted. Those who were adopted, as observers noted, probably had proved themselves worthy of special recognition but not necessarily of full Comanche status (otherwise, the term denoting an adopted captive would not have existed at all). Comanches, moreover, also have distinguished between *nʉmʉnaitʉ* (those who live as Comanche) and *nʉmʉ rʉborarʉ* (those born of Comanches). Thus, even as Comanches recognized some captives as adopted family, they still retained an outsider, (possibly) stigmatized status.[98] Kin incorporation need not be a totalizing process; being an enslaved family member was not oxymoronic. Kin making and slavery could complement one another in Comanche society.

Within Spanish society, slavery was sustained by violence and processes of kin incorporation as well. The aforementioned María Gertrudis de la Peña's story is particularly illustrative of the roles of violence and family making within Spanish slavery. In addition to her experiences being bought and sold by four different men, her life was circumscribed by sexual violence and strategic economic deprivation. Her first slaver, Pedro de la Peña, was both her "adoptive father" and the father of her late child. According to her own account, Pedro had raised her "since my early years until the age of sixteen, when I left because of being pregnant." She did not charge Pedro explicitly with rape, but she felt ashamed and violated enough to leave his home and "agreed to go with" her next slaver, Antonio Oquillas, "under the name of daughter and not of slave." Oquillas was similarly exploitative, as "he took away from me all the clothes I owned which he had given me, and he tried to sell me to the said Don Angel Corzio, who told me at the time of the contract that if I were to go to serve in his house for a period of three years, he would give me my freedom." Of course, this was yet another ruse to gain access to de la Peña's body and labor, as her time in the home of Corzio was also filled with "ill-treatments." Overall, de la Peña's lived experiences over the course of nearly two decades reveal how the violence and exploitation of Spanish slavery easily slipped in and out of the language of "family," just as her subjugated status as a slave simultaneously made her vulnerable to forced family making in a very real sense (i.e., sexual violence).[99]

The discourse of family gained special currency in the context of Spanish slavery because Spaniards clung to the idea that their presence in the borderlands—and in the Americas at large—was ordained by God. During the first half-century of Spanish settler colonization in

Texas, most Spanish slavers procured slaves directly through slave raids, and in order to legitimate their slaveholdings slavers often baptized their captives into the holy family of Christ. This broader impulse to "save" enslaved Native people persisted during the half-century that followed, but the shift in slave acquisition (i.e., primarily through the Norteño/Comanche slave trade) required Spaniards to return to an older tradition, one that prevailed during the earliest days of the Spanish conquest of Mexico, in order to justify the illegal enslavement of Native people. The tradition was the *rescate*, or "rescue," of prisoners held by heathens, and as their Norteño/Comanche slave-trading connections grew, Spaniards returned to the language of the *rescate* to frame their involvement. Initially, Spaniards in Texas focused primarily on rescuing captives who were known to be Christian, because to them the simple presence of Christian women and children among "barbarous" Indian men was an affront to Spanish manly honor. The fear was that the unrestrained and "lascivious" lifestyle of "barbarous" society—combined with the supposedly wicked nature of Indian men—would lure Christian women and children away from a righteous and obedient way of life. Spanish manly honor demanded that they protect and defend their family members as best they could, even if it meant paying a "ransom." So what was in effect participation in a slave trade was understood to be a manly duty that preserved the sanctity of the Christian family.[100]

Yet by the end of the eighteenth century, as Comanches and other Norteños made slaves more available to Spanish buyers, the distinction between Christian and non-Christian captives became virtually meaningless when "rescuing" slaves: eventually, Spaniards were willing to "rescue" *anybody* held in bondage by Native people.[101] Just as Christian captives could be saved from a descent into barbarism, Native captives could be pulled out of barbarism through purchase. Here Spanish processes of kin incorporation dovetailed with the kin-defending practice of the *rescate*. In Spanish records, captives *rescatado* were not slaves; they were, rather, *criados*, outsiders who were raised as family members and "educated in the Catholic faith" by Spanish residents. The term initially was derived from the verb *criar*, meaning "to rear," but in Spanish Texas it was the preferred term to describe Native individuals who were enslaved in Spanish households.[102] By marking enslaved individuals as members of the family unit, Spaniards could flout the legal structures that were supposed to protect Native people from enslavement, even as they made essentially no effort to hide the fact that *criados* were raised "in the service" of their masters.[103] In fact, the term *criado* became so popular for its ability to convey both a Christianizing familial relationship and the status of servitude that *all* who served a superior in Spanish Texas—Spanish, Black, and Native individuals—became known, at least in the documentary record, as *criados* by the 1790s.[104]

Slavery's ties to processes of kin making also accounted for some of the differences between the slaving systems of Comanches and Spaniards in the Texas borderlands. Available evidence strongly suggests that the slavery systems of Spaniards and Comanches differed in at least one important aspect: the question of the inheritance of slave status. In Comanche society, enslaved individuals did not seem to pass on the curse of slave status from generation to generation; instead, the children of slaves likely had the same opportunities to contribute to Comanche society as the children of nonslaves. I have found only one incident during the half-century period covered in this chapter that suggests slave stigmas crossed generations in Comanche society. This incident occurred during John Sibley's interactions with Comanche visitors at Natchitoches in 1807—and possibly tells us more about Sibley's worldview than about Comanche social customs. What impressed Sibley most about the Comanche emissaries during this interaction was that "The Complexion of this Nation is fairer than that of Any Other of the Numerous Tribes I have ever seen." In traditional colonialist fashion, Sibley was especially captivated by the physical features of Comanche women, many of whom "have light Brown or Auburn Hair & Blue or light Grey Eyes." When he inquired about those who "were So white," a Comanche *paraibo* said "he believ'd they possess'd no Mixture of Blood." Yet, one of these "light-haired" women "Blush'd and hid her face" when she overheard this conversation between Sibley and the Comanche *paraibo*. According to the Comanche leader, the young woman turned away because she was "Asham'd of her White Skin." Although we may never know with much certainty why this young woman believed "White Skin" was shameful, this episode seems to indicate that at least some Comanches ascribed meaning to particular physiognomic differences (in this case, skin color). But did skin color somehow signify slave status to those living within Comanche society? Or was her skin color little more than an indication to others that she could not claim full Comanche ancestry? We might assume that given the prevalence of slaving and kin incorporation among Comanches, the women Sibley encountered were either slaves themselves or the offspring of slaves. It is unclear, however, if the young woman "with light hair" was herself a slave or the child of a slave. Either way, it is possible that it was the recognition of her ties to a stigmatized outsider status—such as that of a slave (*tiri?aiwapI* or *kwʉhʉpʉ*)—that upset and embarrassed her. If so, this would suggest that Comanches did associate certain physiognomic features with slave status and that it was possible for such a status to linger beyond a single generation. We must consider, however, the possibility that Sibley's remarks about hair and skin color were simply the racial fixations of an Anglo-American man who came from a highly racialized society, where physiognomy often circumscribed a person's life chances.[105]

Other well-documented Comanche social, political, and economic mechanisms and conventions—specifically, those central to male meritocracy—lend credence to the idea that slave status was *not* multigenerational in Comanche society. When the sexual violence of Comanche slavers against enslaved women resulted in part-Comanche offspring, these slaver-fathers had no reason to fear the loss of political, social, or economic privileges to these part-Comanche children. Although Comanche society was chiefly patrilineal and patrilocal, custom dictated that Comanche children could not inherit privileges from their fathers. The male meritocracy of Comanche society—which bestowed social, economic, and political status to men who proved their worth through personal actions and behaviors in war—prevented inheritance from being a socially divisive issue. In other words, parentage entitled Comanche children to neither property nor office. Therefore, the part-Comanche offspring of enslaved people could inherit essentially nothing from their slaver-fathers. Instead, they would have to gain power, status, and fortune on their own, either through war honors, wife accumulation, or personal raiding. To the extent that heritable slave stigma exists for the fostering and protection of slaver wealth and accumulation (economic, political, social, or psychic), Comanche slavers did not need slave stigma to be transgenerational. Slaver-fathers could favor their children of choice (slave or nonslave), without fearing the economic or political repercussions of inheritance customs.[106]

This was not the case in Spanish society, where slaves could not be kin *and* be spared a heritable slave stigma. As in Comanche society, the question of slave status inheritance seems to have been related to the social, economic, and political mechanisms that governed Spanish society. But unlike Comanche society, Spanish inheritance customs controlled the allocation of property, office, and status from generation to generation. According to Spanish custom, all *hijos legítimos*, or legitimate children, inherited some of their parents' property. This meant that even though Spanish women had limited opportunities to own property (and greater restrictions in general), they nonetheless were entitled to *some* inheritance. Therefore, kin relations—specifically those between a parent and a legitimate child—had material consequences. To be an *hijo legítimo* was to be an individual with a future tied to one's parents' estate. Simply put, family inheritance in Spanish Texas had the potential to limit or enhance significantly a person's success and status.[107]

The incorporation of enslaved people as kin—through metaphorical rituals or through sexual violence—could have created major inheritance problems for Spanish slavers (and those interested in accumulating wealth through slavery) if enslavement was not accompanied by heritable slave status. Thus, both *criados* and (Black) *esclavos* were illegitimate kin. *Criados* were nowhere to be found in the wills of Spaniards in Texas, except possibly as property to be inherited by their legitimate children, for a *criado* could inherit her slaver's name but not his material legacy.[108] Ultimately, *criados* existed in Spanish homes primarily to be exploited. This was why, in 1822, slavers like Joaquín de Almaguer and Francisco Xavier Chávez could openly dispute in court the ownership of an eleven-year-old boy, the son of an enslaved Lipan woman. The boy was an *hijo natural*, an illegitimate child, who was "raised" in the Chávez household, but Almaguer, as the biological father, believed he had "the right to collect the child." Chávez turned away Almaguer and instead petitioned for his own custody of the *hijo natural*. The two men bickered over who was the rightful "father," but not because they felt some inherent parental bond to the young boy; rather, the men wanted him under their power "with the goal of having him help with work." Because they understood the boy to be a stigmatized, illegitimate child, they could easily claim fatherhood without fearing he would be in line to inherit their wealth.[109]

For de jure, chattel slaves—who were almost always Black people in Spanish Texas—the issue of family inheritance was skirted by maintaining the tradition of *vientre libre*, or the principle of the "free womb."[110] This practice of ascribing the legally sanctioned *esclavo* status of the mother to her children functioned primarily as a way to preserve chattel slaveholder property rights and to excuse Spaniards of any obligations that may have stemmed from sexual exploitation of enslaved Black women. So although the baptismal records document the existence of enslaved "illegitimate" Black children who may have had Spanish fathers, because the children were cursed by their mothers' status, Spanish men were absolved of any and all fatherly responsibilities, including the passing on of an inheritance. Spaniards did not have to fear losing property through inheritance to such offspring.[111] The matrilineal inheritance of *esclavo* status in Spanish society also helps to explain the enduring stigmatization of Blackness in Spanish Texas. With Black slave status heritable, Spanish society would not limit or curtail the stigmas of Blackness, although many residents may have preferred to deny their African heritage. To be Black, or *negro*, was to be a dishonored, social outcast in Spanish Texas. For enslaved Afro-Mexicans, this was made evident by the suffering and exploitation they endured on a daily basis. But anti-Blackness could be leveled against other nonslave Hispanic residents as well. José Miguel Games and his brother, Francisco, experienced (and participated in) anti-Blackness firsthand in 1778, when they attempted to halt the marriage of their niece Ana María de la Trinidad Hernández to Urbano Hinojosa, because he was an *indio*. The Games brothers appealed to government authorities to settle the matter, "in view of the dishonor that would accrue to them and their families if their niece, the sister of their nephew, should wed an *indio*, from a mission and of unknown parents." Unfortunately for them, Spanish residents found their lineage to be equally questionable, and Hinojosa, with the help of a local priest, responded to their claims of racial superiority with an indictment of *their* racial status: "It is well known, public knowledge, that they are *mulatos*—by all four bloodlines; and being *mulatos*, their being soldiers does not make them *españoles* or persons of better *casta* or of better or cleaner blood than that of an *indio*. They themselves carry the blemish which gives them their own existence, and they will carry it to their graves. Therefore, no stain whatever accrues to them if a person of better *casta* or bloodlines than themselves should enter their family." Admitting that Blackness *was* part of their lineage, the Games brothers countered by arguing that their military service against *indios bárbaros* should have freed them from their burdensome racial status: "Even if I were *mulato*, to my rank must be added the excellence of having shed whatever [impure] blood I might have had, in service to the king my lord." For them, violence against Indians—war honors—was what made their family *español*. Here the cleansing of blood was both literal and metaphorical because on the battlefield, the Games brothers claimed, they had bled out their Blackness. Ultimately, the entire dispute was moot on a practical level, as Hernández elected to not marry Hinojosa; however, the incident demonstrates the enduring salience of anti-Blackness within Spanish Texas, even as violence between Spaniards and Native people framed much of this history.[112]

Residents also made it clear that Blackness was a debased social condition in their use of the terms *negro* and *mulato* as insults. A number of incidents in which residents insulted one another with accusations of Blackness reveals the level of stigmatization of Blackness within Spanish society. Governor Cabello, for instance, was so fed up with the Menchaca family's influence in San Antonio that he accused them of being "nothing but wretched *mulatos* from the Presidio of Río Grande." Luis Mariano Menchaca, perhaps aware of the rumors about his own Blackness, later deployed the insult against Fernando Arocha, accusing him and his family of being "worthless *mulatos*." Such insults sometimes led to bizarre legal proceedings. In one case, the wife of Francisco Rodríguez was beaten by a man named Manuel Padrón, but when San Antonio authorities gathered testimony, Rodríguez's only concern was with the accusation from Padrón and another woman that his wife was a *mulata*. Apparently being Black was such a debased condition in Texas that racist insults against one's spouse trumped concerns about her physical well-being. As such, Rodríguez petitioned authorities to examine the accusers and find out why they thought she was part-Black, "for I married her trusting that she was *español*."[113]

For all the fictitiousness, subterfuge, and exploitation inherent in Spanish kin incorporation, family ties were not unimportant to enslaved people in Spanish Texas. Instead, both Native and Black bondspeople seem to have done the best they could with the limited opportunities they had, ascribing their own meaning to *familia*. The family history of Candelaria del Fierro, a Black slave of Antonio Baca, for instance, demonstrates the remarkable resilience of some enslaved people in spite of their subjugated condition. Fierro first shows up in the documentary record in November 1783, when she and her husband, José Manuel Gonzáles, baptized their six-day-old son, Clemente. Over the next twelve years, she and Gonzáles would baptize an additional six children. What appears most remarkable is the fact that the two parents lived in separate households—as Gonzáles was the slave of Leonor Delgado—but still managed to maintain a shared life. Also impressive was Fierro's ability to recruit important Béxar families as godparents of her children. Among these were members of the well-known Leal and Arocha families, whose affiliation probably indicated Fierro's determination to create for her children beneficial social connections.[114] And some enslaved men and women, such as Antonia Galbán and Tomás Reyes, took it upon themselves to serve as the godparents of other enslaved people. This could not have been an easy decision, considering the fact that it would have been their responsibility to care for the *ahijado* if something happened to the parents. Moreover, the parents of the child certainly must have valued the relationships fostered with the godparents, because as slaves they could not have offered much in terms of social, economic, or political influence in the community. For these enslaved people, this did not matter as much as the bonds created between the various families.[115] At least here we see kinship ties functioning in a sincere, resourceful way for enslaved people in Spanish Texas. But these relationships existed solely at the interstices of slavery in the Texas borderlands. In general, family making was a coercive process, a means to solidifying slaver authority in a violent, unstable place.

Summary

The collision of generations-long Spanish and Comanche slave raiding in Texas, although resulting in considerable collaboration at times, could not have ended in peace. Neither Spaniards nor Comanches were willing to accept the hegemonic rule of the other, and when the economic, political, and cultural prerogatives of the two groups no longer converged, peace collapsed. Unfortunately for the Spaniards of Texas, Comanches outmatched them in both military might and regional economic influence. Even Spanish slavery catered to a more prominent Comanche model. Thus, when peace between Comanches came to an end, so did the Spanish sway in Texas. Comanche violence drove Spanish officials to look elsewhere, and elsewhere brought them to schemes of Anglo-American colonization. By the 1820s, Spanish rule officially had given way to Mexican authority, but the events of the 1810s had unleashed historical forces that ultimately would undermine the new Mexican system. And although the descendants of the Spanish regime would remain important agents of change in Texas, Texas borderlands slavery would be driven henceforth by Comanche and Anglo-American imperatives more so than those of Hispanic people. The days of Hispanic-dictated slaving in the Texas borderlands were nearing their end.

But Spaniards still had contributed much to the shaping of Texas borderlands slavery. As before, Spanish men raided Native communities for slaves, but they also opened up new avenues for slave acquisition by expanding their slave-trading ties with neighboring Native groups, especially Comanches. By engaging Native merchants in the trading of enslaved bodies, Spanish slavers fostered bonds of friendship and alliance with historically hostile peoples, and their committed efforts to the enslavement of shared enemies—specifically Ndé people—also helped to cement peace between warring communities. Just as important, Spanish slavers continued to find ways to justify and normalize their illegal slaving practices. By tying their slaving tendencies to larger Christianizing and civilizing impulses, Spanish slavers made the forced incorporation of outsiders as kin a commendable activity, deserving not of reproach but of admiration. Entangled in a web of geopolitical concerns, economic opportunities, and ideological sensibilities, Spanish slavery became as flexible as ever.

Spanish slavers' active involvement with their Comanche counterparts—through both the slave trade and joint slave raiding—meant that Spanish and Comanche systems of slavery sometimes overlapped. Like Spanish slavery, Comanche slavery was geopolitical in nature; it shaped Comanche relationships with allies and enemies. Sometimes the exchange of slaves built trust between Comanches and their allies, but at other times the raiding of communities for slaves exacerbated intergroup conflicts. Moreover, like Spanish slaveholders, Comanche slavers incorporated their slaves as ostensible kin, which provided Comanches with labor for the principal unit of production in their economy: the household. Through both the domestic and reproductive work of enslaved people, particularly women and children, Comanche slavers enhanced the productive capacity of their communities. And this is to say nothing of slave contributions to the Comanche pastoral economy. Without the exploited labor of enslaved people, Comanches likely would not have dominated the commerce and politics of the Texas borderlands.

For the slaves of Spaniards and Comanches, concerns about diplomacy, commerce, and civilization paled in comparison to the violence of their slavers and host communities. Being the kin of one's slaver meant little if violence and exploitation were the defining characteristics of that familial relationship. Instead, slave work—whether household labor, skin manufacturing, herding, or farming—and the physical and psychological abuse of slavers circumscribed life as an enslaved person. In Spanish society (and possibly in Comanche society), stigmatization followed enslaved people and their children. While the children of slaves in the meritocratic society of Comanches may have had greater opportunities to advance economically, politically, and socially, in general enslaved people were treated as dishonorable outsiders. In Spanish Texas, this was especially the case for enslaved Afro-Mexicans and their descendants, who continued to endure the curse of anti-Blackness. Nevertheless, the enslaved Native people of Spanish Texas remained exploitable, marginalized members of society too, evidence of Spanish colonialism's ongoing consumption of Native bodies and lives.

5 / "Honest People . . . from Hell Itself": Anglo-American Colonization and the Rise of Chattel Slavery in Texas, 1800–1836

In June 1806, a small group of Black men arrived at Nacogdoches, the northeastern-most settlement of Spanish Mexico. The men had come a long way, traveling perhaps as many as eight hundred miles from Kentucky, on the western fringes of the United States, where they procured a pass from a local Anglo-American administrator. The pass, it seems, placated the local Spanish officials for the time being, although they could not be certain if these ambitious travelers were there for legitimate colonial business or if they were fugitives who had made their way to Texas in search of freedom. Then, just over a month later, in late July, news arrived in the form of a petition from a man by the name of Jacob Bean that a number of his "*negro* fugitive slaves" had escaped to Texas. For the weary journeymen, it seemed, the jig was up. Their visible Blackness, now combined with a formal petition from a White man, gave local Spanish officials plenty of evidence to assume their slave status. Yet fortunately for them, diplomatic tensions between Spain and the United States made local officials wary of acquiescing to the request of a random Anglo-American slaveholder from the East. So instead of surrendering the men to their slaver, they decided to stand pat "until a new royal resolution is received." While the Black fugitives remained in Spanish Texas, officials elected to keep them "occupied in field work or in any other kind of work, so that they may earn their subsistence." This may not have been the freedom they expected, but it was likely better than their condition as slaves under the authority of Bean.[1]

At the time, in 1806, the arrival of a small group of enslaved Black people in Spanish Texas hardly would have registered on the radar of most Spanish residents of the borderlands. Aside from the handful of people who processed their arrival, housed them, and benefited from their paid labor, few people likely even noticed their presence in Texas, where it was not entirely unusual for people enslaved in other Euro-American communities to seek asylum.[2] But as unremarkable as the appearance of these enslaved men was at the time, their arrival portended a new epoch in the Texas borderlands: the rapid expansion of the Anglo-American cotton frontier. The small group of fugitives was just the beginning of the massive transfer to Texas of enslaved Black people and their Anglo-American slavers. Although Anglo-American slavery seemed far away in 1806, by the 1830s Anglo-Americans would drive their cotton frontier well into the heart of the Texas borderlands.

This chapter situates Anglo-American settler colonization in Texas through the end of official Hispanic rule in 1836 within the context of generations of borderlands violence. The intrusion of Anglo-Americans into the borderlands, although not entirely unprecedented, was unlike the respective conquests of Spaniards and Comanches in at least one significant way: while slave raiding brought Spaniards and Comanches to Texas, the prospects of slave*holding* motivated Anglo-Americans. At a fundamental level, Anglo-Americans invested in their colonial project for purposes of expanding an economic system that was already dependent upon chattel slavery. Thus, slavers relocated to Texas *with* substantial numbers of enslaved people already under their power, in hopes of producing cash crop commodities, especially cotton, that held incredible value in markets far beyond the Texas borderlands. By virtue of its Atlantic orientation, Anglo-American chattel slavery introduced slaving practices that were unique to previous forms of borderlands slavery. Specifically, the Anglo-American emphasis on the property status of slaves, coupled with a virulent Anglo-American version of anti-Blackness, made life particularly precarious and oppressive for enslaved people in Anglo-Texas. Although anti-Blackness had pervaded the Hispanic-influenced borderlands for a century, Anglo-American slavers' fostering of a widespread slave-trading network made prominent—as never before—the commodification and accumulation of Black bodies. This pervasive accumulative commodification, along with the violence slavers wielded to extract Black labor, further exacerbated anti-Black thought and practice.

Nonetheless, despite the importance of transregional connections in the development of Anglo-American colonialism, Anglo slavery still had to contend with local realities: the thick historical web of borderlands relations, customs, and conventions. Fortunately for Anglo-American settler colonists, their slaving practices found inviting circumstances in the borderlands, where Hispanic and Comanche people had for generations built their dominion through the violence of slaving. Like its predecessors, Anglo-American slavery rested on the subjugation of stigmatized outsiders, and like their Hispanic and Comanche counterparts, Anglo slavers attempted to naturalize and legitimate the violent exploitation of their slaves through processes of kin incorporation. As had been the case for a century, family making operated as a form of social control, a way to balance the practical concerns of physical, economic integration with the social (and psychic) impulses to stigmatize and justify slaver dominance.

The violence of Anglo-American settler colonialism, of course, was multipronged, as the Anglo-American expansion of their anti-Black cotton frontier necessitated the violent displacement of Native peoples. This was the very reason Hispanic officials accepted the broader project of Anglo-American colonization in the first place; Hispanic authorities turned to Anglo-Americans in an effort to assert *their* dominion over *el norte* of Mexico. On the eve of Anglo-American colonization during the early 1820s, Native people still reigned over their Texas homelands, and, as before, Hispanic officials hoped to secure the region through the colonization of like-minded (i.e., anti-Native) Euro-American people. In this regard, Anglo-Americans fit the bill. Mexican officials also authorized Anglo-American colonization because they were excited about the possibility of developing the industries, commercial networks, and communities of the Northeast in ways that reflected their new nation's emphasis on liberal state building. Anglo-American colonization, it seemed, was the first step toward throwing off the legacies of the old, oppressive mercantilist policies of the Spanish colonial government. With the aid of Anglo colonists a new era of prosperity and political freedom lay on the horizon.

At first, Anglo-American colonists *did* help to realize this vision. Agricultural output and commerce increased exponentially in Texas, and many of the Hispanic residents of Texas cherished the new economic opportunities made available by their new Anglo-American neighbors. Moreover, Anglo-American colonists were willing, if not eager, to participate in anti-Native campaigns alongside their Mexican counterparts. But not all was copacetic in the colonial marriage of Hispanic and Anglo-American communities. Despite their shared enthusiasm for the vilification and exploitation of Black and Native people, by the middle years of the 1830s Hispanic and Anglo-American leaders had come to disagree on *how* to handle and subjugate these debased populations properly. To the Anglo-American colonists, Hispanic dealings with Native people had become too inconsistent and forgiving; unmanly capitulation and conspiracy, they believed, had become the qualities of the Mexican model. Just as troubling to Anglo-Americans, moreover, was the Mexican government's escalating insistence on regulating the violent exploitation of Black people. Believing that Mexican officials had known from the beginning that such violence was an integral part of their colonial program, Anglo-Americans felt betrayed and ultimately rebelled. From this perspective, the Anglo-American rebellion against Mexico in 1835 and 1836 represented the ultimate divergence of Mexican and Anglo-American monopolies on violence in the Texas borderlands. The ensuing Anglo-American victory spelled the ultimate doom of Hispanic dominion in the region.

Sowing the Seeds of Anglo-American Expansion, 1800–1820

While Spaniards pushed northward to reach Texas and Comanches headed south, Anglo-Americans cast their gaze to the West. The "West" had long been the Anglo-American frontier, where generations of prospective colonists and speculators had set their sights and hitched their fortunes, the eager residence of the Anglo-American settler colonial imagination. Events throughout the second half of the eighteenth century, especially the overthrow of British imperial rule, only seemed to embolden Anglo-American West-seekers, who came to see the West as a vast, open land that awaited their settlement.[3] Then, in 1803, the United States purchased the Louisiana Territory from France, which in turn unleashed a torrent of Anglo-American movement westward. Anglo-American colonists poured into the Lower Mississippi Valley from all over the Atlantic seaboard—from North Carolina, South Carolina, Virginia, Georgia, Maryland, New England, New Jersey, and Connecticut. Although regional and ethnic variations characterized many of these English-speaking colonists, they had much in common, as all arrived with hopes for future personal prosperity, and all had little to no regard for the territoriality and sovereignty of Native people. Thus, with the creation of each Anglo settler community necessarily came the potential for violence and disruption, and the cumulative effect of widespread Anglo-American relocation ultimately meant the mass displacement of Native communities.[4] But these were rarely the concerns of individual colonists. To them, the fertile soils of the West held promises of riches and success, if only they could seize it. So seize it they did. By 1820, nearly 300,000 agents of Anglo-American colonialism populated the Lower Mississippi Valley: 153,000 in Louisiana, 75,000 in Mississippi, and another 66,000 in Missouri.[5]

The transfer of so many Anglo-American people into the Native homelands bordering the eastern parts of Texas was the result of economic transformations both within and beyond the United States. By the end of the eighteenth century, developments in English textile manufacturing and a rising demand for cotton cloth, coupled with the invention of cotton seed removal (ginning) machines, had provided new incentives for crop producers in North America. Across the United States (but particularly in South Carolina, Georgia, and the Mississippi Valley), cash-crop cultivators switched from tobacco to cotton, and almost immediately cotton production skyrocketed. Export statistics reflected this. In 1800, the United States exported seventy-three thousand bales of cotton; by 1820, the country was exporting ten times that amount. Moreover, it was that same year that the United States surpassed India in production output, becoming the world's leading producer of the crop.[6]

The mass production of cotton was not, however, the sole work of individual farmers and their families, nor was it the fruit of wage labor. The cotton industry thrived in the early nineteenth-century United States because Anglo-American slavers violently marshaled the productive capacities of enslaved Black people, converting their labor into the cash-crop commodity. Thus, slavery was at the heart of these economic transformations. In many respects, the system of slavery that Anglo-American people constructed by the start of the nineteenth century was not unique to human history. Anglo-American slavers, particularly those from the southern United States, drew heavily from Roman law and philosophy to fashion their form of slavery and based it on the idea that slaves were the chattel property of slave owners. But unlike ancient systems of slavery, Anglo-American slavery was unabashedly anti-Black; it was dependent upon the violent exploitation of African-descended people, whom Anglo-American slavers believed were inherently inferior, deserving of their condition as slaves.[7] Furthermore, Anglo-American slavery was linked to a larger globalized economic system that connected the production of cash crops and manufactured goods to the enslavement of Black people. In the context of Anglo-American westward movement during the first two decades of the nineteenth century, cotton-producing slavers thus positioned themselves to profit within this broader economic system. The fertile lands of the Mississippi Valley had proven ideal for cotton cultivation, and it did not take long for Anglo-American slavers to ponder the possibilities of expanding their cotton-oriented conquest farther westward. By 1820, Texas existed just beyond the cotton frontier.[8]

As it lurked ominously on the eastern margins of the Texas borderlands prior to the 1820s, the Anglo-American system of slavery indirectly influenced social, economic, and political circumstances in Texas. Although very few Anglo-American slaveholders and their slaves relocated to Texas prior to the 1820s, agents of Anglo-American colonialism laid the commercial and ideological groundwork for future endeavors. Anglo-American trade connections were especially important. Merchants like Philip Nolan had sought to exploit the vast horse herds that covered much of the Texas plains through trade as early as the 1790s, and with the Louisiana Purchase Anglo-Americans invested even more resources and manpower into the burgeoning trade in animals and goods. By 1820, a number of overland trade routes linked the people of the United States with Texas borderlanders, especially Comanche and Wichita traders. One such trade artery was constructed by Spanish–Anglo-American revolutionary filibusters during the early 1810s. After failing to oust Spanish imperial leaders from Texas in 1812, these Hispanic and Anglo-American rebels relocated to Natchitoches, where—with their strong commercial ties to New Orleans—they began trafficking various goods, including horses, mules, and guns, to and from Texas. Another prominent trade route, which ran "by way of the River Kansas to the Missouri," supplied Native people with arms and ammunition in exchange for horses, mules, and other Texas animals. Trade became so lucrative during the 1810s that entire communities of Native people relocated to nearby areas to profit more directly from the commerce. Thus by the 1820s, a great number of Yamparika Comanches had migrated to the Red River, where they traded with Anglo-American merchants alongside their Kotsoteka counterparts.[9]

To an extent, both Comanche and Anglo-American slaving systems contributed to these thriving trade networks. Within the United States, slaveholding cotton farmers benefited from the healthy supply of draft animals, and within Comanchería Comanche slavers discovered novel, if not familiar, incentives for slaving. As before, Comanches found willing buyers of slaves and the goods they produced (or cared for) among the traders of Louisiana, which in turn offered Comanche slavers new opportunities to profit from slave raids elsewhere. Greater access to eastern markets corresponded with a vast growth in Native livestock acquisition, horse herding, and skin manufacturing in general. Even though such activities were nothing new to Native communities, the increase in scale encouraged Native people to augment their slaving operations. This expansion was felt most poignantly during the second half of the 1810s, when Comanches and other Native rangers raided northern Mexico for over two thousand Hispanic men, women, and children.[10] Later observers would confirm these broader connections between Comanche slave raiding south of the Río Grande and the opening of the eastern markets: "The main cause of these [slave-raiding] atrocities is the iniquitous traffic carried on with some of the borderers, inhabitants of the State of Louisiana and its vicinity, who encourage these Indians, and purchase from them the fruits of their robberies."[11] Although Anglo-Americans were not directly responsible for slavery's seemingly exponential growth from 1800 to 1820 in Comanchería, the opening decades of the nineteenth century foreshadowed the immense gravitational pull of eastern commercial connections in Texas slavery's ascension from the 1820s through the 1860s.

One final trade network linked Texas to Anglo-American slavery prior to 1820: the illegal trade in enslaved Africans. The Texas Gulf Coast in particular served as an important region for the flow of enslaved Africans from the Atlantic to the United States. Located only three to five days away by boat from Cuba and other Caribbean slave-trading centers, the Texas Gulf Coast became an ideal spot for pirates and privateers to smuggle Black bodies from the Atlantic into the United States. Such slave-trading activities began during the 1810s, when anti-Spanish rebels established a base camp on Galveston Island. There these rebels recruited the services of various pirates, including the Frenchmen Louis Michel D'Aury and Jean Lafitte, to help launch attacks against Spanish strongholds in Mexico. These men were most successful when they turned their attention to the commercial vessels that sailed the nearby waters, which often carried dozens, sometimes hundreds, of enslaved Africans destined for the Euro-American colonial world. After stealing these slaving vessels, the rebels smuggled the African captives into Louisiana through the eastern Texas coast or New Orleans. When trafficking through Texas, slavers (such as the Bowie brothers, John J., Resin P., and James) marched the bondspeople from the coast to Lake Sabine, where they met other traders and planters who were eager to procure smuggled Africans at reduced prices. Everybody involved—except, of course, the commodified Black people—made plenty of profit, but the Bowie brothers especially made a fortune, earning over $65,000 in just two years of involvement. Although Texas may have been only a thoroughfare for enslaved Africans and slave smugglers during the period, the trading connections presaged a new era of Anglo-American slavery and economic integration.[12]

Thus by 1820, Anglo-American slavery had spread far west to the margins of Texas; it had infiltrated Native trade networks; and it had encouraged the smuggling of African bodies through Texas entry points. Anglo-American slavery was not, however, the predominant system of slavery in the region. With widespread Native dominion and a committed Spanish military and colonial presence, the central catalyst to Anglo-American slaveholder transplantation—access to fertile lands—stood squarely beyond the grasp of enterprising colonizers and slaveholders. Few Anglo-American people relocated to the Texas borderlands, and those who did were men on the move: traders, smugglers, administrative agents, criminals, and filibusters. Texas may have served as the edge of the rapidly developing cotton frontier, but European and Euro-American imperial geopolitical uncertainties—in addition to a profoundly adaptive trans-Mississippian Native resilience—left anxious cotton-producing speculators and slavers with few options but to wait and dream.

"The Texas Fever Prevails": Slavery and the First Wave of Anglo-American Colonization, 1820–1835

The Anglo-American conquest of Texas began with the blessings of the Mexican government. As discussed previously, petitions for planned settler colonization of Texas were nothing new for the bureaucrats of colonial Mexico, but the efforts of Moses Austin and his son Stephen Fuller would prove the most enduring. In late 1820, the elder Austin rode out for Béxar from Missouri with one gray horse, a mule, $50 in cash, and an enslaved Black man named Richmond. Moses was no stranger to Spanish colonial administration, as he had gained Spanish citizenship after procuring a land grant and license in Missouri (which at that time, in 1797, was part of the Spanish province of Louisiana). His experiences and connections proved vital immediately upon his arrival in Béxar on December 23. With the assistance of another enterprising foreigner with vast Spanish colonial connections, the Dutch Baron de Bastrop, Felipe

Enrique Neri,[13] the senior Austin convinced Spanish authorities of both the viability and the efficacy of a program of Anglo-American colonization. Spanish officials granted Austin his application on January 17, 1821.[14]

Moses Austin's colonization plan echoed those of earlier petitioners by fusing promises of "civilized," agricultural development with declared commitments to anti-Indian violence.[15] He made himself responsible for colonizing three hundred families who would "settle in this province [of Texas] . . . in the place best suited for the cultivation of cotton, wheat, sugar cane, corn, etc." He assuaged the fears of Anglo-wary officials by claiming that these prospective colonists were industrious and of "good character and conduct," who would "bind themselves by oath to take up arms in defense of the Spanish government." In other words, not only would agricultural settlement deter Indian influence by virtue of land confiscation and consolidation; Austin's colonists would be active in administering violence against Indians on behalf of the Spanish king.[16]

Unfortunately for the elder Austin, sickness prevented him from seeing his plans through. When Moses died in June 1821, Texas colonization fell to his son, who took up his father's mantle. Only weeks after Moses's passing, Stephen made his way to Texas, where he convinced Governor Antonio Martínez to reaffirm the broader vision of his father's colonization program, with important modifications. The younger Austin proposed a system of land distribution based on colonist status and gender, designating 640 acres per colonizing male head, with an additional 320 acres if married. Moreover, colonists would be allotted another sixty acres for each child and another eighty for each slave brought with them. The implications of Austin's modified plan were clear: Euro-American male-headed families *and* slaveholders were to receive privileged status in his new Texas colony.[17]

Stephen F. Austin's colonization program stirred up fellow expansionists. In October 1821, Austin had contracted with Josiah H. Bell for 2,080 acres of land "on the Brassos or Colorado." Several days later, William Kencheloe agreed to colonize several hundred acres of land and to build a mill in Austin's colony. By the end of the year, Austin had convinced fifty or more Euro-American families to relocate to his colony, and within another two months some fifty men were living on the Brazos River, with another hundred or so colonizing the Colorado River region with log cabins and cornfields.[18] Austin's colonization program would have progressed unimpeded had government officials in Monterrey not suddenly suspended his colonization grant, so during the spring of 1822

Austin headed south to Mexico City on a mission to save his colony. Once there he defended his enterprise by pointing out his colonists' collective commitment to anti-Indian campaigns, as well as the prospects of his people controlling the vast Native-Anglo trade that was crippling Mexico's North. His pleas found somewhat sympathetic audiences, and in the summer of 1822 José Antonio Gutierrez de Lara defended Austin's colonial vision before the Mexican Congress, tying the colonization impulse to a larger project of nation-building, conquest of the *indios bárbaros*, and the expansion of markets. His only reservation was the reality of Austin's stated commitment to protecting the slave property of his colonists, which in Gutierrez's view "dishonors the human race."[19]

Rising Mexican antislavery sentiment notwithstanding, the crisis-stricken Mexican national government ultimately sanctioned Austin's settler colonial project. Under Agustín de Iturbide's short-lived imperial regime, a colonization bill passed, allowing for the existence of slavery "for a moment in any form whatever," and by the middle of 1823 the Mexican Congress had confirmed Austin's colonization application. Then, in 1825, the state of Coahuila y Tejas, a recent administrative construct, passed its own colonization law, unleashing settler colonialism as never before. This official colonization program reflected the changing interests and outlooks of the new federal system enacted in Mexico, which attached the province of Tejas to Coahuila to create a single sovereign state. Specifically, it built off Congress's national colonization law by parceling out and administering its *baldíos*, or "vacant" lands, to settlers, who would "augment the population of its territory [and] promote the cultivation of its fertile lands, the raising and multiplication of stock, and the progress of the arts, and commerce." Although Mexican citizens were preferred, the state law allowed for foreign settlers, provided they could "prove their Christianity, morality, and good habits" in the pursuit of "any branch of industry." *Empresarios*, or land distribution agents, were to be in charge of gathering and organizing colonists, with the obligation of finding one hundred or more families per contract. State officials, moreover, put an emphasis on family settlement, especially families "whose sole occupation is cultivation of land," by offering extra land privileges. Just as important, the law was vague enough regarding the status of slavery's future in Texas: "The new settlers as regards the introduction of slaves, shall subject themselves to the existing laws, and those which may hereafter be established on the subject."[20] Fortunately for the slaveholders who intended to colonize Texas, Mexico's newest national law regarding slavery, which ostensibly prohibited the slave trade, did not make it clear if immigrating *with* one's slaves constituted a violation of this prohibition.[21] Suffice it to say that the state colonization law of 1825 opened the door to massive Anglo-American slaveholder settlement.

Immediately, a number of enterprising individuals sought out *empresario* contracts, many of whom were Anglo-American, and within one month the governor of Coahuila y Tejas had contracted for the colonization of 2,400 families.[22] Among these early *empresarios* were Haden Edwards, Green DeWitt, Frost Thorn, and James Wilkinson—all Anglo-Americans.[23] With their *empresario* contracts and help from various local newspapers across the United States, these men recruited both families and single men from across the United States, including Pennsylvania, New York, Massachusetts, New Hampshire, Ohio, Kentucky, Mississippi, North Carolina, South Carolina, and Virginia, but most seem to have come from Louisiana, Alabama, Arkansas, Tennessee, and Missouri.[24] Yet in an era in which U.S. public lands suddenly had moved beyond the purchasing capabilities of Anglo-American farmers, regional origins mattered less than the prospects of settler fortunes; scheming colonists perceived Mexican-claimed land in Texas as a proverbial gold mine waiting to be exploited.[25] James A. E. Phelps reported to Austin in January 1825 that excitement over Texas spread like a contagion: "The emigrating, or Texas fever prevails to an extent that your wishes would no more than anticipate—It has pervaded all classes of the citizens of this state [of Mississippi] and the adjoining."[26]

The acquisition of land, however, was not strictly the end goal of the prospective colonists. Land was valuable for the commodities it could yield, and for Anglo-Americans this often meant the production of cash crops like tobacco, sugar, and cotton. But in the minds of these colonists, agricultural production could not thrive without slave labor, so the importation of enslaved Black people became the central tenet of Anglo-American colonization.[27] Although not all of the colonists relocated alongside their slave property (and some, like Austin, had their doubts about the long-term viability of slavery), enslaved people had a notable presence both within the colonies and in the correspondence about colonization, where Austin and prospective Anglo-American colonists revealed their obsession with the legal situation of slavery in Texas.[28] In the short period from October to December 1824 alone, Austin received "more than a hundred letters from private citizens in the country, well known men of character who are inquiring whether the Government would allow free entry to Emigrants, particularly as to whether they will be permitted to bring their slaves." The way they saw it, successful Anglo-American colonization could not occur without their right to accumulate slave property.[29] And Austin concurred. In December 1824, he appealed to an influential Bexareño, claiming that Texas would not witness much Anglo-American immigration if the importation of Black slaves were to be outlawed. He suggested, "Let each colonist have full authority to bring in his slaves for his own use, which shall continue to be slaves here but protected from all violence from their masters by just and wise laws."[30] And to prove his commitment to protecting slaver entitlement to Black bodies, Austin codified slavery in his 1824 civil and criminal codes (especially Articles 10 through 14 of the criminal code) by setting penalties for anyone assisting fugitives, outlining punishments for slave criminality, and instituting a pass system to heighten slave surveillance.[31]

Ultimately Austin's advocacy and assurances, along with the general prospects of slave-based colonization, were enough to convince Anglo-American slavers to tie their future to the Texas project. By 1826, an estimated 1,357 Anglo-Americans had moved to Austin's colony, bringing with them 443 enslaved Black people (who accounted for about 25 percent of the total population). Of the sixty-nine families that owned slaves, Jared E. Groce's family owned ninety enslaved people, ten families owned eleven or more, and fifty-eight owned between one and eight bondspeople.[32] Within two years, the Anglo-American population in Austin's colony had grown to some 1,800 residents or more, with an unknown increase in the enslaved population, because, as Manuel de Mier y Terán remarked, the colonists "conceal the number."[33] By 1834, the numbers had become even more striking. San Felipe alone, the administrative center of Austin's colony, was now home to 2,500 residents, with an additional 400 people living on its margins. The entire Department of Brazos, which included both Austin's colony and that of Green DeWitt, consisted of some 10,100 individuals, of whom at least 1,000 were Black and enslaved.[34] And the Department of Brazos was not the only region to see a dramatic rise in Anglo-American slaveholder colonization; Nacogdoches, which Euro-Americans had abandoned entirely by the close of the 1810s, now touted a population of 3,500 individuals, with another 500 colonists living nearby. Like Austin's colony, Nacogdoches was administratively tied to other colonies, and together (collectively known as the Department of Nacogdoches) they had amassed a population of some 10,600 people. Of that total, about 1,000 were enslaved.[35]

In addition to forcing their slaves to accompany them to Texas, Anglo-American slavers quickly acquired slaves during or after their relocation

Table 2. Anglo-Texas population estimates, 1826–1834

Year	*No. of Anglo-American Colonists*	*No. of Enslaved Black Individuals*	*Total Population*	*Slave % of Total Population*
1826	1,357	443	1,800	24.6
1828	1,800	?	?	?
1834 (Austin Colony)	9,100	1,000	10,100	9.9
1834 (Nacog-doches)	9,600	1,000	10,600	9.4
1834 (Total)	18,700	2,000	20,700	9.7

Note: The population of enslaved people was probably much higher than Almonte's figure of 2,000. See Henry M. Morfit to John Forsyth, August 27, 1836, in U.S. Congress, *Public Documents*, vol. 1, nos. 14, 20; Campbell, *An Empire for Slavery*, 30–31.

to Texas, usually when land was deeded to them. The process by which Anglo-American colonists converted land acquisition into expansion of their slaveholdings moved quickly during the first decade and a half of Anglo colonization. For the entrepreneurial colonists of the lower Brazos River region, the vast tracts of land made available by Mexican officials offered a number of pathways to slave procurement: some purchased slaves with loans obtained with their land as collateral; others sold their land in exchange for cash to buy slaves; and still others directly exchanged their real property for slave property.[36] J. Tate, for instance, hoped to convert his future Texas landholdings into a sugar mill business built on and operated by Black slave labor. "If funds in negro slaves and mony could be obtained by a sale of the land," Tate explained to Austin in 1827, "it would certainly be favorable."[37]

The efforts of Anglo-American colonists to convert real property into human chattel reveal another key aspect of the system of slavery that developed during the early years of Anglo-American colonization in Texas: the slave trade. Scholars have had little success quantifying the domestic slave trade in Texas prior to 1836, but anecdotal evidence provides some clues regarding its nature.[38] As mentioned above, some slaveholders purchased their slaves during or immediately before their relocation to Texas. John Botts, for instance, seems to have acquired some thirty to forty slaves in 1823 when he made a stop at New Orleans, before heading to Texas. Others, however, purchased their slaves after spending some time in the Texas colonies. Such was the case for Asa Hoxey, who, in December 1832, wrote to Robert M. Williamson that he planned "to make a trip to Virginia for the purpose of adding to my Stock of Slaves." Others purchased Black bondspeople as slave traders made them available in Texas; some acquired slaves from other slavers living within Texas; and still others purchased slaves at reduced cost during estate sales.[39] Regardless of when and how slaveholders procured their slaves, the trade in enslaved Black people seems to have been alive and well on the eve of the Texas Rebellion in 1835. It was, after all, the Anglo-American "traffic in human flesh" that so disturbed Juan Nepomuceno Almonte during his visit in 1834.[40]

In addition to purchasing slaves from the United States, Anglo-American colonists acquired hundreds of enslaved Africans through Atlantic trade networks.[41] As previously mentioned, during the 1810s, Texas—particularly the Gulf Coast region—had become a popular staging ground for the trade in enslaved Africans. This trade in African captives, however, slowed considerably after 1821 until 1833, when a ship "laden with negroes recently from the African coast" arrived "direct from the Island of Cuba."[42] Over the next three years, vessels carrying hundreds of African people would continue to deposit them on the Texas coast, and by the end of 1836 Anglo-American Texas had partaken in the illegal importation of several hundred enslaved Africans.[43] The main difference between the trade of the 1810s and that of the 1820s and 1830s was the voracious market that now existed *within* Texas, which merited the attention of outside observers. José María Sánchez y Tapia, for instance, believed that of the 116 slaves owned by Jared Groce, "most . . . were stolen." Six years later, in 1834, Almonte reported "that an individual named [Benjamin Fort] Smith, an Anglo American settled in the [Department] of Brazos for about two years, brought into this country some fifty African slaves that he had purchased on the Island of Cuba for the purpose of cultivating his lands." Perhaps just as upsetting to the antislavery Almonte, however, was the slave trade's growing popularity: "It seems that other individuals are preparing to follow his example, and for this purpose they have sailed from New Orleans for the aforesaid island."[44]

"As Long as They Are Useful": Citizen-Building, the Slavery Question, and the Limits of Mexico-Directed Colonization, 1822–1835

Given the rapid advance of Anglo-American settler colonialism during the 1820s, it is easy to forget that Anglo-American colonization was intended to be only a small part of the larger Mexican equation of Texas settler colonial development. Other colonization programs—those carried out by "trustworthy" Mexican and European-born Catholics—were designed to receive the full extent of Mexican government support. The preference for Mexican and non-U.S.-born Catholics was expressed by Mexican administrators from the earliest days of planning and continued to be repeated well into the 1830s.[45] The logic was rather simple: families from Mexico and Europe did not have the same political and religious ties that Anglo-Americans had to Mexico's aggressive neighbor to the northeast. Moreover, Mexican officials believed that Catholicism was an effective medium for ethnic amalgamation and citizen building. As the Mexican Committee on Colonization theorized in 1822, "The marriages that would take place between the new settlers and the daughters of the country ought also to call your attention; for, since the grave obstacle of a difference in religion does not exist [among Catholics, American or foreign born], it is probable that these may be frequent."[46] Thus, Mexican officials were especially partial to prospective colonization agents—and their followers—who had cultural ties to Mexico and Catholic Europe.

To the delight of colonization advocates, a number of Mexican *empresarios* emerged during the first several years of renewed colonization. Martín de León, for instance, received a colonization contract in April 1824 to settle forty-one Mexican families on the lower Guadalupe River. Four years later, in November 1828, Miguel Ramos Arizpe obtained an *empresario* contract of his own, which covered the settlement of some eight hundred to one thousand square leagues of land along the northern margins of the Río Grande. Lorenzo de Zavala was another Mexican national who was placed in charge of colonizing hundreds of families, securing his contract in March 1829. And these men were not alone; other Mexican *empresarios* and land grantees, including Juan Dominguez, Juan Antonio Padilla, Vicente Filisola, and José Manuel Royuela, also sought to take advantage of the Texas colonization program.[47]

In general, however, Mexican-headed colonization operations saw little success. Zavala sold his grant rights not long after acquiring them. The other Mexican *empresarios*, such as Filisola, simply failed to find enough families to fulfill their contracts.[48] Only de León's colony, which was named Guadalupe de Jesús Victoria after the first president of Mexico, Guadalupe Victoria, proved successful. Although Jean Louis Berlandier would later refer to Victoria as a "mixed colony" with "Americans, Canadians, some Irish, Mexicans, etc.," the fifty or so original colonists who settled on the Guadalupe River under de León's grant were Mexicans from Cruillas, Tamaulipas. Yet Victoria grew slowly; by 1826, the colony consisted of only eighty-eight people, "among whom were to be numbered only three slaves." Matters apparently worsened in de León's colony over the next two years, and by 1828 the population had dropped to seventy individuals, with "a larger number of men than women, a constant phenomenon which all the budding colonies present." But by 1830, the colony had experienced renewed growth, with 238 people in residence. Most of the colonists were engaged in ranching—as Hispanic colonists had been doing for decades—and even during less prosperous times, such as the year 1828, the small settlement was still home to a respectable collection of animals: 523 head of large livestock, 150 head of small livestock, 58 horses, 70 mules, 159 mares, and about 400 pigs.[49] In any case, Victoria did not draw the same kind of agriculturally oriented colonists that the other, more eastern colonies had recruited, and very few Victoria residents invested in direct ownership of human chattels until after the Texas Rebellion, when Anglo colonists displaced and dispossessed many Hispanic locals.[50]

A few other non–Anglo-American colonial projects received the blessings of the Mexican government, and their colonies saw some success prior to the mid-1830s. The "Irish colony" of John McMullen and James McGloin, located near the Nueces River, was home to about six hundred colonists by 1834, and with its main town of San Patricio, the McMullen-McGloin colonists were said to be "animated with the certain prospect of plenty and independence."[51] Various German-born men, including Friedrich Ernst, also sought to establish colonies in Texas throughout the 1820s and 1830s.[52] In 1831 Ernst moved to Texas on his own, and over the next several years he would be one of the more active promoters of European colonization in Texas, eventually earning a reputation as "the father of immigrants." In Texas, Ernst built a tobacco plantation and lobbied for the establishment of the German-friendly town of Industry, which by 1860 became home to about 85 percent of Texas's total German population.[53] Nonetheless, to the consternation of Mexican officials,

Irish and German colonization occurred too slowly to offer much of an alternative to the burgeoning Anglo-American colonies.

Such was the state of Mexico's non–Anglo-American Texas colonization program in the 1830s. If at the heart of colonization was meant to be a process by which foreign colonists were incorporated en masse into the Mexican national body politic, Texas colonization was largely a failure. With thousands of Anglo-American colonists making their way to Texas during the 1820s, Texas was succumbing rapidly to the influences of foreign Euro-American people. The process, of course, was not entirely unilateral or unforgiving for the Hispanic people of Texas, but certain trends—specifically, rising Anglo-American population rates and increasing U.S. economic penetration—indicated a strong shift in Texas borderlands geopolitics. Yet, it is important to note that much of this shift was the result of Mexico's own doing. Various Mexican leaders across Coahuila y Tejas saw the changes wrought by Anglo-Americans in Texas as key to the broader transformation of the Mexican North and the nation at large. The decision to fuse together the destinies of Tejas and Coahuila as a single state—epitomized by a political alliance between Texas native Erasmo Seguín and Coahuilan politician Miguel Ramos Arizpe—demonstrated a larger Mexican commitment to incorporate *el norte* as a functioning component of an emerging modern, liberal Mexican nation.[54] As Ramos Arizpe understood the decision, "The Texas representative and I have agreed to unite our provinces and are of one mind about parceling out our *baldíos* in such a way that this policy will become a powerful lever working in favor of our two provinces."[55] From an economic perspective, a colonized Texas meant greater access to and production of goods and foodstuffs; from a geopolitical perspective, dense population centers translated into a stronger defense against Native frontier penetration and incursions.[56] Francisco Ruíz laid out the broader rationale in 1830: "I will not . . . cease to talk about the advantages, which, in my opinion, would result if we would admit hardworking, honest people, regardless of the country they come from, as you say, or from hell itself, as long as they are useful, for otherwise the country . . . will be inhabited only by Indians and wild beasts that will devour us. This is the truth. The truth."[57] In short, settler colonization promised a better, more secure way of life for Mexicans in Texas. After all, a "settled," commercially connected, and defensible Texas was what generations of Hispanic administrators had longed for—even if the agents of change were "from hell itself."

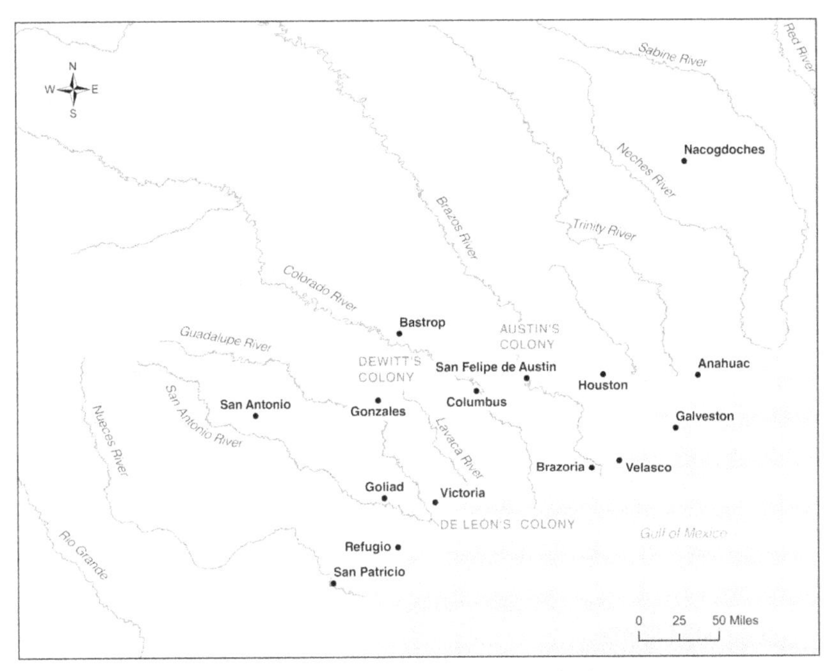

Map 7. Euro-American Texas, mid-1830s. Cartography by Luyang Ren.

And Mexican leaders had reason to be optimistic. A number of influential Anglo-American colonists, Stephen F. Austin in particular, had demonstrated a lukewarm commitment to a reinvigorated Hispanicization of Texas. From the moment he set foot in Mexican Texas, Austin made sure to forge meaningful relationships with local Euro-American elites. José Antonio Navarro, Erasmo Seguín, and Juan Nepomuceno Seguín were among the influential Hispanic men whom Austin befriended, and their close relationships illustrated the degree to which he sought to assimilate to Mexican culture.[58] Furthermore, Austin was a staunch supporter of bilingualism in Texas and frequently impressed upon his fellow Anglo-American colonists the importance of learning Spanish. Finally, Austin regularly repeated his dedication to maintaining Catholicism throughout Texas. He may not have always agreed with Mexican leaders and their policies, but he seems to have offered an honest effort to meet official expectations. At the very least, he represented the potential for a Mexican–Anglo-American synergy.[59]

Ultimately, however, geopolitical fears and general Anglo-American defiance undermined political tranquility in Texas. Gen. Manuel de Mier y Terán was among the most important to first sound the alarm of a budding Anglo-American usurpation of Texas.[60] He, along with Sánchez y Tapia and Berlandier, toured Texas in 1828 to assess the transformations wrought by Anglo-American colonization and to determine the best ways to secure Mexico's northern frontier.[61] What Terán and his followers found disturbed them. To President Guadalupe Victoria, Terán reported intransigent, rebellious Anglo-American colonists with strong political ties to their former homeland:

> If it is bad for a nation to have vacant lands and wilderness, it is worse without a doubt to have settlers who cannot abide by some of its laws and by restrictions that [the nation] must place on commerce. They soon become discontented and thus prone to rebellion and everything becomes graver still if those people have strong and indissoluble connections with a neighboring government that would be lacking in the fine moral qualities that characterize it if it looked with indifference, when necessary, upon the misfortunes of thousands of its subjects, who also would elicit the sympathy of their countrymen.

The situation was in fact dire, Terán warned; if Mexican officials did not act soon, "Tejas will pull down the entire federation."[62] News that U.S. representatives were conspiring to annex Texas only exacerbated such fears.[63]

The solution, as far as Terán was concerned, required three changes in government policy: (1) a greater militarization of Texas, (2) restrictions on Euro-American settlement near the U.S.-Mexico border, and (3) the suspension of all new Anglo-American immigration.[64] The first suggestion was the easiest to implement, and from 1830 to 1831 Mexican officials sent almost a thousand Mexican troops to garrison key military positions throughout Texas, at Nacogdoches, Galveston Bay, and a newly constructed fort on the Brazos River named Tenoxtitlán.[65] The second recommendation was much harder to enforce. To restrict Anglo-American settlement, Mexican officials could refuse, with little difficulty, the colonization proposals that sought to place Anglo-American families along the Louisiana-Texas border; they could not, however, compel violators to abide by such restrictions. The Louisiana-Texas border region had been home to a motley crew of squatters, runaways, criminals, and other unauthorized sojourners since the early years of the nineteenth century, and matters were only worsening by 1830.[66] Nonetheless, the military reinforcements sent to Texas helped to slow such unsanctioned Anglo-American encroachment, even though they could not enforce the restrictions entirely.

Terán's final recommendation proved to be the most difficult to realize—as well as the most divisive. It was, however, quite popular among authorities in Mexico City. President Anastasio Bustamante and Minister of State Lucas Alamán, two of the more powerful figures in national politics at the time, became strong advocates for putting an end to Anglo-American colonial expansion, and with their support Mexico's Congress passed a bill on April 6, 1830, making further Anglo-American immigration illegal and all unfulfilled *empresario* contracts void. National support notwithstanding, the Law of April 6, as it quickly became known, infuriated Anglo-Americans.[67] Sensing such anger, Austin felt compelled to write to the *Texas Gazette* in hopes of convincing the Anglo-American public of "the just and liberal views of the General [Mexican] Government."[68] Ultimately, Austin's call for acceptance, although conciliatory, was ineffective. Mexico's ostracism of prospective Anglo-American colonists, those who had planned to settle in Texas in the near future, would prove to be a source of animosity and conflict for the next several years.

But just as important, the legislation failed to stem the tide of Anglo-American colonial invasion. In fact, colonial encroachment seems to have accelerated after the law's passage. From April 1830 to October 1833 (when the law against Anglo-American immigration was repealed) the number of Anglo-American residents and their slaves doubled. In all, several thousand Anglo-Americans immigrated to Texas illegally during the first three-plus years of the 1830s, and with the resumption of legal Anglo-American colonization in 1834, the flood of Anglo-American settler relocation would reach unprecedented proportions, with an estimated one thousand Anglo-American colonists arriving each month.[69] Legal or not, the Anglos were coming.

The Law of April 6—which sought to restrict Anglo-Americans' commercial and social ties to their homeland—seems to have angered Anglo-Americans more than any other Mexican policies prior to 1835, except, perhaps, Mexico's frequent attempts to curtail Anglo-American slavery.[70] As previously mentioned, Mexican officials and national leaders generally had been reticent about slavery's future in Texas since the beginning of Anglo-American colonization. Although many were actively opposed to the institution, a good number saw it as a "necessary" evil, and still others supported it rather enthusiastically. Matters escalated in 1826, however, when Mexican leaders from the Northeast drafted a new Coahuila y Tejas state constitution. The earliest iteration of the constitution explicitly outlawed slavery in Article 13, which prohibited "absolutely and for all time slavery in all its territory," freeing immediately "slaves that already reside in the state."[71] Needless to say, the article excited the passions of Texas's Anglo-American colonists, and although Anglo-American leaders and their Mexican allies successfully lobbied constitutional delegates to change the antislavery language in the constitution from immediate to gradual emancipation, their victory was short-lived.[72] On September 15, 1829, President Vicente Guerrero commemorated Mexican independence by officially declaring the abolition of slavery throughout Mexico.[73] With Guerrero's proclamation, slavery no longer had legal standing in Texas.

In the years following abolition, Mexico's attack on slavery shifted toward enforcement of the new laws. When Juan Nepomuceno Almonte was charged with investigating the circumstances of Texas in 1834, for instance, his secret orders instructed him to encourage enslaved Black people to resist their Anglo-American slavers by "seeking refuge in the law." Moreover, Almonte was to convince "blacks, mulattoes, quadroons, and all others who are despised in the United States of the North" that the Mexican government was unprejudiced and open to their settlement. Yet, aside from offering his tacit support to the abolitionist Benjamin Lundy (and his efforts to create a colony of free African Americans), little came of Almonte's orders to exploit Black discontent in the Texas sphere.[74] In the end, the Mexican official would assist the enslaved people of Texas only through his rhetoric. As Almonte learned, by then the Mexican administrative capacity was much too weak and slavery much too entrenched in the Texas borderlands.

Exploited Kin: Masters and Slaves in Anglo-American Texas, 1820–1836

With the limited ability of the Mexican government to undermine and abolish slavery, the institution prevailed in Anglo-American Texas during the first decade and a half of colonization. Much of this had to do with Anglo-Americans' deep-seated commitment to the exploitation of Black people as they relocated from the United States to Texas, but the success of slavery was also the result of Anglo-American efforts to reframe the institution. The Anglo-American reframing of slavery was characterized by two discursive strategies: (1) a change in the de jure status of slaves (from *slaves* to *debt laborers* or *indentured servants*) and (2) a social redefinition of the slaver-slave relationship (from *slaver-slave* to *parent-child*). To an extent, the two strategies were contradictory: if slaves were to be understood as family members (who were bonded through social obligations), why was there a need to strike up contractual agreements (as was the case with debt laborers and indentured servants)? Of course, not all slavers forced their slaves to sign a contract with them, and not every slaveholder explicitly articulated the slaver-slave relationship as one of kinship; thus, many Texas slavers may not have viewed such strategies as contradictory. In any case, if a contradiction existed, it mattered not. In practice, enslaved people were neither employees nor family. They were, rather, integral figures of the Anglo-American colonial apparatus, and colonists were keen on exploiting them in Texas. As such, Anglo-Americans went to great lengths to assure slaves' continued presence throughout colonization—even if it meant morphing their institution into a system of slavery that suited the borderlands more than the strict, law-based society that many Anglo-Americans envisioned.

The campaign to convince Mexican officials that their bondspeople were actually not slaves but life-long contracted laborers was the most obvious attempt by Anglo-American colonists to skirt antislavery laws. The idea was hatched as early as July 1826 by Peter Ellis Bean in a letter to Austin. "Gow in Presens of and Alcalde," Bean suggested, "stating that this nigro cost you so much and when he Pays it by labor Don you have no charge against him he Discounts so much a month as any other hirid Persons a small sum so that he will be the same to you as Before." As fears of abolition worsened, Bean's strategy caught on. The *ayuntamiento*, or town council, of San Felipe de Austin petitioned state officials in March 1828 to recognize the legality of contracts between slaves and their employer-slavers, and on May 5, 1828, the state congress issued a decree in support of indentured servitude. A slave, the decree confirmed, could be converted into an indentured laborer if her slaveholder drew up a contract with the slave in front of a public notary, indicating that the slave was free upon entering Texas but bound to her slaver until paying off the debt from the cost of her original purchase, relocation, and daily subsistence. Moreover, the children of this indentured laborer were to serve the slaver until the age of twenty-five, and then at that age they had their *own* debts to pay off. Slaveholders rejoiced at the legal acceptance of this strategy. "[I] am induced to believe the Law will be of great service to this Country," Frost Thorn argued upon learning of the state decree. "It has made a material change in the feelings of many valuable Emigrants and I will have it published in N. Orleans, that it may have publicity in the U.S."[75]

More subtle than the legal rebranding of slavery were Anglo-Americans' claims that their slaves were part of their family. This argument was made as early as 1824 and was advanced by the most influential people of Austin's young colony. On June 5 that year, the leaders of Austin's colony held a general meeting to discuss the news that the Mexican national government hoped to restrict or abolish slavery in Texas. Five days later, a committee, which included Austin, Jared Groce, James Cummings, and John P. Coles, forwarded to Mexico's Congress an appeal from the Anglo-American colonists. In it the committee explained both the importance of their slaves' labor to "civilizing" the Texas wilderness and their supposedly intimate relationships with them: "These Inhabitants respectfully represent to your sovereignty that the Slaves introduced into this establishment by the emigrants were not brought here for the purpose of Trade or speculation neither are they Africans but are the family servants of the emigrants and raised by them as such from their infancy and were intended to aid in clearing the Land and establishing their farms which these Colonists Could not have effected without them for this Province is entirely uninhabited and great Labor required in Opening farms."[76] Even though they could not deny the economic underpinnings of their slaveholding, the Austin colonists made an emotional appeal: slaves and their slavers had family connections that would be threatened by abolition.

But was this claim regarding the kin ties of slaves strictly rhetorical? Or was the family unit *actually* a means by which Anglo-American colonists structured their lives with respect to their slaves? These are difficult questions to answer definitively, especially when we consider the fact that the voices of enslaved people were significantly muted, thrashed out of existence, under the violence of slavery. Nonetheless, available evidence makes it apparent that the metaphor of family resonated on multiple levels for both Anglo-American colonists and their Mexican hosts when it came to slavery. In other words, for our analytical purposes, it does not matter if Anglo-American slavers believed that their slaves were family in the same way that they believed their biological mothers, fathers, sisters, brothers, and children were family (although in some cases their slaves *were* biological kin); what matters is that Anglo-American slaveholders deployed and acted on the metaphor and that Mexican locals and officials interpreted the metaphor according to their own frameworks, expectations, and motives. Moreover, it is worthwhile to consider how an Anglo-American commitment to the slave-as-kin metaphor circumscribed the experiences of Black people under slavery. By no means did enslaved individuals have to accept slaveholder impositions of the family metaphor willingly; at times, however, it could offer them ways to mitigate their suffering as enslaved, subjugated people.

Rhetorically, the slave-as-kin claim was a shrewd strategy for Anglo-American colonists seeking to placate the concerns of suspicious Mexican officials. From day one, Mexican (and Spanish) colonization schemers believed that it was imperative that the colonization of Texas be carried out by families, not single men.[77] The family unit—which was headed by both husband and wife—had been the central building block of Hispanic communities for centuries and remained a chief instrument in the propagation of Hispanic society elsewhere.[78] Nothing expressed this sentiment clearer than Emperor Iturbide's colonization law of 1823. In it Mexican officials spotlighted families as the prime agents of colonization: families were to be sought out by *empresarios*; families were allowed to emigrate on their own; "the union of many families at one place, shall be called a village, town or city"; "a sufficient number of families" was required before a local government was to be established; *empresarios* were rewarded for recruiting families; and foreigners could become citizens of Mexico upon marriage into families. And other colonization laws would continue to emphasize the importance of the family unit in the colonization of Texas. The 1825 state colonization law, for instance, offered more land to married men than to unmarried men.[79] Thus, when Anglo-American colonists claimed that their slaves were part of their family, they were making an appeal to Mexican expectations of a family-based colonization program. As far as they were concerned, their slaves fit well within the Hispanic model of colonial community building.

Moreover, the slave-as-kin metaphor was an idea to which the local Hispanic populations in the Texas borderlands could relate. For a century, Spaniards in Texas had made claims that their slaves were members of their family, and although slavery may have faded as a widespread domestic tradition in Hispanic Texas on the eve of Anglo-American colonization, former and current slaveholders and their families still lived in Texas during the 1820s and 1830s. The widely disseminated radical ideologies of the Independence era may have converted some to the antislavery cause, but much more influential than budding antislavery sentiments were calls for liberalizing economic practices in the region.[80]

Mexican residents in Texas wanted little more than to extend their trade reach to include not only the rest of Mexico but also parts of the United States and even Europe. Slave labor—as their Anglo-American neighbors were reminding them—could be a major contributor to the vibrancy of those commercial connections. Erasmo Seguín recognized as much when he wrote to Austin in 1825, "The great development of your colony, and of the other colonies of Texas, depends among other things, upon permitting their inhabitants to introduce slaves." Furthermore, the fact that a sizable number of Mexican residents personally chose to invest in enslaved Black people during the 1820s and 1830s suggests that a universal disdain for slavery did not exist among the Hispanic people of Texas. Instead, it is likely that a significant portion of the Mexican population saw slavery as an acceptable institution for enhancing the economic prosperity of Texas.[81] Anglo-American people did not invent slavery in Texas, and they certainly were not the first to articulate its structure by using metaphors of kinship.

But the slave-as-kin metaphor was not solely a borderlands adaptation to the local circumstances of Texas. When James F. Perry expressed concern over the fact that his "whole family white and black have been sick," he drew from a White southern tradition of what scholars have referred to as slave master paternalism.[82] Paternalism was an ideology that attempted to obscure the violence of slavery in the nineteenth-century South by claiming that a sense of benevolence undergirded slaveholder relations to their slaves. According to this framework, slavers were bound to care for their slaves as a father was obligated to care for his children. In exchange, enslaved people were to offer to their slaver-parent their labor, dedication, and fidelity. With the slaver as the central paternal figurehead, the slaver-slave relationship took the form of a familial relationship. Slaveholder paternalism seems to have been especially popular among small slaveholding yeomen farmers, who, as Stephanie McCurry has argued, "were defined, above all else, by the social relations of the household, and particularly by the necessity of family labor."[83] Thus, it was neither contradictory nor peculiar in the eyes of most slavers to associate family with labor. And as many early Anglo-American Texas slaveholders owned no more than several slaves, we might even assume that some actually convinced themselves that their slaves were their children and therefore supposedly deserving of parental guidance, rewards, and punishments.[84]

Slaveholder paternalism need not be understood, as some scholars have argued, as the absolute governing framework by which enslaved Black people and their Anglo-American slavers interacted.[85] Certainly, adherence to the fiction that slavers were caring providers may have offered some enslaved people opportunities to enhance their day-to-day lives, just as explicitly refuting a slaver's claims to paternalistic benevolence may have resulted in punitive violence. But paternalism did not account for the entirety of life experiences under slavery. For slaveholders, it was one way to naturalize an inherently violent and unnatural process: the continued exploitation and subjugation of a stigmatized outsider. For enslaved people, it was but one of many ways to interface with and to interpret the conditions of enslavement. At times paternalism hinted at the human connections fostered by close proximity and the shared experiences of transplanted life in an unstable, foreign world. Most of the time, however, it represented attempts "to reconcile the contradictions of the master-slave relationship" and the perverted logic of the violence that slavers imposed upon their exploited, debased bondspeople.[86] In this way, Anglo-American slavers were not too different from their Hispanic slaving predecessors, who also sought to incorporate enslaved people as family in an effort to mask the violence of their condition as slaves.

Moreover, like their Hispanic predecessors, Anglo-American slaveholders sometimes took the slave-as-kin metaphor literally; that is to say, Anglo-American slavers made families with enslaved people through coercive sexual encounters. In his study of the Brazos River Valley, Sean Kelley discovered that "quite a few Anglo men had long-term sexual and even emotional relationships with women who were enslaved to them." One such man was Columbus R. Patton, who was well known for his affair with one of his slaves, Rachel. Apparently, Rachel was Patton's most prized slave, as he regaled her with fancy clothing and permitted her to sit with him in the Whites-only section at church. Moreover, Patton, who owned a sugar plantation and more than fifty enslaved people, even entrusted Rachel with running certain matters on the plantation, including the violent chastisement of bondspeople.[87] Other evidence of Anglo-American colonists making literal kin of their slaves lay in the enslaved biracial men, women, and children who dotted the Anglo-American Texas landscapes, their physiognomic features bespeaking slaver sexual violence.[88]

The fact that Anglo-American slaveholders forcefully made literal family out of their slaves points to the central aspects of Anglo-American slavery in Texas: violence. Supposed family member or not, enslaved Black people were subject to both the threat and the administration of extreme violence. Outside observers who traveled across Anglo-American Texas frequently commented on slaveholder violence. Noah Smithwick, for instance, remembered an incident in which the son of slave owner John McNeal shot dead one of his father's slaves, Jim, after he "threw down his hoe" and walked away from him. During his 1828 tour of Texas, Terán observed all sorts of "barbarities" committed against enslaved people: "[Slaveholders] pull their teeth, they set dogs upon them to tear them apart, and the mildest of them will whip the slaves until they are flayed." His traveling compatriot, Sánchez y Tapia, also claimed that the Anglo-Americans he encountered "treat [their slaves] with considerable harshness." Sánchez y Tapia was especially unforgiving in his remarks about Jared Groce, whom he believed "treats his slaves with great cruelty." Anglo-American slaver violence at times reached atrocious proportions. In 1835, Anglo-Americans themselves admitted as much when one colonist reported that dozens of enslaved Black people were "whipd nearly to death" after authorities determined that they were plotting to rebel.[89] In Anglo-American Texas, violence and slavery were inseparable.[90]

Enslaved people also suffered from extreme stigmatization—or "bitter prejudices," as Benjamin Lundy described it.[91] As was the case in Hispanic Texas, in Anglo-American Texas anti-Blackness prevailed: to be Black was to be cursed with social inferiority and fungibility. But bearing Blackness was a much less contested process in Anglo-American Texas than it was in Hispanic Texas. While Afro-Mexican residents could challenge accusations of their *negro*-ness in court (and were less likely to be enslaved simply based on their perceived race), *any* sign of personal Blackness, whether related to physiognomy or known heritage, put inhabitants in Anglo-American Texas at risk for ostracization, violence, and even enslavement. The practice of enslaving legally free Black people had a long history in North America, and little changed when Anglo-American colonists transplanted their slavery to Texas. Even men with supposedly "light skin," such as William Goyens, were subject to illegal enslavement.[92] But the danger of reenslavement was only one consequence of anti-Blackness in Anglo-American Texas. Anti-Blackness was written into the law and extended even to matters *among* Black people. Enslaved people in Anglo-American Texas, for instance, were not permitted to marry, and slave families were not legally recognized. These restrictions had everything to do with the property status of slaves: marriage tied enslaved people to specific geographical and social contexts, which necessarily curtailed slavers' rights to sell or trade their slave property at will. In the Anglo-American slave system, the property rights of slaveholders always trumped the personal prerogatives of bondspeople. Furthermore, the legal denial of marriage and family life to enslaved Black people reinforced their status as legally nonsocial entities. In both the Mexican and Anglo-American structures of government, marriage was a central feature of citizenship; without the legal ability to marry, enslaved people were not to be considered part of the body politic.[93] In Anglo-American Texas, colonists believed that Black people were, by definition, part of an enslaved class, whose primary function was to enhance the productive capacity of Anglo-American families. For a Black person to operate outside of that governing framework (i.e., the male-headed White family) was to live precariously—if not in perpetual terror.

The slave trade exacerbated anti-Blackness in Anglo-American Texas. As previously mentioned, scholars have had great difficulty estimating the extent of the slave trade in Texas prior to 1836, but scholarly uncertainty regarding statistical calculations should not be cause for dismissal of the slave trade's influence on the day-to-day dynamics of Anglo-Texas slavery. First and foremost, the selling and buying of people destroyed families and friendships by ripping child from parent, lover from lover, brother from sister, and friend from friend. But the slave trade also reinforced the fungibility of Black bodies, because on the slave market Black people became replaceable, ever-exchangeable commodities, with a price that fluctuated according to the shifting desires and imperatives of slavers. And as Walter Johnson has demonstrated, enslaved people were acutely aware of their commodification, the reality that their bodies existed as vessels of slaver imagination.[94] In Anglo-American Texas, the propertied nature of slavery and the prevalence of a slave market guaranteed that enslaved individuals constantly worried about the possibility of being sold away from friends and family. Undoubtedly, many slaveholders manipulated those fears to their advantage through explicit threats and orchestrated spectacles of violence.[95]

A prominent slave trade would serve as one of the defining features of Anglo-American slavery in Texas, especially when compared to the slaving systems of Hispanic and Comanche people. While both Comanche and Hispanic people were active and willing slave traders, their systems of slavery were also sustained by the slave raiding of other nearby communities; thus, the process of enslavement differed significantly for slavers and the enslaved. In the Comanche and Hispanic contexts, slavers were more often directly involved in the process of forcefully removing enslaved individuals from their communities of origins. There was a geopolitical context to the initial act of enslavement, and this accounted for notable differences in the structuring of life as an enslaved person. Escape, for instance, offered the real possibility of returning to one's family or community of origin, and diplomacy—although rarely successful—sometimes resulted in the freeing of enslaved kinspeople. In Anglo-American Texas, the slave trade made it more likely that bondspeople would have to suffer from the process of displacement and community relocation multiple times throughout their (usually young) lives. And with each exchange, enslaved people were pulled farther and farther away from their places of origin. It is difficult, if not fundamentally impossible, to imagine the kind of psychological damage caused by such continual reenslavement and reconditioning, but there can be no doubt that it existed. The slave trade made life under Anglo-American slavers highly oppressive and disorienting.[96]

Yet physical and psychological violence at the hands of slavers entailed only part of the abuse inherent to slavery. For Anglo-Americans in Texas, slavery functioned as a labor system—a means to realizing economic prosperity in a supposedly untamed, wild land. As such, land clearing stole the time and energy of many enslaved people during the early years of Anglo colonization. As Terán observed in 1828, enslaved people were vital instruments in the taming of the so-called Texas wilderness, which included "forests so thick that only with *negro* labor can they be cleared." Terán himself witnessed such tree clearing: "All over this country they use the word *cincho* for a big stretch of thick trunks from which they have stripped the bark, epidermis, etc., until they leave the bare wood, wherein, the tree, being deprived of the vessels through which its juices pass, dies and rots within a few years." Killing trees by stripping them bare was but one method by which enslaved Black laborers cleared the land. Some cleared terrain by setting fire to the timber and brush, while others worked in gangs to chop down the many trees that covered prime agricultural lands.[97]

Land clearing was the prerequisite to crop cultivation. Once enslaved people had cleared their slavers' lands of intrusive trees and brush, most were forced to work hard tilling the land and planting crops.[98] Although the early generation of enslaved people first cultivated corn for food production, it was typically the ultimate aim of Anglo-American slaveholders to develop their land for the production of cash crops like cotton and sugar. It made sense for early Anglo-American colonists to invest in corn production before cotton, because the colonial markets in Texas—foodstuffs included—had been terribly limited for decades. Colonial restrictions on trade and frequent Native raids had made commerce in food commodities a risky business, so when Anglo-American farmers arrived in Texas during the 1820s they found an urgent demand for such basic food commodities across the region, not just within their colonies. The frontier markets in foodstuffs, nevertheless, paled in comparison to the great transatlantic markets in cotton, which, for Anglo-American slavers, promised great fortune and prosperity.[99]

And cotton fortunes *were* made in Texas.[100] Jared Ellison Groce was probably the most successful and well-known cotton-producing slaver in Texas prior to 1836. Born in Halifax County, Virginia, in 1782, Groce took a long and circuitous path to Texas. Throughout his early life, he moved from southern state to southern state, amassing substantial real and human property along the way, until finally reaching the Brazos River Valley in January 1822 with ninety enslaved Black people. There, just south of present-day Hempstead, Texas, Groce forced his slaves to build a plantation, known eventually as Bernardo Plantation. Soon Bernardo Plantation became a money-making machine. There and elsewhere, enslaved people harvested "much cotton, which they comb [gin] in a water mill used for grinding cornmeal." According to Terán, Groce's slaves had harvested quite the bounty, with "more than 400 quintals of cotton . . . being dispatched for Orleans" at the time of his visit in May 1828. By January the following year, Groce's slaves, "whose estimated worth is 100 thousand pesos," reportedly had produced six hundred bales of cotton for market, each weighing some five hundred pounds. Even if these estimates were inflated, it is evident that enslaved Black people catapulted Groce to unprecedented wealth.[101]

But not all slavers needed to own dozens of slaves to exploit their labor successfully in Texas. John Williams, a native of Tennessee, impressed Terán with his wealth despite his small slaveholdings: "He enjoys some prosperity, to judge by the agricultural assets he has accumulated through his own industry and the labor of two or three slaves." Others, such as the residents of Nacogdoches, drove their slaves to produce less profitable crops like corn, beans, squash, watermelons, cantaloupes, *chiles*, and potatoes.[102] Regardless of their choice in crop, many Anglo-American colonists believed that slave labor was necessary to cultivate anything at all. In Anglo-Texas, the road to prosperity was paved by the extraction of labor from enslaved Black bodies.

Even when enslaved Black people were not actively engaged in land clearing or agricultural production, they contributed to the vitality of the budding Anglo-American colonies in other ways. A number of enslaved people, for instance, seem to have been assigned labor related to transportation, such as ferry rowing, loading and unloading merchant goods, and shipping.[103] Enslaved Black people, moreover, worked alongside their slavers in various artisan and craft fields; twenty-two-year-old Nosere and eighteen-year-old Andrés, for instance, labored in the household of the blacksmith James Boulter.[104] Even the aforementioned William Goyens, "a light-skinned mulatto businessman," exploited slave labor in his blacksmith shop. According to an 1835 census, Goyens lived with his wife, two children, and six Black slaves: Sallie, Louisa, Juliana, Haire, John, and James.[105] But merchants, coachmakers, and blacksmiths were not alone in stealing the time and energy of enslaved Black people; mechanics, like twenty-seven-year-old E. F. Hanks, sometimes included slaves in their workshops as well.[106]

In short, Black slave labor kept the economic engines of Anglo-Texas firing during the 1820s and early 1830s. Most Anglo-American colonists, unlike their Hispanic predecessors, entered Texas with vast commercial connections to highly profitable markets in the East, and upon arrival they immediately exploited Texas lands for the purpose of producing cash crops and other highly coveted commodities.[107] Steadily, the commercial output of Anglo-Texas rose. In 1828, cotton output from Austin's colony amounted to several hundred bales. By 1831, it was well over a thousand bales. According to Almonte, in 1833 the Department of Brazos exported some two thousand bales of cotton, "each bale about 400 or 500 pounds," and in 1834 "there were not less than five thousand" bales exported. Terán could not hide his admiration for the Anglo-American economic system that had emerged across Texas by 1828: "Industry in this colony is outstanding, not only in the cultivation of the land for the harvesting of cotton and other cereals except wheat, and for raising cattle, but also in artisanry. They make wool and cotton textiles of fair quality; they have machines to gin cotton and to saw lumber to make planks. They sell their products in Béjar, La Bahía, and Nacodoches, and they also go to the sea by the Brazos River."[108]

As productive as enslaved African Americans were in Texas, they were not simply passive instruments of colonial development. Instead, enslaved Black people responded to their condition as slaves in a number of ways. Some, like the slaves of Francis Berry, took advantage of the Anglo-American colonies' proximity to the rest of Mexico—where residents were generally more vigilant in enforcing antislavery legislation—by running away "to the Spaniards."[109] Others escaped the violence of their slavers by fleeing to Native country, although their experiences there probably varied considerably based on the values, priorities, and labor systems of their host Native communities.[110] And on at least a handful of occasions, enslaved Black people attempted to rise up in revolt against their Anglo-American slavers. The arrival of Mexican troops in 1835 and 1836 during the Texas Rebellion, for instance, inspired a handful of slave insurrection conspiracies, and Anglo-American colonists often feared that a slave revolt was inevitably lurking around the corner.[111] When direct resistance proved to be an untenable option, however, bondspeople sometimes sought out other opportunities for freedom, as Tomas Morgan did in 1834, when she "purchased her freedom with the proceeds of her own labor."[112]

Most, however, just tried to minimize their suffering and live as best as they could under the oppression of slavery. One common way to cope with slavery was to build meaningful relationships with other enslaved people. Although families that existed outside of the slaveholder family structure were not legally recognized, enslaved people struggled mightily to keep together the families they did make. In 1837, for instance, a group of eight hired-out enslaved men refused to work when they realized that they were being tricked into separating from their spouses. Others found meaning in the nonfamilial relationships they forged with their enslaved counterparts, some of which would have been structured by the various African cultural customs that they brought with them to Texas. The influence of the illegal slave trade in African people would have contributed to this phenomenon. Both Sánchez y Tapia and Berlandier, for instance, commented on the "expressive" singing of three African-descended rowers whom they encountered during their tour of Texas in 1828. The men probably were not related, but their sense of cultural commonality would have offered them some comfort, especially as their use of a non-European language offered them space to communicate independent of the watchful eye of slaver society.[113]

As in Hispanic Texas and Comanchería, enslaved people in Anglo-Texas experienced slavery in a multitude of ways. Yet, the structures of Anglo-American society—specifically, slaveholder property rights, an agriculture- and market-oriented infrastructure, and a racially homogeneous enslaved population—made life under Anglo-American slavery notably different from enslaved life within Hispanic or Comanche communities. The slave trade stands out as especially oppressive in Anglo-American Texas, although it may have operated with some similarities in Comanche and Hispanic society. Moreover, slave labor clearly was tied to agricultural development, and the slave production of agricultural commodities, particularly cotton, contributed to both individual slaveholder and Anglo-American community prosperity. Finally, the lines between slaver and the enslavable were much more definitive. Blackness was more than just a social stain in Anglo-Texas; it was a liability that could result in the enslavement or reenslavement of legally free people, as well as a daily reminder of slave fungibility. This meant that avenues to a meaningful freedom were severely limited.

But slavery in Anglo-Texas was not entirely unique. Just as it was in Hispanic and Comanche society, violence was at the heart of the slaver-slave relationship. Sometimes Anglo-American slaveholders forced incredible physical violence against their slaves; at other times they traumatized their slaves through psychological affliction. Similarly important was the fact that slaves *always* lived under the threat of violence; even if it appeared gratuitous to some, violence was the modus operandi of Anglo slavery. And like Comanche and Hispanic slavers, Anglo-American colonists employed metaphors and processes of kin to help naturalize the innately violent relationship between slave and slaver. Patriarchs were the rulers of households and communities; enslaved people may have resided at the very bottom of these hierarchies, but Anglo-American men—like Comanche and Hispanic slavers—believed that they belonged to these hierarchies nonetheless.[114] And although the slave-as-kin metaphor may have been chiefly imaginary, it certainly framed much of the Anglo-American imagination.

Anglo-Mexican Manliness and the "Indispensable Campaigns against the Savages," pre-1836

The economic, political, and cultural ascension of Anglo-American slavers in the Texas borderlands ushered in yet another era of slavery, but like the earlier iterations of borderlands slavery in Texas, the violence of slavers during this period did not operate in a vacuum. Colonization itself was a program initiated only with the blessings of Mexican government officials and local community leaders. Furthermore, Native people still controlled vital resource domains throughout the region, and their presence only seemed to be growing, as tens of thousands of displaced Native people, including Cherokees, Choctaws, Creeks, Seminoles, Alabamas, Coushattas, Kickapoos, Delawares, Shawnees, and others, made their way to the Texas borderlands from various parts of the United States.[115] Although Anglo-Americans often characterized Texas as a vast virgin land that was ripe for the taking, their sudden colonial intrusion into the homelands of various Native peoples set the stage for immediate, violent confrontation. To the Anglo-American newcomers, settler colonization demanded the clearing—the annihilation—of Native people from the land.[116] Fortunately for them, the Hispanic people of the borderlands were similarly invested in such an endeavor and early on would be all too willing to lend a hand in the persecution of Native people. Not surprisingly, violence against Native communities would be the principal means by which Hispanic and Anglo-American colonists collaborated and shared in the broader experience of a rejuvenated settler colonialism.[117]

For those willing to recognize the actual geopolitics of the Texas borderlands, the situation by the 1820s must have been sobering, especially as it belied Anglo representations of an "empty" Texas. San Antonio and La Bahía, for instance, remained Hispanic strongholds, with population figures hovering between 1,500 and 2,400 people at San Antonio and between 600 and 700 at La Bahía. To the west of San Antonio and ranging from the San Sabá River south to the Río Grande were communities of Lipan Apaches, totaling about 1,000 people. Along the Gulf Coast, 1,000 or so Karankawas remained entrenched as the principal inhabitants of the vast strip of land stretching (roughly) from the Brazos River to the Nueces River. Just north of the Karankawa communities were bands of Tonkawas numbering about 1,500, who during the nineteenth century had abandoned their decades-long hostility toward Ndé people and had become one of their more important allies in Texas. North of the Tonkawas were various Wichita communities—still agriculture-based and commerce-oriented—stationed near the Trinity, Brazos, Colorado, and Red Rivers. The principal Wichita groups consisted of some 2,000 Taovayas, 900 Wacos, 200 Kichais, and another 600 Tawakonis, together accounting for around 3,700 people. Finally, Caddos—among the longest tenured people in the Texas borderlands—were spread out into two main groups across the central and northeastern river valleys of Texas. Sadly, the warfare, epidemics, and economic changes resulting from the past century and a half of colonization had been particularly devastating for the Caddo people of the Texas borderlands: numbering as many as 40,000 during the late seventeenth century, their total population had dwindled to some 300 families by the 1820s.[118]

Much of Texas Native country, of course, also included Comanchería, and during the 1820s and 1830s the 7,000 to 8,000 or so Comanches living in the Texas sphere maintained their pronounced influence across the region. Although Comanchería underwent significant changes during this period, the core of Comanche society remained intact and influential. As Pekka Hämäläinen has argued, during the 1820s and 1830s Hispanic Texas reverted to its earlier status as a "colonial appendage" of Comanchería. In exchange for peace, Comanches reestablished their system of tribute extraction, collecting gifts from Hispanic residents at San Antonio and Nacogdoches. And just as before, when the trade proved insufficient or disadvantageous to Comanches, they extracted their supplies by other means—that is, through horse thefts, slave raids, and individual attacks.[119]

Slavery also remained an important component of Comanche society. The slave raiding of the 1810s actually expanded during the 1820s and 1830s, and even though the main Hispanic communities in the Texas borderlands—San Antonio, Nacogdoches, and La Bahía—managed to escape the brunt of Comanche slave-raiding violence, the flow of slaves into Comanchería increased steadily. During the period, most slave raids occurred near or beyond the Río Grande, as was the case in 1820, when Dionisio Santos, Fernando González, and about two dozen other children were stolen from their community at Lampazos, Nuevo León. Some slave raids, like the one experienced by these unfortunate children, resulted in the enslavement of dozens of individuals, but most seem to have ended in the enslavement of no more than several individuals.[120] In any case, by the late 1820s Comanche slaves numbered in the several hundreds if not thousands. These enslaved people, "who are forced to perform all the work," undoubtedly contributed to the economic well-being of Comanchería.[121] Their robust presence within Comanche communities was evidence of Comanches' continuing ability to exercise incredible military and geopolitical power across the region.

The broad influence of Native people in the Texas borderlands meant that Anglo-American colonization necessarily disrupted the status quo of the region. But most Anglo-American colonists failed to recognize this reality, or they framed their disruptive operations as a natural part of the "development" of a vast wilderness. Clearly self-serving, Anglo-American interpretations of their colonial project provided an ideological foundation for the persistent use of violence against Native communities, as their characterization of Texas as "an entire and howling wilderness" prior to colonization allowed the colonists to view their own activities as benevolent, righteous, and providential.[122] Thus, Native resistance to Anglo-American colonization was, in the Anglo mind, necessarily the work of "marauding savages" with no appreciation for "civilized" life. By default, the Indian was the enemy, the menace, and the Anglo-American the hero, the redeemer.

Anglo-American slaver-colonists brought with them to Texas cultural traditions that buttressed their collective sense of settler colonial prerogative. On the one hand, Anglo-Americans drew from a centuries-long history of violently displacing Native communities in the service of carving out purportedly autonomous, self-contained colonies of settlers. The "march of progress," as they saw it, dictated a continuous and inevitable westward expansion of White settler communities, at the expense of Indigenous people, who were little more than obstacles to overcome.[123] On the other hand, with many Texas colonists arriving from the southern portions of the United States, Anglo-American newcomers also carried with them a unique set of ideas about honor and manhood. Nineteenth-century White southerners were a rather self-conscious people, and their perceived image was integral to their identity. At the center of this image was the glorification of personal valor; White southern men believed that they were the bravest lot in the world. For the preservation of their integrity and image, it was incumbent upon White southern men to protect both their families and their communities, for family and community were one and the same: "threat to community was danger to home and vice versa." White men, were, therefore, by nature the principal agents of southern honor. When women and children were victimized, their victimization was a reflection of male weakness, and when women and children were protected, their safety was the result of manly valor. The honor of men also extended to the larger community: a prosperous community was evidence of honorable men; a flailing community was proof of male impotence.[124] In the context of the borderlands, the only appropriate and honorable response to any threat to Anglo-American families or communities by Indians was violence. Austin articulated this logic in a May 1826 call to arms: "You are . . . now called upon to protect your own homes, your own property, to shield your wives and children from the arrows of a savage and merciless enemy. . . . Every honorable and ardent impulse . . . that can animate the bosoms of free men burns in yours and urges you forward to meet the enemy."[125] This martial mentality structured Anglo interpretations of the so-called Indian problem in Texas, and it would play itself out over and over again as Anglo-Americans expanded their settler colonial project over the course of the century.[126]

Anglo-American colonists, of course, were not alone in their condemnation of Native people. Like their Anglo-American immigrant neighbors, many of the Mexican residents of Texas viewed Indians as a scourge, the bane of their existence. Their experiences as victims of Native violence during the opening decades of the nineteenth century did little to alter their long-held biases against *el indio*, and throughout the 1820s and 1830s Mexican residents frequently voiced their anger and resentment regarding so-called Indian depredations. Ramón Músquiz summed up Hispanic frustrations in a letter to José María Letona in September 1831:

> Permit me to call the occupied attention of Your Excellency to the people living along the Northern Frontier of this Department, and to stress the sacrifices of various kinds which, for more than a century of years, the inhabitants have had to make, and the benefits which they have produced for the people living in the interior. They are of such a nature that, without the barrier which they afford against the *indios bárbaros* who are enemies of civilized man, their present situation would be very unfortunate, just like the one in which these people find themselves now, for, despite the resources and elements with which nature has enriched it, they have not been able to enjoy such estimable benefits for lack of peace with the savages, and consequently at no time either have they been able to enjoy the precious rights to safety and property which in every society that is even half way regulated are guaranteed to its individuals. They are already tired of waiting for the situation to improve, and they cannot resist assassination, robbery, and finally, the complete devastation of the country by the *indios bárbaros* who are making war on them.[127]

The Mexican inhabitants of Texas, like their Anglo-American counterparts, interpreted their war against Indians as an honorable, manly endeavor.[128] In Mexican Texas, as in other frontier regions in Mexico, an honorable man was an autonomous man who could provide for others but depended on no one else. Similar to their Anglo-American colonial neighbors, Mexican men believed that it was their duty to protect their families and communities from external dangers, and in the context of the Texas borderlands this meant defense against Native violence and "corruption." As discussed in previous chapters, violent excursions against Native people had long been a barometer for Hispanic men's worth and at times reaped substantial economic and social benefits.[129] Conversely, the "honorable" nature of Hispanic men also operated in discursive opposition to the weak, dishonorable character of Indian men. Thus, when José María Moreno reported to Antonio Elosúa the success of an expedition against Tahuacanos in July 1831, he contrasted the "valorous" efforts of the Mexican soldiers with the "shameful flight" of Indian men. Little better embodied the Hispanic ideology of manliness than the praise and recognition frequently bestowed upon Mexican volunteers and professional soldiers by their superiors for their brave service against Native people.[130]

With similar codes of martial manliness, Mexican and Anglo-American anti-Indian efforts aligned rather seamlessly in the Texas borderlands during early Anglo-American colonization.[131] As mentioned above, Austin was from the earliest days a major proponent of anti-Indian campaigning, and his advocacy for an active anti-Indian policy persisted throughout the 1820s and 1830s. In March 1822, he wrote to Gen. Anastasio Bustamante, explaining his commitment to the subjugation of Native people: "If the government will grant me the privilege . . . I will obligate myself . . . to organize the settlers into Rifle Companies and arm them, and to hold them in readiness at all times to march against the Indians within said Province whenever called on—These companies will be sufficient in conjunction with the regular troops and militia of the Province to subdue the Indians and keep them at peace." Austin proved his dedication to this program as early as October 1823, when he and a party of Anglo-American men tracked down a band of Tonkawas after they had stolen a number of horses from the colonists. Austin's volunteer party, forerunners to the Texas Rangers of a later period, "surprised their camp . . . and compelled the captain to deliver to me all the stolen animals, and to inflict with his own hands in my presence a severe lashing on the marauders." His report of successful expeditions to Luciano García later that month undoubtedly pleased Mexican authorities.[132]

Over the next few years, and with the active support of Mexican authorities, Austin continued to lead or authorize campaigns against Native people. In June 1824, he sent Amos Rawls and his followers to attack another camp of Tonkawas, where they were to "punish the thieves by whipping them severely and shaving the head." Over a year later, in September 1825, Austin ordered militia forces "to pursue and kill all those [Karankawa] Indians wherever they are found" near the Brazos and Colorado rivers.[133] With the blessing of Col. Mateo Ahumada, a group of armed Anglo-American men massacred a Karankawa village at the mouth of the Colorado River. In the massacre, at least forty Karankawa men, women, and children were murdered in minutes, while some of those who managed to escape death were enslaved by the campaigners, later to be exploited sexually and as servants. Thus, it did not take the Anglo-American colonists long to become active participants in a more traditional form of Texas borderlands slavery.[134] Months later, in March 1826, Austin reported that his fellow colonists were itching for more genocidal violence: "[They] are now agitating the spirits of young men to make a campaign. . . . I have learned that their real objective is to kill Indians and carry off their horses."[135]

Anglo-American violence against Native people continued into the closing years of the 1820s, with plenty of support from both Mexican and Anglo-American authorities. In August 1827, Austin drew up an elaborate plan for the military subjugation of Comanches. His plan was designed to coordinate efforts by both Mexican soldiers and Anglo-American militia men. According to Austin, "Three divisions of troops shall be formed: the 1st in Bexar; the 2nd shall be composed of troops from New Mexico and Chihuahua, and the 3rd, of volunteers from Austin's Colony, from Nacogdoches, and from Pecan Point." With each division of troops advancing from different directions, the Indians ultimately were to "find themselves hemmed in and completely surrounded." Austin's grand campaign never came to fruition, but Mexican authorities remained enthusiastic about joint Mexican–Anglo-American expeditionary activities. In March 1829, for instance, General Bustamante requested the assistance of Austin and his militiamen for a campaign against Taovayas, who reportedly were "committing frequent thefts and assassinations in the vicinity of Béjar and the other frontier establishments." According to Bustamante, "it has become indispensable to destroy that perverse Tribe by attacking their own village and annihilating it." By May of that year, Mexican lieutenant colonel Francisco Ruíz and several dozen Anglo-American militiamen were out searching for Taovayas and other Wichitas on the Southern Plains. With the seasoned Native-language interpreter Ruíz at the helm, this particular expedition did not end in violence, but a later expedition by some two hundred Anglo-American men was less interested in diplomacy. When the large Anglo-American party discovered a Waco village in September 1829, the militiamen pillaged what remained, enslaved a handful of women and children, killed an old man, and burned the village to the ground. Although the village was mostly abandoned, this kind of one-sided violence apparently was the honorable thing for Anglo-American men to do.[136]

Even when Hispanic and Anglo-American men were not out campaigning alongside one another, the broader coordination of Mexican and Anglo-American exterminationist violence demonstrated their converging interests. Various Wichita groups, for instance, were subjected to the violence of both Mexican and Anglo-American military men throughout 1829, 1830, and 1831.[137] In June 1831, Francisco Ruíz received word that "the Americans are getting interested in going out against the Wacos, Tawakonis, and Tahuayases," so, naturally, he decided to "encourage everybody I have seen to do so, for it would be to our advantage." By August of that year, Anglo-American militiamen had embarked on yet another campaign. When Ruíz learned of this expedition of forty men, he prayed for the annihilation of the Wichita targets: "May it be God's will that not a one of them will be left." But when Native attacks persisted into the closing months of the year, Mexican officials organized their own expedition. Músquiz recruited from all over Texas, including Gonzales and Green DeWitt's colony, who "might want to join up as volunteers, and at their own expense, for the campaign." In Elosúa's later instructions, he ordered the campaigners to "go to the villages of the Huecos and Tahuacanos in order to attack them in them, so energetically that they will be left so severely punished that they can never be hostile to us again." When the campaigners eventually tracked down a community of Wichitas and Comanches located near the San Gabriel River on November 13, they "marched on the village, and, as soon as we drew near, we opened fire with a dense volley, and we continued to pour bullets into them so fast that within a few minutes it was necessary to cease fire because the field had been completely abandoned by savages." In the end, the expeditioners confiscated over two hundred horses and left dead at least four Wichitas and two Comanches, including a well-known Comanche *paraibo*, Barbaquista.[138]

The Anglo-Mexican campaigns of the 1820s and 1830s also hint at the ways in which anti-Native violence sometimes converged with Anglo-American anti-Black slavery. Some Anglo-American slaveholders, for instance, forced their slaves to accompany them on their anti-Indian expeditions. Jared Groce was one such man. On a number of occasions, Groce armed his Black slaves to campaign against Native people, with one expedition flaunting some thirty enslaved fighters. Another like-minded slaveholder was the former slave smuggler James Bowie. In 1831, Bowie forced at least two of his slaves to attack a community of Native people near the San Sabá River.[139] Given the oppressive context of the enslaved fighters' bondage, it is pointless to attempt to assess the complicity of these enslaved individuals in attacking and destroying Native communities; nonetheless, these examples are illustrative of how the violence of Anglo-American slavers could reverberate on multiple levels, from Anglo-American slaveholder to enslaved African American to Native victim. In this regard, Anglo-American slavers had much in common with their Mexican neighbors.

"To Wrest the . . . Valuable Territory of Texas from the Mexican Republic": Slavery, Euro-American Violence, and the Texas Rebellion, 1835–1836

When it came to the use of violence against "the Indian," Mexican and Anglo-American men were of the same mind. Through the shared vilification and destruction of Native people, both the Mexican and Anglo-American people of Texas saw themselves as carrying out the work of civilization. Not only were they protecting their families; they were also protecting their plans for future development of industries, trade networks, and communities. There was, nonetheless, an undercurrent of distrust in these collaborative efforts. As much as both Mexicans and Anglo-Americans believed that Indians were a menace to their communities, they also believed that Indians were innately opportunistic, a group of mercenaries-in-waiting who, if bribed adequately, could be manipulated to advance the interests of any devious party. It was also not difficult for representatives from both communities to manufacture evidence of supposed duplicity and collusion. The Cherokee immigrants of the northeastern Texas borderlands were a perfect example, as both Mexican and Anglo-American agents sought to exploit their precarious position as displaced migrants to their own benefit.[140] It mattered little, however, if Cherokee leaders were *in actuality* collaborating with one side or the other; what mattered was that charges of Indian conspiracies had remarkable rhetorical resonance.[141] By 1836, even Austin—a man who strove tirelessly to make Mexican rule congruent with Anglo-American colonization—was willing to conflate Mexicans and Indians: "A war of extermination is raging in Texas—a war of barbarism and of despotic principles, waged by the mongrel Spanish-Indian and Negro race, against civilization and the Anglo-American race."[142] Charges of Indian treachery were cheap—and an easy way to malign an enemy.

Of course, Native people were not just waiting idly to be recruited and manipulated by their colonial neighbors, as Mexican and Anglo-Americans claimed. Generally, Native decisions to collaborate with Euro-American colonists reflected internal prerogatives and community-oriented calculations. But the perception of their opportunism served as yet another source of distrust between Anglo-American colonists and Mexican authorities. The supposed deviousness of Indians only added fuel to the fires that were the persistent legal controversies concerning settlement and slavery. Therefore, when President Antonio

López de Santa Anna dismantled the federal system in Mexico—thereby quashing any hope for Anglo-American colonists to control key legal and economic circumstances relating to their Texas colonies—frustrations erupted into political rebellion.[143]

The general narrative of the Texas Rebellion is well known and often mythologized.[144] Important events included antitaxation protests and scuffles between Mexican troops and Anglo-American militiamen at Anahuac in the summer of 1835; Austin's September 1835 call for war against Mexico (which quickly won support from a number of prominent Bexareños); the first military engagement during the October 1835 Battle of Gonzales; the November 1835 Anglo-American siege of Béxar; the appointment of Sam Houston as commander in chief of the regular Texas Army on November 14, 1835; President Santa Anna's arrival in Béxar with some six thousand troops in February 1836; the signing of the Texas Declaration of Independence on March 2, 1836; the March 6, 1836, attack on Anglo-American forces at Mission San Antonio de Valero, where two hundred or so rebels, including William B. Travis, David Crockett, and James Bowie, were killed; the March 27, 1836, execution of James Fannin and nearly four hundred Anglo-American soldiers at La Bahía (also known as Goliad); the Battle of San Jacinto on April 21, 1836, in which Sam Houston scored a decisive victory over Santa Anna's forces; the capture of Santa Anna the following day; and, finally, the signing of the Treaties of Velasco by officials of the Republic of Texas and General Santa Anna on May 14, 1836, which effectively ended the war.[145] While elaboration of these events is unnecessary for our purposes here, there is at least one aspect of the Texas Rebellion that merits discussion in some detail: slavery's role in framing Anglo-American calls for political independence.

Slavery's role in the Texas Rebellion is one of the oldest controversies in the historiography of (Anglo) Texas. Benjamin Lundy, perhaps as much as any other author, was responsible for the earliest interpretation of the Anglo-American revolt. To Lundy, the intentions of the Anglo-American rebels were plain enough: "*The immediate cause and the leading object of this contest originated in a settled design, among the slaveholders of this country, (with land speculators and slave-traders,) to wrest the large and valuable territory of Texas from the Mexican Republic, in order to re-establish the* SYSTEM OF SLAVERY; *to open a vast and profitable* SLAVE-MARKET *therein; and, ultimately, to annex it to the United States.*" As far as Lundy was concerned, the Texas Rebellion had three components: (1) it was instigated by a conspiracy among Anglo-American slaveholders;

(2) it was motivated by the desire to expand both the institution of slavery and the slave trade; and (3) it was the first step toward Texas's annexation by the United States, which would have enlarged the political influence of slaveholders in the United States. Central to Lundy's interpretation was the role of powerful slaveholders in the United States—the so-called slaveocracy—in orchestrating the rebellion and eventual annexation of the territory. Anglo-American claims regarding the "sacred principles of Liberty, and the natural, inalienable Rights of Man" were, therefore, strictly rhetorical and manipulative; they were attempts to mask the true intentions of the Anglo-American colonists. In short, slavery and the history of the Texas Rebellion were inexorably intertwined.[146]

Later analysts discounted Lundy's conspiratorial charges as bombastic, exaggerated, and misguided. Lester Bugbee, for instance, argued in 1898 that the Rebellion had very little to do with U.S. sectional politics and everything to do with the quest for rights and political representation in the context of Mexico: "They [the Anglo-American colonists] believed that their constitutional rights as Mexican citizens had been trampled upon and, as Mexican citizens, they stood ready to defend those rights."[147] As an admirer of Stephen F. Austin, Eugene Barker was probably the most forceful in his rejection of Lundy's thesis, proclaiming on numerous occasions that "the Texas revolution was precipitated . . . as a result, largely, of Santa Anna's determination to centralize the government of Mexico"; slavery was thus only a marginal concern of the rebels. In Barker's estimation, Lundy's interpretation was nothing more than "reckless" propaganda; "its charges are brief, pointed, and without qualification."[148]

A growing number of modern-day scholars, however, have agreed that slavery *was* a critical factor in the conflict that led up to the Anglo-American revolt against Mexico. Paul D. Lack, for instance, argues, "The conflict with Mexico raised before Anglos the spectre of slave revolt, created for blacks other avenues to freedom beside rebellion, generated forces that weakened the hold of masters over bondsmen, and placed the very survival of the institution in Texas on the success of Texas arms."[149] For our purposes here, the question of whether or not concerns over slavery were *the absolute* cause of the Texas Rebellion matters not. Available evidence makes it clear that Anglo-American colonists believed the Mexican government threatened slavery in Texas—and thus threatened the economic prosperity of the colonies. None other than Austin himself—a man who vacillated on the slavery question throughout his career as spokesman for the Anglo-American colonies—agreed with such a formulation: "The best interests of the United States require that Texas shall be effectually, and fully, *Americanized. . . . Texas must be a slave country. It is no longer a matter of doubt.*"[150] Above all, the Texas Rebellion should be understood as an exercise in political-economy building. More precisely, the Texas Rebellion was an attempt to craft a political economy conducive to Anglo-American slavery, one reminiscent of that of the United States. As was the case in the United States during the nineteenth century, government-derived pressures to limit the economic viability of slavery weighed heavily on the minds of slavers. Even if the government directly attacked not the institution itself but instead the infrastructure in which it thrived—such as land acquisition opportunities, a limited tariff system, and transportation privileges—slaveholders still feared for the safety of their institution.[151] The political system that the Anglo-American rebels constructed in the immediate aftermath of the war, which was codified in the Constitution of the Texas Republic, put an end to those fears by securing slavery's place and future in the economy of an independent Texas.[152]

There is, however, a flipside to this interpretation regarding Anglo-American political-economy building. In many ways, the Texas Rebellion was rooted in the shortsightedness of Mexican officials. The Mexican government's turn to Anglo-American settler colonization as a panacea for their northern frontier Indian problem sowed the seeds of their own undoing. Leaders of the new Mexican nation bought into the generations-old Hispanic belief that they were destined to civilize the great wilderness of Texas. The program may have shifted in tone from monarchical subjugation to national unification, but the substance of the program was the same: conquer the *indios bárbaros* and settle the land. Agricultural development, specifically the kind spearheaded by Euro-American colonists, was to work hand in hand with efforts to pacify the frontier, especially as land acquisition and boundary making squeezed Native people out of long-held (if not ancient) territorial domains. That Anglo-Americans relied upon Black slave labor for such agriculture-based colonization was an issue tangential to the broader vision; what mattered most was ending Native resistance to the Hispanic settler colonial project. Slavery, nevertheless, was *not* an inconsequential issue to the Anglo-American colonists who relocated to Texas—not in the least. "Without it [slave labor]," the colonists claimed, "it is difficult to clear the wilderness." Even local Hispanic leaders recognized this.[153]

Thus, the Texas Rebellion was as much a contest over monopolies on violence as it was a fight over political systems and cultural hegemony.

When Mexican national officials attempted to clamp down on slavery, the Anglo-American colonists of Texas felt as though they had suffered from a great betrayal. The Mexican government had put them in an irreconcilable bind: they were charged with civilizing the wilderness without one of their defining instruments of civilization. As far as Anglo-Americans were concerned, *they* had accomplished what Hispanic people had struggled to do for decades; they had "settled on unappropriated land . . . [and] with great labor and cost opened farms, built houses, mills, and cotton gins, and introduced horses, & cattle, & hogs, & sheep, into the wilderness."[154] Why were they to be punished? The violence of Anglo-American slavers and military men was worthy of commendation, not chastisement and political suppression. As far as Anglo-American observers were concerned, a political system that treated its citizens this way was no political system worth maintaining or defending.

The Anglo-American declarations of independence in 1835 and 1836 articulated the predicament in which they believed the Mexican government had placed them. At Goliad in December 1835, Anglo-American colonists justified their call for an independent nation by connecting their perceived mission to civilize the Texas wilderness to their betrayal by the Mexican government: "The laws and guarantees under which we entered the country as colonists, tempted the unbroken silence, sought the dangers of the wilderness, braved the prowling Indian, erected our numerous improvements, and opened and subdued the earth to cultivation, are either abrogated or repealed, and now trampled under the hoofs of the usurper's cavalry."[155] A few months later, in March 1836, the colonists clarified their argument in a more systematic fashion with a formal, delegate-approved declaration. In it they claimed that the Mexican government had "invited and induced the Anglo American population of Texas to colonize its wilderness under the pledged faith of a written constitution" but now had reneged on their promises to protect Anglo-American "life, liberty, and property." Among other transgressions, they argued (in typical Anglo revolutionary fashion), the Mexican government also "has, through its emissaries, incited the merciless savage, with the tomahawk and scalping knife, to massacre the inhabitants of our defenceless frontiers." Thus, in the eyes of the Anglo-American rebels, it was not *they* who were abandoning the original cause of Texas colonization but the Mexican government. So corrupted had the Mexican government become, they reasoned, that they could not even agree upon the destruction of their longtime mutual enemy: the savage Indian. Rather, as the rebels claimed, Mexicans had crossed over to the enemy's side.[156]

Summary

When viewed from a century-long perspective, such was a fitting end to Hispanic rule in the Texas borderlands. So much of the history of Spanish and Mexican people in Texas was colored by the violence of punitive campaigns, slaving expeditions, and personal domination against Indigenous people in an effort to conquer, colonize, and "civilize" the territory. Yet such efforts yielded only a tenuous hold on the region. Certainly, countless Native people suffered immeasurably at the hands of Hispanic colonists, but other Native groups thrived in spite of Hispanic violence. Ultimately, Spanish and later Mexican officials were desperate. When they pinned their hopes for a so-called civilized Texas on the settler colonization programs of Anglo-Americans, they made a gamble that a shared Euro-American ethos to dominate, colonize, and expand would prevail over substantially different political and cultural heritages. And prospects for a shared development of Texas looked encouraging during the first few years of Anglo-American colonization. As never before, Euro-American people populated the Texas borderlands and integrated their communities within the larger Atlantic-world commercial network. A prosperous Texas was finally well within reach for its Euro-American inhabitants.

Yet the Hispanic-sanctioned Anglo colonization program was a Faustian bargain. As Austin's colonists made obvious, their dreams of prosperity were tied to the collective acceptance of anti-Black chattel slavery as a tool for colonial development. Mexican authorities, who had become more antislavery over the years, thus had to contend with this impulse if they were to see their vision of frontier development realized. And Anglo-American slavers were persistent in defending their institution. They were willing to reframe slavery—as both a form of remunerated servitude and a familial institution—to meet local imperatives, but they were not willing to abandon it entirely. The labor of enslaved Black people was, after all, the lifeblood of virtually every Anglo-American economic enterprise in Texas.

Although the violence that Anglo-American and Mexican men administered against Native people reminded both communities of their shared sense of purpose, these experiences had their unifying limits. Anglo-American colonists sought monopolies on violence against both Native *and* Black people. Making land available through the destruction of Native communities was only one part of the equation of development; the other was the exploitation of enslaved Africans and African

Americans. Mexican authorities could agree completely with only the first part of the formula. Thus, when the broader goals of Mexican officials and Anglo-American colonists no longer converged—that is, when the shared desire to "civilize" Texas was overpowered by competing visions of political and economic formation—something had to give. Unfortunately for Mexico, by the mid-1830s the Anglo-American capacity for coordinated violence outstripped that of Mexico. The end result was the rise of Anglo-American slaver-colonial supremacy throughout much of the Texas borderlands.

Part III
Violent Confluences in the Age of Anglo-Slaving Supremacy, 1836–1860

Rose Williams lived the mid-nineteenth-century transformations of the Texas borderlands. Her pleading, tears, and trembling made human the effects of the cotton-generating machine that had taken over the region. She was, strangely, both its engine and its product. Forced to endure the humiliation of the auction block, she stood exposed alongside several other enslaved human beings, to be pricked and prodded by Anglo-American fortune seekers. When she learned that the man who had purchased her mother and father also decided to purchase her, for $525, she was overcome with relief. As she remembered decades later, at that moment she was "glad and 'cited! Why, I's quiverin' all over."[1]

Williams's sale from William Black to Hall Hawkins in 1860 epitomized the new norm for enslaved people in the Texas borderlands in the aftermath of the Anglo-American Texas Rebellion. The years prior to the Rebellion foretold the increasing integration of Texas within the broader transatlantic system of cotton production, credit expansion, technological advancement, manufacturing, and slavery, but the tearing away of Texas from its Hispanic colonial roots unleashed the full force of the North American cotton frontier upon the region and its populations. Anglo-American colonists flooded the eastern and central Texas borderlands with their families and their slave property. They cleared more forests, drained more swamplands, and planted lots of cotton seed. With each tree felled and each seed deposited, the future of Texas became more and more tied to the mass enslavement of humans, Black people in particular. Thus, the commerce in slaves grew exponentially, as did anti-Black violence. Cotton-loving slavers drove their slaves, through torture, to labor with unprecedented efficiency. The cotton-generating machine swallowed these enslaved people whole.

As part of the larger history of the North American cotton frontier, this story of slavery was not unique to Texas. Since the turn of the nineteenth century, as the English-speaking residents of the Atlantic seaboard spread their slaving empire westward, the desire to extract and ship millions upon millions of pounds of cotton fibers inspired innovations in colonizing, financing, technology, politics, and violence. Historians have worked hard to detail and explain this history.[2] But the expansion of the cotton frontier was not the entire experience of slavery and enslavement in Texas, even by 1860, when hundreds of thousands of exploited people were living proof of the omnipotence of King Cotton. Anglo-American slavers found a comfortable home in the Texas borderlands, with its long past of slavery and manly violence. Here in Texas, Anglo-American slavery would continue to experience a kind of resonance—and in some cases a profound synergy. Part III is thus an examination of the slaving confluences that emerged in tandem with the ascendance of the Anglo-American cotton frontier. In these final chapters I argue that although Anglo-American slaving violence—and its long, enveloping shadow of anti-Blackness—ultimately ushered in an era of Anglo supremacy during the middle decades of the nineteenth century, this violence did not operate in a vacuum. Other borderlanders, especially Comanches, continued to forge their own paths in the broader region by adapting to the transformative changes wrought by long-term Anglo-American colonization. These adaptations reminded Anglo-Americans that within the borderlands their dominion remained contested, subject to local imperatives.[3]

As before, Anglo-American slavers sought to entangle coercion, violence, exploitation, and family making. Rose Williams was, after all, purchased strictly for her ability to expand her slaver's family of slaves. As her first slaver explained, she was a "portly, strong young wench . . . [who had] never been 'bused and will make de good breeder." Her new owner, Hawkins, concurred. At the young age of sixteen years, Williams was forced to mate with a slave by the name of Rufus. Hawkins warned her, "Woman, I's pay big money for you and I's done dat for de cause I wants yous to raise me chillens. . . . If you doesn't want whippin' at de stake, yous do what I wants." This was slaver rape by proxy, and for Williams it was the "one thing Massa Hawkins does to me what I can't shunt from my mind." Yet what was singular in the mind of Williams was typical of slavery in the Texas borderlands, where slavers grew and fostered their enslaved "families" by coercion and violence. The principal difference was that *individual* enslaved people, like Williams, had become more expendable than ever. Anglo-American slaving operations grew so enormous that Anglo slavers assessed the usefulness of individual Black people according to ever-shrinking parameters of value—specifically, the extent to which they could directly contribute to slaver cash-crop fortunes. Anglo-American slavers wielded extreme violence to extract the utmost utility from their slaves, which in turn reinforced the fungibility and extinguishability of Black bodies. The middle decades of the nineteenth century thus represented the height of anti-Blackness in Texas, even as Anglo-American slavers remained interested in integrating enslaved people as "family." Anglo-American family could be a mechanism of social control (as it was for Hispanic and Comanche people in Texas), and as controlling Black bodies was the premier objective of Anglo slavers, the Anglo family sustained anti-Blackness.[4]

This partly explains why a number of Hispanic Texans elected to partake in the evolving Anglo-American cotton kingdom. Anglo-American chattel slavery may have been first and foremost a system designed to maximize Anglo cash-crop wealth, but in the borderlands it was flexible enough as a slaving system to allow for creative adaptation. The enslavement of *negro* and *indio* people was as old as Hispanic colonization, especially in the Texas borderlands, so direct participation in the broader system of buying, selling, abusing, driving, exploiting, and integrating enslaved people was not an unusual practice for certain Hispanic residents. Moreover, some Mexican people of the region—themselves facing unprecedented levels of racial animosity and economic, political, and social displacement—found engagement on behalf of the Anglo-American system a boon to their economic, political, and social fortunes. Their role in clearing Texas of the obstacles of Anglo-American slaving progress, including Native people, demonstrated their continued commitment to subjugating so-called lesser peoples and at times proved their social worth to Anglo-American colonists. Anglo-Americans particularly appreciated their assistance chasing down and apprehending the many Black fugitives who sought to escape their unbearable conditions. Unfortunately for the Hispanic residents of Texas, their complicity in the rising Anglo regime would prove insufficient, and many Anglo-Americans would actually view Mexicans themselves as a degraded, conquerable race.[5]

If Anglo-Americans dismantled Hispanic dominion rather steadily in the wake of the Rebellion, contending with Comanche power would be an entirely different matter, as the late 1830s and 1840s represented the apogee of Comanche slaving. During those years, Comanches expanded their slaving operations both in scope and in scale, with Comanche fighters sweeping across the Mexican northern frontier and even leading campaigns deep into the heart of the young republic. These expeditions, which sometimes included several hundred rangers, devastated the Mexican North, as Comanches stole and slaughtered livestock, enslaved women and children, and struck down desperate defenders. For the Comanche communities of the Texas borderlands, however, these campaigns preserved their broad regional influence in the face of a genocidal, Anglo colonial threat. Not only did they supply Comanche communities with the necessary livestock to maintain their massive transregional commerce; the steady enslavement of Mexican northerners provided Comanche slavers with critical labor, commodities for trade, social currency, and a degree of demographic sustenance.[6]

Despite their continuation of raiding and slaving violence in the late 1830s and throughout the 1840s, Comanches found themselves largely displaced from Texas by 1860. During the 1850s, the combination of disease epidemics, diminishing bison herds, and an aggressive Anglo-American settler colonial program of annihilation finally caught up with the Comanche people of the Texas borderlands. As Anglo-Texas grew economically, demographically, and militarily, so did its capacity to undermine Comanche dominion. Thus, the mass expulsion of Comanches from Texas in 1859 would be the culmination of Anglo-American power in the mid-nineteenth century. Not coincidentally, the late 1850s and opening years of the 1860s also would be the apex of Anglo-American slaving supremacy.

6 / "De Overseer Shakes a Blacksnake Whip over Me": Consolidating an Anti-Black Colonial Regime, 1836–1860

In 1851, Lucky decided that he could bear his slaver's violence no more. For nearly forty years, Lucky had worked endlessly for the benefit of White men and their families. In exchange, he received lashings, verbal berating, threats of more violence, and a price tag on his head of $1,000, reminding him that although slavers valued him for his productive capacities, he was also a commodity: a wealth-producing object to be exchanged at his slaver's whim. Lucky also had to endure witnessing the violence that his slaver, John Story, and his proxies used against the six other enslaved Black people on the Story farm in Burleson County—six people who were likely Lucky's family. As an inhabitant of Burleson County (which lay on the more western part of Anglo-Texas), Lucky knew that Native country was not far off—perhaps a hundred or so miles away. So on the Fourth of July, 1851, the seventy-fifth anniversary of Anglo-American independence from Britain, he took his chances and set off on his escape to freedom.[1]

Lucky's travels took him as far west as Austin. There, on the edge of Anglo-controlled territory, he ran into a White couple by the name of Baker, who took it upon themselves to capture Lucky and return him to his slaver. Yet on this occasion, Lucky would not abide. Resisting their claims to his Black body, he killed the man and his wife and continued his journey westward. Unfortunately, his travels would not last much longer, as local Anglo-Americans soon tracked him down, ending his escape for good. But instead of returning Lucky to his owner, who regarded him as a "well conditioned and . . . valuable slave," or sending him to local authorities, the Anglo mob took "justice" into their own hands. It was thus in the town of Austin, before a crowd of onlookers, that "the people of Travis County" lynched Lucky. Months later, his slaver, John Story, begged the Texas state legislature to compensate *him*, arguing that the loss of his property "falls heavily upon" him and his net worth.

As Lucky's story of slaver exploitation, slave commodification, Black resistance, and anti-Black violence suggests, much of this chapter takes readers to familiar, if still haunting places in the history of Anglo-American slavery. In the literature on slavery in Texas, the themes of Lucky's story remain most prominent—and for good reason. In many ways, from 1836 to 1860 Anglo-Americans transformed much of the Texas borderlands into an extension of the U.S. South, where slave-produced cotton reigned, White slavers asserted vast political and social authority, and enslaved Black people struggled to survive the onslaught of slaver torture.[2] Anglo-American colonists' collective ability to marshal and exploit eastern capital, Atlantic trade connections, and Black bodies ushered in an unprecedented era of Anglo slaving supremacy in the Texas borderlands. Several hundred thousand people would come to inhabit Anglo-Texas by 1860, and for the first time in the history of the Texas borderlands, Euro-Americans would outnumber Native people in the region. To demonstrate their expansive dominion, Texians—as Anglo-Americans called themselves—sought to subsume the borderlands into the apparatus of the burgeoning Anglo state, creating the Republic of Texas in 1836, and then incorporating with the United States in 1845.

Yet Anglo state-building remained a fraught endeavor. Even as Anglo-Americans established government frameworks, passed laws, and appointed state agents, the vicissitudes of transregional markets, competing national claims to the borderlands, and the imperatives of local communities limited the power of the Anglo state.[3] Significant were the several thousand Hispanic people, endowed with their own colonial heritage, still residing throughout the larger colonialist domain, as well as the tens of thousands of Native people who claimed the borderlands as their homeland. Thus, Anglo-American slavery remained flexible, and slavers forced their slaves to labor—as herders, land clearers, builders, mechanics, cooks, carpenters, and in-home servants—in whatever capacity suited their colonial project in the borderlands. Kin incorporation, moreover, remained a useful mechanism of Anglo social control. Forced family making gave Anglo men both a practical framework for asserting their manly dominance and an effective instrument of bondage, anchoring enslaved women especially to the offspring of sexual violence. The power of kin incorporation was particularly poignant in light of the fact that Anglo-Texas's southern and western borders were as porous as ever. When Lucky ventured westward for freedom in the summer of 1851, he may not have known what to expect from the Native inhabitants of the region, but he *did* know that Native country represented the geographical limits of Anglo slaver authority. The immediate, extralegal violence of the Austin locals suggests that they too were aware of this. Their lynching of Lucky was as much a message to other enslaved people as it was a reminder to the Anglo population that they had to stay vigilant in the borderlands.

Ultimately, what accounted for Anglo-American supremacy during the quarter-century from 1836 to 1860 was the meteoric expansion of anti-Black slavery. The great potential of cotton-based fortunes inspired wave after wave of Anglo-American settlers to further colonize Texas, and as Anglo colonization grew, so did slave-derived cotton production and the Anglo economy at large. Anglo-American slavery itself also changed. The feverish emphasis on cotton production concentrated the laboring activities of enslaved people, and slavers more readily employed torture to extract maximum compliance and output from their slaves. This, along with the expansion of the slave trade, further objectified Black bodies, thereby enhancing anti-Blackness. By the middle decades of the nineteenth century, Anglo-Americans collectively had made Blackness not just a stigma of social dishonor but also a prima facie rationale for Black subjugation.

Anti-Blackness also would serve as a tool of colonial consolidation, a prime way to incorporate or reject the vestiges of the previous colonial order.[4] The process whereby Anglo-Americans supplanted their Hispanic neighbors as the primary force of colonialism in Texas required more than the simple transferring of official state authority from a Mexican to an Anglo government; colonial consolidation took time, operating slowly and cumulatively on multiple economic, social, and political levels. As was the case prior to the Texas Rebellion, some Hispanic locals became determined to collaborate with their Anglo colonial counterparts and entrenched themselves in the new regime by renewing their investment in violence against Black people, as slaveholders and slave hunters. Others, usually the less well connected, forged ahead as best as they could, eking out a humble existence on the pastoral and commercial peripheries of the regional economy. And still others subverted the new colonial-slaver apparatus, challenging the Anglo regime's ethos of anti-Blackness in both subtle and overt ways.[5]

Nonetheless, for most of the Hispanic people of Texas, the new Anglo establishment brought dispossession, vilification, and violence. No matter how hard some tried to acclimate themselves to the rising Anglo order, Hispanic borderlanders were, in the eyes of Anglo settler colonists, generally a conquered people. Anglo-Americans expected them to capitulate or move out of the way. Those who would not (or could not) bolster their slaver-colonial project became its enemies, and it was as perceived detractors, obstacles, and racial interlopers that Hispanic people became *Blackened* within the Anglo mind. By 1860, with the Hispanic population either denigrated, servile, and displaced or actively complicit in anti-Black violence, the long shadow of anti-Blackness had proven itself an effective means to colonial consolidation, the fulcrum upon which Anglo slaver supremacy rested in a long-colonized Texas.

"Hurrah for Texas!" The Cotton Boom

The smashing success of the Texas Rebellion proved to Anglo-American colonists that between the two combatant parties of Mexico and Anglo-America only the latter deserved a monopoly on violence in the Texas borderlands. Evidence of their merit, they argued, lay in their struggle and performance during the war. As David Burnet declared in his first presidential address to the congress of the new Republic of Texas, "Many citizens have suffered an entire devastation of their personal goods; others have had their dwellings destroyed by the enemy; others again have seen theirs given to the flames, by their own countrymen, for purposes connected with the public defence." But in the end, Texian violence and determination prevailed: "It was a triumph not only of arms, but of soul: not of mere animal power, but of intellectual and moral impulse." In the words of lawyer-turned-rebel Colin De Bland, Texas was "rendered illustrious, by the Chivalry of her sons."[6]

With their victory came the spoils. Immediately at the conclusion of the Rebellion, as the new congress of the Republic got to work, Anglo-American officials sought to translate the honor of manly military violence into economic prosperity. Legislators proposed granting vast tracts of land to the men who fought on behalf of the Texian Army, regardless of their status as "foreigners" or as longtime residents of Texas. Soon fighting men like William Steele, Burton H. Freeling, and John W. Robertson were receiving grants of between 320 and 1,280 acres for "having served faithfully and honorably." Anglo-American officials also set out to unleash U.S. capital on the Republic's budding economy because, as they proclaimed, once aided by U.S. capitalists, Anglo-Texas "will soon develop its immense internal resources, and population and wealth, and commerce and agriculture and a prosperous and happy people will be the result."[7]

Anglo-American entrepreneurs had reason to be optimistic about their prospects for prosperity. In the few years immediately preceding the Texas Rebellion, cotton had boomed. According to Andrew Torget's estimates, from 1831 to 1835 cotton production increased from about 450,000 pounds annually to more than 3.15 million, a growth intimately tied to the insatiable demand for raw cotton in Britain.[8] And this, of course, was during a period of supposed Mexican governmental "tyranny"; naturally, many Anglo-American colonists believed that the success of the Rebellion would open the flood gates of cotton-based wealth. As merchant and investor Thomas McKinney wrote in 1839, "There never has been such a universal feeling in favor of raising cotton in Texas as at present."[9]

Early on, U.S. investors expressed considerable interest in Texas. Anglo-American development of the Texas cotton frontier had been dependent upon U.S. capital prior to the Rebellion, as merchants, especially those in New Orleans, regularly extended lines of credit for the purchase of items that were rare or unavailable in the borderlands; with Texians' political independence from Mexico, merchants and banks were more eager to offer their services. Stephen F. Austin figured as much when he planned in late 1836 to seek a "Merchant in N. Orleans" to finance the improvement of a cotton plantation the following year. An anonymous writer penned a letter to Republic president Sam Houston in 1837, stating, "There has at no time been any want of disposition in capitalists in the U S to furnish Texas with large sums of money." Investors were anxious to claim a piece of the Texas pie, and some even promised to lend money for a few years without "any rate of interest, not even at 30 pr Cent per annum." Notably, a handful of German slavers and their plantations were financed by a number of well-connected, wealthy individuals from their homeland. By the late 1850s, over three thousand lenders had invested more than $3 million in Texas.[10]

The fortunes of Anglo-Texans—and some European colonists—were inextricably tied to the expanding credit system of North America and the Atlantic world. During the earliest days of independent Anglo-Texas, government officials, including Branch T. Archer, William H. Wharton, and Stephen F. Austin, worked hard to secure loans to keep the young, massively indebted government afloat, and Republic commissioners continued to seek enormous loans for the next several years. But loans were not just for the government; individuals relentlessly sought credit opportunities as well. Credit, after all, offered exponential benefits to those willing to take risks. Farmers, who needed land to cultivate and machinery and labor to harvest and transport their wealth-generating yields, took out loans. Land speculators borrowed money to purchase land that was to be sold at inflated prices to other loan recipients. Slave traders, whose operations were linked to the ebbs and flows of cotton and chattel slave prices, purchased and sold enslaved people, sometimes without ever seeing a single cash payment exchange hands. And merchant firms, based both in Texas and throughout the United States, moved credit and goods around to keep this system functioning, especially when cash flow was limited. George Woolfolk has offered an astute explanation of this web of cotton, capital, credit, and slaves at the Texas plantation level: "At most stages of the slave's life from birth to death, planters found it possible to mortgage him for moderate or large sums of money or credit to get supplies, merchandise, or other necessities to carry on the economics of plantation existence. Slave labor created the crops of cotton, corn, and sugar and thus demonstrated its function as producer's capital. At the same time, then, that slave labor was being used as an instrument of production, that labor was also creating capital." For most Anglo-American colonists, credit was one of the main ways in which they reoriented Texas toward the Atlantic world.[11]

As the credit system grew, so did the Anglo-Texas built environment. Many of the towns hyped by speculators never materialized, especially in the depression years of the late 1830s, but some did take hold. By the 1850s, Anglo-Texas consisted of scores of towns, settlements, and forts, spread out across the diverse terrain of the Texas borderlands to demarcate a region bounded by the Red River in the East and North, the Río Grande in the South, and the Southern Plains in the West. The two most important Anglo-American towns of the post-Rebellion era were Galveston and Houston, and both illuminated the roles of cotton, capitalists, and credit in the making of Anglo-Texas. Galveston had long been a desired pit stop to and from the Texas markets but did not become an established town until 1837. The town benefited from the deep channel at the Galveston Bay entrance, which could accommodate large sea vessels, and from the Trinity and San Jacinto rivers, the most navigable water routes of the area. Within two years the *Daily Picayune* declared, "It is no longer a misnomer, to call this the *city* of Galveston"—as opposed to simply a *town*. In the mid-1840s, commentators described Galveston as "the most thriving town upon the sea coast, and rapidly increasing in commercial importance." Eventually, Galveston would become home to some of the most important cotton-moving and -financing firms and commission houses of Texas, including R. & D. G. Mills & Company, Ball, Hutchings, Sealy & Company, T. H. McMahon & Company, E. B. Nichols & Company, Hewitt, Swisher & Company, and W. B. Sorley & Company. By 1860, some 7,300 people lived in the town, and over two-thirds of all cotton produced in Texas, about 200,000 bales, were prepared for export in Galveston.[12]

The town of Houston, Galveston's rival, was planned out in late 1836 and then heavily populated during the first half of 1837. Like Galveston, the town was financed by investors, with "at least One Million Dollars of capital," and designed to be "the great interior commercial emporium of Texas," connecting cotton producers of the region to New Orleans, New York, and the rest of the globe. The founders, New Yorker brothers John and Augustus Allen, envisioned Houston as the heart and soul of Texas development: "As the country shall improve, rail roads will become in use, and will be extended from this point to the Brazos, and up the same, also from this up to the headwaters of San Jacinto, embracing that rich country, and in a few years the whole trade of the upper Brazos will make its way into Galveston Bay through this channel." Only months after its founding, John Dancy believed it to be "the most animated looking town I have seen in Texas." By the spring of 1839, after just two years, Houston was inhabited by over 2,000 people residing in some 400 houses, and by 1860 the town proper had grown to 4,800 residents (with over 8,000 countywide). Short railway lines would not appear in the vicinity until the 1850s, but steamships proved instrumental for transporting products, supplies, and people in the meantime.[13] Thus, even though the two towns of Galveston and Houston paled in comparison to the other major North American cities of the era, as sites of significant trade, enterprise, industry, and urbanization they suggested that Anglo-Texas was no longer solely a series of colonies but also part metropolis.

Building a cotton kingdom based on credit came with significant risks, though, and changes in the global price of cotton could enhance or curtail economic growth at a moment's notice. The Panics of 1837 and 1839 revealed the precarious nature of a cotton-centric economy. With an economy propped up by small banks, short-term notes, and anticipated yields, the sudden drop in cotton prices in 1837 (from 15 to 8 cents a pound) and again in 1839 (from 14.5 to 6.5 cents a pound) had wide-ranging consequences.[14] Planters and farmers could hardly sell their crops or pay back their loans; merchants could not move their products; banks lost their international sponsors; and consumers were left with essentially worthless banknotes. On a transnational scale, from Mississippi to New York to London, cotton producers, investors, and movers—as well as their ancillary industries—felt the strain of economic depression. In April 1839, Samuel A. Plummer claimed that "the times are harder here than ever known," even predicting "a dreadful revolution throughout Europe & the U. States."[15] But there was a safety net built into Anglo-Texas's economic system that protected the financial well-being of many: human chattels. Although banknotes sometimes depreciated under inflation (and with distance and failed contracts) and real estate fell victim to wild speculation, chattel slaves were a form of moveable property that maintained a steady increase in value throughout the mid-nineteenth century, more than doubling in cost from 1840 to 1860.[16] Naturally, Anglo-American colonists held firm to their slave property. "Texas lands will not sell for any thing," one Anglo-American declared in 1842. "There seems to be no kind of property here now that would answer in the place of money except good work Mules or Negroes at a fair price."[17]

Fortunately for the young Republic, financial devastation throughout the slaveholding portion of the United States during the late 1830s and after turned out to be an economic and demographic boon to the Anglo-Texan cotton kingdom. As debt collectors swept across Alabama, Mississippi, Tennessee, and other southern states, White slaveholding debtors ran away to Texas, where their state laws had no jurisdiction. It was thus during this era that the acronym GTT, "Gone to Texas," grew in popularity (and infamy). Julien Devereux, the son of Alabama planter John Devereux, exemplified this desperate but shrewd strategy. By 1839, Devereux the younger had found himself mired in massive debt, facing a $10,000 creditor lawsuit. After selling his land and a number of his chattel slaves and moving in with his father, Devereux still owed a fortune. In 1841, with court summonses mounting, he gave up on repaying his creditors and headed to Mobile with his father. From Mobile, the Devereux men sailed to New Orleans and then to Galveston. With them they dragged along their slave property—the key to their new fortunes in the borderlands.[18] Julien and John Devereux were by no means alone in escaping their debt by going to Texas. A German traveler named Gustav Dresel, for instance, met a colonizing Mississippi planter "who owned a considerable number of slaves [and] had contracted debts the payment of which would have entailed the sale of all his possessions." So instead of surrendering his slave property, "he decided to run his slaves to Texas." Local Texians took note of these debt runaways. "The embarrassments of the planting interests in Mississippi and Alabama," Abner S. Lipscomb wrote to James Hamilton in January 1840, "has thrown among us . . . a large amount of slave population, and it will still continue to flow in, and must result most beneficially for us."[19]

Overall, the period from 1836 to 1860 witnessed an unprecedented expansion of the Anglo-Texas economy. Untethered from the restraints of Mexican bureaucracy and buoyed by U.S. capital, Anglo-American setter colonists built a slave-based cotton kingdom that showed few signs of collapsing by the start of the U.S. Civil War in 1861. Export figures of Texas cotton, "unequaled by other varieties, both in strength and in length," tell part of the story. From about 3.15 million pounds of cotton produced in 1835, production in 1850 increased to 57,596 bales, or 23.04 million pounds. Then in 1860, the annual figure of cotton production reached 431,463 bales, weighing a total of 172.59 million pounds. Overall from 1835 to 1860, cotton production increased by an astounding 5,300 percent. In terms of profitability (as opposed to productivity), the profits received from slave-based cotton production in relation to slaveholder investments were at least "reasonable." In his study of slaveholding cotton farmers in Texas, Randolph Campbell found that "with the exception of small slaveholders (1–9 slaves), all groups enjoyed rates of return (that is, profits as a percentage of investment) of approximately 6 percent or better in 1850 and 1860. By 1860, assuming 9-cent cotton, even these smallest slaveholders were over the 6-percent mark." The cotton-producing machine that Anglo-American slavers had built in Texas also proved capable of accommodating supplementary crops, such as sugar, corn, peas, beans, and potatoes, as well as sufficient animal industries, especially hog and cattle raising. And as mentioned above, the value of enslaved people continued to rise throughout the period.[20]

Cotton-producing slavers were thus the wealthiest men of the Texas borderlands during this era. In 1850, 30 percent of Euro-American heads of household owned slaves, yet they controlled 72 percent of real property. Ten years later, the percentage of real property they controlled grew slightly, even though the percentage of slaveholding heads of household dropped to 27 percent. Not all slaveholders produced cotton, but slavers certainly dominated its production: one-third of all slaveholders produced 89 percent of the cotton in 1850 and 91 percent in 1860. And their economic monopoly extended to the realm of politics, as 58 percent of all Texas officeholders were slavers in 1850. Their influence grew to 68 percent of all offices by 1860, revealing a trend toward slaver political consolidation. Moreover, Anglo-American slaveholders tended to concentrate in specific regions, especially in the old Austin colony (along the Brazos and Colorado rivers), eastern Texas, and the far Northeast, which had the effect of amplifying their sway.[21] Not surprisingly, Anglo-Americans were enthusiastic about their slaveholding influence in Texas. As John M. Lewis proclaimed in 1845, "If there is one passion which predominates over all others in the citizens of this country, it is the desire to hold slaves. They regard them as more valuable than money, and when a man acquires a sufficient amount to allow of the purchase of slaves, that is the first investment he thinks of." Even nonsoutherners could be impressed with Anglo-American slaveholding dominance in Texas. The usually critical New Yorker Teresa Griffin Vielé declared in the 1850s, "Texas stands among the slave-holding states unrivalled in cultivation and production, in energy and enterprise, in intelligence and morality." And when "a Mr Dupree from Georgia" passed through Nacogdoches with ninety-six enslaved Black people in tow, the longtime German colonist of the town, Adolphus Sterne, exclaimed, "Hurrah for Texas!"[22]

"Elbowed to One Side": Hispanic Displacement

For the Hispanic residents of the Texas borderlands, the Anglo victory in 1836 presaged the demise of their already limited dominion in the region. San Antonio, the Hispanic heartland of Texas, emerged from the Texas Rebellion in tatters. Juan Seguín remembered his people's return to San Antonio after the war as a tragic affair, with residents finding "their houses in ruins, their fields laid waste, and their cattle destroyed or dispersed." One Anglo-American traveler who visited San Antonio in 1837 was similarly struck by the ruinous state of the town: "The walls are indented in a thousand places with marks of bullets and cannon balls. . . . The houses in the suburbs, as well as many on the principal streets near the center of the town . . . have the most shabby and ragged appearance and are not in any respect superior to the temporary huts of the savage. . . . The ravages and waste of civil war are seen even upon the churches, and many of them are in ruins." As years passed and war with Mexico persisted, San Antonio continued to hemorrhage Hispanic residents. When Edward Still visited the town during the U.S.-Mexico War, he found it virtually depopulated, "not exceed[ing] 1,000 souls," with "much of the property here, as well as in the country . . . confiscated."[23] Other towns fared worse. Goliad, formerly La Bahía del Espiritu Santo, lay desolate for years. John Russell Bartlett, who traveled through the town in 1850, noted that its population had been reduced to "about two hundred inhabitants," while only personal dwellings and a handful of stone buildings, "with nothing but their walls standing," remained.[24]

Hispanic residents had to make do with the new colonial regime, to varying degrees of success. The San Antonio River Valley, for instance, remained the breadbasket of Hispanic Texas. "Both cotton and corn flourish in the valley, especially the latter, which forms the principal agriculture of the country," one observer noted. "It is the only breadstuff of the [Hispanic] natives, and each family has a little patch for this necessity of life." Mexican residents, moreover, continued to excel at raising and caring for their *ganado mejor*, their huge herds of horses, mules, and cattle.[25] And a significant number of Bexareños maintained the ox-driven supply trains from northern Mexico and the Gulf Coast to San Antonio—a trade that Anglo-Americans frequently sought to exploit and co-opt for themselves. As Bartlett observed, "The business of freighting almost entirely supports the Mexican population of the city and its vicinity."[26]

Some Hispanic people, particularly those from the landed and military elite, adapted to the new regime by inserting themselves within the higher ranks of the rising Anglo-oriented social order. Seguín, for instance, demanded social recognition for "the Mexican-Texians [who] were among the first who sacrificed their all in our glorious Revolution." He and dozens of others had fought on behalf of the rebels, so they curried the "high regard" bestowed upon "patriots and soldiers" for their "honor and chivalry."[27] Moreover, some Hispanic patriots who had lost much of their property during the Rebellion worked hard to prove publicly their sacrifices for an independent Texas.[28] Others attempted to draw into *their* already established social order—through marriage—the more influential and ambitious men among the quickly expanding Anglo-American community. To an extent, this reflected "an early accommodation between old and new elites," David Montejano has argued.[29] With such high-class mingling, it was not unusual for Anglo-American commentators to laud aspects of Hispanic upper-class society. Mary Ann Maverick, for instance, was quick to note, with admiration, the conspicuous lifestyle of elite Hispanic women in San Antonio: "The principal citizens lived in the plazas or within two blocks of them on Flores, Acequia, Soledad, Commerce and Market streets. Very few of the Mexican ladies could write but they dressed nicely and were graceful and gracious of manner. We exchanged calls with the Navarros, Sotos, Garzas, Garcias, Zambranos, Seguins, Veramendis and Yturris."[30]

Marriage was one of the easiest ways Hispanic residents could align their interests with elite Anglo-American colonists. For Mexican Texans, this offered a degree of assurance to family members that their social, economic, and political interests would be considered—if not actively fostered—by the Anglo-American newcomers. These connections certainly helped Hispanic residents exercise some political influence in places like San Antonio, Brownsville, and El Paso. For Anglo-Americans, marriage into an elite Hispanic family provided important social capital and often direct access to local wealth. Spanish, Mexican, and even Texan law recognized and protected women's property rights more than traditional Anglo-American law did, so hardnosed Anglo men could not simply appropriate such property from their new wives upon marriage.[31] Nonetheless, marriage usually meant that otherwise single Anglo-Americans were able to amass a sizable amount of livestock and land quickly and with few expenses. And when marriage into Hispanic families was not an available option, many Anglo-Americans cemented their bonds of alliance through fictive kinship. As was the case in Spanish colonial Texas, residents forged relationships through *compadrazgo* and other forms of religious sponsorship. Anglo-Americans, of course, were not made slaves by these ritual-based familial relationships, but they were still brought into the world of Hispanic Texas. To a degree, a number of Anglo-Americans reshaped their own identities to fit into the existing Hispanic social order.[32]

But local accommodation could go only so far to stem the tide of Anglo colonial aggression. The Anglo slaver regime required, first and foremost, control of the land, and Anglo colonists feverishly acquired land after the Rebellion, displacing much of the Hispanic population in the process.[33] Although Hispanic elites sometimes contributed to Hispanic dispossession (e.g., through speculation), Anglo-Americans were systematic in their efforts to acquire land, displacing local Hispanic people through manipulation, fraud, squatting, intimidation, and outright expulsion.[34] As Edward Dwyer suggested to a Texian military officer, Thomas Jefferson Green, in October 1836, Anglo colonists were willing to marshal military resources for their purposes: "The people [of San Antonio] . . . are not sufficiently scared to make an advantageous sale of their lands. In case two or three hundred of our troops should be stationed there, I have no doubt but a man could make some good speculations with Gold and Silver."[35] Moreover, Anglo-American buyers had a budding legal system on their side, which could be used to deem illegitimate the land claims of Hispanic residents. As one 1850s legislative committee explained, San Antonio *vecinos* were to blame for their own dispossession, because *they* had failed to clarify their property rights for the Anglo state. If they had lived "for many years within a stone's throw of [state] tribunals open for the granting of headrights" yet delayed their applications for so long, the committee reasoned, they did not deserve the land on which they resided. Plus, they argued, their fidelity to the Anglo state was suspect, as among them were "many who adhered to the [Mexican] enemy."[36] And when legislative committees were insufficient mechanisms for removal, Anglo-American lawmen and vigilantes manufactured criminal charges, like horse theft and slave insurrection conspiracy, as justification for forcefully expelling Hispanic locals. After mass "punitive expulsions" from Travis, Guadalupe, Matagorda, Colorado, and Uvalde counties throughout the 1850s, the Hispanic population of Texas generally entered the 1860s as a dispersed people. Pedro Gonzáles spoke for his people in Ysleta, Texas, as well as many other Hispanic residents, when in 1852 he explained to Governor P. H. Bell that "without any kind of commission, court, process warrant and etc. there are some men, who, under the disguise of surveyors, survey their lands, dispossess them of their property . . . [and] make a complete fun and ridicule of the constituted authorities that they beat them, and even threaten them with pistols when they try to enforce any law or command."[37]

Dispossession during the 1830s, 1840s, and 1850s heightened the economic precarity of a great number of Hispanic borderlanders, creating "a working underclass."[38] Farm acreage and production figures offer some clues regarding their diminishing economic opportunities. In their study of socioeconomic change in nineteenth-century Texas, Kenneth L. Stewart and Arnoldo de Léon found that Mexicans controlled just over seven thousand acres of improved farmland in 1850, which was equivalent to a mere 1.1 percent of the total improved farm acreage in Texas. They also discovered that farmers and ranchers from the predominantly Hispanic communities of Texas accounted for only 1.1 percent of the state's livestock products, 2.0 percent of the corn and grain produced, and 0.5 percent of the cash crops.[39] Thus, more and more Mexican Texans found themselves making a living through menial labor as field hands, ranch hands, herders, and servants.[40] Even Hispanic freighters, who had monopolized much of the supply transportation business from San Antonio to northern Mexico and the coast for decades, faced immense pressure from Anglo-Americans by the late 1850s. Anglo frustrations with cheaper Mexican freighting prices eventually escalated to widespread violence in 1857, when Hispanic-led cart trains were attacked "by a body of mounted men, disguised and armed." The violence, which stretched from Goliad to Karnes County, became known as the Cart War, but the "war" was mostly unilateral, a series of organized assaults on the *arriero* business specifically and Hispanic economic influence in general.[41]

The broader trajectory of social change in Euro-American Texas was clear: English-speaking White Americans were taking over. Although historically Hispanic locales like San Antonio and Nacogdoches still bore cultural, political, and demographic marks of their Hispanic colonial origins, the Anglo-Mexican fusions of the mid-nineteenth century revealed the mounting influence of Anglo-America. During her 1852 stay in Brownsville, Teresa Griffin Viele observed that even though Fort Brown had been built directly on "the estate of a Spanish nobleman," it was rapidly losing its Hispanic flair. "Consequently," she claimed, "some fine trees are growing in the neighborhood, as it was once an exquisite garden, filled with plants and irrigated from the Rio Grande, by means of stone aqueducts, now falling into decay."[42] Other places similarly gave way to the Anglo-American invasion. An Anglo-American traveler who visited Nacogdoches in 1840 noticed, "Most of the Spanish and Mexican inhabitants have left it, and it is becoming an English town."[43] Bartlett claimed in 1850 that San Antonio was "essentially American in its character," with Anglo-American arrivals constantly "elbowing the old settlers to one side." Perhaps the most famous Hispanic marker in Texas, Mission San Antonio de Valero, had also shed much of its Catholic-colonial origins. After the notorious Mexican siege in the early months of 1836, the longtime mission-settlement-turned-fort became the ultimate symbol of Anglo-American colonial perseverance and destiny. Here Anglo-Americans would pin their claims of ownership over the whole of Texas and carve out their justifications for war and Mexican dispossession. It was also here that they built the U.S. Quartermaster's Department storehouse—both a symbol and an instrument of Anglo-American supremacy—in the aftermath of annexation. Thus, for most Hispanic residents, the mission-fort served as a physical reminder of how remarkably times had changed.[44]

Under the Blacksnake Whip: A New Age of Anti-Black Slavery

The coerced acquisition of Hispanic property, the usurpation of commercial networks, and the destruction and replacement of colonial markers were all functions of the massive transfer of people from the United

States to the borderlands. From 1836 to 1860, the population of Texas exploded. This generation of Anglo colonists continued to ride the coat-tails of their English-speaking predecessors, traveling from all over the United States, but most relocated from the South, especially Tennessee, Alabama, Georgia, and Mississippi. By 1860, the overall population of Texas—not including the independent Native people of the region—had swelled from 38,000 to 604,000. Included among them, of course, were 183,000 enslaved Black people, whose forced migration represented the vast scale of human movement during the era as a chain of violence and exploitation. In many respects, Anglo-Texas had become by 1860 a land of foreign invaders and tethered people.[45]

Texians pinned the fortunes and future of their cotton-based paradise to the ever-growing transplantation of Anglo colonists. As Governor Bell explained in his message to the Texas state legislature in 1853, "The past year has been distinguished by an unusual yield of the agricultural products of the State; and the superabundant returns of the husbandman find a ready demand in the tide of immigration now swelling to an unexampled extent. With few exceptions, general health has been enjoyed by the citizens of every section." Others concurred. "Again, we want population," declared Congressman Pendleton Murrah in 1857. "We want more of our rich lands in cultivation; and every inducement, however slight it may be, ought to be held out to emigrants."[46] In general, the economic benefits were quite extensive for the Anglo colonial project, as movement itself propped up Anglo development. The gateway towns of Natchitoches, Shreveport, and Fulton grew as colonists funneled their way into Texas through the Gulf of Mexico and the Red River. With overland travel growing, especially along the northeast trails, portions of Texas were increasingly dotted with impromptu campsites, travelers inns, and urban hotels. Port towns and way stations like Galveston and Houston benefited economically from the flow of people who traveled by river and by sea, with local establishments charging fees for all sorts of services, including lodging, boarding, wagon repair, horse stabling, and resupplying. For instance, the cost of travel to Montgomery County, Texas, for two Alabama families, numbering fifteen people, with fifty enslaved African Americans and various draft animals, was about $120; with tens of thousands of people making their way to Texas, the accumulated value of such expenses meant Anglo-American locals reaped significant profits. Texian commentators thus had reason to laud "the tide of immigration."[47]

But even as Anglo-American newcomers received the credit for growing the economy and for developing the built environment of Texas, enslaved Black people were the primary engines of economic change, the major suppliers of colonial labor. The midcentury reality that Texian writers would often skirt (or treat euphemistically) was the fact that wherever Anglo-Americans went, enslaved people toiled. The sugarcane fields that dotted the eastern and Gulf portions of Texas, for instance, were made profitable only by slave labor. There African Americans did everything: they prepared the land, planted the stems, gathered and rolled the cane, and boiled the sugar until crystallization. They also took care of the many cornfields that sustained the growing population of Anglo-Texas, and still others labored as domestic servants for the rich and the (relatively) poor.[48] And when slaveholders had surplus slaves or were in need of a quick influx of cash, they hired out their slaves for all sorts of purposes. Hired-out enslaved people worked as cultivators, pickers, builders, mechanics, cooks, carpenters, and in-home servants. Their presence was widespread, evidence of "slavery's flexibility and functional utility" in Texas.[49]

As further evidence of that flexibility, Anglo-Americans also forced enslaved Black people to care for their herds of animals, especially on the vast grasslands of the region. After touring Texas in 1839, Gaillardet noticed that "Texians keep no pastures or stables for these animals [horses]; they mark them with their branding iron and leave them on the open plains. They send out their home slaves, the Negroes, to retrieve these prairie slaves whenever they want to use them." Daniel Phillips remembered how as a boy on his slaver's ranch in San Marcos "de men cotches de wild horses and I has to drive 'em so's dey won't git wild again." And Phillips was not alone; Jack Bess had similar memories of his enslavement in Goliad. But pastoral labor was not confined to the western portions of the Texas borderlands; even on plantations in the easternmost parts of Texas, such as the one Wash Anderson was forced to work on in Orange County, enslaved Black people spent significant time tending to animals: "Dey had plenty of hosses and mules and cows on de ol' plantation. I had to look atter some of de hosses but dem what I hatter look atter was s'pose to be de bes' hosses in de bunch." Herding was one way for slavers to exploit young enslaved people before they forced them to do backbreaking labor as field hands.[50] In Texas there were few laboring roles enslaved people could not fill.

The diversity of slave labor notwithstanding, in an economy increasingly dominated by cotton, most enslaved people were forced to dedicate their labor to cotton production. Cotton production, however, did not simply involve the planting and harvesting of cotton; there were multiple labor-intensive steps along the way that converted uncultivated land to lucrative cotton yields. Black slave labor was essential at each step. From clearing the land to tilling the soil, from picking the cotton to removing the fibers for baling and transport, Black slave labor made the cotton-producing machine run in Texas. Even the clothes enslaved people wore to survive their exploited condition were supplied by their own labor. William Bollaert noticed the diversity of cotton-related slave labor when he visited a Texas plantation in the 1840s: "They spin and weave all their cotton and woolen clothing on this plantation and make the bagging and rope of cotton, for baling upon the cotton for market." In fact, Anglo-American slavers kept their enslaved workforce so occupied that labor shortages abounded: "Much more planting, particularly cotton, would go on if there was more 'force' (hands); as it is, many of the planters and farmers plant more than they can gather in or pick."[51]

Although enslaved Black people could be found toiling in every aspect of cotton production, slave labor was most valuable for cotton picking. Not only was it grueling, tedious, and painful work; it was the one part of the cotton-integrated system that struggled to measure up to transnational demands. As Edward Baptist has explained, during the first several decades of the nineteenth century technological innovations across the Atlantic world allowed for the easier accumulation of capital, the faster transportation of goods, and the more efficient manufacturing of textiles. But during that same period, "there was no mechanical innovation of any kind to speed up the harvesting of cotton." Thus, Black people were driven to reinvent themselves and to expand their laboring capacities to meet ever-increasing output expectations—or face the torture of their slavers.[52]

Enslaved African Americans were highly productive when it came to collecting cotton fibers from the field. In terms of output, estimates vary, but all are astounding—and testament to the extreme exploitation and violence endured by enslaved people. Contemporary observers measured *individual* Black cotton picking in the thousands of pounds. In 1843, Bollaert learned that "a good working hand in fine weather will pick 1,000 pounds of cotton per week." More than a decade later, Frederick Law Olmsted met a Mr. Strather in eastern Texas who averaged "seven and a half bales to the hand"—or about three thousand pounds per slave—on his two plantations in one season. Formerly enslaved people, remembering in the 1930s the tens of thousands of hours they and their counterparts spent in the cotton fields, put their estimates in the hundreds of pounds per day. Mary Kincheon Edwards recalled, "Us pick 'bout 100 pound cotton in one basket. I didn't mind pickin' cotton, 'cause I never did have de backache. I pick two and three hunnert pounds a day and one day I picked 400."[53]

Given these remarkable output figures, enslaved Black people were, first and foremost, perceived as economic assets by Anglo-Americans. They were the means by which Anglo-American slaver-colonists could translate the marshaling of capital into personal wealth and economic expansion. And as cotton output figures grew exponentially, so did Anglo-American dehumanization of Black bodies. The numbers that Anglo slavers ascribed to their chattels' painful labor worked to divorce these enslaved people from their personhood. In the context of Anglo slaver profit making, slave bodies were predictable machines that could be input into a larger system of cotton production and wealth accumulation. The endurance of twentieth-century informants' memories regarding particular cotton-picking measurements speaks to their awareness of their role in the broader cotton calculus; they knew that their identity was tied inexorably to the ever-shifting numbers on a scale. The economics of Anglo-American slavery in Texas therefore cannot be discounted—especially when considering how the cotton economy provided the fulcrum for the making and remaking of anti-Blackness. Cotton output figures—monetized calculations—increasingly became the measure of most Black people's worth in Anglo-Texas society. This helps to explain how and why slavers made Black bodies even more fungible: as long as these bodily "machines" could satisfy the economic desires of slavers, the individual identities of enslaved people were meaningless. Here Black *lives* did not matter; slavers concerned themselves only with net Black *productivity*.

Yet to characterize Anglo-American slavery as *solely* an economic system is to dismiss other equally dynamic, interactive components of Texian slavery (as well as Anglo-generated anti-Blackness). Anglo-American slavers, like their Hispanic predecessors, imagined the spread of their form of slavery as part of a broader civilizing mission. In this sense, slaveholding had immense symbolic, cultural value to the slaver communities that relocated and then re-created themselves in the Texas borderlands. Specifically, in the minds of Anglo-Americans, slaveholding was indicative of an ordered community, one that placed honorable White men at the head of society above all others, especially slaves. Subjugated slaves were socially valuable as a reminder of an appropriately structured, civilized world. Mid-nineteenth-century Anglo-American supremacy hinged upon this logic, and Anglo colonists and their descendants worked hard to implement their social vision.

While the lived conditions of the Texas borderlands shaped the culture of Anglo-Americans over time, most of the settlers who peopled the Texas borderlands during this era transplanted their value systems from the U.S. South. In the words of one observer, the "morals and ideas of propriety differ but little from the standard upon such subjects adopted in the states of the South."[54] As was the case during the first generation of Anglo-American colonization, southern ideas about manly honor were especially prominent. White men were to be in charge at every level of society: governmental, communal, and familial. The ideal, honorable man was one who could secure the prosperity of his people while protecting them from danger. If a firm hand was necessary, so be it; violence was justified if administered for the purpose of protecting his people. But violence was supposed to be limited, a means to control and to teach. The honorable man was therefore fatherly, ambitious, loyal, honest, strong, and protective. Yet he was also fiercely independent and unflinchingly violent, especially when facing supposedly inferior people.[55]

So-called honorable men abounded in mid-nineteenth-century Texas. Hiram G. Runnels, a major slaver and former governor of Mississippi who relocated to Texas in 1842, was one such man. Although his financial problems were likely the main cause for his relocation to Texas, he purportedly first came "under a call for volunteers," receiving the "authority to raise a regiment for the service of Texas." Soon after, he "settled in Brazoria, with the view of building up his shattered fortune," in part through the exploitation and sale of dozens of enslaved Black people. Eventually Runnels made his way to Harris County, where he managed a moderate-size estate that included eight of his own slaves and a number he rented for hire. By the time of his death, his holdings amounted to about $18,000, most of it tied to his slaves and their labor. According to his peers, he was a man of great "moral worth": "In all the relations of life, either as a public or private man, there was much to admire; he was brave, generous, confiding—his hand and purse were ever open to a friend; he was a kind parent, a devoted and affectionate husband." In short, Runnels was the ideal fatherly figure, and when he died, state legislators made it a point to send his family resolutions of condolence.[56] There was also Anson Jones, the last president of the Republic of Texas and a slaver who was, in the words of his contemporaries, "so well known for his talents, his patriotism, and his devotion to the South and to the whole of our beloved country." He, like Runnels, committed to Anglo-Texas "his talents and his blood whenever necessary" and was "noble" in his military service. If he was stern in his public persona, he was gentle on a personal level: "In his private associations, he was kind, courteous, and hospitable; as a husband, he was kind and affectionate; as a father, he filled the whole duties of that significant word; as a master, he was kind."[57] And then there was Edward Burleson, the longtime Indian and Mexican fighter (and slaver), who may have been the archetype of the honorable Texian man. Upon Burleson's death Guy M. Bryan declared, "Brave without rashness, cautious without timidity, benevolent without weakness, he was the friend of the vanquished, as he was the terror of the enemy." But the flipside of Burleson's bravery was his "softness and delicacy of feeling"—because it was equally important for an Anglo-American man to be "kind and gentle in his family" as well as "benevolent and humane."[58]

These ideal traits undergirded the paternalism that Anglo-Americans sought to impose on the Texas borderlands during the mid-nineteenth century. This paternalism, of course, was most visible in the context of their enslavement of Black people. Slavers created the fiction that their slaveholding was for the good of themselves, their families, their community, *and* their slaves. According to this logic, the model slaveholder cared for slaves and resorted to violence only for purposes of discipline, like a father would with his children.[59] This ideal colored the commentary of many Anglo-American observers. "Opinion stigmatizes persons who maltreat their Slaves," claimed the Texas booster William Kennedy, "and the general tendency is to feed them sufficiently, and to use them without rigour. Scanty fare and harsh treatment are generally confined to the Slaves of impoverished owners. . . . The Negroes of Slaveholders in easy circumstances are considered to enjoy as good health, and to live as long as free persons." Bollaert, a friend of Kennedy, offered a similar assessment of the paternalism of the Anglo-American slaver: "Generally speaking . . . the Negroes are well treated, and I can bear witness that they are not over-worked or ill-used."[60]

As was the case during the early years of Anglo colonization, the slaves-as-family metaphor was foundational to slaver ideology. It provided a justification for the enslavement of people while reinforcing the core organizing principle of White manly dominance within Anglo-Texan society. Needless to say, Anglo-Americans worked tirelessly, through emotive language, to craft an image of a paternalistic society.[61] Contemporaries spoke of "family Negros," who were "brought up by their owners" and "reared in my family with my own little children." They made claims to "family feelings" and memories of shared upbringings among slaves and masters. "I have three slaves," explained William

Beck Ochiltree during the Texas constitutional convention of 1845, "two of them a father and mother, the property of my ancestor, which came to me endeared by all the recollections which will grow up between master and slave brought up together from childhood, and tended in infancy by the same black 'mammy.'" And they frequently emphasized the importance of a firm fatherly approach toward their slaves. "It is our duty to be humane at the same time that it is our duty to be just," Ochiltree's colleague James Love professed. "And he would not permit inhumanity towards a slave nay more than towards a child; but would place them on the same footing." Supposed slave love and loyalty were the hallmarks of their paternalism. Samuel Maverick, for instance, was so moved by the bravery of his slave Griffin, who would "do anything for his master," that he believed Griffin deserved a monument.[62]

In the realm of public discourse, Anglo-American slaveholders were devout paternalists. They always strove to be "humane" toward their children-slaves, and any violence directed toward them could be explained away as appropriate punishment and discipline. Yet, as numerous scholars have demonstrated, paternalism hardly reflected the lived experiences of enslaved African American people. Mid-nineteenth-century Anglo-American slavery was above all a system of violence and humiliation, designed to exploit the labor of dehumanized Black people. Nonetheless, the twentieth-century testimony of formerly enslaved people suggests that the slaves-as-family fiction *did* shape the experiences of enslaved people, especially in mid-nineteenth-century Texas. Naming practices are revealing. Slaves, slavers, and other members of the "home" wore the titles of kin. Formerly enslaved Laura Cornish, for instance, was "Aunt Laura," while her slaver, Isaiah Day, was "Papa Day." To Milly Forward, Master Jason Forward and Mistress Sarah Ann Forward were "je' like dey us pappy and mammy," and to Lou Turner, "old missy" was "mama." Even Sarah Ford's overseer, who would "whip de slaves so much dat some like my papa what had spirit was all de time runnin' 'way," was known as "Uncle Jake."[63] Slavers, moreover, often forced their slaves to take their surnames, and in the aftermath of emancipation some decided to keep their former slaver's name. As the daughter-in-law of Martin Jackson, a formerly enslaved person, explained, "The master's name was usually adopted by a slave after he was set free . . . because it was the logical thing to do and the easiest way to be identified [rather] than . . . through affection for the master."[64] But the voluntary taking of a former slaver's surname also reflected the enduring nature of slaver influence and power. Slaveholders (and then former slaveholders) framed

Black social significance in Anglo-Texas. This was intentional: by making slaves family, they indicated that even their slaves' natal identities were dependent upon them. John McCoy explained the predicament of enslaved (and formerly enslaved) people when it came to understanding their familial and natal connections: "All a slave have to go by am what de white folks tells him 'bout his kinfolks."[65] In other words, slavers *did* recognize a "personhood" of enslaved people; it was simply a personhood that could not exist outside of the authority of the slaver.[66]

As in the earlier pre-Rebellion period, Anglo-American slaver family making was not just metaphorical. In addition to providing an ideological framework for their exploitation and subjugation of Black people, slaver kin incorporation offered a vehicle for physical domination of their slaves. Forced family making, or sexual violence, was perhaps one of the most effective ways in which Anglo-Americans solidified their rule in Anglo-Texas. By sexually exploiting their slaves, slavers reiterated their complete dominance while forging familial connections that bound their slaves to the slave system *and* expanded their slaveholdings.[67] Forced family making revealed the depths of Anglo-American slaveholder depravity, as well as their ability to consolidate their dominion in the Texas borderlands.

Enslaved Black women endured the brunt of Anglo slaver sexual violence. In many cases, slavers themselves violated the enslaved women they owned. As a number of formerly enslaved people explained, slavers like Albertus Arnwine exploited enslaved women to fulfill their sexual or perverse desires, especially when they were unmarried. At times, the wealthier slaveholders used enslaved women as showpieces, adorning them in the finest dresses and jewelry available to them.[68] But few examples exist of such symbols of conspicuous sexual consumption; for the most part, these forced "partners" were clothed and fed like the rest of the slavers' human property, and they all suffered from the same forces of White male aggression, slaver domination, and Black vulnerability. And when slaveholders did not perpetrate sexual violence on their own, they induced proxies to do their bidding.[69] Few formerly enslaved people could forget how slaveholders would force couples together for purposes of increasing their slave "stock." As Katie Darling remembered, "Niggers didn't cou't then like they do now, massa pick out a po'tly man and a po'tly gal and jist put 'em together. What he want am the stock." And when enslaved women like Silvia King would not capitulate to slaver breeding schemes, slavers resorted to more conventional forms of violence: "I fit him good and plenty till de overseer shakes a blacksnake whip over me."[70] The fact that so many Anglo-American slavers controlled the sexual partnerships of their slaves speaks to the predominance of slaveholder proxy violence. Even in the more banal instances, when slavers simply demanded that their slaves receive permission for their relationships with other slaves, the slaver's control over his slaves' sexual behavior was implied.[71] Overall, slaveholder sexual violence, both direct and proxy, reinforced the slaver's utter, unquestionable authority over his slaves. In the words of Betty Powers, "Dey thinks nothin' on de plantation 'bout de feelin's of de women and dere ain't no 'spect for dem. De overseer and white mens took 'vantage of de women like dey wants to. De woman better not make no fuss 'bout sich. If she do, it am de whippin' for her."[72]

Sexual violence also had consequences for enslaved children, even if available evidence does not indicate that they were direct victims. The children of slavers and "breeders" often were deprived of relationships with their biological fathers and had difficulty keeping track of their siblings. In the absence of explicit father figures, some, such as William Byrd, were taught to believe they were originally "a stray in the woods." Others discovered early in life the psychological pain and disorientation that came with exposure to the logic of Anglo-American heritable slavery, which taught children that their slave status was inherited from their mother. As they looked around and surveyed their enslaved counterparts, children had to create their own familial and social schemata. Sexual violence, as Adeline Marshall recalled, fostered natal alienation: "Dat de reason so many 'No Nation' niggers 'round. Some call dem 'Bright' niggers, but I call dem 'No Nation' 'cause dat what dey is, ain't all black or all white, but mix."[73] Compounding this psychological suffering was the grim fact that all enslaved children served as genealogical anchors for their enslaved family members. As long as children were an integral part of the lives of enslaved people, it was harder and riskier for them to rebel or escape from slavery. In this way, the human offspring of slaveholder sexual violence, direct or proxy, had two simultaneous effects: (1) it expanded the wealth of the slaveholder (by adding to his property holdings), and (2) it further bound his slaves to him (through the creation of new genealogical ties).[74] In the borderlands, where state-level authority could be fleeting, these mechanisms added a layer of security to the broader Anglo colonial project.

Even if the Anglo-American paternalist ethos could (rhetorically) accommodate forced family making and sexual violence, it failed when it came to accounting for the inherent violence of Anglo-American slavery. As cotton-picking demands grew decade by decade, so did slaver violence. Accounts from contemporaries tracked the escalation of violence in Texas. In 1840, the British emissary Francis Sheridan heard from Texas locals during his visit that "the great demand for labor, the immense price it fetches, the poverty & covetousness of the proprietors, all militate against the poor nigger, and I fear his leisure moments are few & his lashes frequent." Over a decade and a half later, Olmsted, a New Englander who toured Texas for evidence of the demoralizing effects of anti-Black slavery, was surprised to see how slavers and slaves were in a constant "state of war": "Damn 'em, give 'em hell, frequent expressions of the ruder planters towards their negroes, appeared to be used as if with a meaning—a threat to make their life infernal if they do not submit abjectly and constantly. There seemed to be the consciousness of a wrong relation and a determination to face conscience down, and continue it; to work up the 'damned niggers,' with a sole eye to selfish profit, cash down, in this world." In 1860, the cruelty of one Coryell County slaver became such a spectacle that a witness believed he had never seen draft animals treated so poorly.[75] Given the violent context of the Texas borderlands, such an indictment speaks volumes.

Newspaper advertisements regarding fugitive enslaved people also revealed the extreme violence of Anglo-American slavery in Texas, albeit unintentionally. Although the authors of these advertisements intended to offer descriptive information to aid in recapturing a slave or reuniting her with her slaver, their detailed descriptions also exposed the kind of physical and psychological violence slaveholders and their proxies inflicted upon Black people. Such newspaper notices were replete with references to physical abuse: superficial scars, missing teeth, branded initials, facial deformations, and bodily mutilation.[76] At times the details were ghastly, like those in the Austin *City Gazette* regarding one fugitive by the name of Joe, whose "little finger of the right hand has been cut off," or those in the Clarksville *Northern Standard* describing the fugitive Bob, who was "very dark, both ears bit off . . . with black teeth much scattered." Other advertisements were more suggestive of psychological violence. The not uncommon mention of speech impediments, stammers, and anxiety problems among fugitives may have reflected what Eugene Genovese refers to in his seminal study on master-slave relations as "accommodation to paternalism," where seemingly weak or servile characteristics were actually subversive actions akin to resistance.[77] Or it may have signified the role that fear and trauma played in the everyday interactions of enslaved people and slaveholders. Tom, a thirty-year-old fugitive who "holds his head down mostly; and stammers considerably," for instance, evidently was not a passive man; the fact that he tried to escape from Anglo-American slavery reveals this. But with "the end of one of his thumbs . . . smashed . . . and disfigured," he was also a man who suffered from horrendous violence.[78] As enslaved people faced the threat of violence on a day-to-day basis, it does not seem unreasonable to assume that some struggled to find the words, cadence, and grammar necessary to appease their slavers and Anglo-Americans in general. Rather, an appreciation of their struggles to endure slaver violence makes their surviving testimony—often vivid and articulate—that much more impressive.

The verbal expression of slaver violence was no easy task for enslaved people—even decades after they suffered from it. The Federal Writers' Project narratives, which recorded the spoken testimony of formerly enslaved people during the latter part of the 1930s, serve as reminders of the long, transtemporal reach of Anglo-American slaver violence. A survey of the more than two hundred former slave testimonies can give the impression that Anglo-American paternalism bred truly benevolent masters. Scores of testimonies in fact say just that: "Old massa was kind and good"; "massa give us plenty to eat; fact, he treated us kind-a like he own boys"; "Massa was purty good." These were the transcribed words of people who were once enslaved in Texas by Anglo-Americans.[79] But a close, systematic reading of these narratives makes it obvious that a "kind" or "good" master was hardly a nonabusive one. Following nearly every claim regarding a benevolent slaveholder was a description of a punishment meted out by the slaver or his proxy. Or the formerly enslaved informant displaced the violence of Anglo-American slavery onto others, explaining how atrociously violent a neighbor, slave patroller, or driver was. Perhaps the interviewees sometimes skirted personal stories of slaver abuse so as to not offend the racist sensibilities of their often White interviewers during the era of Jim Crow.[80] Or perhaps reliving the violence they endured decades earlier, through verbalization, was too much to bear. In any case, such a strategy was so common that the testimonials of formerly enslaved people appear somewhat formulaic. Hagar Lewis's discussion of Anglo-American violence was typical: "I can't say we were treated bad, 'cause I'd tell a story. I've always been treated good by whites, but many of the niggers was killed. They'd say bad words to the bosses and they'd shoot 'em."[81]

As evasive as many formerly enslaved people were, a good number were unflinchingly candid about the slaver violence they experienced and observed. Most of them spoke of the frequent use of the whip—the "black snake," many called it. For slaveholders, the black snake was inducement for faster and more efficient cotton picking; it was the direct and implied violence that forced individuals to collect hundreds of pounds of cotton every single day. As Austin Grant explained it, "They tasked us. They would give us 200 or 300 pounds of cotton to bring in and you would git it, and if you didn' git it, you better, or you would git it tomorrow, or your back would git it." Yet whippings were hardly the extent of it. In addition to the sexual violence previously discussed, Anglo-Americans pushed human cruelty to its limits. Slaveholders and their proxies poured salt and pepper into the open wounds they created; they humiliated their slaves by attaching bell contraptions to their heads; they chained them to trees overnight; and they dragged enslaved people for miles from the back of their buggy. Slavers, seeking to maximize the productive output of their chattels, tortured Black people with virtually no regard for their sentience; some slavers were even willing to undermine their own financial well-being by murdering their slaves.[82] In such moments, claims of Anglo-American paternalism could not have been further from the truth.

If rape, torture, and murder were not enough to undermine the Anglo-American paternalist fiction, slaver participation in the separating of mothers, fathers, children, and siblings—the slave trade—should have. Some tried to reconcile the paternalist contradiction by claiming that the trade was small in scale and confined to the dealings of desperate slaveholders or unseemly characters.[83] Others, like W. Steinert, were less convinced by such logic, even as they still adhered to the myth of the benevolent slaver: "In general the slaves are well kept . . . [but] no matter how good the treatment may be and how much the laws protect the slaves, it is still cruel enough that the very noble white people leave their black brothers uneducated, tear apart family bonds by buying and selling slaves, and that they allow slave traders to drive chained Negroes to market where they are inspected before the sale like cattle." Regardless of how contemporaries framed the slave trade, it—along with day-to-day slaver violence—was one of the defining features of slave experiences. The trade was, above all, a vivid reminder that they were chattels, "like steers," as John Barker recalled. Beyond shattering families, it also fostered the utterly humiliating experience of the auction block. Stearlin Arnwine captured the essence of the slave trade in his testimony: "I seed slaves for sale on de auction block. They sol' 'em 'cordin' to strengt' and muscles. They was stripped to de wais'. I seed the women and little chillum cryin' and beggin' not to be separated, but it didn' do no good. They had to go."[84]

Although evidence suggests that the majority of enslaved Black people arrived in Texas alongside their colonizing slavers, tens of thousands came by means of slave traffickers. Atlantic shipping ties helped, as boatloads of bound Africans and African Americans poured in through the Gulf ports.[85] So did newspapers, which frequently advertised "Negroes for sale," public auctions, and trader deals. Men like the members of Sampson & Co., Shaben & Bro., G. F. Rogers & Bro., and Vance & Bro., who made their living by buying and selling people, were most prominent in the slave trade, but the commerce would not have functioned without the active involvement of nonprofessionals. Slave patrollers, town sheriffs, their deputies, and Texas Rangers caught and sold unclaimed fugitive slaves, often for a handsome fee. Town officials sold human chattels with other property when acting as administrators during estate sales. And editors disseminated news of impending sales by printing notices in their papers. This, of course, is to say nothing of the thousands of slaveholders who bought and sold slaves as labor investments or to turn a quick profit.[86] The world that Anglo-Americans built in Texas—its transportation network, financial connections, print culture, and law enforcement apparatus—all worked together to facilitate the forced movement of enslaved Black people. With prices ranging from several hundred to several thousand dollars per slave, there was a lot of money to be made in slave commerce, and many Anglo-Americans made sure to partake in it.[87] This also meant that the commodification of Black bodies was a widespread enterprise, not just the work of a handful of shrewd slave traders.

Thus, the climate of violence nurtured by Anglo-Americans was made possible by the collective efforts of tens of thousands of individual slavers and their proxies. Each slaving participant, with his personal infliction of pain upon Black individuals, contributed to the general dehumanization and subjugation of Black people in Texas. But slaveholders also marshaled the embryonic state apparatus for essentially the same purposes. Their ability to reshape government and law so completely in favor of the oppression of Black people was unprecedented in the history of the Texas borderlands. While their Hispanic predecessors (and contemporary counterparts) also stigmatized Blackness, previous governmental strictures were hardly as comprehensive as they were in midcentury Anglo-Texas. The Texas Rebellion was, after all, a rejection of Mexican governmental efforts to control Anglo-American slaving violence, and it ushered in a distinctly anti-Black legal culture into Texas. After their victory, Anglo-Americans wrote into law the permanent subjugation of Black people. From day one, legislators excluded "Africans" and "the descendants of Africans" from national citizenship. They sought to devise a constitutional framework that would prevent African Americans from "passing" as White men, thereby strengthening the racial barrier between White and Black populations. And they worked tirelessly to enforce the primary tenet of their emerging social order: the notion that in Texas Black people were—and could be—nothing more than commodified chattel property. As Guy M. Bryan reminded his congressional colleagues in 1851, "In legislating, we should never loose [*sic*] sight of the fact, that the negro in the eye of the law, is property—as much the property of the owner as his cow, or his horse."[88]

Little captured the emergent age of state-backed anti-Black racism in Anglo-Texas as well as Anglo-American treatment of Black people who were not slaves. The supposed problem of the "free Negro" was among the most vexing public issues in Anglo-Texas during the mid-nineteenth century. To many leaders, the very existence of nonslave African Americans—who were not bound to the direct authority of a slaver—was antithetical to the new Anglo-Texan social order, so even before the Rebellion was over, Anglo-Americans embarked on criminalizing Black freedom. The efforts would continue for decades, resulting in laws and city ordinances that excluded nonslave Black people from permanent residence in Texas, prevented the manumission of slaves without congressional approval, and threatened the enslavement of nonslaves who resided in the Republic or State.[89] Anglo-Americans were explicit in their rationale: nonslave Black people disrupted the racial order they were crafting because free African Americans proved to the enslaved that Black people were not innately servile. To have a population of nonslave Black people would have subjected Anglo-Texas to various "evils," Anglo-Americans reasoned. "It is well known," declared Governor Elisha Pease, "that their intercourse with slaves tends to corrupt them and make them dissatisfied, and ought by all means to be avoided."[90] Ultimately, the idea of "free negroes" living within the boundaries of Anglo-Texas was anathema to Texian formulations of social being, and Anglo leaders could not abide them.

"They Was Goin' to Be Mexicans": Fugitive Freedom and the Shadow of Anti-Blackness

Forced into a system that rested upon the administration of extreme manly violence, collective Anglo investment in the economic value of slave property, and, to a lesser extent, the marshaling of state powers, enslaved Black people faced the apex of slaver power in the Texas borderlands. Their lives and well-being were, for the most part, subject to the whims of slaveholders, drivers, and their proxies. Yet, as so many scholars have argued for the past several decades, Anglo-American slavery did not create strictly passive, infantilized, or wholly subservient slaves. Enslaved Black people, rather, responded to the anti-Black regime as they and their ancestors had for generations, by adapting, refusing, surviving, moving.[91] Across the borderlands they established meaningful kin relationships with one another, subverting the slaver class's attempt to wield family as a mechanism of bondage. Others carved out their own spaces within an ever-broadening Black community, confounding or frightening Anglo observers, whose collective ethnographic eye failed to discern the complex tapestry of Black social relations.[92] Still others were more outwardly resistant, like those who poisoned their slavers and their families, axed their overseers to death, or smashed the heads of slave hunters with blacksmith anvils and sledgehammers. Black uprisings, small and large, always put Anglo-Americans into a frenzy, with Anglo officials enacting laws and ordinances to further criminalize Black behavior and newspaper editors decrying the supposedly lax treatment of Black people. But even as retribution for offenders was often swift and extralegal, Black refusal and resistance continued through the middle decades of the nineteenth century.[93] Although Anglo-American slavery attempted to strip and recast the personhood of enslaved people, African Americans did all they could to preserve it in ways that were meaningful to them.[94]

Ultimately the most common form of explicit resistance to Anglo-American slavery was flight, attempted escape.[95] Newspapers, filled with scores of fugitive advertisements, bore witness to the pervasiveness of this strategy. Notices of "Ranaway," "A Runaway Negro," and "Fifty Dollars Reward!" were regular features of Texian periodicals, evidence of both slavers' commitment to restoring their escaped property and Black dedication to personal freedom. Most fugitives seem to have attempted to flee from Anglo-American slavery on their own, but from time to time notices indicated larger parties of escapees, like the eight enslaved Black individuals who absconded from the Smith County slaveholder Lewis Todd in September 1850. This group included two men named John and Kye; a pregnant woman named Rachael; two young girls; and three boys, one a toddler. John and Kye had acquired firearms, and Todd suspected that they were all "making for the Wichita Mountains and aim to get with the Indians." What made this group particularly unusual was the inclusion of women and children. Most reported fugitives were men—partly because it was more dangerous to travel with children—but this party bucked the trend. Clearly the freedom of their families was a priority for Rachael, John, and Kye.[96]

There were other reports of fugitives heading to Native country, but most of the discussion about Black escapees revolved around slaveholder suspicions that their slaves were heading across the southern border into Mexico.[97] In the eyes of Anglo-American contemporaries, the Mexican border became a specter, a reminder of the geographical limits of Anglo-American slaver-colonial authority. And to a large degree, they were right. Even the eastern portions of Texas, the heart of Texian dominion, were susceptible to Mexico's fugitive lure. One of the more elaborate escape attempts was organized in the winter of 1850–51 by four or five dozen enslaved Black people living in and around Brenham. According to a young enslaved boy who was implicated in the plot, a number of fugitives were recruiting enslaved locals "to depart for Mexico" that February and "nearly every one of the negro fellows of this place and vicinity were in the conspiracy." The plotters, it seems, were planning to fight their way toward the border if they had to, as "they had taken several guns, a keg of powder, etc." in preparation for their escape. The fortuitous (for Texian slavers) capture of the young boy, as well as the interrogation of about fifteen or twenty other enslaved individuals, ultimately foiled their plans for mass liberation, but two "negro fellows" still slipped away on their own, despite the investigation. White locals also received word that a similar plot had been discovered in Columbus, about forty miles south of Brenham. With Mexico on their minds, enslaved Black people ensured that the whole of Texas would remain part of the borderlands, even well into the mid-nineteenth century.[98]

Fugitive populations south and west of the Río Grande thus grew over the decades as fugitives built "a clearly established network that . . . even rivaled the Underground Railroad in the upper South."[99] In 1842, Thomas Green found a number of Black escapees just across the border. Their presence was so prominent that he speculated, "The interference of the former [Mexico] with the rights of negro property of the latter [Texas], and many other opposite interests, would keep up between the two perpetual excitement, which would result in perpetual war."[100] Two years later, the Clarksville *Northern Standard* reported "some thirty fugitive slaves from Texas in and about Matamoras," and in 1850 the ever-scheming Indian agent Marcellus DuVal knew of over one hundred Black fugitives who were living around the Río Grande with the support of the Seminole leader Coacoochee.[101] During the mid-1850s, Olmsted noted that "runaways were *constantly* arriving" at Negras Piedras in Coahuila, and John "Rip" Ford, as editor of the Austin *Texas State Times*, claimed that there were four thousand fugitives—worth $3.2 million to Anglo slavers—living across the national border.[102] Matters became so urgent to Anglo-American slaveholders that legislators sought extradition treaties with Mexico.[103] But the prospect of freedom was too great an inducement to slow the tide of Black refugees in Mexico. "There wasn't no reason to run up North," Felix Haywood explained during the 1930s. "All we had to do was to walk, but walk South, and we'd be free as soon as we crossed the Rio Grande. In Mexico you could be free. They didn't care what color you was, black, white, yellow or blue. Hundreds of slaves did go to Mexico and got on all right. We would hear about 'em and how they was goin' to be Mexicans. They brought up their children to speak only Mexico."[104]

Across the border, Black escapees largely fended for themselves, navigating a complex milieu of Mexican political, economic, and cultural interests. With anti-Texian sentiment rising among the ranks of Mexican officials south of the border, the questions of extradition, official colonization of fugitives, and Black military enlistment for protection of the border took on both national and international significance.[105] With varying degrees of support, Black fugitives inserted themselves into local communities, like Matamoros, Tamaulipas, where by 1853 the Black population swelled to some 450 people, or 4.5 percent of the population. At Piedras Negras, another popular destination, escapees learned Spanish and devoted their labor and skills to whatever capacity could keep them economically afloat, while some acclimated themselves to northern Mexican society by joining churches or marrying into local families. After Olmsted visited the town during his tour of the borderlands, he convinced himself that in Piedras Negras Black men "could live very comfortably," especially if they "were industrious and saving." Others pinned their fortunes on government-sponsored colonization schemes, such as the one established in Coahuila at Hacienda de Nacimiento. Eventually known as Nacimiento de los Negros, this Black settlement emerged in 1852 out of Mexican government collaborations with Coacoochee and his Black partners, the "Mascogos" (as they were known in Mexican discourse). Under the leadership of John Horse, the residents of Nacimiento proved to the national government the possible benefits of a Black barrier to Texian and Native incursions into the North, even leading an effective campaign against Comanches in 1856. Recognizing the geopolitical worth of Black fugitives, the Mexican state codified Black freedom in its constitution a year later, indicating, at least on paper, that fugitives "who set foot in national territory recover, by this fact alone, their liberty," and were thus protected by the government against efforts, internal and external, to reenslave them.[106]

Fugitive freedom was, nevertheless, often ephemeral if not entirely illusory for many. In practice, fugitivity meant confiscating and repurposing slaver property and tools, constantly moving and evading the surveillance system of slavers and their proxies, charting new routes and landscapes of refuge, forging new personal connections, and establishing a sense of home in a historically unstable region. From a broad perspective, it represented Black dedication to "survivance," as well as the limits of slaver authority. Yet for all its symbolism as a declaration of Black agency, fugitivity was an ongoing condition that could offer only the prospects of Black freedom. Anti-Black threats lurked around nearly every corner, and even geography and distance could not shield Black fugitives fully from the long tentacles of slaver machinations. The most obvious dangers were the forays of Texas slave hunters into the Mexican North, which, despite their illegality, occurred with surprising frequency throughout the 1840s and 1850s. Even with defensive support from various Mexican locals, who usually saw Texian slave hunting as a violation of Mexican sovereignty, Black fugitives often fell prey to slave catchers. Slave-hunting expeditions sometimes dovetailed with other transborder endeavors, like the Anglo "punishing" of rebellious Native people, but any Anglo-American presence across the border tended to endanger Black refugees. Given the omnipresent threat of slaver invasion, Olmsted's account of meeting a "startled" and guarded Black man on the streets of Piedras Negras speaks to the precariousness of Black freedom in Mexico. According to James Nichols, "No black was secure from this illegitimate use of violence, and even in Mexico African Americans could not completely escape the reduction of blackness to servility."[107]

The draw of Mexico did not necessarily carry all Black fugitives across the Mexican-Texas border. Because the cross-border mobility of Anglo and Hispanic traders, multiethnic "bandits" and traffickers, Mexican laborers, and Native communities made the zone closest to the Mexican border an especially unstable space (even by borderlands standards), in some cases enslaved Black people found a degree of security and independence in the company of the more impoverished Hispanic people of the southern and western portions of Texas, who were known to "harbor . . . them in their camps at night," socialize with them, and even aid in their escape.[108] These Texas-located Black-Hispanic collaborations grew particularly in the aftermath of the U.S.-Mexico War, as the political boundary between the two countries ossified, at least in national imaginations, along the Río Grande. Whereas prior to the war, the so-called Nueces Strip (the land between the Río Grande and the Nueces River) was disputed territory in the eyes of Hispanic and Texian officials, when the United States beat Mexico into submission during the war, the region fell, per international law, within the boundaries of the United States. Although the Hispanic state apparatus had struggled to assert some measure of control for centuries, even its nominal authority dried up by the late 1840s, and for thousands of exploited Mexican laborers, the trans–Río Grande region suddenly became a place of opportunity and new beginnings.[109] In Texas, these Hispanic—or perhaps Hispanicized—"runaways" became known as *peones*, and they would simultaneously present Anglo-Texans with a source of cheap labor and yet another borderlands menace. Their fraternization with and support of enslaved Black people undermined the project of Anglo slaver supremacy, spawning more fears of Black insurrection and possible Hispanic subversion.[110]

Considerable scholarly uncertainty surrounds the origins of the *peones*, whose presence swelled throughout the Texas borderlands during the late 1840s and 1850s. Some scholars have posited that most were descendants of the Native people missionized in, transplanted to, or enslaved in northern Mexico during earlier periods, while others have identified them simply as members of a poor, transient *mestizo* class.[111] Either way, the lives of the *peones* of northern Mexico were circumscribed, like those of their Black counterparts in Anglo-Texas, by the coercive mechanisms of powerful men and their proxies. Bound to *hacendados* (great estate owners) by perpetual debt, *peones* controlled neither their labor nor their mobility and, in many instances, passed on their debt to their children upon death. Unlike enslaved Black people, the bodies of *peones* could not be sold or purchased on the market, but with the commodification of their debt, *peones* had little control over where they worked or for whom. Perpetuating debt peonage, of course, was their meager wage, which in practice often arrived in rations or more credit, to be expended at the *tienda de raya*, the estate store. Violence kept many *peones* subservient and immobilized, as *hacendados* were not afraid to mete out severe "punishments" for defiant workers.[112]

The main problem for their exploiters, especially in the aftermath of the U.S. takeover of Mexico in the 1840s, was the contested nature of the trans–Río Grande region. As long as the Mexican state struggled to establish its authority in the North, *peones* could seize opportunities for a better life by embracing their mobility and confounding national boundaries. In Texas, *peones* garnered higher wages for their labor, especially as muleteers, teamsters, and carters in the trans–Río Grande trade, which according to one south Texas legislator-promoter, was "worth millions of dollars to the State per annum." Yet their mobility unsettled Anglo commentators, and they often emerged in Anglo discourse as opportunists: "thieves," "prowlers," "murderers," and "plunderers." Still, what troubled Anglo colonists most was their association with Black fugitives. As cheap labor "willing to carry goods at a lower price than American citizens can carry them for," *peones* were a nuisance to some Anglo colonists while a boon to others.[113] But as resources for Black escapees, as supporters of a precarious Black freedom, *peones* threatened the very fabric of Anglo society. Although the scope of Black-*peón* cooperation may not have been great, Anglo slavers feared the worst: multiracial rebellion. Gonzales County residents grew so restless in October 1854 that they called for a special convention to outline remedies for the "evil resulting from the transient *peon* population in our midst," who placed themselves "on equality with the slave . . . stir[ring] up among our servants a spirit of insubordination." In Seguin County, Anglo-Americans passed a series of resolutions, demanding the expulsion of all *peones* and promising "prompt measures" for the offense of trading or even communicating with enslaved Black people. Extralegal violence, moreover, was not out of the question: "In the absence of a prompt and efficient remedy through the laws, this abuse will be corrected by the citizens themselves as a matter of self preservation."[114]

In their quest to locate and celebrate a shared history of multiracial resistance to White supremacy, scholars may have overemphasized the influence of the Black-*peón* partnership at midcentury.[115] As outcasts themselves, *peones* were not representative of a general Tejano rejection of Anglo domination. Their treatment at the hands of Texians nonetheless does speak to how Anglo-Texas operationalized their expanding anti-Black regime, particularly over communities that regularly spurned the (imagined) authority of the state. In general, Anglo-American observers understood the "rascally" *peón* to be a unique kind of Mexican, hardly anything like the Hispanic people who had been consorting with Anglo colonists for over a generation. "We do not wish to be understood as favouring the idea of proscribing the entire Mexican population now among us, as a class," explained the affronted Gonzales slaver-colonists. "There are a few worthy Mexicans in every county who have identified their interests with the country, by permanently settling and engaging with laudable enterprise, in industrial pursuits; all should be protected." The *peón* of whom they and many others spoke, rather, was "the half-negro, half Indian greaser, who runs away from his master in Mexico." "Don't compare the respectable Mexican with those of 'low degree,'" clarified the editor of the *Gulf Key*. "There is a wide difference between a Mexican of Castillian descent and that of a peon, mixed with negro and Indian blood."[116]

By distinguishing between "half-negro, half Indian" *peones* and "worthy Mexicans," Anglo commentators not only expressed their parsing of borderlands social dynamics; they also articulated the capaciousness of their anti-Black formulations. On the one hand, they implicitly recognized the distinct historical experiences of these oppressed, transient Hispanicized people, who, along with their ancestors, had been marginalized by the transgenerational reach of Spanish colonialism. On the other hand, they were racializing these defiant interlopers as Black, marking them guilty by association. Anglo-American observers could not understand *peón*-Black collaboration as anything but dangerous insurrectionist activity. If fugitives seeking freedom and a degree of autonomy were criminal for defying the Anglo slaver order, these *peones* were their accomplices, their co-conspirators. That they were also "runaways" from their own "masters" only reinforced their criminal association. The residents of Goliad believed this behavior stripped them of any semblance of Whiteness: "The continuance of the '*greasers*' 'as citizens' . . . is '*an intolerable nuisance*.'" In this way, the long shadow of anti-Blackness could engulf, at least at a discursive level, people on the margins. The violence that *peones* and other "low-degree" Hispanic people faced—branding, whipping, ambush, rape, and murder—was its natural outgrowth.[117]

Black fugitivity thus brought into stark relief the changing landscape of racialization in the Anglo-dominated borderlands of the midcentury. With the Anglo victory over the Mexican government in 1836 and the mass influx of Anglo colonists in the decades that followed, Texas's hegemonic racial regime naturally evolved along an Anglo-American axis. Incessant Texian war with Mexico, the general impoverishment of Hispanic residents, and a rising reputation for Black collusion inspired constant accusations of Hispanic treachery, subversion, indolence, and overall debasement.[118] As if by reflex, many Hispanic people—supposedly docile and exploitable yet untrustworthy and unruly—were Blackened in the minds of Anglo-American colonists. Physiognomic characterizations fused with moral condemnations, which, collectively, created the image of a Black-like "greaser" population.[119] "Mexicans—particularly men, . . . if their Hair would be a little curly would be taken any where for Negroes," claimed Adolphus Sterne. Speaking of the Hispanic women of San Antonio, Robert Weakley Brahan made a similar, if sexualized, comparison: "Many of these 'greasers,' [are] of fine figures & good features, the color of a mulatto."[120] Whether their perceived Blackness was an outgrowth of their subjugation or partly its cause, Anglo observers found their servile status suitable to their racial makeup. This helps to explain why, in the aftermath of the Anglo victory at San Jacinto in 1836, some of the Mexican soldiers captured by the Texas Army were distributed across Texas as "servants," held in bondage and forced to labor in the homes and on the plantations of Anglo "masters" for years. These servile ex-soldiers may not have been "slaves" by Anglo standards, but their treatment and representation suggest that they might as well have been. According to one commentator, these men were "effeminate, squalid, and unsoldierlike"—and thus hardly manly at all. Unmanly and with "complexions [that] varied from the African jet to the copper color of the North American Indian," these ex-soldiers, like all Black people in the Anglo-Texas world, were justifiably enslavable.[121]

If Black fugitives exposed Hispanic experiences of the debasing logic of Anglo anti-Blackness, rejection of their liberationist ambitions served as a means to benefit from that logic. It was not, after all, a coincidence that so many Anglo speakers and writers were quick to qualify their condemnations of *peones* and other "low-degree" Mexicans with celebratory comments about "worthy" Hispanic residents. This all too frequent discursive move partly reflected Anglo-American recognition of Texas's Hispanic colonial roots, which, although repugnantly "tyrannical" and "monkish" to Anglo-Americans, still deserved their respect as a "civilizing" force during an earlier era.[122] But Hispanic value also derived from an elite Tejano embrace of the ascending anti-Black, Anglo-American political economy. Influential men like José Antonio Navarro, José Francisco Ruíz, and Juan Seguín had, to varying degrees, supported the Texas Rebellion, and their shared interests in integrating Texas (and the

Mexican North) into the Atlantic-oriented market economy persisted in the years that followed. On a practical level, elite Tejanos protected and expanded their landholdings, doubled down on ranching enterprises, consolidated their control over regional commerce, secured municipal positions of authority (e.g., as justices of the peace, county commissioners, and tax collectors), and directly subjugated enslaved Black people.[123] To avoid the charge of Blackness, certain Tejanos made it clear that they could be useful instruments, if not equal benefactors, of the new anti-Black regime. Thus, when Navarro argued during the 1845 state constitutional convention that Hispanic people should not be excluded from definitions of Whiteness and citizenship, he made this argument in contradistinction to the inferior status of Blackness. As Navarro explained, he "was as much opposed to giving the right of suffrage to Africans or the descendants of Africans as any other gentleman."[124]

Navarro himself benefited from the personal exploitation of an enslaved twelve-year-old, and he was not alone.[125] U.S. census materials, including the 1850 and 1860 slave schedules, offer some details. According to available records, Bexar County, for instance, was home to at least seven different Hispanic slaveholders, who collectively owned thirteen or more enslaved Black people in 1850. The largest chattel slaveholder was probably Juan Montes, a fifty-three-year-old farmer who claimed ownership of a twenty-seven-year-old woman, a twelve-year-old boy, a toddler, and an infant. By 1860 Montes seems to have passed away, and his slave property went to three of his children, Alegos, Susana, and Antonio. By then, holding Black people in bondage had become slightly more popular among Bexareños, with at least fifteen residents owning a total of twenty-seven Black individuals. Under the violence and power of their Hispanic slavers, enslaved Black people likely worked as field hands, artisan assistants, and house servants. Others did not directly own Black bodies but, like Pedro García, found employment as overseers and labor "managers." Most lucrative and widespread for non-slaveholders, however, was the business of slave catching, the antithesis of Black freedom seeking.[126]

Hispanic slave catching began during the Rebellion, when Juan Seguín and his men were charged with reacquiring the enslaved people who escaped to the Mexican Army, and continued well into the 1850s, especially as fugitives became a more regular feature of the southern Texas borderlands. As the *San Antonio Ledger* reported in September 1853, for at least a handful of Mexican residents in southern Texas slave hunting was profitable enough that they worked alongside "a regularly organized band of slave catchers."[127] As late as 1860, Hispanic citizens were still aiding slaveholders in finding and seizing their human property. In March of that year, Rodrigo Hinojosa earned the "merited praise" of the *Corpus Christi Ranchero* editor for capturing two fugitives.[128] Several months later, José de los Santos Benavides led ten armed men across the Río Grande to arrest a fugitive who was posing as a free man in Nuevo Laredo. Although the party of vigilantes faced some resistance from Mexican soldiers—presumably for violating Mexican sovereignty—they were able to overtake and jail the Black refugee. This apparently was not the first time Santos Benavides had engaged in slave hunting, as the *Ranchero* noted he had "distinguished himself in restoring runaway slaves to their owners."[129]

For Hispanic people at midcentury, the long shadow of anti-Blackness simultaneously propped up and tore down their value within Anglo-American society. Regardless of where they positioned themselves, as supporters of Black fugitive freedom or as its enemies, most Hispanic people of Texas were now caught in the Anglo slaver web of anti-Black violence. As a governing structure, the new Anglo anti-Black regime drew its energy from historical precedent (i.e., Hispanic legacies of anti-Blackness), mass participation, and a racial logic that could recruit just as it excluded. Still, Black fugitives fought on. In this context of Black fugitive commitment, the state, as represented by national boundaries, diplomats, government agents, and legal mechanisms, mattered less than the relentless violence, abuse, and pressures of slavers and their proxies. When Felix Haywood explained that Black fugitives escaped to Mexico "to be Mexicans," he spoke not just of Black ingenuity, determination, and adaptability; he also spoke of the Hispanic dilemma that emerged amid the long shadow of anti-Blackness in the borderlands. Increasingly, what it meant "to be Mexican" depended on one's reactions to both anti-Black violence and the broader pursuit of Black freedom.

Summary

Anglo-American slaving violence built mid-nineteenth-century Texas. Driven by dreams of cotton fortunes, Anglo-Americans relocated to the borderlands by the hundreds of thousands. They brought with them enslaved Black people who cleared lands, tilled fields, planted seeds, harvested crops, packaged cotton, and transported the goods that inspired further investment in a transnational system of credit, trade, and violence against Black bodies. By 1860, with cotton output figures reaching over 170 million pounds a year, the Anglo slaving regime had reached unprecedented economic heights. A torrent of wealth flowed through Texas. Enslaved Black people suffered.

Torture was the means by which slavers extracted maximum production from enslaved people, and along with the increasing prevalence of the slave trade, Black people experienced objectification at unprecedented levels. But as slavers escalated their attacks on Black personhood, they also found merit in explicitly framing Black people's social existence as a function of the slaver family. Slavers thus characterized slaves as "family," which offered Anglo men a familiar patriarchal logic for social control and a direct mechanism for Black subjugation. Sexual violence, especially in the context of the borderlands, became a valuable way to enhance slaver wealth and further bind enslaved people to slaver authority.

As overwhelming as Anglo slaving violence was for the 183,000 enslaved Black people of Texas, Anglo-American slaving supremacy hinged on more than just violence against Black bodies. Because the borderlands were inhabited by tens of thousands of Hispanic and Native people, Anglo-Americans also had to figure out how to control or displace local populations if they were to make their dominion widespread and long lasting. In the aftermath of the Texas Rebellion, in which Anglo-Americans prevailed over the Mexican national government, Texians generally ostracized and displaced their Hispanic neighbors. Yet Hispanic influence remained, both within the old structure of Hispanic colonialism and on the margins of Anglo-American rule. To consolidate their ascending slaver-colonial regime, Anglo-Americans offered Tejanos opportunities to pledge their allegiance to anti-Blackness, with varying degrees of success. Black fugitivity pressed the issue of Hispanic complicity in or resistance to Anglo colonists' anti-Black paradigm, and in response Anglo slaver-colonists doubled down on their anti-Black logic of conquest. In the borderlands, if family structured personal domination, anti-Black violence structured communal domination.

7 / "They Should Have Been Entirely Destroyed": Comanche Raiding, Slaving, and Trading in the Age of Anglo Colonial Ascendance, 1836–1860

Juan Vela Benavides certainly would have met his maker on that fateful day in October 1848 had the already enslaved Bernabé Rodríguez not interceded on his behalf. At sixteen years old, Vela Benavides was, by default, too old to be dragged along with the Comanche campaigners, who, numbering fourteen, were in the midst of scouring the Mexican North just south of the Río Grande for livestock and enslavable people. Vela Benavides counted himself lucky because, he would later remember, "the *indios* would have killed him" without Rodríguez's merciful intervention. But evading death did not save him from his tribulations in the months that followed. Forced to accompany his slavers for several weeks as they attacked and raided his people's borderlands communities, Vela Benavides eventually made the long trek north toward (and eventually past) "*el lomerío de San Sabá*," into the heart of Comanchería. There, after two months of coerced travel, Vela Benavides "occupied himself in the care of horses," most of which had just been confiscated from his own people hundreds of miles away. He quickly learned the language of his Comanche hosts and began to discern the broader logic of Comanche society, economy, and politics. Fundamental to his understanding was the Comanche world of commerce, specifically their involvement at *la casa del Rescate*, an Anglo-American trading house located "not very far" to the northeast of where his hosts had stationed themselves that winter. It was there that Comanches unloaded the animals and people they had appropriated from the Mexican North into the Anglo sphere in exchange for "weapons, munitions, and other things." *La casa del Rescate* was also where a party of German colonists found Vela Benavides and offered to purchase him from his slavers. Ultimately they rejected the Germans' offer, and it would not be until the end of 1849 or early 1850 that Vela Benavides would free himself, by escape to Santa Fe, from the bondage of his Comanche slavers.[1]

Whether or not Vela Benavides fully appreciated the extent to which his very personal story intersected with larger historical forces, his sufferings—a narrow escape from certain death, having to witness his enslavers tormenting his compatriots, an exhausting trek to Comanchería, exploitation of his labor, and commodification of his person—nonetheless symbolized Comanche perseverance in an age of Anglo ascendance. By the late 1840s, the Comanche defense of their Texas homelands had been long underway. Only months prior to Vela Benavides's initial enslavement, in February 1848, the Comanche *paraibos* Mopechucope, Pahayuko, Ohois, Puhacawakis, and Chipeseah had sat in council with Anglo government representatives, negotiating ever-evolving peace terms. "I this day," explained Puhacawakis to U.S. officials, "see you, and my heart is filled with joy and I have the words of our Great Father in my heart, and my people from now, shall listen to his Talk."[2] Talk with agents of the Anglo settler colonial apparatus was, of course, a perilous exercise, but it did pave the way to enhanced commercial relations. And for Comanches, market opportunities drove their dynamic economic system; supplying livestock to voracious buyers, like those at the trading house Vela Benavides discovered, was their specialty. Thus, *la casa del Rescate* was one of the more tangible symbols of Comanche adaptation, a place where Comanches converted the fruits of their own borderlands dominion into colonial currency. Given the vast scope of mid-nineteenth-century Comanche raiding activities, the pastoral labor of enslaved people like Vela Benavides maintained the viability of this dynamic, adaptive system. Their potential on the colonial market as human commodities only buttressed their value.

Adaptation to the expanding influence of the Anglo slaver-colonial regime was at the heart of Comanche slavery's changing nature at midcentury. If anti-Blackness consolidated Anglo rule in the context of Texas's long-standing colonial apparatus, elevating Anglo colonial wealth to unprecedented levels along the way, their program of Native annihilation paved the way for these intrusive processes of consolidation. During the middle decades of the nineteenth century, the Texas borderlands remained Native homelands, with large portions still under Lipan Apache, Mescalero, Tonkawa, Caddo, and Wichita dominion.

Tens of thousands of dispossessed eastern Native people, moreover, were relocating to Texas and its margins, and still others, Arapahoes and Cheyennes included, eyed the borderlands' economic and political opportunities from the North, adding another layer of Native contestation to Euro-American machinations. Comanches, of course, remained entrenched as a governing, gravitational force of borderlands economy, society, and culture, even expanding their sphere of influence deep into the heart of Mexico. Nonetheless, the Anglo slaver-colonial machine churned as never before, marshaling against Native people in toto their Black-generated wealth, the driving logic of anti-Native hatred, unrelenting violence, and the resources of an embryonic but growing state apparatus. As much as the Anglo rise to Texas supremacy was a function of anti-Black violence, it also rested on the concerted Anglo campaign to manipulate, control, and ultimately extinguish the Native people of the borderlands.

The Anglo anti-Native program escalated from the mid-1830s through 1860. In many regards, Anglo violence followed the settler colonial model that they and their colonial forebears had been fashioning since the start of the seventeenth century, combining cries of White victimization at the hands of "savage," "transient" enemies with calls for manly, genocidal retribution.[3] But in the context of the borderlands, Anglo-American colonists were especially adept at leveraging local resources, including Hispanic support, to undermine and dismantle Native autonomy. Some even recognized the relative power of Comanches in the borderlands and sought to diffuse it elsewhere or channel it into "civilizing" enterprises, where Comanche "settler" converts could model for others the supposed blessings and benevolence of a paternalistic White government. Yet militarized "punitive" campaigns, with annihilation as their end goal, would remain the primary mode of Anglo conquest. By 1860, under the weight of Anglo death-dealing violence, Comanches faced expulsion from Texas.

This chapter explores Comanches' expanding slaving violence against the backdrop of Anglo programs of conquest and Native genocide.[4] Comanches' perseverance in the context of Anglo colonial ascendance hinged in many ways on their ability to convert raiding and slaving violence into widespread economic opportunity. Demographic challenges, stemming from the twin scourges of disease epidemics and colonial intrusion, threatened to unravel Comanchería at various points throughout the 1840s and 1850s, creating labor shortages, community fragmentation, and a dwindling class of fighting men. As forced family members, herders, domestic workers, goods manufacturers, and even warriors, enslaved people checked many of these dangers. Comanche kin incorporation of enslaved people—or, as much of the literature terms it, "adoption"—became especially pressing during this period. From this perspective, Comanche integration of enslaved people as family was further proof of adaptation and not, as some scholars have implied, evidence that Comanche slavery was necessarily benign or soft.[5] Violence and exploitation remained integral components of Comanche slavery, and like Anglo-Americans (and their Hispanic predecessors), Comanche slavers regularly objectified enslaved bodies as commodities for trade and accumulation. Those who experienced Comanche slavery firsthand, like Vela Benavides and so many others, knew that Comanche slaving violence helped to sustain their regional power amid the rise of an anti-Black slaver-colonial order.[6]

Reconciling "the Line between Our Countries": Violence and the Settler Colonial Imperative, 1836–1845

In the fall of 1837, about a year and a half after Anglo colonists emerged victorious in their war against Mexico, the young Republic's new government offered one of its earliest official assessments of the "Indian problem" in Texas. In this report by the Standing Committee on Indian Affairs, Texian representatives claimed that dangers lurked everywhere. As before, Caddos were living in the northern and eastern parts of Texas, "some hav[ing] returned to their old homes" in Nacogdoches County, yet all were heavily invested in commerce with the "Hostile tribes" of the "Praries." Stationed on the headwaters of the Trinity, Brazos, and Colorado rivers, Wichitas and their allies continued to "commit most horrible outrages" against Anglo colonists, just as they had "for 5 years past." Lipan Apaches and Tonkawas, moreover, were said to "occupy the Western Part of Texas," where they supposedly acted as agents of the Mexican state and thus were "no longer to be considered as a different People from that nation." Even the relative newcomers to the borderlands, the resident Kickapoos, Shawnees, and Delawares, could be found "roam[ing] the Praries in perfect confidence," adding yet another element of insecurity to the Anglo frontier. Perhaps most disconcerting were the activities of Cherokees settled along the Angelina, Neches, and Sabine rivers, where they were "taking the lead and forming an union of the different tribes of Texas," essentially picking up where they left off as a stubbornly autonomous community—and an obvious colonial headache. The long-influential Comanches, the committee decided, might be the Republic's best bet for tipping the balance of power to their favor: "Your Committee had not any evidence of hostile feelings on the part of these indians towards the People of this Republick and do not entertain a doubt but that a treaty of amity between this Govt and those Indians might be effected if presents and energetic measures were adopted for that purpose by Executive and Congress of this Republick."[7]

If anything, the committee's report revealed that, although Anglo colonists had built for themselves in Texas a new independent nation, with all of the bureaucratic pomp and ritual of an elaborate government structure, the borderlands were still very much Native country. Victory over Mexico displaced one colonial regime, but it did not erase the colonial context altogether; Native people did not suddenly vanish when the captured Mexican president, Antonio López de Santa Anna, effectively signed away Mexican claims to Texas on May 14, 1836. Instead, the transfer of colonial power meant that Native subversion of and resistance to colonialism were, for the most part, now Anglo-American problems. Responding to Native dominion and resilience would become the defining task of the new Anglo slaver-colonial regime.

The Standing Committee members knew this. "In making up their report," they declared, "your committee have been guided by a singular and anxious wish to recommend that course of Policy that will redound to the Honor and safety of our Country as well as the securing to the Indians their just claims." That course of policy, they explained, was resolution of the question of "vested rights" in the land. If the Mexican government "previous to our declaration of Independence" had recognized their legal claims to their homelands *and* they had "not subsequently forfeited [them] by overt acts against the Peace of this Republick," the new government was to recognize Native dominion as "sacred and inviolable." But, as the committee concluded, no such claims existed: "Your Committee have not upon the most mature consideration and the most assiduous inquiry been able to ascertain that a vested right of any kind had accrued to or been obtained by any tribe or tribes of Indians, other than *Prima Facia* right of Occupancy to those tribes *natives* of the Country." In other words, for all legal purposes, the Texas borderlands were a tabula rasa, an empty, virgin land awaiting further Anglo colonial penetration and development.[8]

It was, of course, one thing to declare Native dominion null and void and another to actualize it. Thus, during the earliest years of the Texas

Republic, Texians scrambled together a mixed approach of boundary making, commercial partnership, tribute payments, expulsion, and sheer violence to secure their new claims. In a November 1837 agreement with Tonkawa diplomats Ouchcala, Gosata, and Harshokena, Texians delineated trading protocols and Anglo boundaries, also attempting to bring them into the fold of their criminal "justice" system.[9] A month and a half later, Anglo officials treated with Ndé leader Cuelga de Castro, "promis[ing] and solemnly pledg[ing] themselves to be and remain . . . perpetual friends," while assuring tribute payments in exchange for the "deliver[y] over to the Citizens of said Republic all Cattle, Horses, Mules or other property which may come into their hands." As was the case with the Tonkawa treaty, the Ndé agreement ostensibly limited their mobility and conceded Anglo authority over criminal matters and even passage through Native territory. Perhaps most important, though, was the "Treaty of Peace and Amity" forged with Comanche diplomats Muguara, Muestyah, and Muhy in Houston on May 29, 1838. Although some early Anglo commentators deluded themselves into believing that Comanches offered no threat to the young Republic, by 1838 Texian officials could not ignore Comanche commitments to defending and securing their homelands, which, according to one Anglo report, were "a portion of the finest country in Texas." The Comanche treaty skirted the issue of boundaries—despite Comanche demands for "full and undisturbed possession of the country north of the Guadaloupe Mountains"—but it did secure Comanche promises to "bring to just punishment" those who "may commit any depredations," to return property confiscated from Anglo colonists, and to "stand by the White Man and be his friend against all his enemies."[10]

These treaties were, nonetheless, essentially placeholders, stopgap measures to prevent an imagined, all-out campaign of unified Native people against the young and fragile Texian nation.[11] With a limited state apparatus in place, enforcement of these treaties rested principally on Native acquiescence, as virtually all colonial agreements in the borderlands had since the late seventeenth century. Yet Anglo officials never truly entertained the possibility of long-term amicable relations with Texas's Native inhabitants. As Thomas Rusk, the Republic's first secretary of war, explained to an emissary he sent to Native country in the late summer of 1837, "In your talk with them you will be careful not to promise them Lands at any particular place and be cautious you make no promise however slight that cannot be strictly complied with."[12] Negotiating land in favor of Native sovereignty was a nonstarter; Texians fully expected to extend their dominion outward in the years that followed, regardless of local claims. But as Native communities collectively rejected this assumed settler entitlement to their homelands, Anglo-Americans ultimately would default back to an orchestrated program of vilification, coercion, and violence—the essence of colonialism.

As ominous as it was, the threat of Texian colonial expansion did not define life across Native country in the mid- to late 1830s. Colonialism had long revolutionized the economies, politics, and societies of Native people in the Texas borderlands, and this generation of Anglo-American invaders was, to an extent, simply the newest iteration of centuries-old processes. There still remained, despite Euro-American attempts to quash it, an internal logic to Native country, one forged by historical connections and rivalries that circumvented, subverted, and betrayed colonial imperatives. Ndé people continued to live off the raiding and trading of livestock north and south of the Río Grande, defying colonial pronouncements of national boundaries between Mexico and Anglo America. Hainais, Kichais, Kadohadachos, Nadacos, Tawakonis, and Wacos remained intimately fixed to their homelands, planting their sedentary communities along the banks of the Brazos and Trinity rivers, while still maintaining a broad commercial influence across the Southern Plains. Even the peoples forcefully displaced and expelled by Euro-American intruders did not surrender their autonomy or capitulate to the demands and dictates of colonial agents and operatives. In the borderlands, these recent migrants included Delawares, Shawnees, Creeks, Cherokees, Alabamas, Seminoles, Osages, Chickasaws, Choctaws, and others, totaling some twelve thousand individuals by the mid-nineteenth century. Many had ties to—and even lived among—the Native communities removed and relocated to Indian Territory by the U.S. federal government, and in general they all adapted to the political economy of the Southern Plains quickly and effectively. Anglo fears of Cherokee, Shawnee, and Delaware overtures to the "Prairie Indians" reflected this adaptation, as did colonial promises to "punish" the migrants for trading with plainspeople. The commerce forged by these displaced Native people, which spiked during the 1840s and 1850s, would confound and frustrate Anglo officials for decades.[13]

Few groups exemplified Native autonomy in the post-Rebellion period better than the Nʉmʉnʉʉ. By the mid-nineteenth century, Comanches had rearranged themselves into at least four principal divisions: Yamparikas, Kotsotekas, Tenawas, and Penatekas. As in previous eras, these divisions were not fixed groupings but were instead relatively fluid political organizations, which allowed individuals and families to move from community to community, depending on their own economic, social, and political prerogatives. Furthermore, in terms of geographic distribution, the divisions did not assign themselves to fixed regions within Comanchería; rather, most communities embraced mobility as a means to creative market engagement and widespread resource extraction. With frequent cross-divisional coordination efforts, Comanche dominion thus spread far and wide across the Southern Plains and the Texas borderlands. And Comanche power would be reinforced during the middle decades of the nineteenth century, as new alliances—especially those with Kiowas and Naishans—brought various military and economic resources within the fold of Comanchería. "These connections," Brian DeLay has argued, "created the potential for the coordination of formidable offensive power; and offense was the key to territorial security."[14]

The middle years of the 1830s were, nonetheless, a critical moment for Comanches. Although they successfully expanded, through raiding, trading, and warfare, the reaches of their dominion in the decade and a half prior, by the mid-1830s massive waves of eastern Native immigration coupled with Arapaho and Cheyenne territorial encroachment from the north were beginning to box them in. The borders of Comanchería, which now extended from the Cross Timbers to the Pecos River (east to west) and from the Arkansas River to the Balcones Escarpment (north to south), had become too vast for even the region's horse-mounted rulers to enforce on a regular basis. Slowly but steadily, Comanches began to cede hunting grounds in exchange for political alliances and new trade relationships. In 1835, they gave permission to Osages and many of the eastern Native immigrants to hunt within the boundaries of Comanchería, and five years later peace between Comanches, Kiowas, Naishans, Cheyennes, and Arapahoes resulted in a major escalation of Cheyenne and Arapaho hunting on the Southern Plains.[15] The net effect of these concessions—in addition to the decades-long agreement between Comanches and New Mexicans that allowed for New Mexican hunting on the Llano Estacado—was the rapid destruction of available bison herds. In response, Comanches sought out new modes and routes of resource acquisition, strengthening their already robust system of raiding and trading.[16]

Comanche raiding was two-pronged, with a Texian and a Mexican extraction field. The Texian raiding field was as much a defensive response to heightened post-Rebellion Anglo colonial aggression as it was a function of Comanche economic endeavors. With Texians assuming that the victory over Mexico gave them settler entitlement over the central and western portions of the borderlands, Comanches immediately attacked these colonial settlers as both economic opportunities and invaders. The most well-known attack occurred in May 1836, when Comanches sacked John Parker's colonial outpost near the headwaters of the Navasota River, killing five and enslaving five others, and it was followed by several others throughout the summer.[17] After Anglo colonists responded with a few Ranger-led campaigns of their own, general war broke out, with only a brief reprieve between the 1838 treaty and the Republic's presidential election of Mirabeau Lamar, an unabashed anti-Indian exterminationist. By the summer of 1839, the Anglo press was sharing reports that the plainspeople were "hostile to all white Americans, and particularly to Texians."[18] As had been customary over the past century-plus, borderlanders drove themselves into yet another cycle of violence.

The campaigns against Anglo colonial encroachment funneled horses, mules, and enslaved bodies into Comanchería, but the scale of those operations paled in comparison to the havoc Comanches wreaked in the Mexican raiding field. What began as episodic excursions into the frontier communities of the Mexican North during the 1820s became by the 1840s a massive invasion deep into the Mexican countryside. Comanche war parties—some numbering over eight hundred men and women—hit settlements located in Chihuahua, Tamaulipas, Coahuila, Nuevo León, and Durango, with a number of attacks ranging as far south as Zacatecas and San Luis Potosí. From these raids Comanches procured thousands of animals and hundreds of slaves—while leaving behind a remarkable trail of death and destruction, a symbol of their dominion in the region.[19] According to the Standing Committee's 1837 report, Comanches had made themselves "the natural enemies of the Mexican whom they contemptuously discriminate their *stockkeepers* and out of which nation they procure slaves." In short, what Comanche rangers could not acquire along the Texian frontier they readily obtained in Mexico, through violence and coercion.[20]

To Anglo-Americans, Comanche manipulation of colonial resources and Euro-American national borders was an intolerable contravention of colonialist authority, and in 1840 the still young Anglo colonial regime put to the test its capacity to bear the full force of Comanche power. That January, Comanche emissaries visited San Antonio, reporting that their people had grown tired of the relentless barrage of Texian forces. Henry W. Karnes, who, as a Texas Ranger, personally had led a war party against Comanches the previous summer, received the diplomats, "treat[ed] them well and dismiss[ed] them with presents" but demanded that they return with their "American Captives" and "all stolen property" if they wanted to secure a new peace agreement. As they awaited the arrival of more distinguished Comanche leadership, Karnes and other Anglo officials plotted to flip peace overtures into extortion. Karnes recommended that commissioners should be sent to meet them, "accompanied by a force sufficient to justify our seizing and retaining those who may come in, as hostages." Albert Sidney Johnston, Lamar's secretary of war at the time, expanded on Karnes's counsel, explaining that once they were held hostage, Texians would have the "right . . . to dictate the conditions of [their] residence." Above all, the commissioners were to convince the Comanche *paraibos*, at gunpoint, that Texas "citizens have a right to occupy any vacant lands of the Government, and that they must not be interfered with by the Comanche." In other words, they were to force Comanches into accepting their settler colonial prerogative.[21]

On March 19, the Comanche peace party arrived at San Antonio, numbering sixty-five persons, women and children included. The Anglo commissioners welcomed a dozen *paraibos* to the council house, where they inquired about the location of thirteen White captives, whom they assumed to be held by Comanche slavers. But the Comanche leaders had brought only one Anglo captive with them, explaining that "the rest are with other tribes." Further frustrating colonial officials was the Comanches' customary request for payment in exchange for the enslaved girl, Matilda Lockhart, who, although a potential symbol of a friendship in the making, was still a commodity in their eyes. Finding the Comanches' responses to be the pretext they needed to enact their hostage-taking ploy, Anglo officials ordered the *paraibos* arrested, and the meeting quickly spiraled out of control. Tabetuh, who along with Muguara had led the peace talks on behalf of their people, acted on this treachery by plunging "his butcher knife into the throat of the Texan sitting nearest to him." The other Comanches in attendance "drew their knives or their bows and arrows," and the company of Anglo soldiers unloaded their firearms on the entire party, killing them all. The massacre quickly spilled beyond the walls of the council house, and the remaining Comanche fighters fought in desperation for their lives and those of their families, only to be hunted down by a second company of troops and a number of mounted colonists. Weeks later the press reported, "The loss of the enemy was the whole of their fighting men killed, numbering thirty-two, and three women and two children who fell in the midst of the melee." Twenty-seven women and children were captured, in addition to two elderly men.[22] One San Antonio resident, a Russian phrenologist by the name of Dr. Weideman, who was "universally respected and liked by the Americans," sifted through the lifeless bodies of slain Comanches, dismembering their heads and other body parts to add to his scientific collection of human specimens. "What a day of horrors!" Mary Ann Maverick would recall a half-century later.[23]

Stunned, reeling, and outraged, Comanches nevertheless waited several months before unleashing their fury on the Texian frontier. Their retaliatory assault arrived in early August 1840, when Potsanaquahip—"Buffalo Hump" to many Anglos—led a party of several hundred fighters southward along the western edge of Anglo-Texas. The campaigners slashed, burned, and plundered their way south to the coastal town of Victoria, at the mouth of the Guadalupe River. They targeted symbols of the expanding Anglo colonial program, harassing and killing frontier settlers, horse traders, wagoners, and even enslaved Black people. Once at Victoria, Potsanaquahip and company encircled the town, confiscating hundreds upon hundreds of horses and mules. Their delays on the outskirts of Victoria ultimately allowed for a reinforced Anglo defense to stave off a full-scale sweep of the town, but the Comanche warriors remained undeterred and, after regrouping at Placido Creek, they moved on to the nearby town of Linnville. There the Comanches killed or chased off its residents and then worked methodically to ransack the town, setting ablaze "every house to the number of about twenty, among them some of the finest buildings in Texas." Over the course of just three days, from August 6 to 8, Comanches had devastated the Texian frontier; contemporaries estimated thousands of livestock taken, fifty colonists dead, and several individuals captured, including an enslaved Black woman and a young White girl. On August 12, four days after the storming of Linnville, the Texian press reported "the town destroyed, and the inhabitants butchered."[24]

After burning Linnville, the Comanche campaigners retired inland, camped for the night, and prepared to head home toward the hill country. On their heels, of course, was a predictable party of colonial pursuers, numbering two hundred or more, under the authority of Gen. Felix Huston. With the Comanche campaigners encumbered by their spoils of renewed war, the Anglo volunteers eventually caught up with them on Plum Creek. The ensuing skirmish proved less decisive than the Anglo volunteers had hoped, because instead of facing the well-armed Anglo forces head-on for protracted battle, the Comanches split up and traversed the Texas hills in small, fractured, but mostly secure parties. Still, their quick reprisal yielded several hundred animals recovered, the death of perhaps forty or more Comanches, and the capture of a woman and child. Anglo participants claimed victory in the days that followed, with Huston expressing his admiration for the "cool, deliberate, and prompt courage" of his men, who acted so "gallantly" in the face of such a terrible foe. Others were less enthusiastic. John Linn recalled decades later that although "the Indians were defeated in the engagement . . . they should have been entirely destroyed."[25] Annihilation was the preference of most Anglo settler colonists.

Anglo exterminationists would engineer another opportunity to destroy their defiant Comanche enemies just two months later, when Col. John Moore organized yet another "punitive" colonial campaign into Comanche country. This party, buttressed by a Lipan contingency under the leadership of the *náshneta* Cuelga de Castro, headed northwest along the Brazos River in early October, hoping to surprise an unsuspecting Comanche community as they prepared for the cold winter season. Treacherous snowy weather almost derailed Moore's genocidal plans, but with help from their Ndé auxiliaries, the Texian Rangers finally spotted a vulnerable Comanche *ranchería* planted on the south side of the Colorado River. That night, October 23, the Anglo war party of ninety colonists "beamed with feelings of pride and anticipation of a general engagement" as they prepared for the massacre that would follow. At daybreak, the attackers pounced. "Upon charging the village," Moore later explained, "a general and effective fire was opened upon the enemy." As the panicked Comanche villagers attempted to escape to the river, Moore and his men shot them dead: "Many were slain before they were able to reach the water, in which they took refuge—many of whom were there either killed or drowned." After hunting down the rest, who had fled for their lives, the Texians celebrated their devastation of the Comanche *ranchería*. On November 7, Moore reported 34 Comanches captured and 128 dead, a number "considered by the troops as being too small an estimate of the number actually killed and destroyed."[26]

Scattered, on the run, and grieving, the Comanches faced their nadir in the borderlands, and had the nascent Texian state been endowed with the resources and infrastructure to continue the Anglo genocidal campaign deeper into Comanchería that fall and winter, the Anglo colonial regime might have dismantled Comanche dominion in Texas for the foreseeable future. But in the borderlands, even by 1840, power remained tenuous and diffuse, spread out within and across diverse communities, Native and colonial. Mass Anglo violence solidified their regional rule, but it was neither totalizing nor necessarily singular. After all, Cuelga de Castro and his followers provided the skills and intelligence to track down the targets of Moore's violence. And although the Moore massacre may have represented the apex of Lamar's exterminationist program, coordinated anti-Indian persecution was a costly business, financially, psychologically, and politically.[27] By the time Anglo volunteers had reorganized the following spring, Comanches were on heightened alert—and reinforced by Caddo, Kickapoo, Shawnee, Cherokee, and Choctaw arms and ammunition, which by December 1840 were being funneled into Comanche communities in exchange for horses and slaves.[28] Thus, the volunteers were less successful the following spring, and rather than undermining Comanche power, Texians instead displaced their anti-Indian hatred indiscriminately onto other Native borderlanders. Then, in the late summer of 1841, Sam Houston won the Republic's presidential election. In his inaugural address to Congress the following December, he called for a more conciliatory—and less expensive—approach to the so-called Indian problem: "A thorough knowledge of the Indian character has induced a firm belief on my part that a sum less than one fourth of the amount heretofore annually expended for these purposes, would procure and maintain peace with all the Indian tribes now upon our borders." Trade and treaties, Houston argued, were the solution: "Finding a disposition on our own part to treat them fairly and justly, and dreading a loss of the advantages and facilities of trade, they would be powerfully affected both by feelings of confidence and motives of interest to preserve peace and maintain good faith."[29]

Yet the violence and perfidy of 1840 were still too fresh in the minds of Comanches, and peace talks would not resume until 1843—and only after Delawares, Shawnees, Caddos, Wichitas, and others paved the way for the Texas Republic.[30] Joseph C. Eldridge led Anglo efforts to reopen diplomacy; after months of travel across Comanchería, Eldridge finally negotiated with the *paraibo* Pahayuko a tentative agreement to exchange captives and meet again, with more Comanche leaders in attendance so that, as Pahayuko explained, "there will be no lies spoken on my side." Understandably, tensions ran high during the meetings. Relatives of those massacred at San Antonio in 1840 stalked the Texian diplomats, and Pahayuko refused to smoke the ceremonial pipe with them, fearing that they would be presented with "*poisoned tobacco*." Pahayuko and his people doubted the sincerity of Eldridge, as well as Houston's broader intentions: "When we make a treaty I want it to be a *Strong treaty*, one that shall last as long as this world exists." Comanches understood that Anglo colonialism generated an insatiable thirst for Native homelands; Pahayuko wanted a treaty that would halt Anglo expansionism for good.[31]

Houston would get his chance to confer with the greater Comanche leadership in the fall of 1844. Wisely, he met with the Comanche delegates at the Falls of the Brazos face to face, partly assuaging their fears that the peace overtures were yet another attempt to lure them into a massacre. He set the tone by apologizing for the "bad chief" Lamar's genocidal policies, even admitting that the late Comanche *paraibos* were treacherously "murdered" at San Antonio. Eventually all of the parties agreed to improve their trade relationship, to "deliver up prisoners," and to spare women and children in all affairs of war. The sticking point of the negotiations, of course, was the question of boundaries. Houston wanted to move the trading post line—the practical delineation of geographic dominion—deeper into Comanche hunting territory, and the Comanche *paraibos* resolutely opposed his requests. As Potsanaquahip declared, "I like the Treaty well enough, all but one thing, the line is too far off; too far up the country." Others' claims to their hunting grounds were false and illegitimate, he explained: "The lands belong to the comanche." In the end, all explicit articulations of the boundary line were excised from the treaty.[32]

As such, the agreements from 1843 and 1844 did little to resolve the proverbial elephant in the room—or, rather, the settler colonial imperative in the borderlands: would Anglo colonists respect Comanche territorial claims? The possible delineation of a boundary line, it seems, was one of the major incentives that brought Comanches to the negotiation table in 1844. Mopechucope said as much months before the Houston-led conference: "All I want now is a line run between our countries."[33] But because Texians—the self-declared "owners of all the Land in Texas"—refused to concede Native territoriality as legitimate and real, the peace talks instead fell back on the more practical but still nebulous questions of criminality and property remuneration.[34] Houston continued to seek imposition of Anglo governance on Comanche "criminals" and "depredators," while Comanche *paraibos* pushed for prohibitions on Texian movement in and across their country.[35] The "peace" that followed, then, was as much a rhetorical tool for borderlands leaders as it was evidence that the burgeoning Anglo state had the power to establish and enforce the terms of Native-Texian relations. With the treaties, Anglo officials could say that they were working to protect frontier colonists from Native "depredations," while Comanche (and other Native) signatories could feign ignorance or impotence in the face of independent, disruptive action on the part of their younger community members. By the time the U.S. federal government got involved in 1845 and 1846, a decade of violence and diplomacy had yielded very little. At least there could be no doubt in the minds of Native borderlanders, especially Comanches, that Anglo colonists always teetered on the brink of genocidal.

"Followed into Their Homes, and Well Thrashed": The Comanche Expulsion

When Texians elected to join their Anglo counterparts as the twenty-eighth state of the Union in 1845, they assumed that the powers and resources of the U.S. federal government would help to quash the Indian menace once and for all. "The strong arm of our government," U.S. voices assured Texians, "would be extended over [their land]."[36] The federal government, however, mostly maintained the status quo over the next decade and a half. In the fall of 1845, Thomas H. Crawford, the commissioner of Indian affairs, sent Pierce M. Butler and M. G. Lewis into the borderlands to treat with Comanche leaders. Testament to Comanche skepticism of Anglo intentions, it would be months before Butler and Lewis could gain their audience in council, and in the meantime the two men traversed the broader borderlands region, recruiting various Native guides and interpreters along the way. Among them was the Cherokee representative Elijah Hicks, whose diary of his travels with the commissioners reveals the prevalence of cross-ethnic slaving in the "land of Captives." Hicks reassured his "Brothers the Comanches" that the "hands of the Cherokees & the Comanches are white, we have never done each other any wrong, and what we have to say cannot injure you." With Hicks's support, as well as the assurances of other Native leaders, Comanche *paraibos*, including Potsanaquahip, Pahayuko, Santa Anna, and Mopechucope, finally came to an agreement with the U.S. representatives. As before, "peace and friendship" hinged on the exchange of enslaved bodies, shared recognition of Anglo definitions of criminality, and issues of mobility. Still, territorial claims—the coveted "Boundary line to Separate you and the Whites"—could not be resolved, and the delegates "defered [*sic*] that question until their visit to Washington."

When a newly appointed Indian agent, Robert Neighbors, met with Potsanaquahip and Pahayuko a year later to explain that the U.S. Senate had ratified their treaty but removed two articles (the third, which limited White mobility in Comanchería, and the fifth, which sanctioned Comanche diplomatic travel to Washington "whenever they may think their interest requires it"), the two *paraibos* fumed. "For a long time a great many people have been passing through my country," complained Potsanaquahip. "They kill all the game, and burn the country, and trouble me very much. The commissioners of our great father promised to keep these people out of our country. I believe our white brothers do not wish to run a line between us, because they wish to settle in this country. I object to any more settlements."[37]

Thus, even as U.S. officials orchestrated a remarkable coordination of Native leadership and an elaborate system of trade, Anglo colonial influence postannexation remained ensconced in a web of Native prerogative and dominion. Over the next several years, U.S. federal agents would continue to negotiate terms of amity with the Comanche leadership, with notable agreements in 1848, 1850, and 1851, but on a broader scale little changed.[38] Violence was still the prime agent of change, the lever that could tilt the balance of power in one direction or another. Comanches defended their homelands, regularly attacking surveying parties and settlers who invaded their territory, while Texians ratcheted up their discourse of an inevitable colonial war of extermination.[39] As the Houston *Democratic Telegraph and Texas Register* declared, "It is quite certain that the tide of emigration that is rapidly rolling towards the Rocky mountains will soon compel the Commanches, Arapahoes, Kioways, and other savage tribes that have long held undisturbed possession of the great prairies adjoining the frontiers of Missouri, Arkansas, and Southern Texas, to seek new homes farther west within the territories of Mexico. Wars will almost inevitably arise between these Indians and the Mexicans, or our settlers." Reports of planned massacres and annihilationist campaigns filtered into Comanchería and across Native country in general over the next few years.[40] Constantly on edge, Comanches and other Native borderlanders stemmed the tide of Anglo settler colonial intrusion throughout the late 1840s by raiding settlements for animals and people, killing trespassers, and "waylaying the Roads" that facilitated Anglo expansion. When Anglo officials appealed to Comanche *paraibos* to surrender the perpetrators, these leaders shrewdly reminded them that colonial expansion was the cause of these problems. They also assured them they were doing the best they could; unfortunately, they had only limited authority, as "the late occurrences . . . was [*sic*] confined to a small portion of Comanches, beyond control, and those bands who did not consider themselves in treaty with the United States."[41]

By the turn of the 1850s, Texians, frustrated with the Anglo state's inability to restrict Native influence, had become unequivocally genocidal. U.S. Capt. H. G. Catlett, after surveying the Texas field in 1849, called for the "kind of lesson (a good drubbing) which alone will make them respect their treaties and keep the peace": a destructive campaign into their winter quarters. Texas governor P. H. Bell blamed the U.S. federal government: "The conduct of the Government on the one hand, and the oft repeated aggressions of the Indians on the other, have made the people of Texas almost prepare . . . to engage in a war of extermination, as the only reliable means of self defence." In February 1850, Indian agent John Rollins reported that the exterminationist sentiment was ubiquitous, the essence of Anglo frontier identity: "A desire to fight and exterminate the Indians strongly pervades the minds of the people of Texas. . . . Indian depredations are the very soul of the border without which the blood would stagnate and life bereft of its incident and its charm." The editor of the Victoria *Texian Advocate* believed that only Rangers could be trusted to subjugate or destroy their Comanche enemies: "These red skin rascals will never cease their depredations until a few thousand Texian Rangers get after them. They will then be followed into their homes, and well thrashed."[42]

Despite the frequent calls for a concerted genocidal campaign into the heart of Comanchería, Anglo colonial authorities ultimately settled on Native confinement as the best solution to their self-inflicted Indian problem. With Anglo-Native violence raging across the borderlands, both state and federal officials agreed (naively) that designated reservations would pacify Native borderlanders while opening up lands to colonial settlers. In February 1852, the Texas state legislature authorized the governor to negotiate with the federal government for creation of Indian reservations within Texas, and within months U.S. Indian agents were polling interest among Native leaders, including the Comanche *paraibo* Ketumsee, who already the previous fall had expressed to them his fatigue dealing with Anglo settler colonialism.[43] Early progress notwithstanding, it would not be until February 6, 1854, that the Texas state legislature would designate land officially "for use and benefit of the several tribes of Indians residing within the limits of Texas." With the go-ahead from the State of Texas, Robert Neighbors and Randolph B. Marcy surveyed the designated lands and solidified their plans for

Native "settlement." In December 1854, as Anglo forces were mobilizing for yet another exterminationist campaign, the *paraibo* Ketumsee and his Comanche followers agreed to relocate to a reservation. By March 20, 1855, 180 Comanches had arrived at the Brazos reserve, along with some 800 Caddos, Ionies, Wacos, Tahwaccanos, and Anadarkos, just as word was traveling across the borderlands of an impending colonial attack on Comanches in their winter quarters. Then in May, Neighbors relocated 226 Comanches to their own reserve on the Clear Fork of the Brazos River.[44] Although U.S. officials understood that the Clear Fork reservation community represented only a fraction of the larger Comanche nation, they still believed that the success of their general Indian program in Texas rested on the "progress" of the two reservation experiments. "There can be no doubt of the success of the policy so far as the Texas Indians proper are concerned," declared Neighbors only months after the founding of the reserves. "I would earnestly commend it to the fostering care of the General Government as the most humane and economical that could possibly be followed, and one that in a very short time will relieve our frontier forever from the scenes of murder and theft, that has retarded the extension of civilization for so many years."[45]

That *any* Comanches would be willing to confine themselves to a particular strip of land under the jurisdiction of a foreign authority would have surprised most perceptive observers at the time. During the previous two decades, Comanche influence in the borderlands had been unparalleled. The Comanche commercial reach extended far and wide, connecting parts of the North American West to Mexico, the U.S. South, and even Canada. The scope of their commercial activities was so vast that multiple national governments, including Mexico, the Texas Republic, and the United States, attempted to curtail, accommodate, or exploit it. Comanche traders exchanged horses and mules for manufactured goods with Anglo-American traders on the Arkansas, Canadian, and Red rivers, in New Mexico, and at various forts. They tapped into the St. Louis–Canada network through Pawnee and Osage agents, gaining access to firearms and ammunition, and they adopted the encroaching German colonial settlements, including Fredericksburg, into their trading grid. When thousands of Native people were expelled from the eastern parts of the United States and migrating to Texas and its surrounding regions, Comanches made trading partners of them as well. Some Comanches even managed to find Mexican gun suppliers, whose weapons were then turned against their compatriots during large-scale raids into northern Mexico. Overall, Comanches were able to coordinate supply lines, fields of resource extraction, and willing buyers across a swath of land that extended several hundred miles. Their trade with Anglo-Americans, moreover, connected the Comanche economy to the cash-crop South, where Comanche mules were converted into farming draft animals, creating an indirect bridge between Comanche and Anglo-American slaving systems.[46]

Yet by the 1850s the Comanche system of influence and prosperity stood on the brink of collapse. During the latter part of the 1840s, a years-long drought, at least two major disease epidemics, and persistent colonial aggression threatened to undermine the very foundations of Comanche power. Drought translated into a weakened pastoral economy; disease splintered families and communities, disabling production and destabilizing leadership; and Anglo violence, coercion, and territorial encroachments exposed and exacerbated all of these hazards and uncertainty, as ever-shrinking homelands meant fewer resources and reduced access to commercial opportunities. Ketumsee articulated to U.S. officials his people's troubles in the early 1850s: "They have wandered about for seven years and driven from their homes where their parents are buried and where they raised (maze) corn and still driven back by the white men & have no resting place. We do not wish to do or to take other men or persons land, as the White men, have done." Their hunting grounds, he explained, "are now fast passing away from us." In October 1854, Neighbors connected the harsh ecological conditions that Comanches faced to the spike in reported Comanche raiding and slaving: "The scarcity of game in the country in which they reside, has in many instances drawn them to acts of violence."[47]

Neighbors's fall 1854 observations were astute. In response to mounting ecological, demographic, and geopolitical pressures, Comanches intensified their raiding into Mexico during the 1850s. In 1851, they hit Durango, Coahuila, Sonora, and Sinaloa, and the following year they toured the Mexican North all year long in search of livestock, slaves, and even Ndé scalps to sell in Chihuahua. The raids continued well into the latter years of the 1850s, even after the Comanches lost possibly hundreds of people on multiple occasions during bloody incursions in Chihuahua and Coahuila.[48] With bison herds growing scarce on the Southern Plains, Comanches spent more and more time in northern Mexico, turning to Mexican borderlanders for sustenance by raiding their farms and ranches for animals and foodstuffs. As the *paraibos* Sanaco, Potsanaquahip, Katumsee, and Saviah explained to Neighbors, raiding had become a survival strategy; they would consider halting their raids into Mexico only "provided they can find any other means of subsisting."[49] Comanche slaving also took on an unprecedented urgency during the 1850s. Although Comanches had long targeted women as potential slave-wives, with population figures dropping precipitously captured women became even more valuable. Given the desperate demographic circumstances, incorporating more people into Comanche society, enslaved or otherwise, offered them a fighting chance at maintaining their regional influence—even if their raids posed significant dangers to their own personal safety.[50]

Along the Anglo frontier, Comanches fought off the intrusive colonists as best they could. Their activities were as much a matter of economic survival as they were attempts to restore Comanche dominion. From 1852 to 1854, Comanches raided various Texian settlements for livestock and "committed some serious depredations." In one instance, several Comanche men reportedly attacked a family on the Medina River, killing the father, capturing his son, and violating the mother. In another set of attacks on the Frio and Leon rivers, Comanches seemed to be concerned strictly with acquiring "Horses and Mules." At the northern reaches of the borderlands, Comanches and their Kiowa and Ndé allies seized goods from trains of colonists and merchants heading to California and New Mexico. Raids grew so burdensome that one officer claimed the Comanches were "a people who are at war with our people *in Texas*."[51] By 1855 the Comanche onslaught had grown in intensity, with the German settlements near the Guadalupe River as prime targets. Indian war was thus the talk of Texas. "If . . . robbing murdering and ravishing, and carrying into captivity women and children does not constitute a State of war," exclaimed Bexar County colonists, "we are at a loss to define the meaning of war among barbarians." The frontier had been "almost overrun by the Indians."[52]

But the Anglo military complex was ill equipped to neutralize Native power in its totality in 1855. In March of that year, Gen. Persifor F. Smith, the head commander of U.S. military forces in the Texas field, captured in his report to the adjutant general the sad state of army affairs, lamenting soldier turnover and the recruitment of "inferior men." His Texas forces, he explained, "have had no recruits for over two years, and some of the companies have not over twenty men." Perhaps worst of all, "so many will have their discharges due at the same time, so a large leaven of raw men will come into each company at once." The Texas Rangers, meanwhile, had demonstrated some success "put[ting] a stop to the depredations which the Indians were committing," but coordinating state and federal approaches was proving to be a logistical nightmare, as Texas governor Elisha Pease explained to Smith in September. Despite obvious misgivings by most Anglo colonists, White authorities looked to the reservation experiments—the subsidized confinement of Native communities—as the best course of action for the time being. From this perspective, Clear Fork reservation's Indian agent John Baylor articulated the prevailing sentiment: "It is cheaper to *feed* than *whip* them."[53]

Thus, during the closing half of the 1850s, the U.S. federal government leaned on its reservation program as the panacea for Anglo-Texas's Indian problem. Once certain groups of Indians were persuaded to "settle" on specified plots of land, they figured, the remaining Indians would stand out as obviously "wild" and "hostile." Then the Anglo military could divert its resources toward "punishing" those intransigent "renegades," while still proving to the world—and other Native groups—the "humanity" and philanthropic underpinnings of their Indian approach.[54] Unfortunately for such colonial schemers, Comanches had other plans for the reservation system. The Clear Fork reserve was by no means the first colonial mechanism designed to restrain Comanche independence through collaboration, and like virtually every other attempt Comanches adapted the program to their needs. The Clear Fork enterprise became, at various points, a refuge, a resource domain, a symbol of good faith, a meeting place, and even a staging ground for continued raids into northern Mexico. On the surface—and according to the official (Office of Indian Affairs) party line—the reservation represented the potential for Comanche "civilizing," where "Southern Comanches" under the leadership of Ketumsee could shed their "communistic" practices and embrace a liberalized, enlightened way of life. Here they were to plant corn and grow wheat (when rainfall and grasshoppers allowed for it), build fixed abodes, send their children to school, and learn to abide by the Anglo system of "justice."[55] But even as some engaged in those activities, many spurned Anglo rules, proscriptions, and expectations. The worst offenders, according to Indian agents, were the young men, who frequently "quit . . . the reserve to join in the continued forays made by them both upon our frontier and that of Mexico."[56]

The Clear Fork reservation became, in many regards, another node in the broader Comanche system of commerce and dominion building. The reserve provided significant material benefits for those residing on it, as federal agents agreed to distribute food, tools, draft animals, and other commodities to its residents, who sometimes passed those same goods on to their nonreserve counterparts. U.S. government protection, moreover, was supposed to be a condition of their residence. And in the agricultural fields, where Anglo assimilationists promised that Comanches would be transformed into "civilized" men, the Comanches instead forced their Mexican slave "hands" to labor.[57] In essence, the Clear Fork reserve represented Comanche manipulation of Anglo colonialism at its finest. Even if Ketumsee genuinely wanted to build a future within the Anglo colonial orbit, perhaps because of his falling out with other Comanche leaders, many of his people, including those who resided on the reservation, clearly did not. Federal agents repeatedly explained to them that they were not permitted to leave the reservation grounds, yet Comanches did anyway, especially to join the raiding or war parties that passed nearby and through the reserve. Comanche *paraibos* like Sanaco regularly promised Indian agents, after collecting gifts from them, that they would be settling on the Clear Fork in the near future—only to renege at the last minute. And in August 1856, Baylor noted that other bands of Comanches often visited to traffic in stolen goods and to gather intelligence on Anglo colonial machinations.[58] In the meantime, nonreserve Comanches and their allies escalated their attacks and raids across the borderlands, while Anglo military leaders unleashed their own wave of supposedly punitive violence. Neighbors could do little more than complain about Comanche manipulation of colonial resources and strategies: "Some of the same guns given at Arkansas river [by the U.S. federal government] are now on the reserves in Texas, the Indians (Wacoes) who have them having traded for them from the Upper Camanches but a short time since."[59]

In late 1857 and 1858, the reservation program unraveled. Indian agents continued to report substantial "progress" among the Native "settlers" on the reserves, but widespread Comanche manipulation of colonial policy, mixed with intensifying Anglo frustrations over Native resistance to settler intrusion, pushed Anglo colonists to the edge. Texians saw in Native violence what they had been plotting for decades: a coordinated effort to "exterminate the white settlements," as John Smiley put it. Self-declared citizens' committees petitioned Anglo officials for property remuneration and military protection; state leaders called for more volunteers; and when volunteers appeared "inefficient for the protection of the frontier," authorities called for genocidal campaigns, backed by U.S. troops, into the heart of Comanchería. As Governor Hardin R. Runnels argued in January 1858, "Nothing short of a permanent mounted force of several hundred men will be anything like adequate to the object [of protecting the frontier], unless an expedition is authorised to follow the Indians to their places of retreat, break up their lodges and execute on them that summary vengeance which alone can give permanent peace."[60] Colonists also took it upon themselves, without official sanction from their government, to defuse Native power by organizing a genocidal mob, led, ironically, by one-time reservation enthusiast John Baylor. In February, the "Clear Fork Citizens," as they termed themselves, threatened the immediate destruction of "all Indians found in this vicinity [near the reservations] *with* or *without* passes." Over the next year and a half, Baylor and his men would attack Native borderlanders indiscriminately, their violence culminating in their unabashed massacre of seventeen sleeping men, women, and children from the Brazos reserve and their very public execution and scalping of a Caddo elder in front of U.S. government officials. By June 1865, "vigilante" colonists were warning Indian agents that they had to remove the reserve Indians or expect to face the "utter destruction of all reservations."[61]

But the real damage was done through coordination of Anglo federal and state forces. By the spring of 1858, Anglo-Americans finally had committed the full force of their military infrastructure to the subjugation of Native people in the Texas borderlands. Texas Rangers scoured the frontier for Comanche communities, reassuring each other that "no one, whose opinion is worth asking, expresses any doubt of the speedy termination of hostilities in the event of our being able to meet with the Comanche on their hunting grounds." In May 1858, they, along with the Brazos reserve Indian agent S. P. Ross and over one hundred Native auxiliaries, attacked a Kotsoteka encampment north of the Canadian River, capturing "over three hundred head of horses . . . [and] eighteen prisoners, mostly women and children," and leaving seventy-four warriors and two *paraibos* dead.[62] Emboldened by Ranger successes in May, U.S. military officials prepared to send more detachments into Comanchería "and follow them up winter and summer; thus giving the Indians something to do at home and taking care of their families." Then in September 1858, the Second Cavalry and another party of over a hundred Native fighters hit a large band of Comanches in western Oklahoma, killing dozens of men and at least two women. According to the leading officers of the massacre, Maj. Earl Van Dorn and Capt. Charles J. Whiting, "about one hundred and twenty lodges were burned" to the ground and "some women and children [were] taken prisoners by the friendly Indians."[63] The following spring, Van Dorn and the Second Cavalry marched two hundred miles into Comanchería and decimated a *ranchería* of about one hundred Comanche men, women, and children. The defenders were

Potsanaquahip's people, and they fought to the end, "without giving or asking quarter until there was not one left to bend a bow." Alas, they were outnumbered and ill equipped, victims of the sheer force of accumulative Anglo colonial violence. Thus by mid-1859, the Anglo colonial onslaught had effectively shattered Comanche influence in Texas. At least for the moment, Comanches were expelled from their Texas homeland. The Anglo annihilationist agenda had been fulfilled.[64]

"The Blood of . . . Little Ones Cries for Vengeance": Anglo Honor, Anti-Native Violence

Since at least the seventeenth century, the diverse peoples of the Texas borderlands had forged, to varying degrees, identities along axes of violence and coercion. Whether it was in the service of a broader Christianizing mission, to plead Whiteness, to wrangle defiant communities into the fold of an ever-growing social order, or to make others fungible, accumulable, and exploitable, violence framed and structured social worth. Manly violence, moreover, had long resonated across borderlands communities. In this regard, mid-nineteenth-century Texian violence against Native people was in lockstep with generations of borderlands history. For Anglo-American colonists, conquering "the Indian" was as foundational to their supposedly singular Texian identity as was their deeply pervasive project of anti-Blackness. In the Anglo colonial mind, Native people were—and always would be—inferior savages. Indeed, the term "savage" was used so often during the mid-nineteenth century that it became synonymous with the word "Indian." The conflation reflected how Anglos perceived the essence of their colonial program, their desire to subjugate or "tame" the Texas wilderness and then replace it with Anglo civilization. Per this formulation, the Indian was but a fixture of the wilderness, a dangerous animal awaiting colonial pacification (or extermination). "The Indians are as scattered as the wolves of the prairies," one Anglo legislator explained in 1855, "and like the wolves, come when least expected, in gangs of ten or fifteen or twenty. They rob and murder, and are off again; one can hardly say where."[65] The Indian was inherently depraved, irreligious, uncontrollably violent, and base; he was a cowardly warrior, an opportunistic thief, and sometimes even a cannibal. The women, moreover, had no shame, and the children were corrupted from birth. In short, the Indian represented nearly everything the Anglo-American was not.

This sweeping dehumanization of Native people—and all of its racist tropes—flourished in mid-nineteenth-century Anglo-Texas, especially as Native people resisted Anglo colonial intrusion. That Native people were *rightfully* and *justly* defending their homelands never crossed the collective Anglo mind. Instead, Native borderlanders were the intruders, instigators, and perpetrators, and Anglo settlers the victims. Although men had to be careful to not reveal their own manly impotence, White settlers and travelers alike depicted Native people as an omnipresent menace. "These savages [are] always ready for war upon the whites," one anonymous Anglo-American wrote. "A dark cloud is always lowering in the east, the north, the west, and part of the south which threatens to dart its lightnings and pour out its fury over the plain. . . . The people must expect to be harassed; their homes reduced to ashes; their wives and children will be butchered, and what is worse than all, the whole country kept in perpetual fear and anxiety." Newspapers regularly editorialized about poor, "defenceless" Anglo settlements. Fearmongering also came from the highest reaches of government, as when Governor Bell painted his picture of Texian victimization on the southwestern frontier: "With every precaution, and after employing all the means within their power, they [the colonists] were yet daily subject to the unhappy fate of witnessing the recurrence of the most tragic scenes: their friends butchered—women and children dragged into hopeless captivity—their property destroyed or carried off, and in fine, every other act of rapacity and violence usual with, and characteristic of lawless associations of renegade Mexicans and savage Indians."[66]

Even supposedly sympathetic or philanthropic interpretations of Native people contributed to the anti-Native racism of the period. The Office of Indian Affairs agents, for instance, were the strongest proponents of "gentle" or "benevolent" policies toward the Native communities of the borderlands, seeking out ostensibly peaceable solutions to the so-called Indian problem. Most prioritized demarcating boundaries between Native communities (and their hunting grounds) and White settlements. Others believed it was simply the poverty of Indians that forced them to raid and steal, so they advocated a gift-giving program on the part of the federal government. Of course, all still called for the immediate confinement and assimilation of Native people, and when their "civilizing" projects inevitably fell short of the standards of the larger colonial community, their failures served as more evidence of the hopelessness of Indian assimilation. Revealingly, these same advocates for Native reservations also trafficked in the eliminationist ultimatum:

assimilate or face extermination.[67] Thus, the Anglo man who defended the Clear Fork and Brazos reservations most fervently could be the same man who advocated the extermination of those who disrupted and undermined his program of assimilation. As Neighbors explained to Gen. David Twiggs in a series of pleas for military assistance, "Free intercourse with the Camanches for years has fully convinced me that it is absolutely necessary either to whip them or continually overawe them with a strong military force, in order to hold them in subjection and to make them peaceable." The proper solution, he argued, was to send "a sufficient military force into their country to occupy it or regular campaigns against them until they are reduced to proper subjection or extermination."[68]

Although federal and state authorities often bickered about each other's approach to the ever-present "Indian menace," Anglo-Americans across the board agreed upon the same basic premise: the Indian must give way to the "civilized" settlement of the White man. In December 1857, Congressman Pendleton Murrah explained how, in the end, all Texian men, including state and federal officials, *were* working toward the same goal:

> It has been the policy of the Texas Government, like that of the Federal Government, to keep separate the Indians and white man, and in conformity with this policy, separate lands have been provided for them; this policy is founded upon stern necessity. Humanity demands that the untutored savage shall be protected and cared for, but it would be unwise to extend this provision for the weak and ignorant, so far as to retard the onward march of civilized society—the life of the savage and that of the civilized man are controlled by laws at war with each other. . . . To contend that because the Indian and his forefathers, originally owned this continent, that its broad expanse was his home, his wild hunting ground, his habits cannot be interfered with, the limits of his wild home cannot be diminished, is to contend for the absurd proposition that the progress of intelligence, the spread of religion and civilization shall be arrested at the bidding of savage existence.[69]

This was, in effect, the broader paradigm of Anglo-American slaver-colonial supremacy—the governing assumption that the White patriarch was to dictate and preserve, through benevolent violence and coercion, the new political, economic, social, and cultural status quo—packaged and deployed as the inevitable outcome of the so-called Indian problem.

White men would act with "humanity" toward their lesser, ignorant neighbors, as a responsible father would toward his "untutored" children. Naturally, the metaphor of family emerged as the framework through which Anglo-American government officials tried to interface with the Indigenous people of Texas. "The Great Father," the president of the United States, they argued, was the munificent patriarch of all North Americans, Indians and Whites alike, and it was his duty to guide his "children" toward happiness and prosperity. Here the Anglos' ideology of slaveholder paternalism dovetailed with their colonial imperative of Native subjugation. Colonial representatives hoped to convince Native people that all of the "good" Indians would receive their Great Father's protection, while the "bad" Indians would be disciplined appropriately. From this perspective, the Indian predicament was the same as that of the Black slave: listen to your racially superior father or face his righteous punishment.[70]

The fostering of fictive kinship was a shrewd move on the part of Anglo-American officials, especially those who sought to minimize anticolonial violence. As scholars have demonstrated, Native diplomacy worked best when all involved parties recognized a mutual obligation to one another as metaphorical family. In the Texas borderlands, kinship diplomacy had a long history, with Hispanic colonists and various Native groups forging peace with one another through intermarriage and ceremonies of metaphorical family making.[71] Even Texians before statehood, perhaps taking a cue from their Hispanic predecessors and contemporaries, perceived the value in claiming familial ties during political discussions, often referring to Native delegates as "brothers."[72] Yet as the years went by and as Anglo-American power grew in Texas, the paternalistic ethos would become more and more prominent in federal government discourse, with claims of brotherhood yielding to demands for obedience to an all-powerful father.[73]

There were thus two ways in which Anglo-American men could assert their manly prerogatives in the Texas borderlands when it came to Native people: they could show them the way of "civilization" by means of a gentle, fatherly touch, or Anglo-American men could wield genocidal violence against them to demonstrate their unwavering commitment to the protection of their vulnerable families—women, children, and slaves included. Although calls abounded for "a lively sympathy for the destitute, unhappy tribes of Indians who inhabit our Country," most defaulted to the latter approach. President Lamar explained his people's manly dilemma in 1838:

> As long as we continue to exhibit our mercy without shewing our strength, so long will the Indian continue to bloody the edge of the tomahawk, and move onward in the work of rapacity and slaughter. And how long shall this cruel humanity, this murderous sensibility for the sanguinary savage be practised, in defiance of its tested impolicy? Until other oceans of blood; the blood of our wives and children, shall glut their voracious appetite? I would answer no. If the wild cannibals of the woods will not desist from their massacres; if they will continue to war upon us with the ferocity of Tigers and Hyenas, it is time we should retaliate their warfare, not in the murder of their women and children, but in the prosecution of an exterminating war upon their warriors, which will admit of no compromise and have no termination except in their total extinction or total expulsion.

The argument would be repeated over and over again into the 1840s and 1850s, especially as U.S. federal involvement failed to subjugate or destroy Native communities fully. "Their [the Indians'] audacity is increasing; they approach densely populated neighbourhoods and disturb the sacredness of the country Sabbath by murder and rapine," declared the *Nacogdoches Chronicle* in May 1854. "The blood of a father and his little ones cries for vengeance, and the hardy people of the West have become aroused to answer the call. Blood for blood, destruction for destruction is now the watchword."[74]

In the context of such vitriolic anti-Native racism, campaigning against Native people became a rite of passage for Anglo-American men, and many took the opportunity to prove their manhood through violence against the "savage." Most Indian-fighting operations, especially those involving the Texas Rangers, began with a sighting of "unauthorized" or supposedly suspicious Indian movement in a nearby area or with the official sanction and support of the Anglo government. As word spread of the impending expedition, prospective leaders gathered volunteers, who usually furnished their own weapons, horses, saddles, and other travel supplies. Depending on the size of the campaign, which ranged from dozens to hundreds of men, the expeditioners might bring along a few wagons and several pack mules equipped with extra provisions. Scouts—Hispanic, Native, and Anglo—were essential to these campaigns, as they used their knowledge of local geography, topography, and cultural practices to track the movement of the pursued Indians. The main body of the expedition trailed behind, and after receiving news of a nearby encampment, village, or settlement, the rest caught up. Provided scouts successfully discovered a potential target, the next phase was the attack. Ideally, Anglo-Americans attacked their enemies without warning, rushing them while they were asleep in their abodes and thus most vulnerable. If Anglo leaders feared they would lose the upper hand by delaying an assault, they would seek out a strategically advantageous position and fire on the Indians from there. Indeed, firearm engagement was the preferred method of fighting, especially as their flintlock rifles generally proved more lethal than the clumsier smoothbore muskets that Native people purchased from Arkansas traders. Nonetheless, the slower reload of the flintlock rifle meant that many campaigners had to resort to hand-to-hand combat. The adoption of Samuel Colt's revolving pistol starting in the early 1840s made Anglo anti-Indian fighters even deadlier.[75]

After their attacks, the Anglo-American campaigners confiscated Native property, captured survivors, reassessed the enemy's warring capabilities, and returned home. If they learned of other possible targets in the vicinity or if they believed they could chase down those who had escaped their main attack, the men might continue their campaign. Otherwise, they packed up the spoils of war and headed home. The obligatory report (or set of reports) from the campaign leaders represented the official close to their campaigns. Rare was the report that did not laud the *always* courageous efforts of the Anglo-American fighters or exaggerate the number of enemies killed. Most common was unabashed praise for their violence. As A. Nelson asserted in the aftermath of the Ranger campaign of 1858 against Comanches led by John "Rip" Ford, "It affords me pleasure to bear testimony to the gallantry of both officers & men under my command. . . . [They] bore themselves gallantly & as men sensible they have to maintain the character of 'Texian Rangers.'"[76]

Despite the fact that Texians framed their campaigning as necessary for protecting their families, friends, homes, and property, the violence of Anglo-American campaigners was never strictly defensive or retaliatory. For many Texians, there was a certain value in partaking in the very act of violence itself. This helps to explain why the practice of trophy taking spread throughout the middle decades of the nineteenth century. Although Anglo-Americans often denounced Native people for taking scalps, there is evidence that scalping was just as much an Anglo-American ritual of manliness as it was a Native custom of war. In fact, Anglo-Americans had scalped Native people since the earliest days of colonization in Texas, and the gruesome ritual persisted for decades.[77] Francis Sheridan, for instance, witnessed firsthand in 1838 how men proudly displayed their trophies of human flesh and hair.[78] Twenty years later, Ford and his men returned from their months-long campaign against Comanches with "76 scalps and about ten prisoners and some 300 head of animals." The following year, Indian agent Ross reported news of former Indian agent Baylor "prowling" around Native settlements "with a body of armed men with the avowed object of taking scalps."[79] This resulted in the aforementioned public scalping and murder of an eighty-year-old resident of the Brazos reserve.[80] A year later, Baylor and company, including his brother George, continued their rampage, collecting at least several fresh scalps. After one fight with Comanches, they celebrated with "a regular scalp dance": "We strung the scalps of the Indians and the rest of the trophies on a rope stretched diagonally across the courtroom, and danced under them the greater part of the night."[81]

In the context of the larger history of the U.S.-Mexico borderlands, the proliferation of scalping represents the confluence of various historical forces, including interethnic violence, the entrenchment of systems of manly honor, state building, and a burgeoning market economy. In the aftermath of the Spanish Empire's expulsion from Mexico, the already enervated northern frontier of Mexico became even weaker and more susceptible to the raiding of well-connected and well-armed, commercially oriented Native people. Most of the budding state and local governments of the new Republic had neither national support nor a local military infrastructure to stave off the resurgent Native danger that resurfaced in the 1830s. So instead of acceding to Native rule, Mexican leaders appealed to the honor- and money-seeking sensibilities of the northern frontier people by offering bounties on the ears and scalps of Indian enemies, especially Apaches. The scheme drew enthusiasm from Hispanic locals and even from a number of Anglo-Americans, dispossessed Native people from the U.S. Southeast, and Black fugitives. The rewards for individual scalps varied, from about 75 pesos for the scalp of a woman to 100 or more pesos for that of a man, with bounties for scalps increasing over time.[82] Furthermore, for those accustomed to enslaving Native people, scalping served as an extra incentive to slave-raid, as the Mexican governments typically accepted for payment both scalps and captives, particularly if they were women and children.[83]

With multiple Mexican lower-level governments involved in the scalp-taking business, the practice was naturally oriented southward and westward from Texas. But this did not foreclose Anglo participation. There were, in fact, a number of contracted Texians (some ex-Rangers) who profited handsomely from their involvement. Most of their activity was in the Mexican North, but it sometimes brought them north of the Río Grande into Texas proper.[84] Yet, even those who were not fully committed to the business could make a little money from selling a scalp here or there, as scalping meshed well with the broader Anglo-American program of conquest. The existence of a scalping economy, no matter how distant, was enough to motivate Anglo-Americans to escalate their war of extermination against Native communities. After all, scalp bounties supplemented the booty that Anglo-American campaigners typically plundered from Native people during their attacks, and through both activities Texian men could collect a significant reward for their efforts. Moreover, the exchange of objectified and commodified flesh was a familiar practice to Anglo-Americans, whose system of anti-Black slavery thrived upon that very notion. Native bodies, like Black bodies, became more fungible as the commercial tentacles of the cotton frontier spread ever westward into the borderlands, where indiscriminate violence against Native neighbors was often the measure of a (Euro-American) man.

Many Hispanic Texans readily discerned this social reality. Although Hispanic borderlanders faced their own wave of racist Anglo venom during the midcentury, for some, participation in the decimation of Native communities was their ticket to acceptance—if not success—within the new colonial regime. Violence against Native people was, after all, one of the oldest traditions in Hispanic Texas; their forefathers had, for all intents and purposes, initiated the cycles of violence that continued to curse the borderlands through the middle decades of the nineteenth century. Thus, with or without the prompting of their Hispanic counterparts across the Río Grande, whose government-based bounties offered lucrative opportunities in an era of deteriorating Tejano economic and social circumstances, Hispanic Texans continued their anti-Native campaigning during the post–Texas Rebellion period. When violence exploded between Anglo colonists and Comanches during the late 1830s, for instance, Hispanic residents stepped up for the colonial regime. In the summer of 1839, Juan Seguín, who already had a record of anti-Indian fighting, led a company of more than fifty Hispanic volunteers from San Antonio to chase after a band of "hostile" Comanches deep "into this country, north west and west of San Antonio." Alongside another company of Anglo volunteers, Seguín and his men spent three weeks "hunting the Indians," proving to their Anglo partners their military and social worth. Even though Seguín's activities buttressed Anglo settler colonialism, thereby contributing to his own marginalization in the years that followed, two decades later Seguín made sure Anglo authorities understood that he and his men had fought valiantly, "never expecting to receive pay for said service."[85]

Hispanic anti-Indian campaigning continued, albeit to a lesser degree, into the 1840s and 1850s. In most cases, the fighting was retaliatory, in direct response to raids on homes or property, but in others it was more calculated and premeditated. The citizens of Webb County, for instance, held a public meeting in March 1854 for the purpose of decrying the federal government's failure to protect them and to call for the organization of a force "of not less than two hundred men, who shall be prepared at their own expense." The citizens leading this meeting included E. Garza, Albino Treviño, José María Gonzáles, A. Soto, and Bentura González, and they hoped to muster fighters from the counties of Bexar, Nueces, Star, Hidalgo, and Cameron, locations with sizable Hispanic populations.[86] Other Hispanic residents were more directly involved in anti-Indian fighting. In one skirmish near Corpus Christi, a Mexican man by the name of Juan Ramírez demonstrated his social worth by shooting dead a Native war leader with a double-barreled shotgun and then taking a spear through his own body as he and Henry Kinney stood surrounded by a force of Native fighters.[87] José de los Santos Benavides, the prolific (Black) slave hunter, was probably the most prominent Hispanic anti-Indian fighter of them all during the 1850s, his pursuits taking him back and forth across the Río Grande throughout the decade. When Hispanic Texans were not fighting Native people themselves, they were helping Anglo-American military forces however they could, offering their services as scouts, guides, interpreters, and suppliers of equipment and goods.[88]

Hispanic military performance during the 1830s, 1840s, and 1850s sometimes received recognition and praise from Anglo-American commentators. In October 1837, for instance, Barnard E. Bee, a high-ranking Anglo official, formally recognized the service of Juan A. Zambrano, who had "served . . . with honor to himself and the Country" for the past several months. Bee also signed off on a land warrant for Manuel M. Flores, authorizing the transfer of 1,280 acres of land to Flores for "having served faithfully and honorably." Other Anglo-Americans, like the aforementioned Kinney, had similar praise for their Hispanic counterparts: "I will say here, that I have had as good and faithful soldiers who were Mexicans, as I have had of the Americans." In fact, some war reputations lasted for decades; for instance, José María González's military contributions—against Mexico from 1836 to 1837 and against Comanches in 1839—earned him the public approbation of a state congressional committee in the late 1850s.[89] Thus for Hispanic men, violence against Texian foes, especially Native people, sometimes translated into tangible social, economic, and—in the case of Seguín—political benefits.[90] If the long shadow of anti-Blackness did not offer Hispanic Texans a pathway to social significance, anti-Native violence could serve as a fallback, a way to distinguish themselves from the supposed racial inferiority of the Indian.[91]

But as most Hispanic borderlanders were figuring out, Anglo colonial violence did not follow a simple, two-dimensional, or uniform script. Although paternalistic violence framed much of their colonial engagement with ostensible "outsiders," it was capacious in its manifestations: the massacring of a community, the scalping of a person, the execution of a diplomat, the violation of a woman's body, the sale of a child, the brutal whipping of someone's back. Anglo dominion building and prosperity rested on all of that. And sometimes the violence bled from one Anglo-dominated arena onto another: what was typically anti-Black violence became anti-Native violence and vice versa. The instability of the borderlands, the contested nature of dominion and power, virtually assured that this would happen among an aggressive lot of slaving colonizers. Thus in the mid-nineteenth century, despite their overwhelming reliance upon the enslavement of Black bodies, Anglo-American colonists still readily participated in the more traditional iteration of borderlands slavery: the enslavement of Native people. For Anglo slavers, the enslavement of Native people became yet another way to gain leverage over the Indigenous inhabitants of the borderlands, to fashion their dominion on both personal and cross-communal levels.

Calculating the precise number of enslaved Native people taken and held by Anglo-Americans is all but an impossible task, but numerous instances exist in the historical record to bear out its prevalence. In most cases, anti-Native slaving seems to have been a means for community subjugation, another form of Anglo "punishment." Both the Council House Massacre and John Moore's surprise assault near the Colorado River in 1840 reflected this impulse, as those instances of mass slaving, which together resulted in the enslavement of sixty-four Comanches, were accompanied by genocidal violence. The Anglo message in both of these incidents was essentially the same: live by our rules or die. But little prevented Anglo slavers from exploiting Native bodies once under their personal power, as they did Black people. Notably, in the aftermath of the

Council House Massacre, Adjt. Gen. Hugh McLeod ordered one of his officers "to divide the Comanche women among the respectable families, to be returned when required." There, among the wealthier families of San Antonio, these Comanche women lived as forced guests and served as "domestics." Their hosts may not have considered them slaves per se—as, in their minds, *that* status was reserved for Black people—but they probably treated these purportedly "contented" and "tractable" women as such, especially given McLeod's characterization of them as docile and controllable.[92] Comanches remained enslaved among Anglo colonists for at least several years, and at one point Sam Houston felt compelled to lobby the Texian congress to pass legislation that would force—for purposes of captive diplomacy—Anglo slavers to relinquish their Native bondspeople, who apparently included not just Comanches but also Lipan Apaches, Tonkawas, and Wichitas.[93]

The Anglo colonial extension of their slaving impulses onto Native people was as much a function of the moment and place in which they lived—the mid-nineteenth-century Texas borderlands—as it was a product of their anti-Native imperative. Anglo-American men wore their violent domination of Native people as a badge of honor, as proof of their manly ability to protect both family and country. "It is not the money [for military service] that the frontier man wants . . . but that protection which will enable him to remain at home quietly in his agricultural pursuits," explained D. C. Dickson, a Texas state representative, in 1855. "We do not desire to see the frontier settler *forced* to turn soldier for defence of that family . . . [but he cannot] leave them exposed to the merciless savages that may be lurking about their habitation."[94] His colleague William Edwards similarly thought it necessary to foster "a military spirit . . . among our citizens," especially as he believed that they not rely upon federal assistance. Thankfully, he noted, Texians already had proven themselves worthy: "Texas has heretofore earned for herself, through her Rangers and Riflemen, an enviable reputation for chivalry, and shed a halo of glory around her arms long to be remembered."[95] Native blood brightened the "glorious" halos of Anglo manhood.

"Whatever Children Are Stolen from Their Enemies, Are Incorporated": Comanche Raiding and Slaving in the Age of Anglo Colonial Invasion

The violent onslaught of the Anglo colonial regime was, in many respects, unlike anything Comanches had faced in the Texas borderlands over the previous century or more. Although uneven and contingent, it was unquestionably relentless and, in the minds of its purveyors, inevitable. Annihilationist violence was the ultimate end goal of the Anglo colonial project—at least as far as Comanches and other Native borderlanders were concerned. There was, of course, another part to the colonial equation: the development and expansion of their anti-Black society. Comanches were less familiar with this other part, but it still contextualized Comanche life during the middle decades of the nineteenth century, a period in which Comanches collectively witnessed immense highs and utterly depressing lows. How they responded to the broader world of expanding slaver colonialism largely determined their ability to maintain their autonomy, if not their larger dominion across the borderlands. Midcentury Comanche fortunes thus rested on continued reinvention, geopolitical maneuvering, and exploitation of changing resource opportunities. For the Nʉmʉnʉʉ, raiding and slaving violence remained pivotal instruments of perseverance and regional influence.

Raiding and slaving helped to define and impose the boundaries of Comanchería. As discussed above, Comanche *paraibos* regularly sought demarcation of the borders of their homeland in negotiations with Anglo colonial leaders. Colonial diplomats often attempted to skirt the issue, but land always took center stage in their deliberations, and colonial border crossing—usually by surveying parties, settlers, or migrating travelers—typically sparked violence on the frontier. Thus, Comanche raiding and small-scale slaving in the context of the Anglo-Texas sphere was as much about border enforcement and securing the limits of their dominion as it was a means to wealth acquisition. Certainly Comanches confiscated livestock, clothing, firearms, and other goods in mass quantities during their attacks, but rarely did their raids result in the capture of more than a few individuals. It was, rather, more common for them to wound or execute frontier residents than to enslave them. The main objective of most of these strikes, it seems, was to send a message, to signal to the Anglo colonial world that they would not permit violations of their sovereignty. Even the act of confiscation was geopolitical in nature, as it redistributed material wealth from the colonial world to Comanchería, thereby enhancing Comanche power at the expense of their colonial enemies. This fact was not lost on Anglo contemporaries. "The insecurity for life and property is telling with fearful rapidity upon the prosperity of all our border settlements," contended Bexar County colonists in 1855, "and unless ample protection is soon afforded them, the tide of immigration which has been so suddenly arrested, will flow backwards." Comanche raiding, they explained, subverted the unilateral thrust of Anglo settler encroachment.[96]

Significantly, Comanche resistance to settler intrusion effectively arrested the spread of Anglo-American slavery. Although generations of scholars have focused on the question of whether or not chattel slavery had natural (environmental) limits in North America, most have ignored or dismissed the role of Native people in circumscribing Anglo-American slavery's expansion.[97] What is clear from contemporary commentary and settlement patterns is that there were many Anglo-Americans who truly believed that chattel slavery had a promising future in the western parts of Texas. The fact that it did not thrive in the western borderlands had little to do with a lack of Anglo-American enthusiasm or with annual levels of rainfall (as Charles Ramsdell has famously argued). Anglo-Americans thought of chattel slavery as a flexible institution, one that could be adapted to changing geographical and environmental circumstances. Many contemporaries anticipated slave labor being essential to the grazing business, which would be "unlimited in its capacity" as the western parts of Texas had "naturally the best grass in the world . . . and of course the best pasturage." Others were optimistic that cash crops could be produced in "some of the finest agricultural country" of the state. Even those who *were* skeptical about slavery's westward expansion still believed western Texas could—and would—accommodate the institution as "the last abiding home of the slave on this continent."[98] The very fact that Anglo-Americans never stopped bringing their slave property to western Texas throughout the period indicates that many slaveholders were committed to making their institution work on their frontier.[99]

While colonial commentators may have been hopeful of slavery's possibilities in the western portions of Texas, they all understood that slavery's success there depended upon their ability to curtail Native influence and control. Generally speaking, Anglo-American frontier development had an inverse relationship with Native communities' enforcement of their dominion. Anglo slavery's hold could be only tenuous at best in territory that was claimed and guarded vigilantly by Native people. Thus, Native defensive and offensive violence and resource management established the limits of the Anglo-American slaving frontier. Petition after petition, complaint after complaint, appeal after appeal, all made clear the disruptive nature of the so-called Indian menace. Surveyors could not locate and set aside lands for Anglo-American colonization. Farmers struggled to plant and harvest their crops. Owning horses and cattle, the prime targets of Native raiders, was a risky endeavor, as was owning Black people. Even the Anglo-American imagination was stifled, as dreams of Texas fortunes surrendered to the harsh reality of Native dominion preservation.[100]

Of course, Comanche raiding and slaving were not solely confined to the Anglo frontier. Northern Mexico also experienced its share (and more) of Comanche violence. But in contrast to their efforts on the Texian frontier, Comanches and their allies did not venture into Mexico to chastise Mexicans for intruding upon their territory; instead, they embarked on their extensive, weeks-long sweeps across the northern portions of Mexico almost principally to enhance the well-being of their communities. For Comanches, much of northern Mexico served as an extraction field, a resource domain to be exploited and transformed into Comanche strength, cohesion, and internal prosperity. "They were not fighting for their land or for the safety of their families or in defense of their culture," DeLay has argued. "At bottom they were fighting to win honor, avenge fallen comrades, and grow rich."[101] In Mexico, Comanches and their allies decimated the countryside, "robbing animals from all parts and killing many people," as Macedonio Perales, a former Comanche slave, recalled years later.[102] Certainly their attacks entrenched Comanche communities within ongoing cycles of vengeful, sometimes genocidal violence, but they also supplied Comanches with the commodities necessary to sustain their widespread commercial network.[103] Formerly enslaved people, who in the 1870s offered the Mexican government inside looks into the workings of Comanchería, were perhaps most forthcoming about these connections. Many confirmed government suspicions that the goods and people Comanches forcefully obtained in Mexico regularly made their way into the hands of Anglo and Native borderlands traders, a reallocation of wealth and labor that buttressed and secured Comanche regional influence at the obvious expense of Mexican colonial development.[104]

Comanche slaving, however, was not limited to the transfer of commodified bodies from one context to another. Enslaved people continued to be held in bondage *within* Comanchería, often for years or decades at a time. In fact, their relative presence grew as the middle decades of the nineteenth century progressed: while the total population of Comanches dipped from as many as twelve thousand in 1830 to perhaps nine thousand by 1860, the number of individuals held in bondage within Comanche communities had grown from several hundred to over a thousand.[105] Enslaved people had become so prominent among Comanches during the mid-nineteenth century that Hamilton P. Bee claimed, "Every warrior has more or less captives, generally Mexicans, to wait upon him, and his squaws also generally have one or more captives (girls or women) to aid them in their work."[106] As Bee and other contemporaries (who often had more reliable information than he) explained, these incorporated outsiders were not superfluous additions to static Comanche communities; rather, they—not unlike the enslaved Black people of Anglo-Texas—were instruments and symbols of remarkable midcentury change.[107] Their substantial presence within Comanchería reinforced Comanche patriarchy, broadened the wealth and prestige of various individuals, enhanced the laboring and reproductive capacities of Comanche communities at large, and signaled to borderlands populations that Comanche people were still a formidable power on the Southern Plains. In short, they bolstered and enhanced Comanchería, keeping it afloat during one of the more critical times in Comanche history.

Slaving had long been a significant mechanism in the creation and maintenance of Comanche dominion, both internally (within Comanche society) and externally (vis-à-vis other communities), but the escalation of slaving and the greater urgency with which Comanches gathered slaves meant that slaving grew in importance. In general, the wave of violence that Comanches unleashed upon northern Mexico and parts of the Texas borderlands fortified codes of manliness. During this era, Comanches continued to prize individualism, especially male individualism, and honor remained the barometer of Comanche social and political value. Although women were able to earn honor through their accumulation of *puha*, or spiritual powers (one woman, Tabepete, even rose to the status of war leader in the 1850s), more avenues were available for men.[108] The most honorable men, who claimed the title of *tekwʉniwapI*, or warrior-hero, were those who proved themselves in the arena of war, or, in the words of the twentieth-century informant Quassyah, "he who had killed the most enemies in fighting." Their war deeds were made conspicuous by various pieces of attire and weaponry: striped leggings, headdresses, decorated spears, and notched wooden clubs. To be a *tekwʉniwapI* opened all sorts of opportunities for a man, including marriage partners, wealth, and political influence.[109] In a period in which Comanche populations dwindled, cross-community violence—especially slaving—offered men a way to curry the favor of their communities and to procure potential wives and children, thereby enhancing their individual prestige.

This was partly why kin incorporation and slaving remained inevitably intertwined during the mid-nineteenth century. Although scholars have long argued that Comanche captives were adopted into Comanche society and thus not enslaved, the two processes of adoption and enslavement did not operate exclusively of one another.[110] As was the case during the eighteenth and early nineteenth centuries, Comanches incorporated virtually all outsiders into their communities through metaphors and relations of family. Diplomacy was conducted through metaphors of kinship; commercial ties were forged through fictive bonds of brotherhood; and enslaved people who were not immediately killed were brought into Comanche communities ostensibly as children and wives. During an era of continued male assertiveness, influence, and wealth, the patriarch-directed family remained the framework through which much of Comanche social life was experienced. As in Anglo-Texan society, women and children existed primarily in relation to the men in their lives, so much that "a girl was often teased by others during her husband's absence." Enslaved individuals who remained in Comanche communities had to contend with this social order.[111]

The issue of whether or not these adopted people received full status as members of Comanche society, as some have argued, is a separate question. There is evidence—both from contemporary sources and from the testimony of early twentieth-century informants—suggesting that some enslaved people were accepted fully into Comanche society. Mary Ann Maverick, for instance, wrote about the efforts of enslaved children, Mexican and Anglo-American, who tried to return to their Comanche hosts after being retaken in the early 1840s, and Dolly Webster found an enslaved Anglo "by the name of Lyons, who was taken when young, and raised by the Indians . . . almost a savage." Josiah Gregg, who mingled with thousands of Comanches near the Canadian River, claimed that he met an Anglo woman from Matamoros who "had been married to a Comanche since her captivity." According to Gregg, "She did not entertain the least desire of returning to her people." And Neighbors, writing about a decade later, claimed, "Whatever children are stolen from their [the Comanches'] enemies, are incorporated in the family to whom they belong, and treated as their own children, without distinction of color or nation."[112]

A few Comanche men and women who were interviewed by researchers in the 1930s offered similar interpretations of Comanche "captivity." Herman Asenap, whose father was captured by Comanches, claimed that "captives were adopted by families that had no children." Moreover, he argued that "adopted children had the same privileges of attaining leadership as did full bloods" and were bound to conventional Comanche marriage proscriptions. As far as he understood it, "there were no slaves among the Comanches." Although Asenap may have had personal reasons to deny Comanche slavery (i.e., asserting the adoptive nature of Comanche society preserved *his* claim to full Comanche status), his contention about the full status of captured individuals was not uncommon. Three other informants from that era, Niyah, Nemaruibetsi, and Frank Chekovi, also highlighted the adoptive nature of Comanche bondage. Nemaruibetsi even remembered one incident in which a Comanche man "elevated" his Mexican wife-captive over his Comanche wife after she gave birth to their child.[113] By the latter part of the twentieth century, Francis Joseph Attocknie was documenting oral histories about "captive-companions" who mourned the dead alongside their masters and acted "bravely" and "faithfully" for their slavers.[114]

That some enslaved people—or their descendants—may have become full members of Comanche society highlights a key difference between Comanche, Anglo-American, and Hispanic slaving systems: generally speaking, Comanche slave status was not heritable.[115] This had much to do with the nature of each system of slavery; while enslaved Black people were property, with a monetary value that related *first and foremost* to their potential as laborers and commodities in a cash-crop economy, Comanche slaves were valued for their labor *and* their potential to expand their host communities. Enslaved women who bore children, especially male children, enhanced the fighting, raiding, herding, and trading capacity—and thus the wealth and power—of Comanche communities. Their offspring also provided a degree of biological protection against Eurasian-African diseases through "immune system diversity."[116] Moreover, young enslaved males, although often exploited for their labor as herders, could become valuable fighting men later in their lives. With an economy and social structure so reliant upon the violence of men, Comanches allowed some enslaved boys to join in and prove themselves worthy fighters. If they raided and fought admirably, they were more valuable as peers than as dishonored slaves. This helps to explain why a number of twentieth-century informants emphasized the adoptive nature of Comanche bondage. Herman Asenap explained, "An adopted captive son was as much honored as a natural son if he was a good warrior. A brave man was respected for his ability, not for his ancestry." In Comanche society, manly violence could free an enslaved male from his debased, outsider status.[117]

Yet adoption should not be interpreted solely as a loving or benevolent act. The incorporation of women and children into the domestic realms of Comanche men meant that these enslaved people were bound by Comanche patriarchal authority and violence. Women especially were vulnerable. As in the eighteenth and early nineteenth centuries, Comanche wife-taking created *enslaved* wives. No matter how Comanche men—and their other wives—treated their newly incorporated "wives," these women were married by force. Power, sexual violence, and coercion circumscribed all of their activities with their husband-slavers.[118] Granted, their children likely had greater social opportunities, but that did not necessarily make the forced nature of their relationship any less coercive. In some instances, such as the famous story of Cynthia Ann Parker, who was kidnapped as a child in 1836 and then later married to the Comanche *paraibo* Puhtocnocony, children anchored enslaved women to their slaver-husbands. In the case of Parker, who was named Narua by her Comanche hosts, a return to her natal origins was an unacceptable option once she had her own slavery-induced children to look after. This she explained to Randolph Marcy: "All that she held most dear, were with the Indians, and there she should remain."[119] As in Anglo-Texas, children tethered enslaved women to their host communities. This may have been an even more effective slaveholding device within the context of Comanche society, because the children of enslaved women, like Parker's son Quanah, could become influential members of their communities, limiting their desire to leave. Moreover, Comanche custom bound husband-slavers to their slave-wives. As the twentieth-century Comanche informant Atauvich, explained, "A man could not sell a captive wife if she was the mother of his child."[120] Childbearing could be a curse for the slave-wives of Comanches, especially if they were not fond of their slaver-husbands.

Comanches also exploited the labor of enslaved people, a reality that helped to distinguish them as *slaves* within Comanche society. Even informants like Asenap, who doubted that Comanche-captured individuals were slaves, noted their utility as laborers: "Captive boys . . . looked after the horses." In addition to working as herders, enslaved people were exploited as horse trainers, cooks, blacksmiths, hide tanners, home assemblers, caregivers, child bearers, and even as farmers (during the brief reservation period in the 1850s). Much of the labor Comanches forced enslaved people to do was within the domestic sphere, which yielded the most industrial productivity.[121] The Comanche domestic sphere was structured by the extended family unit, or *nʉmʉnahkahni*, and it was at that level where most manufactured goods were converted from raw materials to commodities. Asenap's characterization of Comanche manufacturing offers some sense of the work done in the home to convert hunted bison and deer into usable products: "The Indians dried the meat, made clothing and shelter out of hides, used the bones to make tools out of and the horns to make decorations. . . . They made robes out of buckskin and decorated them with elk's teeth." These manufactured items were traded, along with enslaved people and livestock, for foreign goods like guns, ammunition, and foodstuffs. From this perspective, it is clear that slave labor was integral to the functioning of the Comanche economy. Even those slaves who ventured outside the immediate domestic realm, such as herders and expedition cooks, contributed, as herders nurtured and maintained the engine of Comanche wealth and military reach (i.e., livestock) while expedition cooks helped to sustain Comanche fighters as they gathered that wealth (and more enslaved individuals).[122] Well-tended raiders and horses translated into expanded holdings of livestock and slaves, which translated into more laborers and manufactured goods for trade. At every step along the way, enslaved people were involved. And in an age in which Comanches saw a net decrease in population figures—as a result of disease epidemics and colonial genocidal violence—the reproductive potential and labor of enslaved women were particularly valuable.

Revealingly, the expansion of Comanche slaving during the middle decades of the nineteenth century helped to forge social cohesion among Comanches amid the disruptions of a resurgent Euro-American colonialism. To an extent, Comanche social hierarchies of the era bifurcated in a way that was reminiscent of Anglo-Texas, with the slaver-host community on top and slaves on the bottom (or the margins). At the very least, slaves were sometimes stigmatized members of Comanche society.[123] Physical violence, including the stripping of hair and clothing, was the most obvious indication of their marginalized status. It came in the form of immediate bodily mutilation—for purposes of attempted natal alienation—or through frequent beatings and abuse, which reinforced the dominance and authority of the slaver society. Macario Leal, who was enslaved in 1847, told Mexican authorities that Comanches "beat him in different ways, torturing him to such a degree that he came to believe that they would kill him." When Maverick described Matilda Lockhart after she was purchased from her slavers, she could comment only on Lockhart's "frightful condition":

> Her head, arms and face were full of bruises, and sores, and her nose actually burnt off to the bone—all the fleshy end gone, and a great scab formed on the end of the bone. Both nostrils were wide open and denuded of flesh. She told a piteous tale of how dreadfully the Indians had beaten her, and how they would wake her from sleep by sticking a chunk of fire to her flesh, especially to her nose, and how they would shout and laugh like fiends when she cried. Her body had many scars from fire, many of which she showed us.

The bodily mutilation of an enslaved person was an important process of the enslavement of outsiders, as it served as a transformation of the captured person's identity, stripping her of her natal connections while imparting a new, slaver-dependent one. The women of the host community would inflict their share of welcoming violence as well, by striking enslaved women when they first arrived at their slavers' camps.[124] Regular, daily violence—or the threat of violence—was just as significant, though, especially for maintaining the unquestioned dominance of the slaver. One unidentified twentieth-century informant, for instance, recalled a slaveholder by the name of Noyuhka who whipped his Mexican slave for misplacing a couple of Noyuhka's horses. Virginia Webster, who was captured along with her mother and brother in 1839, remembered being "whipped" and burned "with live coals" as a young child: "I don't know how I lived the way the Indians tortured me." Ultimately the lives of enslaved individuals were in the hands of their hosts. If slaveholders or other Comanches found them burdensome or useless, they killed them, sometimes in dramatic fashion. Herkeyah, for instance, remembered the custom of slavers tying their slaves to saddles and driving them into a herd. "Eventually," he recalled, "he [the enslaved child] was killed. If the saddle turned, the boy would be trampled."[125]

The ostracization of Comanche slaves could manifest in other forms as well. Enslaved men and women, for instance, were not always protected by Comanche cultural conventions. As Rhoda Asenap explained, the sexual partner or wife of an enslaved man was susceptible to the male sexual violence of her host society in ways that were reminiscent of Anglo-Texas dynamics: "Full bloods could take a captive's wives when they wanted them." In general, enslaved men had to work especially hard at proving their manliness, and Comanche slavers were not always quick to provide such opportunities. Instead, they further humiliated enslaved men by forcing some to do "women's work, [such] as tanning hides." It is impossible to know what percentage of enslaved males were forced to labor alongside women, but Tahsuda's comment that Comanches "made slaves of the older boys" and "adopted the younger ones into the family" might indicate that enslaved males in their teens (or older) who were not killed immediately after capture were forced to do women's labor.[126] In any event, enslaved males laboring as women further stigmatized Comanche slaves as deviators from social norms.

If the expansion of Comanche slavery established a growing underclass of enslaved people, the flip side of this growth was an increasingly visible class of prominent slaving men on the other end of the social spectrum. Men like A Big Fat Fall by Tripping, Tabequena, Pahayuko, and Tutsayatuhovit, known as *tsaanaakatʉ*, personified wealth accumulation and conspicuous consumption. All, like Tabequena, whom the famed painter and traveler George Catlin characterized as an "enormous man, whose flesh would undoubtedly weigh three hundred pounds or more," were unusually overweight, "corpulent" men, who had others labor on their behalf. The respect they commanded within their communities initially may have come from their war exploits as young men, but later in their lives it was derived from their control of and influence over many animals, wives, and slaves.[127]

Enslaved people brought considerable wealth to those Comanche individuals who converted them into tradable commodities. Throughout the 1830s, 1840s, and 1850s, Comanches continued to seek markets for slave trading, and they eventually found several eager buyers throughout the Texas borderlands (and beyond). Although Euro-American observers rarely recognized the trade as an exchange of enslaved people (but instead as the "ransoming" of miserable victims), it ultimately involved members from various segments of the borderlands: Republic officials, Anglo-American and Mexican merchants, federal government agents, other Native traders, and the desperate family members of the enslaved. As discussed above, the trade in people often became a point of contention between Comanches and their neighbors, but even after devastating failures—like the San Antonio Council House Massacre in 1840—Comanches persisted in selling their human commodities. Observers like William Bollaert reported trading expeditions with plans to unload hundreds of slaves at a time. U.S. Indian agents received dozens of enslaved individuals themselves, and trade house owners, like those who ran the *casa del Rescate* mentioned by Vela Benavides at the start of this chapter, made few attempts to hide their involvement in the trade. For those involved, it could be a lucrative business. From 1836 to 1849, for instance, James W. Parker, the uncle of Cynthia Ann Parker, gave traders $3,300 to facilitate the purchase of twelve enslaved people, which translated into $275 per slave, roughly the going rate at Fort Gibson around the same time. In 1857, Neighbors authorized payments of $50 per slave "to satisfy those Indians who willingly deliver up their prisoners." And twentieth-century Comanche informants noted that an enslaved person typically could be exchanged for a few animals on the market.[128]

Given the enormous scope of the Anglo-American traffic in bodies, it is somewhat surprising that only the rarest of Anglo observers ever drew connections between Anglo and Comanche practices of human commodification.[129] To most Anglo-American commentators, the Comanche trade was neither rational nor a clear economic strategy; rather it was little more than an ancient, savage custom. The Anglo-American purchasing of Comanche slaves was, after all, rarely interpreted as a commercial transaction and instead was couched in the language of "redemption," "release," or "ransoming." Yet, the commodified existence of Comanche slaves made Comanche slavery rather similar to Anglo-American slavery. Comanche slavers may not have had the same understanding of property as their Anglo-American counterparts, but they *did* recognize an individual slaveholder's entitlement to his slaves. William Hardee made as much clear in 1851 as he and various other Indian agents sought to purchase (and free) slaves living among Comanches: "Ketumsee has promised to surrender five to Judge Rollins in ten days at Fredericksburg, he has also promised to confer with Yellow Wolf, and to endeavor to induce him to do the same. The Comanches may ask time and it will be necessary to grant it. They live under a Democratic Government and the Chief must confer with their people." In fact, Potsanaquahip warned U.S. officials that Comanche slavers held firm to their bondspeople: "If the Comanches were required to give up their prisoners, they might as well go to war." Just as government agents could not violate the rights of Anglo-American slaveholders by confiscating their slave property, Comanche leaders could not force their followers to relinquish theirs.[130]

Comanche slaver entitlement helps to explain why U.S. government officials struggled mightily to control the Comanche slave trade, even though virtually every cross-community agreement during the 1840s and 1850s included some form of a "prisoner release" clause. It also speaks to the reality that after a century and a half of close contact with Euro-American colonialism, Comanches had adopted, to varying degrees, certain characteristics of colonial society. Mass human commodification, after all, was a function of the ever-augmenting colonial world; it was a historical dynamic that first struck the borderlands amid the Spanish-dictated traffic in Native people, and then over time shifted toward an obvious anti-Black orientation with the invasion of English-speaking colonists. Comanche slavers recognized the immense commercial and geopolitical value of human commodities in this constantly changing context and carved out their own place within it. That Anglo and Comanche processes of human commodification could appear so similar by midcentury meant that both peoples were products—if not drivers—of the same colonial world.

Comanche engagement with the mid-nineteenth-century Anglo project of anti-Blackness reveals, nonetheless, that Comanche adoption of ubiquitous colonial paradigms and logics was a fraught, uneven, and often incomplete process. On the one hand, Comanche resistance to Anglo settler intrusion arrested the spread of the Anglo slaver frontier. By halting the development of Anglo colonies in the western borderlands, Comanches articulated, if only indirectly, a rejection of Anglo dreams of an anti-Black slaving future. Yet on the other hand, in thwarting Anglo advancement, Comanches simultaneously contributed to direct violence against enslaved Black people.[131] From the perspective of Comanche rangers, Black bondspeople labored on behalf of the Anglo colonial project: they cleared their hunting grounds of trees and animals; they built permanent structures in territory that had been claimed by generations of their ancestors; and they transported goods across the borderlands, flouting the clearly demarcated boundaries of Comanchería. Notably, enslaved Black men sometimes even carried firearms, strictly for the purpose of fending off or intimidating Native passersby.[132] They were, in short, little different from the Anglo colonists who violently forced them to engage in all of those activities. Thus, Comanche anticolonial raiders rarely spared the enslaved Black people who inhabited the Anglo frontier, and documented Comanche violence against Black people essentially tracked the larger trajectory of Comanche-Anglo violence during the midcentury. From the mid-1830s through the 1850s, numerous reports dotted Anglo correspondence and newspapers with accounts of enslaved Black people facing the wrath of Native (usually Comanche) anticolonial action: enslaved Black people were "carried off by the Indians," "either killed or taken off," "scalped . . . [and left] for dead," "barbarously murdered."[133] Whether or not Comanches discerned the subjugated, enslaved status of Black people within the Anglo-Texas sphere mattered not. What *did* matter was that Comanches understood them as valuable tools of Anglo colonialism, engines of Anglo colonial prosperity.

But anticolonial violence against Black people did not *necessarily* translate into a Comanche appropriation of Anglo *ideas* and *practices* of anti-Blackness. If Comanches began to perceive the accumulable, fungible, and extinguishable nature of Black bodies (per the Euro-American model), this likely occurred in the context of the Comanche-Anglo slave trade, where anti-Blackness cast its long shadow most prominently for Comanches.[134] Quite possibly, this would have sprouted in the 1850s amid concerted efforts of Anglo officials to impose the exchange of Black bodies during treaty negotiations. Although the exchange of "prisoners" or "hostages" had long governed Comanche-colonial peace negotiations, beginning in December 1850, only months after the U.S. Congress passed and began to institute a new, rejuvenated Fugitive Slave Act, Indian agents attempted to insert anti-Black stipulations within their treaties. In particular, the December 1850 treaty required the delivery of "all white persons or negroes who now are among any of the Indians of Texas as prisoners or runaways." Notably, and reflective of a larger continental effort to curtail Black fugitivity, the treaty also made Comanches and the other Native signers into slave hunters. As Article 9 stipulated, "The said Indian parties hereto agree to deliver as soon as found all runaway negroes that may be seen by them in the Indian country, to the officer commanding the nearest military post, or to the Indian Agent, and not knowingly allow any negro or negroes to pass through the Indian country into Mexico without arresting him or them."[135] Then in October 1851, U.S. agents reinforced their slave-catching expectations, adding to their newest treaty another a clause for the "arrest . . . [of] all fugative [*sic*] slaves or runaway negros." Notably, the Indian agents promised "the sum of fifty dollars for each one taken"—even though the treaty explicitly stated that "the United States is not to pay any ransom or reward for the return or delivery of any such captives" taken from Mexico. In other words, only Black bodies held market value.[136]

Perhaps it was because of these particular, determined U.S. government efforts to protect the property rights of Anglo slavers that Comanches became versed in (degrees of) anti-Blackness. Certainly the Anglo fixation with the capture and exchange of Black people could not have been lost on Comanche diplomats. Either way, their long history with Euro-American colonists in general, and Anglo-Americans in particular, taught them that Black bodies were prized commodities—to be bought and sold on the borderlands market, if not held as slaves within their own households and communities. As such, Black people, known specifically as *tuhpísi* among contemporary Comanches, were not an uncommon feature of Native slaveholdings nor of their commercial transactions.[137] Sadly, the suffering they endured represented one of the many Comanche adaptive responses to Anglo-American slaving supremacy.

Summary

In the crucible of settler colonial expansion, exterminationist violence, transregional market penetration, and the engulfing shadow of anti-Blackness, Comanchería had evolved by the mid-nineteenth century into a land of both anticolonial action and slavery, a country of people driven to secure and maintain their autonomy yet cursed by and trapped in cycles of generations-long violence. From a broad perspective, Comanches withstood the quarter-of-a-century Texian onslaught because their mode of adaptation suited that historical moment. Although the very practices that accounted for Comanche regional power (i.e., raiding, slaving, and trading) further contributed to their vilification at the hands of Anglo-Americans and others, violence was a language that everybody spoke in the Texas borderlands—and Comanches spoke it very well. In the face of an unrelenting Anglo colonial imperative of genocide, Comanches refused to cave in or capitulate. Instead they persevered, converting settlers and the world they were building into uneasy but lucrative opportunity.

For Comanches, the expansion of the Anglo-American frontier onto the Texas borderlands and the Southern Plains in general offered them renewed access to markets and goods, which in turn motivated them to extend the scope of their slaving operations well into the heart of Mexico. Comanche slaving, like Anglo-American slaving, merged the impulses of economic exploitation and commodification with kin incorporation, and many Comanche-enslaved people found themselves entangled in a web of slaver-familial ties. Forcefully driven to raise herds, manufacture goods, maintain households, and bear and rear children, enslaved people sustained mid-nineteenth-century Comanchería—the violence and coercion they endured symbolizing Comanches' collective adaptation to the pressures of annihilationist neighbors. But by 1860 Comanches could not (or were unwilling to) keep up with the scale of violence required to secure their control of their Texas homelands. Although their violence limited the speed and breadth of Anglo-American expansion, the Anglo cotton-yielding machine was too entrenched in Texas, too connected to global networks of money, commerce, and militaristic communities, to allow for a permanent Comanche foiling of Anglo-American colonialism in Texas. By 1860, a new day in the Texas borderlands had arrived.

Epilogue: "A Malady without Cure"

When Elijah Hicks, the Cherokee delegate of the Pierce M. Butler and M. G. Lewis expedition that traveled across parts of the borderlands in 1846, commented that Texas was a country of "cursed and driven" people, he could foresee no end to this slaving violence. "If the heart can Sicken at this Trojan War of human rights, a prostitution of humanity," he lamented, "it is a malady without cure to the philanthropist."[1] His remarks were prescient. The violence of slavery was too ingrained in the people and the history of the Texas borderlands to be expunged by simple acts of philanthropy or even state mandate. Slaving violence had driven the dreams of generations of newcomers and their descendants, and the marks of slavery—branded on the scarred bodies of enslaved people, etched into the exploited landscapes of the region, and woven into the fabric of borderlands culture—had become indelible. Texas was a cursed land, with virtually all of its people implicated, as victims or as perpetrators, in over a century and a half of slaving violence.

The violence of war and conquest proved to be the only remedy to the malady of borderlands slavery, and even then it was an imperfect and incomplete one. Anglo-Americans, the premier agents of slaving violence by 1860, saw their slaving kingdom crumble during the mid-1860s, when the United States, with its White supremacist credo, folded in on itself and then split into two nations.[2] Anglo-Texas, which in 1861 became the western frontier of the Confederate States of America, actually served as the last bastion of Anglo-American chattel slavery during the U.S. Civil War, with thousands upon thousands of White easterners fleeing to Texas with their slave property in tow. The process, which accelerated after 1862, was known as "refugeeing," a term that elicited sympathy for White war escapees while obscuring their efforts to preserve anti-Black slavery. In total, Anglo-American war dodgers forcefully brought with them some fifty thousand (or more) enslaved African Americans.[3] But their efforts to prolong legal anti-Black chattel slavery ultimately would fail, as the Union victory during the spring of 1865 spelled the Confederacy's doom. By June 1865, after the surrender of Confederate general Edmund Kirby Smith at Galveston, Union troops under Gen. Gordon Granger had occupied Texas, and with his June 19 issuing of General Orders No. 3, Granger made emancipation the law of the land. African Americans would henceforth commemorate the day of June 19 as Juneteenth.[4]

Sadly, slavery's death in the Texas borderlands would not arrive in the summer of 1865. Even within Anglo-Texas, where Union troops offered enforcement power of emancipationist policy, Anglo-American slavers remained committed to the enslavement of Black people. Some prevented their slaves from receiving news of emancipation. Many forced or tricked Black locals into signing oppressive contracts that virtually re-created a slave labor system. Others articulated their desire to control Black bodies through passage of laws eventually known as the Texas Black Code. Still others reverted to the familiar mode of borderlands interaction: sheer violence. Starting in the summer of 1865, wave after wave of heightened anti-Black violence swept across Texas. Anglo-American individuals and mobs intimidated formerly enslaved people, murdering hundreds while assaulting thousands more. According to Union general Philip H. Sheridan, the violence and tumult of Texas were "anomalous, singular, and unsatisfactory."[5]

Eventually, ex-Confederate resistance to the budding Union-crafted political order spawned a renewed U.S. federal presence across the former Confederacy, Texas included. Those heading this new federal program, deemed Radical Republicans by their contemporaries, believed that Black political participation was the solution to former Confederate intransigence, so by 1867 Black men were given the franchise. The new state government they built in Texas even heralded an unprecedented era of freedom for the formerly enslaved, with legal provisions for political equality, public education, and autonomous family building.[6] Yet laws never *truly* dictated life in the borderlands.[7] Throughout the final third of the nineteenth century, Anglo-Americans devised new means to subjugate and exploit the non-White residents of Texas, African Americans especially. Some held on to the belief that Black people were family, still coercively bound to Anglo-Americans if not by law then by custom. Others abandoned that sentiment entirely, instead terrorizing Black Texans and treating them strictly as objects of exploitation, profit, domination, and spectacle. And in place of chattel slavery grew a vast system of bondage through criminalization, as Black men in particular became the targets of a rapidly expanding police state during the decades that followed the Civil War. Imprisoned for petty, often manufactured crimes, these post-emancipation bondspeople were leased out by the state to labor on farms, in mines, on railroads, and even on the new capitol building. By the turn of the twentieth century, thousands had been devoured by this convict-leasing system.[8] Writing in 1903, social scientist Charles S. Potts explained that the "system is nothing more nor less than a form of human slavery."[9]

Hispanic complicity in slavery's survival varied during the U.S. Civil War era. On the one hand, some Hispanic people had grown weary of Anglo domination in the borderlands, and their actions undermined the larger program of Anglo conquest. Juan Nepomuceno Cortina, who led a series of uprisings against the Anglo order starting in 1859, represented the more resistant strain of the Hispanic response to Anglo supremacy. Under Cortina, poor and elite Mexicans—from both sides of the Río Grande—repulsed Anglo-American advances southward in the borderlands, even convincing some Anglo observers that they were intent on "murdering and breaking up the white settlements, and exciting insurrection among the slaves."[10] Other Tejanos, however, were more committed to the Anglo-slaving political order, especially the 2,500 or so who joined the ranks of the Confederate Army. José de los Santos Benavides was the most influential of these Confederate Tejanos, and he and his men gained a reputation for their "deeds of valor and patriotism in the Southern cause."[11] Still others propped up the Anglo-dominated slaving regime in more indirect ways. Scholars have noted that Hispanic people made possible the thousands of shipments of Confederate cotton that made their way from Anglo-Texas to northern Mexico.[12] In general, however, the Civil War era (and after) witnessed the resumption of Anglo hostility toward Mexican people. Many Anglo-Americans saw Mexicans as a corrupted, dirty, and Blackened race, deserving of further conquest and subjugation.[13] Thus, defending the colonial (i.e., White) legacy of Hispanic Texans would be one of the primary motivations of generations of elite Tejanos. Acknowledging the slaving violence of Hispanic Texans, of course, would not be part of this mission for historical recognition.[14]

For Comanches, who by late 1859 had found themselves confined to a rather narrow strip of land between the Arkansas and Canadian rivers, the civil war among Anglo-Americans ushered in new opportunities for slaving violence. Drawing Anglo military resources away from Comanchería (and Texas in general), the war opened a window for renewed Comanche raiding, especially along the Anglo-Texas frontier during the mid-1860s. In just two years, from 1865 to 1867, Comanches captured nearly four thousand horses and over thirty thousand head of cattle while reportedly killing 162 people and enslaving 43 others. Their forays southward, moreover, took them back across the Río Grande into Mexico, where they revived their custom of violent resource extraction. Their reinvigorated raiding economy even took them northward across the Smoky Hill River, eastward to Civil War–devastated Indian Territory, and westward into New Mexico. According to Hämäläinen, "Comanche war bands covered a range that extended more than eight hundred miles from north to south and five hundred miles east to west." In the six years that followed, Comanches would steal several thousand more horses and well over ten thousand head of cattle from Texas.[15]

As before, Comanches found ready buyers for their stolen goods across the broader borderlands region. During these years, New Mexico, with its *comanchero* trader infrastructure, emerged as the main commercial connection for Comanches, but U.S. federal agents, equipped with the task of curtailing Native movement and enforcing legal emancipation (i.e., through the Thirteenth Amendment to the U.S. Constitution), unintentionally became implicated in this network as buyers as well. Comanche slave traders, accustomed to dealing with self-righteous, Euro-American captive "saviors" and "ransomers," simply reinterpreted these U.S. federal agents as fellow traders. U.S. officials were aware of this dynamic and clearly frustrated. According to the Indian agent I. C. Taylor, "Every prisoner purchased from the Indians amounts to the same as granting them a license to go and commit the same overt act. They boastfully say that stealing white women is more of a lucrative business than stealing horses. I think it high time that they were made to feel the strong arm of the government, which is the only thing that will bring them to a sense of their duty."[16]

Eventually "the strong arm of the government"—the White American annihilationist imperative—would prevail over the Comanche people. Although federal policy during the late 1860s and (very) early 1870s failed to tackle Comanche exploitation of the borderlands, growing government intolerance of Comanche obstinacy, along with the rising influence of exterminationist rhetoric, ultimately inspired a U.S. Army–led scorched-earth policy against the Nʉmʉnʉʉ. Drawing from both long-held Anglo anti-Indian traditions and the recent army experience of total war against the Confederate-run South, Anglo military men wreaked havoc against the very infrastructure of Comanche life: they destroyed winter camps, slaughtered animal herds, and deprived Comanches of their food sources. By the time Anglo-Americans finally had eradicated the bison population of the Great Plains in 1874, an autonomous Comanchería had all but collapsed. A handful of last-ditch efforts, like Quanah Parker's massive attack at Adobe Walls on the Texas panhandle, demonstrated the determination of Comanches to preserve their dominion in the borderlands, but the end had come. By 1875, virtually all Comanches had given in to federal authority, relocating themselves to reservations at Fort Sill.[17]

Under the watchful eye of the U.S. federal government, Comanches were a conquered people. Yet even with ostensibly antislavery U.S. federal agents framing Comanche life and society on reservations, Comanche slavery did not die easily. When U.S. officials conducted censuses of Comanche bands living on reservations from 1879 to 1901, they reported nearly fifty individuals among them who remained enslaved.[18] By the 1930s, once-enslaved people, like Herkeyah (who offered her vivid testimony of forced family making, slave "punishment," and slaver rape to anthropologists in 1933), still lived within Comanche communities. When, exactly, Comanche slavery ended—a question that continues to vex those interested in the end of anti-Black slavery—is not easily discernible. For those like Herkeyah, who could not—and *would not*—forget the violence of her enslavement, the trauma of slavery had no clean breaks, no real closure.[19]

Texas was, as Hicks explained in the mid-nineteenth century, "a country of freedom [only] in name."[20] "Freedom" may have rolled off the tongues of U.S. federal agents, philanthropists, and boosters and onto the administrative transcripts of military victors, conscientious state builders, and new-age colonial and industrial developers, but making freedom a reality was another matter entirely. In the Texas borderlands, the country of the cursed and the driven, slavery's death—evasive, ambiguous, and opaque—was hardly a catalyst for freedom's beginning.

Notes

Introduction

1. Strobel, *The Old Plantations*, 1–40.

2. For a discussion of White southern sentimental fiction, see Blight, *Race and Reunion*, 222–27.

3. Strobel, *The Old Plantations*, 5.

4. For discussions on the persistence of Texas exceptionalism and Anglo-Texan mythology, see Buenger and Calvert, *Texas through Time*, ix–xxxv; Pekka Hämäläinen, "Into the Mainstream: The Emergence of a New Texas Indian History," in Buenger and De León, *Beyond Texas through Time*, 50–84.

5. Testimony of Sarah Ashley, FWP TXN, part 1, 34–36.

6. Testimony of Abelino Fuentes, Sept. 27, 1873, in Velasco Ávila, *En manos de los bárbaros*, 50–51.

7. Max Flomen's recent work, "Cruel Embrace," which "examines the comingling of slaving practices at the intersection of Indigenous borderlands and the Atlantic World," is a notable exception (2). For other important integrative and comparative efforts, see Mark Allan Goldberg, "Linking the Chains: Comanche Captivity, Black Chattel Slavery, and Empire in Antebellum Central Texas," in Martin and Brooks, eds., *Linking the Histories of Slavery*, 197–216; Goldberg, *Conquering Sickness*. For a discussion of some of these historiographical gulfs, see Truett and Young, *Continental Crossroads*, 1–23.

8. In doing so, it follows in the footsteps of a growing body of scholarship that seeks to integrate and compare the historical narratives of Black, Native, and White people in North America. Their studies have revealed, as Wendy Warren has argued, that colonialism and slavery were not distinct historical processes but, rather, "went hand in hand" to create a "deadly symbiosis (*New England Bound*, 1). Important studies include Miles and Holland, *Crossing Waters, Crossing Worlds*; Newell, *Brethren by Nature*; Baptist, *The Half Has Never Been Told*; Krauthamer, *Black Slaves, Indian Masters*; Carson, *Searching for the Bright Path*; Miles, *Ties That Bind*; Saunt, *A New*

Order of Things; Saunt, *Black, White, and Indian*; Usner, *Indians, Settlers, and Slaves*; La Vere, *Contrary Neighbors*; Perdue, *Slavery and the Evolution of Cherokee Society*; Forbes, *Africans and Native Americans*; Naylor, *African Cherokees in Indian Territory*; Leiker, *Racial Borders*; Leroy, "Black History in Occupied Territory"; King, "New World Grammars"; King, *The Black Shoals*.

9. Foreman, "The Journal of Elijah Hicks," 95.

10. Calloway, *One Vast Winter Count*, 121–26, 132–42.

11. Settler colonial studies scholars, led by Patrick Wolfe and Lorenzo Veracini, have argued that *colonialism* and *settler colonialism* are structurally distinct, that "colonial and settler colonial forms actually operate in dialectical tension and in specific contradistinction" (Veracini, *Settler Colonialism*, 7). I find the literature useful for identifying unique colonial traits, processes, and dynamics but less useful for assessing the interconnectedness of Euro-American practices of conquest in the Texas borderlands. In this context, disentangling settler colonialism from "traditional" colonialism can obscure as much as it clarifies (and even further reify historiographical partitioning), especially as "traditional" colonialism and settler colonialism fed off one another. As Tiffany Lethabo King has noted, the terms "settler colonialism, colonialism, and genocide are specific yet supple and agile analytical foci that are not bracketed off from one another" (*The Black Shoals*, 59). More to the point, the eliminate-to-build framework that partly distinguishes settler colonial definitions particularizes a broader reality: "By definition, conquest is an extermination not a recognition of aboriginal peoples" (Wolfe, "Settler Colonialism and the Elimination of the Native," 388). See also Hixson, *American Settler Colonialism*, 5; Trask, *From a Native Daughter*, 25.

12. *Nʉmʉnʉʉ* is the self-referent of the Comanches and means "the People." Wistrand-Robinson and James Armagost, *Comanche Dictionary and Grammar*, 65.

13. Pekka Hämäläinen, of course, has argued that Comanches built an empire during this period. Hämäläinen, *The Comanche Empire*.

14. "Lipan country." Tamez, "Nádasi'né' nde," 29.

15. "The land of the Comanches," from *Nʉmʉnʉʉ* ("the People") and *sokoobi* ("land, earth"). Wistrand-Robinson and Armagost, *Comanche Dictionary and Grammar*, 65, 90, 342.

16. Those who appreciate Native sovereignty, of course, still recognize Texas as Native country.

17. On the Southwest as a distinct regional political economy, see Anderson, *The Indian Southwest*, 3–6. Also see Hickerson, *The Jumanos*, 215–19; Forbes, *Apache, Navaho, and Spaniard*, 220–23.

18. Jeffrey M. Schulze and advocates of Native sovereignty have argued that Native groups actually belong to nations (*Are We Not Foreigners Here?*, 12–17).

19. Here I borrow from Yi-Fun Tuan's formulation of *places*, which describes places as intimately and directly connected to their inhabitants (*Space and Place*, 4).

20. Barr, "Geographies of Power," 9–11; Cecilia Sheridan, "Social Control and Native Territoriality in Northeastern New Spain," trans. Ned F. Brierly, in de la Teja and Frank, *Choice, Persuasion, and Coercion*, 123 ("set of spaces"). On mapping as a colonial exercise, see King, *The Black Shoals*, 74–110.

21. Foster, *Historic Native Peoples of Texas*, 5–6, 10–14, 30–38, 49–73, 83–100, 107–28, 137–61, 169–89, 195–211, 219–30; La Vere, *The Texas Indians*, 19, 29–30, 59–65,

68–69, 81–86, 88–92, 103–12, 128–34. The group names listed are as recorded in Euro-American documents. See Forbes, *Apache, Navaho, and Spaniard* for discussion of how some of these names may have referred to the same peoples.

22. Hämäläinen and Truett, "On Borderlands," 348–49 ("contact zones," "face-to-face"); Truett, *Fugitive Landscapes*, 8. Also see Radding, *Wandering Peoples*, xvi; Schulze, *Are We Not Foreigners Here?*, 9; Wahlstrom, *The Southern Exodus to Mexico*, 7. My definition departs from those formulations that emphasize the importance of an actual fixed (albeit porous) state border. See, for instance, Baud and Van Schendel, "Toward a Comparative History of Borderlands"; Johnson and Graybill, *Bridging National Borders in North America*, 7–8. For commentary on conceptual borders along the Río Grande, see Leiker, *Racial Borders*, 7–8.

23. To borrow Flomen's incisive observation: "Common challenges faced by peoples living in the same time and space will produce broadly similar solutions, in this case the problem of power relations in a borderland setting" ("Cruel Embrace," 10).

24. Whether the violence of slavery was "gratuitous" or "contingent" mattered not, as slaving violence *always* operated as a mode of domination. My definition of slavery has been informed, at least in part, by the theoretical formulations of the following: Nieboer, *Slavery as an Industrial System*; Patterson, *Slavery and Social Death*; Fogel, *Without Consent or Contract*; Turley, *Slavery*; Hartman, *Scenes of Subjection*; Berlin, *Many Thousands Gone*; Cameron, *Invisible Citizens*; Snyder, *Slavery in Indian Country*; Lovejoy, *Transformations in Slavery*; Martin and Brooks, *Linking the Histories of Slavery*; Wilderson, *Red, White and Black*.

25. Patterson, *Slavery and Social Death*, 13.

26. Here I disagree with Frank Wilderson, who has claimed that exploitation is not an inherent characteristic of slavery (*Red, White and Black*, 10–23). Exploitation (whether in a market economy, in a libidinal economy, or in the realm of geopolitics) can be a capacious construct.

27. According to Igor Kopytoff, from a processual perspective, "slavery is seen not as a fixed and unitary status, but as a process of social transformation that involves a succession of phases and changes in status, some of which merge with other statuses (for example, that of adoptee) that we in the West consider far removed from slavery." Igor Kopytoff, "The Cultural Biography of Things: Commoditization as Process," in Appadurai, *The Social Life of Things*, 65.

28. For a discussion of the transformational (i.e., historical) character of slavery, see Lovejoy, *Transformations in Slavery*, 8–11.

29. As terms that speak to process, they also help me to avoid awkward constructions like "captive slaves," "captive slavery," or "enslaved captives." Kiser, *Borderlands of Slavery*, 13, 15, 19, 24. See below for further discussion of conceptual distinctions between *captivity* and *slavery*.

30. I employ the term "population transfer" not necessarily in the precise way Veracini (*Settler Colonialism*, 33) defines it, but I appreciate the flexibility of the term, as well as its implication of multilateral movement (i.e., movement *into* a region in conjunction with forced movement *out*).

31. Andrew Masich, who has referred to the celebration of manly violence as a "martial credo," also has noted the convergence of Native, Hispanic, and Anglo-American cultures of violence in the North American Southwest Borderlands (*Civil War in the Southwest Borderlands*, 13, 31–35).

32. A number of scholars have analyzed the connections between intimacy and slavery. See especially Bianca Premo, "As If She Were My Own: Love and Law in the Slave Society of Eighteenth-Century Peru," in Berry and Harris, eds., *Sexuality and Slavery*, 71–82; van Deusen, "The Intimacies of Bondage"; Miles, *Ties That Bind*. I agree with Sarah Deer's assessments that "rape is a fundamental result of colonialism, a history of violence reaching back centuries," and that "sexual exploitation is a logical result of enslavement" (*The Beginning and End of Rape*, x, 64).

33. Here I echo Frantz Fanon, for "the arsenal of complexes" that have afflicted "the black man . . . germinated in a colonial situation" (*Black Skin, White Masks*, 1, 14 [quote]).

34. Jared Sexton has argued that much scholarship on comparative racism has functioned to exclude or minimize anti-Blackness. He is especially critical of studies that dismiss the roles of non-White anti-Black victimizers (*Amalgamation Schemes*, 253–54). This book highlights how many groups in Texas trafficked in anti-Blackness in historically specific ways.

35. Miers and Kopytoff, *Slavery in Africa*, 15.

36. In *Captives and Cousins* James Brooks has explained how slavery's ties to male-centered systems of kinship sometimes accounted for the success of long-term intergroup relationships.

37. Important studies that have challenged or complicated this distinction include Cameron, *Invisible Citizens*; Rushforth, *Bonds of Alliance*; Gallay, *The Indian Slave Trade*; Snyder, *Slavery in Indian Country*; Hämäläinen, *The Comanche Empire*; Martin and Brooks, *Linking the Histories of Slavery*.

38. For characterizations of Euro-American enslavement of Native people as integrative captivity, see, for instance, Fray Angelico Chávez, "Comments concerning 'Tomé and Father J.B.R.,'" 70; Elizabeth A. H. John, "Independent Indians and the San Antonio Community," in Poyo and Hinojosa, *Tejano Origins*, 109–10.

39. Igor Kopytoff has referred to this characterization of slavery as "the Western Cultural Model of Slavery" ("Perspectives on Slavery: Definitions," in Finkelman and Miller, *Macmillan Encyclopedia of World Slavery*, 2:676–83). For examples of this model, see Engerman, "Some Considerations Relating to Property Rights in Man"; Davis, *The Problem of Slavery*, 39–43; Bonnassie, *From Slavery to Feudalism*, 17–25.

40. That is, of course, if they are not referring to the chattel-based forms of slavery that Native peoples, particularly the so-called Five Civilized Tribes, had adopted by the nineteenth century vis-à-vis their Anglo-American neighbors. Yet even these studies have made stark distinctions between the apparently "fluid" Indigenous forms of captivity practiced earlier and the rigid chattel systems that flourished in the latter period. Perdue, *Slavery and the Evolution of Cherokee Society*, 4; Miles, *Ties That Bind*, 31–34; Krauthamer, *Black Slaves, Indian Masters*, 18–45. A notable departure from this tendency is Carson, *Searching for the Bright Path*.

41. See, for instance, Kiser, *Borderlands of Slavery*, 18; Basso, *Western Apache Raiding and Warfare*, 284; Curtis, *The North American Indians*, 9:74; Dowd, *A Spirited Resistance*, 9–14. Margaret Ellen Newell does not make explicit the captivity-slavery distinction, but she seems to suggest that Native captivity practices met sociopolitical needs while European slavery evolved over time to meet changing economic needs (*Brethren by Nature*, 39–59).

42. Although Paul Timothy Conrad has used the term *captivity* capaciously, his use of the term reinforces strict definitions of *slavery* based on property status and forced labor ("Captive Fates," 10–11).

43. Even recent, nuanced studies of violence have accepted the notion of kin incorporation uncritically. Lance Blyth, for instance, in *Chiricahua and Janos*, his study on Hispanic-Native violence in northern Mexico, characterizes the violent kidnapping and subjugation of female outsiders as *wife-taking*. Also see Bowe, *The Westo Indians*, 25; Strong, *Captive Selves, Captivating Others*, 78–83; Minor, *The Light Gray People*, 117–26.

44. As Peter Robertshaw and William L. Duncan have argued, "Whether or not captives are considered 'slaves' would appear to be a matter of semantic niceties that one suspects would be incorrigible to the captives themselves" ("African Slavery: Archaeology and Decentralized Societies," in Cameron, *Invisible Citizens*, 57). There is also the likelihood that Indigenous (precolonial) "captivity" became more akin to European slavery during the expansion of Euro-American colonialism. Maintaining the anthropological distinction has the effect of obscuring that historical dynamic (and rendering Native societies static).

45. Mark Goldberg has emphasized the importance of focusing on everyday practices to understand slavery in Texas ("Linking the Chains," 198).

46. Campbell's disregard of enslaved Native people in Texas led him to conclude that "although Negro slavery existed [prior to the 1820s], the number of bondsmen in Spanish Texas was always far too small to give the institution a significant hold on the province" (*An Empire for Slavery*, 11).

47. Hartman, *Scenes of Subjection*, 3.

48. As Hixson has explained, "Indigenous people thus not only confronted the European expansion, but also *participated* in a complex and contested colonial encounter. . . . However, colonialism with its vast disrupted power intensified borderland violence and spurred cycles of conflict" (*American Settler Colonialism*, 13, 15).

49. "As process," Bruce B. Lawrence and Aisha Karim have explained, "violence is cumulative and boundless. It always spills over. It creates and recreates new norms of collective self-understanding" (*On Violence*, 12, 14 ["link-chain"]). Others have emphasized the cumulative nature of historical trauma, particularly regarding Native and Black people; see Bonnie Duran, Eduardo Duran, and Maria Yellow Horse Brave Heart, "Native Americans and the Trauma of History," in Thornton, *Studying Native America*, 64; Smallwood, *Saltwater Slavery*, 198–202; Ann Marie Plane, "Visionaries, Violence, and the Legacy of Trauma on the Maine Frontier during King Philip's War, 1675–1677," in Lee and North, *Globalizing Borderlands Studies*, 105–24. It is also important to draw from Fanon and note that the Native and Black violence discussed here was, ultimately, an outgrowth of European colonialism. According to Fanon, "[Colonialism] is violence in its natural state, and it will only yield when confronted with greater violence" (*The Wretched of the Earth*, 61).

50. On the importance of highlighting the instrumentality of violence in order to not essentialize it, see Karim and Lawrence, *On Violence*, 5–9.

51. Attocknie, *The Life of Ten Bears*, 4.

52. Blackhawk, *Violence over the Land*, 8.

Part I

1. Libro de la Villa de San Fernando de Béxar de bautismos, entierros, confirmaciones, y casamientos, 1731–60, NLBLA, entries 94–108.

2. See chapter 2.

3. Campbell, *An Empire for Slavery*, 2, 18.

4. Gillmer, *Slavery and Freedom in Texas*, 9, emphasis mine. Even the recent borderlands monographs of Andrew Torget (*Seeds of Empire*, 5–6) and Sean Kelley (*Los Brazos de Dios*, 2–4), who have astutely pointed out the contested nature of slavery's political struggle in Texas, emphasize the guiding influence of state powers. Hartman's *Scenes of Subjection* is among the most influential law-based studies of slavery, particularly for its exploration of how law has framed the (non)being of enslaved persons. Also see Finkelman, *Slavery and Law*.

5. Juliana Barr is a notable exception. See especially *Peace Came in the Form of a Woman*.

6. See, for instance, the essays published in Campbell, *The Laws of Slavery in Texas*; Menchaca, *Recovering History, Constructing Race*, 2–3; Williams, *Bricks without Straw*, 41.

7. Hämäläinen and Truett, "On Borderlands," 348–49.

8. This definition of anti-Blackness borrows from the theorizing of Saidiya Hartman, *Scenes of Subjection*, especially 19–25; Frank Wilderson III, *Red, White and Black*, 17–22, 27 ("episodically"); Jared Sexton, *Amalgamation Schemes*, 148–49; P. Khalil Saucier and Tryon P. Woods, *On Marronage*; and Tiffany Lethabo King, *The Black Shoals*, 11, 22–26. Nonetheless, my understanding, unlike that of Sexton and Wilderson, does not presume, as Annie Olaloku-Teriba has critically noted, an "essentialisation of blackness, as a coherent and stable category that was invested with a set of stigmatising values by imperial encounters, rather than being *de facto* created by the imperial encounters themselves" ("Afro-Pessimism and the (Un)Logic of Anti-Blackness"). Admittedly, I tend to think "episodically and not paradigmatically."

9. Its salience during this early period lends credence to Jared Sexton's point that "antiblackness is [not simply] longstanding and ongoing but also . . . unlike other forms of racial oppression in qualitative ways" (*Amalgamation Schemes*, 245).

10. From this perspective, Spanish slaving violence during the eighteenth century was part and parcel of the settler colonial entitlement or "providential destiny" that Lorenzo Veracini (*Settler Colonialism*, 53–74), Walter Hixson (*American Settler Colonialism*, 6, 10), and others have discussed.

11. For a discussion of the reverberations and "boomerangs" of colonial violence in North America, see Blackhawk, *Violence over the Land*, especially 5–7; Hixson, *American Settler Colonialism*, xi, 19–22 ("boomerangs").

Chapter 1

1. A *vecino* was a Spanish townsperson. The term was a formal recognition of the person's status as a member of a civilian community. Mission Indians were not *vecinos*. For a discussion of the role of colonists and their varied status on the northern frontier of New Spain, see Jones, *Los Paisanos*, especially 3–16.

2. In the context of New Spain's northern frontier, the term *ladino* typically referred to Indians who were once members of missionary communities. Ramón referred to

this particular group of enemy Indians as the Pelones and Ladinos, "who were named the same."

3. My discussion of the 1707 Diego Ramón expedition is derived from Diario de la jornada que executo el Sargento Mayor Diego Ramón, Cavo Caudillo de la Companía de Campaña esquadra volante que esta de Assiento en la Misión Principal de San Juan Baptista del Río del Norte, AGN PI, vol. 28. All translations are mine. Also see Weddle, *San Juan Bautista*, 75–86; Wade, *The Native Americans of the Texas Edwards Plateau*, 163; Chipman and Joseph, *Spanish Texas*, 105.

4. Ned Blackhawk has urged the study of violence that has reverberated "outside the view of America's settler and immigrant populations" (*Violence over the Land*, 5).

5. Palmer, *Slaves of the White God*, 2; Bennett, *Colonial Blackness*, 4.

6. See especially Reséndez, *The Other Slavery*; Proctor, *"Damned Notions of Liberty"*; Vinson and Restall, *Black Mexico*; Bennett, *Africans in Colonial Mexico*; Bennett, *Colonial Blackness*; Cramaussel, *Poblar la frontera*.

7. Calloway, *One Vast Winter Count*, 122–42.

8. Powell, *Soldiers, Indians, and Silver*, 3–4.

9. The Mixtón War (1540–42) was the Spanish war with the Caxcanes, a sedentary, agricultural people who sought to curb the advance of Spanish colonization during the mid-sixteenth century. See Bakewell, *Silver Mining and Society in Colonial Mexico*, 5.

10. The term *negro* referred to African-descended people in New Spain. See chapter 2 for a discussion of the term in the context of Spanish Texas.

11. Brading and Cross, "Colonial Silver Mining," 557; Powell, *Soldiers, Indians, and Silver*, 14; Bakewell, *Silver Mining and Society in Colonial Mexico*, 5–31; Chipman and Joseph, *Spanish Texas*, 46–47.

12. For more details on Native resistance and adaptation to the Spanish mining frontier, see Forbes, *Apache, Navaho, and Spaniard*, 29–65.

13. The term "Chichimeca" was an epithet, meaning "dirty, uncivilized dog." Spaniards first learned of this term from the Native peoples of central Mexico. For a description of the four prominent Chichimecan groups, see Powell, *Soldiers, Indians, and Silver*, 33–44.

14. Powell, *Soldiers, Indians, and Silver*, 16–31, 45–54, 59–119; Bakewell, *Silver Mining and Society in Colonial Mexico*, 21–30.

15. Reséndez, *The Other Slavery*, 23–45; Stannard, *American Holocaust*, 62–75.

16. Zavala, *Los esclavos indios en Nueva España*, 1–3; Cramaussel, *Poblar la Frontera*, 187.

17. Enslavement according to Just War (or *bona guerra*) theory was prominent in fifteenth-century Iberia. See Blumenthal, *Enemies and Familiars*, 20–23. For Just War theory, see Zavala, *The Defence of Human Rights in Latin America*, 15–24. For discussion of the acquisition of slaves through war, see Díaz del Castillo, *The History of the Conquest of New Spain*, 236–37; Zavala, *Los esclavos indios en Nueva España*, 1–3. Reséndez, *The Other Slavery*, 62 ("make them slaves").

18. Brooks, *Captives and Cousins*, 23; Kicza, "Patterns in Early Spanish Overseas Expansion," 230–31; Zavala, *Los esclavos indios de Nueva España*, 5–6.

19. Zavala, "Nuño de Guzmán," 411–16; Reséndez, *Land So Strange*, 205–12; Calloway, *One Vast Winter Count*, 124–26.

20. An early bishop of Mexico City, Fray Juan de Zumárraga, for example, estimated that Nuño de Guzmán alone was responsible for the transportation of fifteen thousand

enslaved Native people to the Caribbean islands (Zavala, "Nuño de Guzmán," 414). The Franciscan Toribio de Benavente estimated the enslavement of perhaps 100,000 to 200,000 people in Mexico by 1555 (Reséndez, *The Other Slavery*, 65).

21. According to Obed Lira in "Wonder and the Ethics of Proximity," Las Casas fostered support for his cause through an "ethos of proximity," employing affective language in his writings to bring his readers closer to the Indigenous peoples of the Americas. See also Clayton, *Bartolomé de las Casas*, 112.

22. For a nuanced discussion of how Spanish law interacted with Spanish slaving practices, see Conrad, "Captive Fates," especially 78–110. Also see Reséndez, *The Other Slavery*, 67–75; Cramaussel, *Poblar la frontera*, 187. Published versions of pertinent decrees can be found in Konetzke, *Colección de Documentos*, 1:404–5, 410.

23. Las Casas, however, did repudiate African-based slavery later in his life. Clayton, *Bartolomé de las Casas*, 138–39; Davis, *Inhuman Bondage*, 98 ("solution"); Palmer, *Slaves of the White God*, 7–9 ("this land").

24. For importation figures, see Palmer, *Slaves of the White God*, 27–29. For brief discussion of African origins, see Cramaussel, *Poblar la frontera*, 202. Bennett, *Africans in Colonial Mexico*, 20–27, 29 ("discernable presence").

25. Palmer, *Slaves of the White God*, 43, 51; Bennett, *Africans in Colonial Mexico*, 20–25; Klein, *African Slavery in Latin America and the Caribbean*, 34–36; Proctor, *"Damned Notions of Liberty,"* 14–36.

26. Bennett, *Colonial Blackness*, 30 ("debased status"), 35–57. Also see Frank Proctor III, "Slave Rebellion and Liberty in Colonial Mexico," in Vinson and Restall, *Black Mexico*, 41, 95–97, 109.

27. Palmer, *Slaves of the White God*, 44.

28. Chapters 2 and 4 highlight the significance of Afro-Mexican people, enslaved and "free," in Spanish efforts to colonize the northeastern frontier. A brief survey of statistical figures illustrates the numerical importance of Afro-Mexican people on the northern frontier in general. Per Peter Gerhard's study, for instance, by the mid-seventeenth century Nueva Galicia alone was home to some twenty thousand Afro-Mexicans, approximately one-third of the Spanish-controlled population (*The North Frontier of New Spain*, 50). Ben Vinson III writes, "In no uncertain terms, by the end of the eighteenth century, Afro-Mexicans were deeply embedded within the major occupational arenas available to most colonists." Ben Vinson III, "From Dawn 'til Dusk: Black Labor in Late Colonial Mexico," in Vinson and Restall, *Black Mexico*, 123. For an excellent study on Black military participation in colonial Mexico, see Vinson, *Bearing Arms for His Majesty*.

29. Chantal Cramaussel has made a similar argument in *Poblar la frontera*, 203–4.

30. Powell, *Soldiers, Indians, and Silver*, 50–51.

31. Powell, *Soldiers, Indians, and Silver*, 50–51.

32. Powell, *Soldiers, Indians, and Silver*, 88–89.

33. Powell, *Soldiers, Indians, and Silver*, 204.

34. Spicer, *Cycles of Conquest*, 46–49; Gerhard, *The North Frontier of New Spain*, 5–6.

35. Santa Bárbara was built where Río Conchos joined the Río Grande, a place known as La Junta. It was at La Junta that Jumano groups generally congregated. Jumanos were the architects of a vast sixteenth- and seventeenth-century trade system that stretched from La Junta to the south, the Caddo-Wichita lands of the east, and

the Pueblo region of the northwest. Anderson, *The Indian Southwest*, 9–13; Forbes, *Apache, Navaho, and Spaniard*, 68–70, 194–98.

36. Weber, *The Spanish Frontier in North America*, 78; Gerhard, *The North Frontier of New Spain*, 164.

37. Gerhard, *The North Frontier of New Spain*, 165. In the Santa Bárbara vicinity, Spaniards "punished" local rebels in 1587 by enslaving a thousand Native people. Cramaussel, *Poblar la frontera*, 188.

38. Blackhawk, *Violence over the Land*, 23–25; Forbes, *Apache, Navaho, and Spaniard*, 85–91; Gutiérrez, *When Jesus Came, the Corn Mothers Went Away*, 104; Cramaussel, *Poblar la frontera*, 191–92.

39. Gerhard, *The North Frontier of New Spain*, 163, 170–71.

40. Del Hoyo, *Historia del Nuevo Reino de León*, 100–31; Cuello, "The Persistence of Indian Slavery and Encomienda," 687; Foster, *Texas and Northeastern Mexico*, 9–11; Reséndez, *The Other Slavery*, 76, 81.

41. Palmer, *Slaves of the White God*, 6, 12; del Hoyo, *Historia del Nuevo Reino de León*, 102–3; Reséndez, *The Other Slavery*, 76–80.

42. Del Hoyo, *Historia del Nuevo Reino de León*, 398; Cuello, "The Persistence of Indian Slavery and Encomienda," 688–89, 692.

43. My discussion of slavery in Monterrey is based on the bills of sale, land petitions, wills, and property inventories made available in Guajardo et al., *Slaves of Monterrey*, and University of Texas Institute of Texan Cultures, *Residents of Texas*, vol. 3.

44. Bill of sale of Diego, between Juan Francisco and Juan de Cazares, May 22, 1635; bill of sale of Leonor, between Lorenzo Moreno and Bartólome García, Apr. 6, 1648; bill of sale of Blas, between Margarita Montemayor and Blas de la Garza, Aug. 25, 1673; will of Sargento Mayor Antonio López de Villegas, Feb. 11, 1725, all in Guajardo et al., Slaves of Monterrey, 4, 9, 19, 93–94.

45. As Pat Carroll has found, this was not necessarily the case in the more populated and urban areas of colonial Mexico, where Native-Black relations were more amiable and integrative. Pat Carroll, "Black Aliens and Black Natives in New Spain's Indigenous Communities," in Vinson and Restall, *Black Mexico*, 72–89. Also see Vinson, *Bearing Arms for His Majesty*, 15.

46. Hernando de Mendiola to Juan de Mendiola, Apr. 29, 1651, summarized in University of Texas Institute of Texan Cultures, *Residents of Texas*, 3:84.

47. Also see the manumission document of Jerónimo, the *mulato* slave of Capitán Diego de Ayala, in University of Texas Institute of Texan Cultures, *Residents of Texas*, 3:89–90.

48. Gerhard, *The North Frontier of New Spain*, 327.

49. Forbes, "The Appearance of the Mounted Indian."

50. The Monterrey municipal council provided further evidence of pan-Native antislavery resistance when in the 1630s they claimed that Native refugees from Zacatecas, Fresnillo, Cuencamé, and elsewhere were leading the uprisings on the Spanish frontier. Juan Bautista Chapa, *Historia del Nuevo Reino de León*, in Foster, *Texas and Northeastern Mexico*, 29, 33–35, 37–39, 46, 71–72; Weddle, *San Juan Bautista*, 4–5.

51. Quoted in Weber, *The Spanish Frontier in North America*, 148.

52. Chapa, *Historia del Nuevo Reino de León*, 92.

53. Quoted in Chapa, *Historia del Nuevo Reino de León*, 75, 77–78, 84.

54. Chapa, *Historia del Nuevo Reino de León*, 30, 49 ("all ages"), 67 ("exiled").

55. Weber, *The Spanish in North America*, 148–52; Chipman and Joseph, *Spanish Texas*, 70–71.

56. Jean Géry was a deserter from the ill-fated La Salle expedition of 1685. Wade, *The Native Americans of the Texas Edwards Plateau*, 142, 145; Chipman and Joseph, *Spanish Texas*, 71–77.

57. In May 1693, Gregorio de Salinas Varona found Cacaxtles encamped just south of the Río Grande and several Cacaxtle men hunting between the Colorado and Guadalupe rivers in Texas. Foster, Jackson, and Brierley, "The 1693 Expedition of Gregorio de Salinas Varona," 283, 294; Campbell, "The Cacaxtle Indians of Northeastern Mexico and Southern Texas," 10.

58. Fray Francisco Casañas de Jesús Maria to the Viceroy of Mexico, Aug. 15, 1691, in Hatcher, "Descriptions of Tejas," 212–18.

59. For expeditionary reports and diaries of each campaign, see Alonso de León to the Viceroy, July 12, 1690, in Hadley, Naylor, and Schuetz-Miller, *The Presidio and Militia on the Northern Frontier*, 319–26; and Itinerary and Daily Account Kept by General Domingo de Terán, May 16, 1691–Apr. 5, 1692, in Hatcher, "The Expedition of Don Domingo Terán de los Rios," 10–67. Also see Barr, *Peace Came in the Form of a Woman*, 58–59.

60. Wade, *The Native Americans of the Texas Edwards Plateau*, 2, 6, 9–10, 58, 59.

61. Damián Mazanet to the Conde de Calve, Sept. 1690, in Hadley, Naylor, and Shuetz-Miller, *The Presidio and Militia on the Northern Frontier*, 332.

62. Barr, *Peace Came in the Form of a Woman*, 59, 64–67.

63. Damián Mazanet to the Viceroy, Feb. 17, 1694, in Hadley, Naylor, and Shuetz-Miller, *The Presidio and Militia on the Northern Frontier*, 353–54.

64. Damián Mazanet to Carlos de Siguenza, 1690, in Bolton, *Spanish Exploration in the Southwest*, 382.

65. Quoted in Wade, *The Native Americans of the Texas Edwards Plateau*, 14.

66. According to Chapa, de León "carried out nine expeditions there [in Nuevo León] on various occasions, and more than twelve expeditions to the Pelones. In addition, he led more than six other expeditions to the Tamaulipas Mountains, with famous successes, and he punished many of the evildoers" (Chapa, *Historia de Nuevo Reino de León*, 97, 103, 116). See also Wade, *The Native Americans of the Texas Edwards Plateau*, 136; Chipman and Joseph, *Spanish Texas*, 74.

67. Wade, *The Native Americans of the Texas Edwards Plateau*, 136, 148, 151; Chapa, *Historia de Nuevo Reino de León*, 139–40.

68. Wade, *The Native Americans of the Texas Edwards Plateau*, 148, 151–52; Weddle, *San Juan Bautista*, 44.

69. See, for instance, Diario de la jornada que executo el Sargento Mayor Diego Ramón, AGN PI, vol. 28; Tous, "The Espinosa-Olivares-Aguirre Expedition of 1709," 3–14; Weddle, *San Juan Bautista*, 87–97.

70. Barr, *Peace Came in the Form of a Woman*, 58; Chipman and Joseph, *Spanish Texas*, 109–11; Byrd, *Colonial Natchitoches*, 19–20.

71. Cunningham, "The Domingo Ramón Diary," 42; Weddle, *San Juan Bautista*, 110–13.

72. Two factors influenced the expedition's delay: an investigation of the Ramón family's complicity in illicit French commerce and Alarcón's frustration with Fray Olivares. See chapter 2 for further discussion of the Alarcón expedition.

73. The *auditor general* was a high government judge responsible for military affairs.

74. In 1719, Oliván suggested that *indio* families from Parras should migrate to Texas. Recommendations of Juan de Oliván Rebolledo, July 2, 1719, and Dec. 24, 1717, BAO.

75. For the regenerative nature of settler colonialism, see Veracini, *Settler Colonialism*, 54, 62–66. It is worth noting, however, that Spanish settler colonies functioned within the larger rubric of the Spanish Empire. As Gilbert Cruz has argued, "By establishing towns and cultivating the surrounding land, Spanish settlers secured the territory for their monarchs, who, in turn, not only promised them royal protection but also encouraged their continued cooperation by conferring on them *fueros*, or special privileges, which became a set of rights to self-rule" (*Let There Be Towns*, 6).

76. Recommendations of Juan de Oliván Rebolledo, Dec. 24, 1717, BAO.

77. Recommendations of Juan de Oliván Rebolledo, ca. 1717, BAO.

78. *Casta* was the term for a mixed-race person in New Spain. Chapters 2 and 4 discuss Spanish racial markers in more detail.

79. Recommendations of Juan de Oliván Rebolledo, ca. 1717, and Dec. 24, 1717, BAO.

Chapter 2

1. Enrique Gilbert-Michael Maestas has argued that by the mid-eighteenth century, Apachería del Oriente, or Eastern Apachería, covered most of modern-day Texas ("Culture and History of Native American Peoples of South Texas," 168).

2. Proceedings concerning Barrios y Jáuregui's report on the removal of the presidio of San Xavier, Nov. 3, 1756, BAO.

3. Testimonies of Juan Antonio de Moraín, Phelipe Muñoz de Mora, Ygnacio de Zepeda, Ygnacio Hernández, Antonio Cadeña, Joséph de Castro, Francisco Xavier Hernández, and Bernardo de Miranda, Nov. 3–6, 1756, in Proceedings concerning Barrios y Jáuregui's report on the removal of the presidio of San Xavier, Nov. 3, 1756, BAO.

4. Slaving subjugation (framed as Christian assimilation) might be understood as another settler colonial "transfer," per Lorenzo Veracini's schema, whereby colonists sought to undermine and eliminate local Indigenous communities. Spanish colonists believed they were entitled to the lands and (natural and human) resources of Texas. See Veracini, *Settler Colonialism*.

5. Juliana Barr's excellent *Peace Came in the Form of a Woman* illuminates the importance of women in captive diplomacy. For the ties between anti-Native violence and social worth in the Mexican north, see Alonso, *Thread of Blood*, especially 21–36; Masich, *Civil War in the Southwest Borderlands*, 14–15; Brooks, *Captives and Cousins*, 26–33.

6. Barr, for instance, has repeated the claim that slavery in Spanish Texas was not a labor system. Juliana Barr, "A Spectrum of Indian Bondage in Spanish Texas," in Gallay, *Indian Slavery in Colonial America*, 280; Barr, "From Captives to Slaves." Also see de la Teja, *San Antonio de Béxar*, 122–24.

7. Hoffmann, *Diary of the Alarcón Expedition*, 23.

8. Meacham, "The Population of Spanish and Mexican Texas," 85.

9. Relación de los empleos, méritos y servicios del Sargento Mayor Don Martín de Alarcón, Caballero del Orden de Santiago, Jan. 18, 1721, in Archivo General de la Nación, *Boletín del Archivo General de la Nación*, 401–2, 405; Hoffmann, *Diary of the Alarcón Expedition*, 19. For a list of Spanish settlers from the Alarcón expedition, see Chabot, *With the Makers of San Antonio*, 90; Hoffmann, *Diary of the Alarcón Expedition*, 20–24. For an account of Spanish-Native violence in Nuevo León during the first part of the eighteenth century, see Report of José Antonio Fernández de Jáuregui y Urrutia to the Viceroy, Jan. 11, 1735, BAO.

10. Diary of Fray Francisco Céliz, 1718–19, in Hoffmann, *Diary of the Alarcón Expedition*, 43, 44, 49, 57–8, 66–69, 73, 75–84, 86; Hoffmann, "The Mezquía Diary of the Alarcon Expedition," 318.

11. Diary of Fray Francisco Céliz, 1718–19, in Hoffmann, *Diary of the Alarcón Expedition*, 68, 76, 86.

12. Diary of Fray Francisco Céliz, 1718–19, in Hoffmann, *Diary of the Alarcón Expedition*, 55, 86, 87.

13. Hackett, "The Marquis of San Miguel de Aguayo," 199–200, 202–3.

14. Chipman and Joseph, *Spanish Texas*, 119–20; Marqués de Aguayo to the King, June 26, 1720, in Hackett, "The Marquis of San Miguel de Aguayo," 198, 202, 204; Buckley, "The Aguayo Expedition," 29.

15. For a critical analysis of the routes taken by the Aguayo expedition, see Foster, *Spanish Expeditions into Texas*, 145–62. Also see Hackett, "The Marquis of San Miguel de Aguayo," 204–11; Buckley, "The Aguayo Expedition," 61. For population figures, see Meacham, "The Population of Spanish and Mexican Texas," 85.

16. Diary of Juan Antonio de la Peña, 1721–22, in Santos, *Aguayo Expedition*, 25–26, 33, 51–55, 57, 59, 62–63, 65–66, 70, 76.

17. Account of Sieur Derbanne, Nov. 1, 1717, in Bridges and Deville, "Natchitoches and the Trail to the Río Grande," 251; Diary of Juan Antonio de la Peña, 1721–22, in Santos, *Aguayo Expedition*, 59.

18. Barr makes this argument well in *Peace Came in the Form of a Woman*, 2–4.

19. Diary of Domingo Ramón, 1716, in Cunningham, "The Domingo Ramón Diary," 62; Diary of Fray Francisco Céliz, 1718–19, in Hoffmann, *Diary of the Alarcón Expedition*, 77.

20. Henri de Tonti, "Memoir Sent in 1693, on the Discovery of the Mississippi," and Abbe Cavelier, "Cavelier's Account of La Salle's Voyage," both in Cox, *The Journey of Rene Robert Cavelier*, 1:43–44, 289; Smith, "Account of the Journey of Bénard de la Harpe," 529.

21. Diary of Fray Francisco Céliz, 1718–19, in Hoffmann, *Diary of the Alarcón Expedition*, 83; Barr, "From Captives to Slaves," 24, 25. Also see Diary of Juan Antonio de la Peña, 1721–22, in Santos, *Aguayo Expedition*, 70. For Wichita involvement in the trade, see Juan de Ulibarri, "The Diary of Juan de Ulibarri to El Cuartelejo, 1706," in Thomas, *After Coronado*, 74; Lauber, *Indian Slavery in Colonial Times*, 75.

22. Anderson, *The Indian Southwest*, 60–62.

23. Diary of Domingo Ramón, 1716, in Cunningham, "The Domingo Ramón Diary," 59. For a close analysis of the Spanish expeditions that interacted with the Ranchería Grande, see Foster, *The Historic Native Peoples of Texas*, 36, 37, 66–67, 69–70.

24. Anderson, *The Indian Southwest*, 83–85.

25. Augustina Zuazua outlined this history in the oral history she shared with anthropologist Harry Hoijer. See Hoijer, "The History and Customs of the Lipan, as Told by Augustina Zuazua"; Minor, *The Light Gray People*, 15–26. On the Apache self-referent, see Maestas, "Culture and History of Native American Peoples," 27.

26. Anderson, *The Indian Southwest*, 105–6.

27. These strategies were evident in what Nancy McGown Minor has termed the Lipan "shadow trade economy" (*The Light Gray People*, 71–76).

28. Anderson, *The Indian Southwest*, 106–8, 121; Minor, *The Light Gray People*, 59–81, 87–88.

29. Tamez, "Nádasi'né' ndé," 69 ("heterogeneity"); Anderson, *The Indian Southwest*, 3–5, 112–13. Jack Forbes has noted that this process of Jumano-(Lipan) Apache collaboration may have been underway as early as the 1680s (*Apache, Navaho, and Spaniard*, 195–96).

30. Tamez is generally skeptical of the historical existence of Ndé slaving and has emphasized the European origins and influences of Ndé participation in "commodified human exchange systems" ("Nádasi'né' ndé," 101–6, 110–17). Minor, the late tribal historian of the Lipan Apache Tribe of Texas, interpreted Lipan raiding as resource "harvesting" and argued, "The taking of human captives to be used as slaves or adopted into the tribe had always been a component of Apache raiding culture" (*The Light Gray People*, 74 [quote], 109–12, 117–30).

31. As slaves of Apache raiders during the 1730s, San Antonio residents Juan de Sartuche and Andrés Cadeña, for example, were forced to dress skins. Testimony of Ygnazio Lorenzo de Armas, June 28, 1738, in Proceedings Relative to the Infidelity of the Apaches, June 25, 1738, BAO; Anderson, *The Indian Southwest*, 115–22.

32. Dunn, "Apache Relations in Texas," 217n; Testimony of Juan Santiago de la Cruz, July 12, 1724, AGN PI, vol. 32, part 2.

33. Declaration of Louis Antoine Juchereau de St. Denis, Sept. 1, 1717, in Shelby, "St. Denis's Declaration concerning Texas," 180.

34. Cited Euro-American sources, purportedly based on testimony from Native informants, support this conclusion. Nonetheless, Margo Tamez has argued astutely that "the concept and cognitive of 'Apaches' as perpetual 'enemies' of other tribes, pioneers, settlers, conquistadors, peace, and of each other . . . is a tenet, a theme, and formulation imposed upon Ndé as an imperialist project of reconnaissance" ("Nádasi'né' ndé," 46).

35. The fact that Spanish officials initially advocated an alliance with Apaches is testament to the persuasiveness and geopolitical savvy of their Native enemies in Texas. For Spanish calls for an Apache alliance, see Instructions of Juan de Oliván Rebolledo, July 2, 1719, Recommendations of Juan de Oliván Rebolledo (after June 16,) 1719, and Instructions of Marqués de Valero, June 3, 1719, all in BAO; Diary of Juan Antonio de la Peña, 1721–22, in Santos, *Aguayo Expedition*, 39.

36. Pedro de Rivera's Frontier Inspection, 1724–28, in Naylor and Polzer, *Pedro de Rivera*, 86. For further discussion of the mission-settlements as fortresses, see Diary of Juan Antonio de la Peña, 1721–22, in Santos, *Aguayo Expedition*, 75; Report of Governor Thomas Phelipe de Winthuysen, Aug. 19, 1744, in Magnaghi, "Texas as Seen by Governor Winthuysen," 179; Barr, *Peace Came in the Form of a Woman*, 121–22.

37. Tamez, "Nádasi'né' ndé," 109.

38. Diary of Juan Antonio de la Peña, 1721–22, in Santos, *Aguayo Expedition*, 34; Juan Domingo Arricivita, *Cronica seráfica*, in Hammond and Rey, *Apostolic Chronicle*, 2:26–27 ("distributed"); Account of Nicolas Flores y Baldés, 1724, AGN PI, vol. 32, part 2; Marqués de Aguayo to the Viceroy, Feb. 26, 1724, AGN PI, vol. 32, part 2; Opinion of Juan Oliván de Rebolledo, Jan. 27, 1724, ASFG, vol. 10; Dunn, "Apache Relations in Texas," 206–7.

39. Robinson, *I Fought a Good Fight*, 54; Testimony of Juan Santiago de la Cruz, July 12, 1724, AGN PI, vol. 32, part 2; Dunn, "Apache Relations in Texas," 211–12, 212n; Report of Christóval Carabaxal, Nicolas Gutiérres de Lara, Francisco Xavier Maldonado, and Santiago Seguín, Jan. 6, 1724, ASFG, vol. 10 ("take *muchacho*"). Notably, in their report the soldiers quoted the Ndé diplomat using the masculine nouns *muchacho* and *eso*, even though the authors referred to the girl as "*una muchacha*" when describing the incident.

40. The use of violence was authorized formally in the instructions that the viceroy, the Marqués de Valero, left for the Spanish settler colonists of Texas, and Flores's coercion garnered support from his religious peers. See Instructions of the Marqués de Valero, June 3, 1718, BAO; Testimony of Fray Nuñez, June 14, 1724, in Leutenegger et al., *The San José Papers*, part 1, 43.

41. Dunn, "Apache Relations in Texas," 218.

42. Pedro de Rivera's Frontier Inspection, 1724–28, in Naylor and Polzer, *Pedro de Rivera*, 161, 191.

43. The Reglamento de 1729, in Naylor and Polzer, *Pedro de Rivera*, 278–79, 328–29. Transferring a corporate body (i.e., the Isleños, who immediately saw themselves as specially endowed *vecinos*) into the Texas field while physically and discursively (i.e., through assimilation) removing Native people from the region followed a globally budding settler colonial blueprint. Veracini, *Settler Colonialism*, especially 16–26, 53–61.

44. Arricivita, *Cronica seráfica*, 2:31; Dunn, "Apache Relations in Texas," 226–28; Fray Mariano de los Dolores y Viana to Juan Joséph de Montes de Oca, Oct. 8, 1745, in Leutenegger, *Letters of Dolores y Viana*, 47–48.

45. Dunn, "Apache Relations in Texas," 228–30.

46. Nancy McGown Minor has claimed that Caddos (represented as the "Chenti") were among the Ndé when the Spanish party ultimately attacked their *ranchería* (*Turning Adversity to Advantage*, 18).

47. Governor Domingo Cabello claimed in his 1784 report that the Spanish-led forces seized thirty-eight Apaches and about seven hundred horses. According to Ygnazio Lorenzo de Armas, the ordinary *alcalde*, or magistrate, of San Fernando de Béxar, Manuel de Sandoval, the governor who took office after Bustillo y Ceballos, "distributed the booty among those who went on the said campaign." Report of Domingo Cabello, Sept. 30, 1784, AGI PI, vol. 64, part 1; Testimony of Ygnazio Lorenzo de Armas, June 28, 1738, in Proceedings Relative to the Infidelity of the Apaches, June 25, 1738, BAO; Testimony of Juan Antonio Moraín, Nov. 3, 1756, in Proceedings concerning Barrios y Jáuregui's Report on the Removal of the Presidio of San Xavier to San Saba River and Jurisdiction of San Saba, Nov. 3, 1756, BAO; Dunn, "Apache Relations in Texas," 230–33.

48. The Marqués de Altamira to Viceroy Conde de Fonclara, July 4, 1744, in *Documentos para la historia de Texas*, 153; Order of Marqués de Casafuerte, July 18, 1733, BAO; Dunn, "Apache Relations in Texas," 237–39.

49. Captain Urrutia charged Cabellos Colorados with the Apache hostilities of the past decade, and after Governor Prudenzio de Orobio Basterra conducted what likely amounted to a sham investigation, authorities condemned the *capitán* and his companions to serve a bitter, agonizing sentence in Mexico City. Ygnazio Lorenzo de Armas, June 28, 1738, in Proceedings Relative to the Infidelity of the Apaches, June 25, 1738, BAO; Asensio del Rasso, June 28, 1738, in Proceedings Relative to the Infidelity of the Apaches, June 25, 1738, BAO; Proceedings Relative to the Infidelity of the Apaches, June 25, 1738, BAO; Testimony of Joséph de Urrutia, June 26, 1738, in Proceedings Relative to the Infidelity of the Apaches, June 25, 1738, BAO; Dunn, "Apache Relations in Texas," 240–42, 244–45; Barr, *Peace Came in the Form of a Woman*, 169–70; Robinson, *I Fought a Good Fight*, 63–65; Britten, *The Lipan Apaches*, 82–85.

50. Fray Fernández de Santa Ana to Fray Guardian Barco, Feb. 20, 1740, in Leutenegger et al., *The San José Papers*, part 1, 64.

51. Capt. Toribio Urrutia described the poor conditions of San Antonio in 1740, declaring the infrastructural need for a villa church, soldiers' quarters, and other public buildings "due to the poverty of its settlers." By 1743, the material welfare of San Antonio residents had hardly improved, as supply shipments from the South arrived with rotten and spoiled goods. Francisco Hernández of San Fernando de Béxar lamented that "conditions here had been impossible, and instead of improving were growing worse." Toribio Urrutia to the Viceroy, Dec. 17, 1740, in Leutenegger et al., *The San José Papers*, part 1, 84–85; Testimony of Francisco Hernández, May 7, 1743, BAO.

52. Capt. Toribio Urrutia to the Viceroy, Dec. 17, 1740, in Leutenegger et al., *The San Jose Papers*, part 1, 78; Maestas, "Culture and History of Native American Peoples of South Texas," 218.

53. Service Record of Don Vizente Rodríguez, Nov. 2, 1764, AGN PI, vol. 25, part 2; Minor, *Turning Adversity to Advantage*, 28; Dunn, "Apache Relations in Texas," 250–51; Hadley, Naylor, and Schuetz-Miller, *The Presidio and Militia on the Northern Frontier of New Spain*, 478.

54. Fray Benito Fernández de Santa Ana to Viceroy Pedro Cebrián, Conde de Fuenclara, May 16, 1745, in Leutenegger, *Letters of Fernández de Santa Ana*, 49–50; Libro de la Villa de San Fernando de Béxar de bautismos, entierros, confirmaciones, y casamientos, 1731–60, NLBLA, entries 94–108; Arricivita, *Cronica seráfica*, 2:33–34; Minor, *Turning Adversity to Advantage*, 28.

55. Arricivita, *Cronica seráfica*, 2:35.

56. Arricivita, *Cronica seráfica*, 2:34 ("not give her up"), 35–36.

57. Fray Benito Fernández de Santa Ana to the auditor of war, Feb. 23, 1750, in Hadley, Naylor, and Schuetz-Miller, *The Presidio and Militia on the Northern Frontier*, 484, 493.

58. Fray Benito Fernández de Santa Ana to Fray Guardian Alonso Giraldo de Terreros, Dec. 4, 1745, in Leutenegger, *Letters of Fernández de Santa Ana*, 55–56.

59. Hadley, Naylor, and Schuetz-Miller, *The Presidio and Militia on the Northern Frontier*, 476–77.

60. Proceedings concerning Joachín de Orobio y Bazterra's Order for Investigation of French Settlements in Texas, Oct. 1, 1745, BAO.

61. Fray Mariano de los Dolores y Viana to Governor Pedro del Barrio Junco y Espriella, July 16, 1749, in Leutenegger, *Letters of Dolores y Viana*, 50–55; Fray Benito Fernández de Santa Ana to Viceroy Conde de Revillagigedo, Mar. 10, 1749; Fray Benito

Fernández de Santa Ana to Governor Pedro de Barrio Junco y Espriella, July 5, 1749; Fray Benito Fernández de Santa Ana to Governor Pedro de Barrio Junco y Espriella, July 6(?), 1749; Fray Fernández de Santa Ana to Viceroy Conde de Revillagigedo, July 26, 1749; and Fray Fernández de Santa Ana to Viceroy Conde de Revillagigedo, Nov. 11, 1749, all in Leutenegger, *Letters of Fernández de Santa Ana*, 87–160.

62. Proceedings concerning Barrios y Jaurgeui's Report on the Removal of the Presidio of San Xavier to San Sabá River and Jurisdiction of San Sabá, Nov. 3, 1756, BAO; Robinson, *I Fought a Good Fight*, 78–80.

63. Fray Benito Fernández de Santa Ana to the auditor of war, Feb. 23, 1750, in Hadley, Naylor, and Schuetz-Miller, *The Presidio and Militia on the Northern Frontier*, 484–85, 494.

64. Dunn, "Apache Relations in Texas," 260; Arricivita, *Cronica seráfica*, 2:39–40.

65. Evidence indicates that Spaniards distributed captives to residents from Los Adaes and the Río Grande outposts. According to Governor Cabello, writing in 1784, the men were imprisoned at the presidio, while the women and children were distributed among the *vecinos* and missionaries. Report of Domingo Cabello, Sept. 30, 1784, in AGN-PI, vol. 64, part 1; The Cabildo of San Fernando vs. Antonio Rodríguez Mederos, June 17, 1750, BAO; Arricivita, *Cronica seráfica*, 2:39–41.

66. Escrito de Fray Mariano Francisco de los Dolores, Nov. 25, 1749, in *Documentos para la historia de Texas*, 171–72; Arricivita, *Cronica seráfica*, 2:41–42.

67. Robinson, *I Fought a Good Fight*, 72; Escrito de Fray Mariano Francisco de los Dolores, Nov. 25, 1749, in *Documentos para la historia de Texas*, 176; Ygnacio de Zepeda Testimony, Nov. 4, 1756, in Proceedings concerning Barrios y Jaurgeui's Report on the Removal of the Presidio of San Xavier to San Sabá River and Jurisdiction of San Sabá, Nov. 3, 1756, BAO; Report of Domingo Cabello, Sept. 30, 1784, in AGN-PI, vol. 64, part 1 ("treat each other"); Maestas, "Culture and History of Native American Peoples of South Texas," 236.

68. Fray Fernández de Santa Ana to the auditor of war, Feb. 23, 1750, in Hadley, Naylor, and Schuetz-Miller, *The Presidio and Militia on the Northern Frontier*, 485, 487–88.

69. Fray Mariano de Dolores y Viana to Capt. Toribio Urrutia and Lt. Joséph Eca y Musquiz, Sept. 17, 1750, in Leutenegger, *Letters of Dolores y Viana*, 123; Minor, *Turning Adversity to Advantage*, 37.

70. Arricivita, *Cronica seráfica*, 2:48; Robinson, *I Fought a Good Fight*, 83–84.

71. Wade, *The Native Americans of the Texas Edwards Plateau*, 183–87; Robinson, *I Fought a Good Fight*, 83–84; Diligencia de Col. Diego Ortiz Parrilla, May 30, 1757, ASFG, vol. 23.

72. Deposition of Juan Leal, Mar. 22, 1758; Deposition of Father Fray Miguel de Molina, Mar. 22, 1758; and Deposition of Andres de Villareal, Mar. 22, 1758, all in Nathan, *The San Sabá Papers*, 69–70, 73, 85–86.

73. The Auditor Don Domingo Calcarcel to the Viceroy, Apr. 6, 1758, in Nathan, *The San Sabá Papers*, 32–33.

74. Don Angel de Martos y Navarrete to Don Vicente Rodríguez, Mar. 23, 1758; Deposition of Juan Leal, Mar. 22, 1758; and Deposition of Father Fray Miguel de Molina, Mar. 22, 1758, all in Nathan, *The San Sabá Papers*, 21–22, 73–74, 85–87.

75. See chapter 3 for the origins of the Norteño confederation. Spaniards actually received a number of warning signs regarding the dangers of a Spanish-Apache alliance,

but few, if any, paid heed to these events. See, for instance, Fray Francisco Aparicio to Col. Diego Ortiz Parrilla, Apr. 5, 1758, in Nathan, *The San Sabá Papers*, 127.

76. Col. Diego Ortiz Parrilla to the Marqués de las Amarillas, Apr. 8, 1758, in Nathan, *The San Sabá Papers*, 139.

77. Included in the expedition were Native fighters from the San Antonio and Río Grande River mission-settlements and a number of Tlascaltecas. Diary of Juan Angel de Oyarzún, 1759, in Limpscomb, *After the Massacre*, 132.

78. Diary of Juan Angel de Oyarzún, 1759, in Limpscomb, *After the Massacre*, 107–8, 115–16, 120.

79. Diary of Juan Angel de Oyarzún, 1759, in Limpscomb, *After the Massacre*, 120–24, 126–27.

80. Diary of Juan Angel de Oyarzún, 1759, in Limpscomb, *After the Massacre*, 126–27, 129.

81. Meacham, "The Population of Spanish and Mexican Texas," 116; Castañeda, *Our Catholic Heritage in Texas*, 4:131–32. Libro de la Villa de San Fernando de Béxar de bautismos, 1731–60, NLBLA, entries 477, 481, and 483.

82. Historians have been harsh on Colonel Ortiz Parrilla for his performance during the Red River campaign. As Donald Chipman has argued, however, the captain's poor reputation was more the result of another Spanish officer's smear campaign than an accurate assessment of his abilities as a military commander (Chipman and Elizondo, "New Light on Felipe de Rábago y Terán," 173–74).

83. Barr, *Peace Came in the Form of a Woman*, 121–31, 156–57.

84. Schuetz, "The Indians of the San Antonio Missions," 246.

85. Veracini, *Settler Colonialism*, 53–74.

86. Arricivita, *Cronica seráfica*, 2:32–33. Also see Petition of Pedro de Oconitrillo, 1745, BAO.

87. Enslaved Black labor was critical to the operations of *obrajes* (workshops), mines, and plantations across New Spain. This is not to mention the many enslaved Black people forced to serve as domestic workers. See Proctor, "Afro-Mexican Slave Labor"; West, *The Mining Community in Northern New Spain*, 48–51; Kris Lane, "Africans and Natives in the Mines of Spanish America," in Restall, *Beyond Black and Red*, 159–84; Palmer, *Slaves of the White God*, 65–83; Cope, *The Limits of Racial Domination*, 13–14. For discussion of the rumors surrounding the Almagres silver mines near the San Sabá outposts, see Patten, "Miranda's Inspection of Los Almagres."

88. Itinerary and Daily Account Kept by Gen. Domingo de Terán, in Hatcher, "The Expedition of Don Domingo Terán de los Rios," 38; Reséndez, *Land So Strange*, 56.

89. See, for instance, bill of sale between Josepha Flores y Valdés and Justo Voneo y Morales for Luis, slave, Oct. 29, 1743, and bill of sale between Josepha Flores y Valdés and Justo Voneo y Morales for Francisco Joséph, slave, Oct. 29, 1743, both in BAO.

90. Asensio del Rasso, June 28, 1738, in Proceedings Relative to the Infidelity of the Apaches, June 25, 1738, BAO; Ygnazio Lorenzo de Armas, June 28, 1738, in Proceedings Relative to the Infidelity of the Apaches, June 25, 1738, BAO.

91. Libro de la Villa de San Fernando de Béxar de bautismos, 1731–60, NLBLA, entries 94–108; Fray Benito Fernández de Santa Ana to Fray Guardian Alonso Giraldo de Terreros, Dec. 4, 1745, in Leutenegger, *Letters of Fernández de Santa Ana*, 55–56; de la Teja, *San Antonio de Béxar*, 19; Meacham, "The Population of Spanish and Mexican Texas," 78, 80, 85; Schuetz, "The Indians of the San Antonio Missions," 349–50.

92. De la Teja, *San Antonio de Béxar,* 19–20; Meacham, "The Population of Spanish and Mexican Texas," 99–100, 102.

93. The baptismal records of San Fernando de Béxar support this estimate. Of the approximately 520 entries in the 1731–60 records, 58 involved the baptism of an Indian, the child of an Indian, or an enslaved Black person. Of these 58 entries, only 6 do not offer identifiable evidence that the child was a captive or the offspring of a captive. See Libro de la Villa de San Fernando de Béxar de bautismos, 1731–60, NLBLA.

94. Meacham, "The Population of Spanish and Mexican Texas," 78, 80, 85, 99–100, 102. For evidence of the presence of enslaved Black people, see Libro de la Villa de San Fernando de Béxar de bautismos, 1731–60, NLBA; bill of sale between Josepha Flores y Valdés and Justo Voneo y Morales for Luis, slave, Oct. 29, 1743, BAO; bill of sale between Josepha Flores y Valdés and Justo Voneo y Morales for Francisco Joséph, slave, Oct. 29, 1743, BAO; bill of sale between Carlos Vélez de la Torre and Diego Ortiz Parrilla for María Josepha, slave, and Joséph Alexo, slave, Mar. 22, 1760, BAO. Arricivita, *Cronica seráfica*, 2:39 ("not wanted");

95. Chabot, *San Antonio and Its Beginnings*, 91; Chabot, *With the Makers of San Antonio,* 58.

96. Libro de la Villa de San Fernando de Béxar de bautismos, 1731–60, NLBLA, entries 68, 227, 423; bill of sale between Josepha Flores y Valdés and Justo Voneo y Morales for Luis, slave, Oct. 29, 1743, bill of sale between Josepha Flores y Valdés and Justo Voneo y Morales for Francisco Joséph, slave, Oct. 29, 1743, both in BAO.

97. San Antonio actually lacked a public granary. Only the missions housed surplus storage containers, as mission Indians typically produced much more than their *vecino* counterparts. De la Teja, *San Antonio de Béxar,* 93.

98. De la Teja, *San Antonio de Béxar,* 75–81, 89–93, 110.

99. De la Teja, *San Antonio de Béxar,* 111–17, 121–23.

100. Chantal Cramaussel too has turned to baptismal records to uncover the prevalence of *la esclavitud de los indios* on the Mexican frontier (*Poblar la frontera*, 199–200).

101. Libro de la Villa de San Fernando de Béxar de bautismos, 1731–60, NLBLA, entries 325, 367, 368, 385, 423, 442.

102. The Marqués de Aguayo prioritized the segregation of Spanish colonists and mission Indians immediately upon establishing Mission San José. Report of the Founding of San José by Captain Juan Valdéz, Mar. 13, 1720, in Leutenegger et al., *San José Papers,* part 1, 40.

103. See, for instance, Report of Joséph Antonio Fernández de Jáuregui Urrutia to the Viceroy, Jan. 11, 1735, BAO.

104. Fray Fernández acted on this civilize-through-bondage mentality when he baptized the daughter of the *capitán grande* of the Ypande Apaches in 1745. After cleansing the Ypande child in *los oleos santos*, the holy oils, the friar made known his intentions to keep the young girl unless her father agreed to religious conversion. Fray Fernández reasoned that once brought into the fold of Christian civilization through baptism, the Apache girl could not be surrendered back into the barbarous world of her kinspeople. But what was ostensibly a creative attempt to coerce the acceptance of a Christian lifestyle in practice had the potential to operate as a tool for physical subjugation. It seems clear that Fray Fernández genuinely was interested in recruiting the Ypande *capitán grande* and his people for Christian conversion; yet his impulse

to coerce through baptism was shared by many others who were less concerned with spiritual guidance and more preoccupied with gaining access to exploitable laborers. Fray Benito Fernández de Santa Ana to Viceroy Pedro Cebrián, Conde de Fuenclara, May 16, 1745, in Leutenegger, *Letters of Fernández de Santa Ana*, 48–50.

105. Broad theoretical overviews of *compadrazgo* can be found in Mintz and Wolf, "An Analysis of Ritual Co-Parenthood"; Horstman and Kurtz, "Compadrazgo and Adaptation in Sixteenth Century Central Mexico." A number of scholars also have explored the connections and tensions between slavery and baptism. See, for instance, Beasley, "Domestic Rituals"; Martín Casares and Delaigue, "The Evangelization of Freed and Slave Black Africans"; Glasson, "'Baptism Doth Not Bestow Freedom.'" For an exploration of the Spanish-Native bonds forged through *compadrazgo*, see Charney, "The Implications of Godparental Ties." For a notable example of *compadrazgo* functioning to create bonds of alliance in Texas, see Diary of Fray Francisco Céliz, 1718–19, in Hoffmann, *Diary of the Alarcón Expedition*, 77, 79. According to the diary, Alarcón became godfather to at least four Indians to demonstrate his commitment to their people.

106. Van Deusen, "The Intimacies of Bondage," 22; McKinley, *Fractional Freedoms*, 147. Also see Blumenthal, *Enemies and Familiars*, 122–53.

107. Libro de la Villa de San Fernando de Béxar de bautismos, 1731–69, NLBLA, entry 423.

108. Libro de la Villa de San Fernando de Béxar de bautismos, 1731–60, NLBLA, entries 68, 75, 112, 149, 172, 227, 252, 285, 325, 336, 354, 385, 398, 400, 417, 423, 441, 442, 454.

109. Antonia Lusgardia Hernández vs. Miguel Nuñez Morillo, Aug. 9, 1735, BAO.

110. Arricivita, *Cronica seráfica*, 2:32–33.

111. Dictamen, Fiscal, Nov. 30, 1716, in Archivo General de la Nación, *Boletín del Archivo General de la Nación*, 339; Recommendations of Juan de Oliván Rebolledo, Dec. 1717, BAO.

112. Fray Olivares claimed that "such people are bad people, unfit to settle among gentiles, because their customs are depraved, and worse than those of the gentiles themselves." Quoted in Castañeda, *Our Catholic Heritage in Texas*, 2:87.

113. Buckley, "The Aguayo Expedition," 27–28; Foster, *Texas and North-Eastern Mexico*, 6; Testimony of Juan Curbelo during Residencia of Governor Juan Antonio Bustillo y Zevallos, Aug. 20, 1734, BAO.

114. Records kept by Don Manuel Angel de Villegas Puente, Canary Islanders Records; Mason, *African Americans and Race Relations*, 6.

115. Recommendations of Juan de Oliván Rebolledo, ca. 1717, BAO.

116. Martínez, *Genealogical Fictions*, 142–70.

117. See, for instance, Libro de la Villa de San Fernando de Béxar de bautismos, 1731–60, NLBLA, entries 172, 317, and 327.

118. Vinson, *Bearing Arms for His Majesty*, 200.

119. But this is not to say that the racial hierarchies of central Mexico were fixed. For discussions of the salient yet contested nature of race in colonial Mexico, see especially Martínez, *Genealogical Fictions*; Cope, *The Limits of Racial Domination*.

120. Testimony of Bernardo de Miranda, Nov. 6, 1756, in Proceedings concerning Barrios y Jáuregui's report on the removal of the presidio of San Xavier, Nov. 3, 1756, BAO. Also see Testimony of Phelipe Muñoz de Mora, Nov. 3, 1756, in Proceedings

concerning Barrios y Jáuregui's report on the removal of the presidio of San Xavier, Nov. 3, 1756, BAO; Testimony of Ygnacio Hérnandez, Nov. 4, 1756, in Proceedings concerning Barrios y Jáuregui's report on the removal of the presidio of San Xavier, Nov. 3, 1756, BAO. For a study on the connections between honor, military performance, and anti-Indian violence, see Alonso, *Thread of Blood*, especially 21–36.

121. Although the evidence is scant, there is some indication that this racial flattening occurred for enslaved people as well, but with different, socially negative consequences. Native and Black bondspeople shared a dishonorable status. This may have been the reason enslaved Native and Black people, like Tadeo Gonzáles, "a *negro* servant of Marzelino Martinez," and Luisa Martinez, an "Apache Indian," could marry one another. Libro de la Villa de San Fernando de Béxar de bautismos, 1731–60, NLBLA, entries 172, 252, 400, 423, 441, and 454.

122. Testimony of Ygnacio Hérnandez, Nov. 4, 1756, in Proceedings concerning Barrios y Jáuregui's report on the removal of the presidio of San Xavier, Nov. 3, 1756, BAO.

Chapter 3

1. A *náshneta* or *nanitá* was the leader of a Lipan band, who usually was selected based on merit and charisma. In Spanish documents, observers refer to a *náshneta* as a *capitán* or *capitán grande*. Minor, *The Light Gray People*, 101.

2. This anecdote is a dramatization of an incident reported by Fray Diego Ximénez and Fray Antonio de Cuevas on separate occasions from 1763 to 1764. Report of Fray Diego Ximénez and Fray Manuel Antonio Cuebas to the Viceroy, Jan. 24, 1763, in Arricivita, *Cronica seráfica*, 2:80–82; Report of Fray Diego Ximénez and Fray Antonio de Cuevas, Feb. 25, 1763, and Report of Fray Diego Ximénez, Dec. 26, 1764, both in Minor, *Turning Adversity to Advantage*, 68–70.

3. The fact that Comanches referred to Lipan Apaches as "the gray-rumped" is revealing of the expansionist nature of Comanches' historical experiences with Lipan communities. By focusing on their backside, Comanches claimed that Lipanes were always fleeing from them. Comanches called Lipanes *gray* because Lipan people identified themselves as "the light gray people," a people toward the east. Attocknie, *The Life of Ten Bears*, 16; Minor, *The Light Gray People*, 5–7.

4. Few scholars have attempted to detail in narrative form the migration of Comanches during the first two-thirds of the eighteenth century, and even fewer have sought to explicate the importance of slavery in that migration. For brief accounts, see Wallace and Hoebel, *The Comanches*; Kavanagh, *Comanche Political History*; Kenner, *The Comanchero Frontier*; Noyes, *Los Comanches*; Anderson, *The Indian Southwest*; John, *Storms Brewed in Other Men's Worlds*. For discussion of the role of slave raiding during Comanche migration, see Hämäläinen, *The Comanche Empire*; Reséndez, *The Other Slavery*, 180–81.

5. I have found no study that effectively chronicles and analyzes Comanche movement and slave raiding in Texas from the 1740s through 1760s. Hämäläinen, for instance, dedicates only twelve pages to this history, even though he recognizes it as an important era in the history of Comanche expansion (*The Comanche Empire*, 55–66). For a better understanding of this period, I have consulted a little-used manuscript collection at the University of Texas at Austin's Dolph Briscoe Center for American History, called the Archivo General de San Francisco el Grande.

6. Nick Estes has been critical of historians' characterizations of Native peoples as "expansionist," claiming that such accounts create a false equivalence between Native societies and U.S. settler colonies, which were "driven . . . by purely economic motives" in their quest to violently displace locals (*Our History Is the Future*, 70). Nonetheless, territorial, economic, political, and cultural expansions were obvious outcomes of Comanche machinations during the eighteenth century. Whether the Comanche ascendance is best understood as a function of adaptation to a European colonial context, however, is a different matter. This chapter seeks to demonstrate that Comanche expansion hinged upon successful manipulation of a European-influenced world.

7. Notably (and contrary to Euro-American scholarship), the Comanche historian Francis Joseph Attocknie has stated that "only the Comanches, like the buffalo, were native to the South Plains" (Attocknie, *The Life of Ten Bears*, 28).

8. This Little Ice Age argument, of course, is highly speculative and not without its serious skeptics. Douglas B. Bamforth, for instance, has noted the methodological difficulties of gauging precipitation levels, particularly when speaking relatively (i.e., comparing one period of time to another). He also argues that "referring to the long periods of time by terms such as the 'Little Ice Age' and describing them as 'wetter' or 'colder' than other periods of time is conceptually convenient, but obscures the actual pattern of variation with which human beings had to cope" ("An Empirical Perspective on Little Ice Age Climatic Change," 363–64). See also Hämäläinen, *The Comanche Empire*, 20–21; Flores, "Bison Ecology and Bison Diplomacy," 468; Hodge, *Ecology and Ethnogenesis*, 77–85.

9. Anthropologists Ernest Wallace and E. Adamson Hoebel were most responsible for the interpretation that *Comanche* meant "enemy." According to James A. Goss, "their interpretation is just plain wrong." Goss, who spent some thirty-five years working with Numic-speaking consultants, argues, "In Nuutsiyu, 'Kumantsi' was not a generic term for enemy; it was a term for their 'other' relatives." James A. Goss, "The Yamparikas, Shoshones, Comanches, or Utes, or Does It Matter?," in Clemmer et al., *Julian Steward and the Great Basin*, 79–80; Hämäläinen, *The Comanche Empire*, 22–24; Flores, "Bison Ecology and Bison Diplomacy," 468; Hodge, *Ecology and Ethnogenesis*, 87; Brooks, *Captives and Cousins*, 59; Wistrand-Robinson and Armagost, *Comanche Dictionary and Grammar*, 28.

10. Hämäläinen, *The Comanche Empire*, 22–27.

11. Comanche slavery's early commercial character almost certainly was a direct result of the Spanish-influenced slave markets of New Mexico. Ned Blackhawk has argued that the slavery and violence that predominated in Native intercommunity relations after Spanish colonization of the North American Southwest were much more expansive and intense than the slavery and violence that existed prior to Spanish arrival. According to Blackhawk, "violence remained largely a local phenomenon" during the precolonial era. Attempts to understand precolonial Native violence, moreover, are methodologically obstructed by "the violent shock waves accompanying colonial expansion" (*Violence over the Land*, 22–23).

12. Forbes, *Apache, Navaho, and Spaniard*, 41–106; Simmons, *The Ute Indians*, 29; McNitt, *Navajo Wars*, 13.

13. There is reason to believe that Spanish slaving was a major source of the great Native discontent that ultimately led to the Pueblo Revolt of 1680, as early on, rebels

demanded that the governor return all enslaved Apaches. Kenner, *The Comanchero Frontier*, 14–15, 19.

14. In 1681, the Spanish Crown promulgated the Recopilación de 1681, detailing yet again the terms in which Spaniards were permitted to trade in enslaved Indians. According to the code, Spaniards were obligated, as Christians, to ransom or "rescue" those enslaved in other Native communities. The Recopilación de 1681 received further clarification in 1694. Magnaghi, "Plains Indians in New Mexico," 87; Kenner, *The Comanchero Frontier*, 16–18.

15. Simmons, *The Ute Indians*, 29–31.

16. Blackhawk, "The Displacement of Violence," 725–26; Blackhawk, *Violence over the Land*, 25.

17. Attocknie claimed that Comanches began "developing the horse culture" around 1675. Attocknie, *The Life of Ten Bears*, 38; Hämäläinen, *The Comanche Empire*, 25–27.

18. Diary of Juan de Ulibarri, 1706, in Thomas, *After Coronado*, 61, 76.

19. For an explicit reference to this trade, see Governor Antonio Valverde Cosio to the Marqués de Valero, Nov. 30, 1719, in Thomas, *After Coronado*, 141. In *Navajos in the Catholic Church Records*, David Brugge has noted that seventy-four non-Ute-Comanche captives were baptized by Spaniards in New Mexico from 1700 to 1710.

20. Council of War, Aug. 19, 1719, in Thomas, *After Coronado*, 101–10; Noyes, *Los Comanches*, 11.

21. Council of War, Aug. 19, 1719, in Thomas, *After Coronado*, 102, 104.

22. Hämäläinen, *The Comanche Empire*, 27; Council of War, Aug. 19, 1719, in Thomas, *After Coronado*, 105, 107.

23. Moreover, the fact that there were only five Utes living among the Spaniards of New Mexico—when scholars know that Spaniards enslaved 350 Ute women in 1716—suggests that Spanish residents made sure to sell all Ute captives, perhaps out of fear of upsetting the commercial status quo. Simmons, *The Ute Indians*, 31; Brugge, *Navajos in the Catholic Church Records*, 30; McNitt, *Navajo Wars*, 23.

24. Late seventeenth-century reports by Diego de Peñalosa Briceno and Alonso de Posada identified Native individuals who had been held captive for prolonged periods of time in Teguayo, near the homeland of the Utes. Tyler, "The Myth of the Lake of Copala," 320–21; Tyler and Taylor, "The Report of Fray Alonso de Posada," 305; Sánchez, *Explorers, Traders, and Slavers*, 11.

25. Diary of Governor Antonio de Valverde Cosio, 1719, in Thomas, *After Coronado*, 127; Noyes, *Los Comanches*, 318–19n4.

26. Hämäläinen, *The Comanche Empire*, 240–46.

27. Governor Antonio de Valverde Cosio to the Viceroy, the Marqués de Valero, Nov. 30, 1719, in Thomas, *After Coronado*, 142.

28. Diary of Governor Antonio de Valverde Cosio, 1719, in Thomas, *After Coronado*, 110–15, 128.

29. Diary of Governor Antonio de Valverde Cosio, 1719, in Thomas, *After Coronado*, 114.

30. Opinion of Capt.-Maj. of War José Naranjo, Council of War, Santa Fe, May 27, 1720, in Thomas, *After Coronado*, 156–57; Governor Antonio Valverde Cosio to the Marqués de Valero, Nov. 30, 1719, in Thomas, *After Coronado*, 144.

31. The sweeping successes of the Comanche campaigns against the Jicarilla and Carlana Apaches were partly the result of the semisedentary nature of their

communities. Governor Valverde Cosio commented on their farms in 1719: "I found these people very close to embracing our holy faith. . . . They lack only missionaries who may instruct and convert them. They work hard, gather much Indian corn, squashes, and kidney beans, lay out ditches to irrigate their crops, and have always maintained and at present maintain friendship with us." Coincidently, the Ndé quality that impressed Valverde Cosio the most (i.e., their agricultural abilities) was one of their greatest liabilities in the face of a mounted, highly mobile Comanche threat. Governor Antonio Valverde Cosio to the Marqués de Valero, Nov. 30, 1719, in Thomas, *After Coronado*, 142.

32. Decree of Governor Juan Domingo de Bustamante for Council of War, Nov. 8, 1723, in Thomas, *After Coronado*, 194; Governor Juan Domingo de Bustamante to Juan de Acuña, the Marqués de Casa Fuerte, Jan. 10, 1724, in Thomas, *After Coronado*, 201.

33. The Ndé *capitán*, Churlique, told Governor Bustamante in November 1724, for instance, that he and his people were plotting to attack "the Comanche nation, because they found themselves suffering from the havoc they had wrought on one of their rancherías." Although the overall picture indicates severe net losses for Ndé communities, the fact that they brought enslaved Comanches to Santa Fe in at least one instance suggests that they found some success against their Comanche foes. Diary of Governor Juan Domingo de Bustamante, Nov. 17–27, 1724, in Thomas, *After Coronado*, 199; Governor Juan Domingo de Bustamante to Juan de Acuña, the Marqués de Casa Fuerte, Apr. 30, 1727, in Thomas, *After Coronado*, 257; Governor Juan Domingo de Bustamante to Juan de Acuña, the Marqués de Casa Fuerte, May 30, 1724, in Thomas, *After Coronado*, 208.

34. Report of Governor Domingo Cabello, Sept. 30, 1784, AGN PI, vol. 64, part 1. It should be noted that Cabello's point about Ndé migration in 1723 was a rhetorical move on his part: if Apaches were invading Spanish-controlled territory, per his claim, anti-Apache violence was justified. See Maestas, "Culture and History of Native American Peoples," 190–92.

35. Pedro de Rivera to Juan de Acuña, the Marqués de Casa Fuerte, Sept. 26, 1727, in Thomas, *After Coronado*, 211–12.

36. According to Quassyah, a Comanche man who was interviewed by anthropologists in the 1930s, a *paraibo* was a chief: "There was no separate term for subchief, of whom there were two or three in each band. All chiefs were paraibo. If the principal chief was absent, one of the remaining subchiefs was appointed as acting chief." Notes on Quassyah, July 5, 1933, in Kavanagh, *Comanche Ethnography*, 56; Hämäläinen, *The Comanche Empire*, 37–38.

37. The Comanche-Ute alliance deteriorated around midcentury, when Comanches built new political and commercial ties with Wichitas and other eastern-oriented peoples. During the latter part of the eighteenth century, Utes actually joined Spanish and Ndé fighters in campaigns against Comanches. Kavanagh, *Comanche Political History*, 68; Hämäläinen, *The Comanche Empire*, 49–52.

38. Declaration of Fray Miguel de Menchero, May 10, 1744, in Hackett, *Historical Documents relating to New Mexico*, 3:401. For the New Mexican slave trade, see Kavanagh, *Comanche Political History*, 67; Brugge, *Navajos in the Catholic Church Records*, 30. For Spanish attempts to regulate the New Mexico–Comanche trade in 1735 and 1737, see Twitchell, *The Spanish Archives of New Mexico*, 2:205, 209.

39. Magnaghi, "Plains Indians in New Mexico," 87–89; Brooks, *Captives and Cousins*, 127–38; Hämäläinen, *The Comanche Empire*, 39.

40. "Extract of the Journal of the Expedition of the Mallet Brothers to Santa Fe, May 29, 1739, to June 24, 1740," in Blakeslee, *Along Ancient Trails*, 48.

41. Hämäläinen has estimated this population number based on a late 1730s observation of some fifty to sixty villages "scattered about" in the Arkansas valley (*The Comanche Empire*, 39). Kavanagh, however, is less convinced of the authenticity of this account (*Comanche Political History*, 68). A smallpox epidemic swept across Comanchería from 1737 to 1739. Rivaya-Martínez, "Captivity and Adoption among the Comanche Indians," 54.

42. Quoted in Kavanagh, *Comanche Political History*, 66–67.

43. See chapters 4 and 7.

44. In the 1720s, Pedro de Rivera noted that Comanches traded tanned skins at the New Mexican trade fairs. It is possible that enslaved people contributed to the production of such goods, particularly as many enslaved bodies were already flowing in and out of Comanchería at the time. Kavanagh, *Comanche Political History*, 67; Flores, "Bison Ecology and Bison Diplomacy," 471.

45. Adam Hodge has argued that the Comanches' ancestors, the Numu, established "a remarkable level of gender 'complementarity'" and "what might be called gender equality" hundreds of years earlier (*Ecology and Ethnogenesis*, 57, 65). See also Flores, "Bison Ecology and Bison Diplomacy," 471.

46. Governor Marín del Valle was among the first to note the effects of warfare on Comanche social status. Quoted in Kavanagh, *Comanche Political History*, 76.

47. Hämäläinen, *The Comanche Empire*, 39, 246–55; Brooks, *Captives and Cousins*, 59–60.

48. In 1521, King Carlos V prohibited the giving or trading of arms to Indians in his Recopilación de leyes. On May 2, 1735, New Mexico authorities issued a *bando*, outlawing the sale of firearms to Indians, including Comanches. Weber, *The Spanish Frontier in North America*, 428, n28; Twitchell, *Spanish Archives of New Mexico*, 2:205.

49. There is some speculation that French traders had begun trading with Comanches as early as 1719. During Bénard de la Harpe's expedition across the Southern Plains in 1718–19, the Frenchman and his followers encountered a large Native settlement, consisting of several villages, on the western bank of the Arkansas River. According to la Harpe, "These villages make only one village, the houses adjoining one another, running from east to west a league through the most beautiful location that one might possibly see." Among the several thousand predominantly Wichita inhabitants that la Harpe saw were people of the "Caumuche" nation. As editor of la Harpe's diary, Ralph A. Smith considered these people Comanches, but later French accounts indicate that French traders had not established trade or diplomatic ties with Comanches. If these folks were in fact Comanche visitors, evidently la Harpe and his followers failed to impress them. Smith, "Account of the Journey of Bénard de la Harpe," 526–29; Weber, *The Spanish Frontier in North America*, 177; Schilz and Worcester, "The Spread of Firearms among the Indian Tribes," 2; Smith, *The Wichita Indians*, 20–28.

50. Governor Valverde Cosio observed the French-Pawnee trade in firearms during his 1719 campaign across the Plains. Diary of Governor Antonio de Valverde Cosio, 1719, in Thomas, *After Coronado*, 132–33.

51. During the first two decades of the eighteenth century, Pawnee traders sold Ndé plainspeople as slaves to French merchants, likely in exchange for firearms and other manufactured goods. See, for instance, Diary of Juan de Ulibarri, 1706, in Thomas, *After Coronado*, 74.

52. White, *The Roots of Dependency*, 179.

53. Hämäläinen has claimed that the Aa nation "probably refers to the Arapahoes" (*The Comanche Empire*, 40, 377n51). According to Rivaya-Martínez, however, "the Spanish term *Aa* is clearly a borrowing from Comanche *AɁaa*, the denomination for the Crow Indians, meaning literally 'horn'" ("Captivity and Adoption among the Comanche Indians," 163).

54. Aron, *American Confluence*, 22–28.

55. Smith, *The Wichita Indians*, 24–26; Hämäläinen, *The Comanche Empire*, 42.

56. Hämäläinen, *The Comanche Empire*, 40–42; Kavanagh, *Comanche Political History*, 69–74; Report of Governor Tomás Vélez Cachupín, Nov. 27, 1751, in Thomas, *The Plains Indians*, 68–75. Also see Testimony of Fray Lorenzo Antonio Estremera, 1748, in Lummis, "Some Unpublished History," 74–78

57. Report of Thomás Vélez Cachupín, Nov. 27, 1751, in Thomas, *The Plains Indians*, 75–76; Smith, *The Wichita Indians*, 26.

58. Testimony of Antonio Treviño, Aug. 13, 1765, in Proceedings concerning the return of Antonio Treviño by the Taovaya Indians, Mar. 20, 1765, BAO; Smith, *The Wichita Indians*, 28; Kavanagh, *Comanche Political History*, 72; Hämäläinen, *The Comanche Empire*, 43.

59. Governor Joaquín Codallos y Rabál to the Viceroy, Mar. 4, 1748, in Lummis, "Some Unpublished History," 127; Report of Thomás Vélez Cachupín, Nov. 27, 1751, in Thomas, *The Plains Indians*, 76.

60. Opinion of Señor Auditor, June 2, 1752, in Thomas, *The Plains Indians*, 79–80. Also see Juan Francisco de Güemes y Horcasitas to the Marqués de Enseñada, June 28, 1753, and Instructions of Thomás Vélez Cachupín, Aug. 12, 1754, both in Thomas, *The Plains Indians*, 111–12, 132–34; Report of the Reverend Father Provincial of the Province of El Santo Evangelico to the Viceroy, Mar. 1750, in Hackett, *Historical Documents relating to New Mexico*, 3:449.

61. Aron, *American Confluence*, 36; Smith, *The Wichita Indians*, 27.

62. Testimony of Luis Fuesi, Aug. 8, 1752, in Thomas, *The Plains Indians*, 107.

63. In 1765, Antonio Treviño offered a detailed account of the Wichita fort, claiming that the relocation of the Wichita communities on the Red River was the result of Osage attacks around 1757. The permanent nature of the fort, however, suggests that the Wichitas were confident in their new location, which was strategically positioned between Comanchería and French Louisiana. Testimony of Antonio Treviño, Aug. 13, 1765, in Proceedings concerning the return of Antonio Treviño by the Taovaya Indians, Mar. 20, 1765, BAO; Smith, *The Wichita Indians*, 28.

64. It is worth noting, however, that Caddo-Wichita ties seem to have existed since the first decades of the eighteenth century, when epidemics, droughts, war, and agricultural failures forced various Caddo groups to relocate west. Anderson, *The Indian Southwest*, 146–49.

65. Spanish officials likely exaggerated the role of French traders in forging the alliance between Comanches, Wichitas, and Caddos, but it is clear that the distribution of French goods helped to cement the alliances between the various communities.

By the 1750s, Spanish authorities in Texas were learning that French merchants were trading "shirts, blankets, loin cloths, fusils, powder, bullets, beads, vermillion, and other effects valued by those nations" of Caddo country in east and northeast Texas. Like the Wichitas, the Caddos would have been able to serve as middlemen in the French-Comanche commerce. Proceedings of Junta de Guerra y Hacienda relative to the French moving the presidio of Natchitoches, Jan. 21 and 22, 1754, BAO.

66. It should be noted that Bonilla's brief discussion of Ndé-Comanche relations in 1743 failed to mention at least one documented Ndé victory over a band of Comanche fighters early that year. According to Fray Benito Fernández de Santa Ana, the Ndé rout was so one-sided that only one courageous Comanche man survived. The Ndé victory was short-lived, however, as the survivor immediately led a new force of Comanche fighters against the Ndé communities near the Red River. According to Castañeda, these attacks put an end to the Ndé presence in the Red River Valley (*Our Catholic Heritage in Texas*, 3:343–44). See also West, "Bonilla's Brief Compendium," 45–46.

67. For (brief) discussions of the conflicts between Comanches and Apaches during the 1743–53 period, see Hämäläinen, *The Comanche Empire*, 55–59; Anderson, *The Indian Southwest*, 123; Britten, *The Lipan Apaches*, 91–92; Robinson, *I Fought a Good Fight*, 66, 77–80; Castañeda, *Our Catholic Heritage in Texas*, 3:343; Minor, *Turning Adversity to Advantage*, 24–32.

68. Quoted in Minor, *Turning Adversity to Advantage*, 50.

69. Notably, Moraín also attributed Ndé geopolitical weakness to dwindling game populations and relentless Spanish campaigning (Testimony of Juan Antonio Moraín, Nov. 3, 1756, in Proceedings concerning Barrios y Jauregui's Report on the Removal of the Presidio of San Xavier, Nov. 3, 1756, BAO). See also Castañeda, *Our Catholic Heritage in Texas*, 3:371–73; Arricivita, *Cronica seráfica*, 2:54.

70. Fray Francisco Aparicio to Diego Ortiz Parrilla, Apr. 5, 1758, in Nathan, *The San Sabá Papers*, 127.

71. Report of Bernardo de Miranda y Flores to Jacinto de Barrios y Jauregui, Mar. 29, 1756, in Patten, "Miranda's Inspection of Los Almagres," 249; Decree of Viceroy Agustín de Ahumada y Villalón, the Marqués de Amarillas, Feb. 12, 1756, in Proceedings concerning the Junta de Guerra y Hacienda's Report on the Building of New Mission at Mouth of Trinity River, Feb. 4, 1756, BAO.

72. Miguel de Sesma y Escudero to Viceroy Agustín de Ahumada y Villalón, the Marqués de Amarillas, Sept. 14, 1756, AGN PI, vol. 25, part 1.

73. Castañeda, *Our Catholic Heritage in Texas*, 3:396; Maestas, "Culture and History of Native American Peoples of South Texas," 268.

74. Declaración del teniente Don Juan Galván, June 10, 1757, ASFG, vol. 23.

75. Testimony of Bernardo de Miranda y Flores, Nov. 6, 1756, in Proceedings concerning Barrios y Jauregui's Report on the Removal of the Presidio of San Xavier, Nov. 3, 1756, BAO.

76. Castañeda, *Our Catholic Heritage in Texas*, 3:400.

77. Arricivita, *Cronica seráfica*, 2:60–61; Diligencia sobre que el capitán Chiquito, May 30, 1757, ASFG, vol. 23.

78. A few weeks after the massive attack on the San Sabá mission on April 5, Fray Francisco Aparicio articulated what he should have known long before: "I find this reluctance [of the Apaches to settle here], in large part, to be attributable to the

Apaches' awareness of the great number of their enemies, who can easily invade this territory whenever they so desire, and lay waste and wipe out any Apache settlement. This is undoubtedly the reason why the Apaches stay away and live along the Medina, San Antonio, San Marcos, and Guadalupe." Fray Francisco Aparicio to Col. Diego Ortiz Parrilla, Apr. 5, 1758, in Nathan, *The San Sabá Papers*, 127. Also see chapter 2 for Spanish interpretations of the attack.

79. Deposition of Juan Leal, Mar. 22, 1758; Deposition of Father Fray Miguel de Molina, Mar. 22, 1758; Deposition of Andres de Villareal, Mar. 22, 1758; Deposition of Joseph Gutiérrez, Mar. 21, 1758; Deposition of Sgt. Joseph Antonio Flores, Mar. 21, 1758, all in Nathan, *The San Sabá Papers*, 44–45, 47, 52–56, 69–70, 73, 85–86.

80. Arricivita, *Cronica seráfica*, 2:71.

81. Castañeda, *Our Catholic Heritage in Texas*, 4:114–17; Arricivita, *Cronica seráfica*, 2:73–74

82. Castañeda, *Our Catholic Heritage in Texas*, 4:151–52, 154–55.

83. Castañeda, *Our Catholic Heritage in Texas*, 4:160, 163–64, 166–67; Arricivita, *Cronica seráfica*, 2:76–79.

84. Castañeda, *Our Catholic Heritage in Texas*, 4:169.

85. Testimonio de una india Lipan, Apr. 4, 1763, ASFG, vol. 18.

86. Viceroy Joaquín de Montserrat, the Marqués de Cruillas, to Lorenzo Cancio, Dec. 24, 1762, AGN PI, vol. 22.

87. Informe del gobernador, Oct. 6, 1762, ASFG, vol. 13.

88. Testimonio de una india Lipan, Apr. 4, 1763, ASFG, vol. 18.

89. Informe de Luis Antonio Menchaca, Jan. 31, 1764, ASFG, vol. 12.

90. Castañeda, *Our Catholic Heritage in Texas*, 4:182; Fray José de Calahorra to Governor Ángel de Martos y Navarrete, May 8, 1764, ASFG, vol. 12.

91. Viceroy Joaquín de Montserrat, the Marqués de Cruillas, to Governor Ángel de Martos y Navarette, Sept. 10, 1764, BAO.

92. Arricivita, *Cronica seráfica*, 2:84; Castañeda, *Our Catholic Heritage in Texas*, 4:178–79. In July 1765, Eyasiquiche, the *capitán grande* of the Taovayas, told Fray Joseph de Calahorra y Sanz that their Tehuacana allies recently had been victims of an Apache raid. During the raid, Apaches "killed and seized Indians, and took all of the horses they could find." Testimony of Eiasiquiche, taken by Fray Joseph de Calahorra y Sanz, July 30, 1767, in Proceedings concerning the Return of Antonio Treviño by the Taovaya Indians, Mar. 20, 1765, BAO.

93. In addition to their conflict with the Ndé residents of Texas, Norteños were at war with Osages to the east in 1765. Fray Joseph de Calahorra y Sanz to Governor Ángel de Martos y Navarrete, July 16, 1765, in Proceedings concerning the Return of Antonio Treviño by the Taovaya Indians, Mar. 20, 1765, BAO.

94. Informe de Luis Antonio de Menchaca, Mar. 2, 1766, ASFG, vol. 13; Relación de Felipe de Rábago y Terán, Oct. 18, 1766, ASFG, vol. 20.

95. Arricivita, *Cronica seráfica*, 2:84–86; Castañeda, *Our Catholic Heritage in Texas*, 4:183.

96. Arricivita, *Cronica seráfica*, 2:86; Castañeda, *Our Catholic Heritage in Texas*, 4:183–84.

97. Arricivita, *Cronica seráfica*, 2:86–87.

98. Castañeda, *Our Catholic Heritage in Texas*, 4:184–85.

99. Norteño slaving against Ndé communities was so great that in 1753, the governor of Louisiana complained about the traffic in enslaved Apaches, claiming that the importation of Apaches was undermining any possibility for future trade relations with Ndé leaders. Barr, "From Captives to Slaves," 28.

100. Starting around 1750, Ndé communities also made peace with Bidais, Mayeyes, Cocos, and others located in southeast Texas, establishing a vibrant arms trade that solidified Ndé defenses. Minor, *Turning Adversity to Advantage*, 43–44, 55, 75–76; Anderson, *The Indian Southwest*, 105–6; Maestas, "Culture and History of Native American Peoples of South Texas," 275; Minor, *The Light Gray People*, 4–7, 41–42.

101. Minor, *Turning Adversity to Advantage*, 75–76; Minor, *The Light Gray People*, 129; Anderson, *The Indian Southwest*, 106–8, 121.

102. Report of Fray Andrés Varo, 1751, quoted in Report of Fray Pedro Serrano to the Marqués de Cruillas, 1761, in Hackett, *Historical Documents relating to New Mexico*, 3:487.

103. For a midcentury description of the trade fairs of Taos, see Report of Bishop Pedro Tamarón y Romeral to the King, 1765, in New Mexico Office of the State Historian, "Bishop Tamarón's Visitation"; Hämäläinen, *The Comanche Empire*, 45.

104. For thoughts on enslaved women's reproductive labor, see Joseph C. Miller, "Domiciled and Dominated: Slaving as a History of Women," in Campbell, Miers, and Miller, *Women and Slavery*, 2:291–312.

105. For discussion of slaver violence as performance and spectacle, see especially Hartman, *Scenes of Subjection*, 22–25, 32–43.

106. Euro-Americans made note of Comanche hide manufacturing as early as the 1740s. See Antonio Durán de Armijo to Governor Joaquín Codallos, Feb. 27, 1748, in Twitchell, *Spanish Archives of New Mexico*, 1:148.

107. Report of Bishop Pedro Tamarón y Romeral to the King, 1765, in New Mexico Office of the State Historian, "Bishop Tamarón's Visitation."

108. George Catlin noted during the nineteenth century the gendered nature of Comanche lodge-building. Twentieth-century Comanche informants did as well. Catlin, *Letters and Notes*, 2:493–94; Notes on Herman Asenap, June 30–July 1, 1933, in Kavanagh, *Comanche Ethnography*, 39.

109. It is difficult to estimate Comanche horse populations, but evidence suggests that Comanche communities cared for thousands of horses. See, for instance, Report of Governor Tomás Veléz Cachupín, Nov. 27, 1751, in Thomas, *The Plains Indians*, 73–74; Governor Manuel Portillo Urrisola to Bishop Pedro Tamarón y Romeral, Feb. 24, 1762, in New Mexico Office of the State Historian, "Bishop Tamarón's Visitation."

110. On the geopolitical nature of slavery, see Cameron, *Invisible Citizens*, 7–8.

111. See, for instance, Governor Manuel Portillo Urrisola to Bishop Pedro Tamarón y Romeral, Feb. 24, 1762, in New Mexico Office of the State Historian, "Bishop Tamarón's Visitation"; Governor Tomás Vélez Cachupín to the Marqués de Cruillas, June 27, 1762, in Thomas, *The Plains Indians*, 148.

112. For a comprehensive analysis of Comanche political structures from the eighteenth through the nineteenth century, see Kavanagh, *Comanche Political History*. Kavanagh argues that it is inappropriate to think of Comanche political structures as being static or ahistorical. Thus, it would be inaccurate to suggest, as other scholars and observers have claimed, that there were always two or three large Comanche factions. Hämäläinen's work, however, challenges Kavanagh's interpretation to some

extent. By claiming the existence of a Comanche empire, Hämäläinen credits the Comanches of the nineteenth century with developing wide-ranging, coordinated, multigenerational political and commercial systems (*The Comanche Empire*, 2–6).

113. Juan Joseph Lobato to Governor Tomás Veléz Cachupín, Aug. 28, 1752, in Thomas, *The Plains Indians*, 114–17.

114. Quassyah, whom anthropologists interviewed in the 1930s, claimed that Comanche men "could not deprive others of their property by force without the *loss of his reputation*." Notes on Quassyah, July 5, 1933, in Kavanagh, *Comanche Ethnography*, 57. For theoretical discussions of the importance of slaves as property, see Cameron, *Invisible Citizens*, 6; Engerman, "Some Considerations Relating to Property Rights in Man."

115. Herman Asenap emphasized the democratic nature of Comanche political structures. Notes on Herman Asenap, June 30–July 1, 1933, in Kavanagh, *Comanche Ethnography*, 33–36.

116. Later Comanche accounts would emphasize the great significance of bravery during war as well. See, for instance, Attocknie, *The Life of Ten Bears*, 198.

117. Castañeda, *Our Catholic Heritage in Texas*, 4:187–89.

118. Enslaving people was probably not as honorable as killing enemies, however. According to Quassyah, "The *most* honorable man was he who had killed most enemies in fighting. It was also honorable (but less so) to carry off one's wounded friend while under fire." Quassyah also explained that Scalp Dances were held only after a successful raid in which an enemy was killed: "There was *no dance* unless an enemy was killed; even the capture of many horses did not call for a dance, nor did the capture of enemies." Notes on Quassyah, July 5, 1933, in Kavanagh, *Comanche Ethnography*, 58.

119. Notably, Attocknie's chronology begins in the 1790s. Attocknie, *The Life of Ten Bears*, 9.

120. Report of Governor Thomás Vélez Cachupín, Nov. 27, 1751, in Thomas, *The Plains Indians*, 71–73.

121. Notes on Herman Asenap, June 30–July 1, 1933, in Kavanagh, *Comanche Ethnography*, 34.

Part II

1. Rafael Martínez Pacheco to Juan de Ugalde, Jan. 7, 1788, BAO.

2. James Brooks's work remains the most convincing paradigm for interpreting collaboration through violence, as it illuminates how in the U.S. Southwest "Old and New World traditions of honor, violence, and captivity . . . mesh[ed] in a far-flung tapestry of conflict and exchange" (*Captives and Cousins*, 30).

3. Interestingly, many who have noted Anglo-American–Hispanic collaborative violence in Texas have done so for purposes of hero worship (i.e., to demonstrate that Tejanos deserve recognition for their "heroic" contributions to the making of Texas). See, for instance, Rendón Lozano, *Viva Tejas*; Barker, "Native Latin American Contribution." Others have focused on commercial, political, and cultural collaboration. See, for instance, McWilliams, *North from Mexico*; Taylor, *An American-Mexican Frontier*; Alonzo, *Tejano Legacy*, 5–13, 70–74, 124–27; Reséndez, *Changing National Identities at the Frontier*, 67–70, 93–100, 104; Miguel Ángel González-Quiroga, "Conflict and

Cooperation in the Making of Texas-Mexico Border Society, 1840–1880," in Johnson and Graybill, *Bridging National Borders in North America*, 34–52.

4. From the perspective of the long history of Texas borderlands violence, the Texas Rebellion represents a moment of sudden disjuncture rather than the culmination of deeply embedded cultural conflict. For the argument that the Texas Rebellion was rooted in the contest between distinct Hispanic and Anglo cultural traditions, see Barker, *Mexico and Texas*; Lowrie, *Culture Conflict in Texas*; Binkley, *The Texas Revolution*; Miller, "Stephen F. Austin"; De León, *They Called Them Greasers*.

5. Others have commented on these continental connections, particularly during the early nineteenth century. See especially, Reséndez, *Changing National Identities at the Frontier*, 93–104; Torget, *Seeds of Empire*, 36–39.

6. Much of the literature on nineteenth-century Texas, although cognizant of the limits of state power, has spotlighted processes of state formation. Notable examples include Valerio-Jiménez, *River of Hope*, 1–11; Reséndez, *Changing National Identities at the Frontier*, 3–4; Kelley, *Los Brazos de Dios*, 3–4, 8; Torget, *Seeds of Empire*, 6.

7. The relationship between family making and slavery has been ignored in the context of Anglo-Texas. For the role of kin incorporation in Hispanic Texas, see John, "Independent Indians and the San Antonio Community," 109–10. For kin incorporation in Comanche society, see Wallace and Hoebel, *The Comanches*, 241–42; Tate, "Comanche Captives," 234–37; Rister, *Comanche Bondage*, 13; DeLay, *War of a Thousand Deserts*, 93. According Joaquín Rivaya-Martínez, slavery and adoption operated on a sliding scale, as "the status of many captives was promoted to that of full-fledged Comanches through personal achievement, adoption, or marriage to Comanche individuals" ("Captivity and Adoption among the Comanche Indians," 9). Mark Allan Goldberg also has claimed that Comanches "adopted [some] into their communities," although he is generally more critical of the idea that Comanches made "wives" of those enslaved ("Linking the Chains," 204–9).

Chapter 4

1. Domingo Cabello to Jacobo de Ugarte y Loyola, July 3, 1786, BAO. Also see John, *Storms Brewed in Other Men's Worlds*, 698–99.

2. Brooks, "'This Evil Extends,'" 284.

3. By highlighting the significance of kinship in cross-cultural processes of enslavement and social control, this chapter echoes some of the interpretations in Brooks, *Captives and Cousins* and Conrad, "Empire through Kinship."

4. Itinerary of Señor Marqués de Rubí, Field Marshal of His Majesty's Armies, in the Inspection of the Interior Presidios that by Royal Order He Conducted in this New Spain, 1766–68, and Rubí Dictamen of Apr. 10, 1768, both in Jackson and Foster, *Imaginary Kingdom*, 112, 128–30, 181; Castañeda, *Our Catholic Heritage in Texas*, 4:236–38. Monsieur de Pagés, who visited Los Adaes and San Antonio in 1767, was similarly unimpressed with the physical and defensive state of San Antonio. See Pagés, *Travels round the World*, 91–92.

5. Weber, *The Spanish Frontier in North America*, 198–99; Chipman and Joseph, *Spanish Texas*, 174–75.

6. Jackson and Foster, *Imaginary Kingdom*, 71–73, 75–78; Itinerary of Rubí, 1766–68, in Jackson and Foster, *Imaginary Kingdom*, 109–44.

7. Spanish soldiers built El Orcoquizá, or Presidio San Agustín de Ahumada, on the lower Trinity River in the late spring and summer of 1756, after Frenchmen were found in the area trading among Bidais and Orcoquizas. Castañeda, *Our Catholic Heritage in Texas*, 4:52–67.

8. Jackson and Foster, *Imaginary Kingdom*, 79–81; Itinerary of Rubí, 1766–68, in Jackson and Foster, *Imaginary Kingdom*, 128.

9. Rubí Dictamen of Apr. 10, 1768, in Jackson and Foster, *Imaginary Kingdom*, 181–82.

10. The one bright spot in all of Spanish Texas was the San Antonio mission system, which, in Rubí's view, consisted of "very rich missions." It should be noted, however, that the economic successes of the missions were as much a product of Native dedication, sacrifice, and adaptability as they were a result of Spanish efforts. Rubí Dictamen of Apr. 10, 1768, in Jackson and Foster, *Imaginary Kingdom*, 182; Castañeda, *Our Catholic Heritage in Texas*, 4:2–6.

11. By the second half of the eighteenth century, Comanchería had splintered into at least three distinct Comanche communities, known as Yupes, Yamparikas, and Kotsotekas. Although the Yupes, Yamparikas, and Kotsotekas regularly coordinated broader geopolitical and economic objectives, Kotsotekas were the principal rulers of the Texas portion of Comanchería. Kavanagh, *Comanche Political History*, 52, 69, 123–24.

12. Athanase de Mézières to the Baron de Ripperdá, July 4, 1772, in Bolton, *Athanase de Mézières*, 1:297.

13. Athanase de Mézières to Commandant General of Louisiana, Oct. 29, 1770, in Bolton, *Athanase de Mézières*, 1:218–19.

14. According to Governor Domingo Cabello, the Eastern Comanche representatives who visited him at San Antonio during the 1785 peace talks referred to the "Yambericas," or Western Comanches, as "their brothers." Domingo Cabello to José Antonio Rengel, Oct. 3, 1785, BAO. As Kavanagh has contended, it is especially difficult to identify the self-ascribed ethnonym of Western Comanches because most San Antonio residents understood all Western Comanches to be Yamparikas (*Comanche Political History*, 2).

15. Testimony of Antonio Treviño, Aug. 13, 1765, in Proceedings concerning the Return of Antonio Treviño by the Taovaya Indians, Mar. 20, 1765, BAO; Teodoro de Croix to Hugo O'Connor, Sept. 3, 1768, BAO; Athanase de Mézières to Teodoro de Croix, Apr. 19, 1778, in Bolton, *Athanase de Mézières*, 2:209; John, *Storms Brewed in Other Men's Worlds*, 373; Rivaya-Martínez, "Captivity and Adoption among the Comanche Indians," 431; Hämäläinen, *The Comanche Empire*, 90–92.

16. Laredo was established in 1755 and became a villa proper in 1767. By the 1780s it was home to several hundred residents, who generally tended to livestock. Wilkinson, *Laredo and the Río Grande Frontier*, 15–29, 34–39, and 70.

17. The Baron de Ripperdá to Luis de Unzaga y Amezaga, Apr. 17, 1773, in Bolton, *Athanase de Mézières*, 2:31; Testimony of Luis Antonio Menchaca, Apr. 7, 1770, in Proceedings concerning Menchaca's Report on Condition of Ranches and Missions Near Béxar, May 5, 1769, BAO; Baron de Ripperdá to Antonio María de Bucareli y Ursúa, Jan. 6, 1773, BAO; John, *Storms Brewed in Other Men's Worlds*, 380.

18. Extant documents from the 1760s reveal a single successful retaliation campaign, occurring in July 1766, yet even this Spanish victory was successful only with

the help of Native auxiliaries from Mission San José. See Luis Menchaca to Ángel de Martos y Navarrete, Aug. 3, 1773, BAO; John, *Storms Brewed in Other Men's Worlds*, 380.

19. For a report on the depopulation of sixteen ranches surrounding San Antonio, see Petition of Cabildo of San Antonio de Béxar against the Governor, the Baron de Ripperdá, Aug. 4, 1772, AGN PI, vol. 99, part 3.

20. On the importance of gift-giving for early Spanish diplomacy in Texas, see Barr, *Peace Came in the Form of a Woman*, 54–58.

21. Weber, *Bárbaros*, 102–4.

22. Quoted in Weber, *Bárbaros*, 181–83.

23. Luis Unzaga y Amezaga to Athanase de Mézières, in Bolton, *Athanase de Mézières*, 1:171; Deposition of Domingo Chirinos, Oct. 30–31, 1770, in Bolton, *Athanase de Mézières*, 1:222–23; Galán, "The Chirino Boys," 43–47; John, *Storms Brewed in Other Men's Worlds*, 345–47; La Vere, "Between Kinship and Capitalism," 199–205.

24. On the various, ineffective prohibitions, see, for instance, Alejandro O'Reilly to Athanase de Mézières, Jan. 23, 1770, in Bolton, *Athanase de Mézières*, 1:135–6; Instructions for the Traders of the Cadaux D'Acquioux and Hiatasses Nations, Feb. 4, 1770, in Bolton, *Athanase de Mézières*, 1:147–50. On the importance of trade bonds, see Antonio de Ulloa to Hugo O'Conor, 1768, in Bolton, *Athanase de Mézières*, 1:129.

25. Agreement made with the Indian Nations in Assembly, Apr. 21, 1770, in Bolton, *Athanase de Mézières*, 1:157.

26. Athanase de Mézières to Commandant General of Louisiana, Oct. 29, 1770, in Bolton, *Athanase de Mézières*, 1:212; Athanase de Mézières to Luis Unzaga y Amezaga, July 3, 1771, in Bolton, *Athanase de Mézières*, 1:251; Athanase de Mézières to Teodoro de Croix, Apr. 18, 1778, in Bolton, *Athanase de Mézières*, 2:203; Athanase de Mézières to Teodoro de Croix, Apr. 5, 1778, in Hackett, *Pichardo's Treatise on the Limits of Louisiana and Texas*, 255; Hämäläinen, *The Comanche Empire*, 91–94.

27. Quoted in Hämäläinen, *The Comanche Empire*, 97.

28. For Comanche attacks, see the Baron de Ripperdá to Teodoro de Croix, June 7, 1771, AGN PI, vol. 100, part 1; the Baron de Ripperdá to Antonio María de Bucareli y Ursúa, July 4, 1772, in Bolton, *Athanase de Mézières*, 1:314; Petition of Cabildo of San Antonio de Béxar against the Governor, the Baron de Ripperdá, Aug. 4, 1772, AGN PI, vol. 99, part 3; María Bucareli y Ursúa to the Baron de Ripperdá, Feb. 9, 1774, BAO; the Baron de Ripperdá to Luis Unzaga y Amezaga, Apr. 17, 1773, in Bolton, *Athanase de Mézières*, 2:31; Antonio María Bucareli y Ursúa to the Baron de Ripperdá, Mar. 1, 1774, BAO; Antonio María Bucareli y Ursúa to the Baron de Ripperdá, Dec. 21, 1774, and Luis Cazorla to Antonio María Bucareli y Ursúa, Mar. 24, 1775, both in AGN PI, vol. 99, part 3; Teodoro de Croix to the Baron de Ripperdá, July 9, 1777, BAO; the Baron de Ripperdá to Teodoro de Croix, Apr. 27, 1777, in Bolton, *Athanase de Mézières*, 2:127–28; Athanase de Mézières to Teodoro de Croix, Apr. 19, 1778, in Bolton, *Athanase de Mézières*, 2:212; Athanase de Mézières to Teodoro de Croix, Nov. 15, 1778, in Bolton, *Athanase de Mézières*, 2:232–33; Domingo Cabello to Teodoro de Croix, Feb. 9, 1779, BAO; Domingo Cabello to Teodoro de Croix, Aug. 30, 1779, BAO; Domingo Cabello to Teodoro de Croix, Aug. 31, 1779, BAO; Notice of Domingo Cabello, Nov. 5, 1780, in Proceedings concerning Dispositions of Estate of Felipe de Luna, Nov. 5, 1780, BAO; Diario Historico of Fray Cosme Lozano Narvais, in Leutenegger, *Journal of a Texas Missionary*, 17, 19; Monthly Report of the Cavalry Division of Béxar, Nov. 30, 1782,

BAO; Monthly Report of the Cavalry Division of Béxar, Dec. 31, 1782, BAO; Diego de Lasaga to Martín de Mayorga, Apr. 16, 1783, AGN PI, vol. 64, part 1.

29. Hämäläinen, *The Comanche Empire*, 98–99; Tjarks, "Comparative Demographic Analysis of Texas," 303.

30. Domingo Cabello to Teodoro de Croix, July 17, 1780, BAO.

31. The Baron de Ripperdá to Antonio María Bucareli y Ursúa, Apr. 27, 1772, AGN PI, vol. 100, part 2; the Baron de Ripperdá to Unzaga y Amezaga, May 26, 1772, in Bolton, *Athanase de Mézières*, 1:273–74. Also see Barr, *Peace Came in the Form of a Woman*, 230–32. The Reglamentos of 1772 also pushed Spaniards in Texas away from slave raiding and toward a Comanche-based slave-trading model. The Reglamentos created a new administrative structure, the Provincias Internas, to better control frontier activities, and to an extent it did. One effect was the reframing of legal slaving. The Reglamentos dictated that male prisoners of war were not to receive "bad treatment" but were to be deported to Mexico City, where the viceroy "may dispose of them as seems convenient." Apprehended women and children, meanwhile, were to be "treated equally and assisted, in order to procure their conversion and instruction." Brinckerhoff and Faulk, *Lancers for the King*, 6–7, 31 (Reglamentos).

32. Marcelo Valdéz's December 1781 campaign, which left eighteen Comanches dead, was a notable exception. Monthly Report of the Cavalry Division of Béxar, Dec. 31, 1781, BAO. For failed campaigns, see, for instance, the Baron de Ripperdá to Antonio María Bucareli y Ursúa, Apr. 27, 1772, AGN PI, vol. 100, part 2; Journal of J. Gaignard, 1773–74, in Bolton, *Athanase de Mézières*, 2:96; Luis Cazorla to Antonio María Bucareli y Ursúa, Mar. 24, 1775, AGN PI, vol. 99, part 3; Teodoro de Croix to the Baron de Ripperdá, July 9, 1777, BAO; Domingo Cabello to Teodoro de Croix, July 17, 1780, BAO; Monthly Report of the Cavalry Division of Béxar, June 30, 1783, BAO; Domingo Cabello, Ynforme, Sept. 30, 1784, AGN PI, vol. 64, part 1; Kavanagh, *Comanche Political History*, 95.

33. Domingo Cabello to Teodoro de Croix, July 17, 1780, BAO. For a contemporary discussion of Comanche equestrian abilities, see Athanase de Mézières to Commandant General of Louisiana, Oct. 29, 1770, in Bolton, *Athanase de Mézières*, 1:218–19.

34. Hämäläinen, *The Comanche Empire*, 101–2.

35. The Hispanic individuals who *did* fall into the hands of Comanche slavers during the 1760s and 1770s were almost always procured from other slavers or from raids in New Mexico. See, for instance, Baron de Ripperdá to Antonio Maria Bucareli y Ursúa, Apr. 3, 1775, AGN PI, vol. 99, part 1; Antonio María Bucareli y Ursúa to the Baron de Ripperdá, July 26, 1775, BAO. For a detailed history of the ranching industry in Spanish Texas, see Jackson, *Los Mesteños*.

36. Hämäläinen, *The Comanche Empire*, 109–11. For more on disease epidemics during this period, see Goldberg, *Conquering Sickness*, 23–24.

37. Hämäläinen, *The Comanche Empire*, 112–13; John, *Storms Brewed in Other Men's Worlds*, 660–61; Saunt, *West of the Revolution*, 170–82.

38. For a discussion of Ndé economic adaptations and the deterioration of Ndé-Spanish relations in the Texas borderlands from the 1760s to the 1770s, see Anderson, *The Indian Southwest*, 128–44. For Ndé raids and the Lipan-Tejas-Bidais firearms trade, see the Baron de Ripperdá to Luis Unzaga y Amezaga, Dec. 31, 1771, in Bolton, *Anthanase de Mézières*, 1:267.

39. The Baron de Ripperdá to Antonio María Bucareli y Ursúa, Jan. 6, 1773, BAO; Domingo Cabello to Teodoro de Croix, Nov. 2, 1779, BAO; Domingo Cabello to Teodoro de Croix, Feb. 12, 1780, BAO ("quite terrified"); Monthly Report of the Cavalry Division of Béxar, Mar. 31, 1784, BAO.

40. See, for instance, the Baron de Ripperdá to Antonio María de Bucareli y Ursúa, Apr. 28, 1772, in Bolton, *Athanase de Mézières*, 1:269–70.

41. Report of the Council of War at Monclova, Dec. 11, 1777; Report of the Council of War at San Antonio, Jan. 5, 1778; Athanase de Mézières to the Viceroy, Feb. 20, 1778, all in Bolton, *Athanase de Mézières*, 2:150, 163–66, 181–82.

42. Spaniards proved their commitment to a war of Ndé extermination during the years that followed. Under the leadership of Juan de Ugalde, the governor of Coahuila, Spaniards made several campaigns against Apaches in the lower Río Grande Valley. The first was undertaken in late spring 1779, when Spaniards sacked a number of Lipan *rancherías* and seized several hundred horses. During the summer of that year, Ugalde led another campaign against Apaches, this time Mescaleros, and attacked two *rancherías*. Then in 1781, Ugalde, with almost six hundred soldiers and numerous Native auxiliaries, targeted Mescalero and Natagé communities located in the treacherous Bolsón de Mapimí and across the mountainous region of present-day Big Bend, Texas. After some five thousand miles of travel over the course of one year, Ugalde's forces captured three prominent Ndé *capitanes* and approximately 130 fighters. Bolton, *Texas in the Middle Eighteenth Century*, 127; Britten, *The Lipan Apaches*, 142–47; John, *Storms Brewed in Other Men's Worlds*, 633.

43. Pedro Vial and Francisco Xavier Chaves to Domingo Cabello, Diary of their mission, June 17 to Sept. 29, 1785, in John, "Inside Comanchería," 35–44; Hämäläinen, *The Comanche Empire*, 113–16.

44. Hämäläinen, *The Comanche Empire*, 124; Santiago, *The Jar of Severed Hands*, 81–86.

45. Domingo Cabello to José Antonio Rengel, Jan. 24, 1786, BAO; Domingo Cabello to José Antonio Rengel, Feb. 28, 1786, BAO; John, *Storms Brewed in Other Men's Worlds*, 692–93; Hämäläinen, *The Comanche Empire*, 124.

46. Juan de Ugalde to Rafael Martínez Pacheco, Aug. 12, 1789, BAO ("annihilate"); Juan de Ugalde to Rafael Martínez Pacheco, Dec. 19, 1789, BAO; Report of Rafael Martínez Pacheco, Jan. 9, 1790, BAO; Manuel Muñoz to Pedro de Nava Feb. 26, 1791, in Cuaderno Borrador of Muñoz's Letters to Pedro de Nava and Ramón de Castro, Dec. 2, 1790, BAO ("full rigor"); Castañeda, *Our Catholic Heritage in Texas*, 5:16–19.

47. Domingo Cabello to Jacobo de Ugarte y Loyola, July 31, 1786, BAO; John, *Storms Brewed in Other Men's Worlds*, 547, 628, 689, 694–95.

48. Report on Supply and Distribution of Gifts to Indians, Rafael Martínez Pacheco, Sept. 20, 1787, BAO; Report on Indian Expenditures, Manuel Muñoz, Aug. 14, 1792, BAO; Summary and General Settlement of Indian Gift Expenditures, Rafael de Ahumada, Sept. 26, 1801, BAO; Hämäläinen, *The Comanche Empire*, 183–84; Raúl Ramos, "Finding the Balance: Béxar in Mexican/Indian Relations," in Truett and Young, *Continental Crossroads*, 48–49.

49. See, for instance, Pedro de Nava to Manuel Muñoz, Jan. 27, 1795, BAO; Wilkinson, *Laredo and the Río Grande Frontier*, 61; Testimony of Andrés Benito Courbière and Ignacio Pérez, Jan. 24, 1798, BAO; Pedro de Nava to Manuel Muñoz, July 15, 1795, BAO; Petition of Salvador Rodríguez, Vicente Amador, Luis Menchaca, Joaquín Leal,

José Antonio Saucedo, José Hernández, Feliz Ruiz, and Manuel Derbón to the Governor, Sept. 22, 1796, BAO; Manuel Muñoz to Ayuntamiento de Villa de San Fernando, Oct. 5, 1796, BAO; Antonio Cordero's Expedition Instruction to José Menchaca, Apr. 26, 1798, BAO; José Menchaca to Antonio Cordero, Apr. 27, 1798, BAO; Antonio Cordero to Manuel Muñoz, Apr. 28, 1798, BAO; Pedro de Nava to Antonio Cordero, May 29, 1798, BAO; Pedro de Nava to Antonio Cordero, July 10, 1798, BAO; Castañeda, *Our Catholic Heritage in Texas*, 5:118–21.

50. Meacham, "The Population of Spanish and Mexican Texas," 146, 207; Juan Bautista Elguézabal to Salcedo, June 20, 1803, in Hatcher, *The Opening of Texas to Foreign Settlement*, 303–5; Tjarks, "Comparative Demographic Analysis of Texas," 332–33; Meacham, "The Population of Spanish and Mexican Texas," 208–9.

51. Libro de la Villa de San Fernando de Béxar de bautismos, entierros, confirmaciones, y casamientos, 1761–92, NLBLA, entries 1314, 1317, 1371, 1466, 1467, 1489, 1502, 1532, 1573, 1596, 1597, 1604, 1659, 1666, 1701, 1708, 1709, 1769; Libro de la Villa de San Fernando de Béxar de bautismos, entierros, confirmaciones, y casamientos, 1793–1812, NLBLA, entries 1, 16, 57, 58, 60, 98, 103, 159, 182, 231, 269, 270, 272, 275, 324, 398, 417, 523, 537, 544, 551, 563, 593, 626, 645, 670, 686, 688, 740, 777, 780, 840, 846, 849, 906, 1012, 1086.

52. Census of the Jurisdiction of Nacogdoches, José María Guadiana, May 31, 1809, in University of Texas Institute of Texan Cultures, *Residents of Texas*, 2:10–35.

53. Libro de la Villa de San Fernando de Béxar de bautismos, entierros, confirmaciones, y casamientos, 1761–92, NLBLA, entries 1371, 1466, 1467, 1532, 1596, 1597, 1604; Libro de la Villa de San Fernando de Béxar de bautismos, entierros, confirmaciones, y casamientos, 1793–1812, NLBLA, entries 57, 98, 153, 269, 523, 593, 626, 670, 686, 688, 846, 849, 1146.

54. Libro de la Villa de San Fernando de Béxar de bautismos, entierros, confirmaciones, y casamientos, 1761–92, NLBLA, entries 1467, 1659; Rafael Martínez Pacheco to Juan de Ugalde, Feb. 16, 1788, BAO; Libro de la Villa de San Fernando de Béxar de bautismos, entierros, confirmaciones, y casamientos, 1793–1812, NLBLA, entries 98 and 686. For more details on the life and activities of Vial, who was a Frenchman by birth, see Loomis and Nasatir, *Pedro Vial and the Roads to Santa Fe*, xv–xviii.

55. Libro de la Villa de San Fernando de Béxar de bautismos, entierros, confirmaciones, y casamientos, 1761–92, NLBLA, entry 1532; Libro de la Villa de San Fernando de Béxar de bautismos, entierros, confirmaciones, y casamientos, 1793–1812, NLBLA, entries 593, 626, 670.

56. Teodoro de Croix to Domingo Cabello, May 17, 1779, BAO; Qui Te Sain to Bernardo de Gálvez, in Kinnaird, *Spain in the Mississippi Valley*, vol. 2, part. 1, 392.

57. Domingo Cabello to José Antonio Rengel, Jan. 10, 1786, BAO; Rivaya-Martínez, "Captivity and Adoption among the Comanche Indians," 420.

58. Pedro Vial and Francisco Xavier Chaves to Domingo Cabello, Diary of their mission, June 17 to Sept. 29, 1785, in John, "Inside Comanchería," 50; also translated in Kavanagh, *Comanche Political History*, 103.

59. Domingo Cabello, Ynforme, Sept. 30, 1784, AGN PI, vol. 64, part 1; Pedro Vial and Francisco Xavier Chaves to Domingo Cabello, Diary of their mission, June 17 to Sept. 29, 1785, in John, "Inside Comanchería," 50; Rivaya-Martínez, "Captivity and Adoption among the Comanche Indians," 434, 443, 509; Kavanagh, *Comanche Political History*, 101; Manuel Muñoz, Jan. 30, 1791, BAO.

60. Pedro Vial and Francisco Xavier Chaves to Domingo Cabello, Diary of their mission, June 17 to Sept. 29, 1785, in John, "Inside Comanchería," 48; Domingo Cabello to Jacobo de Ugarte y Loyola, Apr. 30, 1786, BAO, emphasis mine.

61. John Sibley to Henry Dearborn, Apr. 10, 1805, in Jefferson, *Message from the President*, 55–57; John Sibley to Henry Dearborn, ca. Jan. 1, 1808, in Abel, *Report from Natchitoches*, 80; Diary of Francisco Amangual from San Antonio to Santa Fe, Mar. 30 to May 19, 1808, in Loomis and Nasatir, *Pedro Vial and the Roads to Santa Fe*, 467–68.

62. Folsom, *Arredondo*, 69–72, 75–76, 87–94; Chipman and Joseph, *Spanish Texas*, 246–52.

63. Salvador Carrasco reported to Antonio Martínez that he "knew for certain they [Anglo traders] had supplied the Comanches with more than 30,000 guns with lances." Antonio Martínez to the Viceroy, Jan. 27, 1818, in Taylor, *Letters from Gov. Antonio Martínez*, 11–12; John Sibley to Henry Dearborn, July 3, 1807, in Garret, "Dr. John Sibley," 382; Hämäläinen, *The Comanche Empire*, 144–49.

64. Kavanagh, *Comanche Political History*, 156–57.

65. Kavanagh, *Comanche Political History*, 155–57.

66. Report of Fray Vallejo, Feb. 11, 1815, in Leutenegger, *The San José Papers*, part 3, 24–26; Antonio Martínez to Commandant General, Oct. 21, 1817, Mar. 25, 1818, June 26, 1818, and June 27, 1818, all in Taylor, *The Letters of Antonio Martínez*, 8, 12, 16–17; Kavanagh, *Comanche Political History*, 158.

67. Antonio Martínez to Commandant General, Mar. 25, 1818, in Taylor, *The Letters of Antonio Martínez*, 12. Also see Antonio Martínez to the Viceroy, June 2, 1818, in Taylor, *Letters from Gov. Antonio Martínez*, 20.

68. On impressment, see Antonio Martínez to Commandant General, June 17, 1818, in Taylor, *The Letters of Antonio Martínez*, 16, no. 289. Regarding requests, see, for instance, Antonio Martínez to Commandant General, June 11, 1817, June 23, 1817, May 28, 1818, July 31, 1817, and Sept. 13, 1819, all in Taylor, *The Letters of Antonio Martínez*, 8, 12–13, 33, 134–35, 263; Antonio Martínez to the Viceroy, May 31, 1817, June 13, 1817, Dec. 10, 1818, all in Taylor, *Letters from Gov. Antonio Martínez*, 3–4, 29–30.

69. Antonio Martínez to Commandant General, Apr. 1, 1819, in Taylor, *The Letters of Antonio Martínez*, 217–18.

70. Antonio Martínez to the Viceroy, May 23, 1818, in Taylor, *Letters from Gov. Antonio Martínez*, 18.

71. Nemesio Salcedo to Juan Bautista Elguézabal, Mar. 27, 1804, BAO; Jacobo de Ugarte y Loyola to Juan Bautista Elguézabal, Apr. 1, 1804, BAO; Jacobo de Ugarte y Loyola to Juan Bautista Elguézabal, Apr. 3, 1804, BAO; Castañeda, *Our Catholic Heritage in Texas*, 5:286–87, 293–95.

72. Fray Juan Brady and Bernardo Martín Despallier to Juan Bautista Elguézabal, Apr. 10, 1804, BAO; Castañeda, *Our Catholic Heritage in Texas*, 5:288, 296–98.

73. See, for instance, Castañeda, *Our Catholic Heritage in Texas*, 5:299–300, 315; Hatcher, *The Opening of Texas to Foreign Settlement*, 102–5.

74. Memoria of José Miguel Ramos de Arizpe, Nov. 10, 1792, Archivo General de Indias, *Audencia de Guadalajara* vol. 62.

75. Antonio Martínez to the Viceroy, Dec. 22, 1813, in Taylor, *Letters from Gov. Antonio Martínez*, 9.

76. Barr, "A Spectrum of Indian Bondage in Spanish Texas," 280; Barr, "From Captives to Slaves," 19–46; de la Teja, *San Antonio de Béxar*, 122–24.

77. See, for instance, Libro de la Villa de San Fernando de Béxar de bautismos, entierros, confirmaciones, y casamientos, 1731–60, NLBLA, entries 368, 385, 417, 423, 442; Libro de la Villa de San Fernando de Béxar de bautismos, entierros, confirmaciones, y casamientos, 1761–92, NLBLA, entries 17, 1000, 1532, 1659; Libro de la Villa de San Fernando de Béxar de bautismos, entierros, confirmaciones, y casamientos, 1793–1812, NLBLA, entries 57, 58, 523, 593, 626, 686, 688.

78. Domingo Cabello to Jacobo de Ugarte y Loyola, July 3, 1786, BAO; Libro de la Villa de San Fernando de Béxar de bautismos, entierros, confirmaciones, y casamientos, 1793–1812, NLBLA, entries 551 and 563; Chabot, *With the Makers of San Antonio*, 60, 95. Domingo Cabello's slaves were in charge of his household economy. Declaration to Gather Testimony, Domingo Cabello, Apr. 20, 1782, Testimony of Macario Sambrano, Apr. 22, 1782, and Testimony of Bartólome de Seguín, Apr. 23, 1782, all in Proceedings of Governor Cabello and the Cavalry Division of Béxar versus Tomás Travieso, Feb. 14, 1782, BAO.

79. The 1793 census listed eighty-eight *labradores*, or farmers, in San Antonio. De la Teja, *San Antonio de Béxar*, 95–96.

80. Juan Bautista Elguézabal to Nemesio Salcedo, June 20, 1803, in Hatcher, *The Opening of Texas to Foreign Settlement*, 303.

81. Juan Bautista Elguézabal to Nemesio Salcedo, June 20, 1803, in Hatcher, *The Opening of Texas to Foreign Settlement*, 304; Testimony of Juan José Hernández, Aug. 21, 1794, in Proceedings against Juan José Hernández, Aug. 16, 1794, BAO. Libro de la Villa de San Fernando de Béxar de bautismos, entierros, confirmaciones, y casamientos, 1793–1812, NLBLA, entries 98, 182. Diego Menchaca and Pedro Flores were also farmers and slaveholders. Census of San Fernando (de Béxar), Dec. 31, 1792, University of Texas Institute of Texan Cultures, *Residents of Texas*, 1:77 and 90.

82. Hämäläinen, *The Comanche Empire*, 243.

83. See, for instance, the Baron de Ripperdá to Antonio María Bucareli y Ursúa, Apr. 3, 1775, AGN PI, vol. 99, part 1; Teodoro de Croix to Domingo Cabello, May 17, 1779, BAO; Rafael Martínez Pacheco to Juan de Ugalde, Aug. 17, 1789, BAO; Manuel Muñoz to Conde de Revilla Gigedo, Feb. 2, 1791, AGN PI, vol. 162, part 3; Ramón de Castro to Conde de Revilla Gigedo, July 12, 1791, AGN PI, vol. 224, part 2; John Sibley to Henry Dearborn, Apr. 10, 1805, in Jefferson, *Message from the President*, 55–57; Diary of Francisco Amangual from San Antonio to Santa Fe, Mar. 30 to May 19, 1808, in Loomis and Nasatir, *Pedro Vial and the Roads to Santa Fe*, 467–68.

84. John Sibley to Henry Dearborn, Apr. 10, 1805, in Jefferson, *Message from the President* 55–56.

85. John Sibley to Henry Dearborn, ca. Jan. 1, 1808, in Abel, *Report from Natchitoches*, 78–79.

86. Journal of J. Gaignard, 1773–74, in Bolton, *Athanase de Mézières*, 2:95; Domingo Cabello to José Antonio Rengel, Jan. 10, 1786, BAO. Domínguez is quoted in Kavanagh, *Comanche Political History*, 130.

87. See, for instance, bill of sale between Nicolas de la Mathe and Toribio Fuentes for negro slave, June 10, 1778, BAO; bill of sale between Antonia Morales and Tomás Lombraña for María Candelaria, slave, Sept. 3, 1779, BAO; and bill of sale between José Vicente Lozano and Isidro Treviño for María del Carmel Ramides, slave, Apr. 11, 1788, BAO.

88. Testimony of María Gertrudis de la Peña, 1785, in Proceedings concerning the Freedom of María Gertrudis de la Peña, Jan. 25, 1785, BAO; Antonio María de Bucareli y Ursúa to the Baron de Ripperdá, Nov. 18, 1772, BAO; Testimony of Juan Nicolás, Jan. 16, 1773, and Testimony of Christobal de Cordova, Jan. 16, 1773, in Proceedings against Citizens of Nuevo Santander, Jan. 16, 1773, BAO.

89. David G. Burnet to John Jamison, Aug. 1818, in Wallace, "David G. Burnet's Letters," 129–30. For other accounts of quick Comanche executions of male captives, see Journal of J. Gaignard, 1773–74, in Bolton, *Athanase de Mézières*, 2:94–95; Antonio Martínez to Commandant General, Mar. 3 and Apr. 26, 1820, both in Taylor, *The Letters of Antonio Martínez*, 308–9, 317.

90. David G. Burnet to John Jamison, Aug. 1818, in Wallace, "David G. Burnet's Letters," 130–31.

91. Athanase de Mézières to the Baron de Ripperdá, July 4, 1772, in Bolton, *Athanase de Mézières*, 1:298; Monthly Report of the Cavalry Division of Béxar, Nov. 30, 1783, BAO; Juan Antonio Padilla, Report on the Barbarous Indians of the Provinces of Texas, Nov. 15, 1820, in Hatcher, "Texas in 1820," 53–55. Anderson has described an incident of ritual adoption, or "seasoning," that occurred in 1768 among Comanche captors (*The Indian Southwest*, 221–22). Also see Rivaya-Martínez, "Captivity and Adoption among the Comanche Indians," 45–53.

92. David G. Burnet to John Jamison, Aug. 1818, in Wallace, "David G. Burnet's Letters," 130–31, no. 3.

93. Padilla, Report on the Barbarous Indians of the Provinces of Texas, Nov. 15, 1820, in Hatcher, "Texas in 1820," 53–55; Anderson, *The Indian Southwest*, 221–22.

94. Domingo Cabello to Jacobo de Ugarte y Loyola, Oct. 8, 1786, BAO; Manuel Muñoz to Pedro de Nava, Feb. 10, 1791, BAO.

95. Hämäläinen, *The Comanche Empire*, 250, 260.

96. Scholars continue to interpret forced wifehood uncritically as little more than the integration of outsiders as family. See especially Blyth, *Chiricahua and Janos*. For discussions of and references to forced wifehood and violence against female captives, see Anderson, *The Indian Southwest*, 222; Rivaya-Martínez, "Captivity and Adoption among the Comanche Indians," 45–48; Brooks, *Captives and Cousins*, 179; Noyes, *Los Comanches*, 70.

97. Manuel Muñoz to Pedro de Nava, Jan. 30, 1791, BAO.

98. Hämäläinen, *The Comanche Empire*, 255–57; Brooks, *Captives and Cousins*, 178–79; Wistrand-Robinson and Armagost, *Comanche Dictionary and Grammar*, 37, 66, 132.

99. Testimony of María Gertrudis de la Peña, 1785, and Declaration of Domingo Cabello, Mar. 5, 1785, in Proceedings concerning the Freedom of María Gertrudis de la Peña, Jan. 25, 1785, BAO. For another revealing account of slaver violence, see Testimony of Juan José Hernández, Aug. 21, 1794, and Testimony of María Martínez, Aug. 21, 1794, in Proceedings against Juan José Hernández, Aug. 16, 1794, BAO.

100. See, especially, Opinion of the Assessor General, May 31, 1780, in Proceedings concerning Proposal for Voluntary Contribution to Ransom Christian Captives among Apaches, June 8, 1780, BAO. Also see Brooks, "'This Evil Extends,'" 291.

101. Notably, even some Spanish authorities understood the rhetorical nature of slavers' supposed Christianizing mission. See, for instance, Domingo Cabello to Teodoro de Croix, May 28, 1780, BAO.

102. Velazquez et al., *The New Velázquez Spanish and English Dictionary*, 286–87. Also see Conrad, "Empire through Kinship," 641.

103. See, for instance, Libro de la Villa de San Fernando de Béxar de bautismos, entierros, confirmaciones, y casamientos, 1761–92, NLBLA, entries 50, 51, 401, 1466, 1467, 1489, 1659; Libro de la Villa de San Fernando de Béxar de bautismos, entierros, confirmaciones, y casamientos, 1793–1812, NLBLA, entries 98, 269, 523, 544, 670, 686, 740, 846, 1146.

104. The 1793 census of San Fernando de Béxar demonstrates the frequent employment of the term *criado* when identifying servants. Census of the Villa of San Fernando (de Béxar), 1793, BAO.

105. John Sibley to Henry Dearborn, ca. Jan. 1, 1808, in Abel, *Report from Natchitoches*, 80. Regarding colonialist fetishization of Indigenous women, see, for instance, McClintock, *Imperial Leather*, 21–31. For a discussion of racial thought in Anglo-American society, see chapters 5, 6, and 7.

106. Hämäläinen, *The Comanche Empire*, 263–67. On heritable slave status, see Wiecek, "The Statutory Law of Slavery and Race," 262–63; Miles, *Ties That Bind*, 59–63.

107. Stuntz, *Hers, His, and Theirs*, 25–26, 31–44, 71–85. This is not to say that Iberians *never* passed on an inheritance to their illegitimate and enslaved family members, for paternalism sometimes inspired such behavior. See, for instance, van Deusen, "The Intimacies of Bondage," 25–26; Blumenthal, *Enemies and Familiars*, 125–27.

108. Their absence is particularly noticeable given the fact that many *criados* were appended to households in various census listings. On enslaved Native people as inheritable property, see Brooks, "'This Evil Extends,'" 296.

109. Petition of Francisco Xavier Chávez, Feb. 18, 1822, and Testimony of Ygnacio Pérez, Feb. 20, 1822, Béxar Archives Manuscripts.

110. Martínez, *Genealogical Fictions*, 145–46.

111. Libro de la Villa de San Fernando de Béxar de bautismos, entierros, confirmaciones, y casamientos, 1761–92, NLBLA, entries 17, 321, 362, 441, 483, 571, 676, 721, 855, 900, 1701, 1769; Libro de la Villa de San Fernando de Béxar de bautismos, entierros, confirmaciones, y casamientos, 1793–1812, NLBLA, entries 103, 272, 324, 398, 551, 740, 840.

112. Petition of José Miguel Games, Francisco de Sales Games, Pedro Hernández, and Carlos Hernández, June 3, 1781, and Petition of Urbano Hinojosa, (Aug. 25,) 1781, in Proceedings Conducted in the Matter of the Opposition Raised by José Miguel Games and Francisco de Sales Games to the Marriage of Ana María de la Trinidad Hernández, June 4, 1781, BAO. For further analysis of purity of blood (*limpieza de sangre*) and race discourses in Iberian and Spanish American culture, see Martínez, *Genealogical Fictions*.

113. Domingo Cabello to Teodoro de Croix, Aug. 16, 1780, BAO; Proceedings of Fernando de Arocha versus Luis Mariano Menchaca, Nov. 5, 1785, BAO; Petition of Francisco Rodríguez, Oct. 23, 1783, in Proceedings of Francisco Rodríguez versus Manuel Padrón, Oct. 20, 1783, BAO.

114. Libro de la Villa de San Fernando de Béxar de bautismos, entierros, confirmaciones, y casamientos, 1761–92, NLBLA, entries 1192, 1291, 1489, 1666; Libro de la Villa de San Fernando de Béxar de bautismos, entierros, confirmaciones, y casamientos, 1793–1812, NLBLA, entries 16, 182.

115. Libro de la Villa de San Fernando de Béxar de bautismos, entierros, confirmaciones, y casamientos, 1761–93, NLBLA, entry 1502.

Chapter 5

1. Manuel Antonio Cordero y Bustamante to Nemesio Salcedo, June 14, 1806, and Nemesio Salcedo to Manuel Antonio Cordero y Bustamante, Aug. 14, 1806, Béxar Archives Manuscripts.

2. Hoonhout and Mareite, "Freedom at the Fringes?," 71–77.

3. On the Anglo-American colonial imagination and the West during the 1770s, see Saunt, *West of the Revolution*, 17–28. Also see Horsman, *Race and Manifest Destiny.* Gary Nash has detailed English and Anglo-American frontier violence throughout the latter part of the eighteenth century in *The Unknown American Revolution.*

4. Long-term displacement was, of course, a contested process, and Native and Euro-American people often collaborated with one another when such a relationship proved beneficial to both parties. See, for instance, Usner, "American Indians on the Cotton Frontier."

5. For a discussion of the regional and ethnic origins of these colonists, see Hamilton, "The Southwestern Frontier," 389–92. For population figures, see U.S. Census, *Census for 1820*, 18.

6. Torget, *Seeds of Empire*, 35–36; Howe, *What Hath God Wrought*, 128; Baptist, *The Half Has Never Been Told*, 80–83; Beckert, *Empire of Cotton*, 84–105. For the history Native possession in these areas, see Ostler, *Surviving Genocide*, especially 191–260.

7. For a classic analysis of Roman slavery, see Hopkins, *Conquerors and Slaves*, especially 99–132.

8. The closest Anglo-American slaveholding community was one that emerged around 1816 along the northeastern margins of Texas at Pecan Point, then part of the Arkansas Territory. Campbell, *An Empire for Slavery*, 12–13. On globalized economic system, see Curtin, *The Rise and Fall of the Plantation Complex*, 128–43; Beckert, *Empire of Cotton*, 199–241; Baptist, *The Half Has Never Been Told*, 42–43, 77–83, 85–92, 126–29; Davis, *Inhuman Bondage*, 27–47.

9. The experience of relocation was so transformative that these Yamparikas crafted a distinct political identity and henceforth were known as Tenawas, or "Those Who Stay Downstream." Stephen F. Austin to Anastasio Bustamante, May 10, 1822, AP, vol. 1, part 1, 507–10. Hämäläinen, *The Comanche Empire*, 150–51; Torget, *Seeds of Empire*, 28.

10. Reséndez, *Changing National Identities at the Frontier*, 51.

11. General Wavel, "Account of the Province of Texas," in Ward, *Mexico in 1827*, 553; Hämäläinen, *The Comanche Empire*, 145–51.

12. McGhee, "The Black Crop," 131–50; Barker, "The African Slave Trade in Texas," 148; Campbell, *An Empire for Slavery*, 11–13.

13. The Baron de Bastrop was born Philip Hendrik Nering Bögel, and although he was not actually a nobleman, he successfully convinced the Euro-American colonists of Louisiana of his importance when he arrived in the 1790s. In the Louisiana province, Bastrop was involved in a number of business ventures, including a colonization program in the Ouachita Valley. After the U.S. Louisiana Purchase in 1803, Bastrop relocated to Spanish Texas, where he expanded his business and political influence. Bacarisse, "Baron de Bastrop," 319–30.

14. Barker, *The Life of Stephen F. Austin*, 9–13, 26–27.

15. See chapter 4 for discussion of earlier colonization schemes.

16. Moses Austin to Governor Antonio Martínez, Dec. 26, 1820, in Hatcher, *The Opening of Texas to Foreign Settlement*, 354–55; Moses Austin to James E. B. Austin, Apr. 8, 1821, AP, vol. 1, part 1, 385–87.

17. Barker, *The Life of Stephen F. Austin*, 31–39.

18. Stephen F. Austin, Permit for Josiah H. Bell to Settle Lands, Oct. 6, 1821; Stephen F. Austin, Permit for William Kincheloe to Settle Lands, Oct. 16, 1821, both in AP, vol. 1, part 1, 415, 421–22; Barker, *The Life of Stephen F. Austin*, 39–43.

19. Stephen F. Austin to Anastasio Bustamante, May 10, 1822, AP, vol. 1, part 1, 507–10; Barker, *The Life of Stephen F. Austin*, 45–49, 51–53, 60–66; Campbell, *An Empire for Slavery*, 15; Torget, *Seeds of Empire*, 57–76.

20. Barker, *The Life of Stephen F. Austin*, 70–76; Campbell, *An Empire for Slavery*, 15–16; Reséndez, *Changing National Identities at the Frontier*, 27–29, 61–65; Weber, *The Mexican Frontier*, 20–24, 162; National Colonization Law of Aug. 18, 1824, in Austin, *Translation of the Laws, Orders and Contracts*, 56–57; Colonization Law of the State of Coahuila and Texas, Mar. 24, 1825, in Austin, *Translation of the Laws, Orders and Contracts*, 58–66.

21. Campbell, *An Empire for Slavery*, 16–17.

22. Many of these *empresarios* were also Freemasons. According to Reséndez, who has illuminated the importance of Mason connections among Texas *empresarios*, more than half of all land grants were issued to Masons (*Changing National Identities at the Frontier*, especially 56–92).

23. Henderson, "Minor Empresario Contracts, Part 1," 298–99.

24. The *Arkansas Gazette*, *St. Louis Enquirer* (Missouri), *Frankfort Argus* (Kentucky), *Edwardsville Spectator* (Illinois), *Richmond Enquirer* (Virginia), *Washington Gazette* (Washington, DC), and other newspapers helped advertise Texas colonization by reprinting some of Austin's early idyllic descriptions of the fertile lands of Texas. Many also emphasized the great availability of cheap land in Texas. Torget, *Seeds of Empire*, 63. The Atascosita Census of 1826 offers a decent sample of Anglo-American immigrants and their locations of origin. See Osburn, *The Atascosita Census of 1826*; Barker, "Notes on the Colonization of Texas," 116–17. Also see Jordan, "The Imprint of the Upper and Lower South."

25. Following the cotton boom of the 1810s and the Panic of 1819, prices for public lands in the United States skyrocketed. During the 1820s, U.S. federal lands sold for $1.25 per acre, and the fertile cotton-producing lands of Alabama and Mississippi were priced as high as $50 per acre. In Mexican Texas, comparable lands could be obtained for a measly surveying fee of 12 cents per acre. Torget, *Seeds of Empire*, 64.

26. James A. E. Phelps to Stephen F. Austin, Jan. 16, 1825, AP, vol. 1, part 2, 1020–21.

27. Austin confessed as much in his warning to Mexican officials in 1826. See Stephen F. Austin to José Antonio Saucedo, Aug. 7, 1826, AP, vol. 1, part 2, 1401; also quoted in Barker, "The Influence of Slavery," 12. Also see Torget, *Seeds of Empire*, 2–3, 7–8; Kelley, *Los Brazos de Dios*, 21–25.

28. See, for instance, William N. Henderson to Stephen F. Austin, Nov. 1, 1821; James Fort Muse to William W. Little, Dec. 1, 1821; G. Pearce to Stephen F. Austin, Dec. 12, 1821; Elijah Noble to Stephen F. Austin, June 29, 1822; all in AP, vol. 1, part 1, 438–39, 445–46, 528. Gregg Cantrell has noted Austin's conflicting views but has argued, "It would be a mistake to characterize Austin as tortured over slavery" (*Stephen F. Austin*, 189–90).

29. Stephen F. Austin to Gaspar Flores, (Dec. 31, 1824), PCRCT, vol. 2, 240–41.

30. Stephen F. Austin to Gaspar Flores, (Dec. 31, 1824), PCRCT, vol. 2, 240–42.

31. Criminal Regulations, Jan. 22, 1824, in Austin, *Translation of the Laws, Orders and Contracts*, 68; Campbell, *An Empire for Slavery*, 18–19; McKnight, "Stephen Austin's Legalistic Concerns," 256–57.

32. Barker, "The Influence of Slavery," 32; Campbell, *An Empire for Slavery*, 19. According to Sean Kelley, about 35 percent of the Anglo-American colonists stationed on the Brazos River owned slaves (*Los Brazos de Dios*, 61, 73).

33. José María Sánchez estimated that the families of Austin's colony accounted for more than 2,000 people. It is unclear if he factored slaves into his estimate. According to census materials, in 1828 Austin's colony consisted of 2,023 residents. If we are to assume that Terán's estimate of 1,800 Anglo-Americans was correct, the census did not properly account for the slave population. J. C. Clopper, as well as Stephen F. Austin himself, reported that same year (1828) that there were 3,000 people in Austin's colony. Diary of José María Sánchez, Nov. 10, 1827, to June 3, 1828, in Castañeda, "A Trip to Texas in 1828," 271; Meacham, "The Population of Spanish and Mexican Texas," 289; Clopper, "J. C. Clopper's Journal," 58; Stephen F. Austin's Description, 1828, in Barker, "Descriptions of Texas," 102. Terán noted in his 1828 report that Groce's holdings had expanded to between 105 and 150 slaves by then. For Groce's slaveholdings, see Manuel de Mier y Terán to President Guadalupe Victoria, Mar. 28, 1828; Diary of Manuel de Mier y Terán, Apr. 13 to Feb. 11, 1829; both in Jackson, *Texas by Terán*, 33–34, 63, 144; Berlandier, *Journey to Mexico*, 2:324.

34. The 1834 slave figures are almost certainly deflated. Juan Nepomuceno Almonte, who journeyed across Texas in 1834, had some difficulties calculating the slave population in the Brazos Department. Before Almonte toured the Department of Brazos for himself, he estimated that there were about six hundred to seven hundred African-descended slaves living there. Apparently his sources underestimated their prominence. Moreover, many Anglo-American colonists were suspicious of Almonte's intentions so may have hid some of their slave property from the view of a man they (rightfully) assumed was antislavery. Juan Nepomuceno Almonte to Secretaría de Relaciones Exteriores, June 14, 1834, in Jackson, *Almonte's Texas*, 133; Juan Nepomuceno Almonte, Statistical Report on Texas, 1835, in Castañeda, "Statistical Report on Texas," 198.

35. Of the four thousand or so Euro-American colonists at Nacogdoches proper, at least four hundred were Mexican. Juan Nepomuceno Almonte, Statistical Report on Texas, 1835, in Castañeda, "Statistical Report on Texas," 206, 210; Juan Nepomuceno Almonte, Secret Report on the Present Situation in Texas, 1834, in Jackson, *Almonte's Texas*, 253.

36. Kelley, *Los Brazos de Dios*, 31.

37. J. Tate to Stephen F. Austin, Feb. 27, 1827, AP, vol. 1, part 2, 1608–9.

38. Scholars have debated the extent of the slave trade in Anglo-American Texas. Randolph Campbell has argued that "most [slaves] came to the state with their owners"; therefore, the domestic slave trade was insignificant (*An Empire for Slavery*, 51). Others, like Fred Lee McGhee, have found evidence that the slave trade was much more prominent ("The Black Crop," 120–33, 156). It is worth noting, however, that most of the data for both interpretations referred to the later, post-1836 period.

39. McGhee, "The Black Crop," 155; Asa Hoxey to Robert M. Williamson, Dec. 2, 1832, in Raines, Bolton, and Barker, "Notes and Fragments," 285–86. On slave traders, see William W. Hunter to James F. Perry, Mar. 21, 1831, James Franklin Perry and Stephen Samuel Papers, vol. 2. For the intra-Texas trade, see bill of sale for Ben, a slave, between Daniel McLean and Josiah H. Bell, Sept. 27, 1831, James Franklin Perry and Stephen Samuel Papers, vol. 2. Newspapers often advertised estate sales and auctions. See, for instance, *Texas Gazette* (Austin), Oct. 3, 1829, and June 12, 1830; *Constitutional Advocate and Texas Public Advertiser* (Brazoria), Sept. 5, 1832; *Texas Republican* (Brazoria), Nov. 8, 1834, May 30, 1835, and June 27, 1835.

40. Juan Nepomuceno Almonte, Secret Report on the Present Situation in Texas, 1834, in Jackson, *Almonte's Texas*, 219.

41. More than any other scholar of Texas history, Sean Kelley has attempted to trace the historical origins of these enslaved people. Kelley has concluded tentatively that the people who were enslaved in Texas came from the Bight of Benin, West Central Africa, Sierra Leone, and the Bight of Biafra (*Los Brazos de Dios*, 48–56).

42. Quoted in Barker, "The African Slave Trade in Texas," 151.

43. Estimates of the number of slaves imported illegally through the Atlantic networks vary widely. The evidence is rather clear, however, that at least several hundred African slaves were imported from 1821 (after Lafitte's expulsion from Galveston Island) to 1836. For examples of these estimates, see McGhee, "The Black Crop," 131; Barker, "The African Slave Trade in Texas"; Kelley, *Los Brazos de Dios*, 208.

44. Diary of José María Sánchez, Nov. 10, 1827, to June 3, 1828, in Castañeda, "A Trip to Texas in 1828," 274; Juan Nepomuceno Almonte to Secretaría de Relaciones Exteriores, June 16, 1834, in Jackson, *Almonte's Texas*, 138–39.

45. See, for instance, Report of the Committee on Colonization (1822), in Kelly and Hatcher, "Tadeo Ortiz de Ayala," 79–83; Manuel de Mier y Terán to Guadalupe Victoria, Mar. 28, 1828, in Jackson, *Texas by Terán*, 38–39; Juan Nepomuceno Almonte, Secret Report on the Present Situation in Texas, 1834, in Jackson, *Almonte's Texas*, 223–24. José Angel Hernández has emphasized the importance of "civilized" Native people in Mexican formulations of colonization policy. José Angel Hernández, "'Indios Bárbaros' and the Making of Mexican Colonization Policy after Independence: From Conquest to Colonization," in Confer, Marak, and Tuennerman, *Transnational Indians in the North American West*, 104–7. On Mexican government coordination with Native groups from the United States, see Everett, *The Texas Cherokees*, 25–48, 57–69.

46. Report of the Committee on Colonization (1822), in Kelly and Hatcher, "Tadeo Ortiz de Ayala," 80.

47. Henderson, "Minor Empresario Contracts, Part 1," 299–300, 309; Reséndez, *Changing National Identities at the Frontier*, 67–69.

48. Henderson, "Minor Empresario Contracts, Part 1," 305.

49. Tijerina, *Tejanos and Texas under the Mexican Flag*, 15–16; Berlandier, *Journey to Mexico*, 2:383–84. For a brief history of de León's colony, see Ana Carolina Castillo Crimm, "Finding Their Way," in Poyo, *Tejano Journey*, 111–23; Henderson, "Minor Empresario Contracts, Part 2," 4–10.

50. Juan Nepomuceno Almonte, Statistical Report on Texas, 1835, in Castañeda, "Statistical Report on Texas," 179–80; Jacoby, *The Strange Career of William Ellis*, 9, 23–29.

51. Holley, *Texas: Observations*, 74 ("Irish colony" and "animated"); Juan Nepomuceno Almonte, Statistical Report on Texas, 1835, in Castañeda, "Statistical Report on Texas," 188; Juan Nepomuceno Almonte, Secret Report on the Present Situation in Texas, 1834, in Jackson, *Almonte's Texas*, 234–35. Also see Lundy, *The Life, Travels and Opinions*, 102.

52. Joseph Vehlein and Johan von Racknitz were two other German *empresarios*. See Brister, "Johann von Racknitz," 48–65; Struve, *Germans and Texans*, 44–53,

53. Kelley, *Los Brazos de Dios*, 42; Biesele, *The History of the German Settlements in Texas*, 43–47. A handful of other German colonists eventually would invest in anti-Black slavery as well. See Struve, *Germans and Texans*, 92–95; Kearney, *Nassau Plantation*, 112.

54. Liberalism—an ideology that spotlighted the importance of individual freedom and industry—had gained much popularity among political and intellectual circles throughout Mexico, including in Coahuila and Texas. Many observers saw the economic and political successes of the United States and believed Mexico was fated to emulate such prosperity. See Reséndez, *Changing National Identities at the Frontier*, 73.

55. Quoted in Reséndez, *Changing National Identities at the Frontier*, 70.

56. And this is to say nothing of the remarkable lucrativeness of careers in the budding administration of the North. As Reséndez has noted, each colonization project required a number of bureaucrats, including commissioners and surveyors, to administer and to organize landholdings (*Changing National Identities at the Frontier*, 71). Many Texas-born Hispanic residents took advantage of these career opportunities. Ramos, *Beyond the Alamo*, 93.

57. Francisco Ruíz to Stephen F. Austin, Nov. 26, 1830, PCRCT, vol. 5, 250.

58. Austin, for instance, had his brother James spend several months with the Seguíns to learn Spanish. Ramos, *Beyond the Alamo*, 81–82, 96–97, 100.

59. See Stephen F. Austin to Colonists, Aug. 6, 1823; Stephen F. Austin to (unknown), Oct. 20, 1823; Stephen F. Austin to the Legislature of Coahuila y Tejas, Dec. 22, 1824; Stephen F. Austin to Emily Perry, May 16, 1830, all in AP, vol. 1, part 1, 679–81, 703–4, 996–1002, and part 2, 275–76; Cantrell, *Stephen F. Austin*, 115–16, 134.

60. Earlier events, of course, had made Mexican authorities aware of the possibility of Anglo-American rebellion. The so-called Fredonian Rebellion of 1826–27, in which one disgruntled *empresario*, Haden Edwards, declared independence from Mexico and created the Republic of Fredonia near Nacogdoches, was ample proof of the potential for Anglo-American revolt. See Everett, *The Texas Cherokees*, 43–48; Barker, *The Life of Stephen F. Austin*, 148–78. For analysis of Mexican national government interpretations of Texas circumstances, see Torget, *Seeds of Empire*, 150–57; Weber, *The Mexican Frontier*, 242–49.

61. Jackson, *Texas by Terán*, 1–3.

62. Manuel de Mier y Terán to Guadalupe Victoria, Mar. 28, 1828; Manuel de Mier y Terán to Guadalupe Victoria, June 30, 1828, both in Jackson, *Texas by Terán*, 33, 36–37, 98–99.

63. U.S. presidents John Quincy Adams and Andrew Jackson were particularly adamant about acquiring Texas from Mexico during the 1820s and 1830s. Howren, "Causes and Origin of the Decree of April 6, 1830," 383–85; Manning, "Texas and the Boundary Issue," 235–39.

64. Manuel de Mier y Terán to Guadalupe Victoria, Mar. 28, 1828, in Jackson, *Texas by Terán*, 38–39.

65. Anderson, *The Conquest of Texas*, 76.

66. See, for instance, Manuel de Mier y Terán to Guadalupe Victoria, June 30, 1828, in Jackson, *Texas by Terán*, 100–101; James Gaines to the Governor of Texas, Aug. (?) 1823, P. L. Buquor Papers.

67. Howren, "Causes and Origin of the Decree of April 6, 1830," 406–22.

68. Stephen F. Austin to *Texas Gazette*, July 3, 1830, in AP, vol. 1, part 2, 437–40.

69. Juan Nepomuceno Almonte to Secretary of State and of the Department of Foreign Relations, Apr. 12, 1834, in Jackson, *Almonte's Texas*, 90; Weber, *The Mexican Frontier*, 177.

70. For a detailed analysis of Texas residents' views regarding government regulation, see Reséndez, *Changing National Identities at the Frontier*, 117–23.

71. Quoted in Andrew J. Torget, "The Saltillo Slavery Debates: Mexicans, Anglo-Americans, and Slavery's Future in Nineteenth-Century North America," in Martin and Brooks, *Linking the Histories of Slavery*, 177. For an analysis of antislavery discourse in Latin America, see Blackburn, *The Overthrow of Colonial Slavery*, 331–75.

72. Torget, "The Saltillo Slavery Debates," 177–84; Constitution of the State of Coahuila and Texas, 1827, in Gammel, *The Laws of Texas*, 1:424; Torget, *Seeds of Empire*, 120–29.

73. Slavery remained legal, however, on the Isthmus of Tehuantepec. Barker, "The Influence of Slavery," 21; Torget, "The Saltillo Slavery Debates," 189.

74. Confidential Instructions Which Sr. Almonte Should Follow in Carrying Out His Commission, 1834, in Jackson, *Almonte's Texas*, 38–44; Juan Nepomuceno to Secretaría de Relaciones Exteriores, Apr. 13, 1834, in Jackson, *Almonte's Texas*, 97. For a discussion of Lundy's plans, see Dillon, "Benjamin Lundy in Texas."

75. Ellis H. Bean to Stephen F. Austin, July 5, 1826, in Barker, *Annual Report*, vol. 1, part 2, 1368–69; Barker, "Minutes of the Ayuntamiento," 311; Frost Thorn to Stephen F. Austin, July 22, 1828, AP, vol. 1, part 2, 74–75; Campbell, *An Empire for Slavery*, 23–24.

76. Although John A. Williams, a slaveholder from Nacogdoches, was not present at the June meeting, he would have concurred with the Austin colonists' interpretation of the slaver-slave relationship. In a letter to Austin written a few months after the general meeting, Williams asked for permission to relocate his family from Nacogdoches to San Felipe: "My family consists of myself, my wife and a few negroes six of which negros are fit for field hands." Stephen F. Austin, Jared E. Groce, James Cummings, and Jno. P. Coles to Federal Congress, June 10, 1824; John A. Williams to Stephen F. Austin, Sept. 8, 1824, both in AP, vol. 1, part 2, 827–28, 892.

77. Kelley, *Los Brazos de Dios*, 60.

78. Stuntz, *Hers, His, and Theirs*, 31–44. The Hispanic emphasis on families as agents of colonialism stemmed in part from (justified) fears that male-heavy colonies would be prone to victimizing local women—and thus undermine the larger colonial project. For an illuminating discussion of these dynamics in California, see Chávez-García, *Negotiating Conquest*, especially, 3–24.

79. Colonization Law of 1823, in Gammel, *The Laws of Texas*, 1:27–30; Colonization Law of the State of Coahuila and Texas, Mar. 24, 1825, PCRCT, vol. 2, 269–85.

80. Vincent, "The Blacks Who Freed Mexico," 259–60; Reséndez, *Changing National Identities at the Frontier*, 93–123.

81. Seguín quoted in Barker, "Native Latin American Contribution," 320. For examples of Mexican slaveholders in Texas during the 1820s and 1830s, see Census Report of Nacogdoches, from Attoyac to Loco, 1828; Census Report of Nacogdoches, Town Proper, 1828; and Census Report of Nacogdoches, from Attoyac to Nacogdoches, June 1, 1828, all in University of Texas Institute of Texan Cultures, *Residents of Texas*, 2:214, 216, 218, 242; Census of the Inhabitants of this City of Nacogdoches, Apr. 30, 1835, and Census Report of Nacogdoches, 1835, both in University of Texas Institute of Texan Cultures, *Residents of Texas*, 3:8, 71. For San Antonio slaveholding, see Ramos, *Beyond the Alamo*, 92.

82. Quoted in Kelley, *Los Brazos de Dios*, 65. Also see Thomas Carter to Stephen F. Austin, Apr. 7, 1830, AP, vol. 1, part 2, 364–65.

83. McCurry, *Masters of Small Worlds*, 56; Kelley, *Los Brazos de Dios*, 58.

84. As census materials are incomplete prior to 1836, it is difficult to know the exact distribution of slaves among slaveholders in Texas during the period of Mexican rule. Nonetheless, anecdotal data suggest that many owned no more than seven or eight slaves. See, for instance, Census of the Inhabitants of this City of Nacogdoches, Apr. 30, 1835, and Census Report of Jasper, Municipality of Bevil, May 1, 1835, both in University of Texas Institute of Texan Cultures, *Residents of Texas*, 3:5–19.

85. Foundational works on the nature of slave master paternalism include Phillips, *American Negro Slavery*; Genovese, *Roll, Jordan, Roll*; Rose, *Slavery and Freedom*; Johnson, *Soul by Soul*. For a brief review and analysis of the historiography, see Lacy Ford, "Reconsidering the Internal Slave Trade: Paternalism, Markets, and the Character of the Old South," in Johnson, *The Chattel Principle*, 143–51.

86. Kelley, *Los Brazos de Dios*, 93.

87. Kelley, *Los Brazos de Dios*, 62, 64.

88. Holley, *Texas: A Facsimile Reproduction*, 166; Smithwick, *The Evolution of a State*, 156; Diary of Manuel de Mier y Terán, Apr. 13, 1828, to Feb. 11, 1829, in Jackson, *Texas by Terán*, 62; bill of sale for Turner, a slave, between Isaac Best and William W. Hunter, Dec. 24, 1832; bill of sale for Clenan, a slave, between John Brown and James F. Perry, Oct. 3, 1833; and Power of Attorney to Sell Chaney, a Slave, between Joshua Fletcher and James F. Perry, Mar. 6, 1834, all in James Franklin Perry and Stephen Samuel Papers, vol. 3.

89. Smithwick, *The Evolution of a State*, 27; Manuel de Mier y Terán to President Guadalupe Victoria, June 30, 1828, and Diary of Manuel de Mier y Terán, Apr. 13, 1828, to Feb. 11, 1829, in Jackson, *Texas by Terán*, 100–101, 145; Diary of José María Sánchez, Nov. 10, 1827, to June 3, 1828, in Castañeda, "A Trip to Texas in 1828," 271, 274; B. J. White to Stephen F. Austin, Oct. 17, 1835, in Barker, *Annual Report*, vol. 3, 190. Also see Account of John G. McNeel, John Salmon Ford Memoirs, 1:179–80.

90. Fugitive advertisements in newspapers sometimes hinted at this violence. See, for instance, *Texas Gazette* (Austin), Feb. 27, 1830.

91. Lundy, *The Life, Travels and Opinions*, 96.

92. There were approximately 150 free Black men, women, and children living in Texas in 1835. Lack, *The Texas Revolutionary Experience*, 248. On the enslavement of free Black people in the United States, see Wilson, *Freedom at Risk*; Devereaux, "William Goyens," 53. For other examples of the illegal enslavement of free Black residents in the Texas borderlands, see John Sprowl to Stephen F. Austin, Aug. 18, 1824, AP, vol. 1, part 1, 876; Lundy, *The Life, Travels and Opinions*, 48.

93. Kelley, *Los Brazos de Dios*, 58.

94. Johnson, *Soul by Soul*, 19–24.

95. The slave trade was also the firmest reminder of the ideological (i.e., rhetorical) character of Anglo-American slaver-slave kinship. No matter how vehement Anglo-American colonists were about the familial nature of their relationships to their slaves, the existence and importance of the slave trade reduced such claims to little more than fiction and fantasy. There was nothing familial about forcefully tearing a child from her parents or a brother from his siblings. For further discussion, see Ford, "Reconsidering the Internal Slave Trade," 143–51.

96. Kelley also has noted the importance of spotlighting the migratory experiences of enslaved Africans and African Americans as unique and often divorced from that of their slavers (*Los Brazos de Dios*, 25, 48–56). For important studies on the experiences of enslaved people during the transatlantic voyage and beyond, see, for instance, Rediker, *The Slave Ship*; Smallwood, *Saltwater Slavery*; Gomez, *Exchanging Our Country Marks*; Hall, *Slavery and African Ethnicities in the Americas*.

97. Smithwick, *The Evolution of a State*, 18–19; Diary of Manuel de Mier y Terán, Apr. 13 to Feb. 11, 1829, in Jackson, *Texas by Terán*, 56–57, 144–45; Kelley, *Los Brazos de Dios*, 103–5; Curlee, "The History of a Texas Slave Plantation," 85.

98. Census data indicate that most slaveholders were farmers. See, for instance, Register of the families introduced by the Citizen Empresario Estevan F. Austin by virtue of . . . the Colonization Law of the State of Coahuila and Texas, 1829, in White, *1830 Citizens of Texas*, 9–42.

99. Tobacco may have been another crop produced largely by enslaved people. It does not seem to have had a large market, though. Berlandier, *Journey to Mexico*, 2:319; Kelley, *Los Brazos de Dios*, 106; Torget, *Seeds of Empire*, 7–8.

100. In an unsigned letter to two men in Philadelphia, a San Felipe resident boasted of cotton's success in Texas: "Many of the Inhabitants have commenced raising cotton this year and many more preparing for raising it next which will bring money among us. . . . Our cotton planters here succeed . . . astonishingly." (Unknown) to Ferguson Jones and Campbell, Sept. 6, 1832, James Franklin Perry and Stephen Samuel Papers, vol. 3.

101. The estimate of six hundred bales probably was an exaggeration. In August 1828, Austin predicted that the total seasonal output of his colony would be equal to "about six hundred bales of cotton and eighty hogsheads of sugar." Stephen F. Austin's Description, 1828, in Barker, "Descriptions of Texas," 102; Diary of Manuel de Mier y Terán, Apr. 13 to Nov. 11, 1828, in Jackson, *Texas by Terán*, 63, 144–45; Bertleth, "Jared Ellison Groce."

102. Diary of Manuel de Mier y Terán, Apr. 13 to Nov. 11, 1828; Diary of Manuel de Mier y Terán, Apr. 13 to Feb. 11, 1829, both in Jackson, *Texas by Terán*, 63, 79, 144–45; Diary of José María Sánchez, Nov. 10, 1827, to June 3, 1828, in Castañeda, "A Trip to Texas in 1828," 271.

103. Diary of José María Sánchez, Nov. 10, 1827, to June 3, 1828, in Castañeda, "A Trip to Texas in 1828," 272; Berlandier, *Journey to Mexico*, 2:322; Census Report of Nacogdoches, Southwest of Nacogdoches, Apr. 25, 1835; Census of the Inhabitants of this City of Nacogdoches, Apr. 30, 1835; and Census of Jasper, Municipality of Bevil, May 1, 1835, all in University of Texas Institute of Texan Cultures, *Residents of Texas*, 3:3–7, 13.

104. Census of the Inhabitants of this City of Nacogdoches, Apr. 30, 1835, and Census of Jasper, Municipality of Bevil, May 1, 1835, both in University of Texas Institute of Texan Cultures, *Residents of Texas*, 3:6–7, 17.

105. Devereaux, "William Goyens," 52–56; Census Report of Nacogdoches, 1835, in University of Texas Institute of Texan Cultures, *Residents of Texas*, 3:70.

106. Census Report of Nacogdoches, 1835, in University of Texas Institute of Texan Cultures, *Residents of Texas*, 3:80.

107. The only manufacturing investments early slaveholders cared to make were the construction of sugar mills and cotton gins. Berlandier, *Journey to Mexico*, 2:319; Clopper, "J. C. Clopper's Journal," 59.

108. Stephen F. Austin's Description, 1828, in Barker, "Descriptions of Texas," 102, 113; Juan Nepomuceno Almonte, Statistical Report on Texas, 1835, in Castañeda, "Statistical Report on Texas," 201, 205; Manuel de Mier y Terán to President Guadalupe Victoria, Mar. 28, 1828, in Jackson, *Texas by Terán*, 34.

109. Smithwick, *Evolution of a State*, 37; Lundy, *The Life, Travels and Opinions*, 44; Francisco Ruíz to Samuel M. Williams, Sept. 13, 1831, in PCRCT, vol. 6, 414; Torget, *Seeds of Empire*, 147. For a broader discussion of the flight of enslaved people to Mexico, see Kelley, "'Mexico in His Head.'" It should be noted, however, that these enslaved people were in some ways extending a runaway tradition that dated back to the early days of the nineteenth century. See, for instance, Captain Turner to James Wilkinson, Oct. 15, 1804, U.S. Congress, *American State Papers*, 2:690; Nemesio Salcedo to Juan Bautista Elguézabal, Jan. 22, 1805, Béxar Archives Manuscripts.

110. Porter, *The Negro on the American Frontier*, 369–407.

111. Lack, *The Texas Revolutionary Experience*, 238–44; Addington, "Slave Insurrections in Texas," 411–13; Account of John G. McNeel, John Salmon Ford Memoirs, 1:179–80.

112. Quoted in Schoen, "The Free Negro in the Republic of Texas, VI," 87.

113. Kelley, *Los Brazos de Dios*, 73; Diary of José María Sánchez, Nov. 10, 1827, to June 3, 1828, in Castañeda, "A Trip to Texas in 1828," 272; Berlandier, *Journey to Mexico*, 2:322–23. On music as a form of Black resistance and militancy, see Stuckey, *Slave Culture*, 9–28; Rucker, *The River Flows On*, 104–7.

114. Thus, to claim that Blackness translated *strictly* into nonbeing or nonpersonhood for enslaved people, as some have argued, is to misread both the lived conditions of enslaved people *and* how slavers envisioned them within their societies. On Blackness as nonbeing, see, for instance, Gordon, "Through the Zone of Nonbeing," 2–3.

115. Berlandier, *The Indians of Texas in 1830*; Anderson, *The Conquest of Texas*, 26–29; Hämäläinen, *The Comanche Empire*, 151–52.

116. For a capacious discussion of settler colonial annihilation, see Ostler, *Surviving Genocide*, 4–5.

117. Although it is my intention here to highlight the role of violence in Anglo-American–Native relations prior to 1836, it is worth noting that significant commerce existed between the colonists and various Native communities. Like their Mexican neighbors, many Anglo-American colonists attempted to profit from the trade in horses, mules, skins, and other manufactured goods. At times these trade relationships could be converted into diplomatic opportunities and foundations for temporary peace. See, for instance, Personal Reminiscences of Moses Austin Bryan, 1889, Moses Austin Bryan Papers; William Rab to the Governor of Texas, (ca. 1835), P. L.

Buquor Papers; Account of Caiaphas K. Ham, John Salmon Ford Memoirs, 1:94–97; Smith, *From Dominance to Disappearance*, 128–29.

118. Castañeda, *Our Catholic Heritage in Texas*, 6:307–55; Ricklis, *The Karankawa Indians of Texas*, 159–75; Smith, *From Dominance to Disappearance*, 121–25; Anderson, *The Conquest of Texas*, 22–26; La Vere, *The Texas Indians*, 107; Berlandier, *The Indians of Texas in 1830*, 99–152; Smith, *The Wichita Indians*, 111–12.

119. Hämäläinen, *The Comanche Empire*, 191–99. Raúl Ramos has interpreted Comanche-Mexican relations during the 1820s as more cooperative, although he also notes the extractive tendencies of Comanches. Raúl Ramos, "Finding the Balance: Bexar in Mexican/Indian Relations," in Truett and Young, *Continental Crossroads*, 52–54.

120. Testimony of Fernando González, July 7, 1873, and Testimony of Dionisio Santos, July 11, 1873, both in Velasco Ávila, *En manos de los bárbaros*, 33–43; Hämäläinen, *The Comanche Empire*, 196; DeLay, *War of a Thousand Deserts*, 320–22.

121. José Francisco Ruiz, Report of Observations and Additional Information about Indians Living in the Department of Texas by the Undersigned, 1828, in Ewers, *Report on the Indian Tribes of Texas in 1828*, 9; Berlandier, *The Indians of Texas in 1830*, 76–77.

122. Stephen F. Austin's Description, 1828, in Barker, "Descriptions of Texas," 113.

123. Veracini, *Settler Colonialism*, 53–74; Horsman, *Race and Manifest Destiny*, 106–14; Pearce, *Savagism and Civilization*; Anderson, *The Conquest of Texas*, 38–41.

124. Wyatt-Brown, *Honor and Violence in the Old South*, 4, 26–39. Also see Spierenburg, *Men and Violence*; Nisbett and Cohen, *Culture of Honor*.

125. Stephen F. Austin to Militiamen, (ca. May 1, 1826), PCRCT, vol. 2, 560–61.

126. Gary Clayton Anderson has characterized this martial mentality as the "Texas Creed" (*The Conquest of Texas*, 36–41). See also Masich, *Civil War in the Southwest Borderlands*, 16–17.

127. Ramón Músquiz to José María Letona, Sept. 26, 1831, PCRCT, vol. 6, 433–34.

128. Andrew Masich also has found cross-ethnic reverberations of "martial masculinity" across the nineteenth-century southwest borderlands (*Civil War in the Southwest Borderlands*, 30–35).

129. Also see Ramos, *Beyond the Alamo*, 92–96; Brooks, *Captives and Cousins*, 7–10; Alonso, *Thread of Blood*, 3–36, 51–100.

130. José María Moreno to Antonio Elosúa, July 27, 1831; Ramón Músquiz to Rafael Manchola, Oct. 12, 1831; and Antonio Elosúa to Manuel de Mier y Terán, Dec. 3, 1831, all in PCRCT, vol. 6, 316, 456, 590–92.

131. For a similar interpretation, see Tijerina, *Tejanos and Texas under the Mexican Flag*, 87–90.

132. Stephen F. Austin to Anastasio Bustamante, May 10, 1822, and Stephen F. Austin to Luciano García, Oct. 20, 1823, both in AP, vol. 1, part 1, 507–10, 701–2; Anderson, *The Conquest of Texas*, 52–54.

133. Stephen F. Austin to Amos Rawls, June 22, 1824, and Stephen F. Austin to Mateo Ahumada, Sept. 10, 1825, both in AP, vol. 1, part 1, 840, 1197–98.

134. Thomas M. Duke's recollections from the turn of the twentieth century hint at Anglo-American treatment of Native women. Of all the interactions Anglo-American men had with Native people, he remembered that some chased after "squaws." Recollections of Thomas M. Duke, in Kuykendall, "Reminiscences of Early Texans," 250;

Anderson, *The Conquest of Texas*, 54. For another example of Anglo-American slave raiding during this period, see Lucy A. Erath, *Memoirs of Major George Bernard Erath* (unedited), 25, George Bernard Erath Papers. For Mexican slave raiding (and kin incorporation), see Nicacio Sánches to Antonio Elosúa, Sept. 19, 1830; Gaspar Flores and Ramón Músquiz, Sept. 19, 1830; Nicacio Sánches to Antonio Elosúa, Sept. 22, 1830; Diary of Nicacio Sánches, Aug. 17 to Sept. 22, 1830, 1830; Diary of Gaspar Flores, Aug. 17 to Sept. 22, 1830, all in PCRCT, vol. 4, 483–84, 495–506, 509–23; Manuel de Mier y Terán to Antonio Elosúa, Oct. 11, 1830; Ramón Músquiz to Antonio Elosúa, Jan. 12, 1831; Manuel de Mier y Terán to Antonio Elosúa, Feb. 19, 1831, all in PCRCT, vol. 5, 59–60, 411–23, 538.

135. Stephen F. Austin to Mateo Ahumada, Mar. 27, 1826, PCRCT, vol. 2, 528–29.

136. Map of Comanche Country by Stephen F. Austin, Aug. 28, 1827; Anastasio Bustamante to Stephen F. Austin, Mar. 23, 1829; Ramón Musquiz to Stephen F. Austin, June 11, 1829, all in PCRCT, vol. 3, 72–74.

137. Manuel de Mier y Terán to Antonio Elosúa, Sept. 4, 1830; Gaspar Flores to Ramón Musquiz, Sept. 19, 1830; Diary of Nicacio Sánches, Aug. 17 to Sept. 22, 1830; José de las Piedras to Antonio Elosúa, Sept. 28, 1830, all in PCRCT, vol. 4, 448, 472, 483, 484, 498–506, 552–53.

138. Francisco Ruíz to Antonio Elosúa, June 11, 1831; Francisco Ruíz to Antonio Elosúa, Aug. 1831; Ramón Músquiz to Green C. DeWitt and the Gonzales Commissar of Police, Oct. 15, 1831; Antonio Elosúa to Manuel Lafuente, Oct. 15, 1831; Diary of Capt. Manuel Lafuente, Oct. 18 to Nov. 26, 1831, all in PCRCT, vol. 6, 268, 335, 468, 470, 557–65.

139. Kuykendall, "Reminiscences of Early Texans," 35; Kelley, *Los Brazos de Dios*, 97; Bertleth, "Jared Ellison Groce"; Smithwick, *The Evolution of a State*, 137.

140. Anderson, *The Conquest of Texas*, 98–107; Everett, *The Texas Cherokees*.

141. Anderson has analyzed the role of Indian conspiracy rumors in the history of the Texas Rebellion (*The Conquest of Texas*, 108–25). My emphasis on the Anglo-American–Mexican treatment of Native people as an important precursor to the Texas Rebellion is a departure from a large body of literature. Many historians have followed in the footsteps of Barker in claiming that the Rebellion was "the inevitable result of the racial inheritances of the two peoples" of Tejas y Coahuila. As I have attempted to demonstrate, Mexican and Anglo-American people had a lot more in common than scholars have recognized, particularly when it came to the administration of violence against Native people. Paul D. Lack has analyzed the endurance of the Barker thesis in "In the Long Shadow of Eugene C. Barker: The Revolution and the Republic," in Buenger and Calvert, *Texas through Time*, 134–64. See Barker, *Mexico and Texas*, 86; Lowrie, *Culture Conflict in Texas*; Binkley, *The Texas Revolution*. For narratives that challenge the culture conflict thesis, see, for instance Stephen L. Hardin, "Efficient in the Cause," in Poyo, *Tejano Journey*, 49–71; Torget, *Seeds of Empire*, 140.

142. Stephen F. Austin to Senator L. F. Linn, May 4, 1836, AP, vol. 3, 344–48.

143. Campbell has offered a more nuanced discussion of Anglo-American responses to Santa Anna's rise to power (*An Empire for Slavery*, 36–43). Torget's (*Seeds of Empire*, 139–41) interpretation of the causes of the Texas Rebellion is similar to mine. Santa Anna's abandonment of federalism meant that Mexican and Anglo-American Texans would be at the mercy of men who had little knowledge of the economic needs of the citizens. The entire battle over slavery's legality in the Mexican Republic was reflective

of the ideological differences between those living on the northeastern periphery and those living at the center. Federalism, however, had provided Texas residents a degree of influence in the outcome of the slavery controversy.

144. See, for instance, James E. Crisp, "¡Mucho Cuidado! Silencing, Selectivity, and Sensibility in the Utilization of Tejano Voices by Texas Historians," in Perales and Ramos, *Recovering the Hispanic History of Texas*, 111–35.

145. For a detailed and critical narrative of the events of the Texas Rebellion, see Lack, *The Texas Revolutionary Experience*.

146. [Lundy], *War in Texas*, 4, Lundy's emphasis.

147. Bugbee, "Slavery in Early Texas," 651–52.

148. Essentially, Barker dismissed the Lundy thesis because the propaganda of the time rarely mentioned slavery: "It seems beyond question that an anxious, excited public sentiment concerning slavery, had one existed, would have been the object of more frequent and elaborate appeals from the war party, which was leaving no stone unturned now to rouse the settlers to resistance" ("The Influence of Slavery," 5, 34–35; *The Life of Stephen F. Austin*, 257). Strangely enough, Barker thought nothing of the frequent Anglo-American use of slavery as a metaphor for their condition under Mexican rule. As Lack has pointed out, "In their view Mexico sought to enslave the only people in the land who still dared to defend the cause of liberty" ("Slavery and the Texas Revolution," 181).

149. Lack, "Slavery and the Texas Revolution," 182. Campbell has argued that "protecting slavery was not the primary cause of the Texas Revolution, but it certainly was a major result" (*An Empire for Slavery*, 48).

150. Stephen F. Austin to Mary Austin Holley, Aug. 21, 1835, AP, vol. 3, 102. For another example, see James H. C. Miller to the People of Texas, in *Texas Republican*, Oct. 3, 1835.

151. Despite traditional arguments that U.S. southerners were antigovernment, it is rather clear that they depended on the national government for economic prosperity. Since the late eighteenth century, White southerners generally had believed that it was the responsibility of national government to protect independent, propertied farmers by securing markets abroad and by expanding opportunities for land acquisition. See especially McCoy, *The Elusive Republic*; Fehrenbacher, *The Slaveholding Republic*; Wright, *Slavery and American Economic Development*; Majewski, *Modernizing a Slave Economy*; Einhorn, *American Taxation, American Slavery*.

152. Article 9 of the Constitution of the Republic of Texas, which protected the institution of race-based slavery, is particularly noteworthy. Constitution of the Republic of Texas, 1836, in Gammel, *The Laws of Texas*, 1:1079. Also see McGhee, "The Black Crop," 162–78.

153. Berlandier, *Journey to Mexico*, 2:319. For local Hispanic recognition of the importance of anti-Black slavery for the economic development of Texas, see Torget, *Seeds of Empire*, 174–76.

154. Benjamin Milam to Henry Smith, in *Texas Republican*, Mar. 28, 1835.

155. The Declaration of Independence, Goliad, Dec. 20, 1835, in Gammel, *The Laws of Texas*, 1:818.

156. The Declaration of Independence Made by the Delegates of the People of Texas, Washington, Mar. 2, 1836, in Gammel, *The Laws of Texas*, 1:1063–66. The similarities between the Texas declarations and the U.S. Declaration of Independence

certainly reveal the Anglo colonists' belief that they were carrying out the legacies of their American Revolutionary ancestors, but they also illuminate the similar circumstances of each context. Both rebellions emerged amid competing visions of settler colonialism and the roles of slavery. Sam W. Haynes, "'Imitating the Example of Our Forefathers': The Texas Revolution as Historical Reenactment," in Haynes and Saxon, *Contested Empire*, 43–71; Byrd, *The Transit of Empire*, xxi; Horne, *The Counter-Revolution of 1776*, 209–40.

Part III

1. Testimony of Rose Williams, FWP TXN, part 4, 176.

2. For an excellent discussion of the ties between the cotton frontier, slavery, transnational credit systems, and U.S. industrial and technological developments, see Baptist, *The Half Has Never Been Told*. Also see Rothman, *Flush Times and Fever Dreams*; Johnson, *River of Dark Dreams*; Beckert, *Empire of Cotton*; Calvin Schermerhorn, "'The Time Is Now Just Arriving When Many Capitalists Will Make Fortunes': Indian Removal, Finance, and Slavery in the Making of the American Cotton South," in Martin and Brooks, *Linking the Histories of Slavery*, 151–70.

3. Mark Allan Goldberg has explored the confluences of Comanche and Anglo-American slaving in central Texas. His work has analyzed the "everyday practices" and material (usually trade) connections that brought these slaving systems together. Goldberg, "Linking the Chains"; Goldberg, *Conquering Sickness*, 98–131.

4. By emphasizing the importance of kinship structures, I am encouraging scholars to assess anti-Blackness beyond the law, which often articulates theoretical social and ideological positions, as opposed to lived conditions.

5. Scholars have been divided on the question of local Hispanic views on anti-Black slavery in nineteenth-century Texas. For Hispanic–African-American solidarity in Texas, see Valerio-Jiménez, *River of Hope*, 185; De León, *The Tejano Community*, 15, 28; Alonzo Salazar, "Don Carlos de La Garza," and Jesús de la Teja, "Juan N. Seguín," both in de la Teja, *Tejano Leadership in Mexican and Revolutionary Texas*, 204, 225. For discussion of Hispanic complicity in anti-Black slavery during the period of Anglo supremacy, see De León, *They Called Them Greasers*, 50; Thompson, *Tejano Tiger*, 75–76; Torget, *Seeds of Empire*, 8, 61, 78–81, 95, 102–3, 141, 145–46, 160–61, 175.

6. Pekka Hämäläinen in *The Comanche Empire*, Brian DeLay in *War of a Thousand Deserts*, and Joaquín Rivaya-Martínez in "Captivity and Adoption among the Comanche Indians" have elaborated on the economic, political, and social logic of Comanche slaving during this period.

Chapter 6

1. I have reconstructed Lucky's story from the following documents: Petition of John M. Story, Nov. 8, 1851, Texas, Memorials and Petitions; U.S. Census Bureau, 1850 Population Schedule, Burleson County, TX; U.S. Census Bureau, 1850 Slave Schedule, Burleson County, TX.

2. Baptist's *The Half Has Never Been Told* captures these themes best across the United States (and Texas). Also see Campbell, *An Empire for Slavery*; Jones, *Texas Roots*, 135–70; Williams, *Bricks without Straw*, 36–44. For Anglo-American investment

in a cotton-based economy, see Torget, *Seeds of Empire*, 181–83, 185–91, 199–202. On the concentration of political and economic power, see Campbell and Lowe, *Wealth and Power in Antebellum Texas*. For Black resistance, see Gillmer, *Slavery and Freedom in Texas*, 53–88.

3. Andrew Torget has detailed many of the struggles the Republic of Texas dealt with as Anglo-Americans became more obviously invested in chattel slavery in the decade after the Texas Rebellion. He has emphasized global conditions, especially markets and international antislavery politics (*Seeds of Empire*, 179–254).

4. This chapter seeks to complicate discussions of settler colonialism as a categorically distinct process of colonialism by spotlighting the power of anti-Black violence to transcend, frame, and fuse regimes of conquest.

5. Generally, scholars have accounted (if only indirectly) for Tejanos' anti-Blackness during this period by highlighting their enthusiasm for liberalism and Texas's integration with Atlantic markets. See Weber, *The Mexican Frontier*, 123–25, 174–78; Reséndez, *Changing National Identities at the Frontier*, 93–100; Torget, *Seeds of Empire*, 102–3, 108–9; Ramos, *Beyond the Alamo*, 92, 117; James E. Crisp, "José Antonio Navarro: The Power of Tejano Powerlessness," in de la Teja, *Tejano Leadership*, 150. This chapter elaborates on Omar S. Valerio-Jiménez's point that "Mexican Texans gained acceptance as legitimate American citizens when they denied freedom to African American slaves" (*River of Hope*, 234).

6. David Burnet, Message to the First Congress of the Republic of Texas, Oct. 6, 1836, PMBL, vol. 3, 459–61; Colin De Bland to Mirabeau Lamar, Nov. 26, 1836, PMBL, vol. 1, 507.

7. Texas Republic Congress, *Journals of the House . . . First Congress, First Session*, 147, 198–99; Land Warrant for William Steele by Barnard Bee, Dec. 8, 1837; Land Warrant for Burton H. Freeling by Barnard Bee, Dec. 11, 1837; Land Warrant for John W. Robertson, Jan. 4, 1838, all in Barnard E. Bee Papers.

8. Torget, *Seeds of Empire*, 157, 189.

9. Quoted in Torget, *Seeds of Empire*, 202.

10. Torget, *Seeds of Empire*, 124; Stephen F. Austin to John A. Merle and Co., Dec. 10, 1836, AP, vol. 3, 474; Anonymous to Sam Houston, Feb. 1837, PMBL, vol. 1, 536–37; Kearney, *Nassau Plantation*, 13–17; Carlson, *A Banking History of Texas*, 4–8, 10–11, 19–21.

11. Woolfolk, "Cotton Capitalism and Slave Labor in Texas," 47–48, 50. For national loan-seeking efforts, see Loan Contract, Apr. 2, 1836, in Stevens, *The Texas Legation Papers*, 3–9; James Hamilton to Mirabeau Lamar, Sept. 4, 1838, PMBL, vol. 2, 212–13; Barnard E. Bee to G. Victoria, May 26, 1839, PMBL, vol. 2, 595. For examples and discussions of the importance of personal credit, see Thomas McKinney and Samuel Williams to Toby and Brother, May 25, 1836, PMBL, vol. 1, 383; Hollon, *William Bollaert's Texas*, 286; Torget, *Seeds of Empire*, 196–201; Hogan, *The Texas Republic*, 35, 81–88; Holbrook, "Cotton Marketing in Antebellum Texas"; Beckert, *Empire of Cotton*, 219–24; Schermerhorn, "Indian Removal, Finance, and Slavery," 160–65; Baptist, *The Half Has Never Been Told*, 267; Jones, *Texas Roots*, 142–44.

12. *Daily Picayune* (New Orleans), Mar. 29, 1839; Hunt and Randel, *A New Guide to Texas*, 55; Fornell, *The Galveston Era*, 5, 14–15, 23; Campbell, *Gone to Texas*, 212–13; McComb, *The City in Texas*, 77.

13. *Telegraph and Texas Register* (Columbia), Aug. 30, 1836 ("One Million Dollars" and "country shall improve"); Diary of John Winfield Scott Dancy, 1836–56, John Winfield Scott Dancy Papers. Also see Hollon, *William Bollaert's Texas*, 110; Hogan, *The Texas Republic*, 6–9, 72–80, 91; Campbell, *Gone to Texas*, 212–13; U.S. Census Bureau, *Population of the United States in 1860*, 472–82; Gaillardet, *Sketches of Early Texas and Louisiana*, 52–53; Potts, *Railroad Transportation in Texas*, 27–32; McComb, *The City in Texas*, 87–90.

14. These are figures of monthly prices of short-staple cotton at New Orleans. Gray, *History of Agriculture*, 1027.

15. Johnson, *River of Dark Dreams*, 281–84; Samuel A. Plummer to Mirabeau Lamar, Apr. 13, 1839, PMBL, vol. 2, 525.

16. In his sample of some 5,700 slave sales, Randolph Campbell found that the mean value of a chattel slave in Texas rose from $345 in 1842–47 to $765 in 1858–62 (*An Empire for Slavery*, 73). For a contemporary discussion of inflation and economic insecurity in Texas, see, for instance, Report of the Committee on Finance, Jan. 20, 1841, in Texas Republic Congress, *Appendix . . . Fifth Congress*, 414; Sam Houston, Message to Congress, Dec. 1, 1842, in Texas Republic Congress, *Journals of the House . . . Seventh Congress*, 16–21.

17. Quoted in Hogan, *The Texas Republic*, 95. Also see McDonald, *Hurrah for Texas*, 136; Hollon, *William Bollaert's Texas*, 288. For an extended discussion of the staying power of slave property during the 1830s depressions, see Baptist, *The Half Has Never Been Told*, 269–307.

18. Pratt, *Galveston Island*, 105; State of Alabama Court Summons, Apr. 26, 1841, and State of Alabama Arrest Warrant, May 22, 1841, both in Julien Sidney Devereux Papers; Baptist, *The Half Has Never Been Told*, 284–88; Rothman, *Flush Times and Fever Dreams*, 295–96; Winfrey, *Julien Sidney Devereux*, 29–30.

19. Freund, *Gustav Dresel's Houston Journal*, 56; McDonald, *Hurrah for Texas*, 27; Abner S. Lipscomb to James Hamilton, Jan. 6, 1840, in Texas Republic Congress, *Appendix . . . Fifth Congress*, 280–81.

20. Gaillardet, *Sketches of Early Texas and Louisiana*, 63; U.S. Census Bureau, *The Seventh Census of the United States, 1850*, 518; U.S. Census Bureau, *Agriculture of the United States in 1860*, 149; Campbell, *An Empire for Slavery*, 74–76. On sugar production, see Few, *Sugar, Planters, Slaves, and Convicts*, 3–20.

21. Campbell, *An Empire for Slavery*, 209–10; Jones, *Texas Roots*, 138–39.

22. Weeks, *Debates of the Texas Convention*, 244; Vielé, *"Following the Drum,"* 240; McDonald, *Hurrah for Texas*, 80.

23. *Personal Memoirs of Juan Seguín*, in de la Teja, *A Revolution Remembered*, 89; Muir, *Texas in 1837*, 97–98; Stiff, *A New History of Texas*, 28–29. Also see Hollon, *William Bollaert's Texas*, 219.

24. Bartlett, *Personal Narrative of Explorations*, 1:25–27.

25. Muir, *Texas in 1837*, 99 (quote), 108–9.

26. Bartlett, *Personal Narrative of Explorations*, 1:40; *Telegraph and Texas Register*, Feb. 10, 1848; Olmsted, *A Journey through Texas*, 152–53, 160.

27. Sequín quoted in de la Teja, *A Revolution Remembered*, 34. For the language of honor, see Stephen F. Austin, Affidavit, Nov. 24, 1835; Muster roll of Juan Seguín's Company at San Jacinto; Muster roll of Juan Seguín's Regiment; Sam Houston to Juan Seguín, Jan. 16, 1827, all in de la Teja, *A Revolution Remembered*, 135–36, 148–51, 153.

28. Committee report on petition of Luciano Navarro, Dec. 9, 1857, in Texas House of Representatives, *Official Journal of the House . . . Seventh Biennial Session*, 293.

29. Montejano, *Anglos and Mexicans in the Making of Texas*, 34–35, 40–41.

30. Green, *Memoirs of Mary A. Maverick*, 48. For other laudatory comments, see, for instance, Weeks, *Debates of the Texas Convention*, 245; E. M. Pease, Message to the Legislature, Nov. 11, 1857, in Texas House of Representatives, *Official Journal of the House . . . Seventh Biennial Session*, 219–20.

31. Stuntz, *Hers, His, and Theirs*, xxiii, 138–69.

32. Dysart, "Mexican Women in San Antonio," 369–74; Montejano, *Anglos and Mexicans in the Making of Texas*, 36–37; Reséndez, *Changing National Identities at the Frontier*, 129–33; Ramos, *Beyond the Alamo*, 194–96. For contemporary commentary, see Robert Weakley Brahan Jr. to John Donelson Coffee Jr., Jan. 20, 1855, in Boom, "Texas in the 1850s," 283. Probate records offer a peek into the familial and property relations between Hispanic women and Anglo men. The Bexar County probate records, for instance, reveal that in 1838 Erastus "Deaf" Smith's widow, Guadalupe Smith, sought to acquire her dead husband's Mississippi property to be used for the betterment of their children. Her petition was pressing, because at the time an Anglo man by the name of Joseph W. Garraty was trying to take control of the Smith estate. Petition of Guadalupe Smith, Nov. 13, 1838, Texas, Wills and Probate Records, Béxar County, vol. A, 178–79.

33. During the six-year period after the Rebellion, the thirteen most prominent Anglo-American buyers acquired almost 1,370,000 acres of land from 358 Hispanic individuals. De León, *The Tejano Community*, 14. Displacement also was an uneven process, as the Hispanic people of south Texas experienced displacement to a lesser degree than those living elsewhere in Texas. Alonzo, *Tejano Legacy*, 95–143.

34. From 1837 to 1842, land purchases by the most active sixty-seven Mexican buyers accounted for almost 180,000 acres, which had the effect of concentrating land wealth into the hands of only a handful of Hispanic elites. De la Teja, *A Revolution Remembered*, 38; Ramos, *Beyond the Alamo*, 196–99.

35. Quoted in Montejano, *Anglos and Texans in the Making of Texas*, 28–29.

36. Texas House of Representatives, *Official Journal of the House . . . Seventh Biennial Session*, 702–4. Also see Valerio-Jiménez, *River of Hope*, 179–81.

37. Montejano, *Anglos and Mexicans in the Making of Texas*, 28–30; Gonzáles petition translated in J. J. Warnes to P. H. Bell, May 26, 1852, IPTS, vol. 3, 166–67.

38. McDonald and Matovina, *Defending Mexican Valor in Texas*, 20, 22, 29.

39. Stewart and de León, *Not Room Enough*, 15, 17.

40. Yet as Omar S. Valerio-Jiménz has noted, some Hispanic residents, even poor, indebted servants, benefited from the changing regional economy of the era (*River of Hope*, 138–40). This was especially the case in the southern portion of Texas, along the Río Grande, where locals earned wages from and sold their goods to the United States troops stationed there. Olmsted, *A Journey through Texas*, 162.

41. Elisha M. Pease, Message to the Legislature, Nov. 11, 1857, in Texas House of Representatives, *Official Journal of the House . . . Seventh Biennial Session*, 218–20; *San Antonio Ledger*, May 1, 1858; De León, *The Tejano Community*, 15–16, 63, 109; Ramos, *Beyond the Alamo*, 222–27.

42. Vielé, *"Following the Drum,"* 107–8.

43. *Texas in 1840*, 211.

44. On the repurposing of the mission, see Bartlett, *Personal Narrative of Explorations*, 1:39–41. Memorializing efforts for the mission-fort were in full force at least by the 1850s. See, for instance, Texas House of Representatives, *Official Journal of the House . . . Seventh Biennial Session*, 539. David Montejano discusses the importance of the quartermaster's store in the conquest of Texas in *Anglos and Mexicans in the Making of Texas*, 41–42. For a scholarly discussion of the mission-fort and Texas myth making, see Roberts and Olson, *A Line in the Sand*.

45. Torget, *Seeds of Empire*, 195–96; Jordan, "The Imprint of the Upper and Lower South," 670; Campbell, *Gone to Texas*, 159, 207.

46. Texas House of Representatives, *Journals of the House . . . Fourth Legislature—Extra*, 12; Texas House of Representatives, *Official Journal of the House . . . Seventh Biennial Session*, 309.

47. Olmsted, *A Journey through Texas*, 86; Freund, *Gustav Dresel's Houston Journal*, 56; Hollon, *William Bollaert's Texas*, 270–71.

48. *Texas in 1840*, 118–20; Olmsted, *A Journey through Texas*, 244–45; Sarah Ford, FWP TXN, part 2, 44; Jordan, "W. Steinert's View of Texas in 1849" (July 1976), 62, 70; Olmsted, *A Journey through Texas*, 88; Kelley, *Los Brazos de Dios*, 114–20.

49. Campbell, *An Empire for Slavery*, 81–92. On hired-out slave labor, see McDonald, *Hurrah for Texas*, 2, 11, 77, 129; Olmsted, *A Journey through Texas*, 114–15; Helen Blair Chapman to Emily Welles Blair, Sept 12, 1848, in Coker, *The News from Brownsville*, 71–72.

50. Gaillardet, *Sketches of Early Texas and Louisiana*, 54; Testimony of Daniel Phillips, FWP TXN, part 3, 183; Testimony of Jack Bess, FWP TXN, part 1, 73; Testimony of Wash Anderson, FWP TXN, part 1, 19. Also see Hollon, *William Bollaert's Texas*, 272–73; John C. Graham to Samuel Maverick, Nov. 25, 1849 in Green, *Memoirs of Mary A. Maverick*, 118; Jordan, "W. Steinert's View of Texas in 1849" (Jan. 1977), 291; Liles, "Slavery and Cattle in East and West Texas," 29–36. Karl Jacoby has explained how slaver-based ranching and cotton production overlapped in Victoria (*The Strange Career of William Ellis*, 25).

51. Hollon, *William Bollaert's Texas*, 208, 287; Olmsted, *A Journey through Texas*, 59–60. Also see, Jordan, "W. Steinert's View of Texas in 1849" (July 1976), 72.

52. Baptist, *The Half Has Never Been Told*, 124–31. As Alan Olmstead and Paul Rhode have noted (in response to Baptist's work), improved cotton seeds also accounted for increased slave output ("Cotton, Slavery, and the New History of Capitalism," 11).

53. Hollon, *William Bollaert's Texas*, 271; Olmsted, *A Journey through Texas*, 66; Testimony of Mary Kincheon Edwards, FWP TXN, part 2, 16; Testimony of Mary Anne Patterson, FWP TXN, part 3, 171; Testimony of John Walton, FWP TXN, part 4, 125; Kelley, *Los Brazos de Dios*, 107–12.

54. Muir, *Texas in 1837*, 134.

55. For a broader discussion of Anglo-American honor (particularly in the U.S. South), see Wyatt-Brown, *Honor and Violence in the Old South*, 25–39.

56. Texas, Wills and Probate Records, Harris County, vol. M, 61–66; Texas House of Representatives, *Official Journal of the House . . . Seventh Biennial Session*, 392–93.

57. Texas House of Representatives, *Official Journal of the House . . . Seventh Biennial Session*, 572.

58. Although Burleson was not celebrated for wielding violence against enslaved people, he did hold some Black people in bondage on his plantation. See, for instance,

City Gazette, Apr. 15, 1840. Guy M. Bryan, Address to the Legislature, Dec. 27, 1851, in Texas House of Representatives, *Journal of the House . . . Fourth Legislature*, 393.

59. It is interesting to see the extent to which scholars have appropriated this idea of slave "discipline," as some have indexed "violence" under "punishment of slaves." See, for instance, Campbell, *An Empire for Slavery*, 303. For a discussion of family and paternalism in mid-nineteenth-century Texas, see Kelley, *Los Brazos de Dios*, 58–91, 93–102.

60. William Kennedy to Lord Aberdeen, Sept. 5, 1843, in Adams, *British Diplomatic Correspondence*, 259; Hollon, *William Bollaert's Texas*, 271–72.

61. Bianca Premo has found similar emotive language in her analysis of slaver society in eighteenth-century Peru ("As If She Were My Own," 71–82).

62. Smither, *Journals of the Sixth Congress*, 2:199; Hollon, *William Bollaert's Texas*, 271; *City Gazette*, Sept. 15, 1841; Weeks, *Debates of the Texas Convention*, 361–62, 365; Green, *Memoirs of Mary A. Maverick*, 66–68; Petition of Edward Teal (1839), Texas Memorials and Petitions; Memorial of Peggy Rankin, Oct. 25, 1841, Texas Memorials and Petitions.

63. Testimony of Laura Cornish, FWP TXN, part 1, 254; Testimony of Milly Forward, FWP TXN, part 2, 47; Testimony of Lou Turner, FWP TXN, part 4, 120; Testimony of Sarah Ford, FWP TXN, part 2, 43; Testimony of James Hayes, FWP TXN, part 2, 128.

64. Testimony of Martin Jackson, FWP TXN, part 2, 192; Testimony of Will Adams, FWP TXN, part 1, 1; Testimony of James Boyd, FWP TXN, part 1, 118; Testimony of Hagar Lewis, FWP TXN, part 3, 5; Testimony of Mollie Taylor, FWP TXN, part 3, 76.

65. Testimony of John McCoy, FWP TXN, part 3, 33.

66. To argue, in the words of Saidiya Hartman, that "kinship and captivity designate radically different conditions of embodiment" is to assume a very rigid definition of kinship. In the Texas borderlands, kinship was regularly a *means* of captivity (*Scenes of Subjection*, 84).

67. The literature on this topic is vast and continues to grow. See especially White, *Ar'n't I a Woman?*; Jennings, "'Us Colored Women'"; McLaurin, *Celia, a Slave*; Hartman, *Scenes of Subjection*, 79–112; Baptist, "'Cuffy,' 'Fancy Maids,' and 'One-Eyed Men'"; Block, *Rape and Sexual Power in Early America*, 65–74.

68. Testimony of Stearlin Arnwine, FWP TXN, part 1, 31; Testimony of J. W. Terrill, FWP TXN, part 4, 80; Testimony of Auntie Thomas Johns, FWP TXN, part 2, 205; Jordan, "W. Steinert's View of Texas in 1849" (Apr. 1977), 408–10. For a discussion of slave "concubines," see Schoen, "The Free Negro in the Republic, III," 98–99, 111–13. Sarah Black accused her slaveholding husband of having "illicit sexual intercourse" with multiple enslaved women on their large plantation in Brazoria. Sarah H. Black vs. James E. Black, Mar. 26, 1855, Brazoria County Courthouse Records, Angleton, TX, Case no. 1835.

69. Stephanie Jones-Rogers has demonstrated how White slaver women were often complicit in this proxy violence. Stephanie Jones-Rogers, "Rethinking Sexual Violence and the Marketplace of Slavery: White Women, the Slave Market, and Enslaved People's Sexualized Bodies in the Nineteenth-Century South," in Berry and Harris, *Sexuality and Slavery*, 109–20.

70. Testimony of Katie Darling, FWP TXN, part 2, 279; Testimony of Silvia King, FWP TXN, part 2, 291.

71. John C. Graham to Samuel Maverick, Nov. 25, 1849, and A. Toutant to Samuel Maverick, July 18, 1856, both in Green, *Memoirs of Mary A. Maverick*, 118–20; Testimony of Jeptha Choice, FWP TXN, part 1, 218.

72. Testimony of Betty Powers, FWP TXN, part 3, 191. Thomas Foster has argued that the "labeling [of] certain enslaved men as 'stock men' or 'bulls'" also reinforced their dehumanization under slavery. Thomas A. Foster, "The Sexual Abuse of Black Men under American Slavery," in Berry and Harris, *Sexuality and Slavery*, 133.

73. Testimony of Lewis Jones, FWP TXN, part 2, 237; Testimony of William Byrd, FWP TXN, part 1, 182; Testimony of Adeline Marshall, FWP TXN, part 3, 47; Testimony of James Green, FWP TXN, part 2, 88. Suggesting the ubiquity of this violence, the 1860 U.S. Census reported 24,987 enslaved people of mixed-race origin. U.S. Census Bureau, *Population of the United States in 1860*, 486.

74. Tiya Miles (*Ties That Bind*, 46–60) has effectively argued both of these points in her work on the life of Doll, a Black woman who was enslaved by a Cherokee man by the name of Shoe Boots.

75. Pratt, *Galveston Island*, 89; Olmsted, *A Journey through Texas*, 123; Campbell, *An Empire for Slavery*, 146–47.

76. See, for instance, *Telegraph and Texas Register* (Houston), Mar. 20, 1839, Apr. 8, 1840; *Austin City Gazette*, May 27 and July 22, 1840, and Sept. 8, 1841; *Northern Standard* (Clarksville), Oct. 28, 1843, Nov. 27, 1844, Aug. 5, 1848, and Apr. 20, 1850; *State Gazette* (Austin), Sept. 7, 1850, Jan. 11, Mar. 1, and Apr. 5, 1851, Oct. 9, 1852; *Texian Advocate* (Victoria), Sept. 26, 1850; *San Antonio Ledger*, Apr. 21, 1853.

77. *City Gazette* (Austin), Apr. 15, 1840; *Northern Standard* (Clarksville), Oct. 21, 1843; Genovese, *Roll, Jordan, Roll*, 597–98.

78. *Telegraph and Texas Register* (Houston), July 10, 1839. Also see *Telegraph and Texas Register* (Houston), June 26 and July 24, 1839, and July 19, 1849; *Morning Star* (Houston), Apr. 3, 1840; *Northern Standard* (Clarksville), Oct. 28, 1843; *Texas State Gazette* (Austin), Oct. 18, 1850, Sept. 13 and Nov. 8, 1851.

79. Testimony of Harrison Beckett, FWP TXN, part 1, 55–56; Testimony of Anderson Edwards, FWP TXN, part 2, 5; Testimony of Harre Quarls, FWP TXN, part 3, 223.

80. Martin Jackson was most candid about the Jim Crow climate that loomed over the Federal Writers' Project interviews: "Lots of old slaves closes the door before they tell the truth about their days of slavery. When the door is open, they tell how kind their masters was and how rosy it all was. You can't blame them for this, because they had plenty of early discipline, making them cautious about saying anything uncomplimentary about their masters. I, myself, was in a little different position than most slaves, and as a consequence, have no grudges or resentment. However, I can tell you the life of the average slave was not rosy. They were dealt out plenty of cruel suffering." Testimony of Martin Jackson, FWP TXN, part 2, 189. For a critical discussion of the program itself (and the context in which it operated), see Musher, "Contesting 'The Way the Almighty Wants It,'" 1–23.

81. Testimony of Hagar Lewis, FWP TXN, part 3, 6.

82. Testimony of Austin Grant, FWP TXN, part 2, 83–84. For the torture of enslaved people, see Testimony of Julia Blanks, FWP TXN, part 1, 95–96; Testimony of Sarah (Sanders) Barclay, FWP TXN, part 1, 39–40; Testimony of John Barker, FWP TXN, part 1, 42; Testimony of Harriet Barrett, FWP TXN, part 1, 49; Testimony of Richard Carruthers, FWP TXN, part 1, 197; Testimony of Green Cumby, FWP TXN, part 1,

260; Testimony of Henry Lewis, FWP TXN, part 3, 9; Testimony of Gill Ruffin, FWP TXN, part 3, 264; Testimony of Bert Strong, FWP TXN, part 4, 71. For the murder of enslaved people, see Testimony of Ben Simpson, FWP TXN, part 3, 27; Testimony of Bill McRay, FWP TXN, part 3, 39.

83. Weeks, *Debates of the Texas Convention*, 363; Texas House of Representatives, *Journal of the House . . . Sixth Legislature*, 217–18.

84. Jordan, "W. Steinert's View of Texas in 1849" (July 1977), 65; Testimony of John Barker, FWP TXN, part 1, 43; Testimony of Stearlin Arnwine, FWP TXN, part 1, 32.

85. Nicholas Doran Maillard to Lord Palmerston, Sept. 15, 1840, in Adams, *British Diplomatic Correspondence*, 27.

86. Texian newspapers were filled with notices regarding the buying and selling of African Americans. See, for instance, *Telegraph and Texas Register* (Houston), Oct. 21, 1837, May 5, 1838, Apr. 10, 1839, Feb. 1, 1843, Oct. 21, 1847, Aug. 16, 1849, Mar. 17 1854; *Civilian and Galveston Gazette*, July 19, 1845; *Texian Advocate* (Victoria), Jan. 20, 1848, June 14, 1850; *San Antonio Ledger*, Oct. 6, 1853, Aug. 17, 1854; *Texas State Gazette* (Austin), Dec. 6, 1853, Feb. 13, 1854. For Ranger involvement in slave catching, see Olmsted, *A Journey through Texas*, 327. For an example of the fees collected by law enforcement agents, see Claim of John Breeding, Dec. 3, 1839, Texas Republic Claims, Audited Claims, Reel 11, No. 2751.

87. Francis Sheridan to Joseph Garraway, July 12, 1840, in Adams, *British Diplomatic Correspondence*, 25; Olmsted, *A Journey through Texas*, 119–20; Testimony of James Jackson, FWP TXN, part 2, 83; Campbell, *An Empire for Slavery*, 72.

88. Texas Republic Congress, *Journals of the House . . . First Congress, First Session*, 105; Weeks, *Debates of the Texas Convention*, 156–59; Guy M. Bryan to D. C. Dickinson, Nov. 19, 1851, in Texas House of Representatives, *Journal of the House . . . Fourth Legislature*, 135–36. The Texas Supreme Court was the only body of Anglo government that tempered Black legal subjugation. Yet even their efforts were on a tiny scale. See Nash, "The Texas Supreme Court and Trial Rights of Blacks."

89. Smither, *Journals of the Sixth Congress*, 2:219–20; Texas House of Representatives, *Journals of the House . . . First Legislature*, 373; Texas House of Representatives, *Journal of the House . . . Sixth Legislature*, 433–34; Texas House of Representatives, *Official Journal of the House . . . Seventh Biennial Session*, 178–79; Constitution of the Republic of Texas, 1836, and Constitution of the State of Texas, in Campbell, *The Laws of Slavery in Texas*, 52–55; Schoen, "The Free Negro in the Republic of Texas, III," 101–13; Schoen, "The Free Negro in the Republic of Texas, IV," 169–99. A city ordinance from Galveston was posted in the *Civilian and Galveston Gazette*, Mar. 17, 1842, and another from Austin was posted in the *Texas State Gazette* (Austin), Oct. 5, 1850. Also see Marks, "Community Bonds in the Bayou City."

90. Texas House of Representatives, *Journal of the House . . . Sixth Legislature*, 434–35.

91. Foundational studies include Stampp, "Rebels and Sambos"; Blassingame, *The Slave Community*; Genovese, *Roll, Jordan, Roll*; Stuckey, *Slave Culture*. Rucker's *The River Flows On* is a more recent but still exceptional intervention in the "slave agency" debate. Scholars from Black studies and other fields have highlighted "fugitivity" and "the politics of refusal" to reconceptualize Black responses to slavery and anti-Blackness in general. Fugitivity in this context speaks of ongoing tensions and aspirations of freedom, which might be impossible "experientially" as the specter of enslavement

always loomed. Elaborating these tensions, Tiffany Lethabo King has argued that under slavery Black bodies are "shifting, moving, and unstable figures that elude full knowability"; Black fugitivity is thus "the unpredictable movement of Black bodies," which, in the context of the borderlands, existed under the direct power of slavers and their proxies as well as outside of it (*The Black Shoals*, 108–24). See also Snorton, *Black on Both Sides*, 73, 82–83; Sojoyner, "Another Life Is Possible," 518; von Gleich, "African American Narratives of Captivity and Fugitivity."

92. The Victoria *Texian Advocate*, July 20, 1848, for instance, lamented the "dangerous and mischievous . . . negro Balls" that prevailed in their community. Campbell, *An Empire for Slavery*, 154–59.

93. Extralegal "punishment" reinforced the reality that in Texas laws were more declarations and spectacles of authority than actual mechanisms of enforcement. For examples of slave resistance and slaver reprisals, see McDonald, *Hurrah for Texas*, 51; *San Antonio Ledger*, Mar. 23, 1854; *Standard* (Clarksville), Aug. 13, 1853; Olmsted, *A Journey through Texas*, 120–21; *Texas State Gazette* (Austin), Sept. 3, 1853; Claim of William B. Gayle, May 19, 1840, Texas Republic Claims, Audited Claims, Reel 34, No. 4067; Claim of William Earl, May 3, 1841, Texas Republic Claims, Public Debt Claims, Reel 150, No. 164; Claim of J. Harris Catlin, Dec. 10, 1841, Texas Republic Claims, Audited Claims, Reel 16, No. 6798; Claim of R. W. Martin (1854), Texas Republic Claims, Public Debt Claims, Reel 170, No. 2853; Petition of William Grinder (1850), Texas Memorials and Petitions; Petition of John M. Story, Nov. 8, 1851, Texas Memorials and Petitions; Petition of James Ward, Oct. 18, 1853, Texas Memorials and Petitions; Memorial of Joseph Dougharty, Dec. 20, 1859, Texas Memorials and Petitions.

94. Campbell, *An Empire for Slavery*, 153–76.

95. Black efforts to escape from bondage during the Texas Rebellion (e.g., by seeking refuge among the ranks of the Mexican Army) presaged the omnipresence of Black flight in the decades that followed. Texas Congress, *Journals of the House . . . First Congress, First Session*, 136–37; Dimmick, *General Vicente Filisola's Analysis*, 88.

96. *Texas State Gazette* (Austin), Dec. 14, 1850.

97. For other accounts and examples of enslaved Black people seeking freedom among the various Native peoples of the Texas borderlands, see A. S. Lipsomb to B. E. Bee, Aug. 8, 1840, in Texas Republic Congress, *Appendix to the Journals of the House . . . Fifth Congress*, 12–13; Barnard E. Bee to John Forsyth, Dec. 15, 1840, PCRCT, vol. 17, 350; John H. Rollins to Orlando Brown, May 8, 1850, OIA LR, Roll 858; *Texas State Gazette* (Austin), Nov. 16, 1850; *Nacogdoches Chronicle*, July 12, 1853; Helen Blair Chapman to Emily Welles Blair, Oct. 1, 1850, in Coker, *The News from Brownsville*, 184; Dolbeare, *A Narrative of . . . Dolly Webster*, 16–17; Wahlstrom, *The Southern Exodus to Mexico*, 41.

98. *Texian Advocate* (Victoria), Mar. 6, 1851.

99. Nichols, "The Limits of Liberty," 43.

100. Green, *Journal of the Texian Expedition Against Mier*, 121–22, 157, 404.

101. *Northern Standard* (Clarksville), May 22, 1844; M. DuVal to P. H. Bell, Oct. 21, 1850, IPTS, vol. 5, 92. DuVal planned to enslave the Black people living among these Seminoles. See Miller, *Coacoochee's Bones*, 113–17.

102. Olmsted, *A Journey through Texas*, 324; *Texas State Times* (Austin), June 2, 1855.

103. Texas House of Representatives, *Journal of the House . . . Sixth Legislature*, 159–61; Texas House of Representatives, *Official Journal of the House . . . Seventh Biennial Session*, 274–75.

104. Testimony of Felix Haywood, FWP TXN, part 2, 132. Also see Kelley, "'Mexico in His Head,'" 717–18; Nichols, "The Limits of Liberty," 20–60; Nichols, *The Limits of Liberty*, 127–29; Tyler, "The Callahan Expedition"; Taylor, *An American-Mexican Frontier*, 33–39.

105. Nichols has deftly detailed the significance of Black fugitives in northern Mexico to Mexican authorities. (*The Limits of Liberty*, 157–60).

106. Nichols has argued that Mexican authorities and locals made the border a hard "line of liberty" for Black people in the borderlands. I am more skeptical, because, as Nichols himself explains, most Mexican authorities saw Black fugitives as tools to wield against an aggressive Anglo neighbor. In effect, Mexican officials valued Black bodies for their perceived fungibility, just like their Anglo-American counterparts. Nichols, *The Limits of Liberty*, 118–22, 127, 134–35, 140–43; Olmstead, *A Journey through Texas*, 323–25; Congreso General Constituyente, *Constitución Federal*, 25.

107. Nichols, *The Limits of Liberty*, 135–40, 155–61, 157 ("No black"), 196–203; Tyler, "The Callahan Expedition"; Olmstead, *A Journey through Texas*, 323; Jacoby, *The Strange Career of William Ellis*, 17.

108. *Texas State Gazette* (Austin), Sept. 9, 1854, Dec. 12, 1857 ("harbor").

109. The region, Alice L. Baumgartner has argued, was "claimed by two countries but effectively belong[ed] to neither" ("The Line of Positive Safety," 1108).

110. Nichols, *The Limits of Liberty*, 162.

111. George W. Hughes, who, as a member of the U.S. Army, marched across northern Mexico in 1846, implied that most *peones* were "of the aboriginal race (pure, or mixed in different degrees with Spanish blood)." George W. Hughes, *Memoir descriptive of the march of a division of the United States Army*, 1846, in U.S. Congress, *Executive Documents, Senate . . . Thirty-First Congress, First Session, No. 32*, 48–40; Nichols, *The Limits of Liberty*, 82; Valerio-Jiménez, *River of Hope*, 35–37; Harris, *A Mexican Family Empire*, 211.

112. Harris, *A Mexican Family Empire*, 58–78, 205–30.

113. *Texas State Gazette* (Austin), Sept. 9, 1854 ("thieves," "prowlers"), Apr. 10, 1858 (as valuable for lucrative trade and as cheap labor); John T. Porter to Editor of the *Sentinel*, Dec. 23, 1857, in Texas House of Representatives, *Official Journal of the House . . . Seventh Biennial Session*, 461–63 ("murderers," "plunderers"); Nichols, *The Limits of Liberty*, 87–90.

114. *Standard* (Clarksville), Sept. 9 and Oct. 21, 1854; *Texas State Gazette* (Austin), Sept. 2, 9, 16, 23, and Oct. 14, 1854; *San Antonio Ledger*, Sept. 21, 1854. Rebellion was not all Anglo-Americans feared, as legislators in 1853 also considered a bill "to prevent Mexicans from keeping negro women slaves as wives." Texas House of Representatives, *Journal of the House . . . Fifth Legislature*, part 2, 34.

115. According to Valerio-Jiménez, "Indebted laborers and runaway slaves shared a common 'weapon of the weak' (flight) and a view of the international border as a tool of freedom" (*River of Hope*, 185). Also see De León, *The Tejano Community*, 15, 28.

116. *Texas State Gazette* (Austin), Sept. 9, 1854 ("rascally"), Oct. 14, 1854 ("worthy Mexicans"), Apr. 21, 1855 ("half-negro"). *Gulf Key* quoted in *San Antonio Ledger and Texan*, June 30, 1860.

117. *Texas State Gazette* (Austin), Sept. 23, 1854, Nov. 28, 1857 ("intolerable nuisance"), Apr. 10, 1858; Petition from the Citizens of Webb and Starr Counties to P. H. Bell, Oct. 14, 1852, IPTS, vol. 5, 141–44; Olmsted, *A Journey through Mexico*, 164; De León, *They Called Them Greasers*, 68; Villanueva, *The Lynching of Mexicans in the Texas Borderlands*, 4; Montejano, *Anglos and Mexicans in the Making of Texas*, 26–27; Valerio-Jiménez, *River of Hope*, 136–37; Jacoby, *The Strange Career of William Ellis*, 18–22.

118. On the role of Texian-Mexico warfare, see Thompson, *Tejano Tiger*, 22–31; Ramos, *Beyond the Alamo*, 177–91; Nance, *After San Jacinto*, 113–41, 120. For accusations of treason, see Texas Republic Congress, *Appendix to the Journals of the House . . . Seventh Congress*, 18; De León, *They Called Them Greasers*, 49–54.

119. Although the origins of the epithet "greaser" are unclear, it obviously was meant to deride the darker skin color of most of the Hispanic people in the region. De León, *They Called Them Greasers*, 16. For other contemporary examples, see, for instance, *Texas Union* (San Augustine), Nov. 6, 1847; *Texian Advocate* (Victoria), Jan. 23, 1851; *Texas State Gazette* (Austin), July 23, 1853, and Apr. 21, 1855; *Southern Intelligencer* (Austin), Sept. 3, 1856.

120. McDonald, *Hurrah for Texas*, 94; Robert Weakley Brahan Jr., to John Donelson Coffee Jr., Jan. 20, 1855, in Boom, "Texas in the 1850s," 284.

121. Muir, *Texas in 1837*, 6–7. Also see Dresel, Journal, 1837–41, in Freund, *Gustav Dresel's Houston Journal*; 33; McDonald, *Hurrah for Texas*, 193; Diary of John Winfield Scott Dancy, 1836–56, John Winfield Scott Dancy Papers.

122. As the many Texian-authored histories of the nineteenth century reveal, the Spanish colonial period was prologue to the age of Anglo supremacy. See, for instance, Kennedy, *Texas*, 205–7, 217–34; Stiff, *A New History of Texas*, 14–19; Yoakum, *History of Texas*, 53–64; Barker, *A History of Texas and Texans*, 3–4.

123. Valerio-Jiménez, *River of Hope*, 65–67, 148–51; De León, *The Tejano Community*, 77–78, 90–96.

124. Weeks, *Debates of the Texas Convention*, 158–59.

125. U.S. Census Bureau, *1850 Slave Schedule*, Guadalupe County.

126. During his short stay in San Antonio, Olmsted noticed that "a few, of old Spanish blood, have purchased negro servants." He somehow knew, however, that "most of them regard slavery with abhorrence" (*A Journey through Texas*, 163). U.S. Census Bureau, *1850 Population and Slave Schedules*, Béxar County; U.S. Census Bureau, *1860 Slave Schedules*, Béxar County. Guadalupe County was also home to a few Hispanic slaveholders. See Gretchen, *Slave Transactions of Guadalupe County*, 5, 42, 96, 144–45, 157. For Tejano slaveholding in Victoria, see Jacoby, *The Strange Career of William Ellis*, 25.

127. Pedro de Ampudia to [Juan] Seguín, May 2, 1836 and Juan Seguín to Pedro de Ampudia, May 3, 1836, both in de la Teja, *A Revolution Remembered*, 137–38; *San Antonio Ledger*, Sept. 22, 1853; Olmsted, *A Journey through Texas*, 331–32.

128. Quoted in De León, *They Called Them Greasers*, 50.

129. Quoted in Thompson, *Tejano Tiger*, 75–76. Even though Taylor has supplied evidence of Mexican participation in slave catching, he claims that their assistance was "unusual" (*An American-Mexican Frontier*, 34).

Chapter 7

1. Testimony of Juan Vela Benavides, Aug. 2, 1873, in Velasco Ávila, *En manos de los bárbaros*, 65–69.

2. Speeches of Ohois and Puhacawakis, Feb. 15 and 16, 1848, in Robert Neighbors to W. Medill, Mar. 2, 1848, OIA LR, Roll 858.

3. On the narrative tropes of settler colonialism, as well as how it is "inevitably premised on the traumatic, that is, *violent*, replacement and/or displacement of indigenous Others," see Veracini, *Settler Colonialism*, 35–36, 75 (quote), 78–81; Hixson, *American Settler Colonialism*, 4, 17–20.

4. Although I believe the term "elimination" *does* have descriptive value in articulating settler colonial processes, I agree with Tiffany Lethabo King that it becomes euphemistic when used synonymously with "genocide" (*The Black Shoals*, 45, 65).

5. Specifically, Michael L. Tate has argued that "a majority of Texas captives were taken with the intention of adoption and were well treated after an initially harsh period of confinement" ("Comanche Captives," 235). Although Joaquín Rivaya-Martínez's analysis of Comanche slavery is certainly the most nuanced, even he has claimed that Comanche victims were "sometimes unexpectedly well treated" ("Captivity and Adoption among the Comanche Indians," 207). For other versions of the Comanche adoption thesis, see Wallace and Hoebel, *The Comanches*, 241–42; Rister, *Comanche Bondage*, 13; DeLay, *War of a Thousand Deserts*, 93–94.

6. In some ways, this point challenges Rivaya-Martínez's argument in "A Different Look at Native American Depopulation" (392) that Comanche raiding was not motivated by a slaving impulse. Even if enslaving people was not the main purpose of Comanche raiding into Mexico during these years, the people they forcefully procured, along with the animal booty, would have contributed to a broader slaving system.

7. Report of Standing Committee on Indian Affairs, Oct. 12, 1837, IPTS, vol. 1, 22–25.

8. Report of Standing Committee on Indian Affairs, Oct. 12, 1837, IPTS, vol. 1, 25–36.

9. Texas officials convinced Tonkawa leaders to sign another treaty several months later, reinforcing previous stipulations while emphasizing Anglo property rights. Treaty between the Republic of Texas and Tonkawas, Nov. 22, 1837, and Treaty between the Republic of Texas and Tonkawas, Apr. 10, 1838, IPTS, vol. 1, 28–29, 46–48.

10. Texians also secured a treaty with Wichitas in September 1838. This agreement emphasized trade relations and promised tribute for the Wichita people. Treaty between the Republic of Texas and Lipan Apaches, Jan. 8, 1838; R. A. Iron to Sam Houston, Mar. 14, 1838; Treaty between the Republic of Texas and Comanches, May 29, 1838; Treaty between the Republic of Texas and Wichitas, Sept. 2, 1838, all in IPTS, vol. 1, 30–32, 43 ("finest country"), 50–54; *Telegraph and Texas Register* (Houston), Mar. 17, 1838 ("full and undisturbed").

11. R. A. Iron articulated this fear to Sam Houston in March 1838, as did the *Telegraph and Texas Register*. R. A. Iron to Sam Houston, Mar. 14, 1838, IPTS, vol. 1, 43; *Telegraph and Texas Register* (Houston), Mar. 17, 1838.

12. Thomas Rusk to Jesse Watkins, Sept. 14, 1837, IPTS, vol. 1, 21–22.

13. H. G. Catlett to W. Medill, May 12, 1849, OIA LR, Roll 858; Robert Neighbors to George Manypenny, Aug. 6, 1853, OIA LR, Roll 859; La Vere, *Contrary Neighbors*, 106–26; DeLay, *War of a Thousand Deserts*, 107–8; Hämäläinen, *The Comanche Empire*, 152–56.

14. Robert Neighbors, "The Na-ü-ni, or Comanches of Texas," in Schoolcraft, *Information respecting the History Condition and Prospects of the Indian*, 126–31; DeLay, *War of a Thousand Deserts*, 47–49; Kavanagh, *Comanche Political History*, 383–86; Hämäläinen, *The Comanche Empire*, 172–73. According to Comanche historian Joseph Attocknie, the Kiowa-Comanche alliance was an act of generosity on the part of Comanches, who believed Kiowas had little to offer at the time of their peace agreement (Attocknie, *The Life of Ten Bears*, 31–38).

15. Attocknie argued that an 1838 repulsion of a Cheyenne attack convinced them of the futility of campaigns against Comanches, resulting in a "lasting alliance." Attocknie, *The Life of Ten Bears*, 39–54.

16. Hämäläinen, *The Comanche Empire*, 293–302; Kavanagh, *Comanche Political History*, 243–48; Attocknie, *The Life of Ten Bears*, 39–54.

17. DeShields, *Border Wars of Texas*, 172–81; Anderson, *The Conquest of Texas*, 129.

18. Anderson, *The Conquest of Texas*, 130–31; Alcée La Branche to John Forsyth, Nov. 10, 1838, in U.S. Congress, *Executive Documents, Senate, Thirty-Second Congress, Second Session, No. 14*, 9; *Telegraph and Texas Register* (Houston), June 12, 1839.

19. Brian DeLay found evidence of the capturing of over 240 Mexican individuals by Comanche raiders from 1831 to 1840 (*War of a Thousand Deserts*, 135–38, 317, 320–27; DeLay, "Independent Indians and the U.S.-Mexican War," 35–68). See also Kavanagh, *Comanche Political History*, 380–81.

20. Report of Standing Committee on Indian Affairs, Oct. 12, 1837, IPTS, vol. 1, 24.

21. Henry W. Karnes to Albert S. Johnston, Jan. 10, 1840, and Albert S. Johnston to William S. Fisher, Jan. 30, 1840, IPTS, vol. 1, 101–2, 105–6.

22. Hugh McLeod to Mirabeau Lamar, Mar. 20, 1840, in Texas Republic Congress, *Appendix to the Journals of the House . . . Fifth Congress*, 138; Attocknie, *The Life of Ten Bears*, 17 ("butcher knife"); *Galvestonian*, Apr. 3, 1840; *Telegraph and Texas Register* (Houston), Apr. 8 ("the rest," "drew their knives," "loss of the enemy") and 29, 1840; Anderson, *The Conquest of Texas*, 181–84.

23. Green, *Memoirs of Mary A. Maverick*, 25–34.

24. Linn, *Reminiscences of Fifty Years in Texas*, 338–42; *Austin City Gazette*, Aug. 12 ("town destroyed") and 19 ("every house"), 1840; Anderson, *The Conquest of Texas*, 187–88.

25. Linn, *Reminiscences of Fifty Years in Texas*, 342–44; *Austin City Gazette*, Aug. 19, 1840; Anderson, *The Conquest of Texas*, 188–89.

26. John H. Moore to B. T. Archer, Nov. 7, 1840, in *Austin City Gazette*, Nov. 11, 1840; Anderson, *The Conquest of Texas*, 190–91.

27. Hämäläinen, *The Comanche Empire*, 216–17.

28. *Austin City Gazette*, Mar. 31, 1841; Attocknie, *The Life of Ten Bears*, 56–59; Barnard E. Bee to John Forsyth, Dec. 15, 1840, in U.S. Congress, *Executive Documents, Senate, Thirty-Second Congress, Second Session, No. 14*, 52; A. M. M. Upshaw to William Armstrong, Sept. 13, 1841, in U.S. Congress, *Executive Documents, Senate, Twenty-Seventh Congress, Second Session, No. 1*, 340.

29. Anderson, *The Conquest of Texas*, 191–94; Sam Houston to the Texas Republic Congress, Dec. 20, 1841, in Smither, *Journals of the Sixth Congress*, 1:135–36.

30. Minutes of Council at Tehuacana Creek, Mar. 28–31, 1843, IPTS, vol. 1, 150–54, 158–60.

31. J. C. Eldredge to Sam Houston, June 2 and 11, and Dec. 8, 1843, and Agreement between Comanches and J. C. Eldredge, Aug. 9, 1843, IPTS, vol. 1, 212–18, 229, 257–58, 266–73.

32. Minutes of Council at the Falls of the Brazos, Oct. 7–9, 1844, and Treaty Signed in Council at Tehuacana Creek, Oct. 9, 1844, IPTS, vol. 2, 103–19.

33. Mopechucope to Sam Houston, Mar. 21, 1844, IPTS, vol. 2, 6–9.

34. Thomas G. Western to J. C. Neill, E. Morehouse, and Thomas I. Smith, Sept. 8, 1845, IPTS, vol. 2, 353–55.

35. Minutes of Council at the Falls of the Brazos, Oct. 7–9, 1844, IPTS, vol. 2, 103–14.

36. *Northern Standard* (Clarksville), May 20, 1845.

37. Foreman, "The Journal of Elijah Hicks," 85–92, 97–98; Treaty between the U.S. and Comanche, Ioni, Anadarko, Caddo, Lipan, Longwa, Waco, Keechi, Wichita, Tonkawa, and Tawakoni Tribes of Indians, May 15, 1846, IPTS, vol. 3, 43–61; Robert Neighbors to W. Medill, June 22, 1847, in U.S. Congress, *Executive Documents, House of Representatives, Thirtieth Congress, First Session, No. 8*, 893.

38. Robert Neighbors to W. Medill, Mar. 2, 1848, in U.S. Congress, *Executive Documents, House of Representatives, Thirtieth Congress, Second Session, No. 1*, 578; Treaty between the United States and Comanches et al., Dec. 10, 1850, and Treaty between the United States and Comanches et al., Oct. 25, 1851, IPTS, vol. 3, 130–36, 149–54.

39. For Comanche defensive attacks, see J. Pinkney Henderson to W. L. Marcy, Aug. 22, 1847, and Robert Neighbors to W. Medill, Aug. 5 and Dec. 19, 1847, OIA LR, Roll 858.

40. *Democratic Telegraph and Texas Register* (Houston), Apr. 20, 1848. For explicit Native awareness of Anglo genocidal efforts, see Robert Neighbors to W. Medill, Sept. 14, 1847, in U.S. Congress, *Executive Documents, House of Representatives, Thirtieth Congress, First Session, No. 8*, 901–903; Robert Neighbors to W. Medill, Mar. 2, 1848, in U.S. Congress, *Executive Documents, House of Representatives, Thirtieth Congress, Second Session, No. 1*, 582.

41. Robert Neighbors to W. Medill, Dec. 19, 1847, OIA LR, Roll 858 ("waylaying"); Robert Neighbors to W. Medill, Mar. 2, 1848, in U.S. Congress, *Executive Documents, House of Representatives, Thirtieth Congress, Second Session, No. 1*, 578–79 ("late occurrences"). For Native attacks, see Robert Neighbors to W. Medill, Aug. 5, 1847, in U.S. Congress, *Executive Documents, House of Representatives, Thirtieth Congress, First Session, No. 8*, 897; R. Jones to Zachary Taylor, June 26, 1848, OIA LR, Roll 858; *Texian Advocate* (Victoria), Oct. 19, 1848; *Democratic Telegraph and Texas Register* (Houston), Dec. 14, 1848, and Apr. 12 and July 5, 1849; George Brooke to R. Jones, Aug. 11 and Sept. 20, 1849, in U.S. Congress, *Executive Documents, House of Representatives, Thirty-First Congress, First Session, No. 5*, 140–41, 148.

42. H. G. Catlett to W. Medill, May 12, 1849, in U.S. Congress, *Executive Documents, Senate, Thirty-First Congress, First Session, No. 1*, 967–68; Bell quoted in *Texian Advocate* (Victoria), June 14, 1850; John Rollins to V. E. Howard, Feb. 26, 1850, OIA LR, Roll 858; *Texian Advocate* (Victoria), Oct. 10, 1850.

43. Negotiations between the United States and Comanches et al., Oct. 26–27, 1851, IPTS, vol. 3, 143; George T. Howard to Luke Lea, June 1 and 2, 1852, and Horace Capron to George T. Howard, Sept. 30, 1852, OIA LR, Roll 858.

44. *Texas State Gazette*, Feb. 28, 1854; Robert Neighbors to Charles Mix, Oct. 30, 1854, OIA LR, Roll 859; Robert Neighbors to George Manypenny, Jan. 8 and Mar. 20, 1855, and George Hill to Robert Neighbors, May 31 and Aug. 31, 1855, OIA LR, Roll 860.

45. Robert Neighbors to Charles Mix, Sept. 10, 1855, OIA LR, Roll 869.

46. Memucan Hunt to John Forsyth, July 18, 1837, in Garrison, *Diplomatic Correspondence of the Republic of Texas*, part 1, 248; Barnard E. Bee to John Forsyth, Dec. 15, 1840, PCRCT, vol. 17, 350; W. Gilpin to R. Jones, Aug. 1, 1848, in U.S. Congress, *Thirtieth Congress, Second Session*, 138; Dolbeare, *A Narrative of . . . Dolly Webster*, 22–24; Testimony of Francisco Treviño, Sept. 21, 1873, and Testimony of Cornelio Sánchez, July 4, 1873, both in Velasco Ávila, *En manos de los bárbaros*, 45–46, 52–53; Jordan, "W. Steinert's View of Texas in 1849" (Jan. 1977), 284; J. Van Horne to George Deas, Nov. 8, 1849, IPTS, vol. 5, 51; Hollon, *William Bollaert's Texas*, 358; A. S. Lipsomb to B. E. Bee, Aug. 8, 1840, in Texas Republic Congress, *Appendix to the Journals of the House . . . Fifth Congress*, 12; Texas House of Representatives, *Journals of the House . . . Extra Session—Third Legislature*, 64–67; John M. Richardson to W. Medill, Mar. 27, 1848, OIA LR, Roll 858; R. H. Chilton to S. Cooper, July 27, 1853, OIA LR, Roll 859; Rivaya-Martínez, "The Captivity of Macario Leal," 400; Kavanagh, *Comanche Political History*, 278–328; Hämäläinen, *The Comanche Empire*, 190, 222–32.

47. Negotiations between the United States and Comanches et al., Oct. 26–27, 1851, IPTS, vol. 3, 145 ("wandered"); George T. Howard to Luke Lea, June 1, 1852, OIA LR, Roll 858 ("fast passing"); Robert Neighbors to Charles Mix, Oct. 30, 1854, OIA LR, Roll 859; Hämäläinen, *The Comanche Empire*, 293–302; Kavanagh, *Comanche Political History*, 243–48.

48. Kavanagh, *Comanche Political History*, 329–31; Robert Neighbors to George Manypenny, Apr. 12, 1854, OIA LR, Roll 859; Attocknie, *The Life of Ten Bears*, 18, 71; Robert Neighbors to Charles Mix, Oct. 8, 1857, OIA LR, Roll 860.

49. Hämäläinen, "The Politics of Grass," 201–3; Robert S. Neighbors to George W. Manypenny, Sept. 16, 1853, in U.S. Commissioner of Indian Affairs, *Annual Report . . . 1853*, 186.

50. According to Rivaya-Martínez in "A Different Look at Native American Depopulation," Comanches experienced a net loss of people during their raids, which suggests that capturing people was not the principal aim of their expeditions. See also Hämäläinen, *The Comanche Empire*, 302–3.

51. *Weekly Journal* (Galveston), June 18, 1852; George Howard to Luke Lea, Mar. 23, 1852, OIA LR, Roll 858 ("Horses and Mules"); R. H. Chilton to S. Cooper, July 27, 1853 ("a people at war"), George Howard to George Manypenny, June 16, 1854, Robert Neighbors to Charles Mix, Oct. 30, 1854, ("serious depredations"), George Howard to Robert Neighbors, Nov. 1, 1854, and George Howard to Charles Mix, Nov. 1, 1854, all in OIA LR, Roll 859.

52. Persifor Smith to Adjutant General, Mar. 10, 1855, OIA LR, 859; W. E. Jones to E. M. Pease, July 5, 1855, IPTS, vol. 3, 222; Citizens of Bexar County petition to E. M. Pease, July 12, 1855, and Bexar County Committee to E. M. Pease, Sept. 1, 1855, IPTS, vol. 3, 224 ("almost overun"), 233 ("robbing").

53. Persifor F. Smith to S. Cooper, Mar. 14, 1855, in U.S. Congress, *Executive Documents, House of Representatives, Thirty-Fourth Congress, First Session, No. 1*, 53; E.

M. Pease to Persifor F. Smith, Sept. 5, 1855, IPTS, vol. 3, 235; John Baylor to Robert Neighbors, Jan. 1, 1856, OIA LR, Roll 860.

54. For the rationale behind the reservation system, see Robert Neighbors to Charles Mix, Oct. 30, 1854, OIA LR, Roll 859; Robert Neighbors to George Manypenny, Jan. 8, 1855, OIA LR, Roll 860; John Baylor to Robert Neighbors, June 30, 1856, OIA LR, Roll 860.

55. On the "civilizing" mission of the reservation system, see, for instance, Thomas Hawkins to Charles Mix, Oct. 30, 1858, OIA LR, Roll 861.

56. Robert Neighbors to J. W. Denver, Sept. 16, 1857, in U.S. Congress, *Executive Documents, Senate, Thirty-Sixth Congress, First Session, No. 11*, 551.

57. *Dallas Herald*, July 5, 1856; Robert Neighbors to George Manypenny, May 14, 1856, and Robert Neighbors to Charles Mix, Oct. 8, 1857, OIA LR, Roll 860.

58. John Baylor to Robert Neighbors, Jan. 1, May 24, and Aug. 10 and 17, 1856, OIA LR, Roll 860.

59. Robert Neighbors to J. W. Denver, Sept. 16, 1857, U.S. Congress, *Executive Documents, Senate . . . Thirty-Fifth Congress, First Session, No. 11*, 551–52.

60. John Smiley to Robert Neighbors, Nov. 3, 1857, OIA LR, Roll 860; Petition of Williamson County Citizens to Jacob Thompson, Dec. 5, 1857, OIA LR, Roll 861; Petition of Wise and Montague Counties Citizens to H. R. Runnels, Sept. 18, 1858, in U.S. Congress, *Executive Documents, House of Representatives, Thirty-Fifth Congress, Second Session, No. 27*, 61–62; E. M. Pease to Thomas C. Frost, Dec. 7, 1857, and H. R. Runnels to the Senate, Jan. 22, 1858, IPTS, vol. 3, 267, 270–71.

61. Robert Neighbors to J. W Denver, Jan. 30, 1859, in U.S. Congress, *Executive Documents, Senate, Thirty-Sixth Congress, First Session, No. 2*, 594; Resolutions of Weatherford Citizens, June 20, 1859, and Petition of Parker County Citizens, June 24, 1859, in U.S. Congress, *Executive Documents, Senate, Thirty-Sixth Congress, First Session, No. 2*, 684–86.

62. John S. Ford to H. R. Runnels, May 22, 1858, in U.S. Congress, *Executive Documents, House of Representatives, Thirty-Fifth Congress, Second Session, No. 27*, 17–21.

63. Report of Earl Van Dorn, Oct. 5, 1858, in U.S. Congress, *Executive Documents, House of Representatives, Thirty-Fifth Congress, Second Session, No. 27*, 51–53; Charles J. Whiting to John Withers, Oct. 2, 1858, in U.S. Congress, *Executive Documents, Senate, Thirty-Fifth Congress, Second Session, No. 1*, 269–70.

64. Earl Van Dorn to David E. Twiggs, May 13 and 31, 1859, in U.S. Congress, *Executive Documents, Senate, Thirty-Sixth Congress, First Session, No. 2*, 365–66, 368–71; Attocknie, *The Life of Ten Bears*, 19–21; Hämäläinen, *The Comanche Empire*, 312–13.

65. Texas House of Representatives, *Journal of the House . . . Sixth Legislature*, 113.

66. Muir, *Texas in 1837*, 168. For editorials, see, for instance, *Texian Advocate* (Victoria), Oct. 19, 1848; *Northern Standard* (Clarksville), July 14, 1849; *Democratic Telegraph and Texas Register* (Houston), Oct. 30, 1850. Texas House of Representatives, *Journal of the House . . . Fourth Legislature*, 14.

67. Prucha, *The Great Father*, 354–66; Harmon, "The United States Indian Policy in Texas." For contemporary examples, see, for instance, Treaty between the United States and Comanches et al., May 15, 1846, IPTS, vol. 3, 43–61; Horace Capron to Luke Lea, Feb. 18, 1853, and Robert S. Neighbors to George W. Manypenny, Aug. 6, 1853, OIA LR, Roll 859.

68. Robert Neighbors to D. E. Twiggs, July 17, 1857, in U.S. Congress, *Executive Documents, Senate, Thirty-Fifth Congress, First Session, No. 11*, 555 ("free intercourse"); Robert Neighbors to D. E. Twiggs, Jan. 18, 1858, OIA LR, Roll 861 ("sufficient military force").

69. Texas House of Representatives, *Official Journal of the House . . . Seventh Biennial Session*, 424.

70. Pierce M. Butler to Pahayuko, Dec. 11, 1843, and George T. Howard to Luke Lea, June 1, 1852, OIA LR, Roll 858; W. Medill to Robert Neighbors, Mar. 20, 1847, in U.S. Congress, *Reports of Committees, Senate, Thirtieth Congress, First Session, No. 171*, 2–3; Randolph B. Marcy and Robert Neighbors to George Manypenny, Sept. 30, 1854, OIA LR, Roll 859.

71. Barr, *Peace Came in the Form of a Woman*, 10; Hämäläinen, *The Comanche Empire*, 15–16; Brooks, *Captives and Cousins*, 17; Patricia C. Albers, "Symbiosis, Merger, and War: Contrasting Forms of Intertribal Relationships among Historic Plains Indians," in Moore, *The Political Economy of North American Indians*, 119–22; Anderson, *The Conquest of Texas*, 187, 223.

72. Minutes of Council at Tehuacana Creek, May 13, 1844, IPTS, vol. 2, 34–42. For Native use of a "brotherly" discourse, see, for instance, Speech of Bintah, Minutes of a Council at Tehuacana Creek, Apr. 27, 1844, IPTS, vol. 2, 21; Speeches of Ohois and Puhacawakis, Feb. 15 and 16, 1848, in Robert Neighbors to W. Medill, Mar. 2, 1848, OIA LR, Roll 858.

73. Contrast, for instance, the 1838 Texian-Comanche treaty (May 1838, IPTS, vol. 1, 50–52) and the comments of Thomas G. Western and James C. Neill during the council meetings in 1844 with Howard's military report in 1852 (Minutes of Council at Tehuacana Creek, Apr. 27 and May 13, 1844, IPTS, vol. 2, 20, 34–35; George T. Howard to Luke Lea, June 1, 1852, OIA LR, Roll 858). Elijah Hicks's journal notes from 1846 suggest a transition from brotherly language to a more paternalistic approach (Foreman, "The Journal of Elijah Hicks," 86–92).

74. P. H. Bell to G. M. Brooke, June 4, 1850, IPTS, vol. 3, 122–23 ("lively sympathy"); Mirabeau Lamar, Message to Both Houses, Dec. 21, 1838, PMBL, vol. 2, 352–53; *Nacogdoches Chronicle*, May 2, 1854. Also see Texas House of Representatives, *Official Journal of the House . . . Seventh Biennial Session*, 472

75. Revealing examples include Report of Col. Edward Burleson's Winter Campaign against the Comanches, Jan. 14, 1840, in Texas Republic Congress, *Appendix to the Journals of the House . . . Fifth Congress*, 128–31; Report of the Battle of Walker's Creek, J. C. Hays to M. C. Hamilton, June 16, 1844, in Texas Republic Congress, *Appendix to the Journals of the Ninth Congress*, 33; A. C. Norton to Captain Howe, Nov. 4, 1846; George M. Brooke to G. T. Wood, Aug. 11, 1849; R. E. Sutton to P. H. Bell, Jan. 8, 1850; W. W. Hudson to John H. King, Feb. 27, 1850; George M. Brooke to P. H. Bell, Mar. 6, 1850; Thomas C. Frost to H. R. Runnels, Feb. 8, 1858; John S. Ford to H. R. Runnels, May 22, 1858, all in IPTS, vol. 5, 20, 43–44, 63–65, 80–82, 86–87, 220–21, 233. Also see Olmsted, *A Journey through Texas*, 74–75; Utley, *Lone Star Justice*, 7–10; Anderson, *The Conquest of Texas*, 8–9.

76. A. Nelson to John S. Ford, May 21, 1858, IPTS, vol. 5, 232.

77. Smith, *From Dominance to Disappearance*, 128.

78. These Galvestonians were not alone; Capt. John Hart was also known for having a personal scalp collection. Pratt, *Galveston Island*, 71; Strickland, "History of Fannin County," 289.

79. Charles E. Barnard to George Barnard, May 25, 1858, OIA LR, Roll 861.

80. S. P. Ross to Robert S. Neighbors, May 1, 1859, and J. B. Plummer to the Assistant Adjutant General, May 23, 1859, both in U.S. Commissioner of Indian Affairs, *Report . . . 1859*, 271–72, 276–77. Around the same time, Capt. John Williams sent scalps to Governor Runnels, as he had promised. John Williams to H. R. Runnels, Jan. 4, 1859, IPTS, vol. 5, 304.

81. Quoted in Klos, "'Our People Could Not Distinguish One Tribe from Another,'" 615. George Baylor defended his scalping of Native people by claiming that it prevented them from reaching their afterlife paradise. Waller, "Colonel George Wythe Baylor," 27–28.

82. Martin, "From Texas to California in 1849," 131; Smith, "The Scalp Hunter in the Borderlands"; Stevens, "The Apache Menace in Sonora," 219–20; Smith, *Borderlander*, 68–124; Anderson, *The Conquest of Texas*, 232–33.

83. Notably, the term *pieza* was used to indicate both individual scalps and captives. Blyth, *Chiricahua and Janos*, 132, 146.

84. Such instances reveal the inherent flaw in this system of bodily mutilation: it was nearly impossible to distinguish between the scalps of one Native community over another. As Indian agent George Crawford astutely observed, the most "quiet and inoffensive" Native groups typically became the primary prey of these scalp hunters. George Crawford to Thomas M. Clayton, Nov. 8, 1849, OIA LR, Roll 858 and IPTS vol. 5, 54–55.

85. Green, *Memoirs of Mary A. Maverick*, 23; Deposition of Juan Seguín, Sept. 28, 1860, in de la Teja, *A Revolution Remembered*, 184. For examples of his previous record of anti-Indian campaigning, see Juan Seguín to Sam Houston, Mar. 9, 1836, and Juan Seguín to Albert Sidney Johnston, Apr. 10, 1837, both in de la Teja, *A Revolution Remembered*, 158, 167.

86. Proceedings of a Public Meeting of the Citizens of Webb County, Mar. 11, 1854, IPTS, vol. 5, 159–63.

87. *Northern Standard* (Clarksville), July 24, 1844.

88. Thompson, *Tejano Tiger*, 46–56. For another example of Anglo-Hispanic anti-Indian collaboration, see John C. Hays to B. T. Archer, July 1, 1841, John Salmon Ford Memoirs, 2:247.

89. Recognition of Service of Juan A. Zambrano by Barnard E. Bee, Oct. 26, 1837, and Land Warrant for Manuel M. Flores by Bee, Feb. 22, 1838, Barnard E. Bee Papers; Weeks, *Debates of the Texas Convention*, 406.

90. De la Teja, *A Revolution Remembered*, 50–51.

91. Nonetheless, escaping Anglo racialization of Hispanic people as Indian "savages" would remain a formidable undertaking. See, for instance, Helen Blair Chapman to Ebenezer Learned, Aug. 5, 1852, in Coker, *The News from Brownsville*, 296; *Texas in 1840*, 227.

92. Hugh McLeod to Mirabeau Lamar, Mar. 20, 1840, in Texas Republic Congress, *Appendix to the Journals of the House . . . Fifth Congress*, 138; Hugh McLeod to Mirabeau Lamar, Aug. 28, 1840, PMBL, vol. 3, 439 ("divide," "contented," "tractable"); Green, *Memoirs of Mary A. Maverick*, 31 ("domestics"). Also see Felix Huston to Branch Archer, Aug. 12, 1840, and Sept. 28, 1840, in Texas Republic Congress, *Appendix to the Journals of the House . . . Fifth Congress*, 141–45; John C. Hays to B. T. Archer, July 1, 1841, John Salmon Ford Memoirs, 2:247; Hollon, *William Bollaert's*

Texas, 229–30; Anderson, *The Conquest of Texas*, 133–34, 182–83, 190–91; Brown, *Indian Wars and Pioneers of Texas*, 83–84.

93. Sam Houston, Message to Congress, Dec. 24, 1842, in Texas Republic Congress. *Journals of the House . . . Seventh Congress*, 116. Elijah Hicks found Comanches enslaved among Anglo colonists in 1846 (Foreman, "The Journal of Elijah Hicks," 95). For a later instance of Anglo captive taking, see John S. Ford to H. R. Runnels, May 22, 1858, in U.S. Congress, *Executive Documents, House of Representatives, Thirty-Fifth Congress, Second Session, No. 27*, 19–20.

94. D. C. Dickson and H. P. Bee, Nov. 27, 1855, Texas House of Representatives, *Journal of the House . . . Sixth Legislature*, 114.

95. William Edwards, Committee on Military Affairs, Dec. 31, 1857, in Texas House of Representatives, *Official Journal of the House . . . Seventh Biennial Session*, 447.

96. Petition of Citizens of Bexar County to E. M. Pease, July 12, 1855, IPTS, vol. 3, 224.

97. The most prominent voice in this debate was Charles Ramsdell, who advanced his "natural limits" thesis in 1929. The Ramsdell thesis had various implications for historical analyses of chattel slavery's profitability, U.S. sectionalism, and the Civil War, but his key point was that slavery's relationship to a cotton-based economy *necessarily* would have prevented the successful spread of slavery to the western portions of North America. In his estimation, the arid (and semi-arid) lands of west Texas marked a geographical barrier that slavery could not cross ("The Natural Limits of Slavery Expansion," 155–56, 166–67). For challenges to the Ramsdell thesis, see, for instance, Dew, *Ironmaker to the Confederacy*; Starobin, *Industrial Slavery in the Old South*. Randolph Campbell is among those who dismiss the role of Native people. Although "Indians appeared to constitute a formidable barrier [to Anglo-American slavery's expansion] on the northwestern frontier," he argues, they were a "threat that could have been overcome in a reasonably short time" (*An Empire for Slavery*, 58–59).

98. *Northern Standard* (Clarksville), July 28, 1849 ("unlimited," "naturally"), and Apr. 13, 1850 ("last abiding home"); *Texian Advocate* (Victoria), June 14, 1850 ("finest"); *Texas State Gazette* (Austin), June 29, 1850; Jordan, "W. Steinert's View of Texas in 1849" (July 1977), 54.

99. Slave ownership statistics for Bexar, DeWitt, Goliad, Gonzales, Medina, and Nueces counties, where extensive Comanche raiding was reported during this period, reveal the determination of slaveholders. In 1850, there were 389 slaves in Bexar, 568 in DeWitt, 213 in Goliad, 601 in Gonzales, 28 in Medina, and 47 in Nueces. In 1860, there were 1,395 slaves in Bexar, 1,643 in DeWitt, 843 in Goliad, 3,168 in Gonzales, 106 in Medina, and 216 in Nueces. U.S. Census Bureau, *The Seventh Census of the United States*; U.S. Census Bureau, *Population of the United States in 1860*, 479–82.

100. Texas Republic Congress, *Journal of the House . . . Third Congress*, 40; Gaillardet, *Sketches of Early Texas and Louisiana*, 56; Abner S. Lipscomb to James Hamilton, Apr. 18, 1840, in Texas Republic Congress, *Appendix to the Journals of the House . . . Fifth Congress*, 279–80; John F. McKinney to H. L. Kinney, Jan. 3, 1849, and H. L. Kinney to William M. Williams, Jan. 11, 1850, both in Texas House of Representatives, *Journals of the House . . . Third Legislature*, 511–12, 493–504.

101. DeLay, *War of a Thousand Deserts*, 138.

102. Testimony of Macedonio Perales, Oct. 8, 1873, in Velasco Ávila, *En manos de los bárbaros*, 71.

103. The scalp bounties sponsored by Mexican states evidenced the genocidal nature of this violence.

104. Testimony of Abelino Fuentes, Sept. 27, 1873, Testimony of Cornelio Sánchez, July 4, 1873, Testimony of Jesus María Guzmán, June 20, 1873, Testimony of Macedonio Perales, Oct. 8, 1873, and Testimony of Macario Borrego, Oct. 4, 1873, in Velasco Ávila, *En manos de los bárbaros*, 50–53, 62, 71, 75.

105. William Bent to A. B. Greenwood, Mar. 17, 1860, in U.S. Congress, *Executive Documents, House . . . Thirty-Sixth Congress, First Session, No. 61*, 12; W. Gilpin to R. Jones, Aug. 1, 1848, in U.S. Congress, *Thirtieth Congress, Second Session. Ex. Doc. No. 1. House*, 139; Hollon, *William Bollaert's Texas*, 174, 191.

106. Bee's assessment, which identified a Comanche preference for enslaving Hispanic people, largely corresponds to comprehensive analyses of documented captive taking during this period (Hamilton P. Bee report, 1843, in Wilbarger, *Indian Depredations*, 45). According to Rivaya-Martínez, who has collected, collated, and interpreted individual reports of Comanche slaving during the nineteenth century, of the more than one thousand individuals whose captivity was documented, about 75 percent were people of Hispanic origin, while about 15 percent were Native people—Apaches, Karankawas, Tonkawas, and others—and the rest English speakers ("Captivity and Adoption among the Comanche Indians," 410).

107. Formerly enslaved individuals often highlighted the prevalence of slavery within Comanchería, as well as their particular roles as bondspeople within their host communities. For illuminating examples, see Robert Neighbors to George Manypenny, Nov. 21, 1853, OIA LR, Roll 859; Testimony of Fernando González, July 7, 1873, Testimony of Cornelio Sánchez, July 4, 1873, and Testimony of Jesus María Guzmán, June 20, 1873, in Velasco Ávila, *En manos de los bárbaros*, 34–35, 53–54, 63.

108. Because males could accumulate honor more easily than women could, "boys were desired rather than girls, as protectors." Notes on Herman Asenap, June 30–July 1, 1933, in Kavanagh, *Comanche Ethnography*, 34. For a discussion of Tabepete, see Rivaya-Martínez, "The Captivity of Macario Leal," 380–81.

109. Notes on Quassyah, July 5, 1933, in Kavanagh, *Comanche Ethnography*, 58; Notes on Tahsuda (undated), in Kavanagh, *Comanche Ethnography*, 420; Kavanagh, *Comanche Political History*, 31–40; Hämäläinen, *The Comanche Empire*, 278–79; DeLay, *War of a Thousand Deserts*, 118–22; Rivaya-Martínez, "The Captivity of Macario Leal," 391.

110. Scholars have begun to rethink the distinctions between *captivity*, *slavery*, and *adoption*, but the emphasis on adoption remains prominent in the literature. For a rethinking of adoption, see Cameron, *Invisible Citizens*; Carocci and Pratt, *Native American Adoption*; Pauline Turner Strong, "Captivity, Adoption, and Slavery Reconsidered," in Deloria and Salisbury, *A Companion to American Indian History*, 339–56. For emphases on the adoptive qualities of Comanche captivity, see Rister, *Comanche Bondage*, 13; Tate, "Comanche Captives," 235–37; Exley, *Frontier Blood*, 69; Anderson, *The Conquest of Texas*, 135–36.

111. Notes on Post Oak Jim, July 19, in Kavanagh, *Comanche Ethnography*, 210. On Comanche patriarchy, see Wallace and Hoebel, *The Comanches*, 234; Hämäläinen, *The Comanche Empire*, 247–50, 259–69. Francis Joseph Attocknie's discussion of Comanche cultural practices adds important nuance to this characterization. In his history, he recognized the prominence of polygyny but noted that "under certain fortunate

circumstances" women could wed more than one man "so long as it was kept within the family." Also, when a man abandoned a wife for another woman, "tribal custom had left a little recourse for a woman humiliated in this manner" (Attocknie, *The Life of Ten Bears*, 100, 153).

112. Green, *Memoirs of Mary A. Maverick*, 41–42; Gregg, *Commerce of the Prairies*, 2:43; Neighbors, "The Na-ü-ni, or Comanches of Texas," 132; Perrine and Foreman, "The Journal of Hugh Evans," 188; Abert, *Expedition to the Southwest*, 63; Rister, *Comanche Bondage*, 159; Wilson, *A Thrilling Narrative*, 15; Dolbeare, *A Narrative of . . . Dolly Webster*, 12.

113. Notes on Herman Asenap, June 30–July 1, 1933, Niyah, July 6, 1933, Frank Chekovi, Aug. 2, 1933, Atauvich, Aug. 7, 1933, Nemaruibetsi, Aug. 8, 1933, all in Kavanagh, *Comanche Ethnography*, 33–37, 67, 327, 351, 363.

114. Attocknie's discussion of "captives" in his oral history is suggestive. He often highlighted the adoptive nature of Comanche slavery while still pointing out the servile nature of captive experiences. His frequent characterization of Comanche captives as "faithful," moreover, echoes Anglo accounts of their "loyal" slaves (Attocknie, *The Life of Ten Bears*, 44, 56, 88–89, 101, 116, 141, 203–4).

115. Banta's comments about a Comanche-enslaved Black woman and her children (who "were born slaves" among the Comanches) challenge this point, although it is not clear if he is imposing his own assumptions about their slave status (*Twenty-Seven Years on the Texas Frontier*, 116).

116. Hämäläinen, "The Politics of Grass," 200.

117. Notes on Herman Asenap, July 7, 1933, in Kavanagh, *Comanche Ethnography*, 91; Attocknie, *The Life of Ten Bears*, 203. Writing in the 1850s, Heinrich Berghaus shared this interpretation: "With every [Comanche] tribe you find Mexicans, who, when they are grown up, have been trained to be brave warriors, and, as Comanches within the tribe, have even turned into worthy tribe members." Heinrich Berghaus, "Geographic Yearbook, 1851," in Gelo and Wickham, *Comanches and Germans on the Texas Frontier*, 104. George Catlin's characterization of Jesús Sánchez (His-oo-san-ches), supposedly a part-Comanche "half-breed," somewhat complicates this, however. According to Catlin, Comanches "generally have the most contemptuous feelings" towards such members of their society. Nonetheless, he admitted that Sánchez's war performance "commanded the highest admiration and respect of the tribe" (Catlin, *Letters and Notes*, 2:76). See also Rivaya-Martínez, "The Captivity of Macario Leal," 397.

118. For examples of the (usually but not always implied) sexual violence of Comanche captors, see H. Clay Davis to H. L. Kinney, Dec. 17, 1849, in Texas House of Representatives, *Journals of the House . . . Third Session*, 506; Banta, *Twenty-Seven Years on the Texas Frontier*, 116; Neighbors, "The Na-ü-ni, or Comanches of Texas," 132; Rister, *Comanche Bondage*, 164; Wilbarger, *Indian Depredations*, 18; Henry Hith to R. Jones, Sept. 4, 1851, OIA LR, Roll 858; Thomas Espy to Sam Houston, Feb. 15, 1860, IPTS, vol. 4, 8; Babb, *In the Bosom of the Comanches*, 34; Notes on Herkeyah, Aug. 14, 1933, in Kavanagh, *Comanche Ethnography*, 380–85. Also see Rivaya-Martínez, "Captivity and Adoption among the Comanche Indians," 207–11; DeLay, *War of a Thousand Deserts*, 121. Tate's ("Comanche Captives," 237) argument that Comanche society "condemned" sexual violence deserves reconsideration in light of Saidiya Hartman's (*Scenes of Subjection*, 81) point about Anglo-American sexual violence and

supposed slave consent: "As the enslaved is legally [i.e., by Anglo custom] unable to give consent or offer resistance, she is presumed to be always willing." Also see Block, *Rape and Sexual Power in Early America*, 63–74, 78–80.

119. Foreman, *Adventure on Red River*, 169. Sarah Ann Horn shared this sentiment: "I felt that the only remaining tie (my dear children) which bound me to this wretched planet, was among them [the Comanches] and while this was the case, I infinitely preferred remaining with or near them, to any other condition" (quoted in Rister, *Comanche Bondage*, 167).

120. The literature on Cynthia Ann Parker is vast. Interestingly, the experiences of her brother, John Parker, who was also captured, reveal how important gender was in determining the opportunities of captives. John was given the opportunity to prove himself as a fighter and accompanied his captors on raiding expeditions in Mexico, where he became a slaver himself. According to John Henry Brown, a contemporary who considered himself an authority on the lives of the Parkers, "he [John Parker] captured a Mexican girl and made her his wife" (*Indian Wars and Pioneers of Texas*, 41–43). Notes on Atauvich, Aug. 7, 1933, in Kavanagh, *Comanche Ethnography*, 351; Becker, "Comanche Civilization," 243–52; Selden, *Return: The Parker Story*; Exley, *Frontier Blood*, 133–44; Lin Holdridge, "Visual Representation as a Method of Discourse on Captivity, Focused on Cynthia Ann Parker," in Carocci and Pratt, *Native American Adoption*, 173–78.

121. Berghaus detailed the vast labors of Comanche women in his 1851 article, "Geographic Yearbook, 1851," 108.

122. Notes on Herman Asenap, July 7, 1933, Post Oak Jim, July 11, 13, 14, and 24, 1933, Niyah, July 27, 1933, Atauvich, Aug. 7, 1933, Tahsuda (undated), all in Kavanagh, *Comanche Ethnography*, 93, 135, 155, 166, 240, 279–80, 351, 407; Green, *Memoirs of Mary A. Maverick*, 39–40; Testimony of Herman Asanap, Oct. 30, 1937, Indian Pioneer Oral History Project, 3:187–88; Testimony of Francisco Treviño, Sept. 27, 1873, and Testimony of Cornelio Sánchez, July 4, 1873, in Velasco Ávila, *En manos de los bárbaros*, 50–53; David G. Burnet to H. R. Schoolcraft, Sept. 29, 1847, IPTS, vol. 3, 91–92; Rister, *Comanche Bondage*, 138, 156–57; Wilson, *A Thrilling Narrative*, 17; Hämäläinen, *The Comanche Empire*, 261, 309; Kavanagh, *Comanche Political History*, 41; DeLay, *War of a Thousand Deserts*, 92–94; Rivaya-Martínez, "The Captivity of Macario Leal," 389, 396–97.

123. Despite his emphases on the adoptive aspects of Comanche slavery, Attocknie sometimes hinted at the dishonored status of enslaved people, as when he discussed the "faithfulness" of a "nameless and usually despised Mexican captive" (Attocknie, *The Life of Ten Bears*, 116).

124. Rivaya-Martínez, "The Captivity of Macario Leal," 395; Green, *Memoirs of Mary A. Maverick*, 38; Notes on Niyah, July 10, 1933, Herkeyah (undated), both in Kavanagh, *Comanche Ethnography*, 124, 463; Vielé, *"Following the Drum,"* 159–60; David G. Burnet to H. R. Schoolcraft, Sept. 29, 1847, IPTS, vol. 3, 91–92; Wilson, *A Thrilling Narrative*, 15, 18; Dolbeare, *A Narrative of . . . Dolly Webster*, 10, 22–23, 25. Also see James S. Calhoun to Orlando Brown, Mar. 31, 1850, in Abel, *The Official Correspondence of James S. Calhoun*, 183.

125. Notes on Unidentified Consultant (undated), Post Oak Jim, July 17, 1933, Herkeyah (undated), all in Kavanagh, *Comanche Ethnography*, 190–91, 463; Testimony of Virginia (Webster) Simmons, Oct. 19, 1912, PCRCT, vol. 17, 358; Petition of Virginia

Simmons (undated), Texas, Memorials and Petitions; Rister, *Comanche Bondage*, 138, 144, 151–52, 155; Rivaya-Martínez, "The Captivity of Macario Leal," 387–88.

126. Notes on Rhoda Asenap, July 12, 1933, Nemaruibetsi, July 31, 1933, Tahsuda (undated), all in Kavanagh, *Comanche Ethnography*, 151, 295–96, 410.

127. Catlin, *Letters and Notes*, 2:75–75; Foreman, "The Journal of Elijah Hicks," 92; Berghaus, "Geographic Yearbook, 1851," 107; Hämäläinen, *The Comanche Empire*, 259–61; Rivaya-Martínez, "The Captivity of Macario Leal," 392.

128. Hollon, *William Bollaert's Texas*, 165–66; Dolbeare, *A Narrative of . . . Dolly Webster*, 24; *Telegraph and Texas Register* (Houston), Dec. 31, 1845; Foreman, "The Texas Comanche Treaty of 1846," 316; Foreman, "The Journal of Elijah Hicks," 70; George Howard to Luke Lea, June 1, 1852, OIA LR, Roll 858; John Rogers to Luke Lea, Dec. 27, 1851, OIA LR, Roll 858; William Hardee to George Deas, Aug. 29, 1851, OIA LR, Roll 858; A. G. Simmons to the Commissioner of Indian Affairs, Mar. 4, 1854, OIA LR, Roll 859; Robert Neighbors to George Manypenny, Apr. 12, 1854, OIA LR, Roll 859; Robert Neighbors to L. Ross, Sept. 24, 1857, OIA LR, Roll 860; Texas House of Representatives, *Official Journal of the House . . . Seventh Biennial Session*, 206–8; Notes on Atauvich, Aug. 7, 1933, Post Oak Jim (undated), both in Kavanagh, *Comanche Ethnography*, 351, 399; DeLay, *War of a Thousand Deserts*, 91–92.

129. James S. Calhoun, an Indian agent in New Mexico, was one of the few to make such a connection. See James S. Calhoun to Orlando Brown, Mar. 15, 1850, in Abel, *The Official Correspondence of James S. Calhoun*, 161.

130. William Hardee to George Deas, May 28, 1851, OIA LR, Roll 858; William Hardee to George Deas, Aug. 29, 1851, in U.S. Congress, *Executive Documents, Senate, Thirty-Second Congress, First Session, No. 1*, 122 ("give up their prisoners").

131. Tiffany Lethabo King's analysis helps to keep this Native-on-Black violence in perspective: "Claims to innocence on the part of Black or Indigenous people are disingenuous and deprive Black and Indigenous life of the agonizing texture and horrific choices that often had to be (and have to be) made to survive under relations of conquest" (*The Black Shoals*, xi).

132. One enslaved Black man used his shotgun to execute the Comanche *paraibo* Peta Nocona in late 1860. Anderson, *The Conquest of Texas*, 332; Green, *Memoirs of Mary A. Maverick*, 19; McDonald, *Hurrah for Texas*, 36; Banta, *Twenty-Seven Years on the Texas Frontier*, 59–60, 62; Sowell, *Early Settlers and Indian Fighters*, 537–38, 704.

133. *Telegraph and Texas Register* (Houston), Dec. 27, 1836 ("carried off"); *National Intelligencer* (Houston), Mar. 1, 1839 ("either killed or taken off"); *Austin City Gazette*, July 8, 1840 ("scalped"); John Forbes to H. R. Runnels, Jan. 13, 1858, OIA LR, Roll 861 ("barbarously murdered"). Also see Brown, *Indian Wars and Pioneers of Texas*, 79–80; Anderson, *The Conquest of Texas*, 187–88; Porter, *The Negro on the American Frontier*, 394–95.

134. Mark Allan Goldberg has pointed out Torrey's Trading Post No. 2 as a major trade hub where "Comanches regularly engaged in trade . . . supplying the local market with buffalo and deer hides, horses, and mules, as well as Mexican, Native, Anglo-American, and African American captives." It was through this trade, Goldberg argues, that Comanches indirectly "fueled black chattel slavery" ("Linking the Chains," 197, 200).

135. Treaty with the Indian Tribes of Texas, Dec. 10, 1850, in Watson, *Indian Treaties*, 5–19.

136. Treaty between the United States and the Comanche, Lipan, Mescalero, and Other Tribes of Indians, Oct. 28, 1851, IPTS, vol. 3, 151–52.

137. For Comanche interactions with the commodification of Black bodies, see Banta, *Twenty-Seven Years on the Texas Frontier*, 116; Brown, *Indian Wars and Pioneers*, 98; Perrine and Foreman, "The Journal of Hugh Evans," 189; Wilbarger, *Indian Depredations*, 269; Rivaya-Martínez, "Captivity and Adoption among the Comanche Indians," 410, 419, 443, 466–67; Dolbeare, *A Narrative of . . . Dolly Webster*, 20; Goldberg, "Linking the Chains," 203). On Comanche vocabulary, see Manuel García Rejón, *Vocabulario del Idioma Comanche* (1866), in Gelo, *Comanche Vocabulary*, 65.

Epilogue

1. Foreman, "The Journal of Elijah Hicks," 95.

2. For the origins of the Civil War as a contest over competing visions of White supremacy, see especially Du Bois, *Black Reconstruction*, 18–30; Baptist, *The Half Has Never Been Told*, 345–58, 366–91.

3. Dale Baum, "Slaves Taken to Texas for Safekeeping during the Civil War," in Grear, *The Fate of Texas*, 83–103; Campbell, *An Empire for Slavery*, 245.

4. Moneyhon, *Texas after the Civil War*, 6–8; Alwyn Barr, "Juneteenth," in Wilson, *The New Encyclopedia of Southern Culture*, 4:239–40.

5. Moneyhon, *Texas after the Civil War*, 21–24, 35–36, 47, 55–61, 80–84, 95; Crouch, *The Dance of Freedom*, 80–81, 95–109, 110 ("anomalous"). Some Anglo-Americans looked abroad, toward Cuba, Brazil, Mexico, and elsewhere, to preserve their exploitative, agricultural kingdom. See Wahlstrom, *The Southern Exodus to Mexico*, xvi–xxi, 11, 16, 21, 31, 34, 37, 55, 70.

6. Moneyhon, *Texas after the Civil War*, 101–2.

7. Barry Crouch's analysis of post–Civil War violence in Texas supports this interpretation: "The army had a difficult job trying to enforce order and protect the ex-slaves" (*The Dance of Freedom*, 100).

8. Blue, "A Parody on the Law," 1021–37; Crouch, *The Dance of Freedom*, 159–74; Blackmon, *Slavery by Another Name*, 92; David M. Oshinsky, "Convict Labor in the Post–Civil War South: Involuntary Servitude after the Thirteenth Amendment," in Tsesis, *The Promises of Liberty*, 104.

9. Potts, "The Convict Labor System of Texas," 88.

10. Thompson, *Cortina*, 61 ("murdering"); Wahlstrom, *The Southern Exodus to Mexico*, 75–76; Thompson, *Vaqueros in Blue and Gray*, 17–23.

11. Jerry Thompson has argued that Tejanos joined the Confederacy "for reasons less to do [with] states' rights or slavery and more with class and economics." It is worth noting, however, that many of the oldest Hispanic families in Texas—with their own histories of slaving and anti-Black violence—were represented in the ranks of the Confederacy. Thompson, *Vaqueros in Blue and Gray*, xii (Thompson quote), 25–31, 46 ("deeds"), 81, 130–92. Also see Thompson, *Tejanos in Gray*, xvi–xxvi.

12. Alonzo, *Tejano Legacy*, 195.

13. Leiker, *Racial Borders*, 36–41; Thompson, *Vaqueros in Blue and Gray*, 58–59; Foley, *The White Scourge*, 36–39.

14. Hispanic historical preservationists and scholars have long attempted to celebrate the role of Hispanic people in the making of Texas. The careers of Adina De

Zavala and Carlos Castañeda are illustrative. Roberts and Olsen, *A Line in the Sand*, 197–229; Cottraux, "Missed Identity," 1–106; Bacarisse, "A Dedication to the Memory of Carlos Eduardo Castañeda." Also see Hinton, "Manifest Destiny Meets Inclusion," 161–64. B. V. Olguín has demonstrated in "'Caballeros' and Indians" how even Tejano critiques of Anglo colonialism have obscured Hispanic complicity in borderlands colonial violence.

15. Hämäläinen, *The Comanche Empire*, 311–14, 315 ("war bands"), 329.

16. Hämäläinen, *The Comanche Empire*, 315–19; Brooks, *Captives and Cousins*, 323–24, 341–43; I. C. Taylor to Thomas Murphy, Sept. 30, 1866, U.S. Commissioner of Indian Affairs, *Report 1866*, 281. Also see Kiser, *Borderlands of Slavery*, 155–69.

17. Hämäläinen, *The Comanche Empire*, 322–41; Brooks, *Captives and Cousins*, 323–24, 338–39, 343–44.

18. Brooks, *Captives and Cousins*, 354.

19. Notes on Herkeyah, Aug. 13, 1933, in Kavanagh, *Comanche Ethnography*, 378–85.

20. Foreman, "The Journal of Elijah Hicks," 95.

Bibliography

Abbreviations

AGN PI	Archivo General de la Nación, *Provincias Internas.*
AP	Barker, ed. *Annual Report of the American Historical Association for the Year 1919: The Austin Papers.*
ASFG	Archivo de San Francisco el Grande.
BAO	Béxar Archives Online.
FWP TXN	Federal Writers' Project, *Slave Narratives.* "Texas Narratives."
IPTS	Winfrey and Day, eds. *The Indian Papers of Texas and the Southwest.*
NLBLA	Nettie Lee Benson Latin American Microforms Collection.
OIA LR	Office of Indian Affairs. *Letters Received by the Office of Indian Affairs.*
PCRCT	McLean, ed. *Papers of Robertson's Colony in Texas.*
PMBL	Gulick and Elliott, eds. *The Papers of Mirabeau Buonaparte Lamar.*

Archival Sources and Manuscripts

Archivo General de Indias, *Audencia de Guadalajara.* Vol. 62. Dolph Briscoe Center for American History, University of Texas, Austin. Box 2Q143.

Archivo General de la Nación, *Provincias Internas.* Vols. 22, 25, 28, 32, 64, 99, 100, 162, 224. Dolph Briscoe Center for American History, University of Texas, at Austin. Boxes 2Q202, 2Q203, 2Q204, 2Q205, 2Q206, 2Q211, 2Q215.

Archivo de San Francisco el Grande. Vols. 10, 12, 13, 18, 20, 23. Dolph Briscoe Center for American History, University of Texas at Austin. Boxes 2Q251, 2Q253, 2Q254, 2Q255.

Barnard E. Bee Papers. Dolph Briscoe Center for American History, University of Texas, Austin. Boxes 2Q432, 2Q433.

Béxar Archives Manuscripts. Dolph Briscoe Center for American History, University of Texas, Austin. Boxes 2S79, 2S81, 2S83, 2S143.

Béxar Archives Online. Dolph Briscoe Center for American History, University of Texas at Austin. http://cah.utexas.edu/projects/bexar/index.php.

Nettie Lee Benson Latin American Microforms Collection, University of Texas at Austin, FILM 24222.

Brazoria County Courthouse Records. Angleton, TX.

Moses Austin Bryan Papers. Dolph Briscoe Center for American History, University of Texas, Austin. Box 2N254S.

P. L. Buquor Papers, 1783–1829. Dolph Briscoe Center for American History, University of Texas, Austin. Box 2Q457.

Canary Islanders Records, trans. J. Villasana Haggard. Dolph Briscoe Center for American History, University of Texas, Austin. Box 2Q232.

John Winfield Scott Dancy Papers. Dolph Briscoe Center for American History, University of Texas, Austin. Box 3N186.

Julien Sidney Devereux Papers. Records of Ante-bellum Southern Plantations from the Revolution through the Civil War: Series G, Selections from the Barker Texas History Center, University of Texas at Austin. Microfilm Reel 36.

George Bernard Erath Papers. Dolph Briscoe Center for American History, University of Texas, Austin. Box 2Q507.

John Salmon Ford Memoirs, Vols. 1, 2. Dolph Briscoe Center for American History, University of Texas, Austin. Box 2Q510.

Indian Pioneer Oral History Project. Works Progress Administration. Western History Collections, University of Oklahoma, Norman. https://digital.libraries.ou.edu/whc/pioneer/.

Office of Indian Affairs. *Letters Received by the Office of Indian Affairs, 1824–81*. Texas Agency, 1847–59. Microcopy No. 234. Rolls 858–60. Washington, DC: National Archives and Records Service General Services Administration, 1958.

James Franklin Perry and Stephen Samuel Papers. Transcripts. Vols. 2, 3. Dolph Briscoe Center for American History, University of Texas, Austin. Boxes 2R135, 2R136.

Texas, Memorials and Petitions, 1834–1929. Texas State Library and Archives Commission. www.ancestry.com.

Texas Republic Claims. Texas State Library and Archives Commission. www.tsl.texas.gov/arc/repclaims/repintro.html.

Texas, Wills and Probate Records, 1833–1974. www.ancestry.com.

Published Sources

Abel, Annie Heloise, ed. *The Official Correspondence of James S. Calhoun,*

While Indian Agent at Santa Fé and Superintendent of Indian Affairs in New Mexico. Washington, DC: Government Printing Office, 1915.

———, ed. *Report from Natchitoches in 1807.* New York: Museum of the American Indian Heye Foundation, 1922.

Abert, James William. *Expedition to the Southwest: An 1845 Reconnaissance of Colorado, New Mexico, Texas, and Oklahoma.* Ed. H. Bailey Carroll. Lincoln: University of Nebraska Press, 1999.

Adams, Ephraim Douglass, ed. *British Diplomatic Correspondence concerning the Republic of Texas, 1838–1846.* Austin: Texas State Historical Association, 1918.

Addington, Wendell G. "Slave Insurrections in Texas." *Journal of Negro History* 35, no. 4 (October 1950): 408–34.

Alonso, Ana María. *Thread of Blood: Colonialism, Revolution, and Gender on Mexico's Northern Frontier.* Tucson: University of Arizona Press, 1995.

Alonzo, Armando C. *Tejano Legacy: Rancheros and Settlers in South Texas, 1734–1900.* Albuquerque: University of New Mexico Press, 1998.

Anderson, Gary Clayton. *The Conquest of Texas: Ethnic Cleansing in the Promised Land, 1820–1875.* Norman: University of Oklahoma Press, 2005.

———. *The Indian Southwest, 1580–1830: Ethnogenesis and Reinvention.* Norman: University of Oklahoma Press, 1999.

Appadurai, Arjun, ed. *The Social Life of Things: Commodities in Cultural Perspective.* Cambridge: Cambridge University Press, 1986.

Archivo General de la Nación. *Boletín del Archivo General de la Nación* 29, no. 3. Mexico City: Secretaria de Gobernación, 1958.

Aron, Stephen. *American Confluence: The Missouri Frontier from Borderland to Border State.* Bloomington: Indiana University Press, 2006.

Attocknie, Francis Joseph. *The Life of Ten Bears: Comanche Historical Narratives Collected by Francis Joseph Attocknie.* Ed. Thomas W. Kavanagh. Lincoln: University of Nebraska Press, 2016.

Austin, Stephen F. *Translation: Laws, Orders and Contracts, on Colonization, From January 1821, up to 1829; In Virtue of Which, Col. Stephen F. Austin Introduced and Settled Foreign Emigrants in Texas. With an Explanatory Introduction.* Columbia, TX: Borden & Moore, 1837.

Austin, Stephen F., ed. *Translation of the Laws, Orders and Contracts on Colonization, From January, 1821, Up to This Time: In Virtue of Which Col. Stephen F. Austin Has Introduced and Settled Foreign Emigrants in Texas: With an Explanatory Introduction.* San Felipe de Austin, TX: G. B. Cotten, 1829.

Ayer, Edward E., trans. *The Memorial of Fray Alonso de Benavides, 1630.* Ed. Frederick Webb Hodes and Charles Fletcher Lummis. Chicago: privately printed, 1916.

Babb, T. A. *In the Bosom of the Comanches: A Thrilling Tale of Savage Indian Life, Massacre, and Captivity.* 2nd ed. Dallas, TX: Hargreaves, 1923.

Bacarisse, Charles A. "Baron de Bastrop." *Southwestern Historical Quarterly* 58, no. 3 (January 1955): 319–30.

———. "A Dedication to the Memory of Carlos Eduardo Castañeda, 1896–1958." *Arizona and the West* 3, no. 1 (Spring 1961): 1–5.

Bakewell, P. J. *Silver Mining and Society in Colonial Mexico: Zacatecas, 1546–1700.* London: Cambridge University Press, 1971.

Bamforth, Douglas B. "An Empirical Perspective on Little Ice Age Climatic Change on the Great Plains." *Plains Anthropologist* 35, no. 132 (November 1990): 359–66.

Banta, William. *Twenty-Seven Years on the Texas Frontier.* Austin: Ben C. Jones, 1893; reprint, Prosser, WA: Ronald L. Curfman, 2005.

Baptist, Edward. "'Cuffy,' 'Fancy Maids,' and 'One-Eyed Men': Rape, Commodification, and the Domestic Slave Trade in the United States." *American Historical Review* 106, no. 5 (2001): 1619–50.

Baptist, Edward E. *The Half Has Never Been Told: Slavery and the Making of American Capitalism.* New York: Basic Books, 2014.

Barker, Eugene C. "The African Slave Trade in Texas." *Quarterly of the Texas State Historical Association* 6, no. 2 (October 1902): 145–58.

———, ed. *Annual Report of the American Historical Association for the Year 1919: The Austin Papers.* Vols. 1, 3. Washington, DC: Government Printing Office, 1924.

———, ed. "Descriptions of Texas by Stephen F. Austin." *Southwestern Historical Quarterly* 28, no. 2 (October 1924): 98–121.

———, ed. *A History of Texas and Texans by Frank W. Johnson, a Leader in the Texas Revolution.* Vol. 1. Chicago: American Historical Society, 1916.

———. "The Influence of Slavery in the Colonization of Texas." *Mississippi Valley Historical Review* 11, no. 1 (June 1924): 3–36.

———. *The Life of Stephen F. Austin: Founder of Texas, 1793–1836; A Chapter in the Westward Movement of the Anglo-American People.* Nashville, TN: Cokesbury Press, 1925.

———. *Mexico and Texas, 1825–1835.* Dallas, TX: P. L. Turner, 1928.

———. "Minutes of the Ayuntamiento of San Felipe de Austin, 1828–1832, I." *Southwestern Historical Quarterly* 21, no. 3 (January 1918): 299–326.

———. "Native Latin American Contribution to the Colonization and Independence of Texas." *Southwestern Historical Quarterly* 46 (January 1943): 317–35.

———. "Notes on the Colonization of Texas." *Southwestern Historical Quarterly* 27, no. 2 (October 1923): 108–19.

Barr, Juliana. "From Captives to Slaves: Commodifying Indian Women in the Borderlands." *Journal of American History* 92, no. 1 (June 2005): 19–46.

———. "Geographies of Power: Mapping Indian Borders in the 'Borderlands' of the Early Southwest." *William and Mary Quarterly* 68, no. 1 (January 2011): 5–46.

———. *Peace Came in the Form of a Woman: Indians and Spaniards in the Texas Borderlands.* Chapel Hill: University of North Carolina Press, 2007.

Bartlett, John Russell. *Personal Narrative of Explorations and Incidents in Texas, New Mexico, California, Sonora, and Chihuahua.* Vol. 1. New York: D. Appleton, 1854.

Basso, Keith H., ed. *Western Apache Raiding and Warfare: From the Notes of Grenville Goodwin.* Tucson: University of Arizona Press, 1971.

Baud, Michiel, and Willem Van Schendel. "Toward a Comparative History of Borderlands." *Journal of World History* 8 (Fall 1997): 211–42.

Baumgartner, Alice L. "The Line of Positive Safety: Borders and Boundaries in the Rio Grande Valley, 1848–1880." *Journal of American History* 101, no. 4 (March 2015): 1106–22.

Beasley, Nicholas M. "Domestic Rituals: Marriage and Baptism in the British Plantation Colonies, 1650–1780." *Anglican and Episcopal History* 76, no. 3 (September 2007): 327–57.

Becker, Daniel A. "Comanche Civilization with History of Quanah Parker." *Chronicles of Oklahoma* 1, no. 3 (June 1923): 241–52.

Beckert, Sven. *Empire of Cotton: A Global History.* New York: Vintage Books, 2014.

Bennett, Herman L. *Africans in Colonial Mexico: Absolutism, Christianity, and Afro-Creole Consciousness, 1570–1640.* Bloomington: Indiana University Press, 2003.

———. *Colonial Blackness: A History of Afro-Mexico.* Bloomington: Indiana University Press, 2009.

Berlandier, Jean Louis. *The Indians of Texas in 1830.* Ed. John C. Ewers. Trans. Patricia Reading Leclercq. Washington, DC: Smithsonian Institution Press, 1969.

———. *Journey to Mexico, during the Years 1826 to 1834.* Vol. 2. Trans. Sheila M. Ohlendorf, Josette M. Bigelow, and Mary M. Standifer. Austin: Texas State Historical Association, 1980.

Berlin, Ira. *Many Thousands Gone: The First Two Centuries of Slavery in North America.* Cambridge, MA: Belknap Press of Harvard University Press, 1998.

Berry, Daina Ramey, and Leslie M. Harris, eds. *Sexuality and Slavery: Reclaiming Intimate Histories in the Americas.* Athens: University of Georgia Press, 2018.

Bertleth, Rosa Groce. "Jared Ellison Groce." *Southwestern Historical Quarterly* 20, no. 4 (April 1917): 358–68.

Biesele, Rudolph Leopold. *The History of the German Settlements in Texas, 1831–1861.* Austin, TX: Press of Von Bockemann-Jones Co., 1930.

Binkley, William C. *The Texas Revolution.* Baton Rouge: Louisiana State University Press, 1952.

Blackburn, Robin. *The Overthrow of Colonial Slavery, 1776–1848.* London: Verso, 1988.

Blackhawk, Ned. "The Displacement of Violence: Ute Diplomacy and the Making of New Mexico's Eighteenth-Century Northern Borderlands." *Ethnohistory* 52, no. 4 (Fall 2007): 723–55.

———. *Violence over the Land: Indians and Empires in the Early American West.* Cambridge, MA: Harvard University Press, 2006.

Blackmon, Douglas A. *Slavery by Another Name: The Re-enslavement of Black Americans from the Civil War to World War II.* New York: Anchor Books, 2008.

Blakeslee, Donald J., ed. *Along Ancient Trails: The Mallet Expedition of 1739.* Niwot: University Press of Colorado, 1995.

Blassingame, John W. *The Slave Community: Plantation Life in the Antebellum South.* Oxford: Oxford University Press, 1972.

Blight, David W. *Race and Reunion: The Civil War in American Memory.* Cambridge, MA: Belknap Press, 2001.

Block, Sharon. *Rape and Sexual Power in Early America.* Chapel Hill: University of North Carolina Press, 2006.

Blue, Ethan. "A Parody on the Law: Organized Labor, the Convict Lease, and Immigration in the Making of the Texas State Capitol." *Journal of Social History* 43, no. 4 (Summer 2010): 1021–44.

Blumenthal, Debra. *Enemies and Familiars: Slavery and Mastery in Fifteenth-Century Valencia.* Ithaca, NY: Cornell University Press, 2009.

Blyth, Lance R. *Chiricahua and Janos: Communities of Violence in the Southwestern Borderlands, 1680–1880.* Lincoln: University of Nebraska Press, 2012.

Bolton, Herbert E., ed. *Athanase de Mézières and the Louisiana-Texas Frontier: 1768–1780.* Vols. 1, 2. Cleveland, OH: Arthur H. Clark, 1914.

Bolton, Herbert Eugene, ed. *Spanish Exploration in the Southwest: 1542–1706.* New York: Barnes & Noble, 1916.

———. *Texas in the Middle Eighteenth Century.* Berkeley: University of California Press, 1915.

Bonnassie, Pierre. *From Slavery to Feudalism in South-Western Europe.* Trans. Jean Birrell. Cambridge: Cambridge University Press, 1991.

Boom, Aaron M., ed. "Texas in the 1850s, as Viewed by a Recent Arrival." *Southwestern Historical Quarterly* 70, no. 2 (October 1966): 281–88.

Bowe, Eric E. *The Westo Indians: Slave Traders of the Early Colonial South.* Tuscaloosa: University of Alabama Press, 2005.

Brading, D. A., and Harry E. Cross. "Colonial Silver Mining: Mexico and Peru." *Hispanic American Historical Review* 52, no. 4 (November 1972): 545–79.

Bridges, Katherine, and Winston Deville, eds. and trans. "Natchitoches and the Trail to the Río Grande: Two Early Eighteenth-Century Accounts by Sieur Derbanne." *Louisiana History: The Journal of Louisiana Historical Association* 8, no. 3 (Summer 1967): 239–59.

Brinckerhoff, Sidney B., and Odie B. Faulk, eds. *Lancers for the King: A Study of the Frontier Military System of Northern New Spain, with a Translation of the Royal Regulations of 1772.* Phoenix: Arizona Historical Foundation, 1965.

Brister, Louis E. "Johann von Racknitz: German Empresario and Soldier of Fortune in Texas and Mexico, 1832–1848." *Southwestern Historical Quarterly* 99, no. 1 (July 1995): 48–79.

Britten, Thomas A. *The Lipan Apaches: People of Wind and Lightning.* Albuquerque: University of New Mexico Press, 2009.

Brooks, James F. *Captives and Cousins: Slavery, Kinship, and Community in the Southwest Borderlands.* Chapel Hill: University of North Carolina Press, 2002.

———. "'This Evil Extends Especially . . . to the Feminine Sex': Negotiating Captivity in the New Mexico Borderlands." *Feminist Studies* 22, no. 2 (Summer 1996): 25–55.

Brown, John Henry. *Indian Wars and Pioneers of Texas.* Austin, TX: L. E. Daniell, 189?

Brugge, David. *Navajos in the Catholic Church Records of New Mexico: 1694–1875.* Window Rock, AZ: Research Section Parks and Recreation Department, 1968.

Buckley, Eleanor Claire. "The Aguayo Expedition into Texas and Louisiana, 1719–1722." *Quarterly of the Texas State Historical Association* 15, no. 1 (July 1911): 1–65.

Buenger, Walter L., and Robert A. Calvert, eds. *Texas through Time: Evolving Interpretations.* College Station: Texas A&M University Press, 1991.

Buenger, Walter L., and Arnoldo De León, eds. *Beyond Texas through Time: Breaking Away from Past Interpretations.* College Station: Texas A&M University Press, 2011.

Bugbee, Lester G. "Slavery in Early Texas, II." *Political Science Quarterly* 13, no. 4 (December 1898): 648–68.

Byrd, Jodi A. *The Transit of Empire: Indigenous Critiques of Colonialism.* Minneapolis: University of Minnesota Press, 2001.

Byrd, Kathleen M. *Colonial Natchitoches: Outpost of Empires.* San Bernardino, CA: Xlibris, 2008.

Calloway, Colin G. *One Vast Winter Count: The Native American West before Lewis and Clark.* Lincoln: University of Nebraska Press, 2003.

Cameron, Catherine M., ed. *Invisible Citizens: Captives and Their Consequences.* Salt Lake City: University of Utah Press, 2008.

Campbell, Gwyn, Suzanne Miers, and Joseph C. Miller, eds. *Women and Slavery.* Vol. 2: *The Modern Atlantic.* Athens: Ohio University Press, 2008.

Campbell, Randolph B. *An Empire for Slavery: The Peculiar Institution in Texas, 1821–1865.* Baton Rouge: Louisiana State University Press, 1989.

———. *Gone to Texas: A History of the Lone Star State.* New York: Oxford University Press, 2003.

———, ed. *The Laws of Slavery in Texas: Historical Documents and Essays.*

Comp. William S. Pugsley and Marilyn P. Duncan. Austin: University of Texas Press, 2010.

Campbell, Randolph B., and Richard G. Lowe. *Wealth and Power in Antebellum Texas.* College Station: Texas A&M University Press, 1977.

Campbell, T. N. "The Cacaxtle Indians of Northeastern Mexico and Southern Texas." *La Tierra: Quarterly Journal of the Southern Texas Archaeological Association* 11 (1984): 4–20.

Cantrell, Gregg. *Stephen F. Austin, Empresario of Texas.* Austin: Texas State Historical Association, 2016.

Carlson, Avery Luvere. *A Banking History of Texas: 1835–1929.* 2nd ed. Ed. Michelle M. Haas. Corpus Christi, TX: Copano Bay Press, 2007.

Carocci, Max, and Stephanie Pratt, eds. *Native American Adoption, Captivity, and Slavery in Changing Contexts.* New York: Palgrave Macmillan, 2012.

Carson, James Taylor. *Searching for the Bright Path: The Mississippi Choctaws from Prehistory to Removal.* Lincoln: University of Nebraska Press, 1999.

Castañeda, Carlos E. *Our Catholic Heritage in Texas: 1519–1936.* Vol. 2. Austin, TX: Von Boeckmann-Jones, 1936.

———. *Our Catholic Heritage in Texas: 1519–1936.* Vol. 3. Austin, TX: Von Boeckmann-Jones, 1938.

———. *Our Catholic Heritage in Texas: 1519–1936.* Vol. 4. Austin, TX: Von Boeckmann-Jones, 1939.

———. *Our Catholic Heritage in Texas: 1519–1936.* Vol. 5. Austin, TX: Von Boeckmann-Jones, 1942.

———. *Our Catholic Heritage in Texas: 1519–1936.* Vol. 6. Austin, TX: Von Boeckmann-Jones, 1950.

———, ed. and trans. "A Trip to Texas in 1828." *Southwestern Historical Quarterly* 29, no. 4 (April 1926): 249–88.

———, ed. and trans. "Statistical Report on Texas." *Southwestern Historical Quarterly* 28, no. 3 (January 1925): 177–222.

Catlin, George. *Letters and Notes on the Manners, Customs, and Condition of the North American Indians: Written during Eight Years' Travel amongst the Wildest Tribes of Indians in North America.* Vol. 2. Philadelphia, PA: J. W. Bradley, 1859.

Chabot, Frederick C. *San Antonio and Its Beginnings.* San Antonio, TX: Artes Graficas, 1936.

———. *With the Makers of San Antonio: Genealogies of the Early Latin, Anglo-American, and German Families with Occasional Biographies.* San Antonio, TX: Artes Graficas, 1937.

Charney, Paul. "The Implications of Godparental Ties between Indians and Spaniards in Colonial Lima." *Americas* 47, no. 3 (January 1991): 295–313.

Chávez, Fray Angelico. "Comments concerning 'Tomé and Father J.B.R.'" *New Mexico Historical Review* 31, no. 1 (1956): 68–74.

Chávez-García, Miroslava. *Negotiating Conquest: Gender and Power in California, 1770s to 1880s*. Tucson: University of Arizona Press, 2004.

Chipman, Donald E., and Harriett Denise Joseph. *Spanish Texas: 1519–1821*. Rev. ed. Austin: University of Texas Press, 2010.

Chipman, Donald E., and Luis López Elizondo. "New Light on Felipe de Rábago y Terán." *Southwestern Historical Quarterly* 111, no. 2 (October 2007): 160–81.

Clayton, Lawrence A. *Bartolomé de las Casas: A Biography*. Cambridge: Cambridge University Press, 2012.

Clemmer, Richard O., et al., eds. *Julian Steward and the Great Basin: The Making of an Anthropologist*. Salt Lake City: University of Utah Press, 1999.

Clopper, J. C. "J. C. Clopper's Journal and Book of Memoranda for 1828." *Quarterly of the Texas State Historical Association* 13, no. 1 (July 1909): 44–80.

Coker, Caleb, ed. *The News from Brownsville: Helen Chapman's Letters from the Texas Military Frontier, 1848–1852*. Austin: Texas Historical Association, 1992.

Confer, Clarissa, Andrae Marak, and Laura Tuennerman, eds. *Transnational Indians in the North American West*. College Station: Texas A&M University Press, 2015.

Congreso General Constituyente. *Constitución Federal de los Estados Unidos Mexicanos sancionada y jurada por el Congreso General Constituyente el día 5 de febrero de 1857*. Mexico City: Imprenta de Ignacio Cumplido, 1857.

Conrad, Paul. "Empire through Kinship: Rethinking Spanish-Apache Relations in Southwestern North America in the Late Eighteenth and early Nineteenth Centuries." *Early American Studies: An Interdisciplinary Journal* 14, no. 4 (Fall 2016): 626–60.

Conrad, Paul Timothy. "Captive Fates: Displaced American Indians in the Southwest Borderlands, Mexico, and Cuba, 1500–1800." PhD diss., University of Texas at Austin, 2011.

Cope, R. Douglas. *The Limits of Racial Domination: Plebeian Society in Colonial Mexico City, 1660–1720*. Madison: University of Wisconsin Press, 1994.

Cottraux, Suzanne Seifert. "Missed Identity: Collective Memory, Adina De Zavala and the Tejana Heroine Who Wasn't." MA thesis, University of Texas at Arlington, 2013.

Cox, Isaac Joslin, ed. *The Journey of Rene Robert Cavelier*. Vol. 1. New York: Allerton, 1905.

Cramaussel, Chantal. *Poblar la frontera: La provincia de Santa Bárbara en Nueva Vizcaya durante los siglos XVI y XVII*. Zamora: El Colegio de Michoacán, 2006.

Crouch, Barry. *The Dance of Freedom: Texas African Americans during Reconstruction*. Ed. Larry Madaras. Austin: University of Texas Press, 2007.

Cruz, Gilbert R. *Let There Be Towns: Spanish Municipal Origins in the American Southwest, 1610–1810*. College Station: Texas A&M University Press, 1988.

Cuello, José. "The Persistence of Indian Slavery and Encomienda in the Northeast of Colonial Mexico: 157–1723." *Journal of Social History* 21, no. 4 (Summer 1988): 683–700.

Cunningham, Debbie S., ed. "The Domingo Ramón Diary of the 1716 Expedition into the Province of the Tejas Indians: An Annotated Translation." *Southwestern Historical Quarterly* 110, no. 1 (July 2006): 38–67.

Curlee, Abigail. "The History of a Texas Slave Plantation, 1831–63." *Southwestern Historical Quarterly* 26, no. 2 (October 1922): 79–127.

Curtin, Philip D. *The Rise and Fall of the Plantation Complex: Essays in Atlantic History.* 2nd ed. Cambridge: Cambridge University Press, 1998.

Curtis, Edward S. *The North American Indian: Being a Series of Volumes Picturing and Describing The Indians of the United States, the Dominion of Canada, and Alaska.* Vol. 9. Norwood, MA, 1913.

Davis, David Brion. *Inhuman Bondage: The Rise and Fall of Slavery in the New World.* Oxford: Oxford University Press, 2006.

———. *The Problem of Slavery in the Age of Revolution, 1770–1823.* New York: Oxford University Press, 1999.

Deer, Sarah. *The Beginning and End of Rape: Confronting Sexual Violence in Native America.* Minneapolis: University of Minnesota Press, 2015.

De la Teja, Jesús. *San Antonio de Béxar: A Community on New Spain's Northern Frontier.* Albuquerque: University of New Mexico Press, 1995.

———, ed., *Tejano Leadership in Mexican and Revolutionary Texas.* College Station: Texas A&M University Press, 2010.

De la Teja, Jesús F., ed. *A Revolution Remembered: The Memoirs and Selected Correspondence of Juan N. Seguin.* Austin: Texas State Historical Association, 2002.

De la Teja, Jesús, and Ross Frank, eds. *Choice, Persuasion, and Coercion: Social Control on Spain's North American Frontiers.* Albuquerque: University of New Mexico Press, 2005.

DeLay, Brian. "Independent Indians and the U.S.-Mexican War." *American Historical Review* 112, no. 1 (February 2007): 35–68.

———. *War of a Thousand Deserts: Indian Raids and the U.S.-Mexican War.* New Haven, CT: Yale University Press, 2008.

De León, Arnoldo. *The Tejano Community, 1836–1900.* Albuquerque: University of New Mexico Press, 1982.

———. *They Called Them Greasers: Anglo Attitudes toward Mexicans in Texas, 1821–1900.* Austin: University of Texas Press, 1983.

Del Hoyo, Eugenio. *Historia del Nuevo Reino de León.* Monterrey: Tecnológico de Monterrey, 2005.

Deloria, Philip J., and Neal Salisbury, eds. *A Companion to American Indian History.* Malden, MA: Blackwell, 2002.

DeShields, James T. *Border Wars of Texas: Being an Authentic and Popular Account, in Chronological Order, of the Long and Bitter Conflict Wages*

Between Savage Indian Tribes and the Pioneer Settlers of Texas. Tioga, TX: Herald Company, 1912.

Devereaux, Linda Ericson. "William Goyens: Black Leader in Early Texas." *East Texas Historical Association* 45, no. 1 (March 2007): 52–57.

Dew, Charles R. *Ironmaker to the Confederacy: Joseph R. Anderson and the Tredegar Iron Works.* New Haven, CT: Yale University Press, 1966.

Díaz del Castillo, Bernal. *The History of the Conquest of New Spain.* Ed. and trans. Davíd Carrasco. Albuquerque: University of New Mexico Press, 2008.

Dillon, Merton L. "Benjamin Lundy in Texas." *Southwestern Historical Quarterly* 63, no. 1 (July 1959): 46–62.

Dimmick, Gregg J., ed. *General Vicente Filisola's Analysis of José Urrea's Military Diary: A Forgotten 1838 Publication by an Eyewitness to the Texas Revolution.* Trans. John R. Wheat. Denton: Texas State Historical Association, 2007.

Documentos para la eclesiástica y civil de la provincia de Texas o Nuevas Philipinas, 1720–1779. Madrid: Ediciones José Porrúa Turanzas, 1961.

Dolbeare, Benjamin, ed. *A Narrative of the Captivity and Suffering of Dolly Webster among the Camanche Indians in Texas, With an Account of the Massacre of John Webster and his Party, as Related by Mrs. Webster.* New Haven, CT: Yale University Library, 1986.

Dowd, Gregory Evans. *A Spirited Resistance: The North American Indian Struggle for Unity, 1745–1815.* Baltimore, MD: Johns Hopkins University Press, 1992.

Du Bois, W. E. B. *Black Reconstruction in America: 1860–1880.* New York: Harcourt, Brace, 1935.

Dunn, William Edward. "Apache Relations in Texas, 1718–1750." *Quarterly of the Texas State Historical Association* 14, no. 3 (January 1911): 198–275.

Dysart, Jane. "Mexican Women in San Antonio, 1830–1860: The Assimilation Process." *Western Historical Quarterly* 7, no. 4 (October 1976): 365–75.

Einhorn, Robin L. *American Taxation, American Slavery.* Chicago: University of Chicago Press, 2006.

Engerman, Stanley L. "Some Considerations Relating to Property Rights in Man." *Journal of Economic History* 33 (1973): 43–65.

Estes, Nick. *Our History Is the Future: Standing Rock versus the Dakota Access Pipeline and the Long Tradition of Indigenous Resistance.* London: Verso, 2019.

Everett, Dianna. *The Texas Cherokees: A People between Two Fires, 1819–1840.* Norman: University of Oklahoma Press, 1995.

Ewers, John C., ed. *Report on the Indian Tribes of Texas in 1828.* Trans. Georgette Dorn. New Haven, CT: Yale University Library, 1972.

Exley, Jo Ella Powell. *Frontier Blood: The Saga of the Parker Family.* College Station: Texas A&M University Press, 2001.

Fanon, Frantz. *Black Skin, White Masks*. Trans. Richard Philcox. Paris: Éditions du Seuil: 1952; reprint, New York: Grove Press, 2008.

———. *The Wretched of the Earth*. Trans. Constance Farrington. New York: Grove Press, 1963.

Federal Writers' Project. *Slave Narratives: A Folk History of Slavery in the United States From Interviews with Former Slaves, Typewritten Records Prepared by the Federal Writers' Project, 1936–1938, Assembled by the Library of Congress Project Work Projects Administration for the District of Columbia Sponsored by the Library of Congress*. Vol, 16, parts 1–4. Washington, DC, 1941.

Fehrenbacher, Don E. *The Slaveholding Republic: An Account of the United States Government's Relations to Slavery*. Oxford: Oxford University Press, 2001.

Few, Joan. *Sugar, Planters, Slaves, and Convicts: The History and Archaeology of the Lake Jackson Plantation Brazoria County, Texas*. Gold Hill, CO: Few Publications, 2006.

Finkelman, Paul, ed. *Slavery and Law*. Madison, WI: Madison House, 1997.

Finkelman, Paul, and Joseph Calder Miller, eds. *Macmillan Encyclopedia of World Slavery*. Vol. 2. New York: Simon & Schuster Macmillan, 1998.

Flomen, Max. "Cruel Embrace: War and Slavery in the Texas Borderlands, 1700–1840." PhD diss., University of California, Los Angeles, 2018.

Flores, Dan. "Bison Ecology and Bison Diplomacy: The Southern Plains from 1800 to 1850." *Journal of American History* 78, no. 2 (September 1991): 465–85.

Fogel, Robert William. *Without Consent or Contract: The Rise and Fall of American Slavery*. New York: Norton, 1989.

Foley, Neil. *The White Scourge: Mexicans, Blacks, and Poor Whites in Texas Cotton Culture*. Berkeley: University of California Press, 1997.

Folsom, Bradley. *Arredondo: Last Spanish Ruler of Texas and Northeastern New Spain*. Norman: University of Oklahoma Press, 2017.

Forbes, Jack D. *Africans and Native Americans: The Language of Race and the Evolution of Red-Black Peoples*. 2nd ed. Urbana: University of Illinois Press, 1993.

———. *Apache, Navaho, and Spaniard*. Norman: University of Oklahoma Press, 1960.

———. "The Appearance of the Mounted Indian in Northern Mexico and the Southwest, to 1680." *Southwestern Journal of Anthropology* 15, no. 2 (Summer 1959): 189–212.

Foreman, Grant, ed. *Adventure on Red River: Report on the Exploration of the Headwaters of the Red River by Captain Randolph B. Marcy and Captain G. B. McClellan*. Norman: University of Oklahoma Press, 1937.

———, ed. "The Journal of Elijah Hicks." *Chronicles of Oklahoma* 13, no. 1 (March 1935): 68–99.

———. "The Texas Comanche Treaty of 1846." *Southwestern Historical Quarterly* 51, No. 4 (April 1948): 313–32.

Fornell, Earl Wesley. *The Galveston Era: Texas Crescent on the Eve of Secession.* Austin: University of Texas Press, 1961.

Foster, William C. *The Historic Native Peoples of Texas.* Austin: University of Texas Press, 2008.

———. *Spanish Expeditions into Texas, 1689–1768.* Austin: University of Texas Press, 1995.

———, ed., *Texas and Northeastern Mexico: 1630–1690.* Trans. Ned F. Brierley. Austin: University of Texas Press, 1997.

Foster, William C., Jack Jackson, and Ned F. Brierley, eds. "The 1693 Expedition of Gregorio de Salinas Varona to Sustain the Missionaries among the Tejas Indians." *Southwestern Historical Quarterly* 97, no. 2 (October 1993): 264–311.

Freund, Max, ed. and trans. *Gustav Dresel's Houston Journal: Adventures in North America and Texas, 1837–1841.* Austin: University of Texas Press, 1954.

Gaillardet, Frédéric. *Sketches of Early Texas and Louisiana.* Trans. and ed. James L. Shepherd. Austin: University of Texas Press, 1966.

Galán, Francis X. "The Chirino Boys: Spanish Soldier-Pioneers from Los Adaes on the Louisiana-Texas Borderlands, 1735–1792." *East Texas Historical Association* 46, no. 2 (2008): 42–58.

Gallay, Alan ed. *Indian Slavery in Colonial America.* Lincoln: University of Nebraska Press, 2009.

———. *The Indian Slave Trade: The Rise of the English Empire in the American South, 1670–1717.* New Haven, CT: Yale University Press, 2002.

Gammel, H. P. N., ed. *The Laws of Texas, 1822–1897.* Vol 1. Austin, TX: Gammel Book Company, 1898.

Garret, Julia Kathryn, ed. "Dr. John Sibley and the Louisiana-Texas Frontier, 1803–1814 (Continued)." *Southwest Historical Quarterly* 45, no. 4 (April 1942): 378–82.

Garrison, George, ed. *Diplomatic Correspondence of the Republic of Texas.* Part 1. Washington, DC: Government Printing Office, 1908.

Gelo, Daniel J., ed. and trans. *Comanche Vocabulary: Trilingual Edition.* Austin: University of Texas Press, 1995.

Gelo, Daniel J., and Christopher J. Wickham, with contributions by Heide Castañeda. *Comanches and Germans on the Texas Frontier: The Ethnology of Heinrich Berghaus.* College Station: Texas A&M University Press, 2018.

Genovese, Eugene D. *Roll, Jordan, Roll: The World the Slaves Made.* New York: Vintage Books, 1976.

Gerhard, Peter. *The North Frontier of New Spain.* Rev. ed. Norman: University of Oklahoma Press, 1991.

Gillmer, Jason A. *Slavery and Freedom in Texas: Stories from the Courtroom, 1821–1871.* Athens: University of Georgia Press, 2017.

Glasson, Travis. "'Baptism Doth Not Bestow Freedom': Missionary Anglicanism, Slavery, and the Yorke-Talbot Opinion, 1701–30." *William and Mary Quarterly* 67, no. 2 (April 2010): 279–318.

Goldberg, Mark Allan. *Conquering Sickness: Race, Health, and Colonization in the Texas Borderlands*. Lincoln: University of Nebraska Press, 2016.

Gomez, Michael A. *Exchanging Our Country Marks: The Transformation of African Identities in the Colonial and Antebellum South*. Chapel Hill: University of North Carolina Press, 1998.

Gordon, Lewis R. "Through the Zone of Nonbeing: A Reading of *Black Skin, White Masks* in Celebration of Fanon's Eightieth Birthday." *C. L. R. James Journal* 11, no. 1 (Summer 2005): 1–43.

Gray, Lewis Cecil. *History of Agriculture in the Southern United States to 1860*. Vol. 2. Washington, DC: Carnegie Institution, 1933.

Grear, Charles D., ed. *The Fate of Texas: The Civil War and the Lone Star State*. Fayetteville: University of Arkansas Press, 2008.

Green, Rena Maverick, ed. *Memoirs of Mary A. Maverick, Arranged by Mary A. Maverick and Her Son Geo. Madison Maverick*. Introduction by Sandra L. Myres. Lincoln: University of Nebraska Press, 1989.

Green, Thomas. *Journal of the Texian Expedition Against Mier; Subsequent Imprisonment of the Author; his Sufferings, and Final Escape from the Castle of Perote*. New York: Harper & Brothers, 1845.

Gregg, Josiah. *Commerce of the Prairies: Or the Journal of a Santa Fé Trader*. Vol. 2. New York: Henry G. Langley, 1844.

Guajardo, Dahlia Rose, et al., eds. and trans. *Slaves of Monterrey Nuevo León Mexico: Hundreds of Notary Documents*. San Antonio, TX: Los Bexareños Genealogical Society, 2010.

Gretchen, Mark. *Slave Transactions of Guadalupe County, Texas*. Santa Maria, CA: Janaway, 2009.

Gulick, Charles Adam, and Katherine Elliot, eds. *The Papers of Mirabeau Buonaparte Lamar*. Vol. 1. Austin, TX: A. C. Baldwin and Son, 1921.

———, eds. *The Papers of Mirabeau Buonaparte Lamar*. Vol. 2. Austin, TX: A. C. Baldwin and Son, 1922.

———, eds. *The Papers of Mirabeau Buonaparte Lamar*. Vol. 3. Austin, TX: Von Boeckmann-Jones Co., 1922.

Gutiérrez, Ramón A. *When Jesus Came, the Corn Mothers Went Away: Marriage, Sexuality, and Power in New Mexico, 1500–1846*. Stanford, CA: Stanford University Press, 1991.

Hackett, Charles Wilson, ed. *Historical Documents relating to New Mexico, Nueva Vizcaya, and Approaches Thereto, to 1773*. Vol. 3. Washington, DC: Carnegie Institution of Washington, 1937.

———. "The Marquis of San Miguel de Aguayo and His Recovery of Texas from the French, 1719–1723." *Southwestern Historical Quarterly* 49, no. 2 (October 1945): 193–214.

———, ed. *Pichardo's Treatise on the Limits of Louisiana and Texas: An Argumentative Historical Treatise with Reference to the Verification of the True Limits of the Provinces of Louisiana and Texas*. Vol. 2. Austin: University of Texas Press, 1934.

Hadley, Diana, Thomas H. Naylor, and Mardith K. Schuetz-Miller, eds. *The Presidio and Militia on the Northern Frontier: A Documentary History*. Vol. 2, part 2: *The Central Corridor and the Texas Corridor, 1700–1765*. Tucson: University of Arizona Press, 1997.

Hall, Gwendolyn Midlo. *Slavery and African Ethnicities in the Americas: Restoring the Links*. Chapel Hill: University of North Carolina Press, 2005.

Hämäläinen, Pekka. *The Comanche Empire*. New Haven, CT: Yale University Press, 2008.

———. "The Politics of Grass: European Expansion, Ecological Change, and Indigenous Power in the Southwest Borderlands." *William and Mary Quarterly* 67 (April 2010): 173–208.

Hämäläinen, Pekka, and Samuel Truett. "On Borderlands." *Journal of American History* 98, no. 2 (September 2011): 338–61.

Hamilton, William B. "The Southwestern Frontier, 1795–1817: An Essay in Social History." *Journal of Southern History* 10, no. 4 (November 1944): 389–403.

Hammond, George P., and Agapito Rey, trans. *Apostolic Chronicle of Juan Domingo Arricivita: The Franciscan Mission Frontier in the Eighteenth Century in Arizona, Texas, and the Californias*. Vol. 2. Berkeley, CA: Academy of American Franciscan History, 1996.

Harmon, George D. "The United States Indian Policy in Texas, 1845–1860." *Mississippi Valley Historical Review* 17, no. 3 (December 1930): 377–403.

Harris, Charles H. *A Mexican Family Empire: The* Latfundio *of the Sánchez Navarros, 1765–1867*. Austin: University of Texas Press, 1975.

Hartman, Saidiya V. *Scenes of Subjection: Terror, Slavery, and Self-Making in Nineteenth-Century America*. New York: Oxford University Press, 1997.

Hatcher, Mattie Austin, trans. "Descriptions of Tejas or Asinai Indians, 1691–1722, I." *Southwestern Historical Quarterly* 30, no. 3 (January 1927): 206–18.

———, trans. "The Expedition of Don Domingo Terán de los Rios into Texas (1691–1692)." *Preliminary Studies of the Texas Catholic Historical Society* 2, no. 1 (January 1932): 3–67.

———. *The Opening of Texas to Foreign Settlement, 1801–1821*. Austin: University of Texas Press, 1912.

———, ed. "Texas in 1820." *Southwestern Historical Quarterly* 23, no. 1 (July 1919): 47–68.

Haynes, Sam W., and Gerald D. Saxon, eds. *Contested Empire: Rethinking the Texas Revolution*. College Station: Texas A&M University Press, 2015.

Henderson, Mary Virginia. "Minor Empresario Contracts for the Colonization of Texas, 1825–1834, Part 1." *Southwestern Historical Quarterly* 31, no. 4 (April 1928): 295–324.

———. "Minor Empresario Contracts for the Colonization of Texas, 1825–1834, Part 2." *Southwestern Historical Quarterly* 32, no. 1 (July 1928): 1–28.

Hickerson, Nancy Parrott. *The Jumanos: Hunters and Traders of the South Plains.* Austin: University of Texas Press, 1994.

Hinton, Kip Austin. "Manifest Destiny Meets Inclusion: Texas Nationalism at the Alamo." *Journal of Tourism and Cultural Change* 11, no. 3 (July 2013): 153–69.

Hixson, Walter L. *American Settler Colonialism: A History.* New York: Palgrave Macmillan, 2013.

Hodge, Adam R. *Ecology and Ethnogenesis: An Environmental History of the Wind River Shoshones, 1000–1868.* Lincoln: University of Nebraska Press, 2019.

Hoffmann, Fritz Leo, ed. *Diary of the Alarcón Expedition into Texas, 1719–1719.* Los Angeles, CA: Quivira Society, 1967.

———. trans. "The Mezquía Diary of the Alarcon Expedition into Texas, 1718." *Southwestern Historical Quarterly* 41, no. 4 (April 1938): 312–23.

Hogan, William Ransom. *The Texas Republic: A Social and Economic History.* Austin: University of Texas Press, 1946.

Hoijer, Harry. "The History and Customs of the Lipan, as Told by Augustina Zuazua." *Linguistics* 161 (1975): 5–38.

Holbrook, Abigail Curlee. "Cotton Marketing in Antebellum Texas." *Southwestern Historical Quarterly* 73, no. 4 (April 1970): 431–55.

Holley, Mary Austin. *Texas: A Facsimile Reproduction of the Original.* Austin, TX: Steck, 1935.

———. *Texas: Observations, Historical, Geographical and Descriptive, In a Series of Letters, Written during a Visit to Austin's Colony, with a View on a Permanent Settlement, in the Autumn of 1831.* Baltimore, MD: Armstrong & Plaskitt, 1833.

Hollon, W. Eugene, ed. *William Bollaert's Texas.* Norman: University of Oklahoma Press, 1956.

Hoonhout, Bram, and Thomas Mareite. "Freedom at the Fringes? Slave Flight and Empire-Building in the Early Modern Spanish Borderlands of Essequibo-Venezuela and Louisiana-Texas." *Slavery & Abolition* 40, no. 1 (2019): 61–86.

Hopkins, Keith. *Conquerors and Slaves.* Cambridge: Cambridge University Press, 1978.

Horne, Gerald. *The Counter-Revolution of 1776: Slave Resistance and the Origins of the United States of America.* New York: New York University Press, 2014.

Horsman, Reginald. *Race and Manifest Destiny: The Origins of American Racial Anglo-Saxonism.* Cambridge, MA: Harvard University Press, 1981.

Horstman, Connie, and Donald V. Kurtz. "Compadrazgo and Adaptation in

Sixteenth Century Central Mexico." *Journal of Anthropological Research* 35, no. 3 (Autumn 1979): 361–72.

Howe, Daniel Walker. *What Hath God Wrought: The Transformation of America, 1815–1848.* Oxford: Oxford University Press, 2007.

Howren, Alleine. "Causes and Origin of the Decree of April 6, 1830." *Southwestern Historical Quarterly* 16, no. 4 (April 1913): 378–422.

Hunt, Richard S., and Jesse F. Randel. *A New Guide to Texas: Consisting of a Brief Outline of the History of Its Settlement, and the Colonization and Land Laws; A General View of the Surface of the Country; Its Climate, Soil, Productions, &c. with a Particular Description of the Counties, Cities, and Towns.* New York: Sherman & Smith, 1846.

Jackson, Jack, ed. *Almonte's Texas: Juan N. Almonte's 1834 Inspection, Secret Report and Role in the 1836 Campaign.* Trans. John Wheat. Austin: Texas State Historical Association, 2003.

Jackson, Jack. *Los Mesteños: Spanish Ranching in Texas, 1721–1821.* College Station: Texas A&M University Press, 1986.

Jackson, Jack, ed. *Texas by Terán.* Trans. John Wheat. Austin: University of Texas Press, 2000.

Jackson, Jack, and William C. Foster, eds. *Imaginary Kingdom: Texas as Seen by the Rivera and Rubí Military Expeditions, 1727 and 1767.* Austin: Texas Historical Association, 1995.

Jacoby, Karl. *Shadows at Dawn: A Borderlands Massacre and the Violence of History.* New York: Penguin Press, 2008.

———. *The Strange Career of William Ellis: The Texas Slave Who Became a Mexican Millionaire.* New York: Norton, 2016.

Jefferson, Thomas. *Message from the President of the United States, Communicating Discoveries Made in Exploring the Missouri, Red River, and Washita, by Captains Lewis and Clark, Doctor Sibley, and Mr. Dunbar; with a Statistical Account of the Countries Adjacent.* New York: Hopkins and Seymour, 1806.

Jennings, Thelma. "'Us Colored Women Had to Go through a Plenty': Sexual Exploitation of African-American Slave Women." *Journal of Women's History* 1, no. 3 (1990): 45–74.

John, Elizabeth A. H., ed. "Inside Comanchería, 1785: The Diary of Pedro Vial and Francisco Chaves." *Southwestern Historical Quarterly* 98, no. 1 (July 1994): 26–56.

———. *Storms Brewed in Other Men's Worlds: The Confrontation of Indians, Spanish, and French in the Southwest, 1540–1795.* College Station: Texas A&M University Press, 1975.

Johnson, Benjamin H., and Andrew R. Graybill, eds. *Bridging National Borders in North America: Transnational and Comparative Histories.* Durham, NC: Duke University Press, 2010.

Johnson, Walter, ed. *The Chattel Principle: Internal Slave Trades in the Americas*. New Haven, CT: Yale University Press, 2004.

———. *River of Dark Dreams: Slavery and Empire in the Cotton Kingdom*. Cambridge, MA: Belknap Press, 2013.

———. *Soul by Soul: Life inside the Antebellum Slave Market*. Cambridge, MA: Harvard University Press, 1999.

Jones, C. Allan. *Texas Roots: Agriculture and Rural Life before the Civil War*. College Station: Texas A&M University Press, 2005.

Jones, Oakah L., Jr. *Los Paisanos: Spanish Settlers on the Northern Frontier of New Spain*. Norman: University of Oklahoma Press, 1996.

Jordan, Gilbert J., ed. "W. Steinert's View of Texas in 1849." *Southwestern Historical Quarterly* 80, no. 1 (July 1976): 57–78.

———, ed. "W. Steinert's View of Texas in 1849." *Southwestern Historical Quarterly* 80, no. 3 (January 1977): 283–301.

———, ed. "W. Steinert's View of Texas in 1849." *Southwestern Historical Quarterly* 80, no. 4 (April 1977): 399–416.

———, ed. "W. Steinert's View of Texas in 1849." *Southwestern Historical Quarterly* 81, no. 1 (July 1977): 45–72.

Jordan, Terry G. "The Imprint of the Upper and Lower South on Mid-Nineteenth-Century Texas." *Annals of the Association of American Geographers* 57, no. 4 (December 1967): 667–90.

Kavanagh, Thomas W., ed. *Comanche Ethnography: Field Notes of E. Adamson Hoebel, Waldo R. Wedel, Gustav G. Carlson, and Robert H. Lowie*. Lincoln: University of Nebraska Press, 2008.

———. *Comanche Political History: An Ethnohistorical Perspective, 1706–1875*. Lincoln: University of Nebraska Press, 1996.

Kearney, James C. *Nassau Plantation: The Evolution of a Texas German Slave Plantation*. Denton: University of North Texas Press, 2010.

Kelly, Edith Louise, and Mattie Austin Hatcher, eds. "Tadeo Ortiz de Ayala and the Colonization of Texas, 1822–1833, I." *Southwestern Historical Quarterly* 32, no. 1 (July 1928): 74–86.

Kelley, Sean M. *Los Brazos de Dios: A Plantation Society in the Texas Borderlands, 1821–1865*. Baton Rouge: Louisiana State University Press, 2010.

———. "'Mexico in His Head': Slavery and the Texas-Mexico Border, 1810–1860." *Journal of Social History* 37, no. 3 (Spring 2004): 709–23.

Kennedy, William. *Texas: The Rise, Progress, and Prospects of the Republic of Texas*. 2nd ed. London: R. Hastings, 1841.

Kenner, Charles L. *The Comanchero Frontier: A History of New Mexican–Plains Indian Relations*. Norman: University of Oklahoma Press, 1969.

Kessel, John L. *Kiva, Cross, and Crown: The Pecos Indians and New Mexico, 1540–1840*. Washington, DC: National Park Service, 1979.

Kicza, John E. "Patterns in Early Spanish Overseas Expansion." *William and Mary Quarterly* 49, no. 2 (April 1992): 229–53.

King, Tiffany Lethabo. *The Black Shoals: Offshore Formations of Black and Native Studies.* Durham, NC: Duke University Press, 2019.

———. "New World Grammars: The 'Unthought' Black Discourses of Conquest." *Theory & Event* 19, no. 4 (2016): https://muse.jhu.edu/article/633275.

Kinnaird, Lawrence, ed. *Spain in the Mississippi Valley, 1765–1794.* Vol. 2, part 1: *The Revolutionary Period.* Annual Report of the American Historical Association. Washington, DC: US Government Office, 1949.

Kiser, William S. *Borderlands of Slavery: The Struggle over Captivity and Peonage in the American Southwest.* Philadelphia: University of Pennsylvania Press, 2017.

Klein, Herbert S. *African Slavery in Latin America and the Caribbean.* New York: Oxford University Press, 1986.

Klos, George. "'Our People Could Not Distinguish One Tribe from Another': The 1859 Expulsion of the Reserve Indians from Texas." *Southwestern Historical Quarterly* 97, no. 4 (April 1994): 598–619.

Konetzke, Richard, ed. *Colección de documentos para la historia de la formación social de hispanoamérica: 1493–1810.* Vol. 1. Madrid: Consejo Superior de Investigaciones Cientificas, 1953.

Krauthamer, Barbara. *Black Slaves, Indian Masters: Slavery, Emancipation, and Citizenship in the Native American South.* Chapel Hill: University of North Carolina Press, 2013.

Kuykendall, J. H. "Reminiscences of Early Texans: A Collection from the Austin Papers." *Quarterly of the Texas State Historical Association* 6, no. 3 (January 1903): 236–53.

Lack, Paul D. "Slavery and the Texas Revolution." *Southwestern Historical Quarterly* 89, no. 2 (October 1985): 181–202.

———. *The Texas Revolutionary Experience: A Political and Social History, 1835–1836.* College Station: Texas A&M University Press, 1992.

Lauber, Almon Wheeler. *Indian Slavery in Colonial Times within the Present Limits of the Unites States.* New York: Columbia University Press, 1913.

La Vere, David. "Between Kinship and Capitalism: French and Spanish Rivalry in the Colonial Louisiana-Texas Indian Trade." *Southern Historical Association* 63, no. 2 (May 1998): 197–218.

———. *Contrary Neighbors: Southern Plains and Removed Indians in Indian Territory.* Norman: University of Oklahoma Press, 2000.

———. *The Texas Indians.* College Station: Texas A&M University Press, 2004.

Lawrence, Bruce B., and Aisha Karim, eds. *On Violence: A Reader.* Durham, NC: Duke University Press, 2006.

Lee, John, and Michael North, eds. *Globalizing Borderlands Studies in Europe and North America.* Lincoln: University of Nebraska Press, 2016.

Leiker, James N. *Racial Borders: Black Soldiers along the Rio Grande.* College Station: Texas A&M University Press, 2002.

Leroy, Justin. "Black History in Occupied Territory: On the Entanglements of

Slavery and Settler Colonialism." *Theory & Event* 19, no. 4 (2016): https://muse.jhu.edu/article/633276.

Leutenegger, Benedict, ed. *Journal of a Texas Missionary, 1767–1802: The* Diario Historico *of Fr. Cosme Lozano Narvais, Pen Name of Fr. Mariano Antonio de Vasconcelos.* Introduction by Marion A. Habig. Documentary Series No. 3. San Antonio, TX: Old Spanish Missions Historical Research Library, 1977.

———, trans. *Letters and Memorials of Fray Mariano de los Dolores y Viana, 1737–1762: Documents on the Missions of Texas from the Archives of the College of Querétaro.* San Antonio, TX: Old Spanish Missions Historical Research at Our Lady of the Lake University, 1985.

———, trans. *Letters and Memorials of the Father President Fray Benito Fernández de Santa Ana, 1736–1754: Documents on the Missions of Texas from the Archives of the College of Querétaro.* San Antonio, TX: Old Spanish Missions Historical Research Library at Our Lady of the Lake University, 1981.

Leutenegger, Benedict, et al., trans. *The San José Papers: Edited Primary Sources for the History of Mission San José y San Miguel de Aguayo, Part I, 1719–1791.* San Antonio, TX: Old Spanish Missions Historical Research Library at San José Mission, 1978.

Leutenegger, Benedict, et al., trans. *The San José Papers: The Primary Sources for the History of Mission San José y San Miguel de Aguayo from Its Beginning in 1720 to 1824, Part 3: July 1810–February 1824.* Ed. Carmelita Casso. Documentary Series No. 2. San Antonio, TX: Old Spanish Missions Historical Research Library, 1990.

Liles, Debbie. "Slavery and Cattle in East and West Texas." *East Texas Historical Journal* 52, no. 2 (Fall 2014): 29–38.

Limpscomb, Carol, trans. *After the Massacre: The Violent Legacy of the San Sabá Mission. With the Original Diary of the 1759 Red River Campaign.* Ed. Robert S. Weddle. Lubbock: Texas Tech University Press, 2007.

Linn, John J. *Reminiscences of Fifty Years in Texas.* Austin, TX: Steck, 1935.

Lira, Obed. "Wonder and the Ethics of Proximity in Las Casas's *Apologética historia sumaria.*" *Hispanic Review* 87, no. 3 (Summer 2019): 309–31.

Loomis, Noel M., and Abraham P. Nasatir. *Pedro Vial and the Roads to Santa Fe.* Norman: University of Oklahoma Press, 1967.

Lovejoy, Paul. *Transformations in Slavery: A History of Slavery in Africa.* Cambridge: Cambridge University Press, 2012.

Lowrie, Samuel Harman. *Culture Conflict in Texas, 1821–1835.* New York: Columbia University Press, 1932.

Lummis, Charles F., ed. "Some Unpublished History: A New Mexican Episode in 1748." *Land of Sunshine* 8 (May 1898): 74–78, 126–30.

Lundy, Benjamin. *The Life, Travels and Opinions of Benjamin Lundy, Including His Journeys to Texas and Mexico; With a Sketch of Contemporary Events, and a Notice of the Revolution in Hayti.* Philadelphia, PA: William D. Parrish, 1847.

[Lundy, Benjamin]. *War in Texas; A Review of Facts and Circumstances, Showing That This Contest Is a Crusade Against Mexico, Set on Foot and Supported by Slaveholders, Land-Speculators, &c* . . . 2nd ed. Philadelphia, PA: Merrihew and Gunn, 1837.

Maestas, Enrique Gilbert-Michael. "Culture and History of Native American Peoples of South Texas." PhD diss., University of Texas at Austin, 2003.

Magnaghi, Russell M. "Plains Indians in New Mexico: The Genízaro Experience." *Great Plains Quarterly* 10, no. 2 (Spring 1990): 86–95.

———, ed. "Texas as Seen by Governor Winthuysen, 1741–1744." *Southwestern Historical Quarterly* 88, no. 2 (October 1984): 167–80.

Majewski, John. *Modernizing a Slave Economy: The Economic Vision of the Confederate Nation.* Chapel Hill: University of North Carolina Press, 2009.

Manning, William R. "Texas and the Boundary Issue, 1822–1829." *Southwestern Historical Quarterly* 17, no. 3 (January 1914): 217–61.

Marks, John Garrison. "Community Bonds in the Bayou City: Free Blacks and Local Reputation in Early Houston." *Southwestern Historical Quarterly* 117, no. 3 (January 2014): 266–82.

Martin, Bonnie, and James F. Brooks, eds. *Linking the Histories of Slavery: North America and Its Borderlands.* Santa Fe, NM: School for Advanced Research Press, 2015.

Martin, Mabelle Eppard, ed. "From Texas to California in 1849: Diary of C. C. Cox." *Southwestern Historical Quarterly* 29, no. 2 (October 1925): 128–46.

Martín Casares, Aurelia, and Christine Delaigue. "The Evangelization of Freed and Slave Black Africans in Renaissance Spain: Baptism, Marriage, and Ethnic Brotherhoods." *History of Religions* 52, no. 3 (February 2013): 214–35.

Martínez, María Elena. *Genealogical Fictions: Limpieza de Sangre, Religion, and Gender in Colonial Mexico.* Stanford, CA: Stanford University Press, 2008.

Masich, Andrew. *Civil War in the Southwest Borderlands.* Norman: University of Oklahoma Press, 2017.

Mason, Kenneth. *African Americans and Race Relations in San Antonio, Texas, 1867–1937.* New York: Garland, 1998.

McClintock, Anne. *Imperial Leather: Race, Gender and Sexuality in the Colonial Contest.* New York: Routledge, 1995.

McComb, David G. *The City in Texas: A History.* Austin: University of Texas Press, 2015.

McCoy, Drew. *The Elusive Republic: Political Economy in Jeffersonian America.* Chapel Hill: University of Carolina Press, 1980.

McCurry, Stephanie. *Masters of Small Worlds: Yeoman Households, Gender Relations, and the Political Culture of the Antebellum South Carolina Low Country.* New York: Oxford University Press, 1995.

McDonald, Archie P., ed. *Hurrah for Texas: The Diary of Adolphus Sterne, 1838–1851.* Austin, TX: Eakin Press, 1986.

McDonald, David R., and Timothy M. Matovina, eds. *Defending Mexican Valor in Texas: José Antonio Navarro's Historical Writings, 1853–1867.* Austin, TX: State House Press, 1995.

McGhee, Fred Lee. "The Black Crop: Slavery and Slave Trading in Nineteenth Century Texas." PhD diss., University of Texas at Austin, 2000.

McKinley, Michelle A. *Fractional Freedoms: Slavery, Intimacy, and Legal Mobilization in Colonial Lima, 1600–1700.* Cambridge: Cambridge University Press, 2016.

McKnight, Joseph W. "Stephen Austin's Legalistic Concerns." *Southwestern Historical Quarterly* 89, no. 3 (January 1986): 239–68.

McLaurin, Melton A. *Celia, a Slave.* Athens: University of Georgia Press, 1991.

McLean, Malcolm D., ed. *Papers of Robertson's Colony in Texas.* Vol. 2. Fort Worth: Texas Christian University Press, 1975.

———, ed. *Papers of Robertson's Colony in Texas.* Vol. 3. Fort Worth: Texas Christian University Press, 1976.

———, ed. *Papers of Robertson's Colony in Texas.* Vol. 4. Arlington: University of Texas at Arlington Press, 1977.

———, ed. *Papers of Robertson's Colony in Texas.* Vol. 5. Arlington: University of Texas at Arlington Press, 1978.

———, ed. *Papers of Robertson's Colony in Texas.* Vol. 6. Arlington: University of Texas at Arlington Press, 1979.

———, ed. *Papers of Robertson's Colony in Texas.* Vol. 17. Arlington: University of Texas at Arlington Press, 1991.

McNitt, Frank. *Navajo Wars: Military Campaigns, Slave Raids, and Reprisals.* Albuquerque: University of New Mexico Press, 1972.

McWilliams, Carey. *North from Mexico: The Spanish Speaking People of the United States.* Philadelphia, PA: J. B. Lippincott, 1949.

Meacham, Tina Laurel. "The Population of Spanish and Mexican Texas, 1716–1836." PhD diss., University of Texas at Austin, 2000.

Menchaca, Martha. *Recovering History, Constructing Race: The Indian, Black, and White Roots of Mexican Americans.* Austin: University of Texas Press, 2001.

Meyer, Michael C., William L. Sherman, and Susan M. Deeds. *The Course of Mexican History.* 7th ed. New York: Oxford University Press, 2003.

Miers, Suzanne, and Igor Kopytoff, eds. *Slavery in Africa: Historical and Anthropological Perspectives.* Madison: University of Wisconsin Press, 1977.

Miles, Tiya. *Ties That Bind: The Story of an Afro-Cherokee Family in Slavery and Freedom.* Berkeley: University of California Press, 2005.

Miles, Tiya, and Sharon P. Holland, eds. *Crossing Waters, Crossing Worlds: The African Diaspora in Indian Country.* Durham, NC: Duke University Press, 2006.

Miller, Howard. "Stephen F. Austin and the Anglo-Texan Response to the Religious Establishment in Mexico, 1821–1836." *Southwestern Historical Quarterly* 91 (January 1988): 283–316.

Miller, Susan A. *Coacoochee's Bones: A Seminole Saga.* Lawrence: University Press of Kansas, 2003.

Minor, Nancy McGown. *The Light Gray People: Ethno-History of the Lipan Apaches of Texas and Northern Mexico.* Lanham, MD: University Press of America, 2009.

———. *Turning Adversity to Advantage: A History of the Lipan Apaches of Texas and Northern Mexico, 1700–1900.* Lanham, MD: University Press of America, 2009.

Mintz, Sidney W., and Eric R. Wolf. "An Analysis of Ritual Co-Parenthood (Compadrazgo)." *Southwestern Journal of Anthropology* 6, no. 4 (Winter 1950): 341–68.

Moneyhon, Carl. *Texas after the Civil War: The Struggle of Reconstruction.* College Station: Texas A&M University Press, 2004.

Montejano, David. *Anglos and Mexicans in the Making of Texas, 1836–1986.* Austin: University of Texas Press, 1987.

Moore, John H., ed. *The Political Economy of North American Indians.* Norman: University of Oklahoma Press, 1993.

Muir, Andrew Forest, ed. *Texas in 1837: An Anonymous, Contemporary Narrative.* Austin: University of Texas Press, 1958.

Musher, Sharon Ann, "Contesting 'The Way the Almighty Wants It': Crafting Memories of Ex-Slaves in the Slave Narrative Collection." *American Quarterly* 53, no. 1 (March 2001): 1–31.

Nance, Joseph Milton. *After San Jacinto: The Texas-Mexican Frontier, 1836–1841.* Austin: University of Texas Press, 1963.

Nash, A. E. Keir. "The Texas Supreme Court and Trial Rights of Blacks, 1845–1860." *Journal of American History* 48, no. 3 (December 1971): 622–42.

Nash, Gary B. *The Unknown American Revolution: The Unruly Birth of Democracy and the Struggle to Create America.* New York: Penguin Books, 2006.

Nathan, Paul D., trans. *The San Sabá Papers: A Documentary Account of the Founding and Destruction of San Sabá Mission.* Ed. Lesley Byrd Simpson. Dallas, TX: Southern Methodist University Press, 2000.

Naylor, Celia E. *African Cherokees in Indian Territory: From Chattel to Citizens.* Chapel Hill: University of North Carolina Press, 2008.

Naylor, Thomas H., and Charles W. Polzer, eds. *Pedro de Rivera and the Military Regulations for Northern New Spain, 1724–1729: A Documentary History of His Frontier Inspection and The* Reglamento de 1729. Tucson: University of Arizona Press, 1989.

New Mexico Office of the State Historian. "Bishop Tamarón's Visitation to New Mexico, 1760." New Mexico History, July 22, 2015. https://newmexicohistory.org/2015/07/22/bishop-tamarons-visitation-to-new-mexico-1760/.

Newell, Margaret Ellen. *Brethren by Nature: New England Indians, Colonists, and the Origins of American Slavery.* Ithaca, NY: Cornell University Press, 2015.

Nichols, James David. "The Limits of Liberty: African Americans, Indians, and Peons in the Texas-Mexico Borderlands, 1820–1860." PhD diss., Stony Brook University, 2012.

———. *The Limits of Liberty: Mobility and the Making of the Eastern U.S.-Mexico Border.* Lincoln: University of Nebraska Press, 2018.

Nieboer, H. J. *Slavery as an Industrial System.* The Hague: Martinus Nijhoff, 1900.

Niles, John M. *History of South America and Mexico.* Vol. 1. Hartford, CT: H. Huntington, 1838.

Nisbett, Richard E., and Dov Cohen. *Culture of Honor: The Psychology of Violence in the South.* Boulder, CO: Westview Press, 1996.

Noyes, Stanley. *Los Comanches: The Horse People, 1751–1845.* Albuquerque: University of New Mexico Press, 1993.

Olaloku-Teriba, Annie. "Afro-Pessimism and the (Un)Logic of Anti-Blackness." *Historical Materialism: Research in Critical Marx Theory* 26, no. 2 (2018): http://www.historicalmaterialism.org/articles/afro-pessimism-and-unlogic-anti-blackness.

Olguín, B. V. "'Caballeros' and Indians: Mexican American Whiteness, Hegemonic Mestizaje, and Ambivalent Indigeneity in Proto-Chicana/o Autobiographical Discourse, 1858–2008." *MELUS* 38, no. 1 (Spring 2013): 30–49.

Olmstead, Alan L., and Paul W. Rhode. "Cotton, Slavery, and the New History of Capitalism." *Explorations in Economic History* 67 (2018): 1–17.

Olmsted, Frederick Law. *A Journey through Texas; or, a Saddle-Trip on the Southwestern Frontier: With a Statistical Appendix.* New York: Dix, Edwards, 1857.

Osburn, Mary McMillan, ed. *The Atascosita Census of 1826.* Liberty, TX: Liberty County Historical Survey Committee, 1963.

Ostler, Jeffrey. *Surviving Genocide: Native Nations and the United States from the American Revolution to Bleeding Kansas.* New Haven, CT: Yale University Press, 2019.

Pagés, Monsieur de. *Travels round the World, in the Years 1767, 1768, 1769, 1770, 1771.* Vol. 1. London: J. Murray, 1791.

Palmer, Colin A. *Slaves of the White God: Blacks in Mexico, 1570–1650.* Cambridge, MA: Harvard University Press, 1976.

Patten, Roderick B., trans. and ed. "Miranda's Inspection of Los Almagres: His Journal, Report, and Petition." *Southwestern Historical Quarterly* 74, no. 2 (October 1970): 223–54.

Patterson, Orlando. *Slavery and Social Death: A Comparative Study.* Cambridge, MA: Harvard University Press, 1982.

Pearce, Roy Harvey. *Savagism and Civilization: A Study of the Indian and the American Mind.* Berkeley: University of California Press, 1988.

Perales, Monica, and Raúl A. Ramos, eds. *Recovering the Hispanic History of Texas.* Houston, TX: Arte Público Press, 2010.

Perdue, Theda. *Slavery and the Evolution of Cherokee Society*. Knoxville: University of Tennessee Press, 1979.

Perrine, Fred S., and Grant Foreman, eds. "The Journal of Hugh Evans Covering the First and Second Campaigns of the United States Dragoon Regiments in 1834 and 1835." *Chronicles of Oklahoma* 3 (September 1925): 175–215.

Phillips, Ulrich Bonnell. *American Negro Slavery: A Survey of the Supply, Employment and Control of Negro Labor as Determined by the Plantation Régime*. New York: D. Appleton, 1918.

Porter, Kenneth W. *The Negro on the American Frontier*. New York: Arno Press, 1971.

Potts, Charles S. "The Convict Labor System of Texas." *Annals of the American Academy of Political and Social Science* 21 (May 1903): 84–95.

———. *Railroad Transportation in Texas*. Austin: University of Texas Press, 1909.

Powell, Philip Wayne. *Soldiers, Indians, and Silver: The Northward Advance of New Spain, 1550–1600*. Berkeley: University of California Press, 1952.

Poyo, Gerald E., ed. *Tejano Journey, 1770–1850*. Austin: University of Texas Press, 1996.

Poyo, Gerald E., and Gilberto M. Hinojosa, eds. *Tejano Origins in Eighteenth-Century San Antonio*. Austin: University of Texas Press, 1991.

Pratt, Willis W., ed. *Galveston Island, or A Few Months Off the Coast of Texas: The Journal of Francis C. Sheridan, 1839–1840*. Austin: University of Texas Press, 1954.

Proctor, Frank T., III. "Afro-Mexican Slave Labor in the Obrajes de Paños of New Spain, Seventeenth and Eighteenth Centuries." *Americas* 60, no. 1 (July 2003): 33–58.

———. *"Damned Notions of Liberty": Slavery, Culture, and Power in Colonial Mexico, 1640–1769*. Albuquerque: University of New Mexico Press, 2010.

Prucha, Francis Paul. *The Great Father: The United States Government and the American Indians*. Vols. 1 and 2, unabridged. Lincoln: University of Nebraska Press, 1984.

Radding, Cynthia. *Wandering Peoples: Colonialism, Ethnic Spaces, and Ecological Frontiers in Northwestern Medico, 1700–1850*. Durham, NC: Duke University Press, 1997.

Raines, C. W., Herbert E. Bolton, and Eugene C. Barker, eds. "Notes and Fragments." *Quarterly of the Texas State Historical Association* 9, no. 4 (April 1906): 282–88.

Ramos, Raúl A. *Beyond the Alamo: Forging Mexican Ethnicity in San Antonio, 1821–1861*. Chapel Hill: University of North Carolina Press, 2008.

Ramsdell, Charles W. "The Natural Limits of Slavery Expansion." *Mississippi Valley Historical Review* 16, no. 2 (September 1929): 151–71.

Rediker, Marcus. *The Slave Ship: A Human History*. New York: Viking, 2007.

Rendón Lozano, Ruben. *Viva Tejas: The Story of the Mexican-Born Patriots of the Republic of Texas.* San Antonio, TX: Southern Literary Institute, 1936.

Reséndez, Andrés. *Changing National Identities at the Frontier: Texas and New Mexico, 1800–1850.* Cambridge: Cambridge University Press, 2004.

———. *Land So Strange: The Epic Journey of Cabeza de Vaca.* New York: Basic Books, 2007.

———. *The Other Slavery: The Uncovered Story of Indian Enslavement in America.* Boston: Houghton Mifflin Harcourt, 2016.

Restall, Matthew, ed. *Beyond Black and Red: African-Native Relations in Colonial Latin America.* Albuquerque: University of New Mexico Press, 2005.

Ricklis, Robert A. *The Karankawa Indians of Texas: An Ecological Study of Cultural Tradition and Change.* Austin: University of Texas Press, 1996.

Rister, Carl Coke. *Comanche Bondage: Beales's Settlement and Sarah Ann Horn's Narrative.* Introduction by Don Worcester. Lincoln: University of Nebraska Press, 1989.

Rivaya-Martínez, Joaquín. "Captivity and Adoption among the Comanche Indians, 1700–1875." PhD diss., University of California, Los Angeles, 2006.

———, ed. "The Captivity of Macario Leal: A Tejano among the Comanches, 1847–1854." *Southwestern Historical Quarterly* 117, no. 4 (April 2014): 372–402.

———. "A Different Look at Native American Depopulation: Comanche Raiding, Captive Taking, and Population Decline." *Journal of the American Society for Ethnohistory* 63, no. 3 (Summer 2014): 391–418.

Roberts, Randy, and James S. Olson. *A Line in the Sand: The Alamo in Blood and Memory.* New York: Free Press, 2001.

Robinson, Sherry. *I Fought a Good Fight: A History of the Lipan Apaches.* Denton: University of North Texas Press, 2013.

Rose, Willie Lee. *Slavery and Freedom.* Ed. William W. Freehling. New York: Oxford University Press, 1982.

Rothman, Joshua D. *Flush Times and Fever Dreams: A Story of Capitalism and Slavery in the Age of Jackson.* Athens: University of Georgia Press, 2012.

Rucker, Walter C. *The River Flows On: Black Resistance, Culture, and Identity Formation in Early America.* Baton Rouge: Louisiana State University Press, 2006.

Rushforth, Brett. *Bonds of Alliance: Indigenous and Atlantic Slaveries in New France.* Chapel Hill: University of North Carolina Press, 2012.

Sánchez, Joseph P. *Explorers, Traders, and Slavers: Forging the Old Spanish Trail, 1670–1850.* Salt Lake City: University of Utah Press, 1997.

Santiago, Mark. *The Jar of Severed Hands: Spanish Deportation of Apache Prisoners of War, 1770–1810.* Norman: University of Oklahoma Press, 2011.

Santos, Richard G., trans. *Aguayo Expedition into Texas, 1721: An Annotated Translation of the Five Versions of the Diary Kept by Br. Juan Antonio de la Peña.* Austin, TX: Jenkins, 1981.

Saucier, P. Khalil, and Tryon P. Woods, eds., *On Marronage: Ethical Confrontations with Antiblackness.* Trenton, NJ: Africa World Press, 2015.

Saunt, Claudio. *Black, White, and Indian: Race and the Unmaking of an American Family.* Oxford: Oxford University Press, 2005.

———. *A New Order of Things: Property, Power, and the Transformation of the Creek Indians, 1733–1816.* Cambridge: Cambridge University Press, 1999.

———. *West of the Revolution: An Uncommon History of 1776.* New York: Norton, 2014.

Schilz, Thomas Frank, and Donald E. Worcester. "The Spread of Firearms among the Indian Tribes on the Northern Frontier of New Spain." *American Indian Quarterly* 11, no. 1 (Winter 1987): 1–10.

Schoen, Harold. "The Free Negro in the Republic of Texas, III." *Southwestern Historical Quarterly* 40, no. 2 (October 1936): 85–113.

———. "The Free Negro in the Republic of Texas, IV." *Southwestern Historical Quarterly* 40, no. 3 (January 1937): 169–99.

———. "The Free Negro in the Republic of Texas, VI." *Southwestern Historical Quarterly* 41, no. 1 (July 1937): 83–108.

Schoolcraft, Henry R. *Information respecting the History Condition and Prospects of the Indian Tribes of the United States.* Philadelphia, PA: Lippincott, Grambo, 1852.

Schuetz, Mardith Keithly. "The Indians of the San Antonio Missions: 1718–1821." PhD diss., University of Texas at Austin, 1979.

Schulze, Jeffrey M. *Are We Not Foreigners Here? Indigenous Nationalism in the U.S.-Mexico Borderlands.* Chapel Hill: University of North Carolina Press, 2018.

Selden, Jack R. *Return: The Parker Story.* Palestine, TX: Clacton Press, 2006.

Sexton, Jared. *Amalgamation Schemes: Antiblackness and the Critique of Multiracialism.* Minneapolis: University of Minnesota Press, 2008.

Shelby, Charmion Clair, ed. "St. Denis's Declaration concerning Texas in 1717." *Southwest Historical Quarterly* 26, no. 3 (January 1923): 165–83.

Simmons, Virginia McConnell. *The Ute Indians of Utah, Colorado, and New Mexico.* Boulder: University of Colorado Press, 2000.

Smallwood, Stephanie. *Saltwater Slavery: A Middle Passage from Africa to American Diaspora.* Cambridge, MA: Harvard University Press, 2007.

Smith, F. Todd. *From Dominance to Disappearance: The Indians of Texas and the Near Southwest, 1786–1859.* Lincoln: University of Nebraska Press, 2005.

———. *The Wichita Indians: Traders of Texas and the Southern Plains, 1540–1845.* College Station: Texas A&M University Press, 2000.

Smith, Ralph A., trans. "Account of the Journey of Bénard de la Harpe Discovery Made by Him of Several Nations Situated in the West." *Southwestern Historical Quarterly* 62, no. 4 (April 1959): 525–41.

———. *Borderlander: The Life of James Kirker, 1793–1852.* Norman: University of Oklahoma Press, 1999.

———. "The Scalp Hunter in the Borderlands, 1835–1850." *Arizona and the West* 6, no. 1 (Spring 1964): 5–22.

Smither, Harriet, ed. *Journals of the Sixth Congress of the Republic of Texas, 1841–1842.* Vols. 1–2. Austin, TX: Von Boeckmann-Jones, Capital Printing, 1940–44.

Smithwick, Noah. *The Evolution of a State, or Recollections of Old Texas Days.* Comp. Nanna Smithwick Donaldson. Austin, TX: Gammel, 1900.

Snorton, C. Riley. *Black on Both Sides: A Racial History of Trans Identity.* Minneapolis: University of Minnesota Press, 2017.

Snyder, Christina. *Slavery in Indian Country: The Changing Face of Captivity in Early America.* Cambridge, MA: Harvard University Press, 2010.

Sojoyner, Damien M. "Another Life Is Possible: Black Fugitivity and Enclosed Places." *Cultural Anthropology* 32, no. 4 (2017): 514–36.

Sowell, A. J. *Early Settlers and Indian Fighters of Southwest Texas: Facts Gathered from Survivors of Frontier Days.* Austin, TX: Ben C. Jones, 1900.

Spicer, Edward H. *Cycles of Conquest: The Impact of Spain, Mexico, and the United States on the Indians of the Southwest, 1533–1960.* Tucson: University of Arizona Press, 1962.

Spierenburg, Pieter. *Men and Violence: Gender, Honor, and Rituals in Modern Europe and America.* Columbus: Ohio State University Press, 1998.

Stampp, Kenneth M. "Rebels and Sambos: The Search for the Negro's Personality in Slavery." *Journal of Southern History* 37, no. 3 (August 1971): 367–92.

Stannard, David E. *American Holocaust: The Conquest of the New World.* New York: Oxford University Press, 1992.

Starobin, Robert S. *Industrial Slavery in the Old South.* Oxford: Oxford University Press, 1970.

Stevens, Kenneth R., ed. *The Texas Legation Papers: 1836–1845.* Fort Worth, TX: TCU Press, 2012.

Stevens, Robert C. "The Apache Menace in Sonora, 1831–1849." *Arizona and the West* 6, no. 3 (Autumn 1964): 211–22.

Stewart, Kenneth L., and Arnoldo de León. *Not Room Enough: Mexicans, Anglos, and Socioeconomic Change in Texas, 1850–1900.* Albuquerque: University of New Mexico Press, 1993.

Stiff, Edward. *A New History of Texas; Being a Narration of the Adventures of the Author in Texas, and a Description of the Soil, Climate, Productions, Minerals, Tons, Bays, Harbours, Rivers, Institutions, and Manners and Customs of the Inhabitants of that Country; Together with the Principal Incidents of Fifteen Years Revolution in Mexico; and Embracing a Condensed Statement of Interesting Events in Texas, from the First European Settlement in 1692, Down to the Present Time: And a History of the Mexican War, including Accounts of the Battles of Pala Alto, Resea de La Palma, the Taking of Monterey, and the Battle of Buena Vista.* Cincinnati, OH: George Conclin, 1847.

Strickland, Rex Wallace. "History of Fannin County, Texas, 1836–1843." *Southwestern Historical Quarterly* 33, no. 4 (April 1930): 262–98.
Strobel, Abner J. *The Old Plantations and Their Owners of Brazoria County, Texas*. Houston, TX: Union National Bank, 1926.
Strong, Pauline Turner. *Captive Selves, Captivating Others: The Politics and Poetics of Colonial American Captivity Narratives*. New York: Taylor & Francis, 1999.
Struve, Walter. *Germans and Texans: Commerce, Migration, and Culture in the Days of the Lone Star Republic*. Austin: University of Texas Press, 1996.
Stuckey, Sterling. *Slave Culture: Nationalist Theory and the Foundations of Black America*. Oxford: Oxford University Press, 2013.
Stuntz, Jean A. *Hers, His, and Theirs: Community Property Law in Spain and Early Texas*. Lubbock: Texas Tech University Press, 2005.
Tamez, Margo. "Nádasi'né' ndé' isdzáné begoz'aahi' shimaa shini' gokal gową goshjaa ha'áná'idiłí texas-nakaiyé godesdzog." PhD diss., Washington State University, 2010.
Tannenbaum, Frank. *Slave and Citizen: The Negro in the Americas*. New York: Knopf, 1946.
Tate, Michael L. "Comanche Captives." *Chronicle of Oklahoma* 72, no. 3 (Fall 1994): 228–63.
Taylor, Paul S. *An American-Mexican Frontier: Nueces County, Texas*. Chapel Hill: University of North Carolina Press, 1934.
Taylor, Virginia, ed. *Letters from Gov. Antonio Martínez to the Viceroy Juan Ruíz de Apodaca*. San Antonio, TX: Research Center for the Arts and Humanities, 1983.
Taylor, Virginia H., ed. *The Letters of Antonio Martínez: Last Spanish Governor of Texas, 1817–1822*. Austin: Texas State Library, 1957.
Texas House of Representatives. *Journal of the House of Representatives. The State of Texas: Fourth Legislature*. Austin, TX: Cushney & Hampton, 1852.
———. *Journal of the House of Representatives of the State of Texas, Fifth Legislature*. Part 2. Austin, TX: J. W. Hampton, 1853.
———. *Journal of the House of Representatives of the State of Texas, Sixth Legislature*. Austin, TX: Marshall & Oldham, 1855.
———. *Journals of the House of Representatives of the First Legislature of the State of Texas*. Clarksville, TX: Standard Office, 1848.
———. *Journals of the House of Representatives of the State of Texas, Extra Session—Third Legislature*. Austin: Texas State Gazette Office, 1850.
———. *Journals of the House of Representatives of the State of Texas. Third Session*. Austin, TX: Gazette Office, 1849.
———. *Journals of the House of Representatives, of the State of Texas, Fourth Legislature—Extra Session*. Austin, TX: J. W. Hampton, 1853.
———. *Official Journal of the House of Representatives of the State of Texas: Seventh Biennial Session*. Austin, TX: John Marshall, 1857.

Texas in 1840 or, The Emigrant's Guide to the New Republic; Being the Result of Observation, Enquiry and Travel in That Beautiful Country. New York: William W. Allen, 1840.

Texas Republic Congress. *Appendix to the Journals of the House of Representatives: Fifth Congress.* [Austin: Gazette Printing Office, 1841].

———. *Appendix to the Journals of the House of Representatives: Seventh Congress.* [Washington, TX:] Vindicator Office, [1843].

———. *Appendix to the Journals of the Ninth Congress of the Republic of Texas.* Washington, TX: Miller & Cushney, 1845.

———. *Journal of the House of Representatives, Republic of Texas: Called Session of September 25, 1837, and Regular Session, Commencing November 6, 1837.* Houston, TX: Niles & Co., Printers, 1838.

———. *Journal of the House of Representatives of the Republic of Texas, Regular Session of Third Congress, Nov. 5, 1838.* Houston, TX: Intelligence Office, 1839.

———. *Journals of the House of Representatives of the Republic of Texas, First Congress, First Session.* Houston, TX: Office of the Telegraph, 1838.

———. *Journals of the House of Representatives of the Republic of Texas: Fifth Congress, First Session, 1840–1841.* Austin, TX: Cruger and Wing, 1841.

———. *Journals of the House of Representatives of the Seventh Congress of the Republic of Texas.* Washington, TX: Thomas Johnson, 1843.

Thomas, Alfred Barnaby, ed. *After Coronado: Spanish Exploration Northeast of New Mexico, 1696–1727.* Norman: University of Oklahoma Press, 1935.

———, ed. *The Plains Indians and New Mexico, 1751–1778: A Collection of Documents Illustrative of the History of the Eastern Frontier of New Mexico.* Albuquerque: University of New Mexico Press, 1949.

Thompson, Jerry D. *Cortina: Defending the Mexican Name in Texas.* College Station: Texas A&M University Press, 2007.

———, ed. *Tejanos in Gray: Civil War Letters of Captains Joseph Rafael de la Garza and Manuel Yturri.* Trans. José Roberto Juárez. College Station: Texas A&M University Press, 2011.

———. *Tejano Tiger: José de los Santos Benavides and the Texas-Mexico Borderlands, 1823–1891.* Fort Worth, TX: TCU Press, 2017.

———. *Vaqueros in Blue and Gray.* Austin, TX: State House Press, 2000.

Thornton, Russell, ed. *Studying Native America: Problems and Prospects.* Madison: University of Wisconsin Press, 1998.

Tijerina, Andrés. *Tejanos and Texas under the Mexican Flag, 1821–1836.* College Station: Texas A&M University Press, 1994.

Tjarks, Alicia V. "Comparative Demographic Analysis of Texas, 1777–1793." *Southwestern Historical Quarterly* 77, no. 3 (January 1974): 291–338.

Torget, Andrew J. *Seeds of Empire: Cotton, Slavery, and the Transformation of the Texas Borderlands, 1800–1850.* Chapel Hill: University of North Carolina Press, 2015.

Tous, Gabriel, trans. "The Espinosa-Olivares-Aguirre Expedition of 1709." *Preliminary Studies of the Texas Catholic Historical Society* 1, no. 3 (March 1930): 2–16.

Trask, Haunani-Kay. *From a Native Daughter: Colonialism and Sovereignty in Hawai'i.* Revised ed. Honolulu: University of Hawai'i Press, 1999.

Truett, Samuel. *Fugitive Landscapes: The Forgotten History of the U.S.-Mexico Borderlands.* New Haven, CT: Yale University Press, 2006.

Truett, Samuel, and Elliott Young, eds. *Continental Crossroads: Remapping U.S.-Mexico Borderlands History.* Durham, NC: Duke University Press, 2004.

Tsesis, Alexander, ed. *The Promises of Liberty: The History and Contemporary Relevance of the Thirteenth Amendment.* New York: Columbia University Press, 2010.

Tuan, Yi-Fu. *Space and Place: The Perspective of Experience.* Minneapolis: University of Minnesota Press, 1977.

Turley, David. *Slavery.* Oxford: Blackwell, 2000.

Twitchell, Ralph Emerson, ed. *The Spanish Archives of New Mexico: Compiled and Chronologically Arranged with Historical, Genealogical, Geographical, and Other Annotations, by Authority of the State of New Mexico.* Vols. 1, 2. Cedar Rapids, IA: Torch Press, 1914.

Tyler, Ronnie C. "The Callahan Expedition of 1855: Indians or Negroes?" *Southwestern Historical Quarterly* 70, no. 4 (April 1967): 574–85.

Tyler, S. Lyman. "The Myth of the Lake of Copala." *Utah Historical Quarterly* 20, no. 1 (January 1952): 313–29.

Tyler, S. Lyman, and H. Darrel Taylor. "The Report of Fray Alonso de Posada in Relation to Quivira and Teguayo." *New Mexico Historical Review* 33, no. 4 (October 1958): 285–314.

U.S. Census Bureau. *Agriculture of the United States in 1860; Compiled from the Original Returns of the Eighth Census.* Washington, DC: Government Printing Office, 1864.

———. *1850 Population and Slave Schedules.* https://www.ancestry.com/search/collections/8055/.

———. *1860 Slave Schedules.* https://www.ancestry.com/search/collections/7668/.

———. *Census for 1820; Published by Authority of an Act of Congress, under the Direction of the Secretary of State.* Washington, DC: Gales and Seaton, 1821.

———. *Population of the United States in 1860; Compiled from the Original Returns of the Eighth Census.* Washington, DC: Government Printing Office, 1864.

———. *The Seventh Census of the United States, 1850: Embracing a Statistical View of Each of the States and Territories, Arranged by Counties, Towns, Etc.* Washington, DC: Robert Armstrong, 1853.

U.S. Commissioner of Indian Affairs. *Annual Report of the Commissioner of*

Indian Affairs, Transmitted with the Message of the President at the Opening of the First Session of the Thirty-Third Congress, 1853. Washington, DC: Robert Armstrong, 1853.

———. *Report of the Commissioner of Indian Affairs, Accompanying the Annual Report of the Secretary of the Interior, for the Year 1859*. Washington, DC: George W. Bowman, 1860.

———. *Report of the Commissioner of Indian Affairs for the Year 1866*. Washington, DC: Government Printing Office, 1866.

U.S. Congress. *American State Papers: Documents, Legislative and Executive, of the Congress of the United States*. Foreign Relations. Vol. 2. Washington, DC: Gales and Seaton, 1832.

———. *Executive Documents, House of Representatives, Twenty-Fourth Congress, Second Session*. Washington, DC: Blair & Rives, 1836.

———. *Executive Documents, House of Representatives, Thirtieth Congress, First Session*. Washington, DC: Wendell and Van Benthuysen, 1848.

———. *Executive Documents, House of Representatives, Thirtieth Congress, Second Session*. Washington, DC: Wendell and Van Benthuysen, 1848.

———. *Executive Documents, House of Representatives, Thirty-First Congress, First Session*. Washington, DC, 1849.

———. *Executive Documents, House of Representatives, Thirty-Fourth Congress, First Session*. Washington, DC: Cornelius Wendell, 1856.

———. *Executive Documents, House of Representatives, Thirty-Fifth Congress, Second Session*. Washington, DC: James B. Steedman, 1859.

———. *Executive Documents, House of Representatives, Thirty-Sixth Congress, First Session*. Washington, DC: Thomas H. Ford, 1860.

———. *Executive Documents, Senate, Twenty-Seventh Congress, Second Session*. Washington, DC: Thomas Allen, 1841.

———. *Executive Documents, Senate, Thirty-First Congress, First Session*. Washington, DC: Wm. M. Belt, 1850.

———. *Executive Documents, Senate, Thirty-Second Congress, First Session*. Washington, DC: A. Boyd Hamilton, 1851.

———. *Executive Documents, Senate, Thirty-Second Congress, Second Session*. Washington, DC: Robert Armstrong, 1852.

———. *Executive Documents, Senate, Thirty-Fifth Congress, First Session*. Washington, DC: William A. Harris, 1858.

———. *Executive Documents, Senate, Thirty-Fifth Congress, Second Session*. Washington, DC: William A. Harris, 1859.

———. *Executive Documents, Senate, Thirty-Sixth Congress, First Session*. Washington, DC: George W. Bowman, 1860.

———. *Public Documents, Printed by Order of the Senate of the United States, Second Session of the Twenty-Fourth Congress, Begun and Held at the City of Washington, December 5, 1836*. Vol. 1. Washington, DC: Gales and Seaton, 1837.

———. *Reports of Committees, Senate, Thirtieth Congress, First Session.* Washington, DC: Wendell and Van Benthuysen, 1847.

University of Texas Institute of Texan Cultures. *Residents of Texas, 1782–1836.* Vols. 1–3. San Antonio: University of Texas Institute of Texan Cultures, 1979–84.

Usner, Daniel H., Jr. "American Indians on the Cotton Frontier: Changing Economic Relations with Citizens and Slaves." *Journal of American History* 72, no. 2 (September 1985): 297–317.

———. *Indians, Settlers, and Slaves in a Frontier Exchange Economy: The Lower Mississippi Valley before 1783.* Chapel Hill: University of North Carolina Press, 1992.

Utley, Robert M. *Lone Star Justice: The First Century of the Texas Rangers.* Oxford: Oxford University Press, 2002.

Valerio-Jiménez, Omar S. *River of Hope: Forging Identity and Nation in the Rio Grande Borderlands.* Durham, NC: Duke University, 2013.

Van Deusen, Nancy. "The Intimacies of Bondage: Female Indigenous Servants and Slaves and Their Spanish Masters, 1492–1555." *Journal of Women's History* 24, no. 1 (Spring 2012): 13–43.

Velasco Ávila, Cuauhtémoc. *En manos de los bárbaros: Testimonios de la guerra india en el noreste.* Mexico City: Breve Fondo Editorial, 1996.

Velazquez, Mariano, et al. *The New Velázquez Spanish and English Dictionary.* Rev. Ida Navarro Hinojosa, Manuel Blanco-González, and R. J. Nelson. El Monte: Velázquez Press, 2003.

Veracini, Lorenzo. *Settler Colonialism: A Theoretical Overview.* London: Palgrave Macmillan, 2010.

Vielé, Teresa Griffin. *"Following the Drum": A Glimpse of Frontier Life.* New York: Rudd & Carleton, 1858.

Villanueva, Nicholas, Jr. *The Lynching of Mexicans in the Texas Borderlands.* Albuquerque: University of New Mexico Press, 2017.

Vincent, Ted. "The Blacks Who Freed Mexico." *Journal of Negro History* 79, no. 3 (Summer 1994): 257–76.

Vinson, Ben, III. *Bearing Arms for His Majesty: The Free-Colored Militia in Colonial Mexico.* Stanford, CA: Stanford University Press, 2001.

Vinson, Ben, III, and Matthew Restall, eds. *Black Mexico: Race and Society from Colonial to Modern Times.* Albuquerque: University of New Mexico Press, 2009.

Von Gleich, Paula. "African American Narratives of Captivity and Fugitivity: Developing Post-Slavery Questions for *Angela Davis: An Autobiography.*" *Current Objectives of Postgraduate American Studies* 16, no. 1 (2015): https://copas.uni-regensburg.de/article/view/221.

Wade, Maria F. *The Native Americans of the Texas Edwards Plateau: 1582–1799.* Austin: University of Texas Press, 2003.

Wahlstrom, Todd W. *The Southern Exodus to Mexico: Migration across the*

Borderlands after the American Civil War. Lincoln: University of Nebraska Press, 2015.

Wallace, Ernest, ed. "David G. Burnet's Letters Describing the Comanche Indians." *West Texas Historical Association Year Book* 30 (October 1954): 115–40.

Wallace, Ernest, and E. Adamson Hoebel. *The Comanches: Lords of the South Plains.* 1952; Norman: University of Oklahoma Press, 1976.

Waller, John L. "Colonel George Wythe Baylor." *Southwestern Social Science Quarterly* 24, no. 1 (June 1943): 23–35.

Ward, H. G. *Mexico in 1827: His Majesty's Chargé D'Affaires in That Country during the Years 1825, 1826, and Part of 1827.* London: Henry Colburn, 1828.

Warren, Wendy. *New England Bound: Slavery and Colonization in Early America.* New York: Liveright, 2016.

Watson, Larry S., ed. *Indian Treaties, 1835 to 1902.* Vol. 22: *Kiowa, Comanche and Apache.* Yuma, AZ: Histree, 1994.

Weber, David J. *Bárbaros: Spaniards and Their Savages in the Age of Enlightenment.* New Haven, CT: Yale University Press, 2005.

———. *The Mexican Frontier, 1821–1846: The American Southwest under Mexico.* Albuquerque: University of New Mexico Press, 1982.

———. *The Spanish Frontier in North America.* New Haven, CT: Yale University Press, 1992.

Weddle, Robert S. *San Juan Bautista: Gateway to Spanish Texas.* Austin: University of Texas Press, 1968.

Weeks, William F. *Debates of the Texas Convention.* Houston, TX: J. W. Cruger, 1846.

West, Elizabeth Howard, trans. "Bonilla's Brief Compendium of the History of Texas, 1772." *Quarterly of the Texas State Historical Association* 8, no. 1 (July 1904): 3–78.

West, Robert. *The Mining Community in Northern New Spain: The Parral Mining District.* Berkeley: University of California Press, 1949.

White, Deborah Gray. *Ar'n't I a Woman? Female Slaves in the Plantation South.* New York: Norton, 1985.

White, Gifford, ed. *1830 Citizens of Texas.* Austin, TX: Eakin Press, 1999.

White, Richard. *The Roots of Dependency: Subsistence, Environment, and Social Change among the Choctaws, Pawnees, and Navajos.* Lincoln: University of Nebraska Press, 1983.

Wiecek, William M. "The Statutory Law of Slavery and Race in the Thirteen Mainland Colonies of British America." *William and Mary Quarterly* 34, no. 2 (April 1977): 258–80.

Wilbarger, John Wesley. *Indian Depredations in Texas.* 2nd ed. Austin, TX: Hutchings Printing House, 1890.

Wilderson, Frank, III. *Red, White and Black: Cinema and the Structure of U.S. Antagonisms.* Durham, NC: Duke University Press, 2010.

Wilkinson, J. B. *Laredo and the Río Grande Frontier.* Austin, TX: Jenkins, 1975.

Williams, Amelia W., and Eugene C. Barker, eds. *The Writings of Sam Houston, 1813–1863*. Vol. 1. Austin: University of Texas Press, 1938.

Williams, David A. *Bricks without Straw: A Comprehensive History of African Americans in Texas*. Austin, TX: Eakin Press, 1997.

Wilson, Carol. *Freedom at Risk: The Kidnapping of Free Blacks in America, 1780–1865*. Lexington: University Press of Kentucky, 1994.

Wilson, Charles Reagan, ed. *The New Encyclopedia of Southern Culture*. Vol. 4: *Myth, Manners, and Memory*. Chapel Hill: University of North Carolina Press, 2006.

Wilson, Jane Adeline. *A Thrilling Narrative of the Sufferings of Mrs. Jane Adeline Wilson during Her Captivity among the Comanche Indians*. Fairfield, WA: Ye Galleon Press, 1971.

Winfrey, Dorman H. *Julien Sidney Devereux and His Monte Verdi Plantation*. Waco, TX: Texian Press, 1964.

Winfrey, Dorman H., and James M. Day. *The Indian Papers of Texas and the Southwest, 1825–1916*. Introduction by Michael L. Tate. Vols. 1–5. Austin: Texas State Historical Association, 1995.

Wistrand-Robinson, Lila, and James Armagost. *Comanche Dictionary and Grammar*. 2nd ed. Dallas, TX: SIL International, 2012.

Wolfe, Patrick. "Settler Colonialism and the Elimination of the Native." *Journal of Genocide Research* 8, no. 4 (December 2006): 387–409.

Woolfolk, George R. "Cotton Capitalism and Slave Labor in Texas." *Southwestern Social Science Quarterly* 37, no. 1 (June 1956): 43–52.

Wright, Gavin. *Slavery and American Economic Development*. Baton Rouge: Louisiana State University Press, 2006.

Wyatt-Brown, Bertram. *Honor and Violence in the Old South*. New York: Oxford University Press, 1986.

Yoakum, H. *History of Texas, From Its First Settlement in 1685 to Its Annexation to the United States in 1846*. Vol. 1. New York: Redfield, 1855.

Zavala, Silvio. *The Defence of Human Rights in Latin America (Sixteenth to Eighteenth Centuries)*. Paris: United Nations Educational, Scientific and Cultural Organization, 1964.

———. *Los esclavos indios en Nueva España*. Mexico City: El Colegio National, 1967.

———. "Nuño de Guzmán y la esclavitud de los indios." *Historia Mexicana* 1, no. 3 (January–March 1952): 411–28.

Index

Page numbers in italics indicate maps.

In the Borderlands and Transcultural Studies series

The Storied Landscape of Iroquoia: History, Conquest, and Memory in the Native Northeast
by Chad Anderson

Country of the Cursed and the Driven: Slavery and the Texas Borderlands,
by Paul Barba

How the West Was Drawn: Mapping, Indians, and the Construction of the Tran-Mississippi West
by David Bernstein

Chiricahua and Janos: Communities of Violence in the Southwestern Borderlands, 1680–1880
by Lance R. Blyth

The Borderland of Fear: Vincennes, Prophetstown, and the Invasion of the Miami Homeland
by Patrick Bottiger

Captives: How Stolen People Changed the World
by Catherine M. Cameron

The Allure of Blackness among Mixed-Race Americans, 1862–1916
by Ingrid Dineen-Wimberly

Intermarriage from Central Europe to Central Asia: Mixed Families in the Age of Extremes
edited and introduced by Adrienne Edgar and Benjamin Frommer

Words Like Birds: Sakha Language Discourses and Practices in the City
by Jenanne Ferguson

Transnational Crossroads: Remapping the Americas and the Pacific
edited by Camilla Fojas and Rudy P. Guevarra Jr.

Conquering Sickness: Race, Health, and Colonization in the Texas Borderlands
by Mark Allan Goldberg

Globalizing Borderlands Studies in Europe and North America
edited and with an introduction by John W. I. Lee and Michael North

Illicit Love: Interracial Sex and Marriage in the United States and Australia
by Ann McGrath

Shades of Gray: Writing the New American Multiracialism
by Molly Littlewood McKibbin

The Limits of Liberty: Mobility and the Making of the Eastern U.S.-Mexico Border
by James David Nichols

Native Diasporas: Indigenous Identities and Settler Colonialism in the Americas
edited by Gregory D. Smithers and Brooke N. Newman

Shape Shifters: Journeys across Terrains of Race and Identity
edited by Lily Anne Y. Welty Tamai, Ingrid Dineen-Wimberly, and Paul Spickard

The Southern Exodus to Mexico: Migration across the Borderlands after the American Civil War
by Todd W. Wahlstrom

To order or obtain more information on these or other University of Nebraska Press titles, visit nebraskapress.unl.edu.

CPSIA information can be obtained
at www.ICGtesting.com
Printed in the USA
LVHW092201221221
707015LV00001B/16